HOME PLANNERS

Encyclopedia of Home Designs

THIRD EDITION

500 HOUSE PLANS

From 1,000 to 6,300 square feet

HOME PLANNERS

Published by Home Planners, LLC
Wholly owned by Hanley-Wood, LLC
3275 West Ina Road, Suite 110
Tucson, Arizona 85741

Distribution Center:
29333 Lorie Lane
Wixom, Michigan 48393

Jayne Fenton, President
Linda B. Bellamy, Executive Editor
Arlen Feldwick-Jones, Editorial Director
Vicki Frank, Managing Editor
Laura Brown, Associate Editor
Nick Nieskes, Plans Associate
Matthew S. Kauffman, Graphic Designer
Sara Lisa, Senior Production Manager
Brenda McClary, Production Manager

Front cover:
Plan HPT830002
Photograph by Scott W. Moore
& Duvaune E. White
See page 6

Back cover:
Plan HPT830006
Photographs by Scott Moore,
MWS Photography
See page 10

Book design by Matthew S. Kauffman

First printing, February 2003

10 9 8 7 6 5 4 3 2 1

Printed in the United States of America.

ISBN 1-931131-12-0 Softcover

Library of Congress Control Number:
2002112990

Contents

Welcome

From the Colonial era to modern day, Americans have embraced a diverse mix of styles to call home—from urbane ranch houses to breezy cottages to stately revivals. Timeless New England and Southern classics recall historic days, while smooth Mediterranean homes sink roots in sun-drenched soil. This fine collection of house plans represents a rich mix of styles that honor the past yet step into the future. Wide selections of rugged mountain retreats, easy seaside pied-à-terre and just-right Caribbean houses take their place alongside familiar farmhouses and cozy bungalows. European influences prevail in an extensive section that includes charming French cottages and inviting Mediterranean manors, estate-sized Normans, and rustic Tudors. Cape Cod, Colonial, Craftsman, Victorian, and Sun Country designs are ready to build now in square footages from 1,000 to more than 6,000. Relaxed and charming or sophisticated and high-tech, the home of your dreams is just a phone call away. When you're ready to order, call 1-800-521-6797 or turn to page 515.

Design HPT830025, see page 29.

This home, as shown in the photograph, may differ from the actual blueprints. For more detailed information, please check the floor plans carefully.
Photo courtesy of Design Basics, Inc.

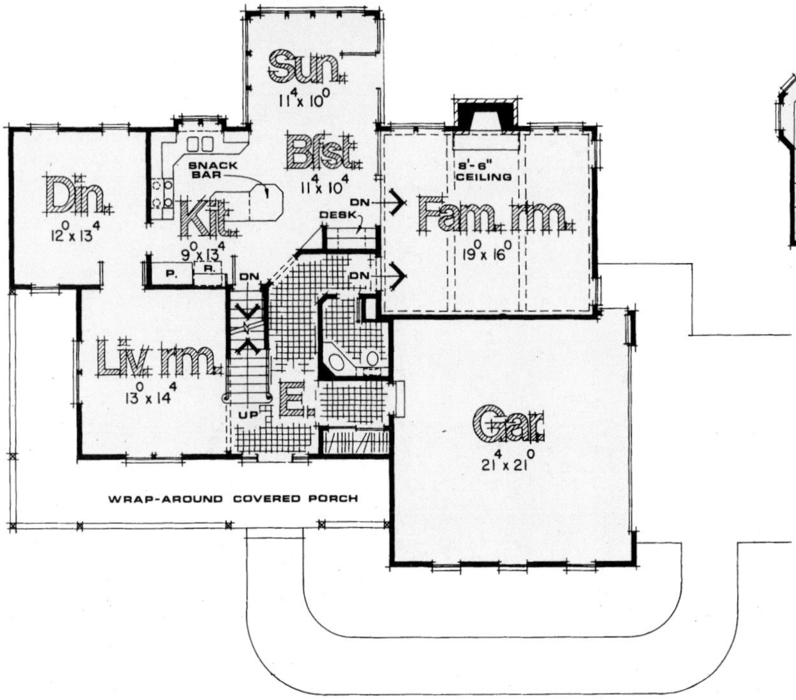

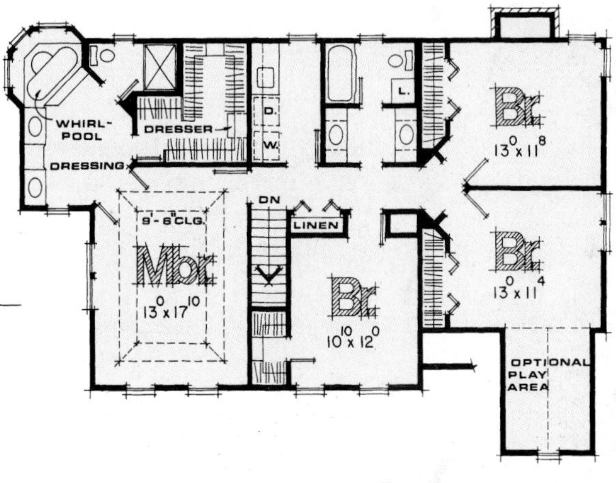

QUOTE ONE®

Cost to build? See page 516 to order complete cost estimate to build this house in your area!

This home has all the comfort you've been looking for! An inviting wraparound porch and sunny breakfast room are just the beginning of this plan's many great features. A sunken family room with a fireplace serves everyday casual gatherings, while the more formal living and dining rooms are reserved for special entertaining situations. The kitchen has a central island with a snack bar and is located most conveniently for serving and cleaning up. Upstairs are four bedrooms, one a lovely master suite with French doors to the private bath and a whirlpool tub with a dramatic bay window. A double vanity in the shared bath easily serves the three family bedrooms.

Design HPT830001

First Floor: 1,322 square feet
Second Floor: 1,272 square feet
Total: 2,594 square feet
Width 56'-0" Depth 48'-0"

This home, as shown in the photograph, may differ from the actual blueprints. For more detailed information, please check the floor plans carefully.
Photo by Scott W. Moore and Duvaune E. White

With five bedrooms and a wonderful stone-and-siding exterior, this country home will satisfy every need. Two sets of French doors provide access to the dining room and foyer. The great room enjoys a warming fireplace and deck access. The kitchen, breakfast bay and keeping room feature an open floor plan. A charming sitting room in a bay window sets off the master bedroom. The master bath features a large walk-in closet, two-sink vanity, separate tub and shower and compartmented toilet. Four bedrooms, an office and two full baths complete the upper level. This home is designed with a walkout basement foundation.

Design HPT830002

First Floor: 2,628 square feet
Second Floor: 1,775 square feet
Total: 4,403 square feet
Width 79'-6" Depth 65'-1"

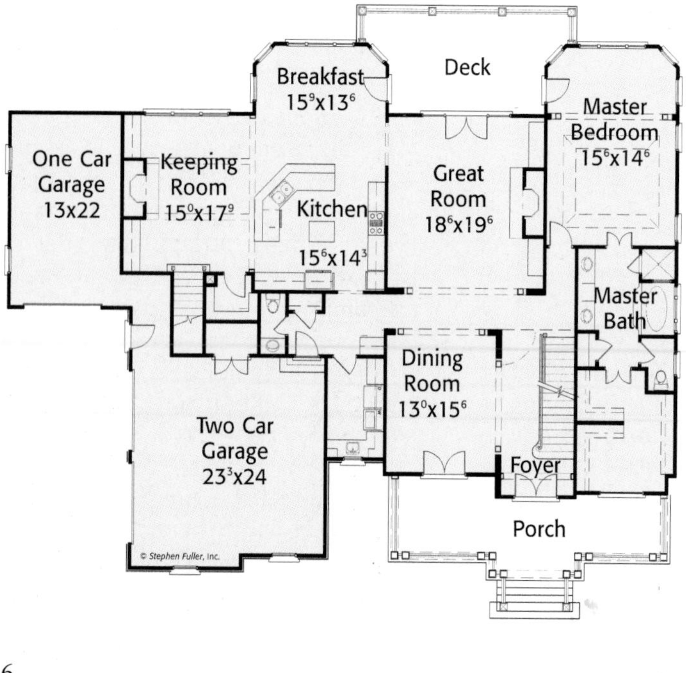

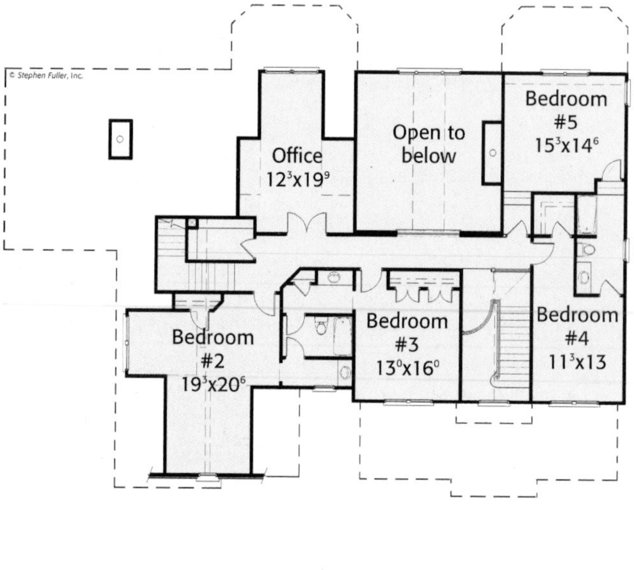

Design HPT830003

First Floor: 2,086 square feet	
Second Floor: 1,077 square feet	
Total: 3,163 square feet	
Bonus Space: 403 square feet	
Width 81'-10"	Depth 51'-8"

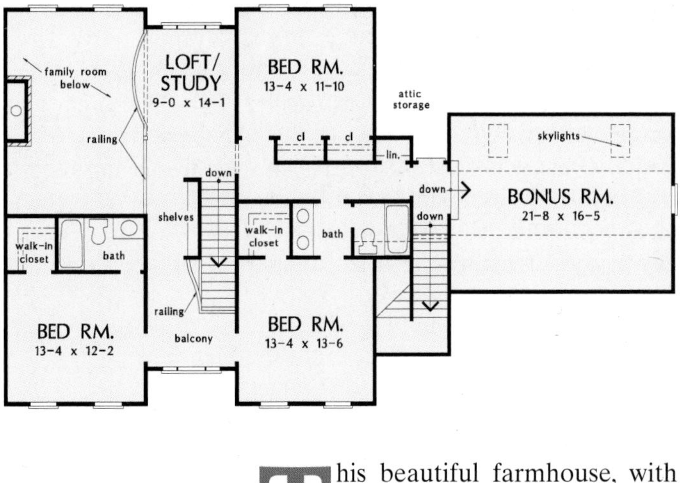

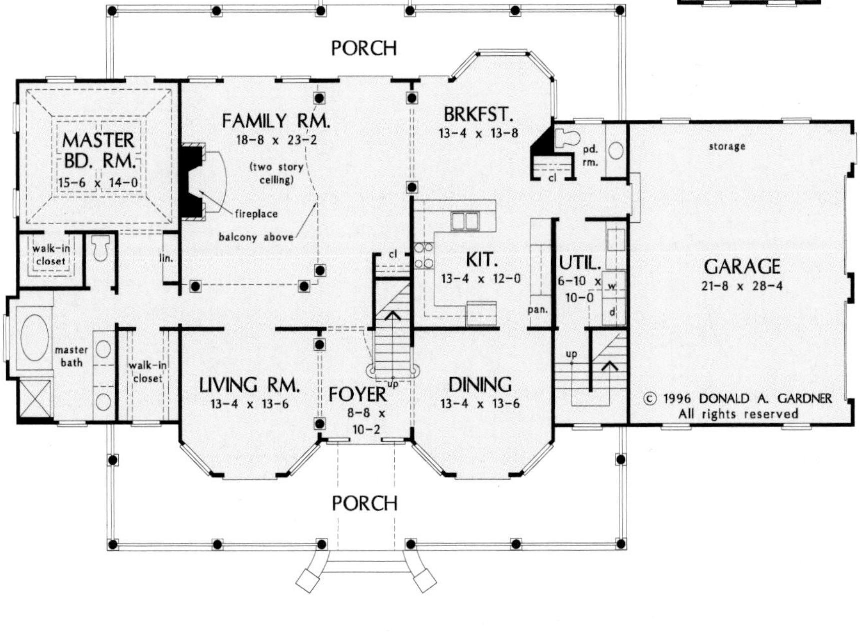

This beautiful farmhouse, with its prominent twin gables and bays, adds just the right amount of country style. The master suite is quietly tucked away downstairs with no rooms directly above. The family cook will love the spacious U-shaped kitchen and adjoining bayed breakfast nook. A bonus room is easily accessible from the back stairs or from the second floor, where three large bedrooms share two full baths. Storage space abounds on this floor with walk-in closets, half-shelves and a linen closet. A curved balcony borders a versatile loft/study, which overlooks the stunning two-story family room.

This home, as shown in the photograph, may differ from the actual blueprints. For more detailed information, please check the floor plans carefully.
Photo by Andrew D. Lautman

With its exceptional detail and proportions, this home is reminiscent of the Queen Anne style. The foyer opens to a living area with a bay-windowed alcove and a fireplace with flanking bookshelves. Natural light fills the breakfast area with a full-length bay window and a French door. Upstairs, the master bedroom offers unsurpassed elegance and convenience. The sitting area has an eleven-foot ceiling with arch-top windows. The bath area features a large walk-in closet, His and Hers lavatories and plenty of linen storage. Plans for a two-car detached garage are included.

Design HPT830004

First Floor: 997 square feet
Second Floor: 1,069 square feet
Total: 2,066 square feet
Width 39'-8" Depth 39'-2"

QUOTE ONE®
Cost to build? See page 516 to order complete cost estimate to build this house in your area!

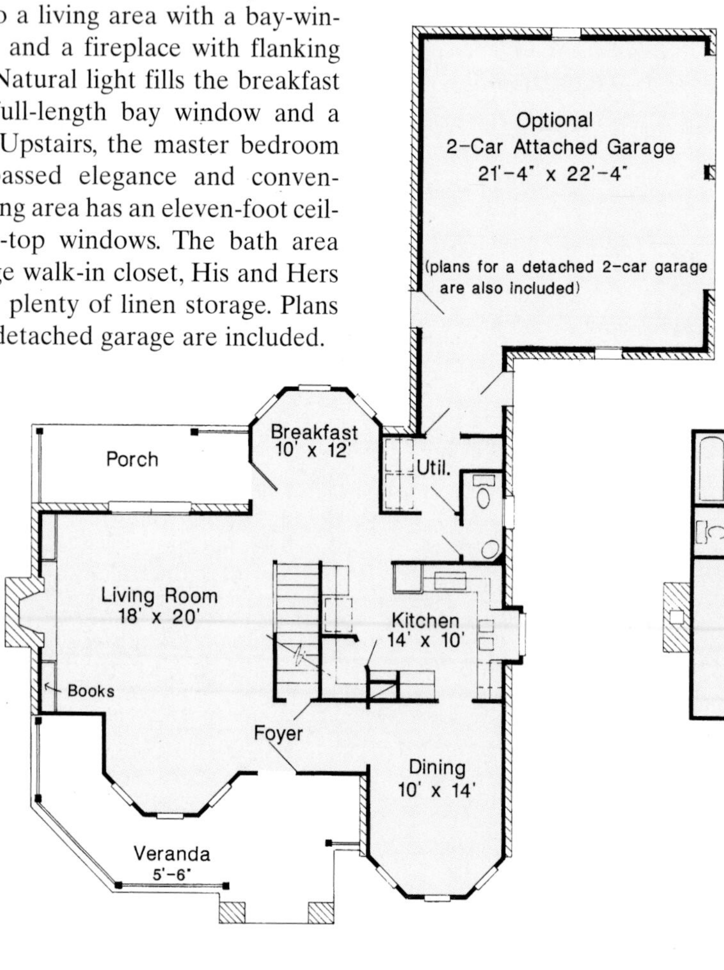
Optional
2-Car Attached Garage
21'-4" x 22'-4"
(plans for a detached 2-car garage are also included)
Breakfast
10' x 12'
Porch
Util.
Living Room
18' x 20'
Kitchen
14' x 10'
Books
Foyer
Dining
10' x 14'
Veranda
5'-6"

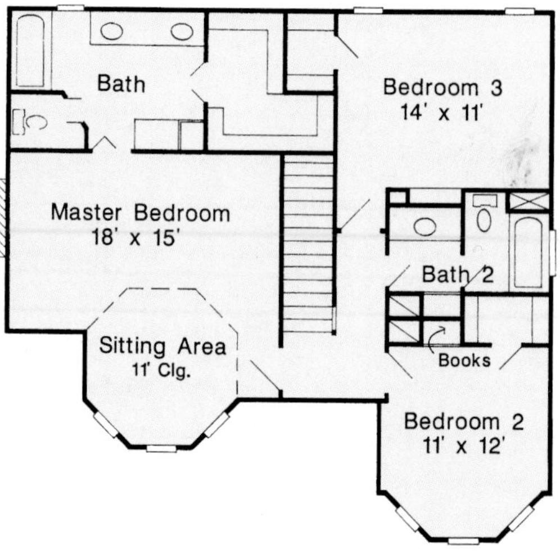
Bath
Bedroom 3
14' x 11'
Master Bedroom
18' x 15'
Bath 2
Sitting Area
11' Clg.
Books
Bedroom 2
11' x 12'

© 1990 Donald A. Gardner Architects, Inc.
B. NATHAN

A wraparound covered porch at the front and sides of this home and the open deck with spa and seating provide plenty of outside living area. A central great room features a vaulted ceiling, fireplace and clerestory windows above. The loft/study on the second floor overlooks this gathering area. Besides a formal dining room, kitchen, breakfast room and sun room on the first floor, there is also a generous master suite with a garden tub. Three second-floor bedrooms complete the sleeping accommodations.

Design HPT830005

First Floor: 1,734 square feet
Second Floor: 958 square feet
Total: 2,692 square feet
Width 55'-0" Depth 59'-10"

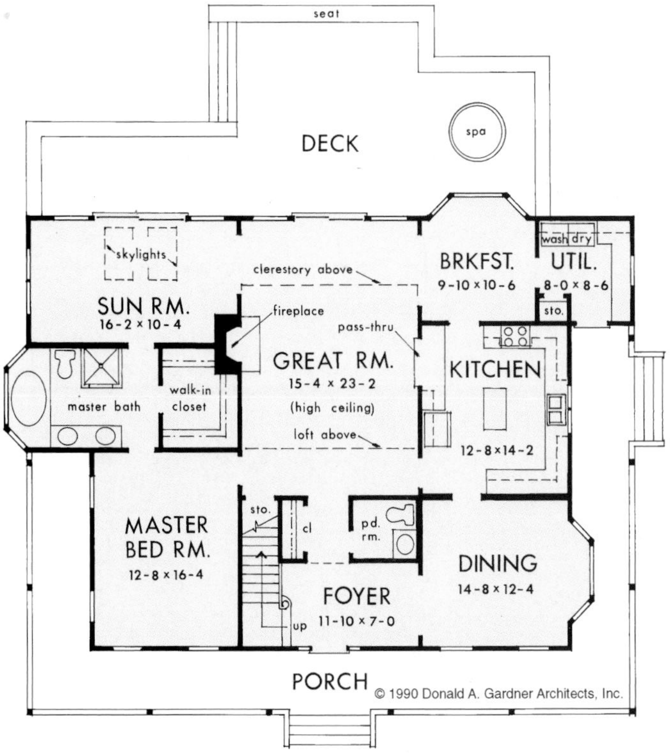
seat
DECK
spa
skylights
clerestory above
SUN RM.
16-2 x 10-4
fireplace
pass-thru
GREAT RM.
15-4 x 23-2
(high ceiling)
loft above
BRKFST.
9-10 x 10-6
wash dry
UTIL.
8-0 x 8-6
sto.
KITCHEN
12-8 x 14-2
master bath
walk-in closet
MASTER BED RM.
12-8 x 16-4
sto.
cl
pd. rm.
FOYER
11-10 x 7-0
up
DINING
14-8 x 12-4
PORCH
© 1990 Donald A. Gardner Architects, Inc.

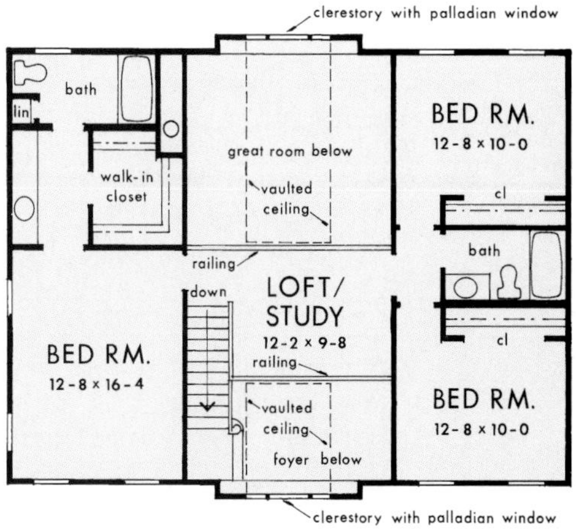
clerestory with palladian window
bath
lin
walk-in closet
great room below
vaulted ceiling
BED RM.
12-8 x 10-0
cl
bath
railing
down
LOFT/ STUDY
12-2 x 9-8
railing
BED RM.
12-8 x 16-4
vaulted ceiling
foyer below
cl
BED RM.
12-8 x 10-0
clerestory with palladian window

This home, as shown in the photograph, may differ from the actual blueprints. For more detailed information, please check the floor plans carefully.
Photography by Scott Moore, MWS Photography

Design HPT830006

First Floor: 1,804 square feet

Second Floor: 1,041 square feet

Total: 2,845 square feet

Width 57'-3" Depth 71'-0"

There's a feeling of old Charleston in this stately home—particularly on the quiet side porch that wraps around the kitchen and breakfast room. The interior of this home revolves around a spacious great room with a welcoming fireplace. The left wing is dedicated to the master suite, which boasts wide views of the rear property. A corner kitchen easily serves planned events in the formal dining room as well as family meals in the breakfast area. Three family bedrooms, one with a private bath and the others sharing a bath, are tucked upstairs. This home is designed with a walkout basement foundation.

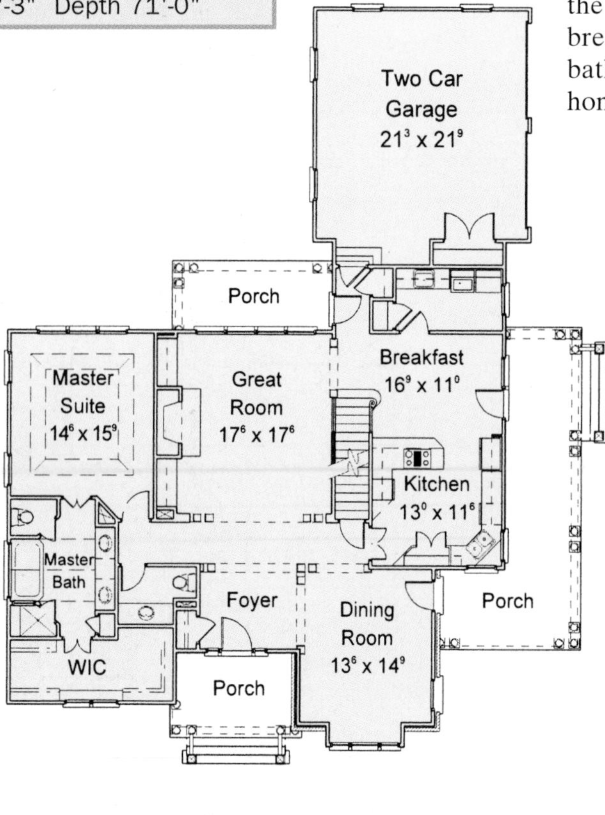

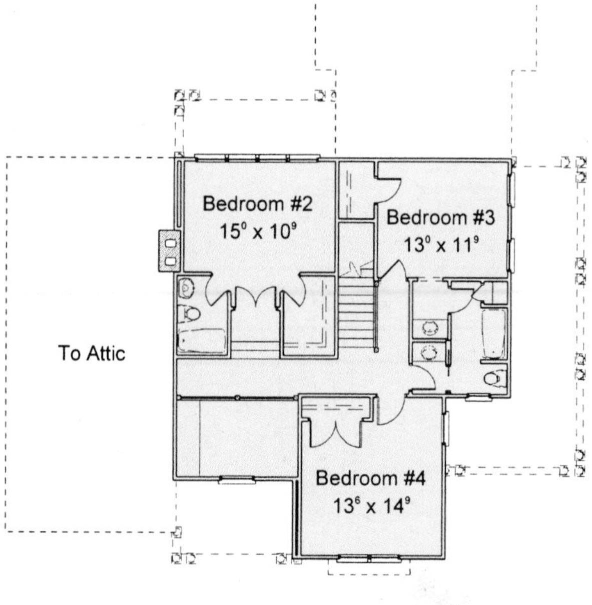

This home, as shown in the photograph, may differ from the actual blueprints. For more detailed information, please check the floor plans carefully. Photo courtesy of Design Basics, Inc.

Growing families will love this unique plan, which combines all the essentials with an abundance of stylish touches. Start with the living area—a spacious great room with high ceilings, windows overlooking the backyard, a through-fireplace to the kitchen and access to the rear yard. The master suite, with a whirlpool tub and walk-in closet, is found downstairs while three family bedrooms are upstairs.

Design HPT830007

First Floor: 1,421 square feet
Second Floor: 578 square feet
Total: 1,999 square feet
Width 52'-0" Depth 47'-4"

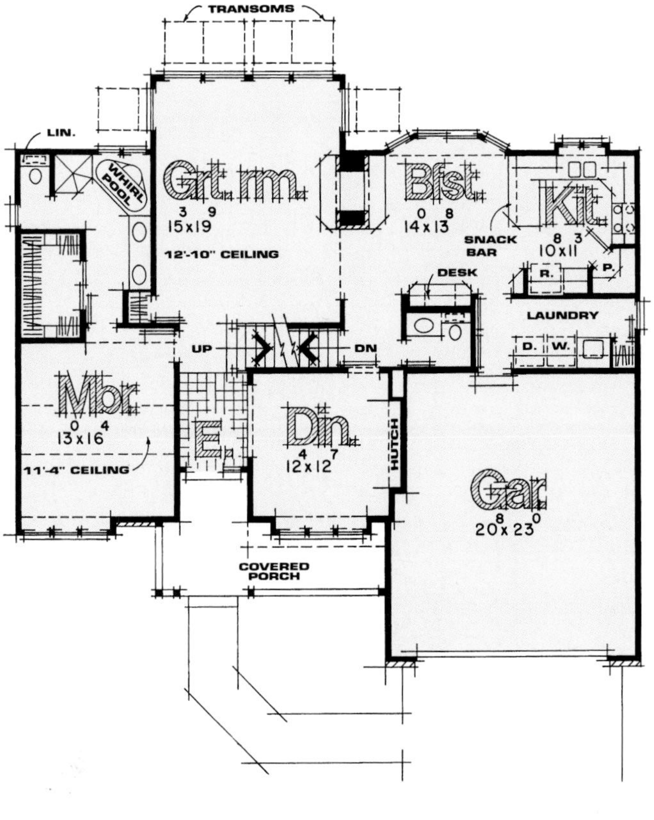

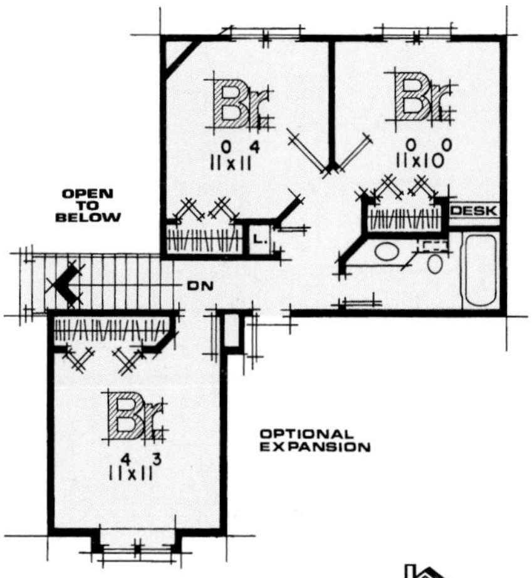

QUOTE ONE®
Cost to build? See page 516 to order complete cost estimate to build this house in your area!

The charming exterior of this beautiful traditional home conceals a perfect family plan. The formal dining and living rooms reside on either side of the foyer. At the rear of the home is a family room with a fireplace and access to a deck and veranda. The modern kitchen features a sunlit breakfast area. The second floor provides four bedrooms, one of which may be finished at a later date and used as a guest suite. Note the extra storage space in the two-car garage. This home is designed with a walkout basement foundation.

Design HPT830008

First Floor: 1,205 square feet
Second Floor: 1,160 square feet
Total: 2,365 square feet
Bonus Space: 350 square feet
Width 52'-6" Depth 43'-6"

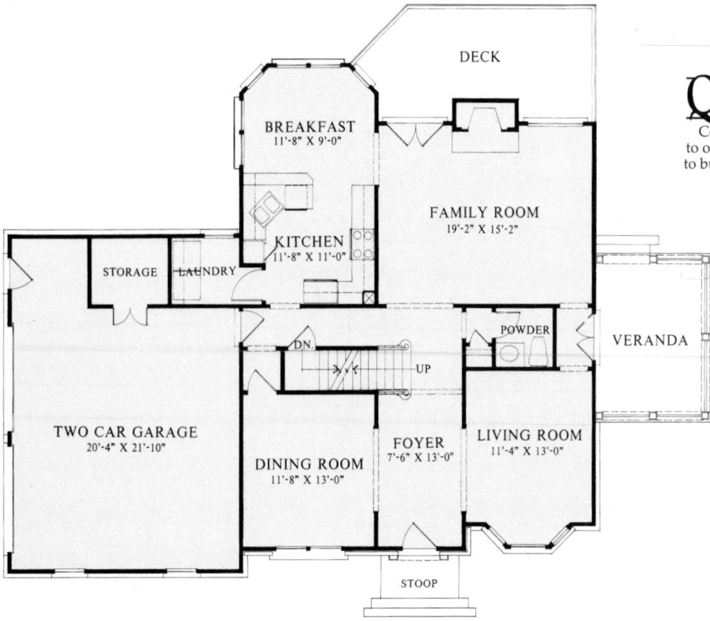

QUOTE ONE®
Cost to build? See page 516 to order complete cost estimate to build this house in your area!

This home, as shown in the photograph, may differ from the actual blueprints. For more detailed information, please check the floor plans carefully.
Photo courtesy of Living Concepts

With a varied facade and European influences, this home has excellent curb appeal. Enter through the foyer to be greeted by an enormous gathering room with an extended-hearth fireplace. To the left, the modified U-shaped kitchen conveniently serves both the breakfast nook and the formal dining room. The first floor also features a living room/study and a pampering master suite with a spa-style bath and tray ceilings. The second floor overlooks the gathering room and includes two family bedrooms with a shared bath and a loft.

Design HPT830009

First Floor: 2,042 square feet
Second Floor: 710 square feet
Total: 2,752 square feet
Width 65'-4" Depth 61'-8"

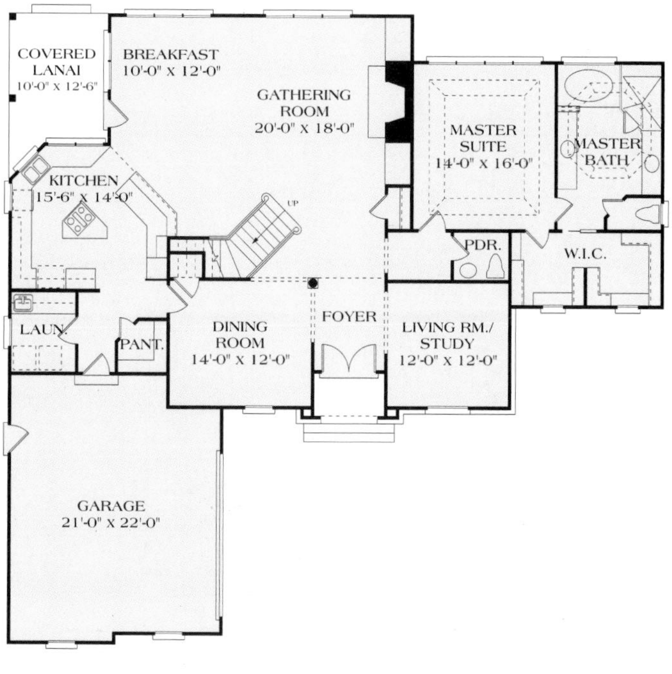

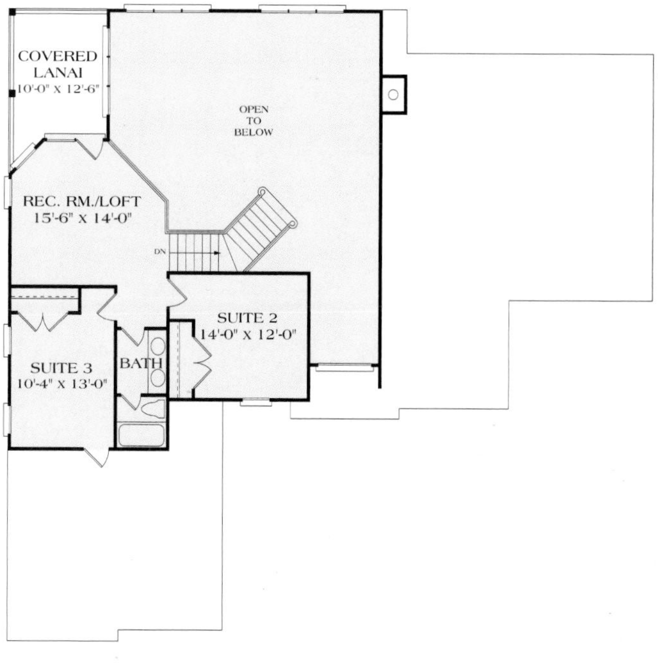

This home, as shown in the photograph, may differ from the actual blueprints. For more detailed information, please check the floor plans carefully.
Photo by Jerry Atnip

The Ashley, a home of elegant Georgian architecture, is reminiscent of the grand homes in the battery section of Charleston, South Carolina. The impressive entry opens to the foyer with its grand staircase. To the right is the library and to the left, the formal dining room. The foyer leads on to the family room where a window wall looks out to the covered porch. A central hall passes the study and proceeds to the luxurious master suite. The left wing holds the breakfast area, kitchen, mudroom and garage. Upstairs three bedrooms enjoy separate and private baths.

Design HPT830010

First Floor: 2,968 square feet
Second Floor: 1,521 square feet
Total: 4,489 square feet
Bonus Space: 522 square feet
Width 82'-6" Depth 81'-8"

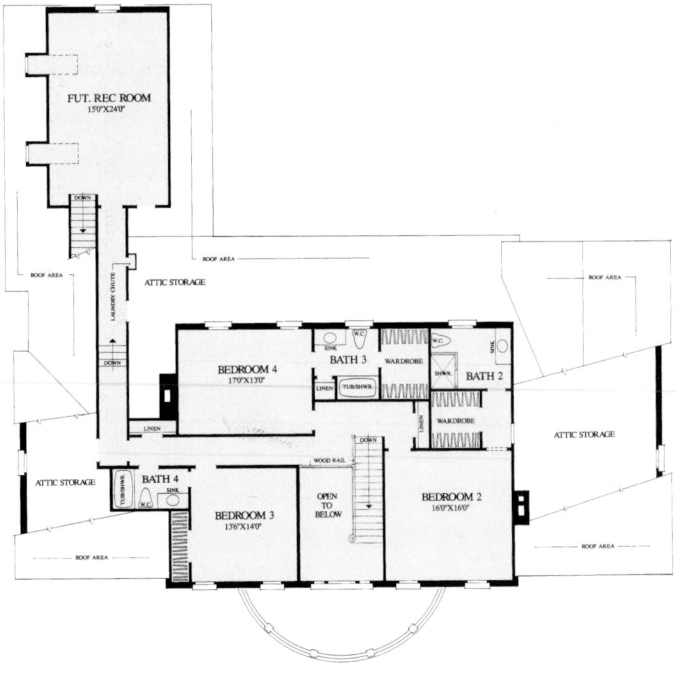

This home, as shown in the photograph, may differ from the actual blueprints. For more detailed information, please check the floor plans carefully.
Photo by Steve Diggs

GARAGE
21'0"X23'0"
TERRACE
STORAGE
UTILITY
WASH
DRY
SINK
BEDROOM 4
11'0"X13'0"
BATH 3
W.C.
TUB/SHWR
BROOM
PORCH
BREAKFAST
AREA
14'6"X12'0"
FAMILY ROOM
18'0"X19'0"
VAULTED TRAY
CEILING
BOOKCASE
ENTERTAINMENT CENTER
DORIC COLUMNS
MASTER BEDROOM
15'0"X19'0"
SHWR.
WHIRLPOOL
TUB
W.C.
MASTER BATH
LINEN
WARDROBE
S.U.
OVENS
KITCHEN
16'0"X13'0"
SINK
SINK
REFG.
PANTRY
DESK
DINING ROOM
16'0"X14'0"
LIVING ROOM
18'6"X13'0"
POWDER
ROOM
W.C.
FOYER
BEDROOM 3
15'6"X13'0"
BEDROOM 2
16'0"X13'8"
BATH 2
LINEN
W.C.
TUB/SHWR
PORTICO

The elegant entry of this Colonial home gives it a stately appearance with its columns and pediment. Inside, the entry opens to the living room where the first of two fireplaces is found. The formal dining room adjoins both the living room and the kitchen. The spacious breakfast area looks out onto the patio. The master suite is found on the right with two additional bedrooms while a fourth bedroom is on the left giving privacy for overnight guests.

Design

HPT830011

Square Footage: 3,136

Width 80'-6" Depth 72'-4"

This home, as shown in the photograph, may differ from the actual blueprints. For more detailed information, please check the floor plans carefully.
Photo courtesy of General Shale Brick, photo by Peter Montanti

Southern grandeur is evident in this wonderful two-story design with its magnificent second-floor balcony. The formal living spaces—dining room and living room—flank the impressive foyer with its stunning staircase. The family room resides in the rear, opening to the terrace. The sunny breakfast bay adjoins the island kitchen for efficient planning. The right wing holds the two-car garage, utility room, a secondary staircase and a study that can easily be converted to a guest suite with a private bath. The master suite and Bedrooms 2 and 3 are placed on the second floor.

Design HPT830012

First Floor: 2,033 square feet
Second Floor: 1,447 square feet
Total: 3,480 square feet
Bonus Space: 411 square feet
Width 67'-10" Depth 64'-4"

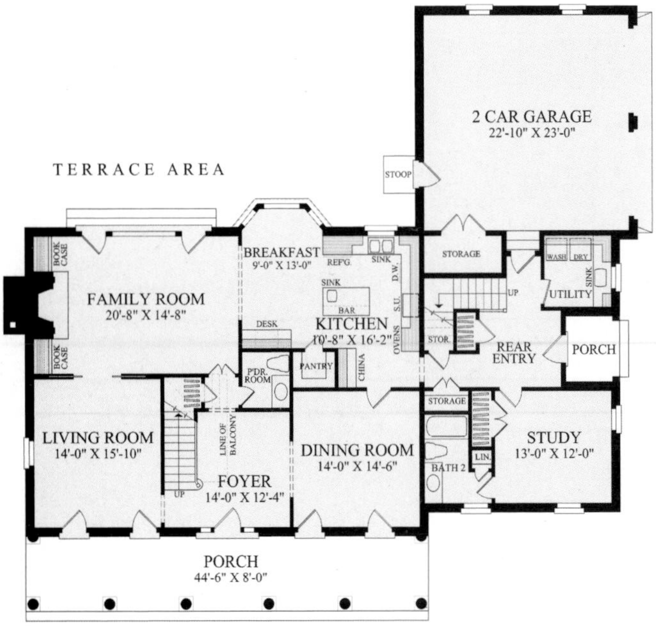

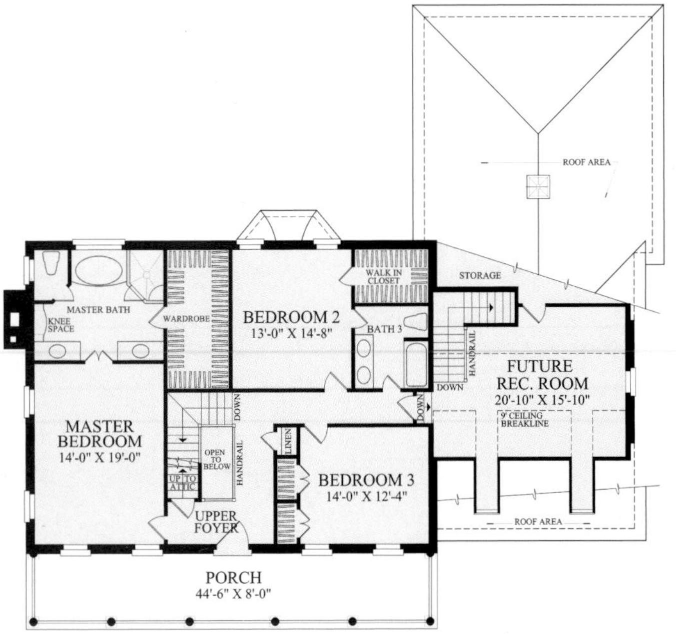

This home, as shown in the photograph, may differ from the actual blueprints. For more detailed information, please check the floor plans carefully.

This two-story home suits the needs of each household member. Family gatherings are not crowded with a spacious family room, which is adjacent to the kitchen and the breakfast area. Just beyond the foyer, the dining and living rooms have a view to the front yard. The master bedroom features its own full bath with dual-vanities, whirlpool tub and separate shower. Three family bedrooms are available upstairs—one with a walk-in closet—and two full hall baths. Extra storage space is found in the two car garage.

Design HPT830013

First Floor: 1,273 square feet
Second Floor: 1,358 square feet
Total: 2,631 square feet
Width 54'-10" Depth 48'-6"

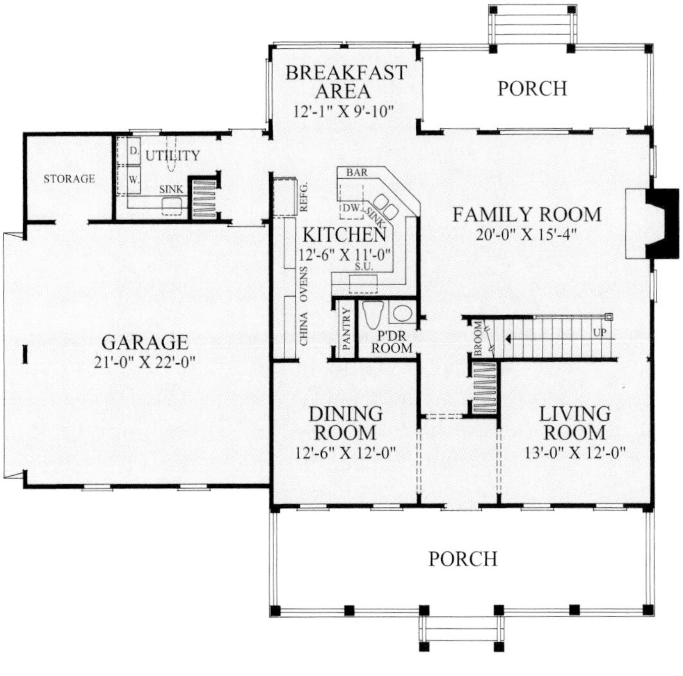

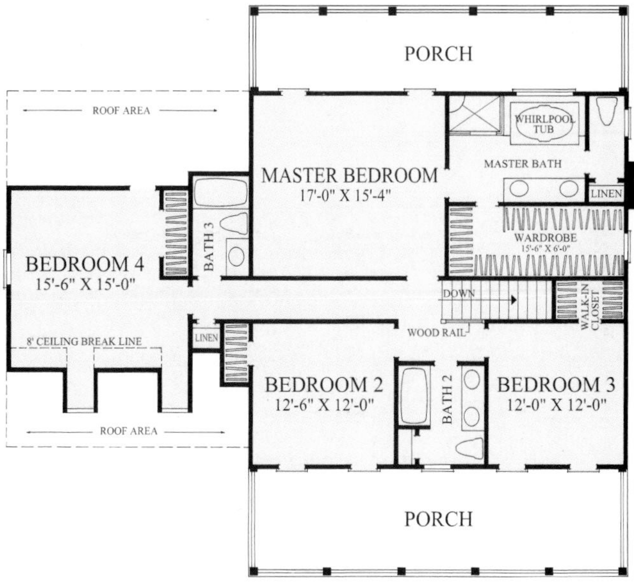

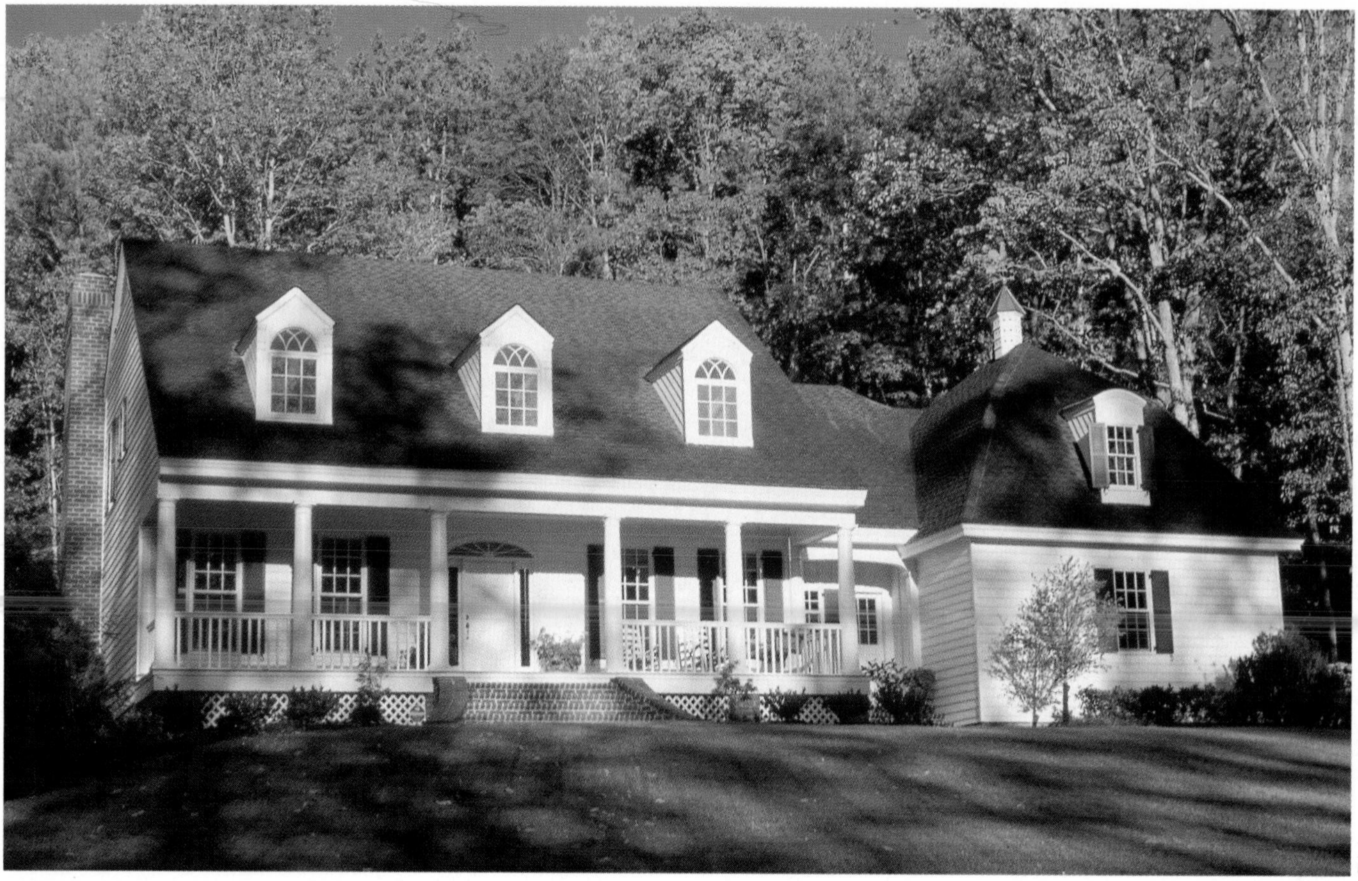

This home, as shown in the photograph, may differ from the actual blueprints. For more detailed information, please check the floor plans carefully.
Photo by Steve Diggs

Design
HPT830014

First Floor: 1,927 square feet
Second Floor: 879 square feet
Total: 2,806 square feet
Bonus Space: 459 square feet
Width 71'-0" Depth 53'-0"

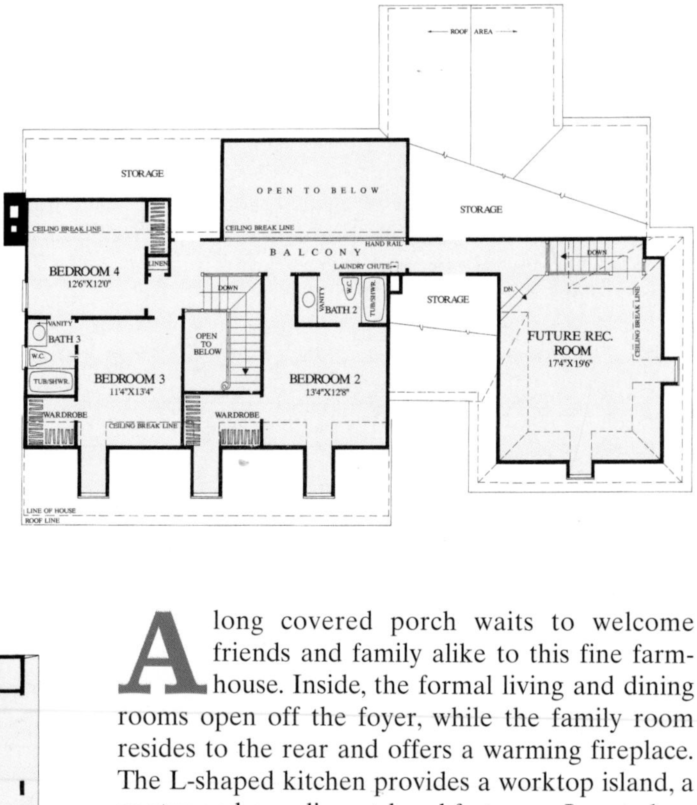

A long covered porch waits to welcome friends and family alike to this fine farmhouse. Inside, the formal living and dining rooms open off the foyer, while the family room resides to the rear and offers a warming fireplace. The L-shaped kitchen provides a worktop island, a pantry and an adjacent breakfast area. Located on the first floor for privacy, the master suite features a huge walk-in closet, lavish bath and private outdoor access. Upstairs, three bedrooms share two full baths and a balcony overlook to the family room. A future space is offered over the two-car garage.

This home, as shown in the photograph, may differ from the actual blueprints. For more detailed information, please check the floor plans carefully.
Photo courtesy of Islands of Beaufort, Beaufort SC

This Bayou Cottage is the perfect setting for festive occasions punctuated by the laughter of friends and family. The inviting front porch announces the foyer that opens to the living room, family room and dining room. The kitchen is conveniently placed between the sunny breakfast area and the formal dining room. Three bedrooms share a full bath on the second floor while the luxurious master suite finds seclusion on the first floor.

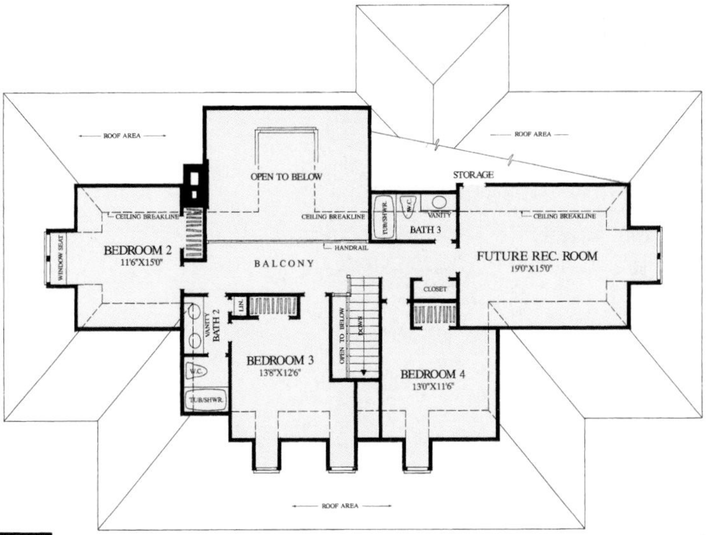

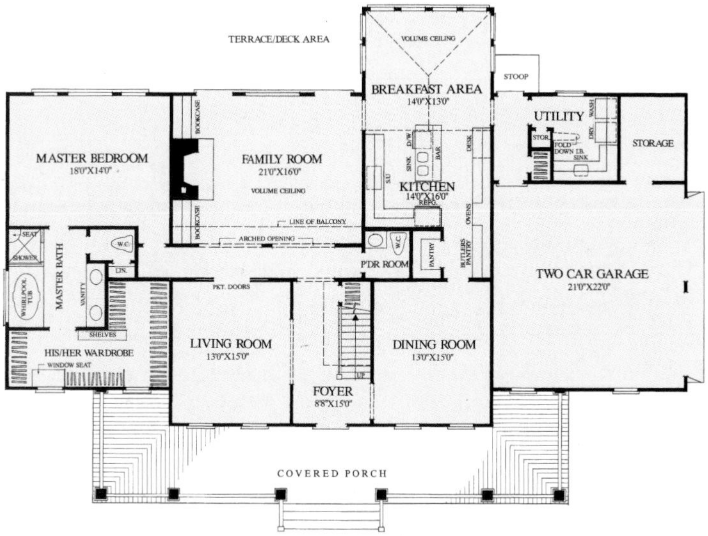

Design HPT830015

First Floor: 2,142 square feet
Second Floor: 960 square feet
Total: 3,102 square feet
Bonus Space: 327 square feet
Width 75'-8" Depth 53'-0"

This home, as shown in the photograph, may differ from the actual blueprints. For more detailed information, please check the floor plans carefully.
Photo courtesy of Islands of Beaufort, Beaufort, SC

Design HPT830016

First Floor: 1,704 square feet
Second Floor: 734 square feet
Total: 2,438 square feet
Bonus Space: 479 square feet
Width 50'-0" Depth 82'-6"

Elegant country—that's one way to describe this attractive three-bedroom home. Inside, comfort is evidently the theme, with the formal dining room flowing into the U-shaped kitchen and casual dining taking place in the sunny breakfast area. The spacious, vaulted great room offers a fireplace and built-ins. The first-floor master suite is complete with a walk-in closet, a whirlpool tub and a separate shower. Upstairs, the sleeping quarters include two family bedrooms with private baths and walk-in closets.

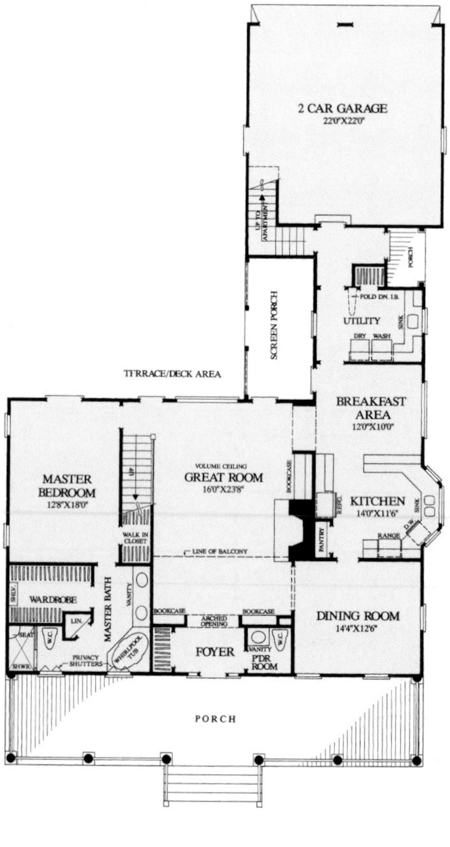

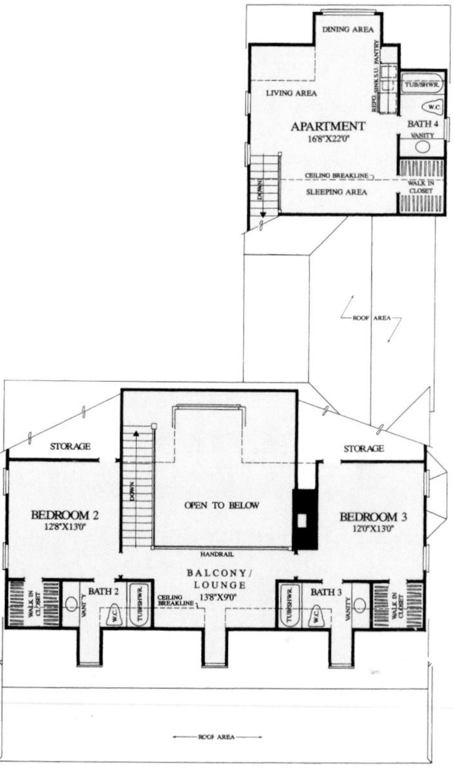

This home, as shown in the photograph, may differ from the actual blueprints. For more detailed information, please check the floor plans carefully.
Photo courtesy of Islands of Beaufort, Beaufort SC

Where creeks converge and marsh grasses sway in gentle breezes, this is a classical low country home. Steep rooflines, high ceilings, front and back porches plus long and low windows are typical details of these charming planters' cottages. The foyer is flanked by the formal dining room, and the living room, which opens to the family room. Here several windows look out to the terrace and a fireplace removes the chill on a winter's night. The sunny breakfast room, which adjoins the kitchen, offers a wonderful space for casual dining. Two bedrooms, the lavish master suite and the two-car garage complete the floor plan.

Design HPT830017

First Floor: 1,883 square feet
Second Floor: 803 square feet
Total: 2,686 square feet
Bonus Space: 489 square feet
Width 63'-0" Depth 81'-10"

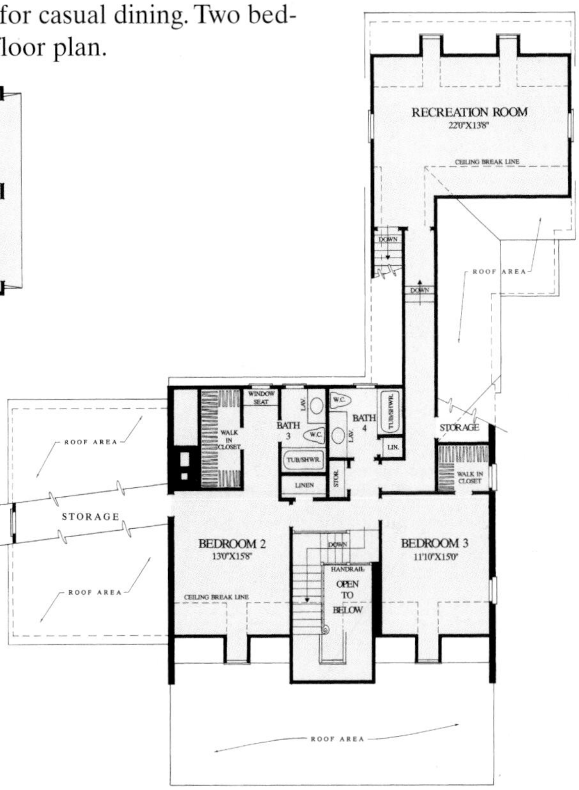

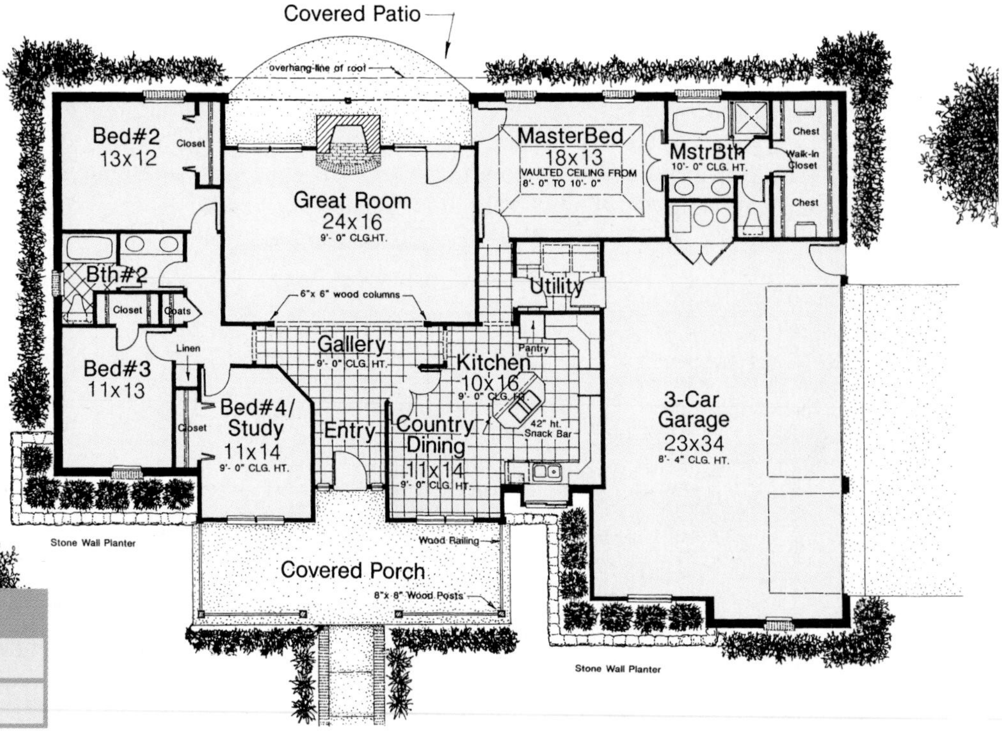
Covered Patio
overhang-line of roof
Bed#2
13x12
Closet
Great Room
24x16
9'- 0" CLG.HT.
MasterBed
18x13
VAULTED CEILING FROM
8'- 0" TO 10'- 0"
MstrBth
10'- 0" CLG. HT.
Chest
Walk-in
Closet
Chest
Bth#2
Closet
Coats
6"x 6" wood columns
Utility
Pantry
Linen
Gallery
9'- 0" CLG. HT.
Kitchen
10x16
Bed#3
11x13
Bed#4/
Study
11x14
9'- 0" CLG. HT.
Closet
Entry
Country
Dining
11x14
9'- 0" CLG. HT.
42" ht.
Snack Bar
3-Car
Garage
23x34
8'- 4" CLG. HT.
Stone Wall Planter
Wood Railing
Covered Porch
8"x 8" Wood Posts
Stone Wall Planter

Design

HPT830018

Square Footage: 2,078

Width 75'-0" Depth 47'-10"

Colonial style meets farmhouse style, furnishing old-fashioned charisma with a flourish. From the entry, double doors open to the country dining room and a large island kitchen. Nearby, the spacious great room takes center stage and is warmed by a fireplace flanked by large windows. Tucked behind the three-car garage, the secluded master suite features a vaulted ceiling in the bedroom. The master bath contains a relaxing tub, double-bowl vanity, separate shower and compartmented toilet. Beyond the bath is a huge walk-in closet with two built-in chests. Three family bedrooms—one doubles as a study or home office—a full bath and a utility room complete the plan.

Design HPT830019

Square Footage: 2,387
Bonus Space: 400 square feet
Width 69'-6" Depth 68'-11"

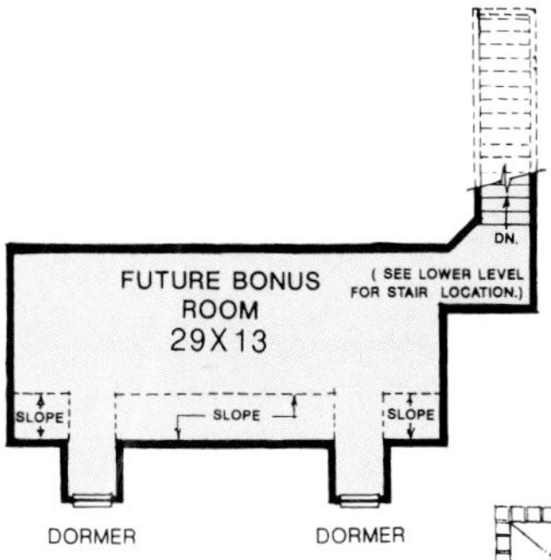

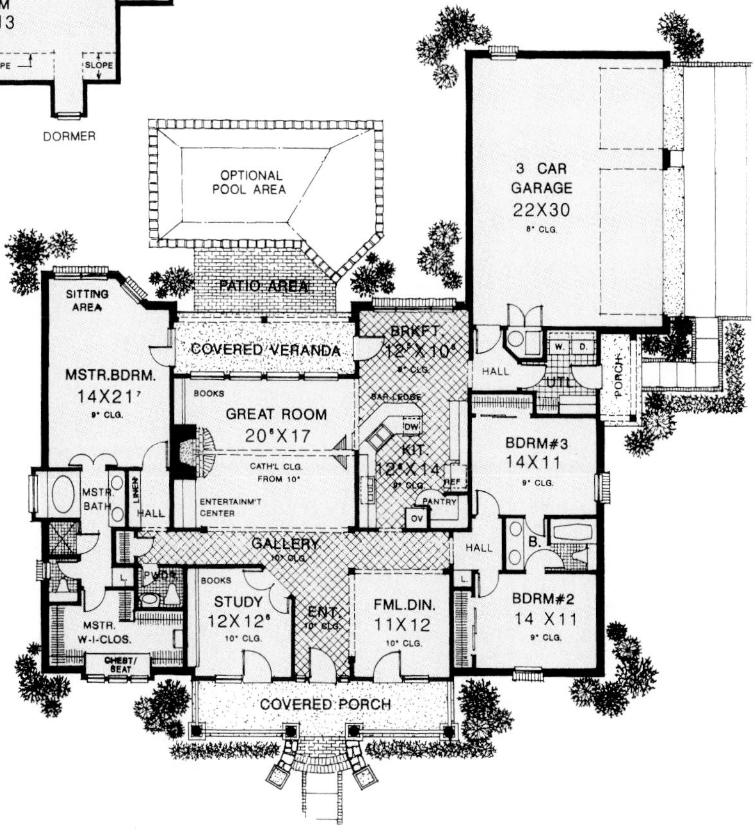

This three-bedroom home brings the past to life with Tuscan columns, dormers and fanlight windows. At the entrance is the dining room and study at either side. The great room boasts cathedral ceilings and a fireplace. The spacious kitchen adjoins a breakfast nook and accesses the rear covered veranda. The master bedroom enjoys a sitting area, access to the covered veranda, a spacious bathroom with a bumped-out tub and a walk-in closet. This home is complete with two family bedrooms.

This traditional design welcomes family and visitors with a bay window, a Palladian window and shutters. The interior plan starts with the formal dining room and the central great room with a fireplace and access to outdoor spaces. The kitchen features an angled eating bar, a pantry and lots of cabinet and counter space. The master suite boasts a high ceiling, a deluxe bath and a walk-in closet with a window. Nearby, Bedrooms 2 and 3 share a hall bath. Please specify crawlspace or slab foundation when ordering.

Design
HPT830020

Square Footage: 1,742

Width 78'-0" Depth 40'-10"

L

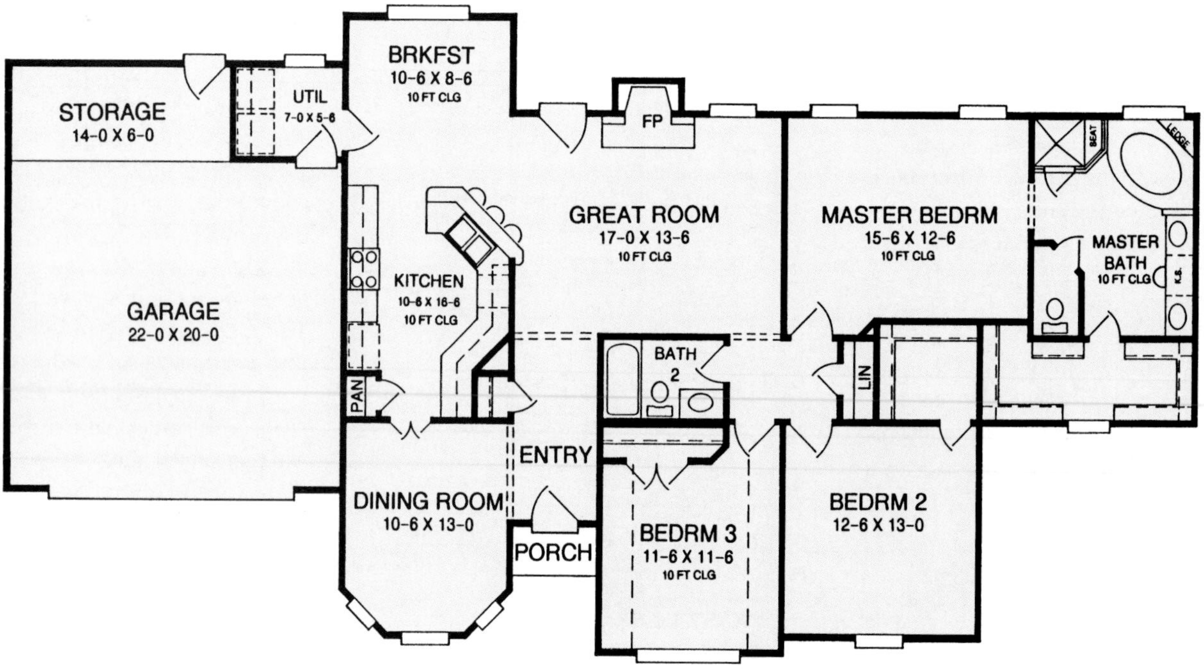
BRKFST
10-6 X 8-6
10 FT CLG
STORAGE
14-0 X 6-0
UTIL
7-0 X 5-6
FP
GREAT ROOM
17-0 X 13-6
10 FT CLG
MASTER BEDRM
15-6 X 12-6
10 FT CLG
MASTER BATH
10 FT CLG
KITCHEN
10-6 X 16-6
10 FT CLG
GARAGE
22-0 X 20-0
BATH
2
LIN
PAN
ENTRY
DINING ROOM
10-6 X 13-0
PORCH
BEDRM 3
11-6 X 11-6
10 FT CLG
BEDRM 2
12-6 X 13-0

Design

HPT830021

Square Footage: 1,849

Width 60'-0" Depth 57'-4"

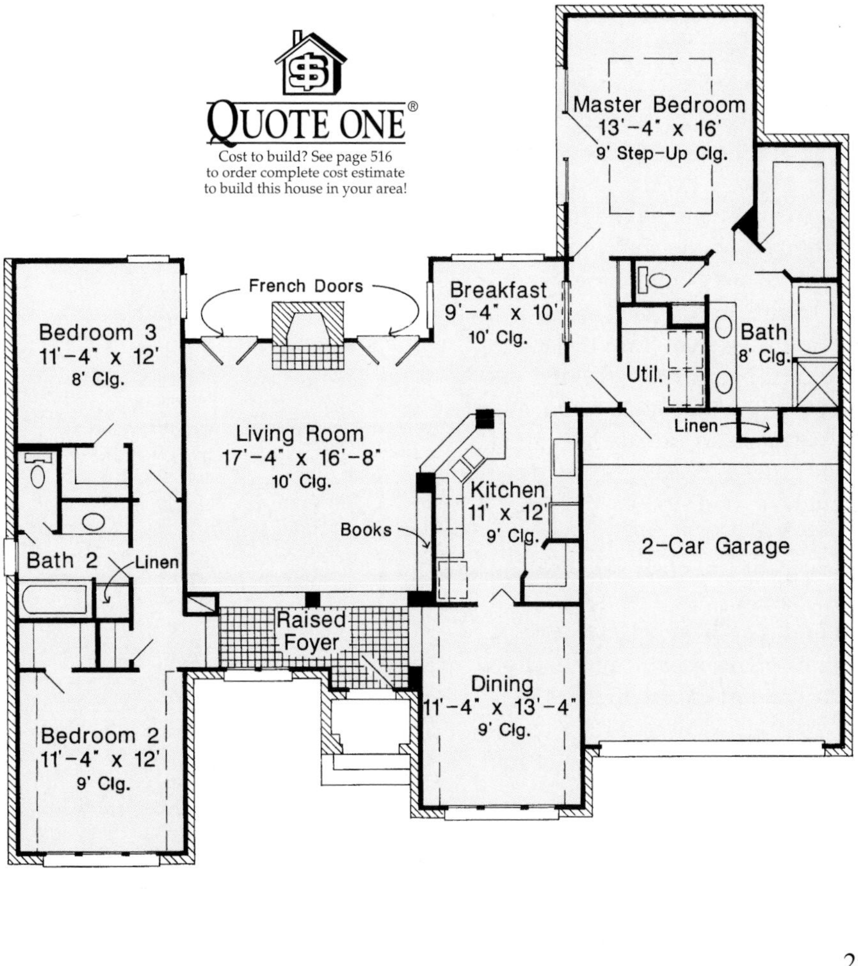
Master Bedroom
13'-4" x 16'
9' Step-Up Clg.
French Doors
Breakfast
9'-4" x 10'
10' Clg.
Bedroom 3
11'-4" x 12'
8' Clg.
Bath
8' Clg.
Util.
Linen
Living Room
17'-4" x 16'-8"
10' Clg.
Kitchen
11' x 12'
9' Clg.
Books
2-Car Garage
Bath 2
Linen
Raised Foyer
Dining
11'-4" x 13'-4"
9' Clg.
Bedroom 2
11'-4" x 12'
9' Clg.

A wonderful floor plan is found on the interior of this cozy one-story plan. The large living room and conveniently placed dining room both open from the raised foyer. In between is the galley kitchen with a huge pantry and an attached breakfast area. French doors flanking the fireplace in the living room open to the rear yard. To the right of the plan is the master bedroom with a walk-in closet and double lavatories. To the left of the plan are two family bedrooms sharing a full bath.

Design

HPT830022

Square Footage: 1,945	
Width 56'-6" Depth 52'-6"	

Corner quoins and keystones above graceful window treatments have long been a hallmark of elegant European-style exteriors—this home has all that and more. This becomes apparent upon entering the foyer, which is beautifully framed by columns in the dining room and the entrance to the vaulted great room. The left wing holds three secondary bedrooms—one doubles as a study—and a full bath. To the right of the combined kitchen and vaulted breakfast room, you will find the private master suite. A relaxing master bath and a large walk-in closet complete this splendid retreat. Please specify basement or crawlspace foundation when ordering.

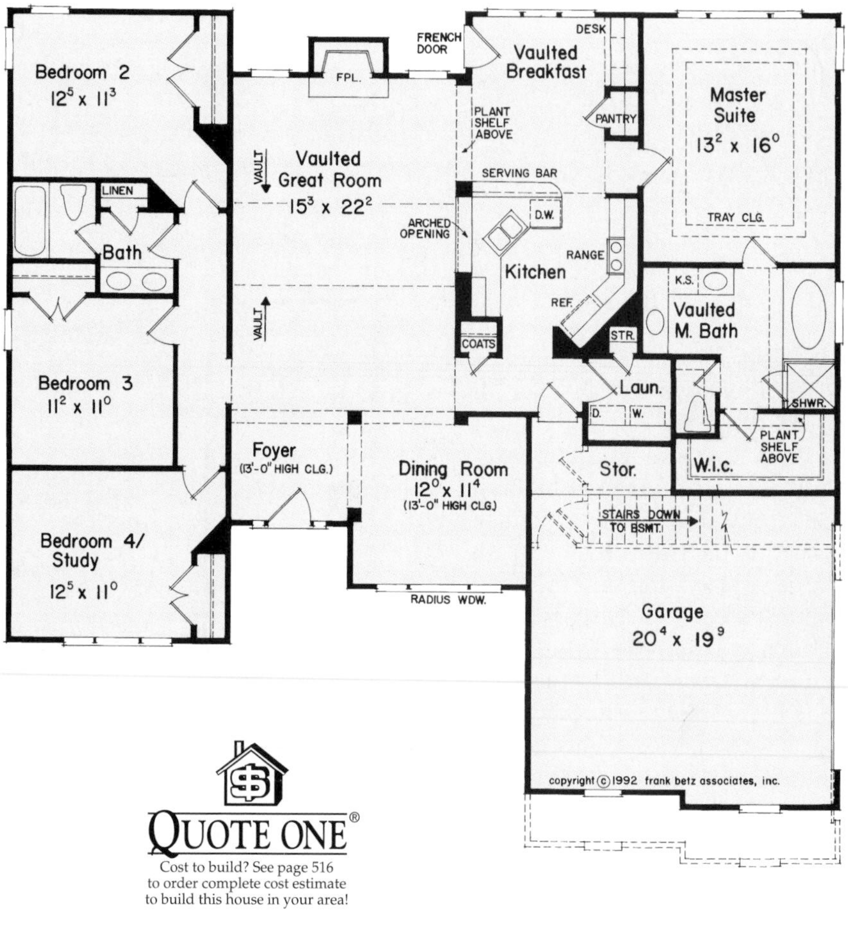

QUOTE ONE®

Cost to build? See page 516 to order complete cost estimate to build this house in your area!

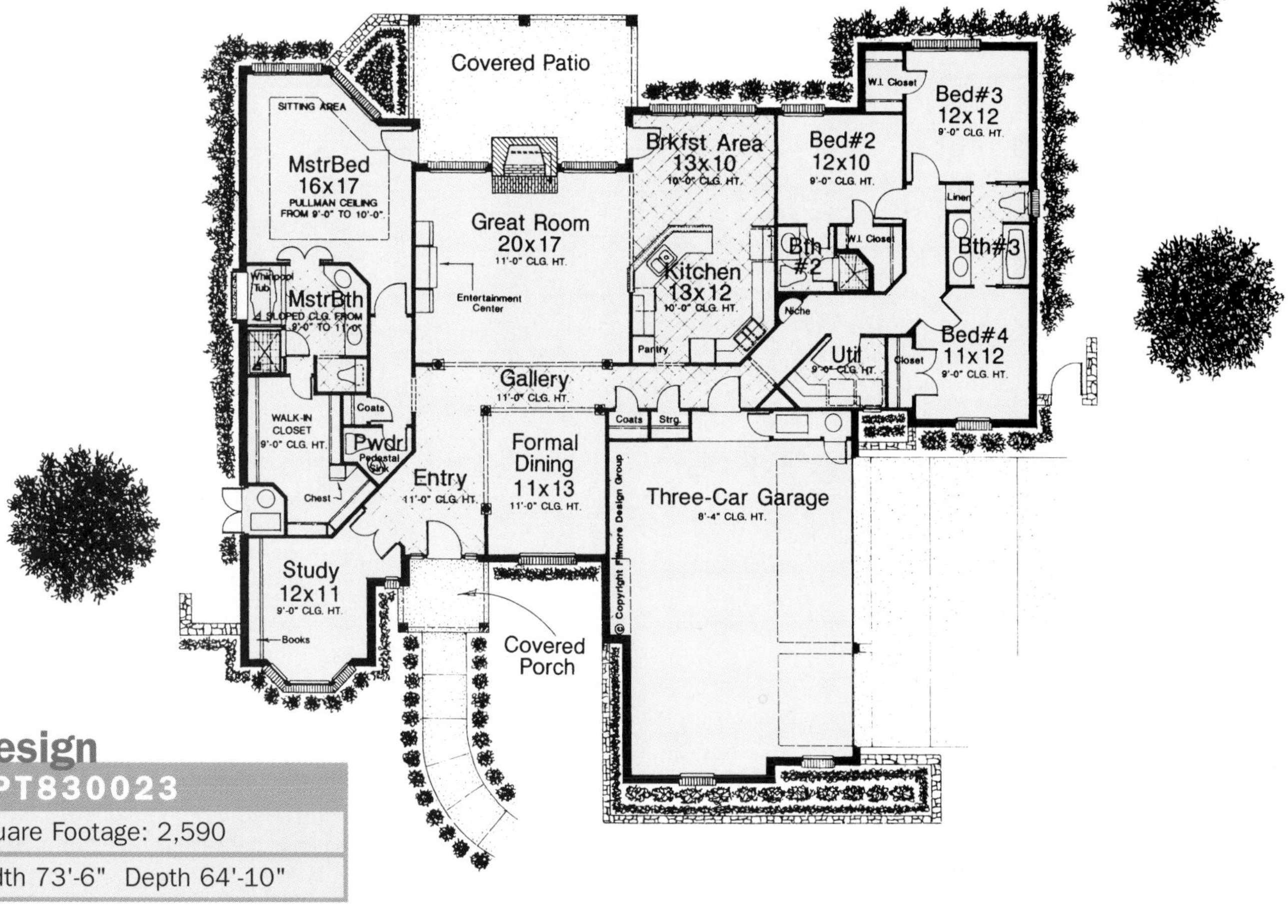

Design HPT830023

Square Footage: 2,590

Width 73'-6" Depth 64'-10"

With a solid exterior of rough cedar and stone, this new French country design will stand the test of time. A wood-paneled study in the front features a large bay window. The heart of the house is found in a large open great room with a built-in entertainment center. The spacious master bedroom features a corner reading area and access to an adjacent covered patio. A three-car garage and three additional bedrooms complete this generous family home.

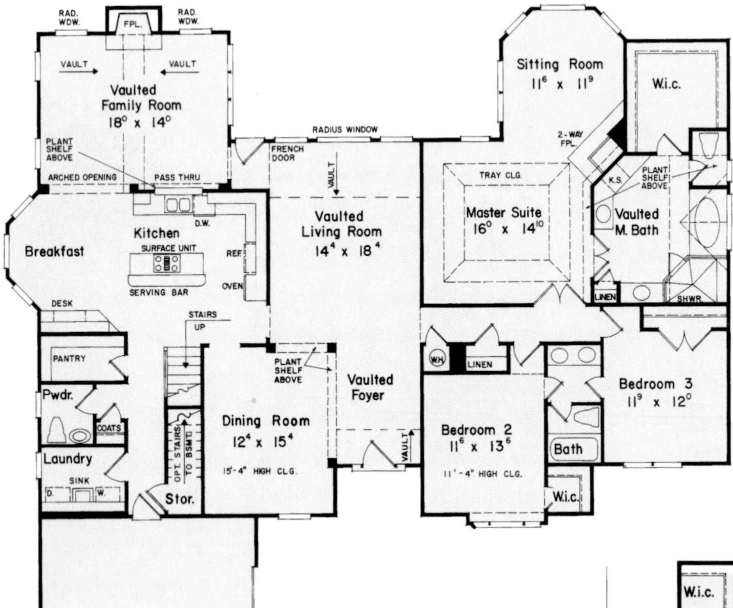

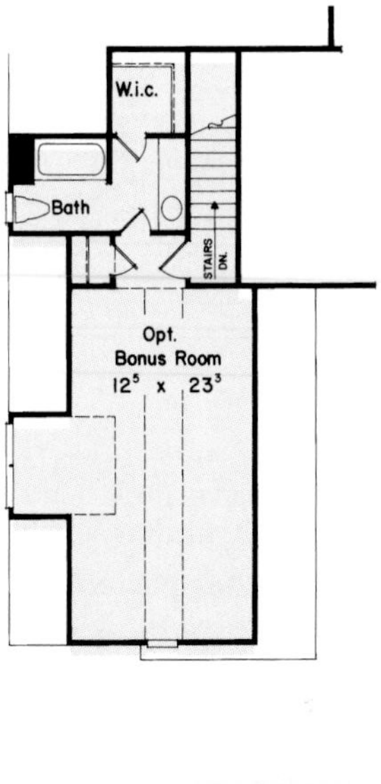

Design HPT830024

Square Footage: 2,622
Bonus Space: 478 square feet
Width 69'-0" Depth 71'-4"

Striking design and an open floor plan contribute to the gracious atmosphere of this one-story home. The front-facing dining room is set off from the foyer and formal living room with columns, creating an open, yet elegant area for entertaining. A vaulted ceiling and fireplace accent the family room. Sleeping quarters are headlined with a luxurious master suite that's designed for relaxing with a sunny sitting room, three-sided fireplace and a spa bath. Two family bedrooms privately access a compartmented bath. The optional bonus room would make a comfortable guest suite. Please specify basement or crawlspace foundation when ordering.

This home, as shown in the photograph, may differ from the actual blueprints. For more detailed information, please check the floor plans carefully.
Photo by Oscar Thompson Photography

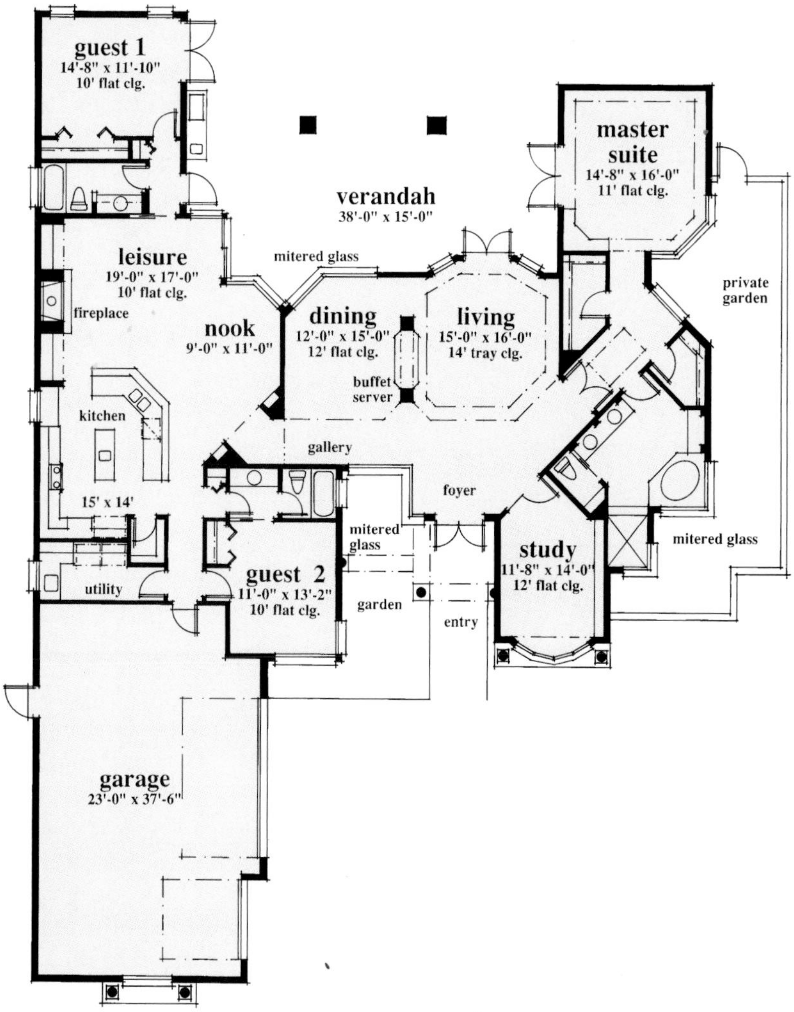

Design

HPT830025

Square Footage: 2,794

Width 70'-0" Depth 98'-0"

L

Classic columns, circle-head windows and a bay-windowed study give this stucco home a wonderful street presence. The foyer leads to the formal living and dining areas. The kitchen, nook and leisure room are grouped for informal living. Two secondary suites have guest baths and offer full privacy from the master wing. The master suite hosts a private garden area, while the master bath features a walk-in shower that overlooks the garden and a water-closet room with space for books or a television.

This home, as shown in the photograph, may differ from the actual blueprints. For more detailed information, please check the floor plans carefully.
Photo by Dave Dawson

Design HPT830026

First Floor: 2,208 square feet
Second Floor: 1,250 square feet
Total: 3,458 square feet
Width 60'-6" Depth 60'-0"

QUOTE ONE®

Cost to build? See page 516 to order complete cost estimate to build this house in your area!

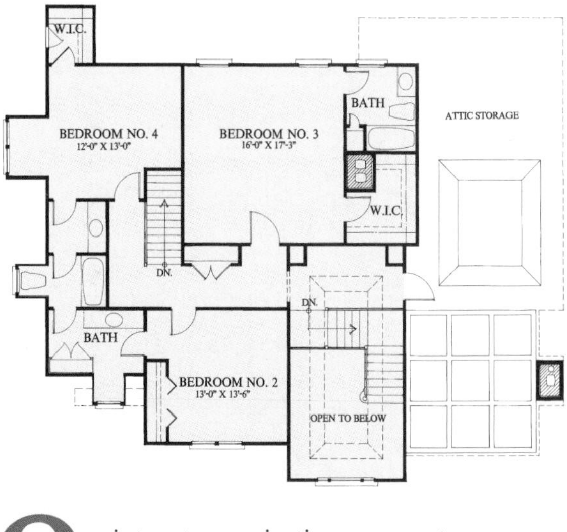

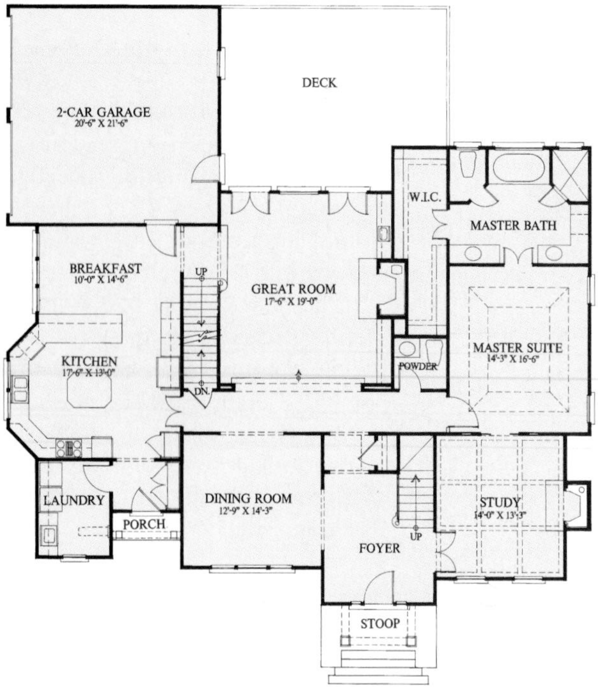

Quaint, yet as majestic as a country manor on the Rhine, this European-style stucco home enjoys the enchantment of arched windows to underscore its charm. The two-story foyer leads through French doors to the study with its own hearth and coffered ceiling. Coupled with this cozy sanctuary is the master suite with a tray ceiling and large accommodating bath. The large sunken great room is highlighted by a fireplace, built-in bookcases, lots of glass and easy access to a back stair and large gourmet kitchen. Three secondary bedrooms reside upstairs. One spacious upstairs bedroom gives guests the ultimate in convenience with a private bath and walk-in closet. This home is designed with a walkout basement foundation.

This home, as shown in the photograph, may differ from the actual blueprints. For more detailed information, please check the floor plans carefully.
Photo by Robert Starling

Sloping rooflines and romantic shuttered windows give this home a chalet feel. Upon entering, the aptly named grand room is straight ahead, complete with a wet bar and opening to the gathering room—with fireplace—and the dining room, set apart by a tray ceiling. The kitchen is a chef's dream, featuring plenty of counter space, a large pantry and an island. The master suite includes a lounge area and a sumptuous bath with a bay window. Upstairs, three family bedrooms—two with private baths—complete the plan.

Design
HPT830027

First Floor: 2,345 square feet
Second Floor: 1,336 square feet
Total: 3,681 square feet
Width 65'-0" Depth 66'-0"

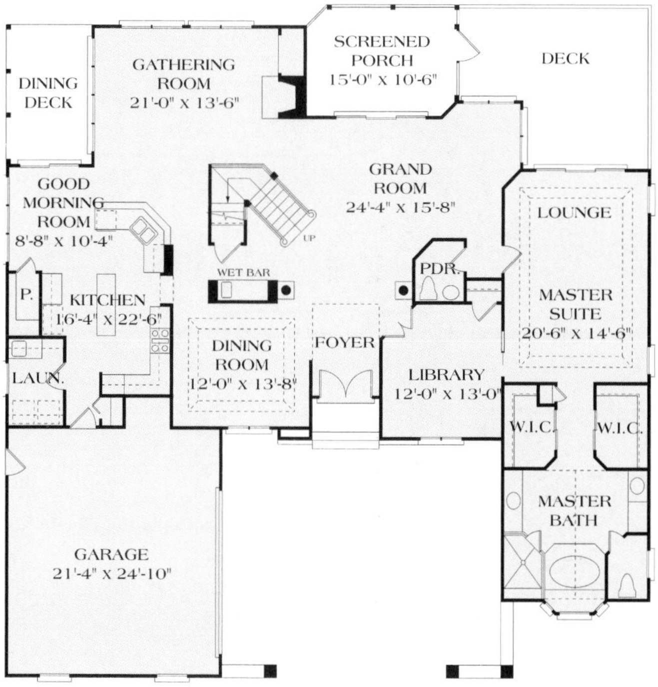

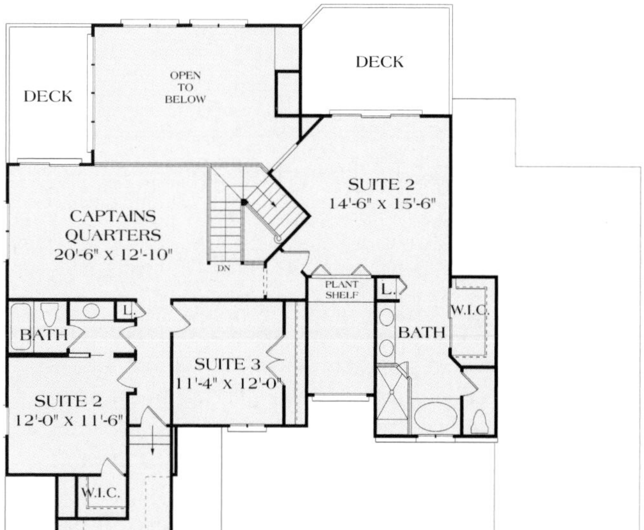

This home, as shown in the photograph, may differ from the actual blueprints. For more detailed information, please check the floor plans carefully.
Photo courtesy of Stephen Fuller, Inc.

SCREEN PORCH
11'-6" X 10'-9"
BEDROOM NO. 3
13'-3" X 12'-6"
W.I.C.
UNFIN. STORAGE
12'-0" X 12'-0"
SITTING ROOM
11'-6" X 11'-6"
MASTER SUITE
18'-3" X 16'-6"
BATH
DN.
HIS
HERS
BEDROOM NO. 2
13'-3" X 12'-0"
OPEN TO BELOW
MASTER BATH

Design HPT830028

First Floor: 1,896 square feet
Second Floor: 1,500 square feet
Total: 3,396 square feet
Other Space: 156 square feet
Width 66'-6" Depth 52'-3"

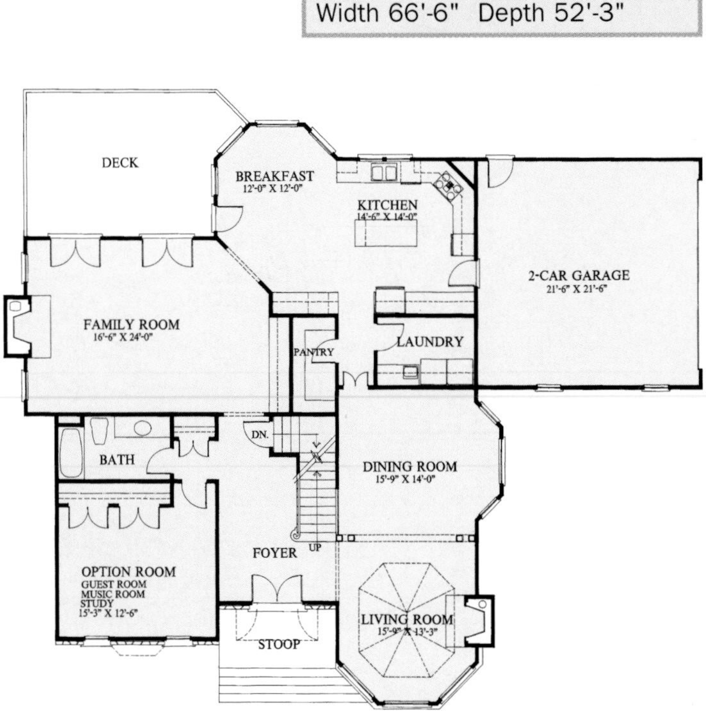

DECK
BREAKFAST
12'-0" X 12'-0"
KITCHEN
14'-6" X 14'-0"
2-CAR GARAGE
21'-6" X 21'-6"
FAMILY ROOM
16'-6" X 24'-0"
PANTRY
LAUNDRY
BATH
DN.
DINING ROOM
15'-9" X 14'-0"
FOYER
UP
OPTION ROOM
GUEST ROOM
MUSIC ROOM
STUDY
15'-3" X 12'-6"
LIVING ROOM
15'-9" X 13'-3"
STOOP

This magnificent home reflects architectural elegance at its finest, executed in stucco and stone. Perhaps its most distinctive feature is the octagonal living room, which forms the focal point. Its attached dining room is bathed in natural light from a bay window. The island kitchen is nearby and has an attached octagonal breakfast room. The family room contains two sets of French doors and a fireplace. An optional room may be used for a guest room, music room or study. The second floor holds two family bedrooms and a master suite with a sitting room. Additional storage space is located over the garage. This home is designed with a walk-out basement foundation.

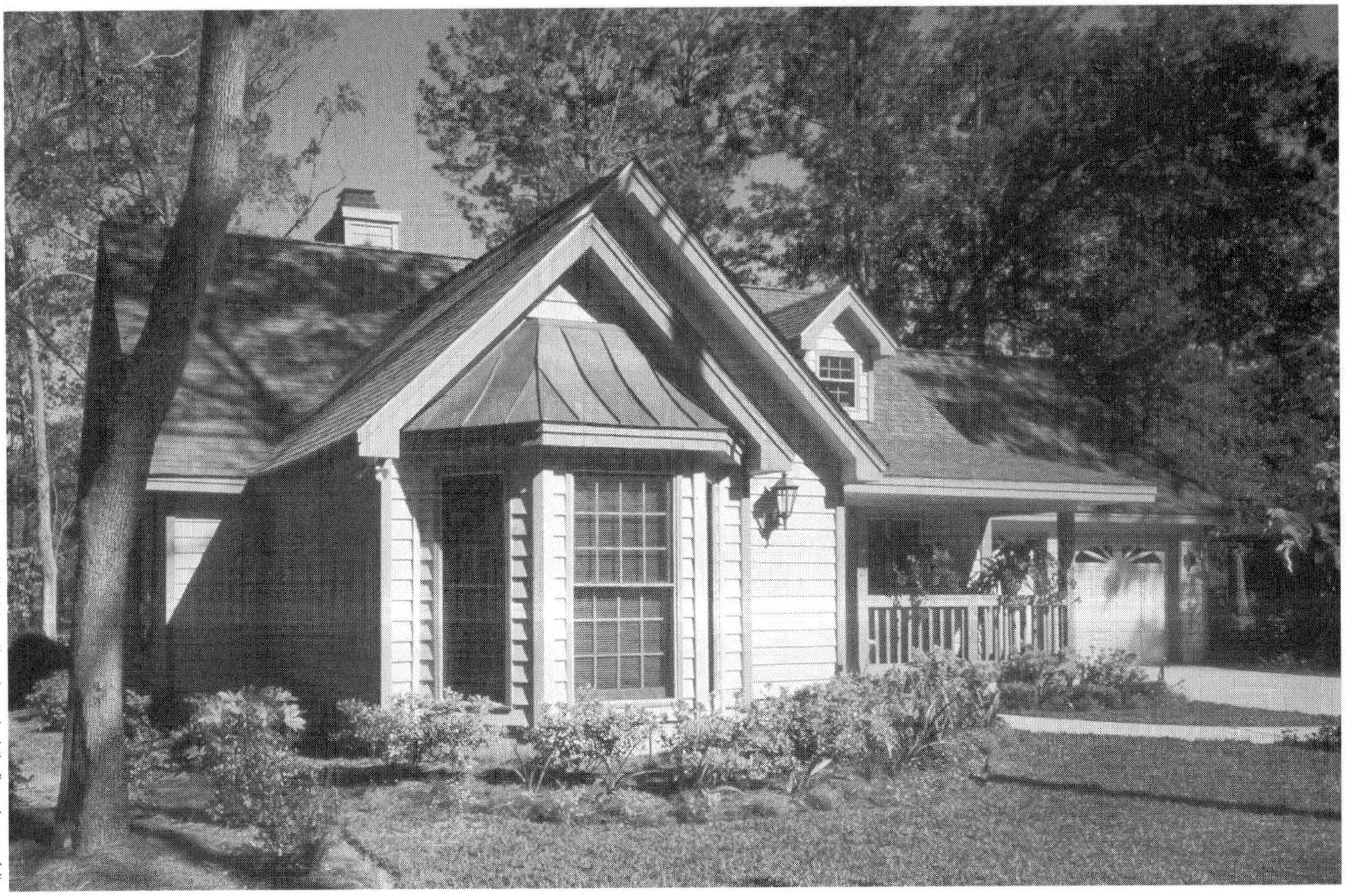

Design
HPT830029

Square Footage: 1,310

Width 61'-0" Depth 51'-5"

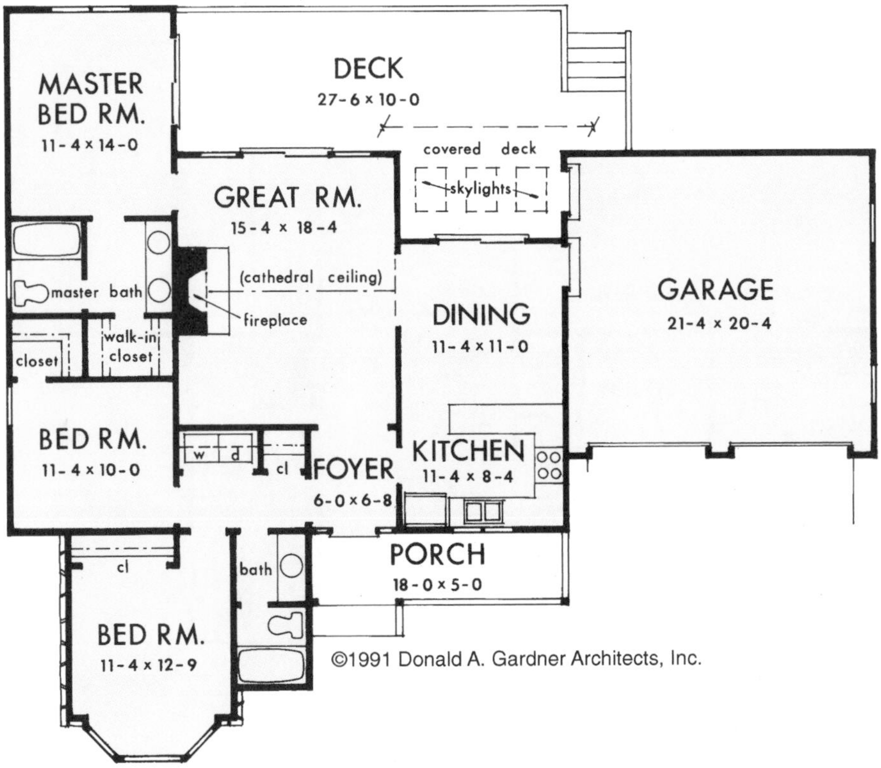
DECK
27-6 x 10-0
covered deck
skylights
MASTER BED RM.
11-4 x 14-0
GREAT RM.
15-4 x 18-4
(cathedral ceiling)
fireplace
master bath
walk-in closet
closet
DINING
11-4 x 11-0
GARAGE
21-4 x 20-4
BED RM.
11-4 x 10-0
w
d
cl
FOYER
6-0 x 6-8
KITCHEN
11-4 x 8-4
cl
bath
PORCH
18-0 x 5-0
BED RM.
11-4 x 12-9

A multi-pane bay window, decorative dormers and a covered porch dress up this one-story cottage. The foyer leads to an impressive great room with a cathedral ceiling and fireplace. The U-shaped kitchen, adjacent to the dining room, provides an ideal layout for food preparation. A large deck offers shelter while admitting cheery sunlight through skylights. The luxurious master bedroom, located to the rear of the house, takes advantage of the deck area and is assured privacy from two other bedrooms at the front of the house. These family bedrooms share a full bath.

Design HPT830030

Square Footage: 1,541	
Width 71'-0"	Depth 59'-0"

This traditional three-bedroom home with front and side porches, arched windows, and dormers projects the appearance of a much larger home. The great room features a cathedral ceiling, a fireplace and an arched window above the sliding glass door to the expansive rear deck. Elegant round columns define the dining room. The master bedroom contains a pampering master bath with a whirlpool tub, separate shower, double-bowl vanity and walk-in closet. Two other bedrooms share a full bath that includes a double vanity.

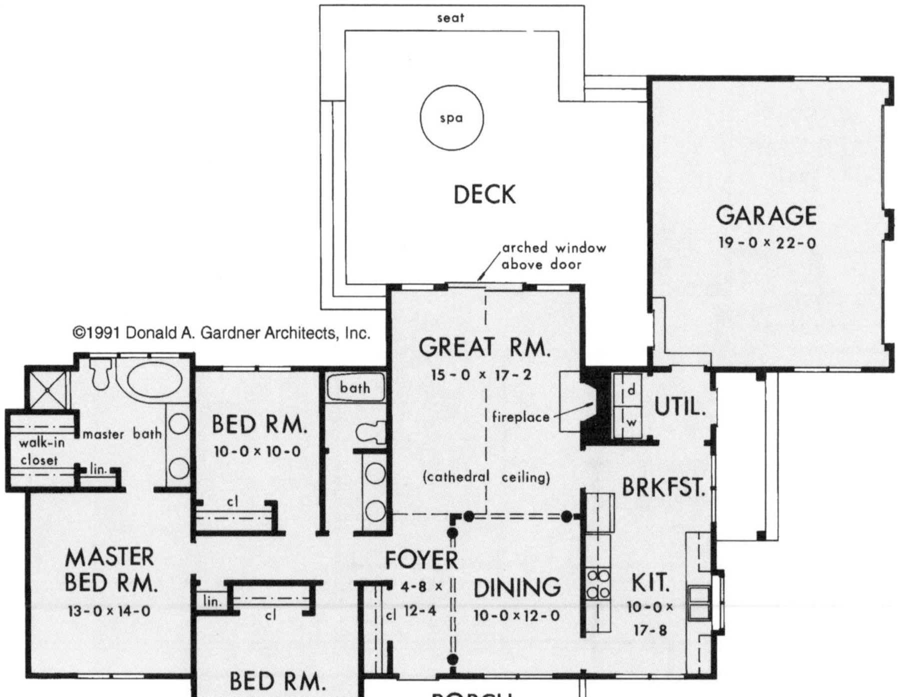
seat
spa
DECK
GARAGE
19-0 x 22-0
arched window above door
©1991 Donald A. Gardner Architects, Inc.
GREAT RM.
15-0 x 17-2
fireplace
(cathedral ceiling)
bath
BED RM.
10-0 x 10-0
master bath
walk-in closet
lin.
cl
UTIL.
d
w
BRKFST.
MASTER BED RM.
13-0 x 14-0
FOYER
4-8 x 12-4
DINING
10-0 x 12-0
KIT.
10-0 x 17-8
BED RM.
13-0 x 11-8
PORCH
17-8 x 6-0

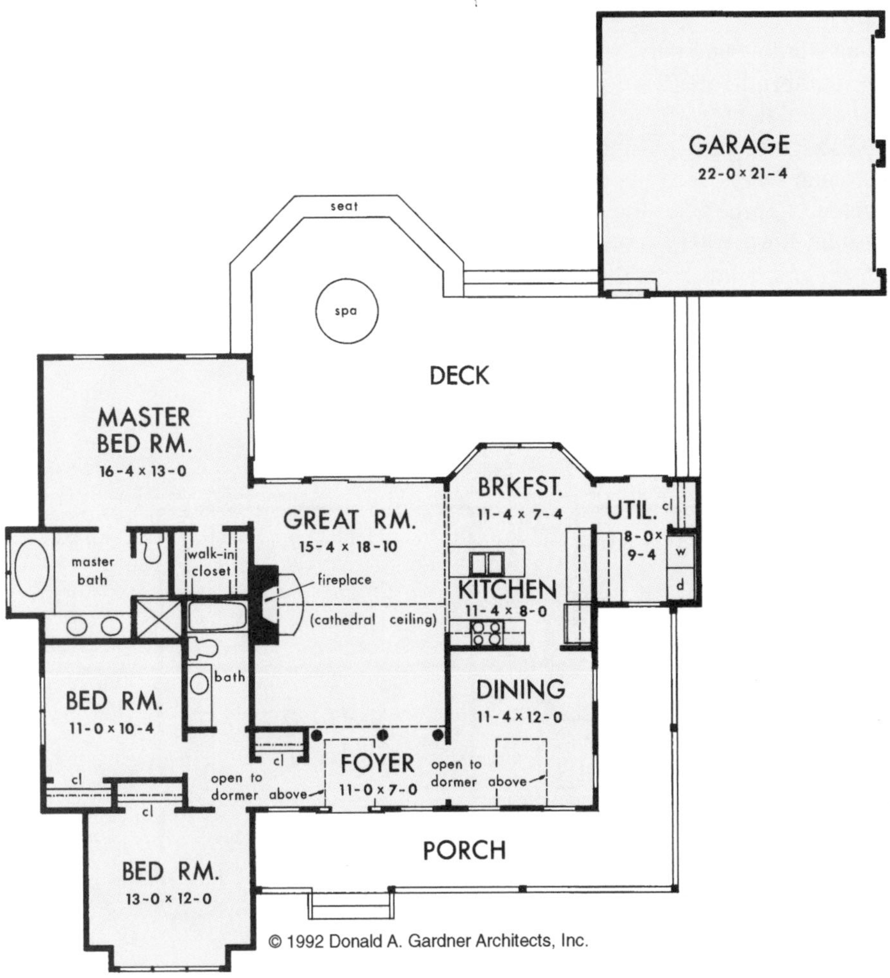

Design HPT830031

Square Footage: 1,590

Width 70'-4" Depth 74'-0"

Columns separate the foyer from the great room with its cathedral ceiling and fireplace. Serving meals has never been easier—the kitchen makes use of direct access to the dining room as well as a breakfast nook overlooking the deck and spa. A handy utility room even has room for a counter and cabinets. Three bedrooms make this an especially desirable design. The master bedroom, off of the great room, provides private access to the deck. This design is flexible enough to be accommodated by a narrow lot if the garage is relocated.

Twin bay windows, an elegant Palladian window and corner quoins help create symmetry to this spectacular Southern home. The formal dining room and living room are filled with natural light from the bay windows that each maintain. The more casual family room also enjoys wonderful views with its generous window wall. The island kitchen serves both the dining room and the breakfast nook with ease and efficiency. Three bedrooms and a full bath join the lavish master suite on the second floor where the master bedroom delights with a tray ceiling. A second staircase leads from the kitchen to the second-floor utility room. A bonus room over the two-car garage offers an option for future development.

Design
HPT830032

Square Footage: 1,400

Width 72'-0" Depth 28'-0"

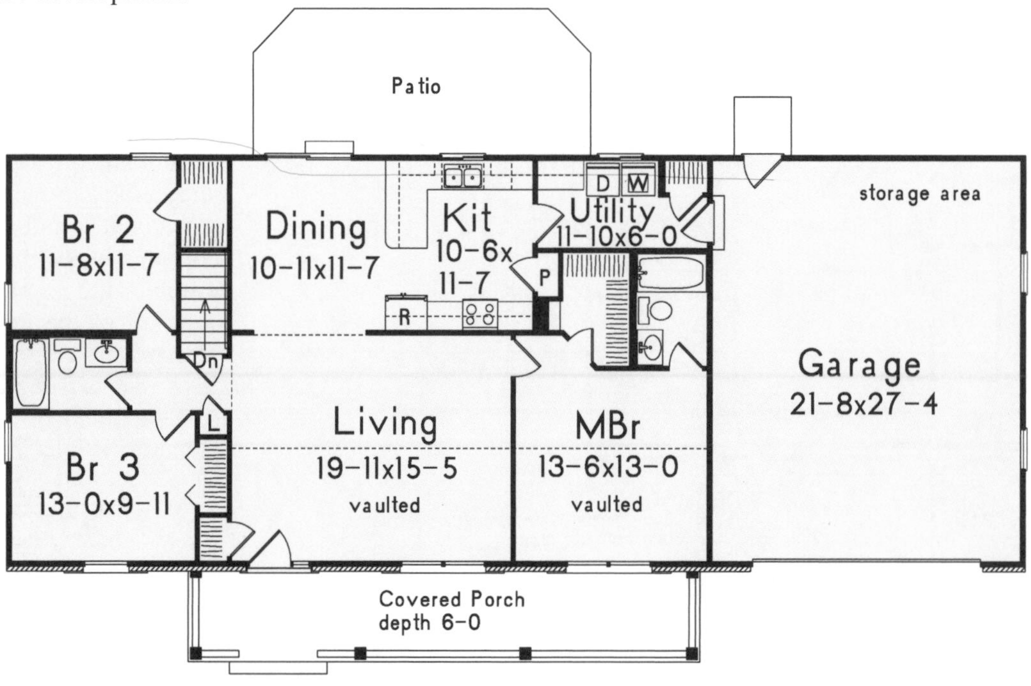

This beautiful brick country home offers style and comfort for an active family. Two covered porches and a rear deck with a spa invite enjoyment of the outdoors. A cathedral ceiling soars above the central great room, warmed by an extended-hearth fireplace and by sunlight through an arch-top clerestory window. The splendid master suite enjoys its own secluded wing and provides a skylit whirlpool bath, a cathedral ceiling and private access to the deck.

Design HPT830033

Square Footage: 1,954
Bonus Space: 436 square feet
Width 71'-3" Depth 62'-6"

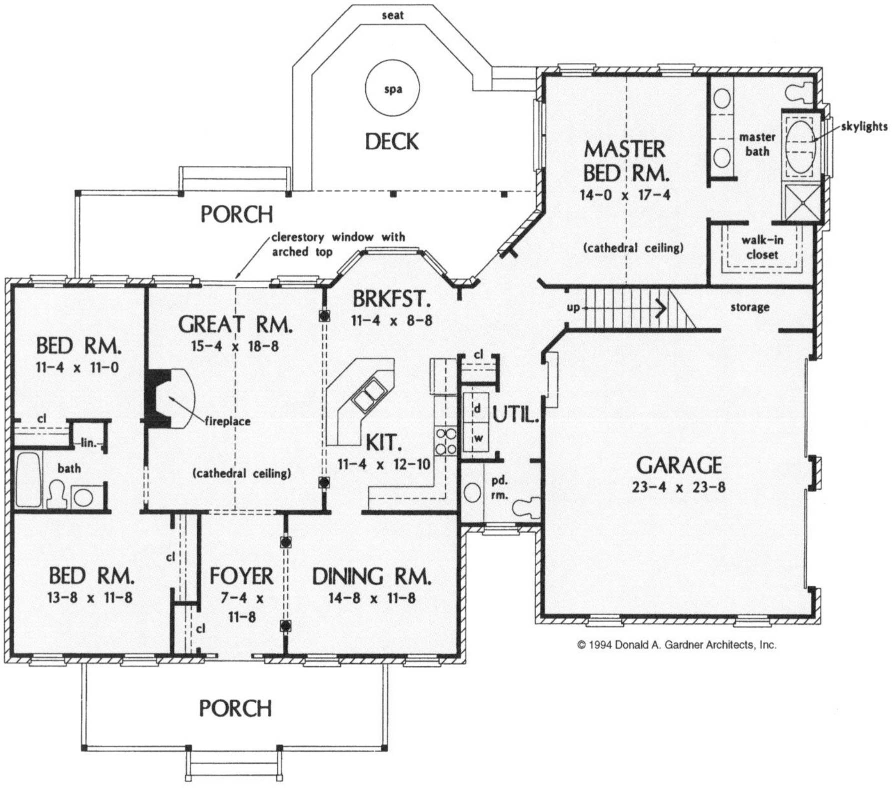

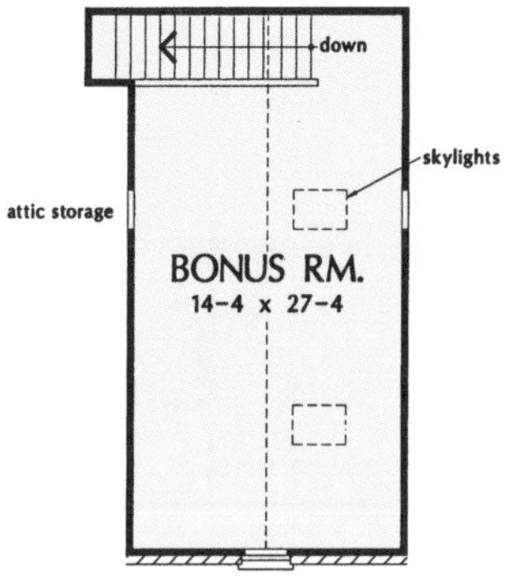

QUOTE ONE®

Cost to build? See page 516 to order complete cost estimate to build this house in your area!

This comfortable country home begins with a front porch that opens to a columned foyer. To the right, enter the formal dining room. Decorative columns define the central great room, which boasts wide views of the outdoors. A breakfast nook nearby accommodates casual dining. The master suite and the great room open to the rear porch. Family bedrooms share a full bath with double lavatories.

Design HPT830034

Square Footage: 1,807	
Bonus Space: 419 square feet	
Width 70'-8"	Depth 52'-8"

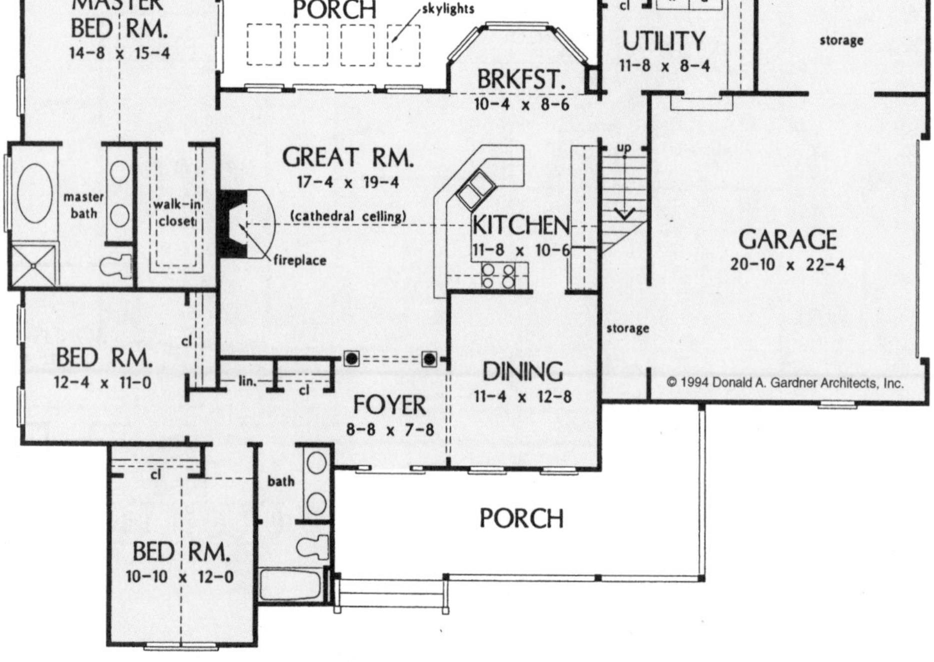

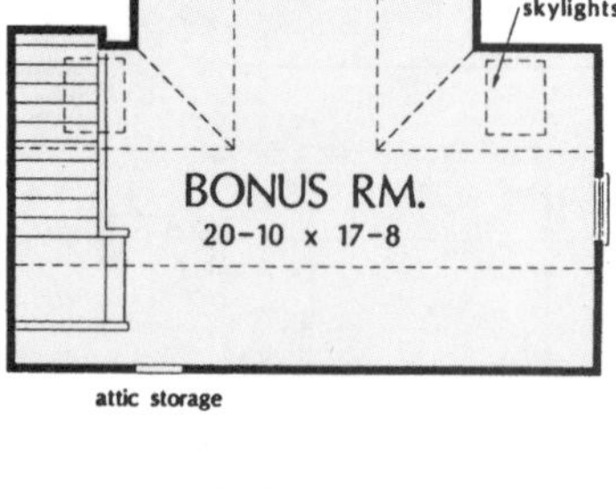

QUOTE ONE®
Cost to build? See page 516 to order complete cost estimate to build this house in your area!

© 1995 Donald A. Gardner Architects, Inc.
S. NATHAN

This charming country home is ready to grow and change as the family's space needs evolve. For example, one of the two family bedrooms would make a fine study and the bonus room upstairs can be finished off to make a great game room or loft. A soaring cathedral ceiling and a cozy fireplace highlight the great room. The kitchen is thoughtfully set between the dining and breakfast rooms. The master bedroom features a walk-in closet.

Design HPT830035

Square Footage: 1,633

Bonus Space: 595 square feet

Width 65'-4" Depth 55'-4"

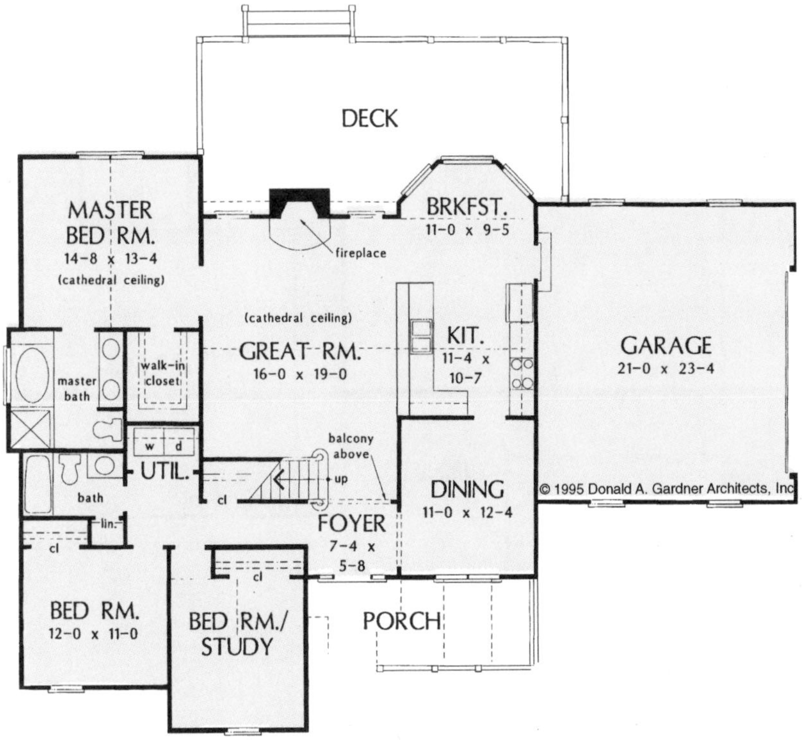

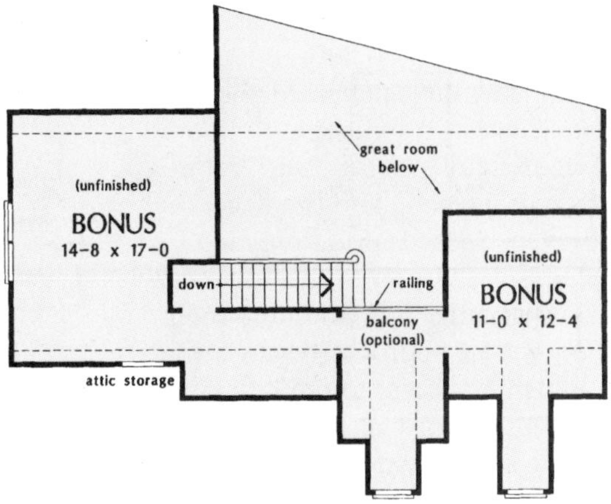

©1995 Donald A. Gardner Architects, Inc.

Design HPT830036

Square Footage: 1,655

Width 61'-0" Depth 49'-8"

Covered front porch dormers and arched windows welcome you to this modified version of one of our most popular country home plans. Interior columns dramatically open the foyer and the kitchen to the spacious great room. The drama is heightened by the great room's cathedral ceiling and fireplace. The kitchen, with its food-preparation island, easily serves the breakfast room and the formal dining room. The master bedroom boasts a tray ceiling and access to the rear deck. Added luxuries include a walk-in closet and a skylit master bath with a double vanity, garden tub and separate shower. Two generous bedrooms share the second bath.

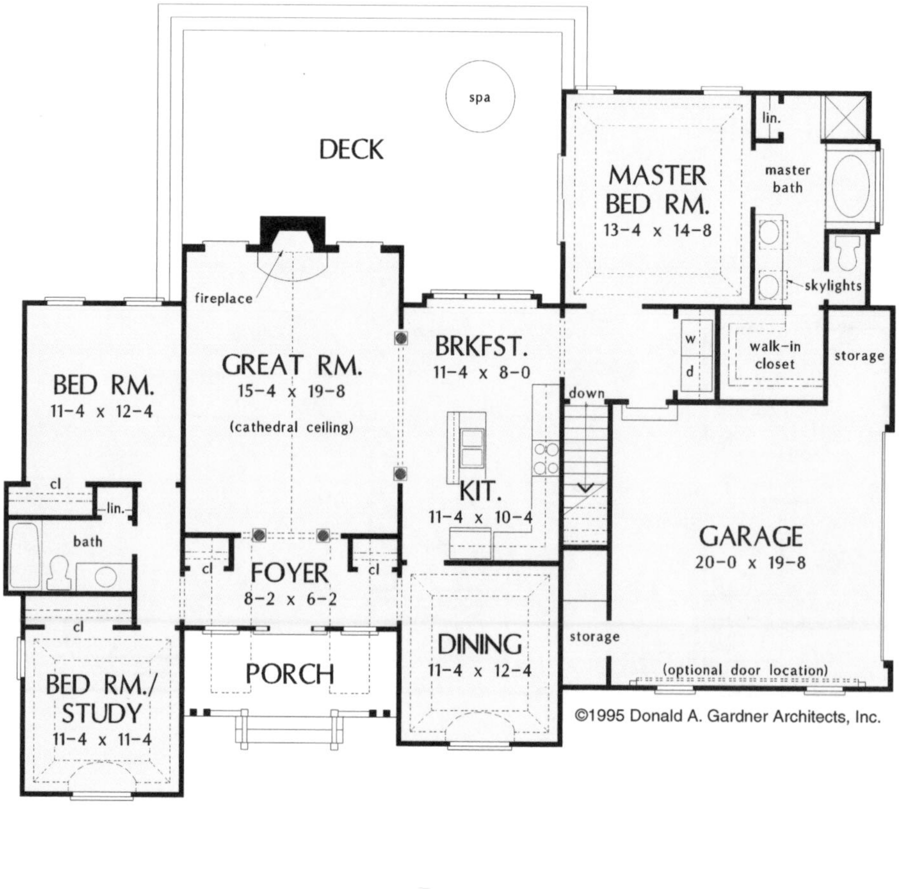

©1995 Donald A. Gardner Architects, Inc.

B. NATHAN

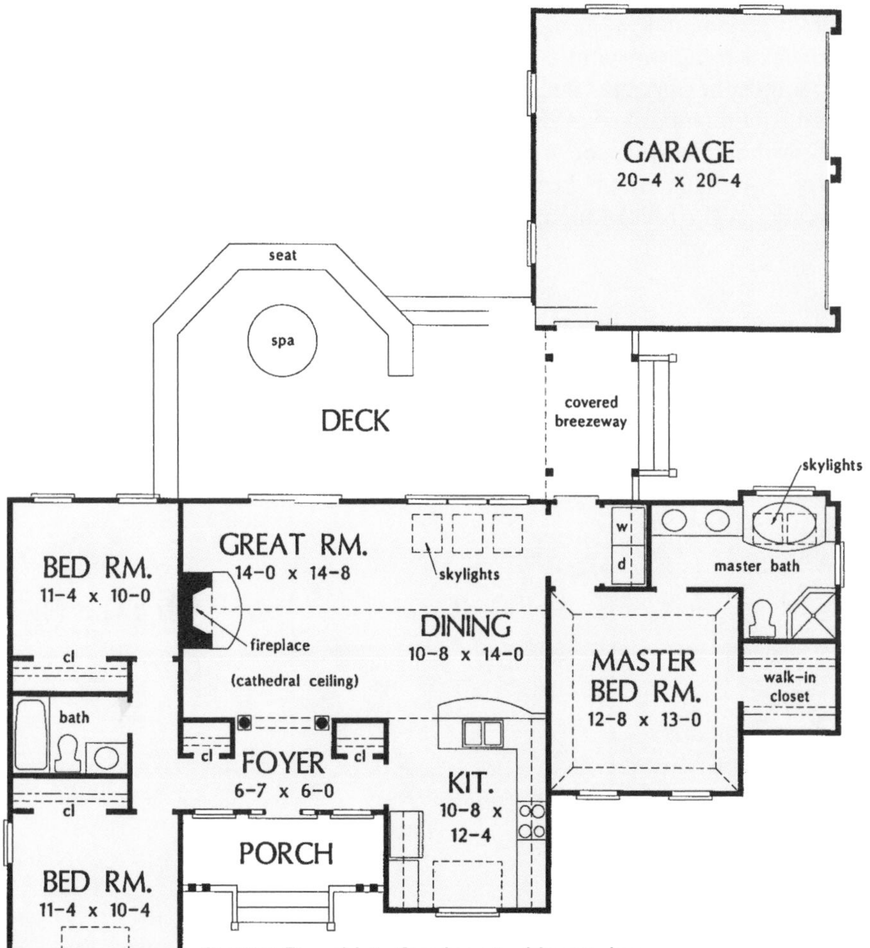
GARAGE
20-4 x 20-4
seat
spa
DECK
covered breezeway
skylights
w
d
master bath
GREAT RM.
14-0 x 14-8
skylights
BED RM.
11-4 x 10-0
fireplace
(cathedral ceiling)
DINING
10-8 x 14-0
MASTER BED RM.
12-8 x 13-0
walk-in closet
cl
bath
cl
FOYER
6-7 x 6-0
cl
KIT.
10-8 x 12-4
cl
PORCH
BED RM.
11-4 x 10-4

Design HPT830037

Square Footage: 1,322
Width 56'-8" Depth 63'-4"

Small doesn't necessarily mean boring in this well-proportioned, three-bedroom country home. A gracious foyer leads to the great room through a set of elegant columns. In this living area, a cathedral ceiling works well with a fireplace and skylights to bring the utmost livability to the homeowner. Outside, an expansive deck includes room for a spa. A handsome master suite has a tray ceiling and a private bath. Two additional bedrooms sit to the left of the plan. Each enjoys ample closet space, and they share a hall bath.

A great room that stretches into the dining room makes this design perfect for entertaining. A cozy fireplace, stylish built-ins and a cathedral ceiling further this casual yet elegant atmosphere. A rear deck extends living possibilities. The ample kitchen features an abundance of counter and cabinet space and an angled cooktop and serving bar that overlooks the great room. Two bedrooms, a hall bath and a handy laundry room make up the family sleeping wing while the master suite is privately located at the rear of the plan.

Design
HPT830038
Square Footage: 1,346
Width 65'-0" Depth 44'-2"

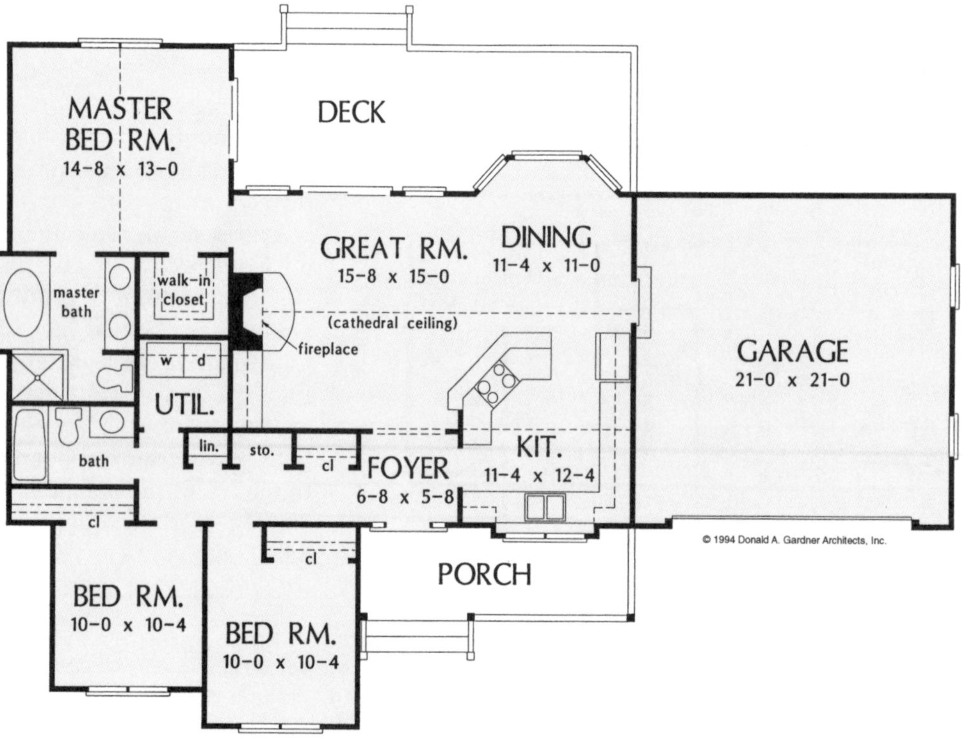
MASTER BED RM.
14-8 x 13-0
DECK
GREAT RM.
15-8 x 15-0
DINING
11-4 x 11-0
master bath
walk-in closet
(cathedral ceiling)
fireplace
w
d
UTIL.
GARAGE
21-0 x 21-0
bath
lin.
sto.
cl
FOYER
6-8 x 5-8
KIT.
11-4 x 12-4
cl
cl
PORCH
BED RM.
10-0 x 10-4
BED RM.
10-0 x 10-4
© 1994 Donald A. Gardner Architects, Inc.

QUOTE ONE®
Cost to build? See page 516 to order complete cost estimate to build this house in your area!

© 1994 Donald A. Gardner Architects, Inc.
B. NATHAN

A covered porch and dormers combine to create the inviting exterior on this three-bedroom country home. The foyer leads through columns to an expansive great room with a cozy fireplace, built-in bookshelves and access to the rear covered porch. To the right, an open kitchen is conveniently situated to easily serve the bay-windowed breakfast area and the formal dining room. The master suite enjoys access to the covered porch, a walk-in closet and a relaxing master bath. A utility room, two secondary bedrooms and a full bath complete the plan. A bonus room over the garage provides room for future growth.

Design HPT830039

Square Footage: 1,575
Bonus Space: 276 square feet
Width 70'-8" Depth 47'-4"

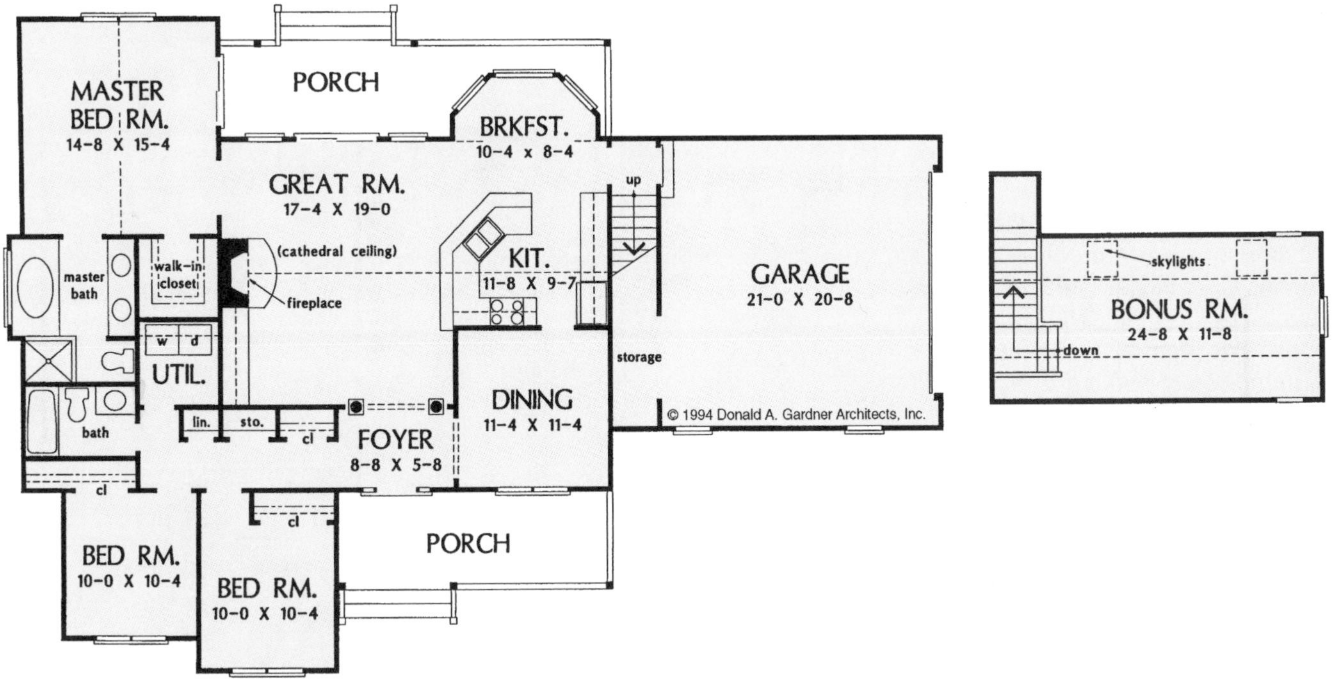
PORCH
MASTER BED RM.
14-8 X 15-4
BRKFST.
10-4 x 8-4
GREAT RM.
17-4 X 19-0
(cathedral ceiling)
fireplace
up
KIT.
11-8 X 9-7
GARAGE
21-0 X 20-8
master bath
walk-in closet
w d
UTIL.
storage
bath
lin.
sto.
cl
FOYER
8-8 X 5-8
DINING
11-4 X 11-4
© 1994 Donald A. Gardner Architects, Inc.
cl
cl
PORCH
BED RM.
10-0 X 10-4
BED RM.
10-0 X 10-4
skylights
BONUS RM.
24-8 X 11-8
down

Design HPT830040

Square Footage: 1,373

Width 50'-4" Depth 45'-0"

A steep gable roofline punctuated with dormer windows and a columned front porch give a traditional welcome to this family home. A vaulted ceiling tops the family and dining rooms, which are nicely accented with a fireplace and bright windows. An amenity-filled kitchen opens to the breakfast room. The master suite has a refined tray ceiling and a vaulted bath. Two family bedrooms, a laundry center and a full bath—with private access from Bedroom 3—complete this stylish plan. Please specify basement or crawl-space foundation when ordering.

QUOTE ONE®

Cost to build? See page 516 to order complete cost estimate to build this house in your area!

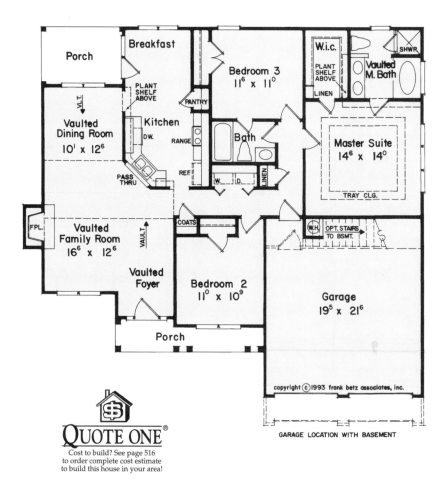

B. NATHAN
© 1996 Donald A. Gardner Architects, Inc.

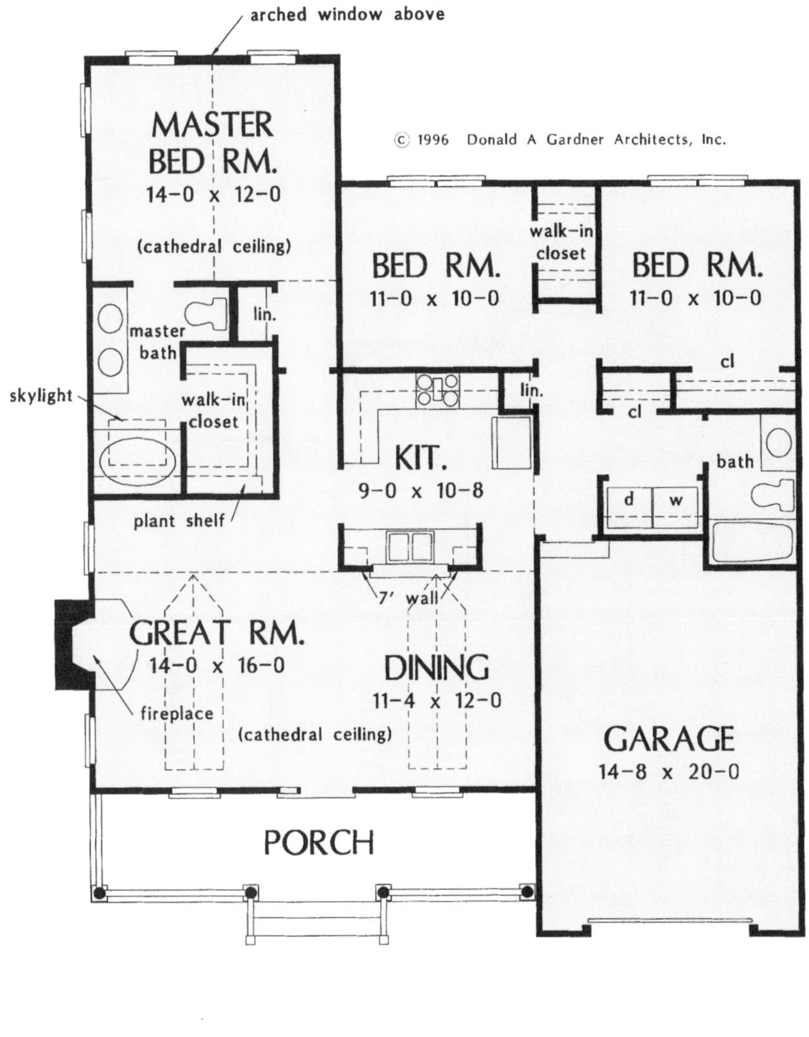
arched window above
© 1996 Donald A Gardner Architects, Inc.
MASTER BED RM.
14-0 x 12-0
(cathedral ceiling)
BED RM.
11-0 x 10-0
walk-in closet
BED RM.
11-0 x 10-0
master bath
lin.
skylight
walk-in closet
lin.
cl
cl
KIT.
9-0 x 10-8
bath
d
w
plant shelf
7' wall
GREAT RM.
14-0 x 16-0
fireplace
DINING
11-4 x 12-0
(cathedral ceiling)
GARAGE
14-8 x 20-0
PORCH

Design HPT830041

Square Footage: 1,306
Width 43'-0" Depth 49'-0"

A central kitchen is the focal point for this country ranch home. It includes a snack bar that is conveniently close to both the living and the sleeping areas. The great room and dining area are combined, offering access to the front porch, a fireplace and a cathedral ceiling. Notice that the washer and dryer are handy to the kitchen as well as to the family bedrooms and the shared full bath. The master bedroom and bath include a cathedral ceiling, a walk-in closet and a skylit whirlpool tub.

Two striking brick gables give a balanced look to this lovely starter home. The living room features a ten-foot ceiling and cozy fireplace. A formal dining room is located to the right of the foyer and has easy access to the kitchen. Ten-foot ceilings throughout the kitchen and breakfast nook give the home a spacious feel. Minimal corridor space in the sleeping zone allows for larger family bedrooms. The master suite features a bath appointed with double vanities, a whirlpool tub and a separate shower. Please specify crawlspace or slab foundation when ordering.

Design HPT830042
Square Footage: 1,553
Width 61'-7" Depth 45'-4"
L

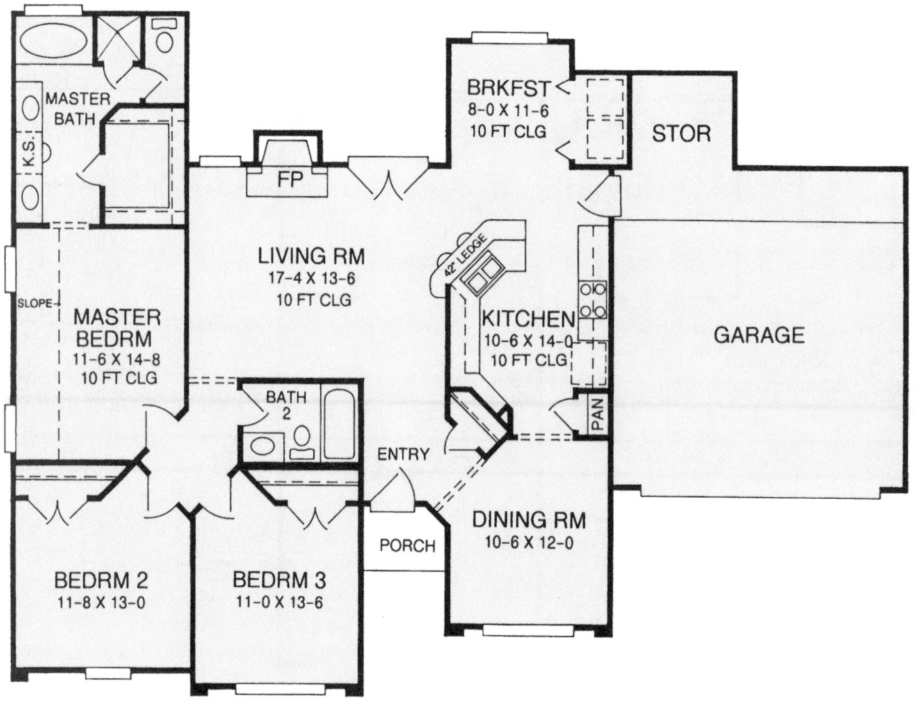

The two dormers draw attention to this home as well as flood the kitchen and breakfast nook with plenty of natural light. The steep rooflines lend vaulted ceilings to the interior of this home. The great room and octagonal dining room enjoy views of the covered patio. The amazingly well-lit kitchen features a pass-through to the dining room, a center island, a walk-in pantry and a breakfast room with a large bay window. The bedrooms align along the right side of the plan.

Design

HPT830043

Square Footage: 1,791

Width 67'-4" Depth 48'-0"

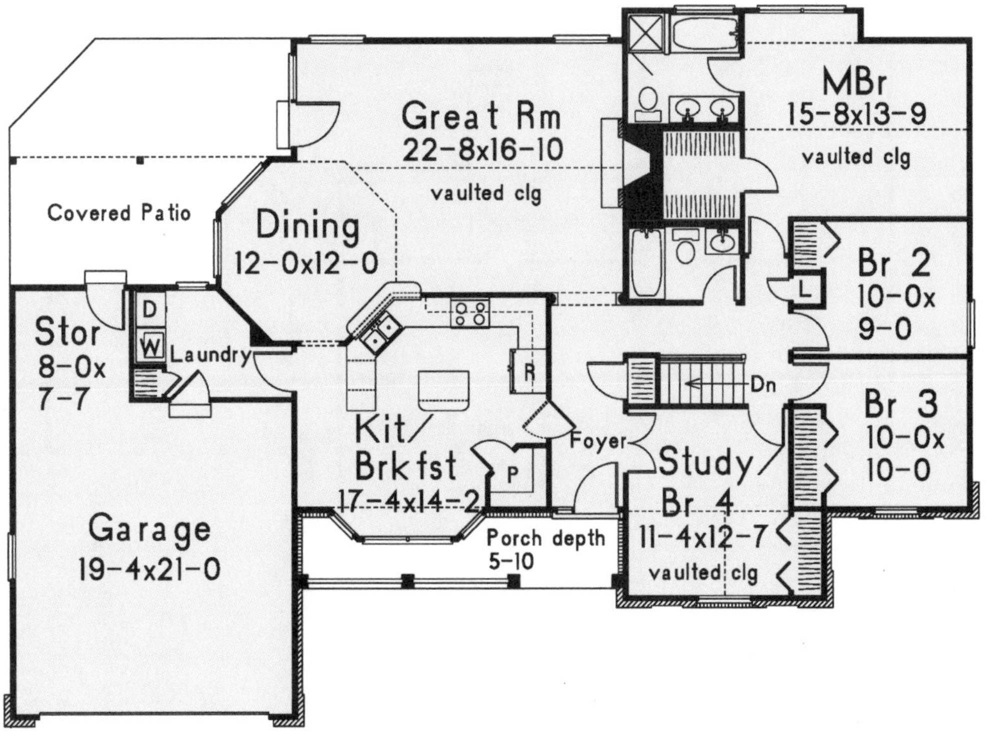
Great Rm
22-8x16-10
vaulted clg
MBr
15-8x13-9
vaulted clg
Covered Patio
Dining
12-0x12-0
Br 2
10-0x
9-0
Stor
8-0x
7-7
D
W
Laundry
R
L
Dn
Br 3
10-0x
10-0
Kit/
Brkfst
17-4x14-2
P
Foyer
Study
Br 4
11-4x12-7
vaulted clg
Garage
19-4x21-0
Porch depth
5-10

Design

HPT830044

Square Footage: 1,671

Width 50'-0" Depth 51'-0"

A symmetrical gables, a columned porch and an abundance of windows brighten the exterior of this compact home. An efficient kitchen boasts a pantry and a serving bar that it shares with the formal dining room and the vaulted family room. A sunny breakfast room and nearby laundry room complete the living zone. Be sure to notice extras such as the focal-point fireplace in the family room and a plant shelf in the laundry room. The sumptuous master suite offers a door to the backyard, a vaulted sitting area and a pampering bath. Two family bedrooms share a hall bath. Please specify basement, crawlspace or slab foundation when ordering.

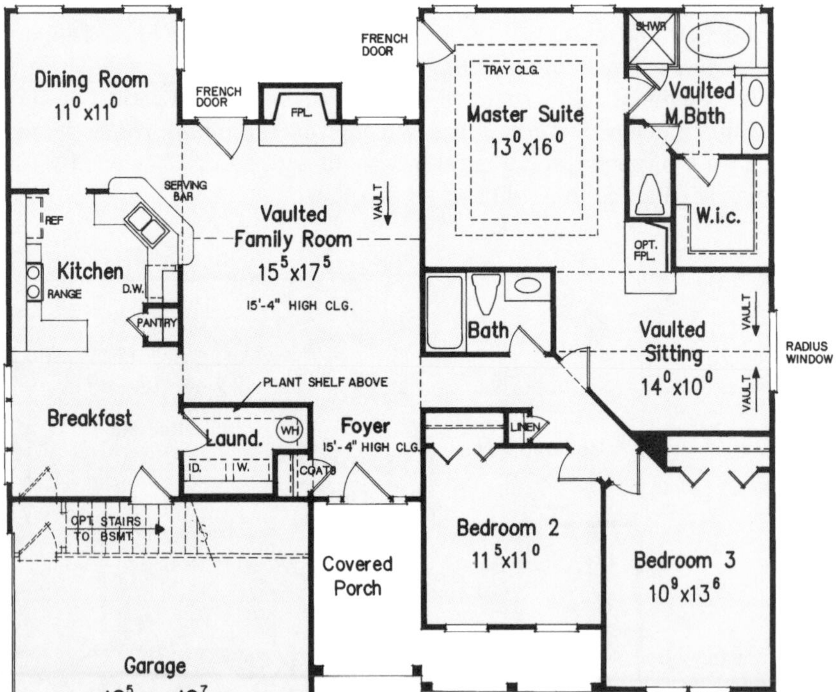

QUOTE ONE®
Cost to build? See page 516
to order complete cost estimate
to build this house in your area!

A lovely traditional facade complements this up-to-date floor plan. Inside, the open angled breakfast bar connects the kitchen and breakfast room to the main living area beyond. Ten-foot ceilings give the home a spacious feel. The master suite features a roomy walk-in closet, double vanities and a separate shower and whirlpool tub. Two family bedrooms have stylish angled entries and share a hall bath. Please specify crawlspace or slab foundation when ordering.

Design HPT830045

Square Footage: 1,628

Width 62'-0" Depth 44'-8"

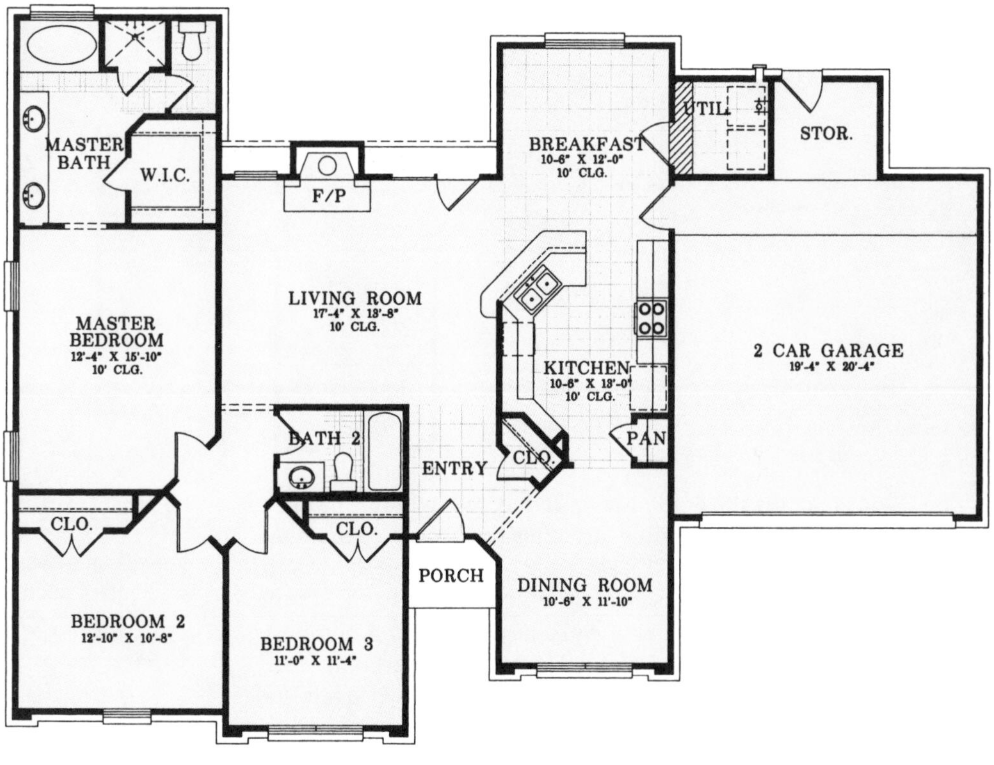

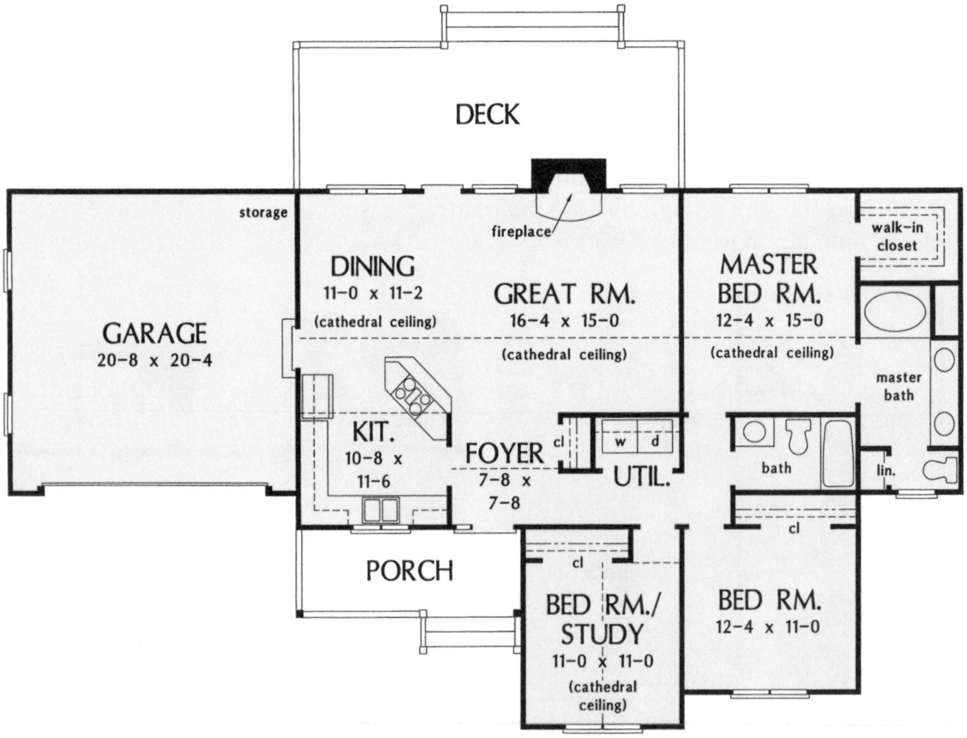
DECK
storage
fireplace
DINING
11-0 x 11-2
(cathedral ceiling)
GREAT RM.
16-4 x 15-0
(cathedral ceiling)
MASTER
BED RM.
12-4 x 15-0
(cathedral ceiling)
walk-in closet
GARAGE
20-8 x 20-4
master bath
KIT.
10-8 x
11-6
FOYER
7-8 x
7-8
cl
w d
UTIL.
bath
lin.
cl
PORCH
cl
BED RM./
STUDY
11-0 x 11-0
(cathedral ceiling)
BED RM.
12-4 x 11-0

A wide-open floor plan puts the emphasis on family living in this modest, single-story home. A cathedral ceiling stretches the length of the plan, stylishly topping the dining room, great room and master bedroom. Cooks will enjoy working in the presentation kitchen that's open to the dining room and great room. The master suite has a walk-in closet and a compartmented bath with a garden tub and twin vanities. One of the two family bedrooms has a cathedral ceiling as well, making it an optional study. A full hall bath and a convenient hallway laundry center complete this plan.

Design

HPT830046

Square Footage: 1,417
Width 69'-0" Depth 39'-0"

3744252

© 1992 Donald A. Gardner Architects, Inc.

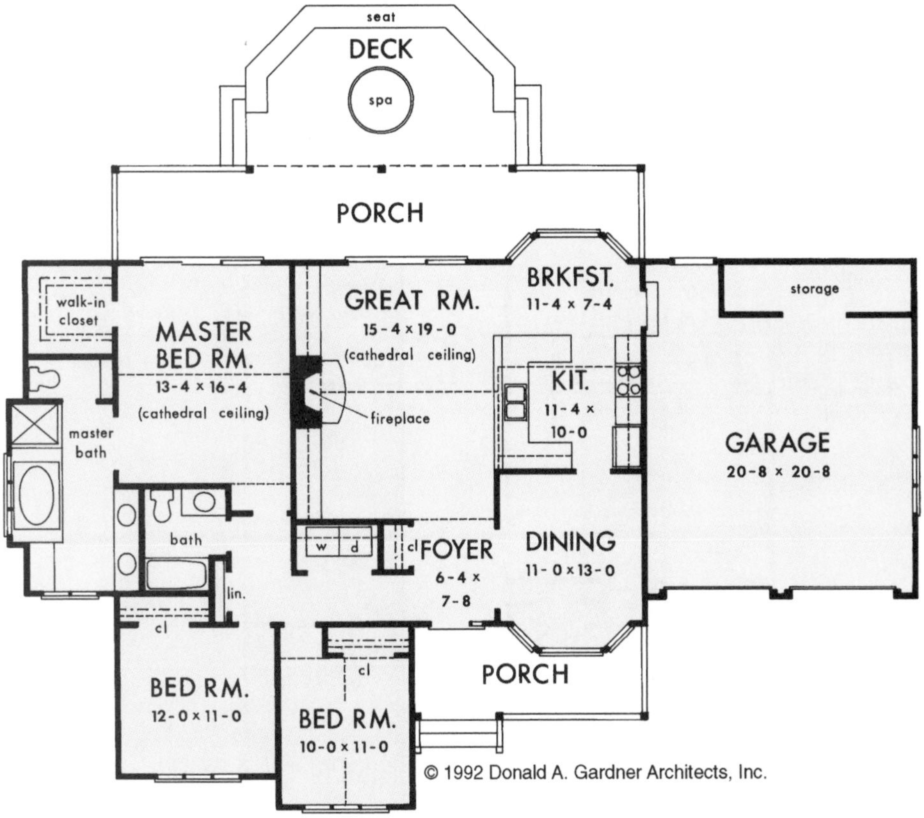

© 1992 Donald A. Gardner Architects, Inc.

Design

HPT830047

Square Footage: 1,625

Width 70'-4" Depth 60'-0"

This family-pleasing design is thoughtful, indeed. Living areas include a kitchen with an efficient work triangle, an adjoining breakfast room, a dining room with bay window and, of course, the great room with fireplace and access to a rear porch. The master bedroom also has porch access, along with a walk-in closet and a lavish bath. One of the two family bedrooms features a half-round transom window, adding appeal to the exterior and interior. The laundry room is convenient to all three bedrooms.

This modest home takes a creative look at space to design an efficient floor plan that's comfortable yet compact. The vaulted family room has a corner fireplace and sliding glass doors to the rear yard. A galley kitchen includes a hidden laundry center and a window over the sink. The breakfast room offers an optional bay window. The master suite has a tray ceiling and a large walk-in closet. Please specify basement, crawlspace or slab foundation when ordering.

Design HPT830048

Square Footage: 1,070

Width 48'-0" Depth 36'-0"

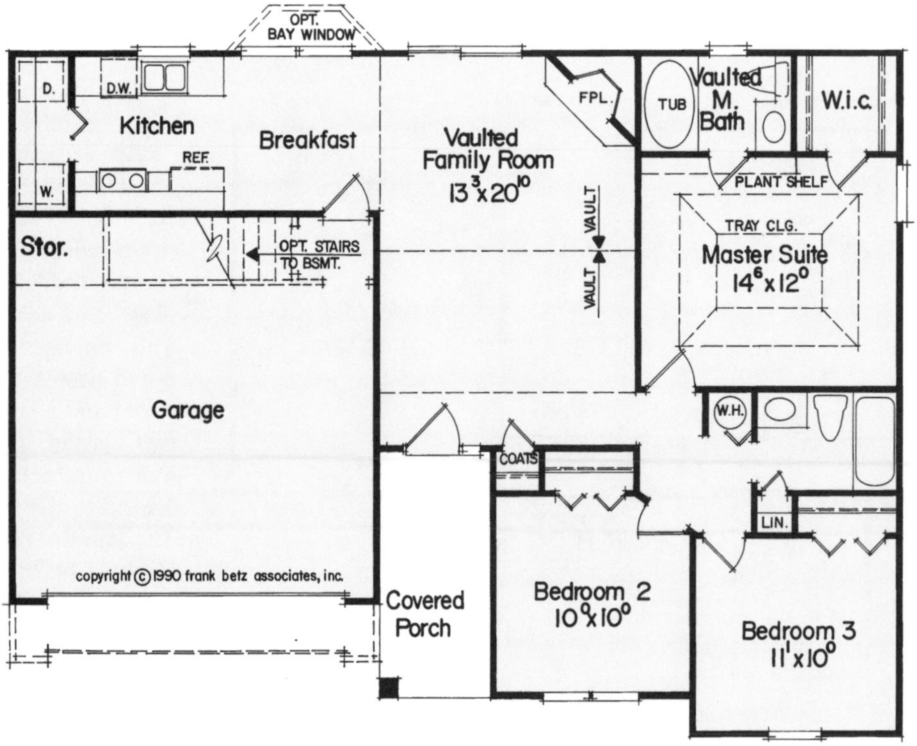

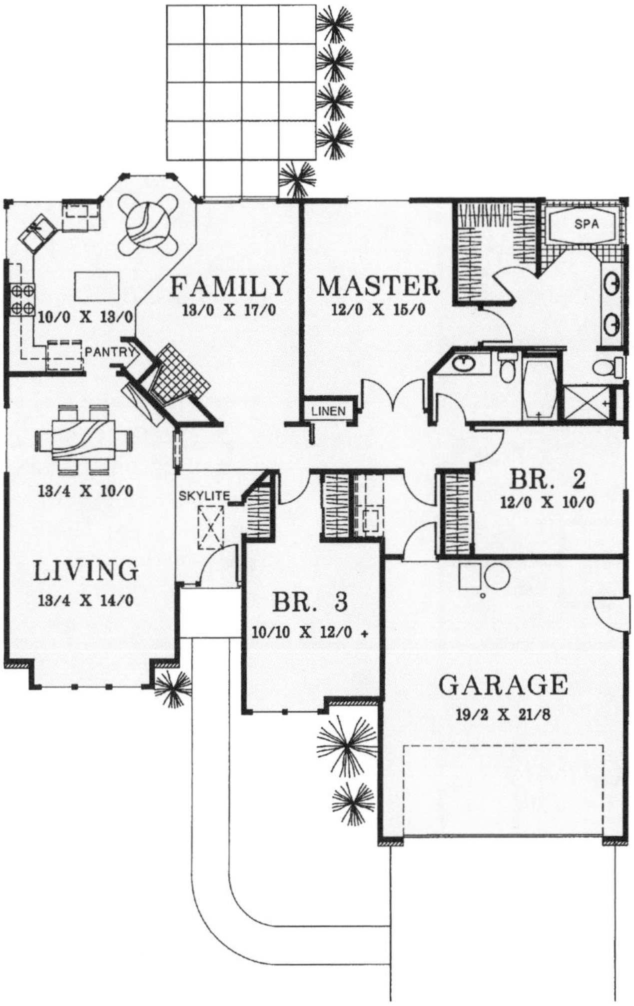

Design HPT830049

Square Footage: 1,687
Width 50'-0" Depth 52'-0"
L

Intriguing rooflines create a dynamic exterior for this home. The interior floor plan is equally attractive. Toward the rear a wide archway forms the entrance to the spacious family living area with its centrally placed fireplace and bay-windowed nook area. An island, mitered corner window and a walk-in pantry complete the efficient kitchen. This home also boasts a terrific master suite complete with walk-in wardrobe, spa tub with corner windows and a compartmented shower and toilet area. Two family bedrooms share a hall bath.

© 1996 Donald A. Gardner Architects, Inc.

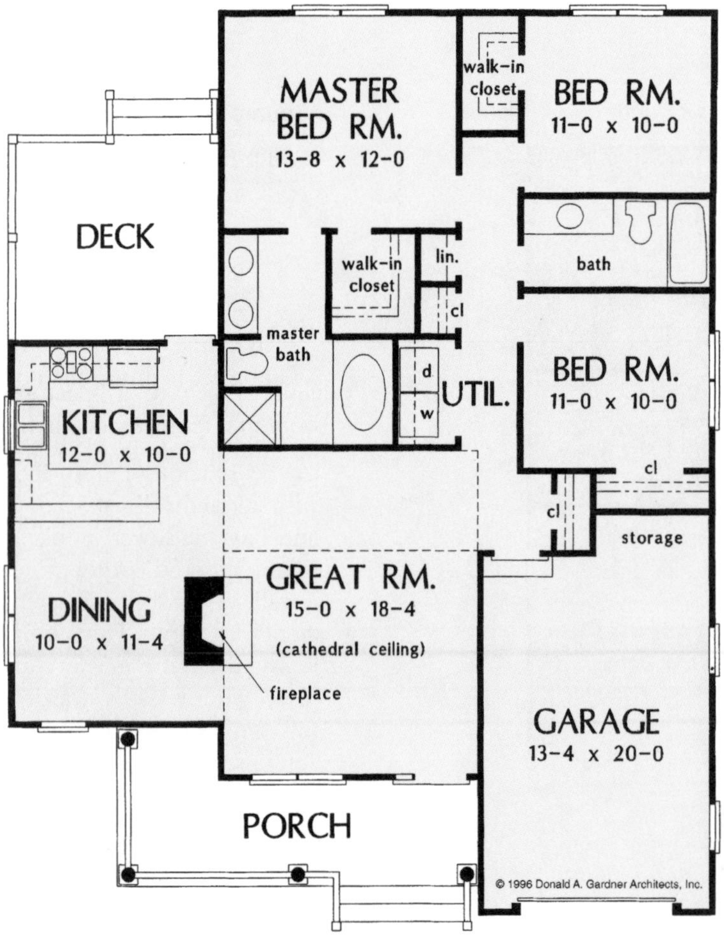
MASTER BED RM.
13-8 x 12-0
walk-in closet
BED RM.
11-0 x 10-0
DECK
walk-in closet
lin.
cl
bath
master bath
d
w
UTIL.
BED RM.
11-0 x 10-0
KITCHEN
12-0 x 10-0
cl
cl
storage
GREAT RM.
15-0 x 18-4
(cathedral ceiling)
DINING
10-0 x 11-4
fireplace
GARAGE
13-4 x 20-0
PORCH
© 1996 Donald A. Gardner Architects, Inc.

Design HPT830050

Square Footage: 1,362	
Width 41'-8"	Depth 51'-4"

This home invites cool summer evenings spent lounging on the front porch or enjoying family gatherings around the fireplace. The central great room, with its cathedral ceiling, opens to the dining room. The efficient kitchen has a door to the rear deck. Three bedrooms include two family bedrooms with a shared bath and a master suite with a walk-in closet and a large master bath. The utility/laundry area is conveniently located by the bedrooms.

This home, as shown in the photograph, may differ from the actual blueprints. For more detailed information, please check the floor plans carefully.

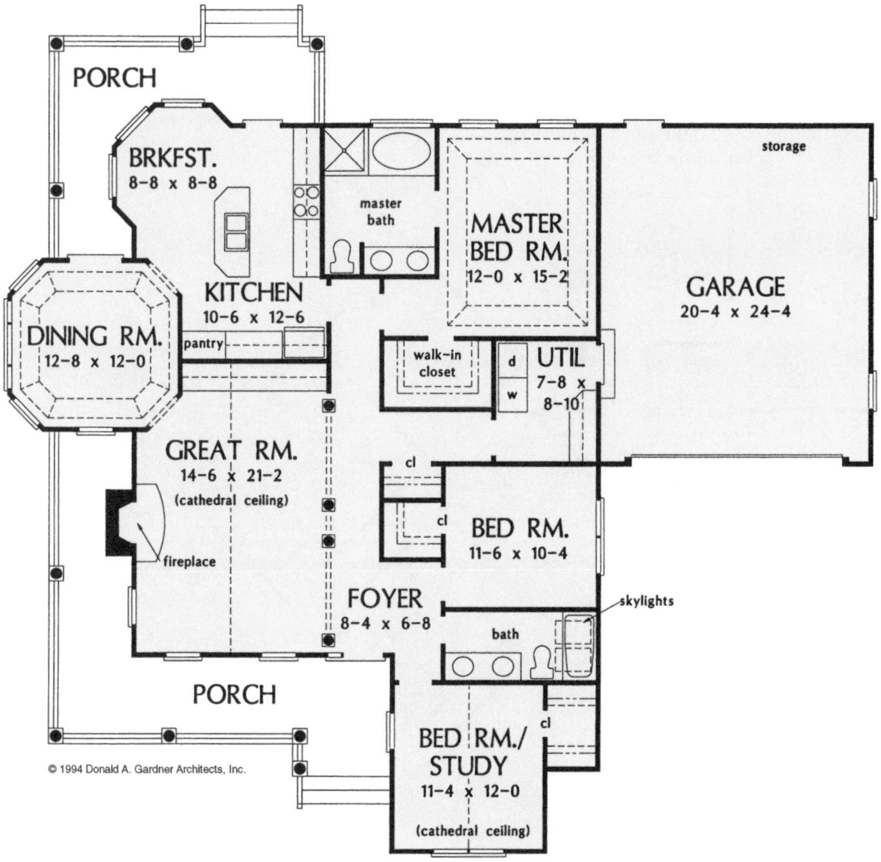
PORCH
BRKFST.
8-8 x 8-8
master bath
MASTER BED RM.
12-0 x 15-2
storage
GARAGE
20-4 x 24-4
KITCHEN
10-6 x 12-6
pantry
DINING RM.
12-8 x 12-0
walk-in closet
d
w
UTIL
7-8 x 8-10
GREAT RM.
14-6 x 21-2
(cathedral ceiling)
fireplace
cl
cl
BED RM.
11-6 x 10-4
FOYER
8-4 x 6-8
skylights
bath
PORCH
cl
BED RM./ STUDY
11-4 x 12-0
(cathedral ceiling)
© 1994 Donald A. Gardner Architects, Inc.

Design HPT830051

Square Footage: 1,737
Width 65'-10" Depth 59'-8"

Inviting porches are just the beginning of this lovely country home. To the left of the foyer, a columned entry supplies a classic touch to a spacious great room that features a cathedral ceiling, built-in bookshelves and a fireplace that invites you to share its warmth. An octagonal dining room with a tray ceiling provides a perfect setting for formal occasions. The adjacent kitchen is designed to easily serve both formal and informal areas. It includes an island cooktop and a built-in pantry, with the sunny breakfast area just a step away. The master suite, separated from two family bedrooms by the walk-in closet and utility room, offers privacy and comfort.

Design
HPT830052

Square Footage: 2,046

Width 94'-8" Depth 64'-4"

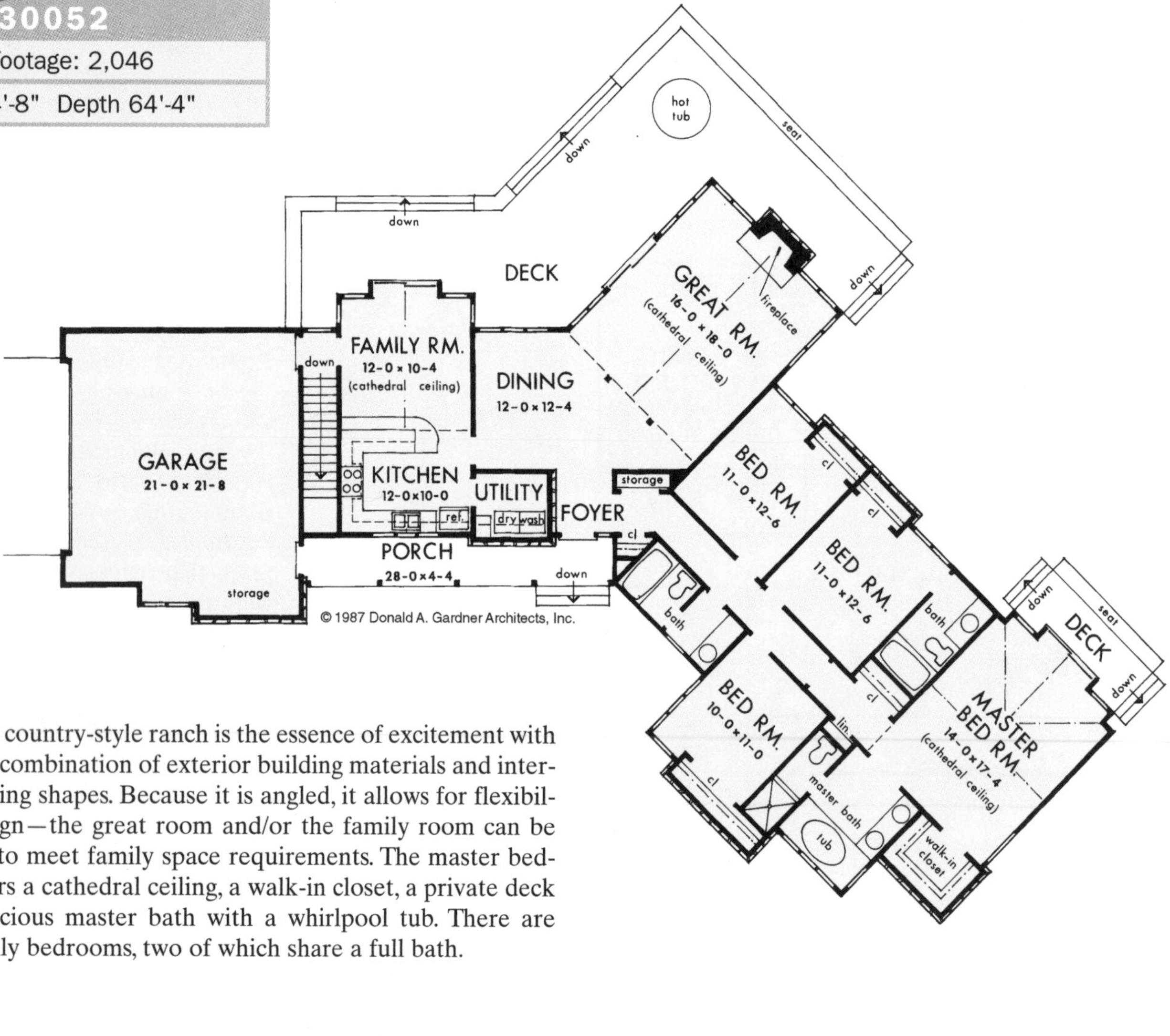
hot tub
seat
down
down
down
DECK
GREAT RM.
16-0 × 18-0
(cathedral ceiling)
fireplace
FAMILY RM.
12-0 × 10-4
(cathedral ceiling)
down
DINING
12-0 × 12-4
GARAGE
21-0 × 21-8
storage
KITCHEN
12-0×10-0
ref.
UTILITY
dry wash
FOYER
storage
cl
PORCH
28-0×4-4
down
© 1987 Donald A. Gardner Architects, Inc.
BED RM.
11-0 × 12-6
cl
BED RM.
11-0 × 12-6
cl
bath
bath
BED RM.
10-0×11-0
cl
lin.
cl
master bath
tub
MASTER BED RM.
14-0×17-4
(cathedral ceiling)
walk-in closet
DECK
seat
down
down

This country-style ranch is the essence of excitement with its combination of exterior building materials and interesting shapes. Because it is angled, it allows for flexibility in design—the great room and/or the family room can be extended to meet family space requirements. The master bedroom offers a cathedral ceiling, a walk-in closet, a private deck and a spacious master bath with a whirlpool tub. There are three family bedrooms, two of which share a full bath.

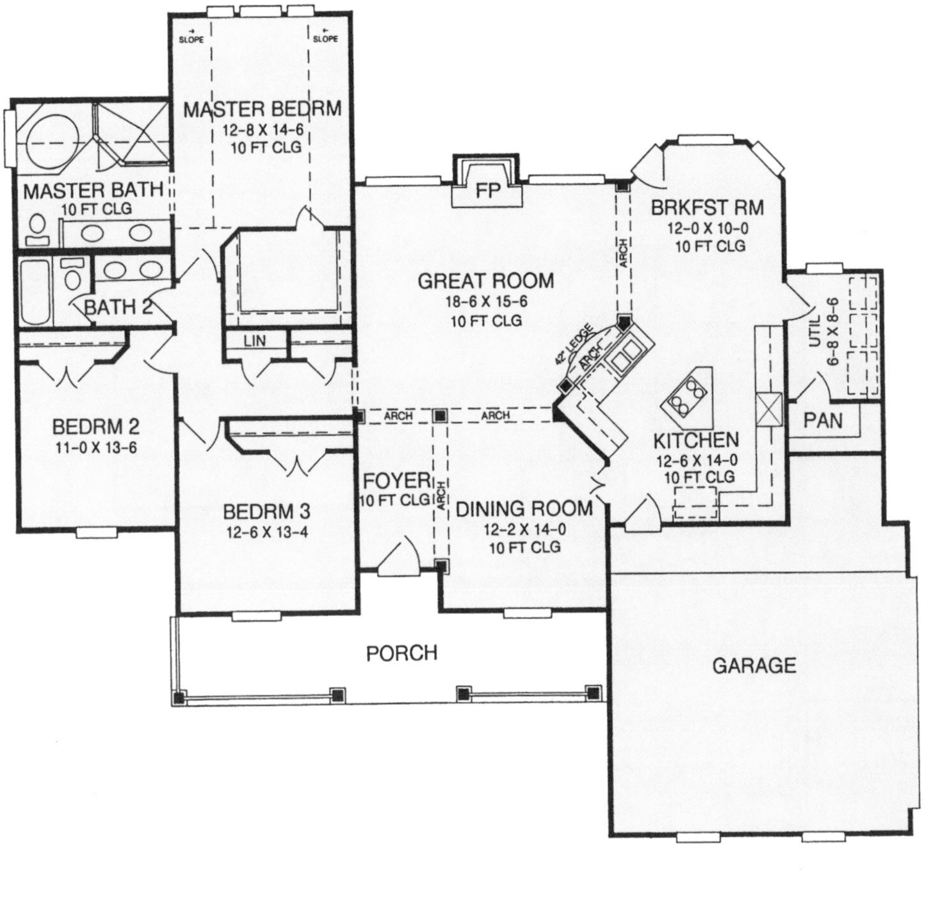

Design HPT830053

Square Footage: 1,955	
Width 65'-0"	Depth 58'-8"

A finely detailed covered porch and arch-topped windows announce a scrupulously designed interior, replete with amenities. Clustered sleeping quarters to the left include a deluxe master suite with a sloped ceiling, corner whirlpool bath and walk-in closet. Picture windows flanking a centered fireplace lend plenty of natural light to the great room. Please specify crawlspace or slab foundation when ordering.

A two-story foyer with a Palladian window above sets the tone for this sunlit home. Columns mark the passage from the foyer to the great room, where a centered fireplace and built-in cabinets are found. Hidden quietly in the rear, the master suite includes a bath with dual vanities and skylights. Two family bedrooms (one an optional study) share a bath with twin sinks.

Design HPT830054

Square Footage: 1,977
Bonus Space: 430 square feet
Width 69'-8" Depth 67'-6"

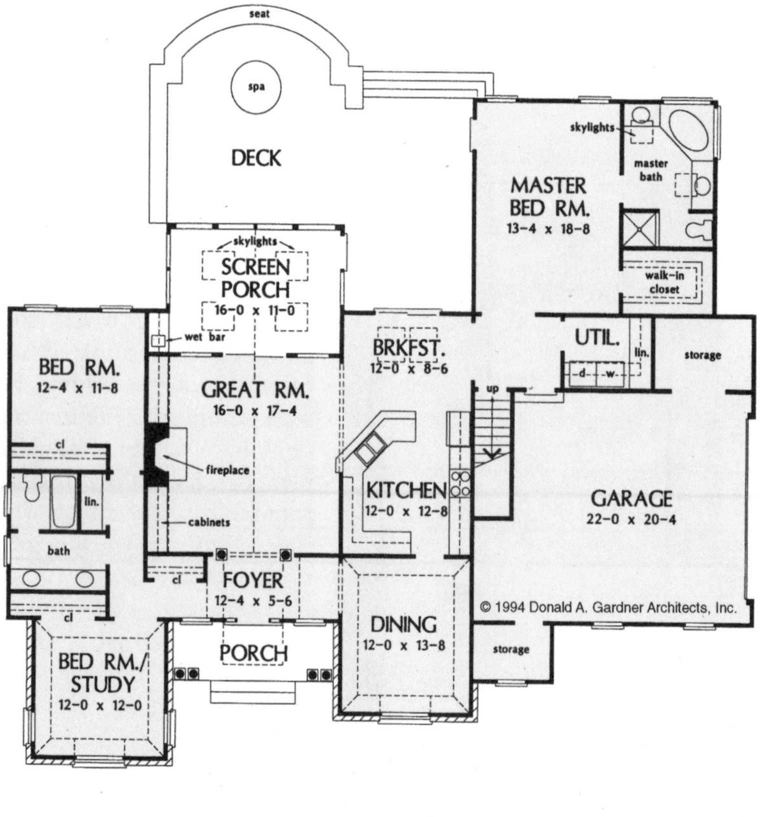

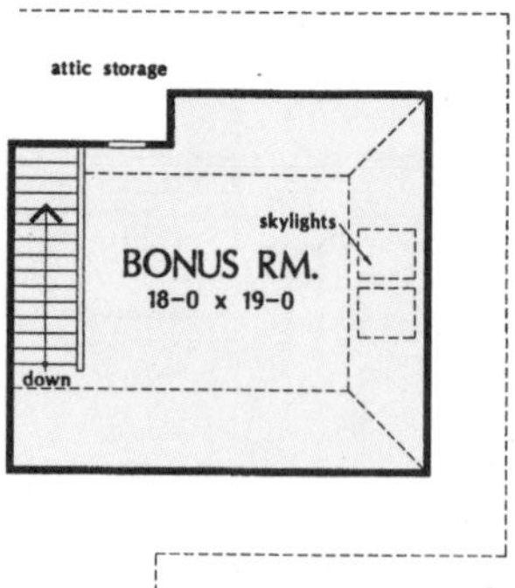

QUOTE ONE®

Cost to build? See page 516 to order complete cost estimate to build this house in your area!

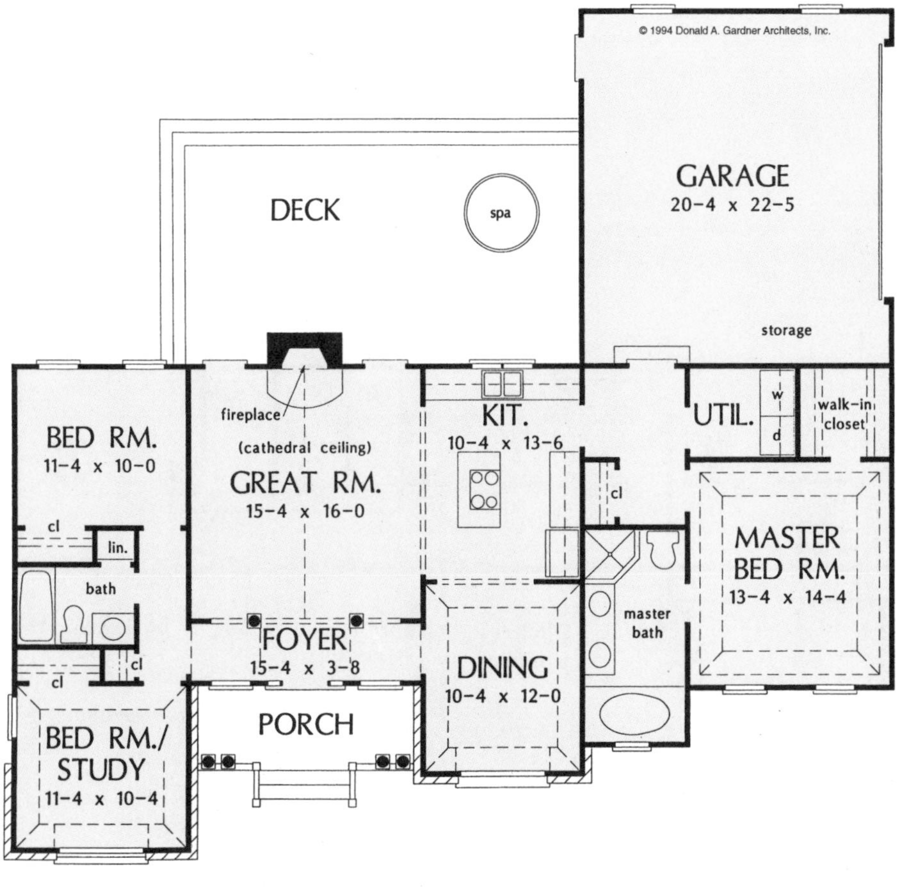
© 1994 Donald A. Gardner Architects, Inc.
GARAGE
20-4 x 22-5
DECK
spa
storage
fireplace
(cathedral ceiling)
GREAT RM.
15-4 x 16-0
KIT.
10-4 x 13-6
UTIL.
w
d
walk-in closet
BED RM.
11-4 x 10-0
cl
lin.
bath
cl
cl
cl
MASTER BED RM.
13-4 x 14-4
master bath
FOYER
15-4 x 3-8
DINING
10-4 x 12-0
PORCH
BED RM./ STUDY
11-4 x 10-4

Design HPT830055

Square Footage: 1,475
Width 59'-6" Depth 54'-7"

This design exhibits timeless appeal. The front porch leads to the columned foyer. A cathedral ceiling in the great room lends height and a feeling of openness. A fireplace is framed by doors leading to a rear deck with a spa. The kitchen easily serves an elegant dining room. In the quiet master bedroom, a tiered ceiling, lavish bath and walk-in closet are appreciated features. Two secondary bedrooms are located on the left side of the plan and share a full hall bath. The two-car garage is positioned at the rear of the plan.

Design
HPT830056

Square Footage: 2,108

Width 68'-9" Depth 68'-7"

Multi-paned windows, dormers, copper-covered bay windows, a covered porch with round columns and brick veneer siding give a sophisticated appearance to this three-bedroom home. A special feature is the sun room with hot tub adjacent to and accessible from both the master bath and great room. The great room has a fireplace, cathedral ceiling and sliding glass door with arched window above to allow plenty of natural light. The spacious master bedroom contains a walk-in closet and a bath with double-bowl vanity, shower and garden tub. Two family bedrooms are located at the opposite end of the house for privacy.

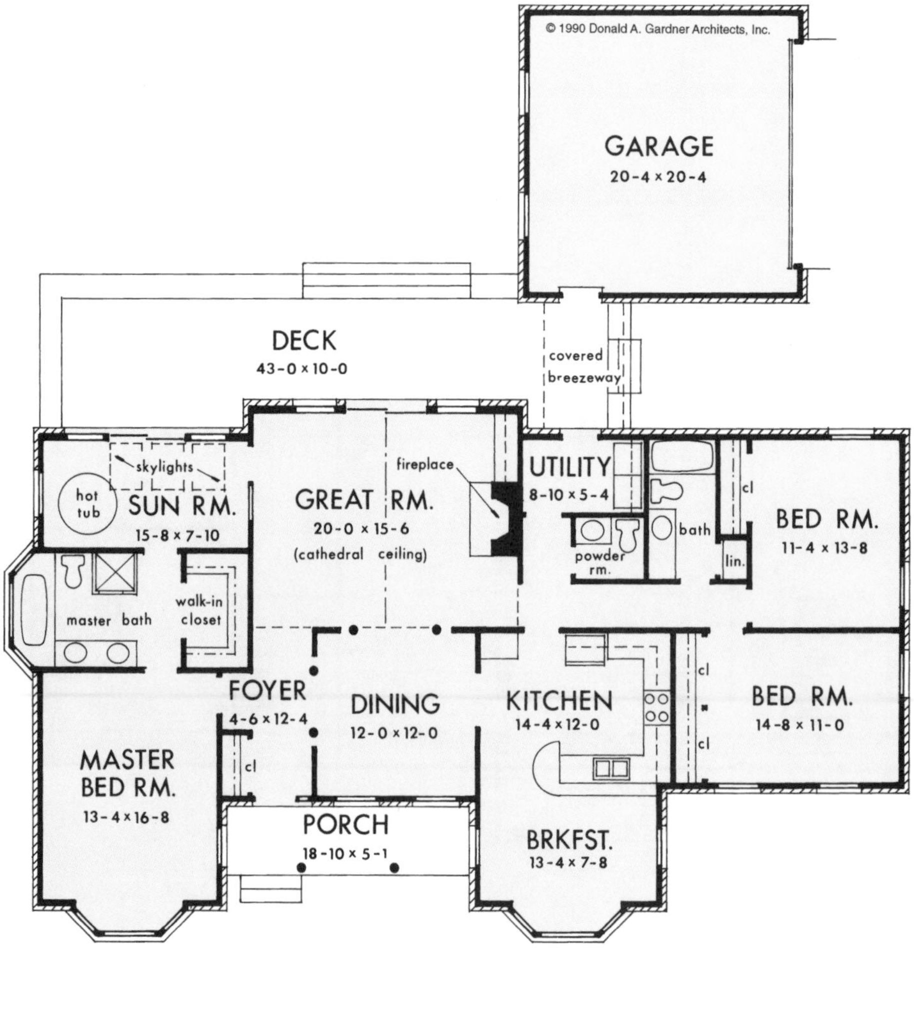

© 1993 Donald A. Gardner Architects, Inc.
B. NATHAN.

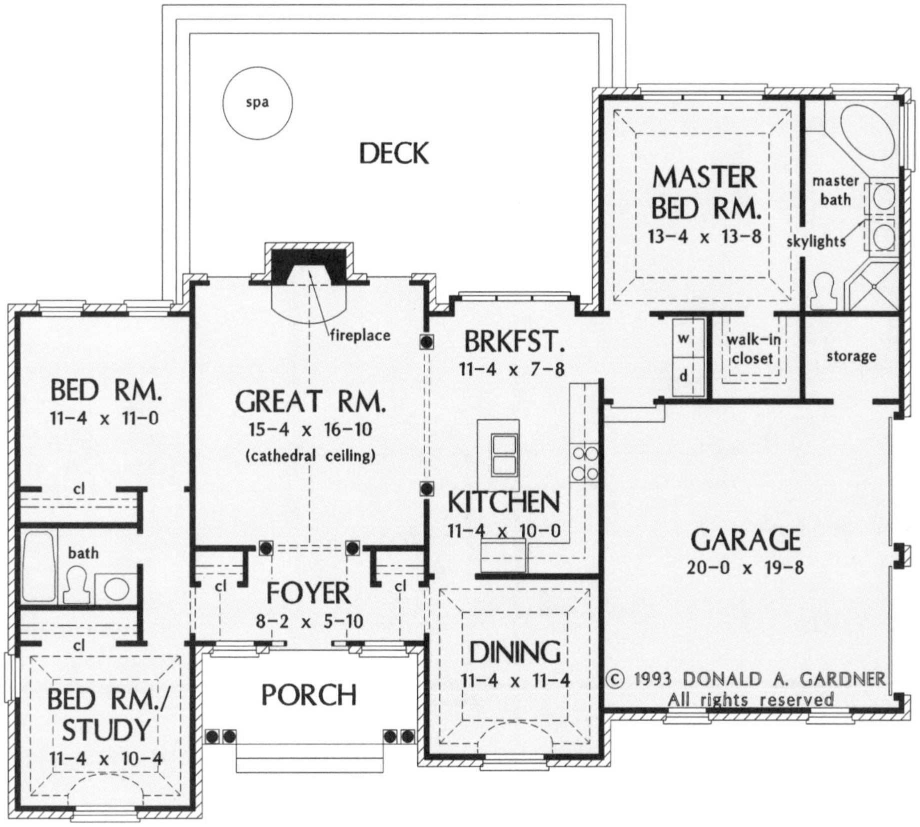
spa
DECK
MASTER BED RM.
13-4 x 13-8
master bath
skylights
fireplace
BRKFST.
11-4 x 7-8
w
d
walk-in closet
storage
BED RM.
11-4 x 11-0
GREAT RM.
15-4 x 16-10
(cathedral ceiling)
cl
KITCHEN
11-4 x 10-0
GARAGE
20-0 x 19-8
bath
cl
FOYER
8-2 x 5-10
cl
cl
DINING
11-4 x 11-4
BED RM./ STUDY
11-4 x 10-4
PORCH
© 1993 DONALD A. GARDNER
All rights reserved

This stately, three-bedroom, one-story home exhibits sheer elegance with its large, arched windows, round columns, covered porch, and brick veneer. In the foyer, natural light enters through arched windows in clerestory dormers. In the great room, a dramatic cathedral ceiling and a fireplace set the mood.

Design
HPT830057

Square Footage: 1,576
Width 66'-0" Depth 43'-3"

Design

HPT830058

Square Footage: 2,090

Width 61'-0" Depth 70'-6"

This traditional home features board-and-batten and cedar shingles in a well-proportioned exterior. The foyer opens to the dining room and leads to the great room, which offers French doors to the rear columned porch. An additional bedroom or study shares a full bath with a family bedroom, while the lavish master suite enjoys a luxurious private bath. This home is designed with a walk-out basement foundation.

QUOTE ONE®

Cost to build? See page 516 to order complete cost estimate to build this house in your area!

Master
Bedroom
16³ x 13⁶
Porch
Breakfast
13³ x 9⁰
Bedroom/
Office
10³ x 11⁰
Great
Room
17⁰ x 17⁹
Bedroom
No. 2
10³ x 12⁰
Kitchen
13³ x 10⁶
Dn
Dining
Room
11³ x 12⁹
Bedroom
No. 3
11³ x 12⁰
Two Car
Garage
20⁶ x 19⁶

Design HPT830059

Square Footage: 2,127

Width 61'-0" Depth 73'-8"

The foyer of this quaint French cottage is set apart from the formal dining room with stately columns. The great room will accommodate easy living with a grand fireplace and doors to the rear porch. A gourmet-style kitchen has a cooktop island and a bayed breakfast nook. The master suite has twin walk-in closets and a luxury bath. Two secondary bedrooms share a hall bath. An additional bedroom and bath off the kitchen would make a nice guest suite or a home office. This house is designed with a walkout basement foundation.

Design

HPT830060

Square Footage: 1,502

Width 51'-0" Depth 50'-6"

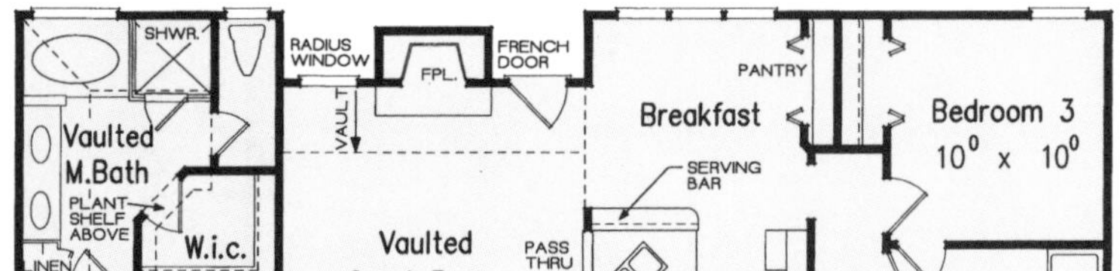

This ambitious plan masterfully combines stylish architectural elements in a smaller square footage. Elegant ceiling details, decorative columns and fancy window treatment prevail throughout this split-bedroom design. The great room is fashioned with a fireplace and has an open view into the breakfast room and serving bar. The modified galley kitchen has a convenient rear entry to the formal dining room and a service entrance through the two-car garage. Two family bedrooms and a full bath are neatly tucked behind the breakfast nook. The master suite is truly an owner's retreat with a cozy sitting room that's accented with a vaulted ceiling and sunny windows. The compartmented bath has a twin vanity and a walk-in closet. Please specify slab, crawlspace or basement foundation when ordering.

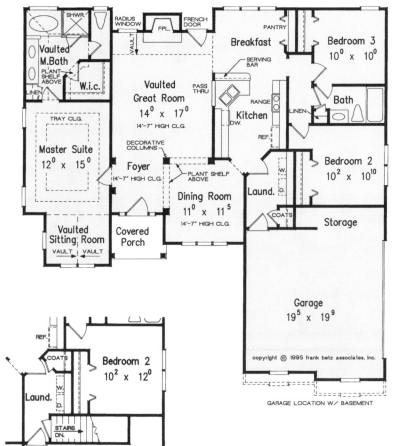

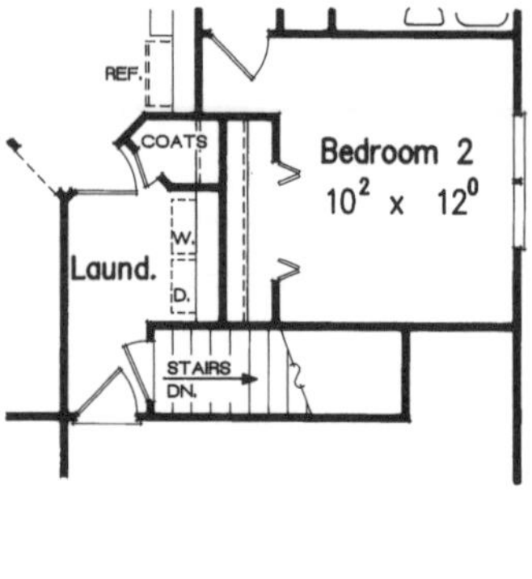

Design HPT830061

Square Footage: 1,884

Width 50'-0" Depth 55'-4"

Arched openings, decorative columns and elegant ceiling details highlight this livable floor plan. The country kitchen has a spacious work area, prep island and breakfast nook. The dining room is set to the rear for gracious entertaining and opens to the great room. The master suite is beautifully appointed with a compartmented bath and walk-in closet. Please specify basement, crawlspace or slab foundation when ordering.

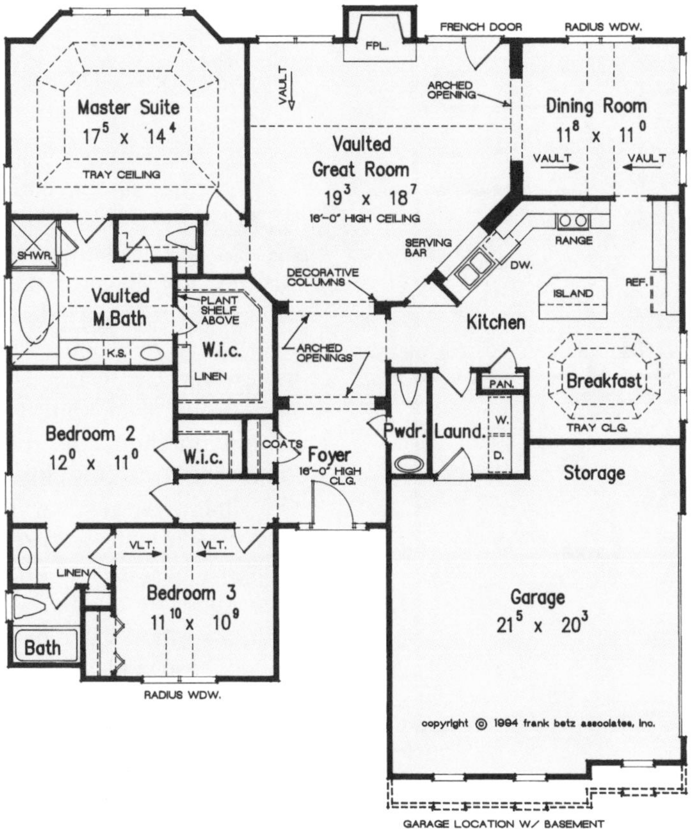
FPL.
FRENCH DOOR
RADIUS WDW.
Master Suite
17^5 x 14^4
TRAY CEILING
VAULT
ARCHED OPENING
Dining Room
11^8 x 11^0
VAULT
VAULT
Vaulted
Great Room
19^3 x 18^7
16'-0" HIGH CEILING
SERVING BAR
RANGE
SHWR.
DECORATIVE COLUMNS
DW.
Vaulted
M.Bath
PLANT SHELF ABOVE
ISLAND
REF.
Kitchen
K.S.
W.i.c.
LINEN
ARCHED OPENINGS
Breakfast
PAN.
TRAY CLG.
Bedroom 2
12^0 x 11^0
W.i.c.
COATS
Foyer
16'-0" HIGH CLG.
Pwdr.
Laund.
W.
D.
Storage
VLT.
VLT.
LINEN
Bedroom 3
11^{10} x 10^9
Garage
21^5 x 20^3
Bath
RADIUS WDW.
copyright © 1994 frank betz associates, inc.
GARAGE LOCATION W/ BASEMENT

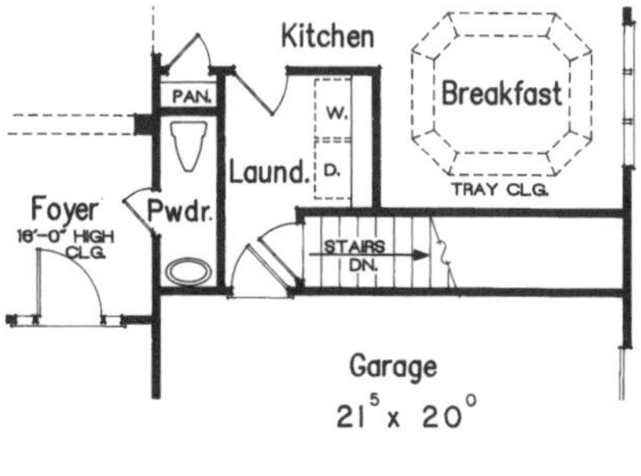
Kitchen
PAN.
W.
D.
Breakfast
Laund.
TRAY CLG.
Foyer
16'-0" HIGH CLG.
Pwdr.
STAIRS DN.
Garage
21^5 x 20^0

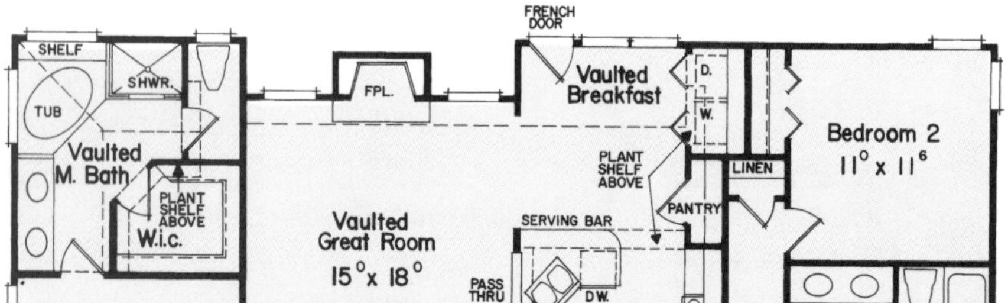
FRENCH DOOR
SHELF
SHWR.
TUB
Vaulted M. Bath
PLANT SHELF ABOVE
W.i.c.
FPL.
Vaulted Breakfast
D.
W.
Bedroom 2
11⁰ x 11⁶
LINEN
PLANT SHELF ABOVE
PANTRY
Vaulted Great Room
15⁰ x 18⁰
14'-0" HIGH CLG.
SERVING BAR
PASS THRU
D.W.
RANGE
Kitchen
Bath
PLANT SHELF ABOVE
REF.
TRAY CLG.
Master Suite
12⁵ x 15⁹
ARCHED OPENING
Bedroom 3
11⁰ x 11⁴
Foyer
14'-0" HIGH CLG.
NICHE
COATS
PLANT SHELF ABOVE
Vaulted Sitting Room
9⁵ x 10³
Covered Entry
Dining Room
10⁹ x 12⁰
14'-0" HIGH CLG.
OPT. STAIRS TO BSMT.
Garage
19⁵ x 22³
copyright © 1992 frank betz associates, inc.

QUOTE ONE®

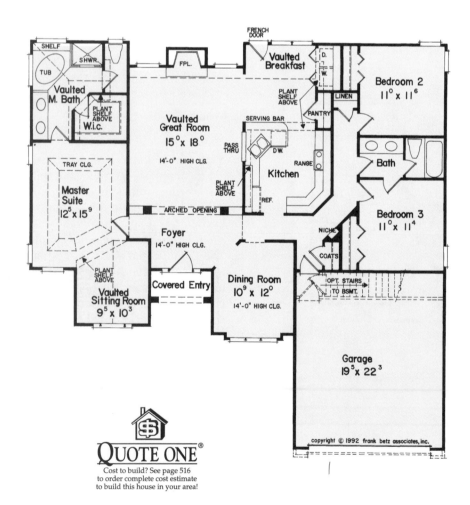

Cost to build? See page 516 to order complete cost estimate to build this house in your area!

Design HPT830062

Square Footage: 1,715
Width 55'-0" Depth 49'-0"

A grand double bank of windows looking in on the formal dining room mirrors the lofty elegance of the extra-tall vaulted ceiling inside. From the foyer, an arched entrance to the great room visually frames the fireplace on the back wall. The wraparound kitchen has plenty of counter and cabinet space, along with a handy serving bar. The luxurious master suite features a front sitting room for quiet times and a large spa-style bath. Two family bedrooms share a hall bath. Please specify basement, slab or crawlspace foundation when ordering.

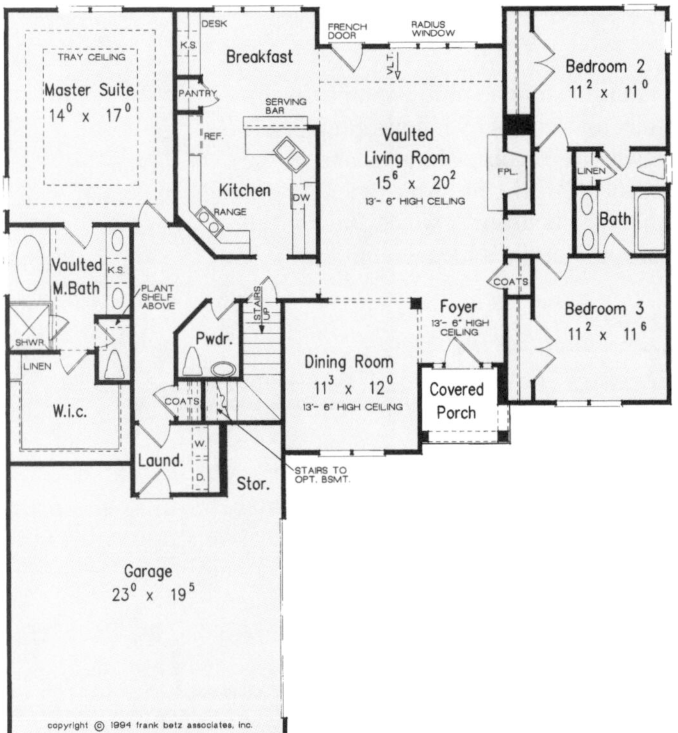

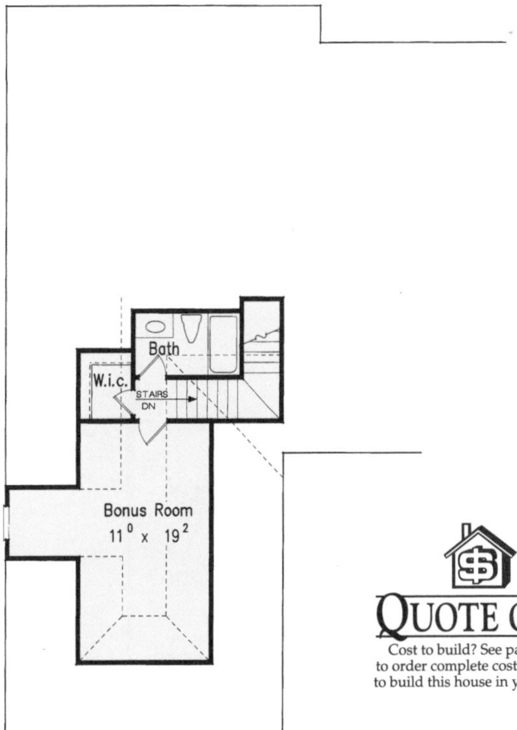

QUOTE ONE®

Cost to build? See page 516 to order complete cost estimate to build this house in your area!

The stucco exterior and combination rooflines give a stately appearance to this traditional home. Inside, the well-lit foyer leads to an elegant living room with a vaulted ceiling, fireplace, radius window and French door that opens to the rear property. Two family bedrooms share a full bath on the right side of the home, while an impressive master suite resides to the left for privacy. A formal dining room and an open kitchen with plenty of counter space complete the plan. Please specify basement, crawlspace or slab foundation when ordering.

Design
HPT830063

Square Footage: 1,845
Bonus Space: 409 square feet
Width 56'-0" Depth 60'-0"

The striking European facade of this home presents a beautiful stone exterior, complete with stone quoins, a shingled rooftop and French-style shutters on the front windows. Step inside the great room where a ten-foot ceiling and fireplace will greet you. A large island in the kitchen provides plenty of much-needed counter space for the cook of the family. An element of privacy is observed with the master suite separated from the other two bedrooms, which share a full bath. An oversized two-car garage and a covered patio are just some of the added amenities.

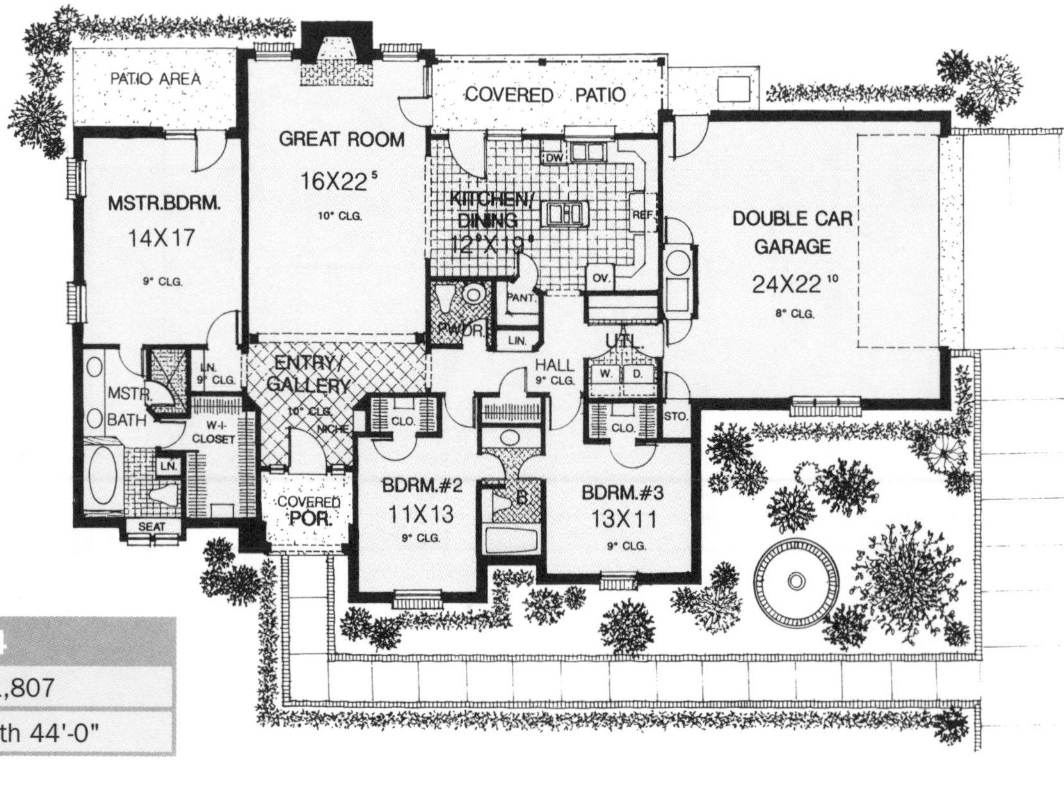

Design
HPT830064

Square Footage: 1,807

Width 74'-0" Depth 44'-0"

The central great room is highlighted with a fireplace and cathedral ceiling. Nearby is a skylit sun room with sliding glass doors to the rear deck and a built-in wet bar. The master suite is separated from the family bedrooms and has access to the rear deck. Family bedrooms share a full bath that includes a double vanity.

Design
HPT830065

Square Footage: 2,099
Width 72'-6" Depth 53'-10"

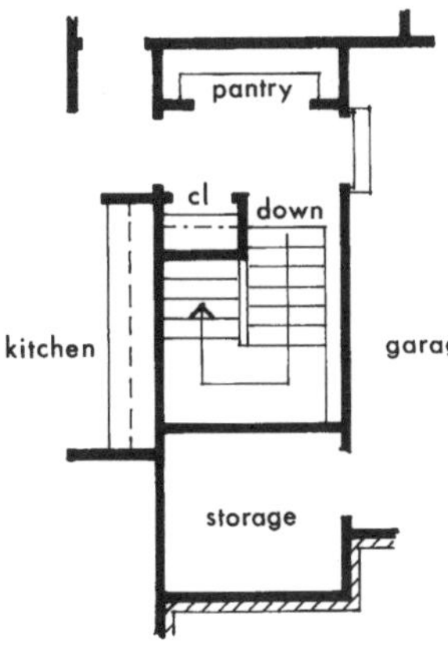

B. NATHAN

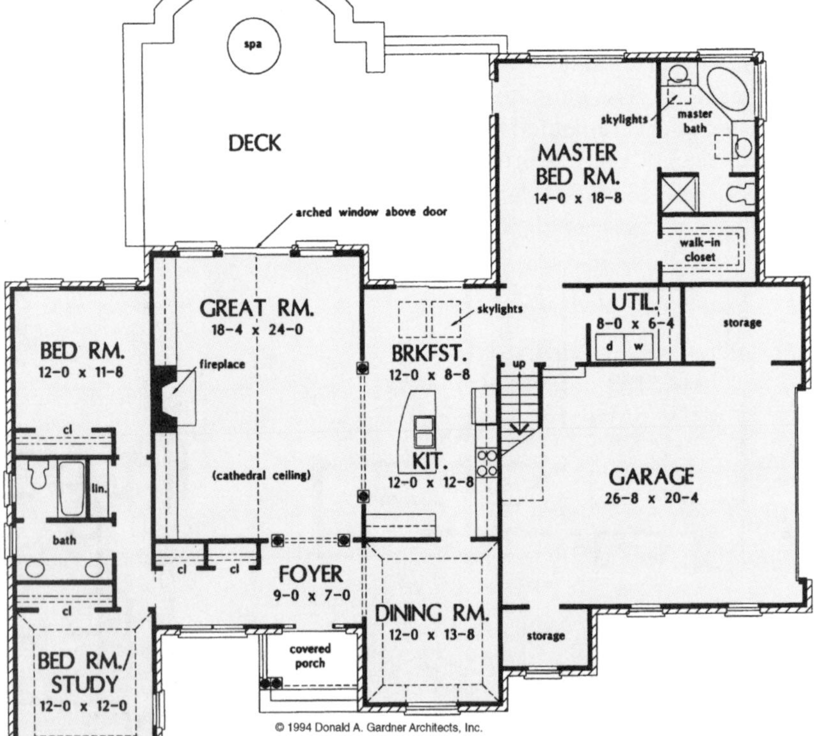
seat
spa
DECK
arched window above door
skylights
master bath
MASTER BED RM.
14-0 x 18-8
walk-in closet
GREAT RM.
18-4 x 24-0
fireplace
(cathedral ceiling)
BED RM.
12-0 x 11-8
cl
lin.
bath
cl
skylights
BRKFST.
12-0 x 8-8
UTIL.
8-0 x 6-4
d w
storage
up
KIT.
12-0 x 12-8
GARAGE
26-8 x 20-4
cl
cl
FOYER
9-0 x 7-0
DINING RM.
12-0 x 13-8
storage
covered porch
BED RM./ STUDY
12-0 x 12-0

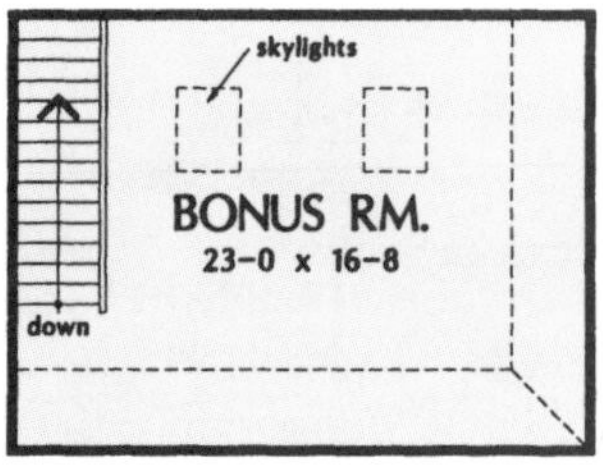
skylights
BONUS RM.
23-0 x 16-8
down

This home is built for entertaining. The large great room is perfect for parties. The kitchen, with sunny skylights and an adjoining dining room, creates a cozy breakfast buffet. Access from both rooms to the expansive deck completes the picture perfectly. The location of the master bedroom and the other bedrooms allows for quiet comfort. You'll love the bonus room, which can be made into a game room or a study.

Design

HPT830066

Square Footage: 2,211
Bonus Space: 408 square feet
Width 71'-7" Depth 59'-11"

Design HPT830067

Square Footage: 1,850

Width 54'-8" Depth 52'-8"

This stately brick one-story home features a side-loading garage, which helps to maintain a beautiful facade. The elegant entry leads to a central hallway, connecting living areas and sleeping quarters, and opens to a formal dining room on the left. A splendid master suite with a coffered ceiling offers private access to the rear deck as well as a pleasant bath with a garden tub, glass-enclosed shower and walk-in closet. This home is designed with a walkout basement foundation.

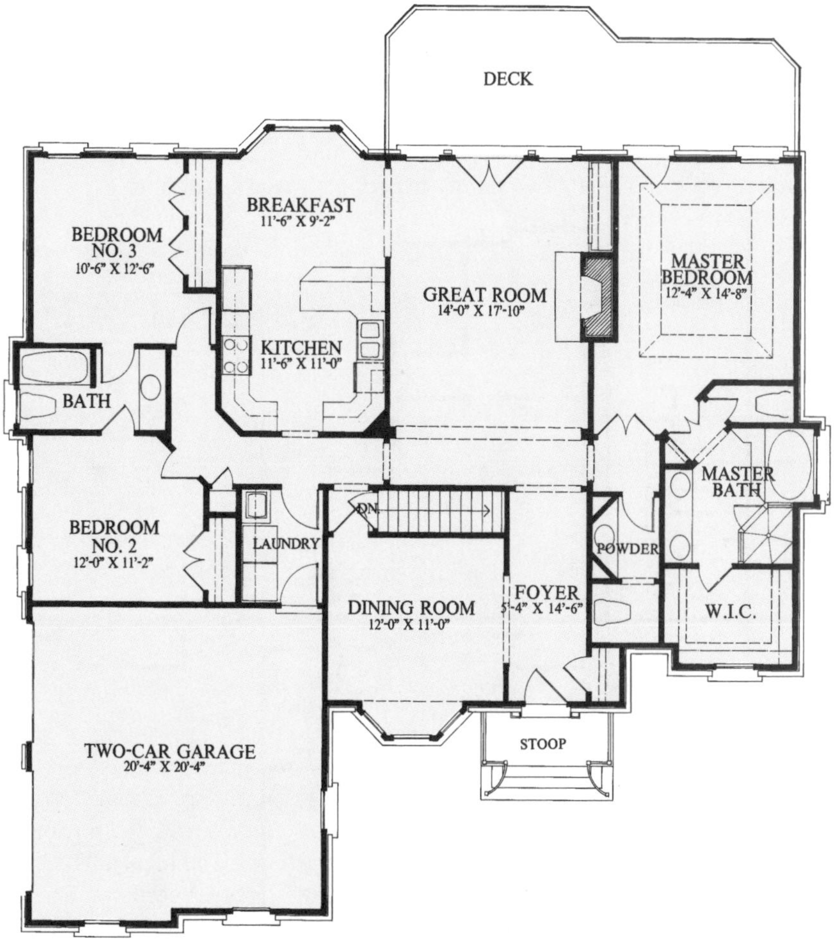

From its hipped rooflines to the corner quoins, this design has plenty of curb appeal. Inside, with large living spaces, this one-story also has plenty of room for great family living. The formal dining room is complemented by an informal eating area, both of which are easily served by the efficient island kitchen. Both connect to the spacious family room, which is complete with a warming fireplace. The large master suite has a compartmented bath and walk-in closet. Two family bedrooms share a hall bath.

Design HPT830068

Square Footage: 1,800
Width 65'-0" Depth 50'-6"

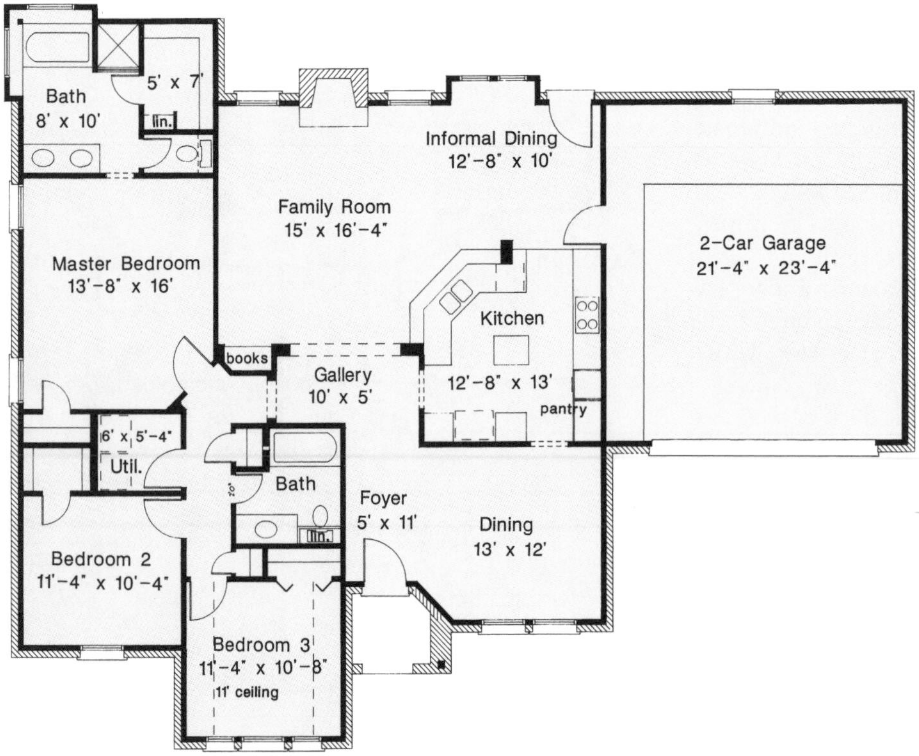

Design HPT830069

Square Footage: 2,120

Width 62'-0" Depth 62'-6"

Arched lintels and fanlight windows act as graceful accents for this design. The formal dining room is to the front of the plan and is open to the entry foyer. A private den also opens off the foyer with double doors. Bedrooms are split, with the master suite to the right side of the design and family bedrooms to the left. This home is designed with a walk-out basement foundation.

QUOTE ONE®

Cost to build? See page 516 to order complete cost estimate to build this house in your area!

ALTERNATE ELEVATION

Two elevations are available for this delightful one-story home. Brick, shutters and corner quoins provide European ambiance, while gables and horizontal wood siding offer a more traditional elevation—the choice is yours. With an eleven-foot ceiling, a warming fireplace and built-in bookcases, the great room will certainly be the family's favorite. The kitchen is bookended by the formal dining room and the sunny breakfast nook, which has an exit to the patio. Three bedrooms cluster on the left with a full bath, while the master suite, with a pair of walk-in closets and a lavish bath, is secluded on the right for privacy.

Design

HPT830070

Square Footage: 2,065

Width 60'-0" Depth 65'-10"

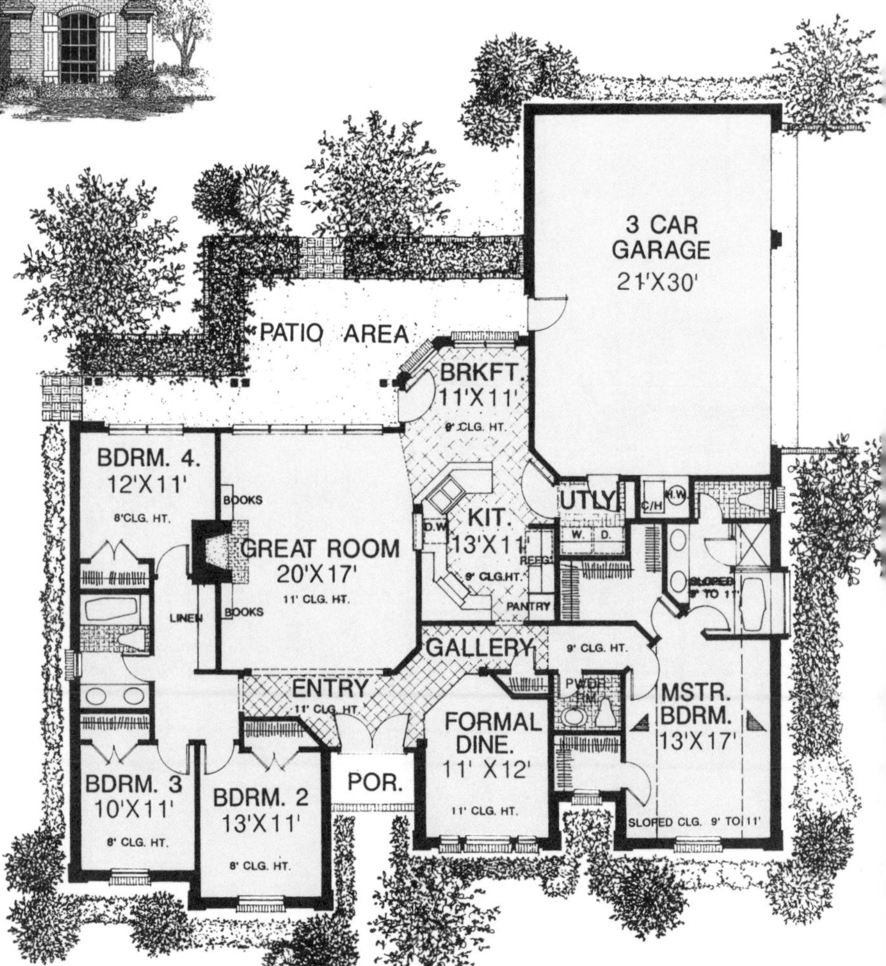

Design HPT830071

Square Footage: 1,733

Width 55'-6" Depth 57'-6"

Delightfully different, this brick one-story home offers everything for the active family. The entry foyer opens to a formal dining room, accented with four columns, and a great room with a fireplace and French doors to the rear deck. The master suite features a tray ceiling, His and Hers walk-in closets, a double vanity and a garden tub. This home is designed with a walk-out basement foundation.

DECK
BREAKFAST
11'-4" X 8'-6"
BEDROOM NO. 3
11'-6" X 11'-0"
GREAT ROOM
14'-0" X 17'-6"
KITCHEN
11'-4" X 10'-0"
MASTER BEDROOM
12'-4" X 15'-6"
BATH
DN.
HIS
FOYER
6'-6" X 6'-6"
MASTER BATH
PWDR.
BEDROOM NO. 2
11'-0" X 14'-8"
DINING ROOM
11'-4" X 10'-6"
LAUNDRY
HERS
TWO-CAR GARAGE
20'-4" X 19'-4"

Design

HPT830072

Square Footage: 2,095

Width 65'-0" Depth 55'-11"

Inside this home, the foyer opens to the living room and the dining room, accented by dramatic window details.The open family room displays a fireplace and built-in cabinetry. In the master suite, a large bath with dual vanities, whirlpool tub and separate shower is complete with a spacious walk-in closet. Two additional bedrooms sit on the opposite side of the home. This home is designed with a walkout basement foundation.

DECK
BREAKFAST
11'-4" X 9'-4"
BATH
BEDROOM NO. 2
11'-0" X 12'-0"
KITCHEN
10'-8" X 12'-2"
FAMILY ROOM
17'-8" X 15'-4"
MASTER BEDROOM
13'-8" X 15'-4"
DN.
BEDROOM NO. 3
11'-0" X 12'-0"
LAUNDRY
POWDER
MASTER BATH
FOYER
6'-0" X 12'-0"
LIVING ROOM
11'-4" X 14'-0"
W.I.C.
DINING ROOM
11'-8" X 15'-0"
STOOP
TWO CAR GARAGE
20'-4" X 19'-10"

QUOTE ONE®

Cost to build? See page 516 to order complete cost estimate to build this house in your area!

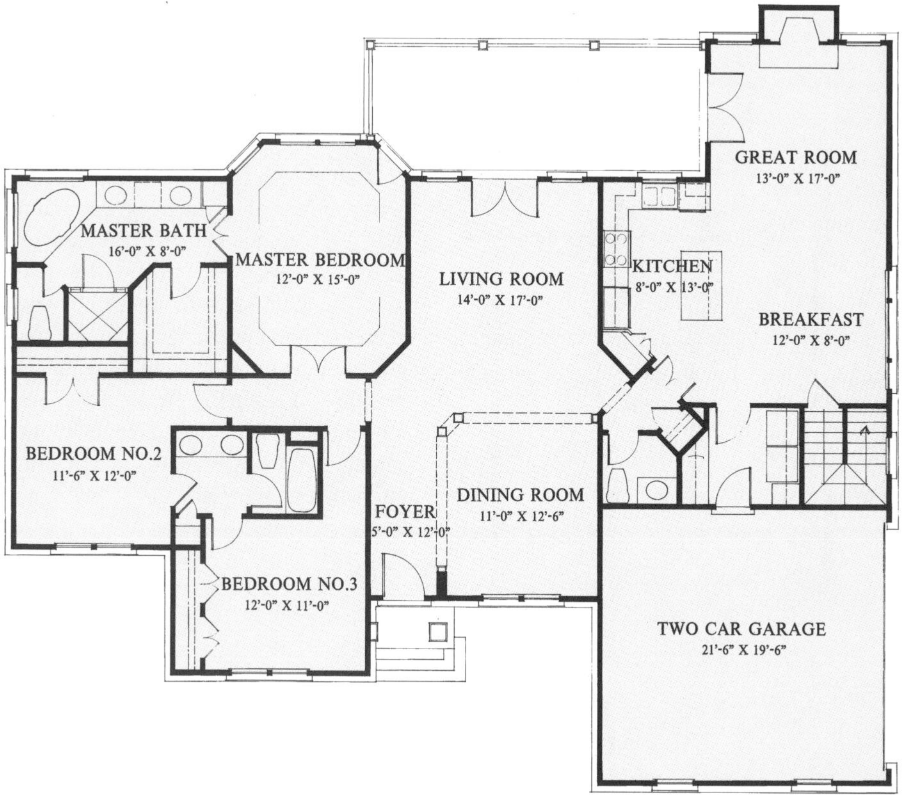

Design HPT830073

Square Footage: 2,077

Width 56'-0" Depth 54'-0"

A porch with column detailing covers the entry to this single-story American classic. Inside, the foyer opens to the living room with a wall of windows and French doors that lead outside. A splendid colonnade defines the banquet-sized dining room. To the right, the spacious kitchen with a work island opens to a sunlit breakfast area and a great room featuring a warming hearth and doors to the rear deck. A hallway just off the foyer leads to the double doors of the master suite. Inside, the special shape of the suite and mirrored ceiling detail make this room unique. The bath accommodates every need with His and Hers vanities, a garden tub and walk-in closet. Two additional bedrooms share a compartmented bath. This home is designed with a walkout basement foundation.

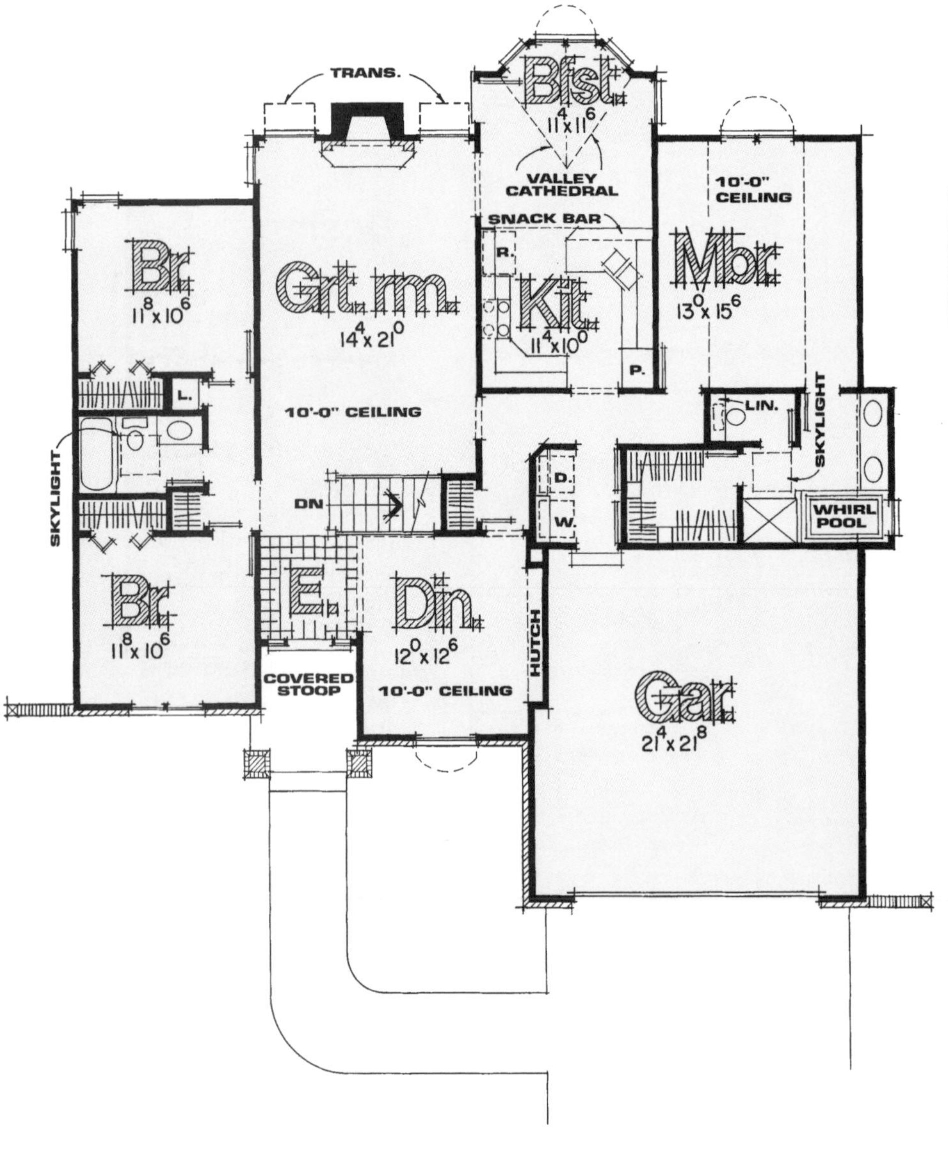

Design HPT830074

Square Footage: 1,697
Width 54'-0" Depth 54'-0"

This volume-look home gives the impression of size and scope in just under 1,700 square feet. The large great room with a fireplace is perfect for entertaining. Its proximity to the kitchen, breakfast room and formal dining room ensures easy serving and cleanup. The master suite includes a luxurious bath. Two family bedrooms offer ample closet space and share a full bath that includes a skylight.

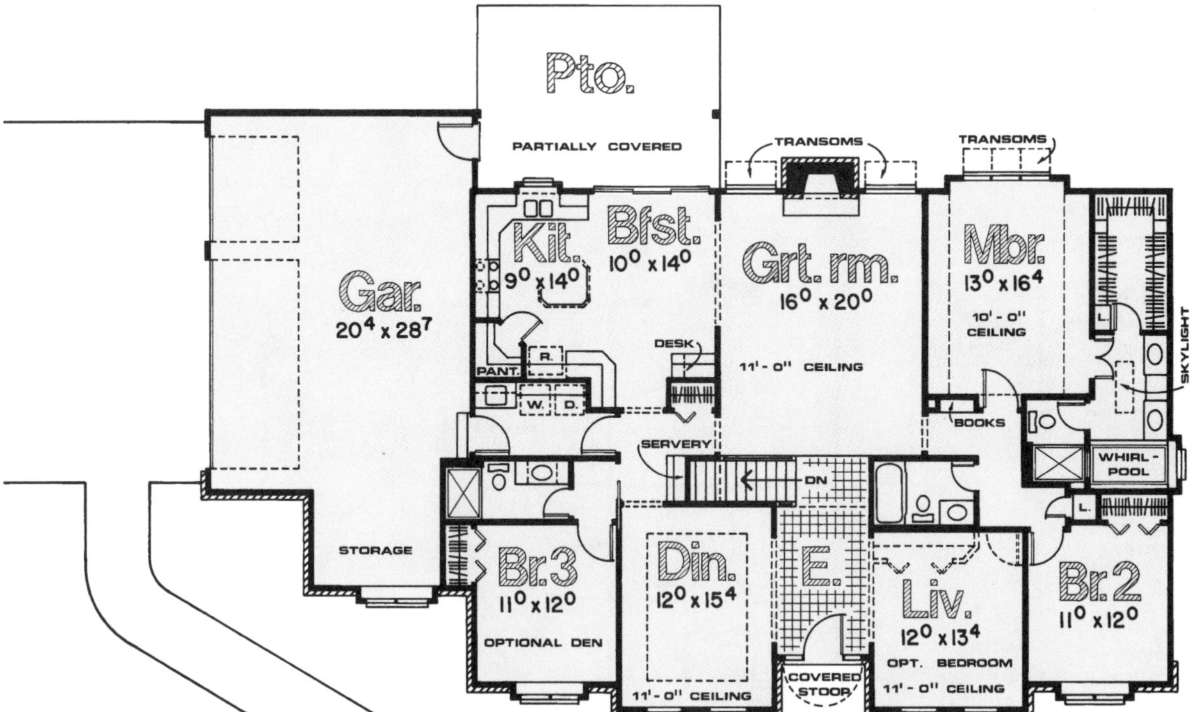
Pto.
PARTIALLY COVERED
TRANSOMS
TRANSOMS
Kit.
9⁰ x 14⁰
Bfst.
10⁰ x 14⁰
Grt. rm.
16⁰ x 20⁰
11'-0" CEILING
Mbr.
13⁰ x 16⁴
10'-0" CEILING
SKYLIGHT
Gar.
20⁴ x 28⁷
DESK
PANT.
R.
W.
D.
SERVERY
BOOKS
WHIRL-POOL
L.
DN
STORAGE
Br.3
11⁰ x 12⁰
OPTIONAL DEN
Din.
12⁰ x 15⁴
11'-0" CEILING
E.
COVERED STOOP
Liv.
12⁰ x 13⁴
OPT. BEDROOM
11'-0" CEILING
Br.2
11⁰ x 12⁰

QUOTE ONE®

Cost to build? See page 516 to order complete cost estimate to build this house in your area!

This one-story home holds a most convenient floor plan. The great room with a fireplace complements a front-facing living room. The formal dining room is convenient to the kitchen. An island, pantry, breakfast room and patio are highlights in the kitchen. A bedroom at this end of the house works fine as an office or guest bedroom. Two additional bedrooms are to the right of the plan: a master suite and a family bedroom.

Design
HPT830075

Square Footage: 2,172

Width 76'-0" Depth 46'-0"

Design

HPT830076

Square Footage: 2,132

Width 72'-0" Depth 58'-0"

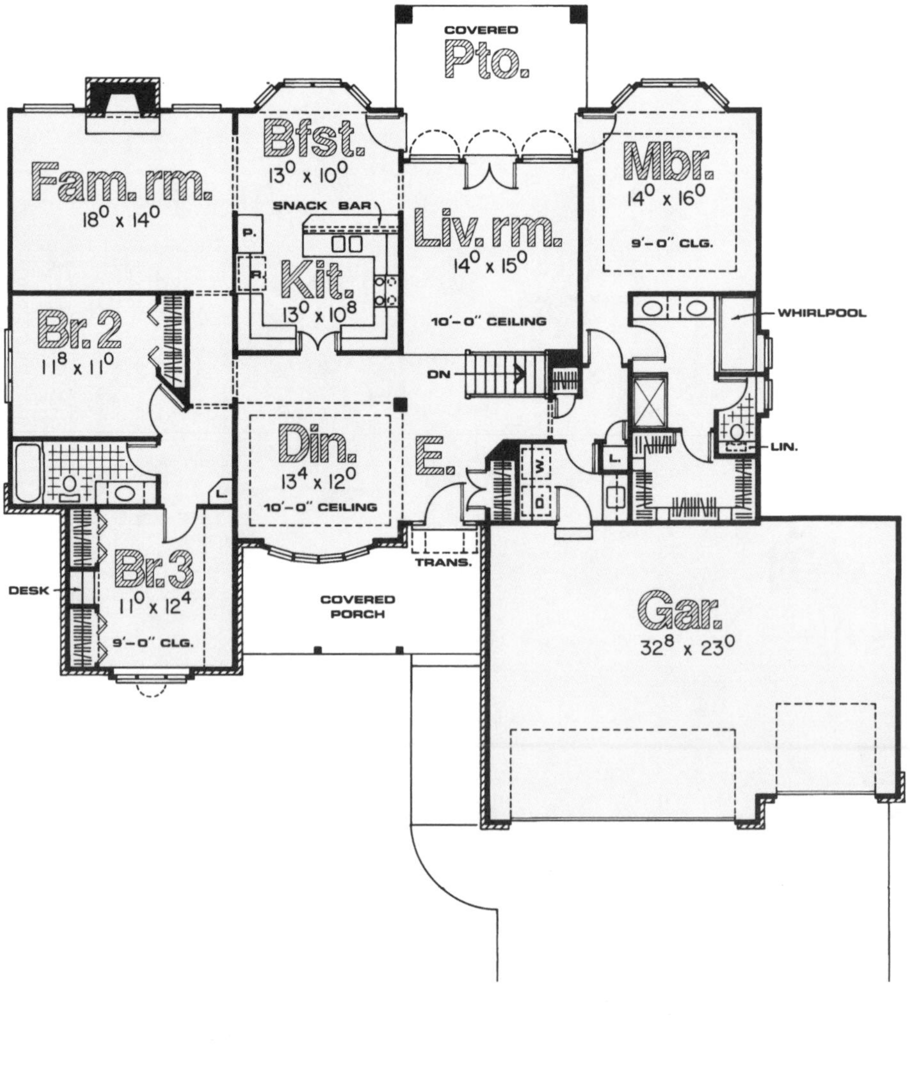

Amenities fill this ranch-style home, from the covered front porch to the covered patio. Upon entering, the foyer opens to a formal dining room enhanced by a bow window. To the rear is a living room filled with light, compliments of a glass wall. Casual times will be enjoyed in the family room with its warming fireplace. The adjacent kitchen is planned for maximum counter space and serves the bayed breakfast room as well as the formal and informal living areas. Separated from the family bedrooms for privacy, the master suite enjoys a bay window.

Design HPT830077

Square Footage: 1,496	
Width 48'-0"	Depth 52'-0"

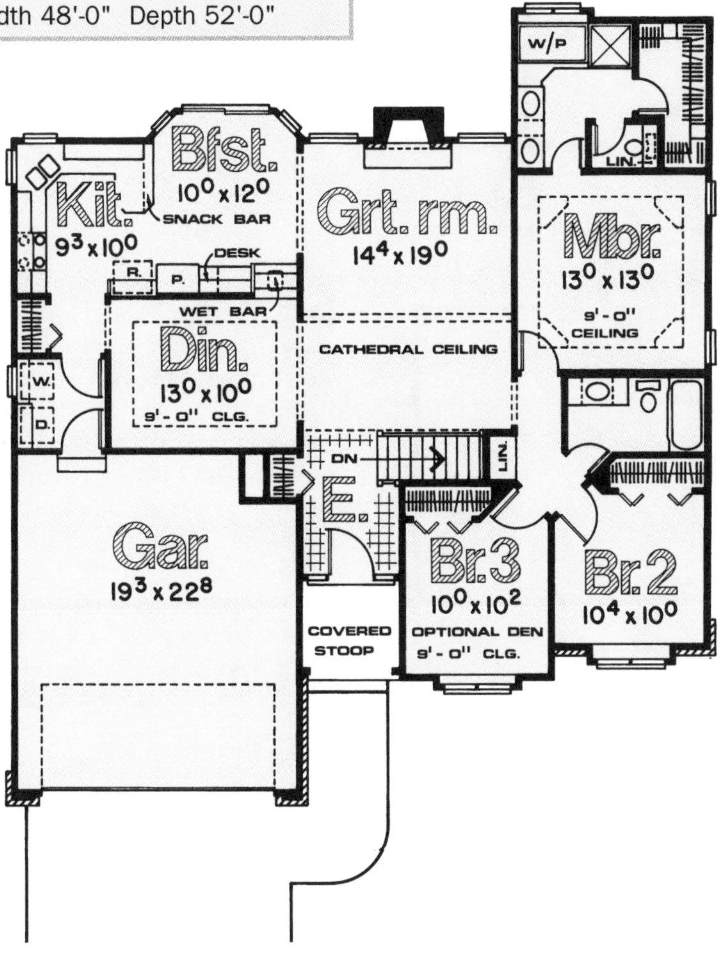

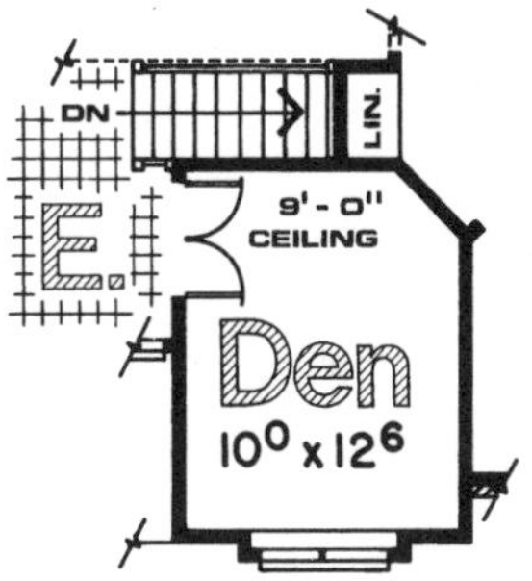

OPTIONAL DEN

Sleek rooflines, lap siding and brick accents highlight the exterior of this three-bedroom ranch home. A tiled entry views the spacious great room featuring a sloping cathedral ceiling and window-framed fireplace. Note the strategic location of the dining room (with a nine-foot boxed ceiling and wet bar/servery), which accommodates formal entertaining and family gatherings. Natural light and warmth add comfort to the bayed breakfast area with its pantry and handy planning desk and the peninsula kitchen. Well-separated sleeping quarters add to the flexibility of this modern floor plan. Both secondary bedrooms share a full bath and linen closet. Bedroom 3 is easily converted to a den or home office. With the nine-foot boxed ceiling, walk-in closet, sunlit whirlpool tub and double vanities, the master suite is soothing and luxurious.

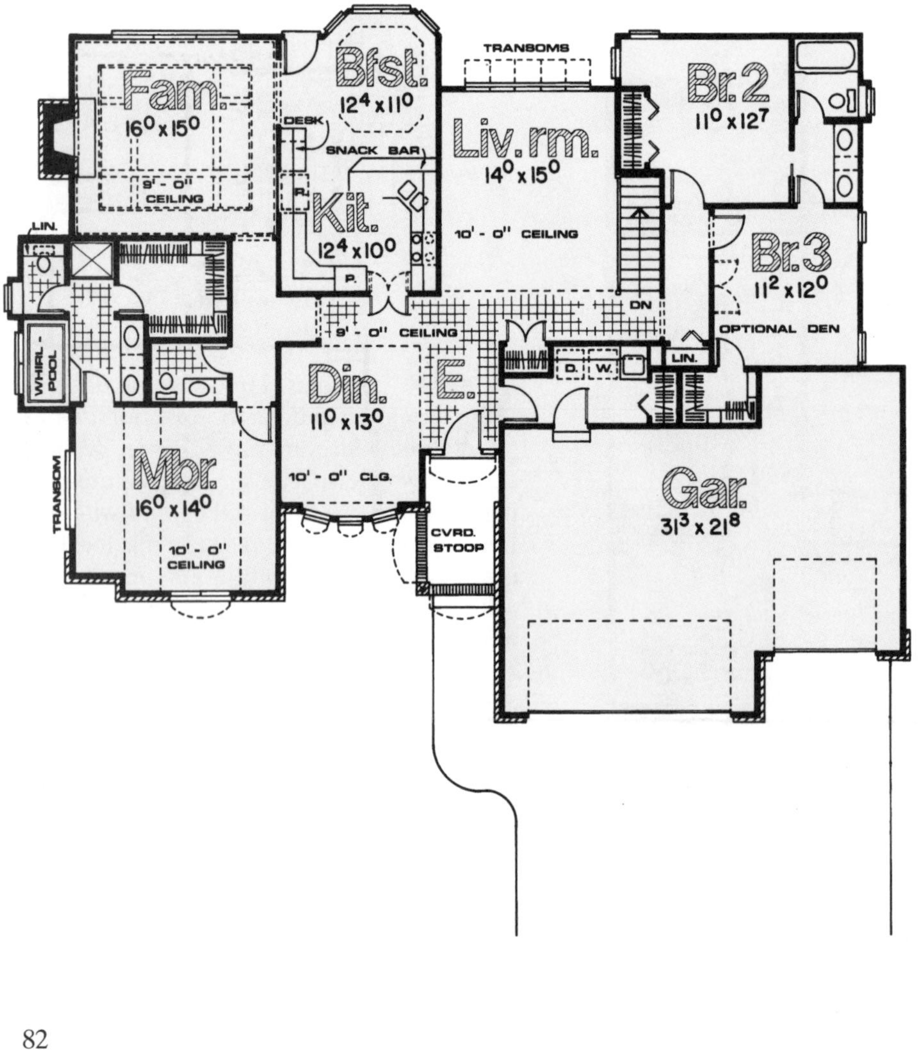

Design HPT830078

Square Footage: 2,149	
Width 70'-0"	Depth 54'-0"

Beautiful and accommodating, this ranch home features open-entry views into formal rooms plus volume ceilings in major living spaces. The beam-ceilinged family room offers a cozy fireplace. The kitchen is equipped with a snack bar open to the breakfast area, a built-in desk and a pantry. Sleeping areas are comprised of three bedrooms, including a master suite with a walk-in closet, double vanity and whirlpool tub. Two additional family bedrooms share a private bath. Bedroom 3 may be used as a den with French doors to the hall.

Drama and harmony are expressed by utilizing a variety of elegant exterior materials on this home. An expansive entry views the private den with French doors and an open dining room. The great room with a window-framed fireplace is joined by the kitchen and bayed breakfast area. His and Hers walk-in closets, a spa-style bath and a built-in entertainment center grace the master bedroom.

Design
HPT830079

Square Footage: 2,276

Width 72'-0" Depth 56'-0"

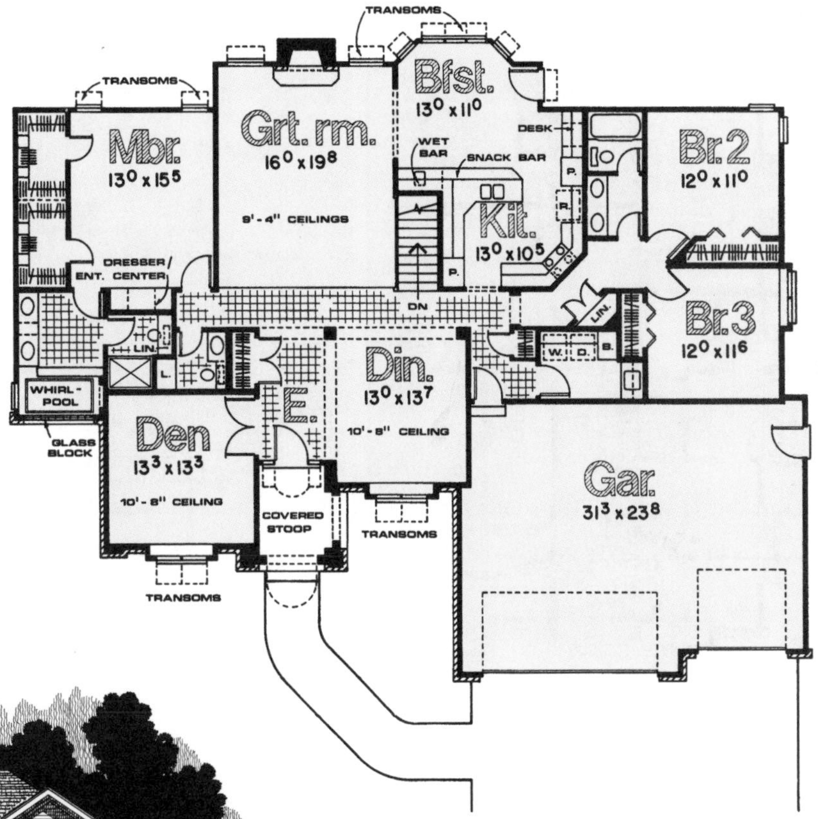

ALTERNATE ELEVATION

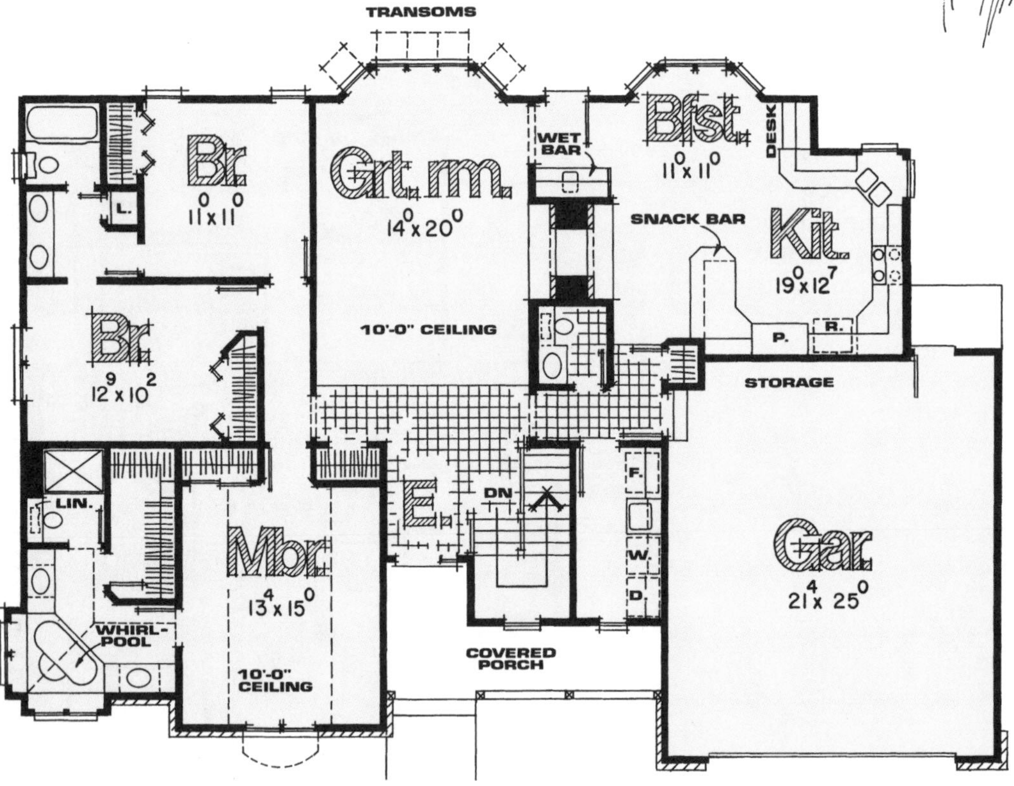

Discriminating buyers will love the refined yet inviting look of this three-bedroom home plan. A tiled entry with a ten-foot ceiling leads into the spacious great room with a large bay window. An open-hearth fireplace warms both the great room and the kitchen. The sleeping area features a spacious master suite with a dramatic arched window and a bath with a whirlpool tub, twin vanities and a walk-in closet. Two secondary bedrooms each have private access to the shared bath. Don't miss the storage space in the oversized garage.

Design
HPT830080

Square Footage: 1,808
Width 64'-0" Depth 44'-0"

Design
HPT830081

Square Footage: 1,735

Width 60'-0" Depth 50'-0"

A covered porch leads to a tiled entry within this three-bedroom home. The great room boasts a fireplace and wide views of the outdoors. An efficient island kitchen provides a center food-prep island. The master suite sports a stunning bay window and an angled whirlpool tub.

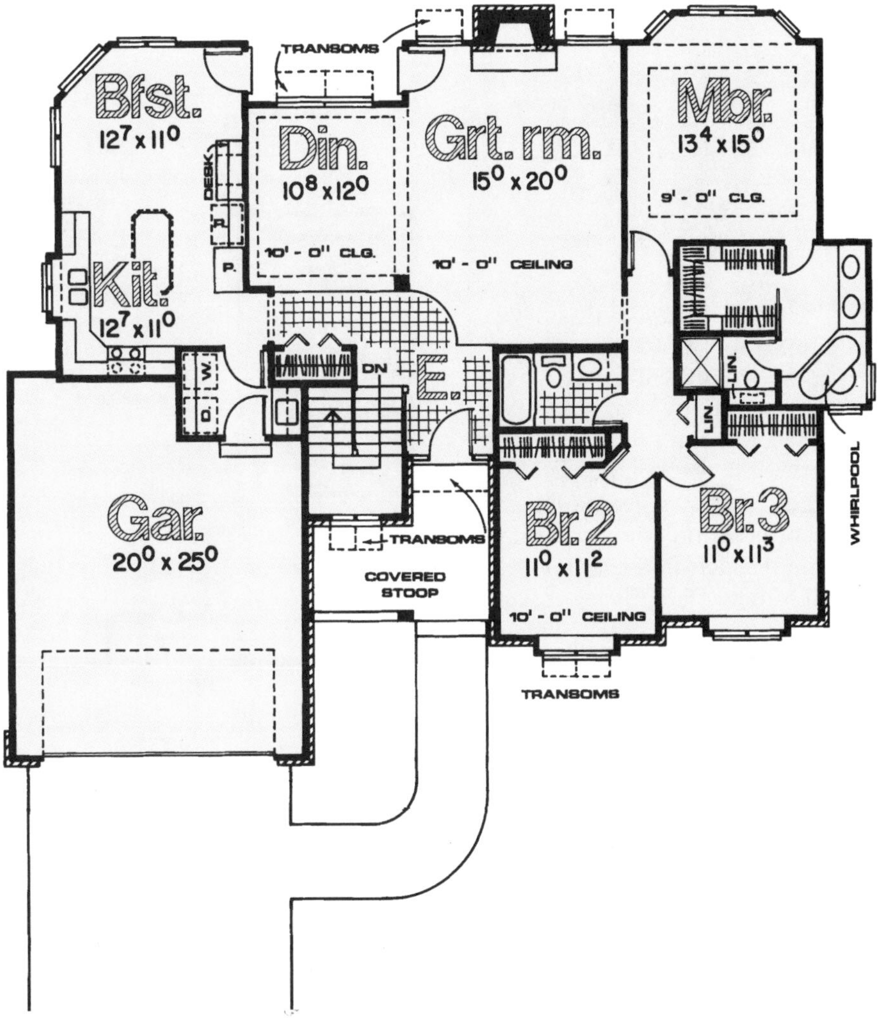

Design HPT830082

Square Footage: 1,911

Width 56'-0" Depth 58'-0"

This sophisticated three-bedroom ranch with a Palladian entry is a welcome addition to any neighborhood. Off the entry are the dining room, with a twelve-foot detailed ceiling and an arched window, and the enormous great room, which shares a through-fireplace with the hearth room. The private master suite features a detailed ceiling, corner windows, a whirlpool bath and a giant walk-in closet.

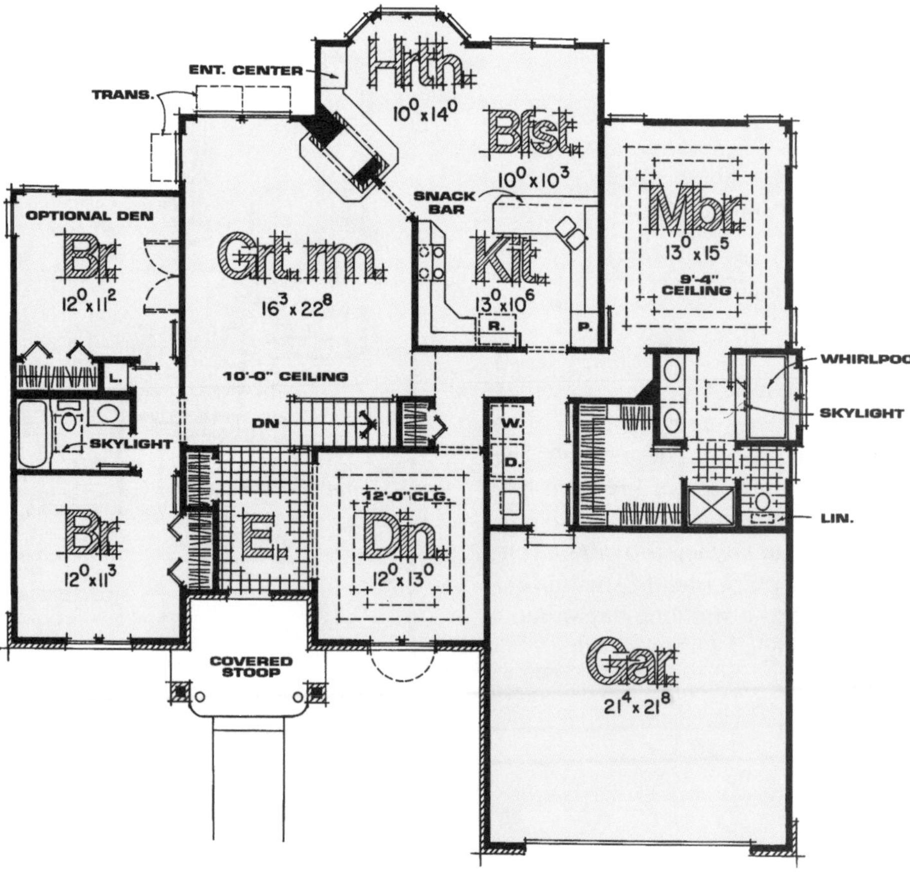

QUOTE ONE®

Cost to build? See page 516 to order complete cost estimate to build this house in your area!

Design HPT830083

Square Footage: 1,996

Width 64'-0" Depth 50'-0"

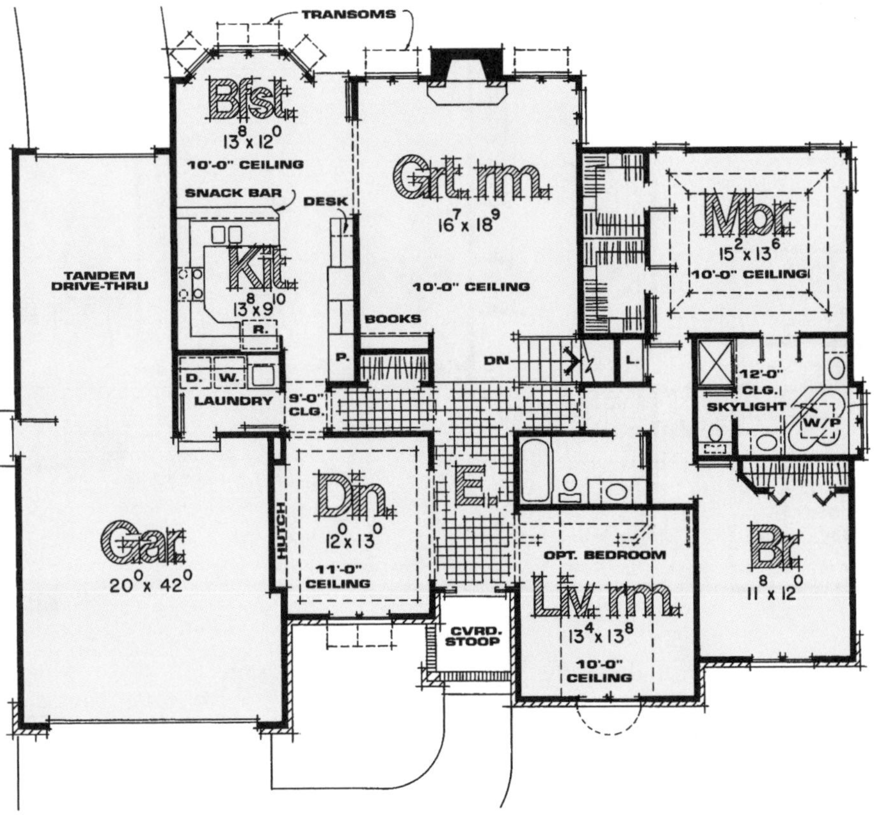

Practical, yet equipped with a variety of popular amenities, this pleasant ranch home is an excellent choice for empty-nesters or small families. The front living room can become a third bedroom if you choose. The great room with a dramatic fireplace serves as the main living area. A luxurious master suite features a ten-foot tray ceiling and a large bath with a whirlpool tub, skylight, plant ledge and twin vanities. The kitchen with a breakfast room serves both the dining and great rooms. A tandem drive-through garage holds space for a third car or extra storage.

QUOTE ONE®

Cost to build? See page 516 to order complete cost estimate to build this house in your area!

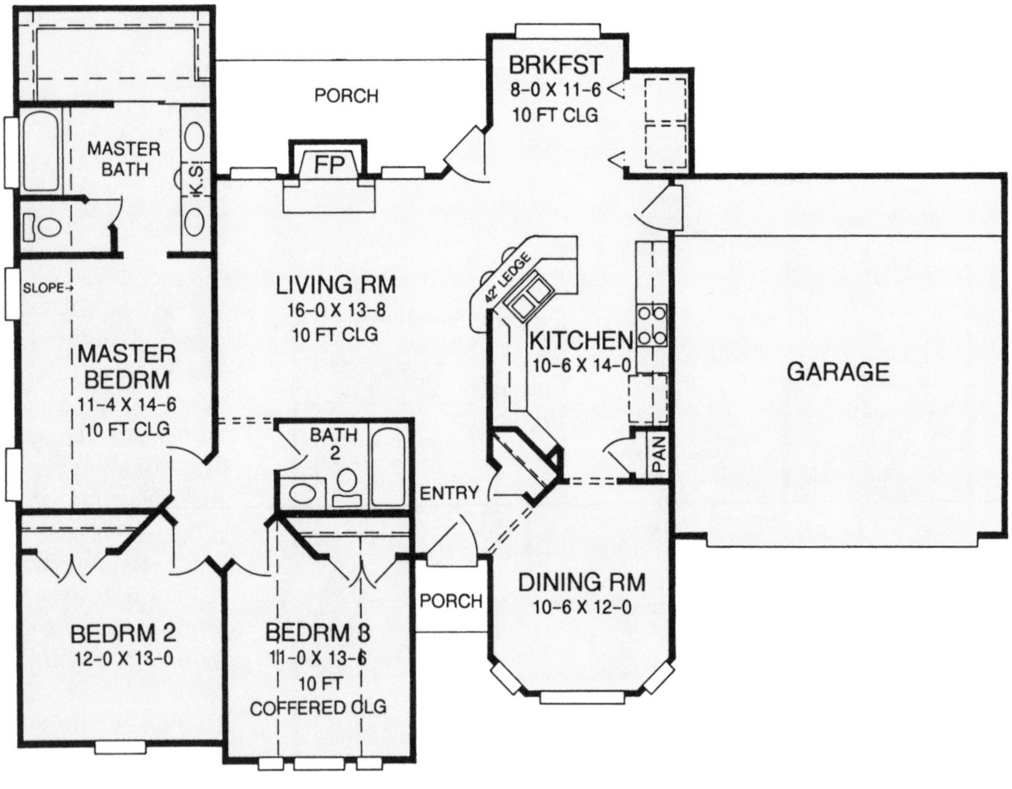

A spacious interior is implied from the curb with the lofty, hipped rooflines of this economical family home. From the entry, the large living room is fully visible, as is the rear yard, through windows flanking the fireplace. The kitchen is partially open to the living room via a snack bar and has full access to the breakfast room. A formal dining room just off the kitchen will serve entertaining needs with style. The master bedroom features a compartment bath with a sit-down vanity. Two family bedrooms share a full hall bath. Please specify crawlspace or slab foundation when ordering.

Design
HPT830084

Square Footage: 1,500

Width 59'-10" Depth 44'-4"

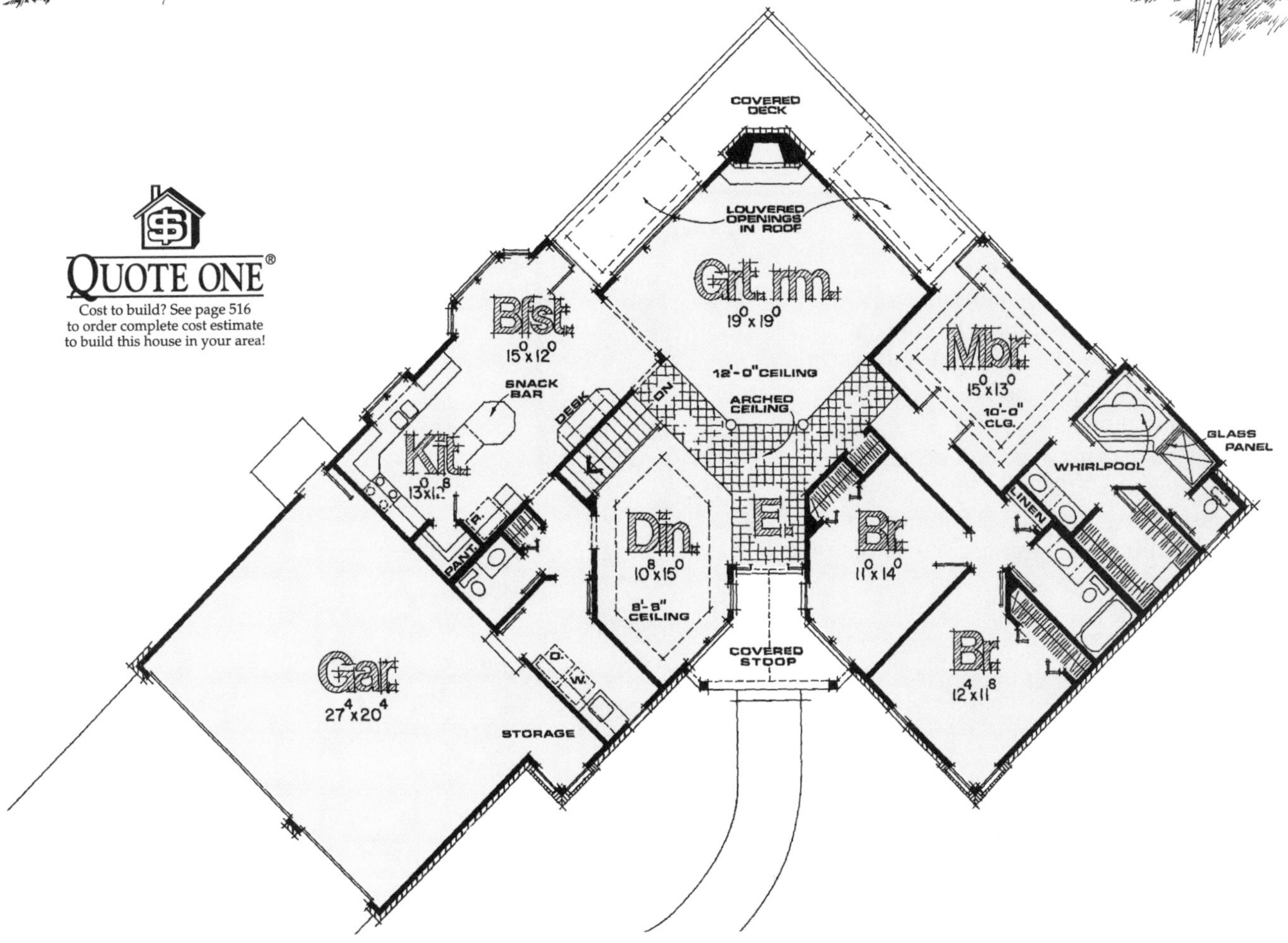

QUOTE ONE®

Cost to build? See page 516 to order complete cost estimate to build this house in your area!

The diagonal nature of this contemporary design makes it a versatile choice for a variety of lot arrangements. Inside, it is quite open visually. From the entry are exquisite views of the great room, with its fireplace flanked by windows, and of the stunning dining room. An island kitchen with a snack bar, planning desk and walk-in pantry adjoins the breakfast area. In the sleeping wing, a romantic master suite is accented with yard access, a whirlpool tub and a tiered ceiling. Two family bedrooms share a full hall bath. The three-car garage holds extra storage space and allows access to the house through the mud/laundry room.

Design
HPT830085

Square Footage: 2,133
Width 74'-4" Depth 58'-0"

A thoughtful arrangement makes this uncomplicated three-bedroom plan comfortable. The living and working areas are grouped together for convenience—a great room with cathedral ceiling, dining room with wet-bar pass-through and kitchen with breakfast room. The sleeping area features a spacious master suite with a skylit bath, whirlpool tub and large walk-in closet. Two smaller bedrooms accommodate the rest of the family. An alternate elevation is available at no extra cost.

Design
HPT830086

Square Footage: 1,604

Width 48'-8" Depth 48'-0"

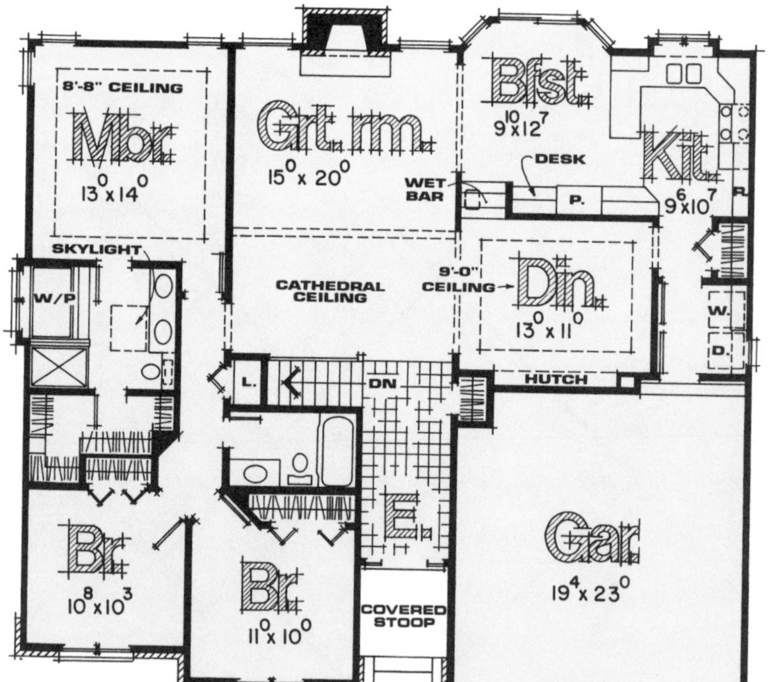

ALTERNATE ELEVATION

QUOTE ONE®

Cost to build? See page 516 to order complete cost estimate to build this house in your area!

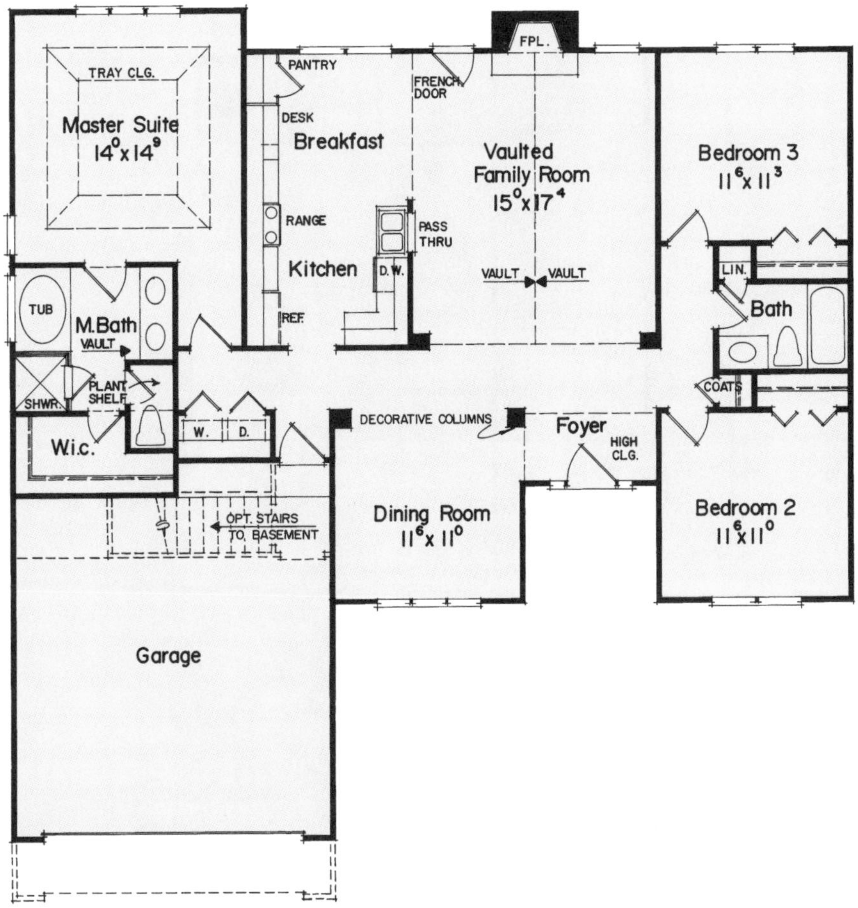

Design

HPT830087

Square Footage: 1,553

Width 52'-0" Depth 49'-6"

This traditional, split floor plan is quite manageable in size while featuring amenities found in much larger homes. Decorative columns frame the entrances to the dining room and the expansive family room, which is fashioned with a vaulted ceiling and a French door to the rear yard. The step-saving kitchen has a planning desk, breakfast area and pass-through to the family room. A dramatic tray ceiling crowns the bedroom of the master suite, which is rounded out with a compartmented bath and walk-in closet. Two family bedrooms, just off the family room, share a hall bath. Please specify basement, crawlspace or slab foundation when ordering.

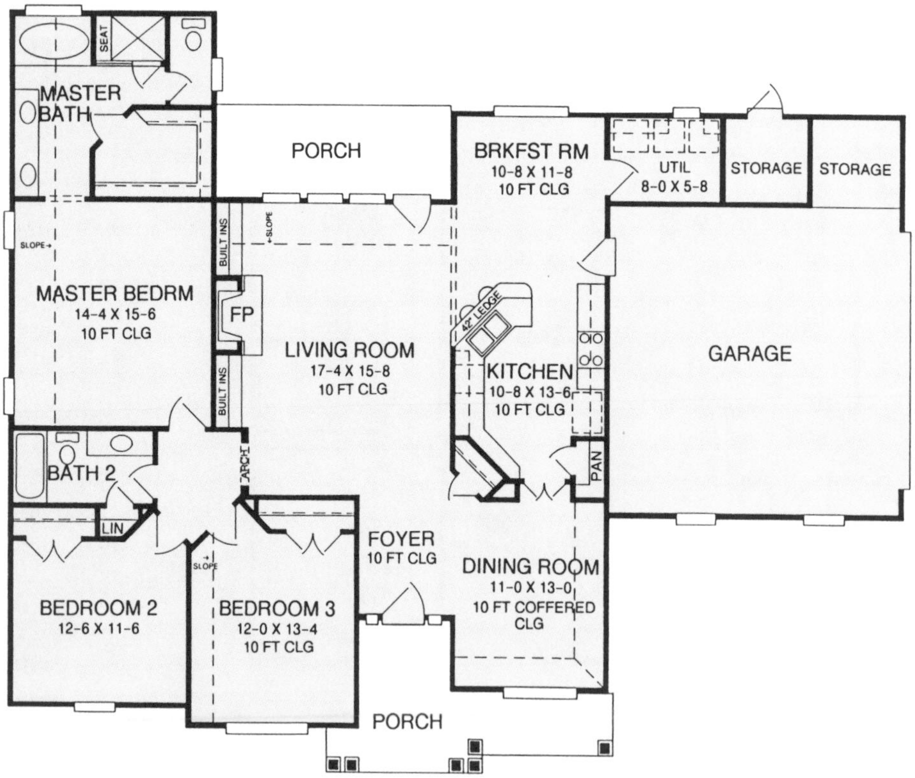
SEAT
MASTER BATH
PORCH
BRKFST RM
10-8 X 11-8
10 FT CLG
UTIL
8-0 X 5-8
STORAGE
STORAGE
SLOPE
BUILT INS
SLOPE
MASTER BEDRM
14-4 X 15-6
10 FT CLG
FP
LIVING ROOM
17-4 X 15-8
10 FT CLG
42" LEDGE
KITCHEN
10-8 X 13-6
10 FT CLG
GARAGE
BUILT INS
BATH 2
ARCH
PAN
LIN
FOYER
10 FT CLG
DINING ROOM
11-0 X 13-0
10 FT COFFERED
CLG
SLOPE
BEDROOM 2
12-6 X 11-6
BEDROOM 3
12-0 X 13-4
10 FT CLG
PORCH

Smaller in size, elegant and classically styled, this home appears larger from the curb. Inside, ten-foot ceilings give the home a spacious feel. The comfortable living room features a lovely fireplace flanked by built-in bookcases. Three bedrooms, including a master suite with a huge walk-in closet, complete this efficiently designed plan. Please specify crawlspace or slab foundation when ordering.

Design
HPT830088

Square Footage: 1,890
Width 65'-10" Depth 53'-5"

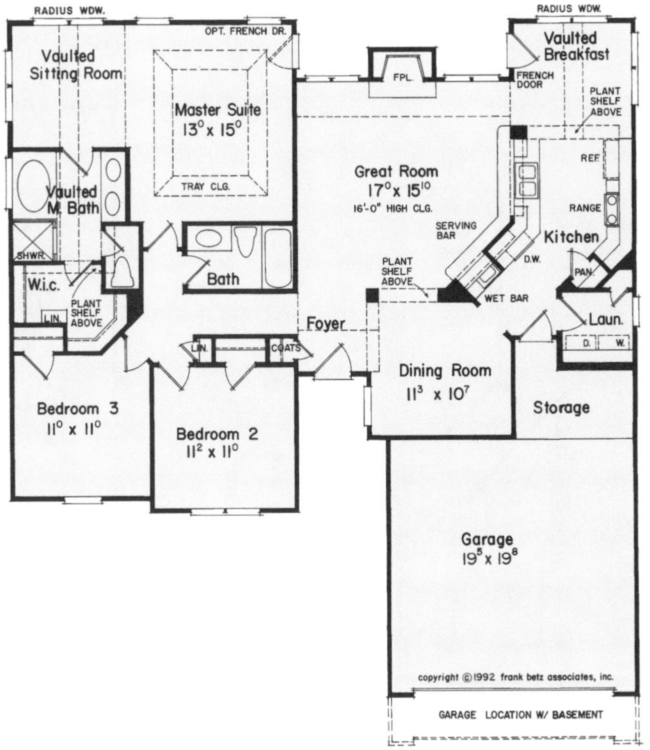

QUOTE ONE®

Cost to build? See page 516 to order complete cost estimate to build this house in your area!

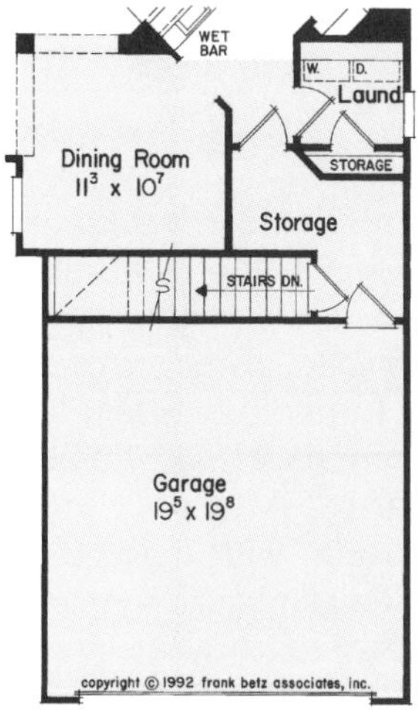

OPT. BASEMENT STAIR LOCATION

Gentle arched lintels harmonize with the high hipped roof to create an elevation that is both welcoming and elegant. This efficient plan minimizes hallway space in order to maximize useable living areas. A favorite feature of this home is the elbow-bend galley kitchen, which has easy access to the dining room and breakfast room—plus a full-length serving bar open to the great room. The master suite has a cozy sitting room and a compartmented bath. Two family bedrooms share a full hall bath. Please specify basement or crawlspace when ordering.

Design
HPT830089

Square Footage: 1,575

Width 50'-0" Depth 52'-6"

Design HPT830090

Square Footage: 2,094

Width 52'-0" Depth 57'-0"

This home offers the perfect combination of traditional formality and casual comfort. A vaulted foyer opens to spectacular formal rooms and leads to the family room. Separated sleeping quarters include an expansive master suite with a vaulted bath that offers an angled spa tub, a knee-space vanity and a large walk-in closet. Two family bedrooms nestle to the right side of the plan and share a full bath. Please specify basement, crawlspace or slab foundation when ordering.

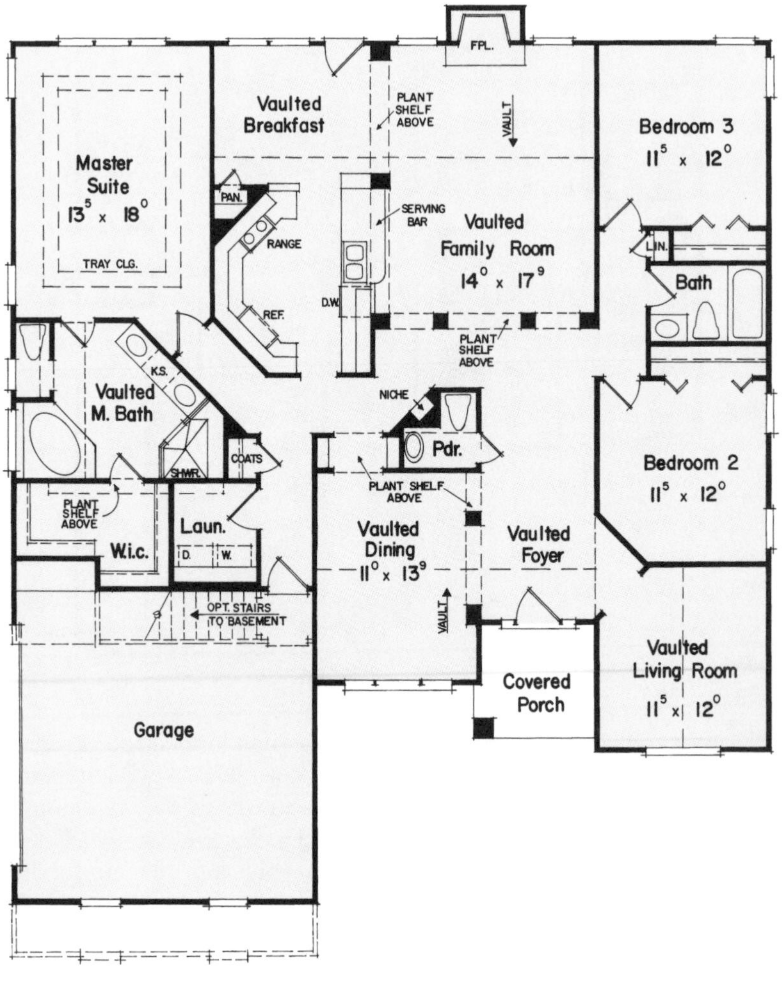

Three arched windows provide just the right touch of elegance and give this home a picturesque appeal. The great room with a corner fireplace is located near the breakfast area and kitchen. Ten-foot ceilings in all major living areas give the plan an open, spacious feel. The master suite includes a luxury bath with a coffered ceiling, large His and Hers closets, a whirlpool tub, a shower with a seat, and twin vanities. A stair leads to an expandable area on the second floor. Please specify crawlspace or slab foundation when ordering.

Design
HPT830091

Square Footage: 2,127
Width 62'-0" Depth 62'-6"

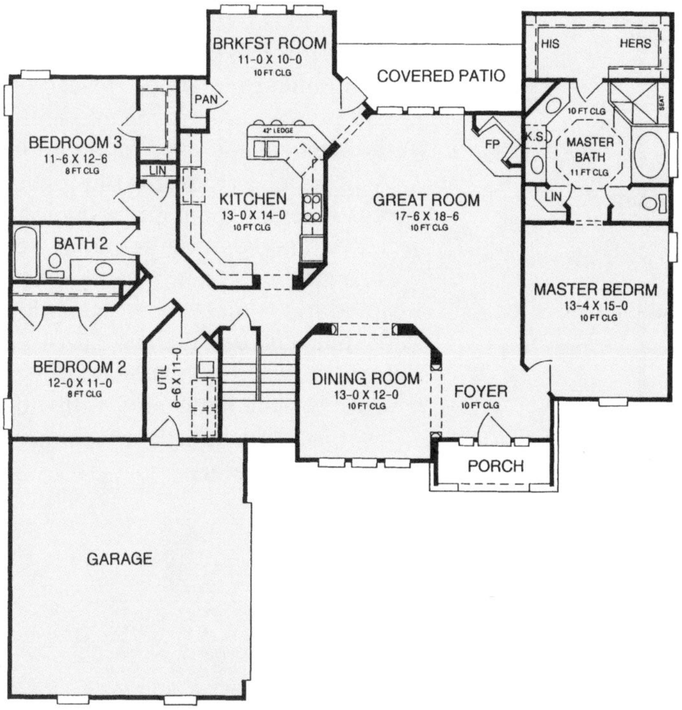

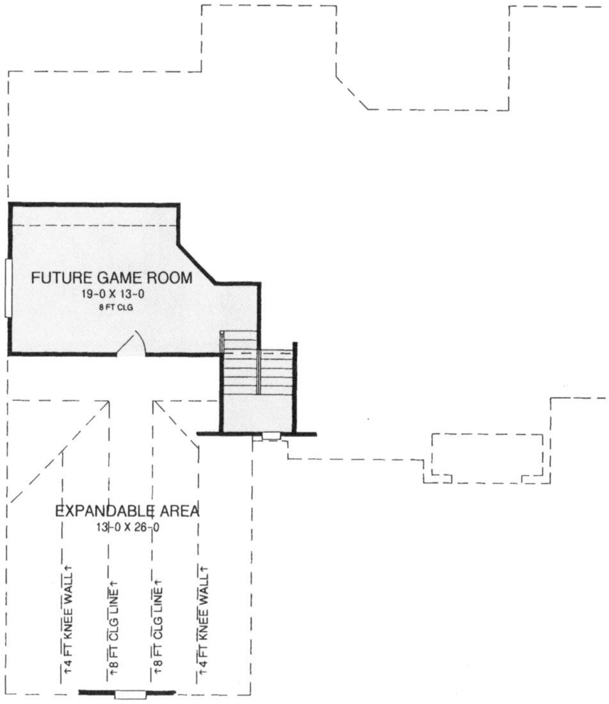

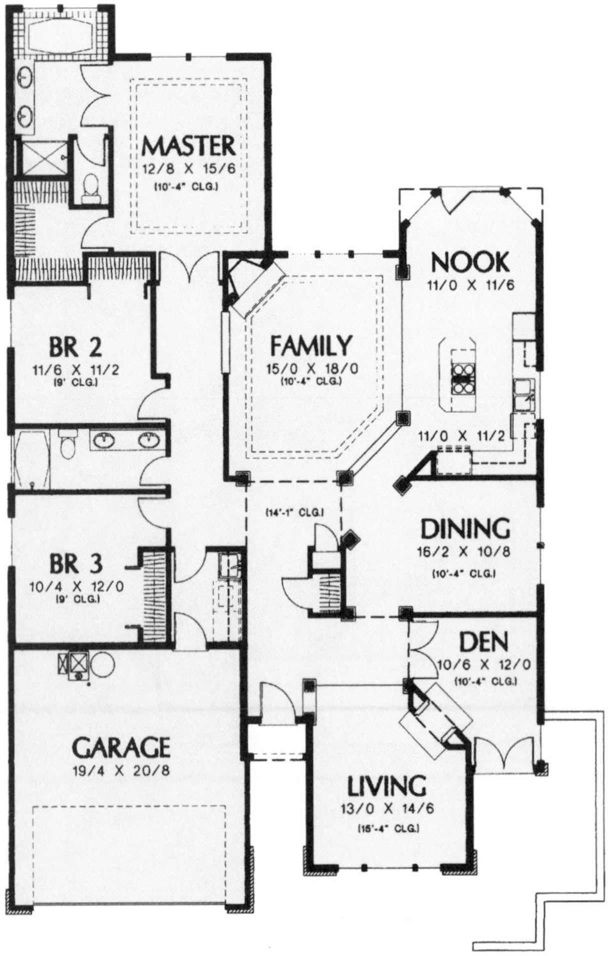

MASTER
12/8 X 15/6
(10'-4" CLG.)
BR 2
11/6 X 11/2
(9' CLG.)
FAMILY
15/0 X 18/0
(10'-4" CLG.)
NOOK
11/0 X 11/6
11/0 X 11/2
(14'-1" CLG.)
DINING
16/2 X 10/8
(10'-4" CLG.)
BR 3
10/4 X 12/0
(9' CLG.)
DEN
10/6 X 12/0
(10'-4" CLG.)
GARAGE
19/4 X 20/8
LIVING
13/0 X 14/6
(15'-4" CLG.)

Design HPT830092

Square Footage: 2,225

Width 45'-0" Depth 73'-0"

The large Palladian window sheds natural light into the living room, which in turn floods through the rest of the house. This home exemplifies clever floor patterning. Casual living takes off in the kitchen, nook and family room. A fireplace here will warm gatherings. A dining room is nearby, as are a den and a living room. A see-through fireplace graces these areas. In the master suite, amenities include a garden tub and dual lavatories. Two secondary bedrooms share a hall bath, also with dual lavatories. A laundry room connects the two-car garage.

QUOTE ONE®

Cost to build? See page 516 to order complete cost estimate to build this house in your area!

Design
HPT830093

Square Footage: 1,875

Width 56'-0" Depth 50'-6"

An oversized picture window gives a cheerful first impression to this well-appointed family home. Boxed columns frame the formal dining room to one side of the foyer. A living room or den is to the other side. A vaulted ceiling soars over the family room. A lovely fireplace flanked by windows and a wrap-around serving bar make this room the heart of family gatherings. The kitchen has all the amenities, including a sunny breakfast nook. The master suite is split from the two family bedrooms and features a lush compartmented bath and walk-in closet. Two family bedrooms, a hall bath and laundry room complete this favorite plan. Please specify basement, crawlspace or slab foundation when ordering.

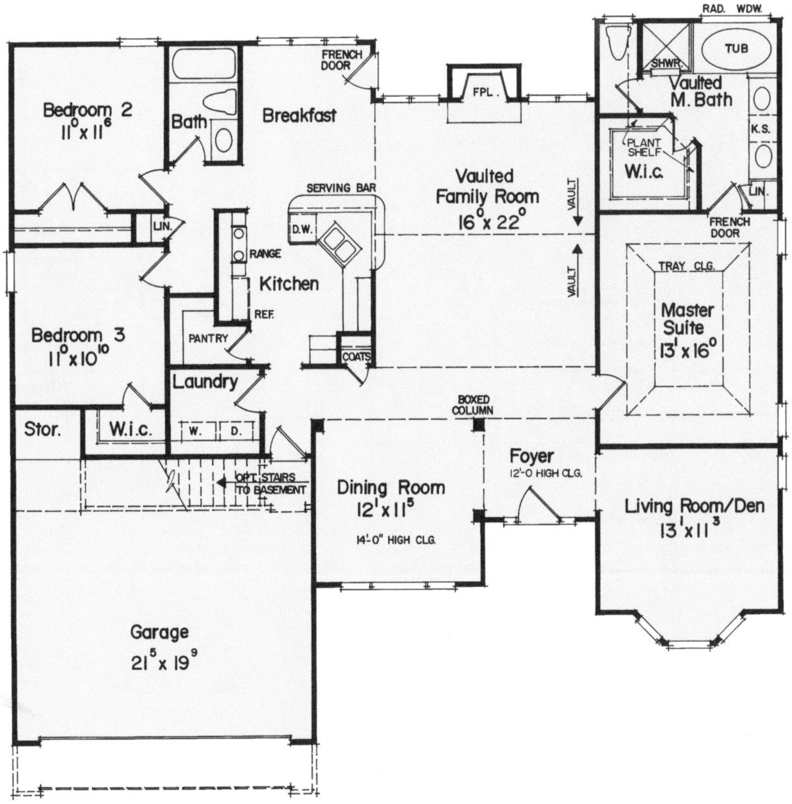

This traditional Southern elevation features an entry flanked by large square columns and dominated by a gable finished with dentil moulding. An angled foyer opens the home to a large great room with fireplace. A formal dining room is defined by a series of columns. The master suite is privately located away from the other bedrooms. Bedrooms 2 and 3 share access to a convenient bath. Please specify crawlspace or slab foundation when ordering.

Design HPT830094

Square Footage: 1,955	
Bonus Space: 240 square feet	
Width 60'-10"	Depth 65'-0"

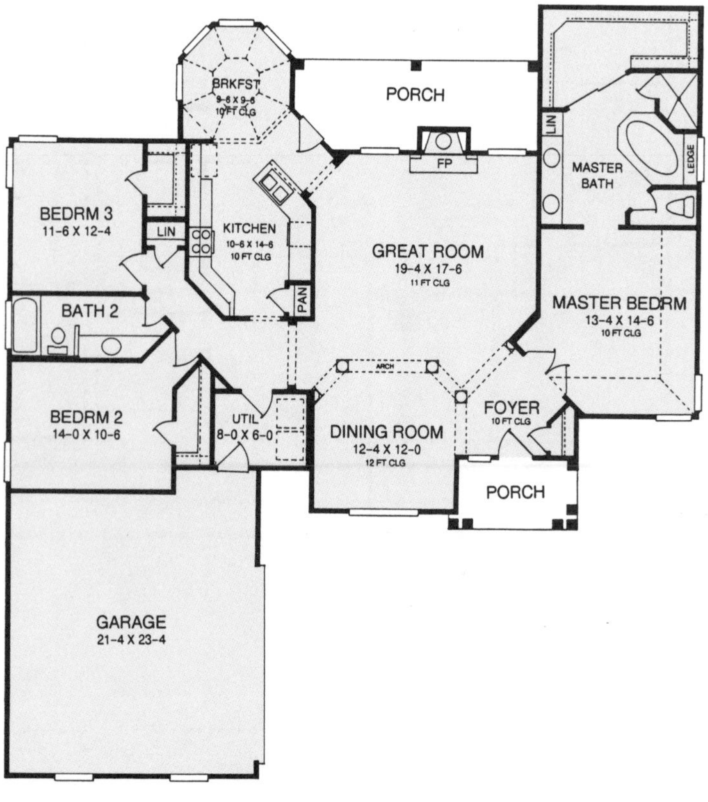

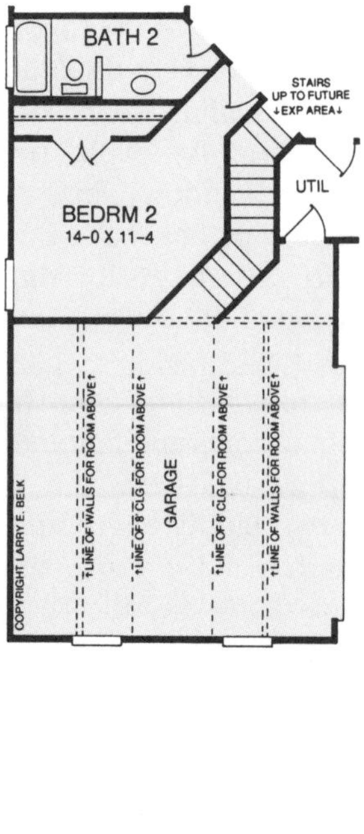

© Design Traditions

Design
HPT830095

Square Footage: 2,721	
Width 69'-3"	Depth 79'-3"

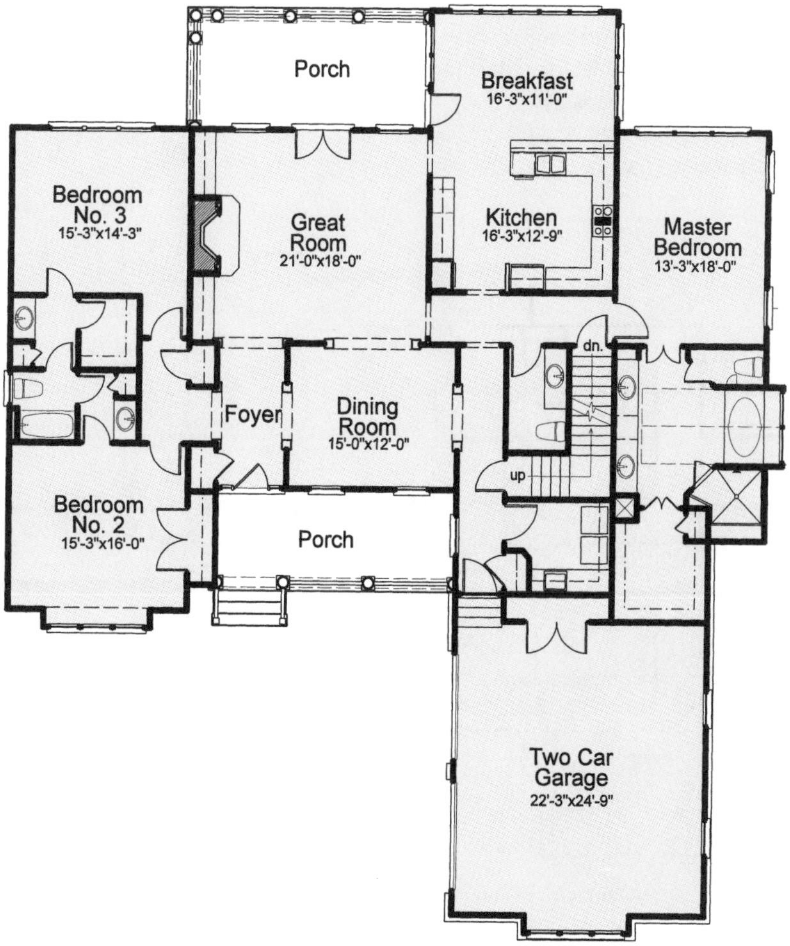
Porch
Breakfast
16'-3"x11'-0"
Bedroom
No. 3
15'-3"x14'-3"
Great
Room
21'-0"x18'-0"
Kitchen
16'-3"x12'-9"
Master
Bedroom
13'-3"x18'-0"
dn.
Foyer
Dining
Room
15'-0"x12'-0"
up
Bedroom
No. 2
15'-3"x16'-0"
Porch
Two Car
Garage
22'-3"x24'-9"

Classic elements play against a rustic shingle-and-stone exterior in this design. Doric porch columns provide elegance, while banks of cottage-style windows let in natural light. The symmetrical layout of the foyer and formal dining room blend easily with the cozy great room. Here, a fireplace creates a welcome atmosphere. The adjacent U-shaped kitchen combines with a sunny breakfast room that opens to a rear porch, making casual meals a pleasure. Separated from family bedrooms for privacy, the master suite enjoys a dramatic private bath. This home is designed with a walkout basement foundation.

Design HPT830096

Square Footage: 2,540

Width 70'-0" Depth 65'-0"

L

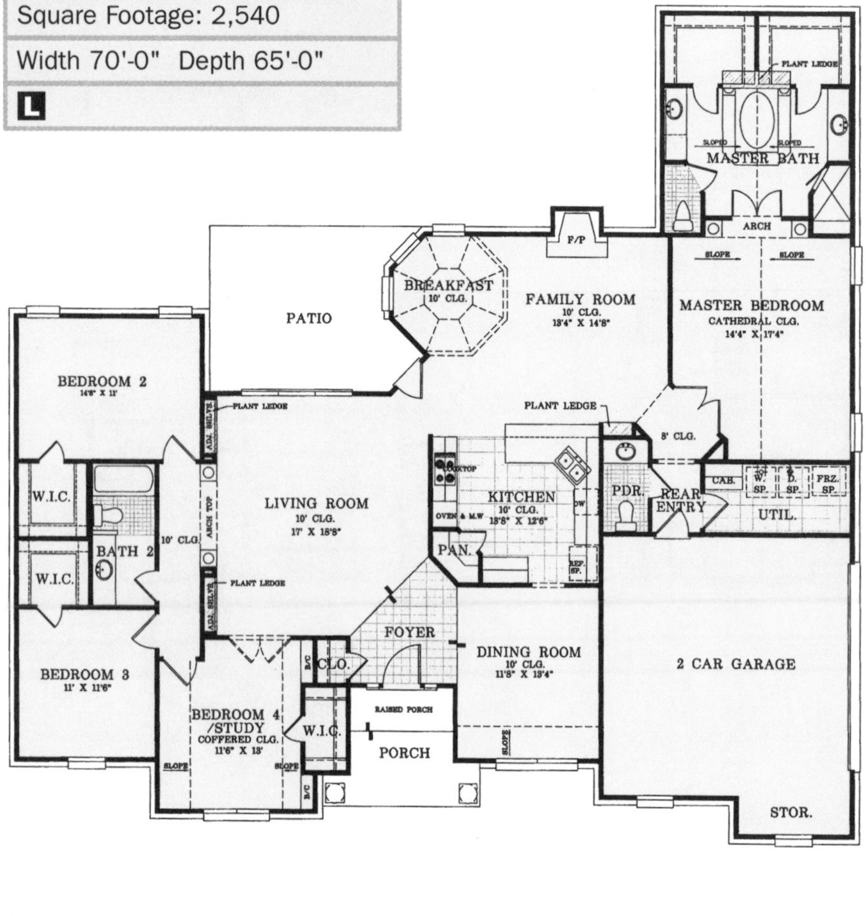

A gabled stucco entry with oversized columns emphasizes the arched glass entry of this winsome one-story brick home. Arched windows on either side of the front door add symmetry and style to this pleasing exterior. An arched passage leads to the three family bedrooms and is flanked by twin bookcases and a plant ledge, providing focal interest to the living room. Bedroom 4 may also be a study, and can be entered from double French doors off the living room. A large, efficient kitchen shares space with an octagonal breakfast area and a family room with a fireplace. Enter the master bedroom through angled double doors and view the cathedral ceiling. Attention centers immediately on the arched entry to the relaxing master bath and its central whirlpool tub. Please specify crawlspace or slab foundation when ordering.

Design HPT830097

Square Footage: 2,561

Width 70'-0" Depth 65'-6"

L

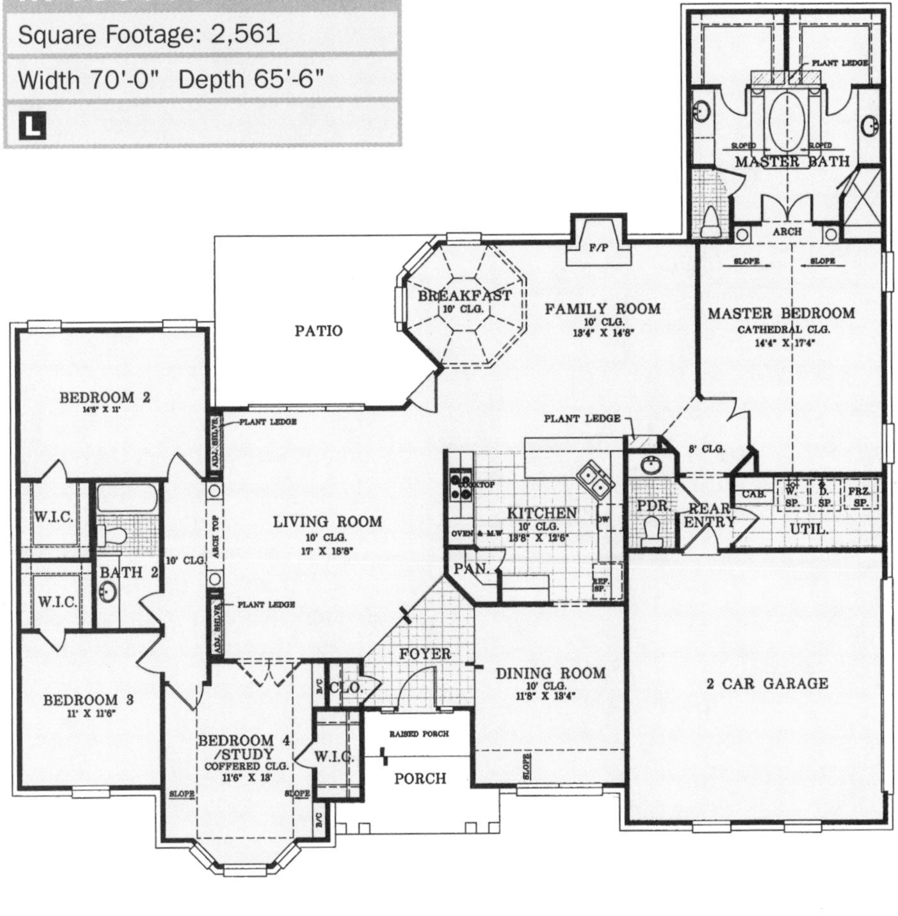

PLANT LEDGE
MASTER BATH
ARCH
SLOPE
SLOPE
MASTER BEDROOM
CATHEDRAL CLG.
14'4" X 17'4"
F/P
BREAKFAST
10' CLG.
FAMILY ROOM
10' CLG.
13'4" X 14'8"
PATIO
BEDROOM 2
14'8" X 11'
PLANT LEDGE
PLANT LEDGE
8' CLG.
W.I.C.
LIVING ROOM
10' CLG.
17' X 18'8"
KITCHEN
10' CLG.
13'8" X 12'6"
PDR.
REAR ENTRY
CAB.
UTIL.
BATH 2
10' CLG.
W.I.C.
PAN.
PLANT LEDGE
FOYER
DINING ROOM
10' CLG.
11'8" X 13'4"
2 CAR GARAGE
BEDROOM 3
11' X 11'6"
CLO.
BEDROOM 4 /STUDY
COFFERED CLG.
11'6" X 13'
W.I.C.
RAISED PORCH
PORCH
SLOPE
SLOPE

Interesting window details and varying rooflines lend this split-bedroom home comfort and elegance. The angled foyer steps down into the living room, where built-in display shelving on either side allows plenty of room for collectibles or books. The family room and kitchen are conveniently grouped with the gazebo breakfast room to provide a large area for family gatherings and informal entertaining. Enter the master suite through angled double doors. The luxury bath awaits with a whirlpool tub as the centerpiece. His and Hers vanities, a separate shower and two large walk-in closets are included. Three family bedrooms with large walk-in closets and a roomy bath complete this best-selling plan. Please specify crawlspace or slab foundation when ordering.

Design
HPT830098

Square Footage: 2,517

Width 69'-0" Depth 63'-6"

L

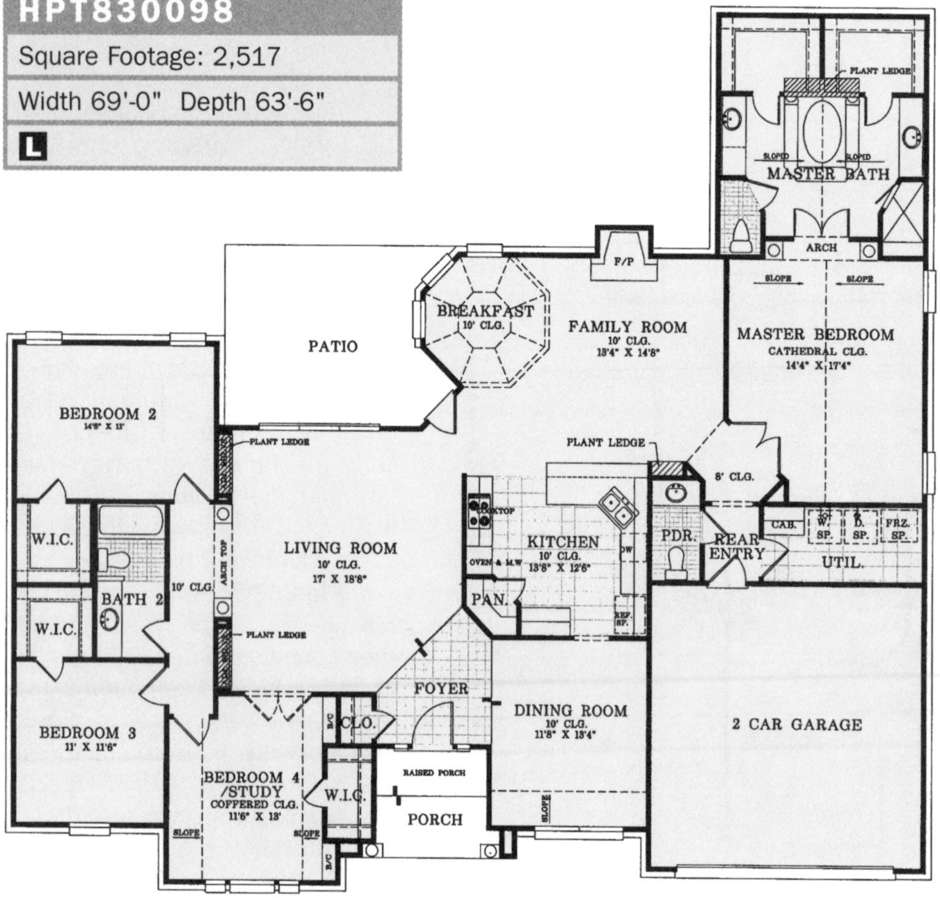

PLANT LEDGE
MASTER BATH
ARCH
MASTER BEDROOM
CATHEDRAL CLG.
14'4" X 17'4"
F/P
BREAKFAST
10' CLG.
FAMILY ROOM
10' CLG.
13'4" X 14'8"
PATIO
BEDROOM 2
PLANT LEDGE
8' CLG.
W.I.C.
LIVING ROOM
10' CLG.
17' X 18'8"
KITCHEN
10' CLG.
13'8" X 12'6"
PDR.
REAR ENTRY
UTIL.
BATH 2
10' CLG.
W.I.C.
PAN.
FOYER
DINING ROOM
10' CLG.
11'8" X 13'4"
2 CAR GARAGE
BEDROOM 3
11' X 11'6"
CLO.
BEDROOM 4 /STUDY
COFFERED CLG.
11'6" X 13'
W.I.C.
RAISED PORCH
PORCH

A graceful stucco arch and quoins accent the traditional brick finish of this gracious home. The angled foyer steps down into the dining room on one side and on the other to the living room with built-in display shelves. The kitchen is conveniently grouped with a sunny bayed breakfast room and the family room, the perfect place for informal gatherings. Upon entering the master suite, the spa-style master bath is the focal point. Three family bedrooms and a full hall bath complete the plan. Please specify crawlspace or slab foundation when ordering.

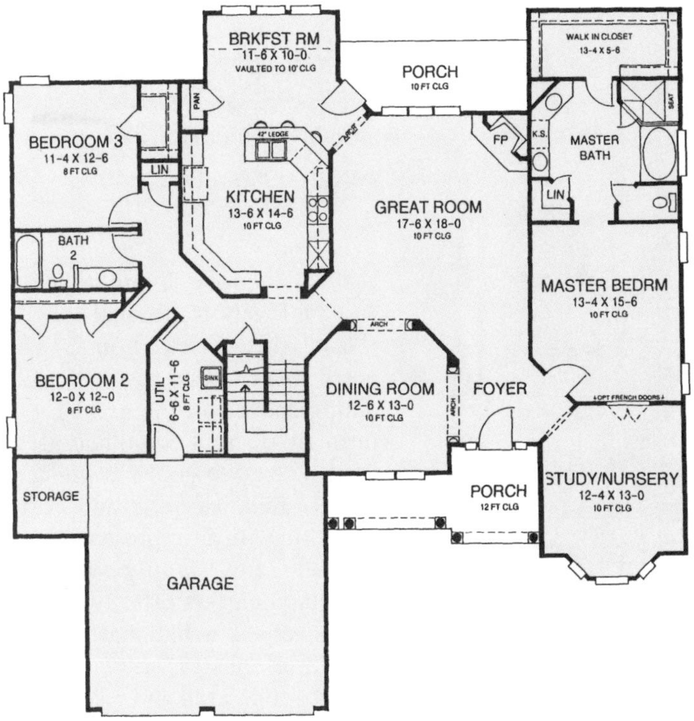

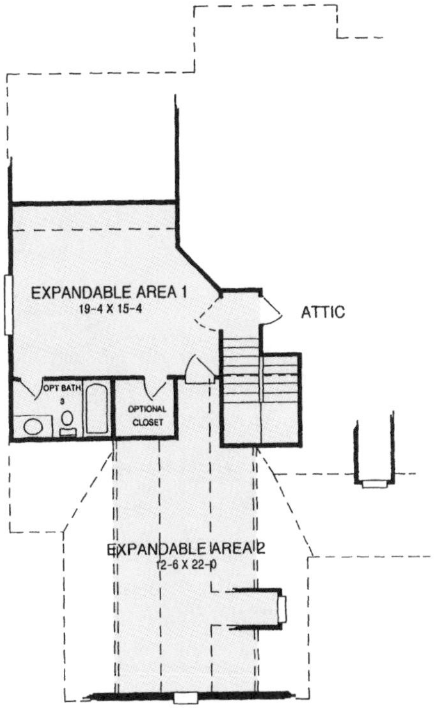

This gracious plan is designed to grow with the family, thanks to the optional nursery/sitting room off the master suite and the expandable area upstairs. A corner fireplace and bright windows to the porch highlight the massive great room. The wraparound kitchen features plenty of cabinet and counter space, a snack bar and a breakfast nook. The luxurious master suite enjoys a large bath that includes a pampering tub and an oversized walk-in closet. Two family bedrooms share a full hall bath. Please specify crawlspace or slab foundation when ordering.

Design
HPT830099

Square Footage: 2,350
Bonus Space: 286 square feet
Width 61'-10" Depth 62'-6"

Design HPT830100

Square Footage: 2,377

Width 69'-0" Depth 49'-6"

DECK
SITTING AREA 12'-0" X 12'-0"
MASTER SUITE 13'-0" X 17'-6"
M.BATH
M.CLOSET
BATH
CLO.
CLO.
LIN.
GREAT ROOM 20'-6" X 19'-0"
BREAKFAST 11'-4" X 10'-0"
KITCHEN 10'-0" X 18'-0"
KEEPING ROOM 11'-4" X 11'-0"
PNTRY
DN.
LAUNDRY
COAT
BEDROOM NO. 3 12'-0" X 11'-8"
BEDROOM NO. 2 13'-10" X 12'-6"
FOYER 8'-0" X 14'-4"
DINING ROOM 12'-0" X 14'-4"
TWO CAR GARAGE 21'-4" X 21'-5"
STOOP

One-story living takes a lovely traditional turn in this brick home. The entry foyer opens to the formal dining room and the great room through graceful columned archways. The open gourmet kitchen, bayed breakfast nook and keeping room with a fireplace will be a magnet for family activity. Sleeping quarters offer two family bedrooms, a hall bath and a rambling master suite with a bayed sitting area and a sensuous bath. This home is designed with a walkout basement foundation.

QUOTE ONE®

Cost to build? See page 516 to order complete cost estimate to build this house in your area!

One-Story Homes Over 2,300 Square Feet

Design HPT830101

Square Footage: 2,592

Width 56'-0" Depth 60'-6"

A blend of contemporary layout with traditional themes places a formal dining room and living room to either side of the foyer, while still allowing an open view to the family room. The efficient kitchen has a welcome walk-in pantry and a serving bar facing both the vaulted breakfast room and the family room. The master suite is located on the opposite side of the plan from the family bedrooms and features twin walk-in closets and a lush bath. Two family bedrooms, both with ample closet space, and a hall bath complete this plan. A two-car garage offers more storage space. Please specify basement, crawlspace or slab foundation when ordering.

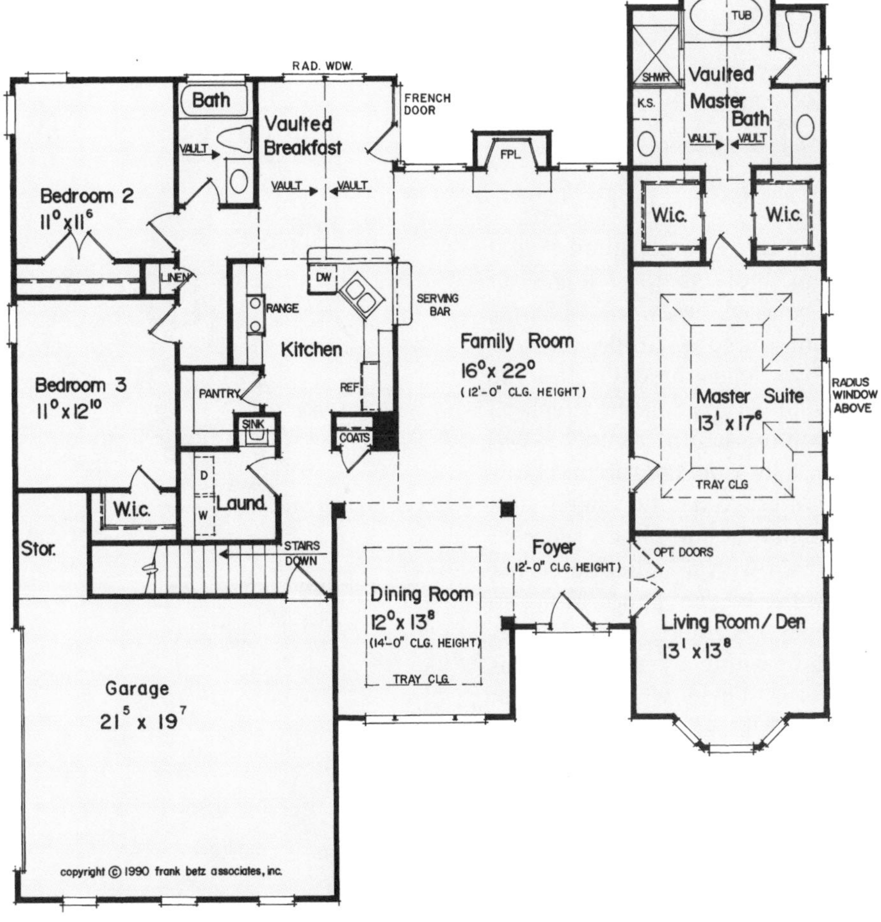

RAD. WDW.
FRENCH DOOR
Bath
Vaulted Breakfast
FPL
TUB
SHWR
Vaulted Master Bath
K.S.
Bedroom 2
11⁰x11⁶
W.i.c.
W.i.c.
LINEN
RANGE
DW
SERVING BAR
Kitchen
Family Room
16⁰x 22⁰
(12'-0" CLG. HEIGHT)
Bedroom 3
11⁰x12¹⁰
PANTRY
REF
SINK
COATS
Master Suite
13'x17⁶
RADIUS WINDOW ABOVE
TRAY CLG
W.i.c.
Laund.
Stor.
STAIRS DOWN
Foyer
(12'-0" CLG. HEIGHT)
OPT. DOORS
Dining Room
12⁰x13⁸
(14'-0" CLG. HEIGHT)
TRAY CLG.
Living Room/Den
13'x13⁸
Garage
21⁵ x 19⁷
copyright © 1990 frank betz associates, inc.

Design

HPT830102

Square Footage: 2,770	
Width 74'-0"	Depth 79'-0"

The European-inspired excitement of this stucco home can be seen in its use of large, abundant windows. Inside, the spacious foyer leads directly to a large great room with a massive fireplace. The banquet-sized dining room receives light from the triple window and features a dramatic vaulted ceiling. The master suite has a separate sitting area with a cathedral ceiling and access to the patio. The two additional bedrooms each has its own vanity within a shared bath. This home is designed with a walkout basement foundation.

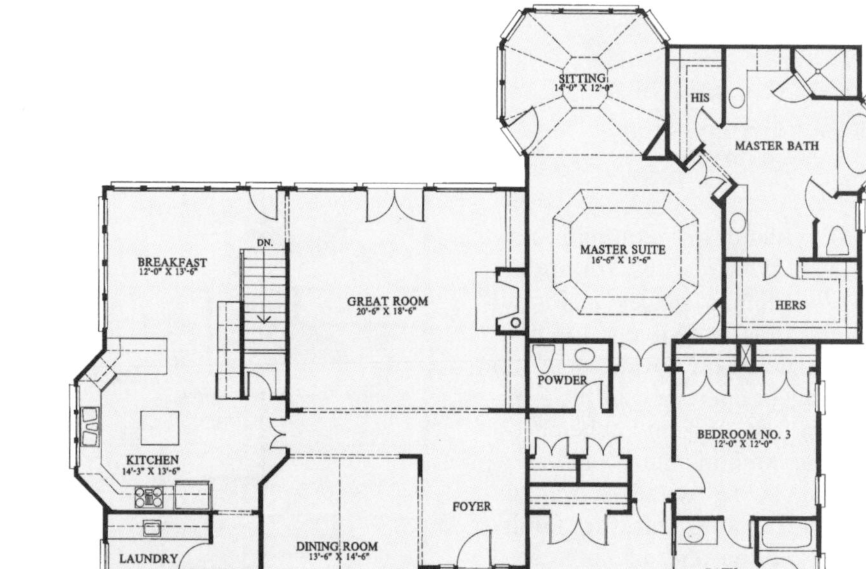

QUOTE ONE®
Cost to build? See page 516 to order complete cost estimate to build this house in your area!

Design HPT830103

Square Footage: 2,902

Width 71'-3" Depth 66'-3"

Arches, transoms and sweeping rooflines blend artfully to highlight this French exterior. The interior starts with a great room that features a tray ceiling, a wet bar and French doors to the outside. Adjoining the kitchen and breakfast room, the spacious keeping room provides a fireplace. The master suite offers a sitting room and a sumptuous bath, while two family bedrooms share a connecting bath. This home is designed with a walkout basement foundation.

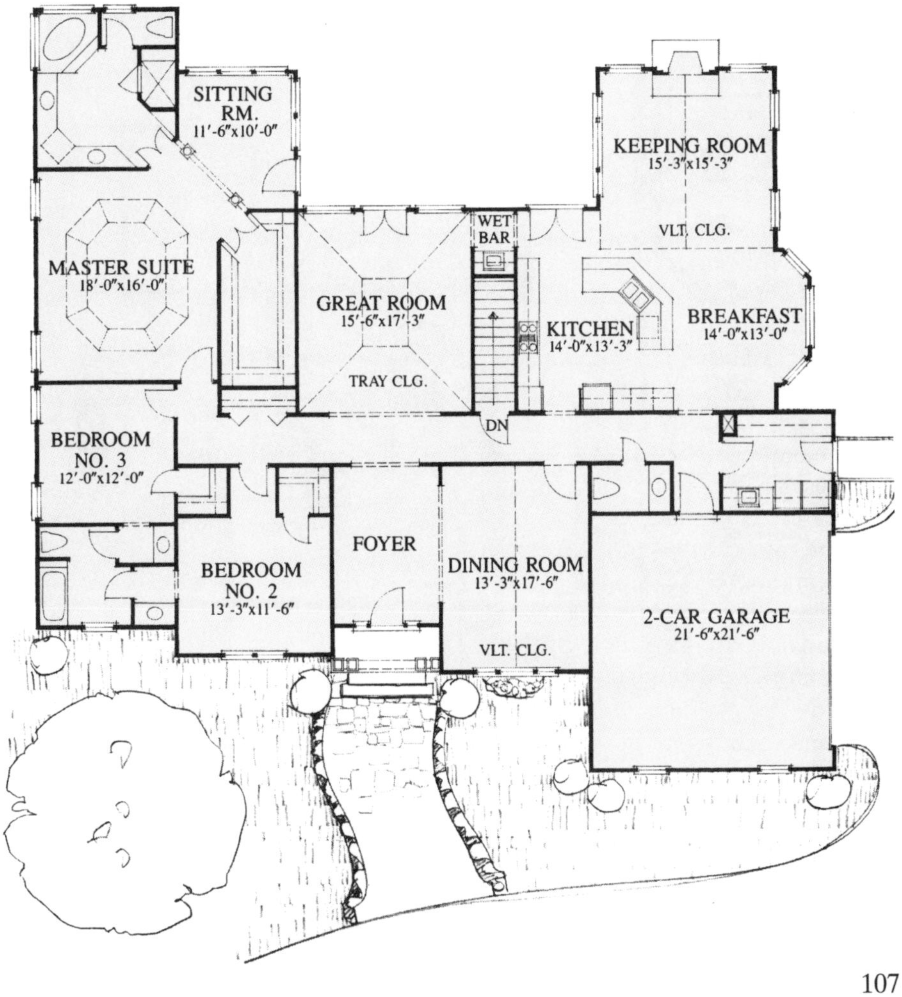
SITTING RM. 11'-6"x10'-0"
KEEPING ROOM 15'-3"x15'-3"
VLT. CLG.
WET BAR
MASTER SUITE 18'-0"x16'-0"
GREAT ROOM 15'-6"x17'-3"
KITCHEN 14'-0"x13'-3"
BREAKFAST 14'-0"x13'-0"
TRAY CLG.
DN
BEDROOM NO. 3 12'-0"x12'-0"
FOYER
BEDROOM NO. 2 13'-3"x11'-6"
DINING ROOM 13'-3"x17'-6"
VLT. CLG.
2-CAR GARAGE 21'-6"x21'-6"

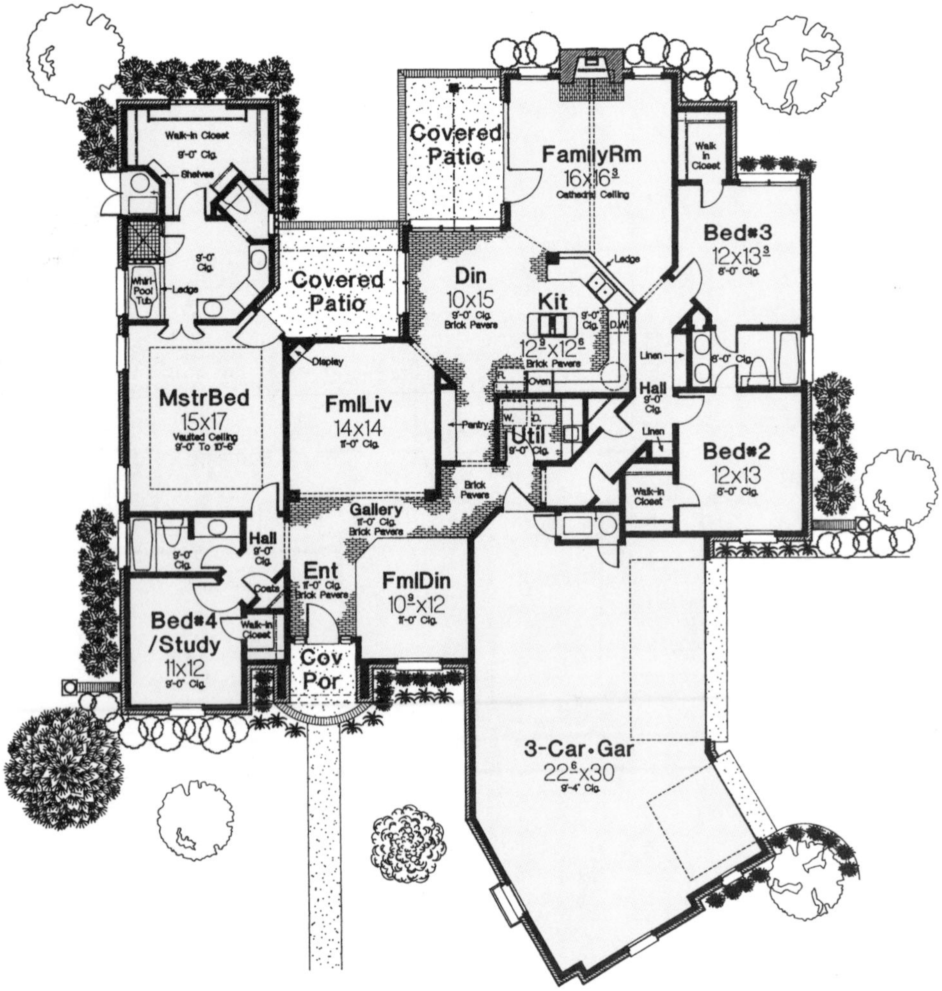

Design HPT830104

Square Footage: 2,526
Width 64'-0" Depth 81'-7"

Interesting angles and creative detailing characterize the exterior of this brick cottage. Inside, the formal dining room is just off the foyer for ease in entertaining. A gallery hall leads to the island kitchen, which opens to an informal dining area with access to two covered patios. Sleeping quarters include two family bedrooms to the right of the plan and another bedroom, which could be used as a study, on the left. The left wing is dedicated to a lavish master suite complete with a vaulted ceiling and sumptuous bath with a whirlpool tub and separate shower.

Design

HPT830105

Square Footage: 2,778
Width 74'-0" Depth 74'-1"

Welcome to a modern home with an outdoor rustic flair! A flagstone facade, a sloping dormer window, an oval window, fanlights above the front door and sidelights flanking it lend this home distinctive charm and character. The sprawling floorplan begins with an entry with wood-plank flooring, which leads through the gallery into a spacious kitchen. With plenty of counterspace, the kitchen can easily serve the dining room, which also has wood flooring. The master bedroom resides on the right side of the plan, and is graced with a vaulted ceiling, luxurious full bath and a large walk-in closet. Bedrooms 2,3 and 4 are on the left side of the plan; each contains its own walk-in closet.

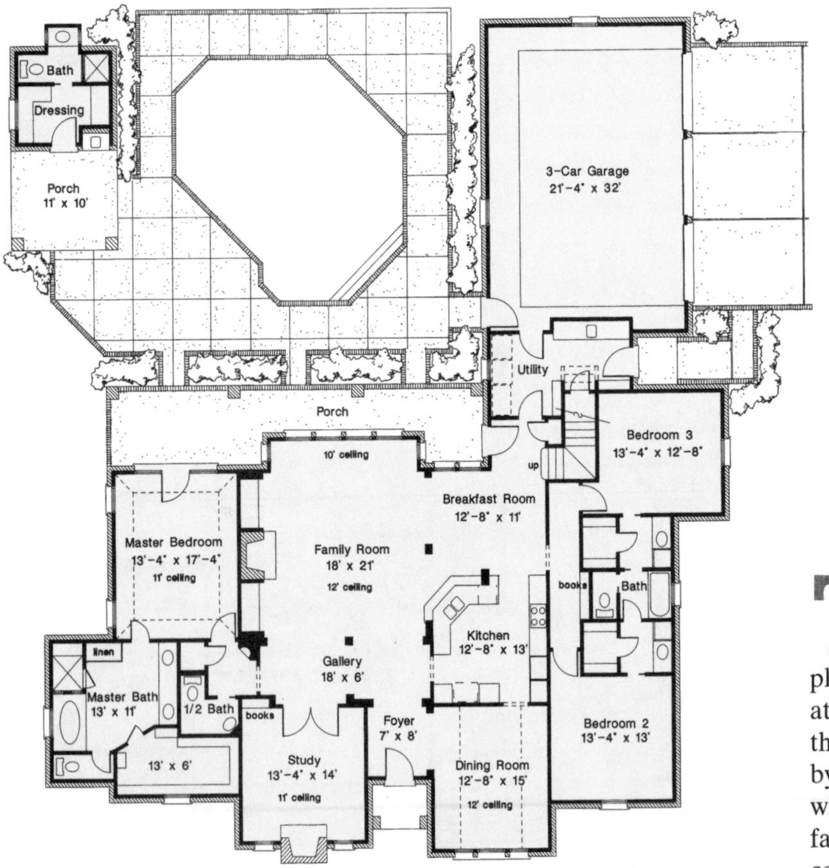

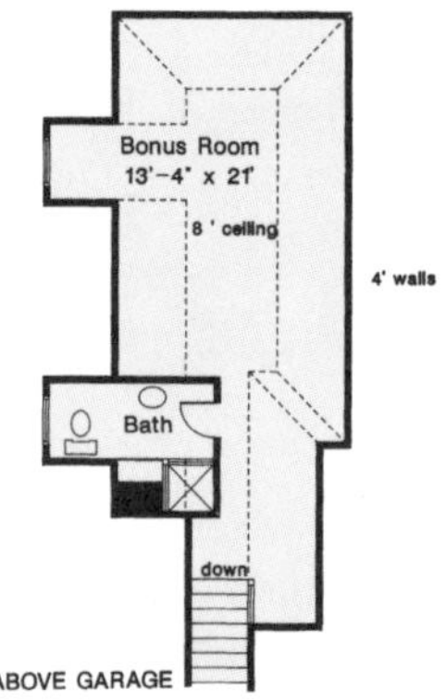

BONUS ROOM ABOVE GARAGE

Design
HPT830106

Square Footage: 2,908

Bonus Space: 479 square feet

Width 75'-2" Depth 88'-6"

The livability presented by this house is outstanding. From a large family gathering area to a cozy study with a fireplace, you're sure to find many pleasing attributes. The formal dining room opens to the right of the foyer. Conveniently accessed by the kitchen, meals will take on a special air when served here. A gallery accentuates the family room, which also sports a twelve-foot ceiling, a fireplace, built-ins and columns. Two bedrooms make up the right side of the house. Both offer ample proportions and superb bath access. In the master bedroom, a private bath, an expansive walk-in closet and outdoor passage create a true retreat. A three-car garage with a bonus room above and a pool cabana complete the plan.

Design HPT830107

Square Footage: 2,481	
Width 75'-4"	Depth 80'-8"

Multiple gables, bay windows and corner windows with transoms above provide an exterior reminiscent of English countryside homes. The formal dining room features an eleven-foot ceiling, bay window, and French doors that open onto a private dining terrace. A spacious kitchen overlooks the breakfast area and the family room, which boasts a corner fireplace and dramatic fourteen-foot ceiling. Another corner fireplace is located in the master bedroom, which also contains a built-in desk and triple French doors. The luxurious master bath has a large walk-in closet and a whirlpool tub inset in a bay window. Two family bedrooms share a hall bath.

A brick exterior, cast-stone trim and corner quoins make up this attractive single-living-area design. The entry introduces a formal dining room to the right and a living room with a wall of windows to the left. The hearth-warmed family room opens to the kitchen/dinette, both with ten-foot ceilings. A large bay window enhances the dinette with a full glass door to the covered patio. A large master suite with vaulted ceilings features a bayed sitting area, a luxurious master bath with double lavatories, and an oversized walk-in closet.

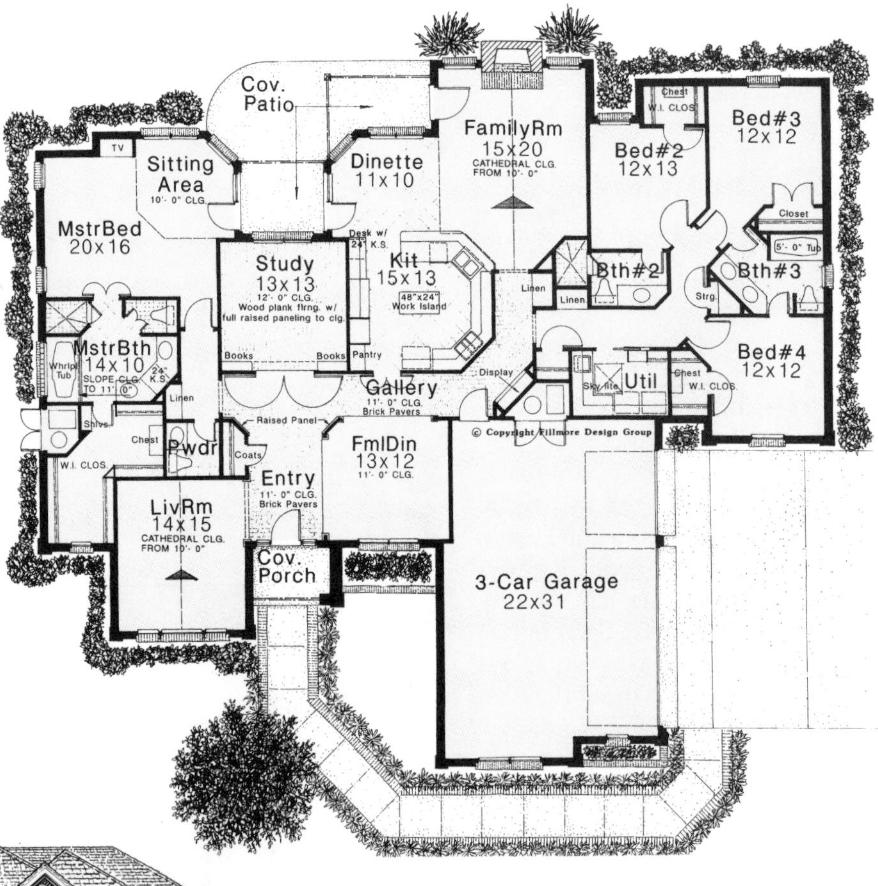

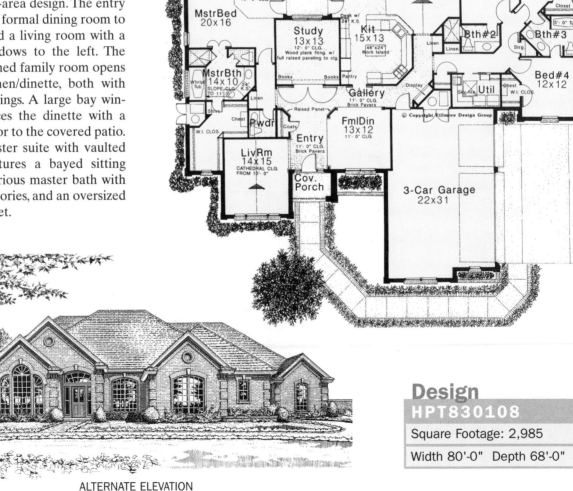

ALTERNATE ELEVATION

Design
HPT830108

Square Footage: 2,985

Width 80'-0" Depth 68'-0"

Design HPT830109

Square Footage: 3,426

Width 78'-6" Depth 82'-4"

L

One-story living takes off in this brick traditional home. Formal living areas flanking the entry are enhanced with ten-foot ceilings and open views to the great room. The great room has a twelve-foot ceiling and is accented by a fireplace and expansive windows. The island kitchen has a sunny breakfast nook and easy passage to the dining room. A luxurious master bedroom has a spa-style bath with a raised corner whirlpool tub and a special exercise room. Three bedrooms share a full hall bath. Please specify crawlspace or slab foundation when ordering.

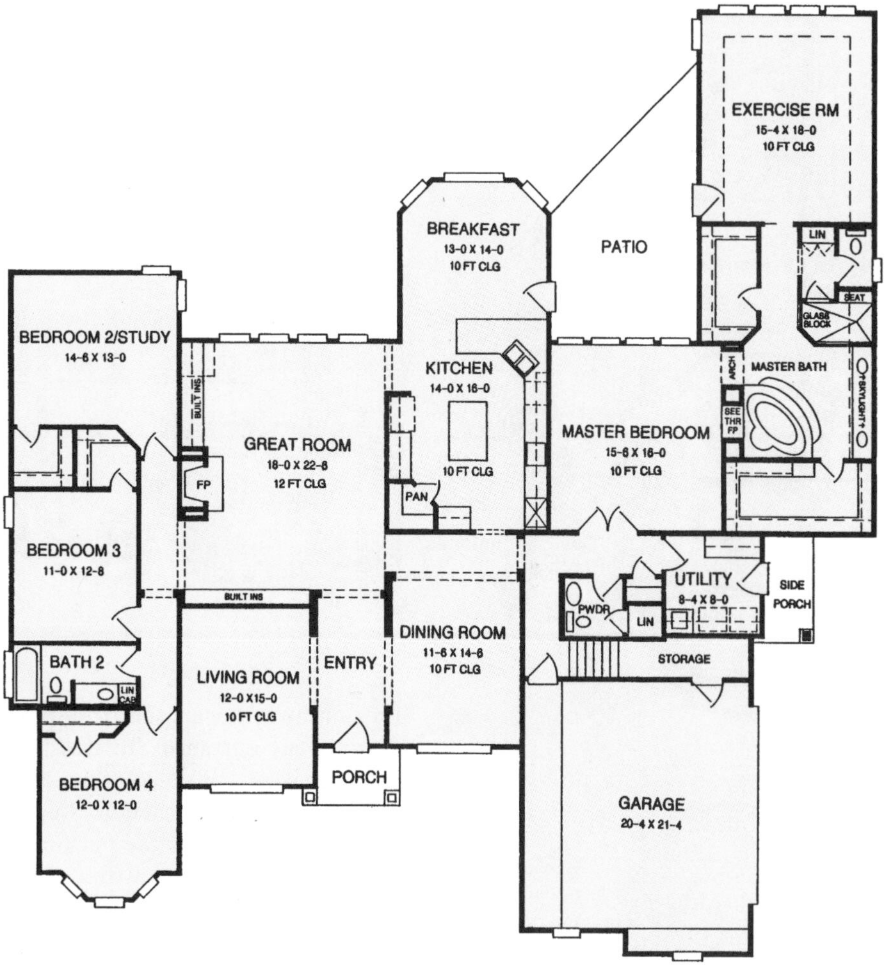

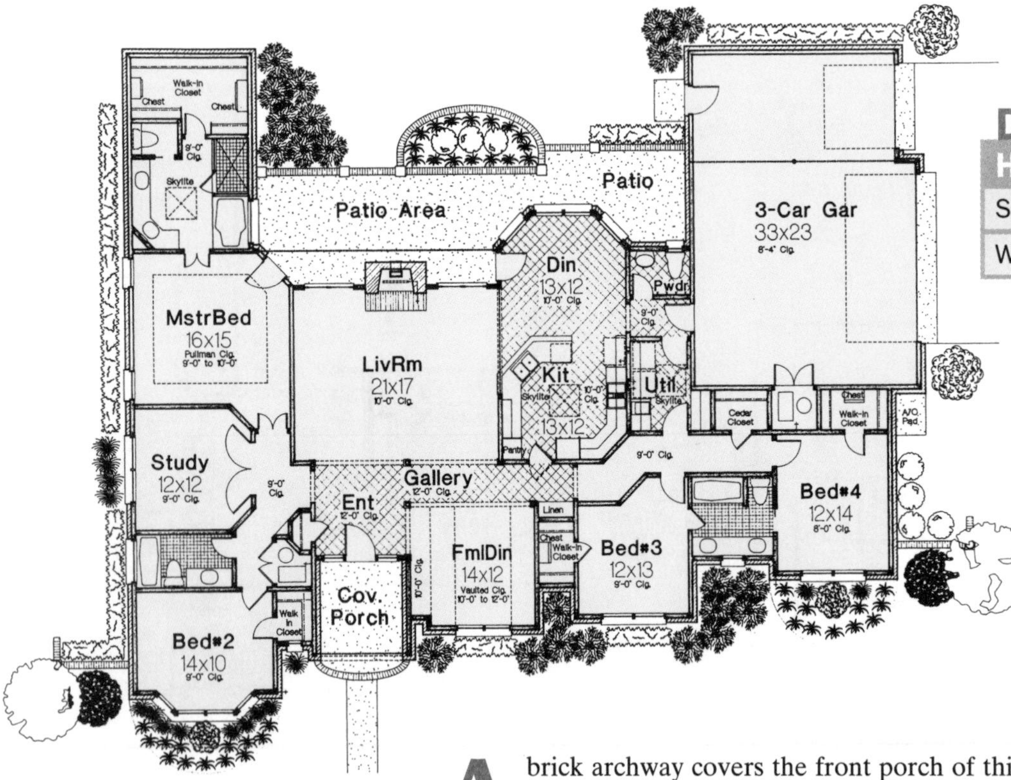

Design HPT830110

Square Footage: 2,696

Width 80'-0" Depth 64'-1"

A brick archway covers the front porch of this European-style home, creating a truly grand entrance. Situated beyond the entry, the living room takes center stage with a fireplace flanked by tall windows. To the right is a bayed eating area and an efficient kitchen. Steps away is the formal dining room. Skillful planning creates flexibility for the master suite. If you wish, use Bedroom 2 as a secondary bedroom or guest room, with the adjacent study accessible to everyone. Or if you prefer, combine the master suite with the study and use it as a private retreat with Bedroom 2 as a nursery, creating a wing that provides complete privacy. Completing this clever plan are two family bedrooms, a powder room and a utility room.

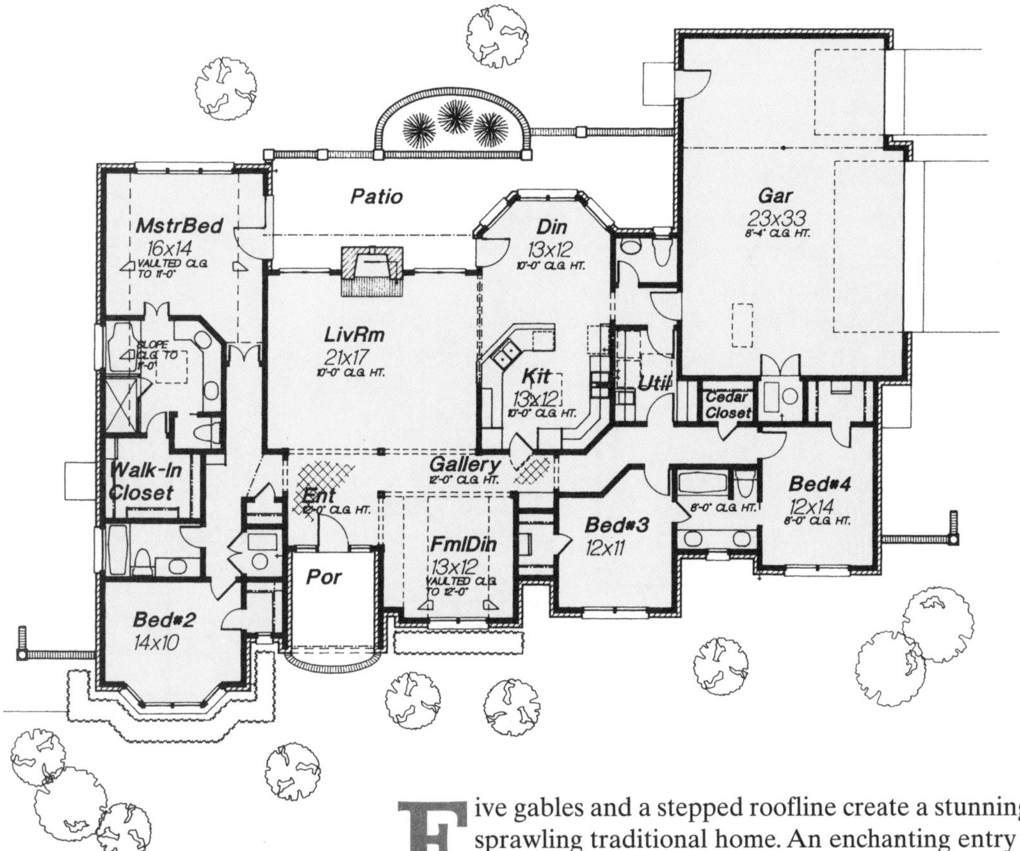

Patio
MstrBed
16x14
VAULTED CLG TO 11'-0"
Din
13x12
10'-0" CLG HT.
Gar
23x33
8'-4" CLG HT.
LivRm
21x17
10'-0" CLG HT.
Kit
13x12
10'-0" CLG HT.
Util
Cedar Closet
Walk-In Closet
Gallery
12'-0" CLG HT.
Ent
12'-0" CLG HT.
Bed#4
12x14
8'-0" CLG HT.
8'-0" CLG HT.
Bed#3
12x11
FmlDin
13x12
VAULTED CLG TO 12'-0"
Por
Bed#2
14x10

Five gables and a stepped roofline create a stunning exterior for this sprawling traditional home. An enchanting entry leads to the long gallery and gracious formal dining area with vaulted ceiling. Wide windows frame the brick fireplace and hearth of the 21' x 17' living room. The master suite features a vaulted ceiling and a French door leading to a covered patio. Relax in the private bath with a skylight in the sloped ceiling. Three additional bedrooms, each with its own walk-in closet and bath, complete this wonderful home.

Design
HPT830111

Square Footage: 2,542

Width 80'-0" Depth 64'-0"

Design

HPT830112

Square Footage: 2,483	
Width 69'-0" Depth 53'-8"	

This elegant traditional home is distinguished by its brick exterior and arched entryway with keystone accent. The entryway opens on the right to a formal dining room with an attractive tray ceiling. On the left, a private study—or make it a fourth bedroom—boasts a vaulted ceiling and a picture window with sunburst transom. Family living space includes a vaulted great room with a corner fireplace and a gourmet kitchen with an adjacent breakfast room. Special features in the kitchen include a breakfast bar, center island, menu desk and pantry. The fabulous master suite enjoys a bay window, large bath, walk-in closet and vaulted ceiling. Two family bedrooms sharing a full hall bath complete the plan. An unfinished basement provides room for future expansion.

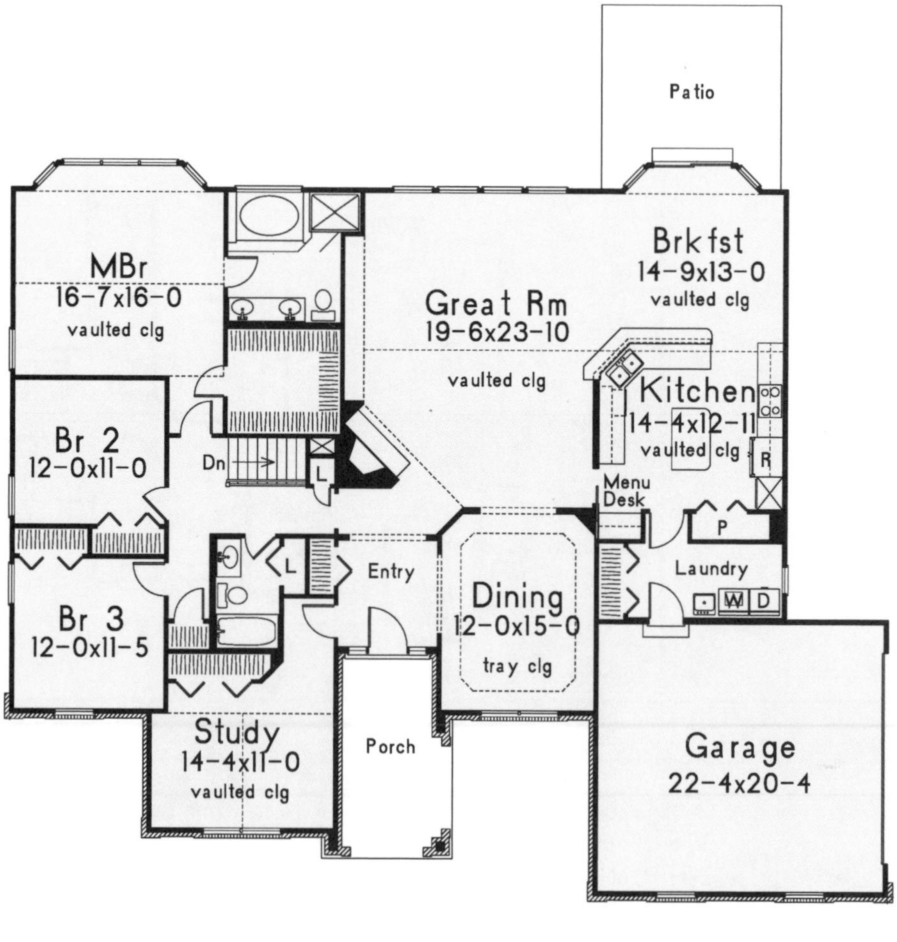

Design HPT830113

Square Footage: 2,349

Finished Basement: 850 square feet

Width 79'-4" Depth 59'-6"

Sunbursts over the entryway and front windows add sophistication to this home. The mix of stone and siding adds a versatile feel to this pleasant home. The rear of this home offers plenty of natural lighting as well as porch space. The grand-scale kitchen features bay-shaped cabinetry overlooking an atrium with a two-story window wall. A second atrium dominates the master suite, which boasts a bayed sitting area and a luxurious bath with a whirlpool tub. The lower level contains a study, family room and unfinished space for future expansion.

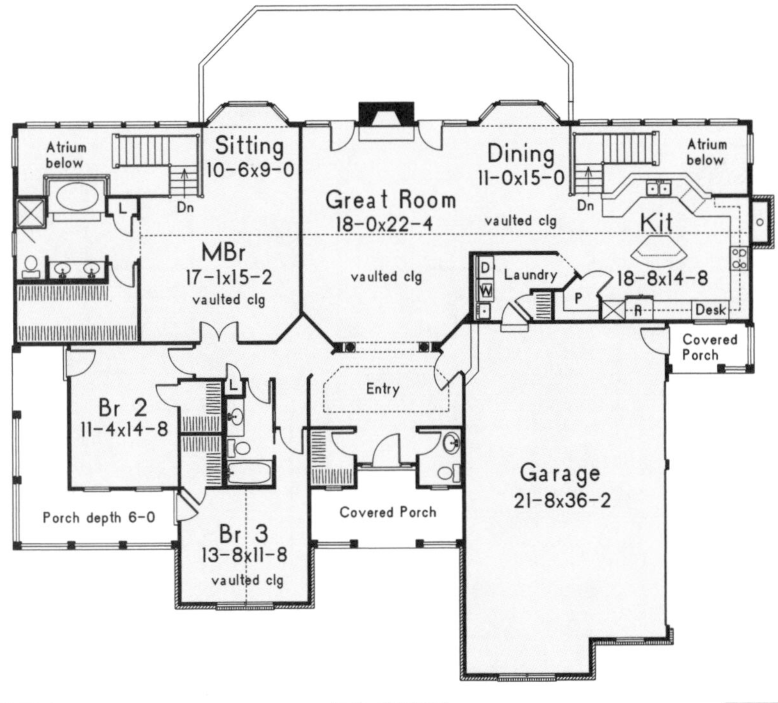

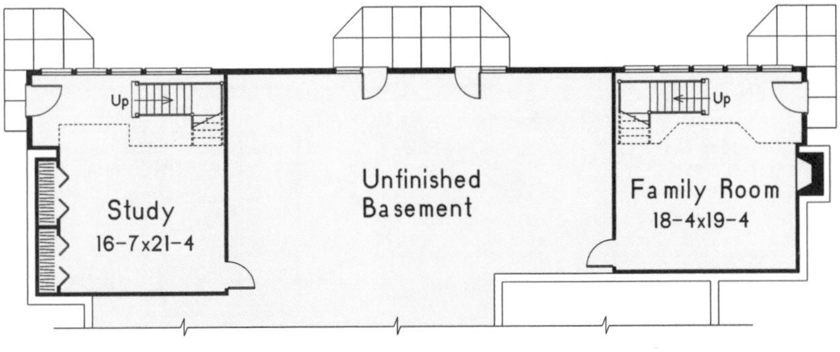

This home, as shown in the photograph, may differ from the actual blueprints. For more detailed information, please check the floor plans carefully.

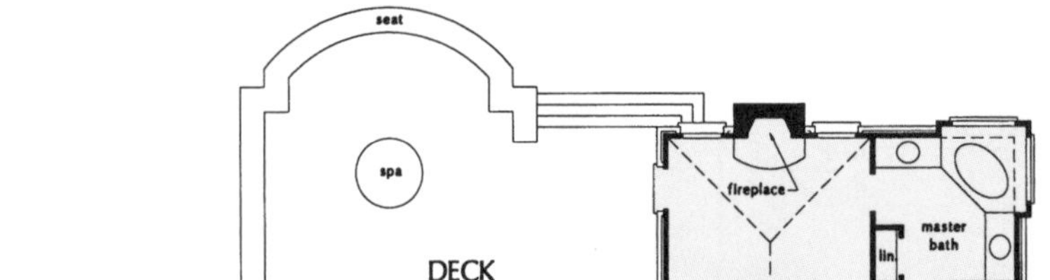

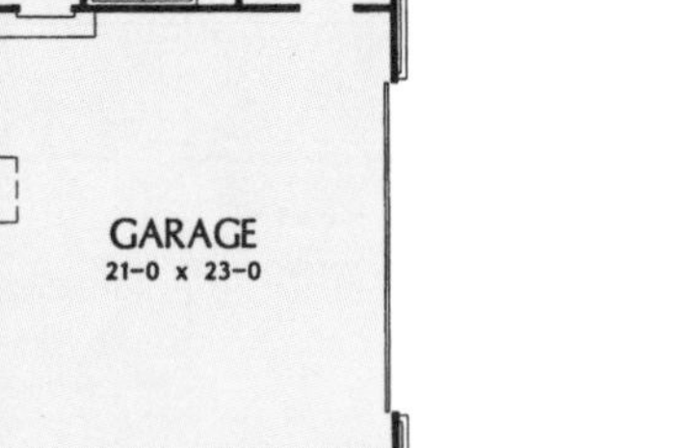

Design
HPT830114

Square Footage: 2,663	
Bonus Space: 653 square feet	
Width 72'-7" Depth 78'-0"	

This home features large arched windows, round columns, a covered porch and brick veneer siding. The arched window in the clerestory above the entrance provides natural light to the interior. The great room boasts a cathedral ceiling, a fireplace, built-in cabinets and bookshelves. Sliding glass doors lead to the sun room. The L-shaped kitchen services the dining room, the breakfast area, and the great room. The master bedroom suite, with a fireplace, uses private passage to the deck and its spa. Three additional bedrooms—one could serve as a study—are at the other end of the house for privacy.

© 1996 Donald A Gardner Architects, Inc.

Design HPT830115

Square Footage: 2,602	
Bonus Space: 399 square feet	
Width 75'-3" Depth 69'-6"	

Classic brick and siding put a fresh face on this traditional home, and introduce a well-cultivated interior that invites planned events as well as relaxed family time. The foyer opens to an expansive great room with a centered fireplace flanked by built-in cabinets. A cathedral ceiling soars above this living space, which leads out to a skylit sun room, then on to a patio. The secluded master suite nestles to the rear of the plan and boasts a vaulted ceiling and a skylit master bath with an angled spa tub and two vanities. Three additional bedrooms—or make one a study—share a full bath and a convenient powder room on the opposite side of the plan.

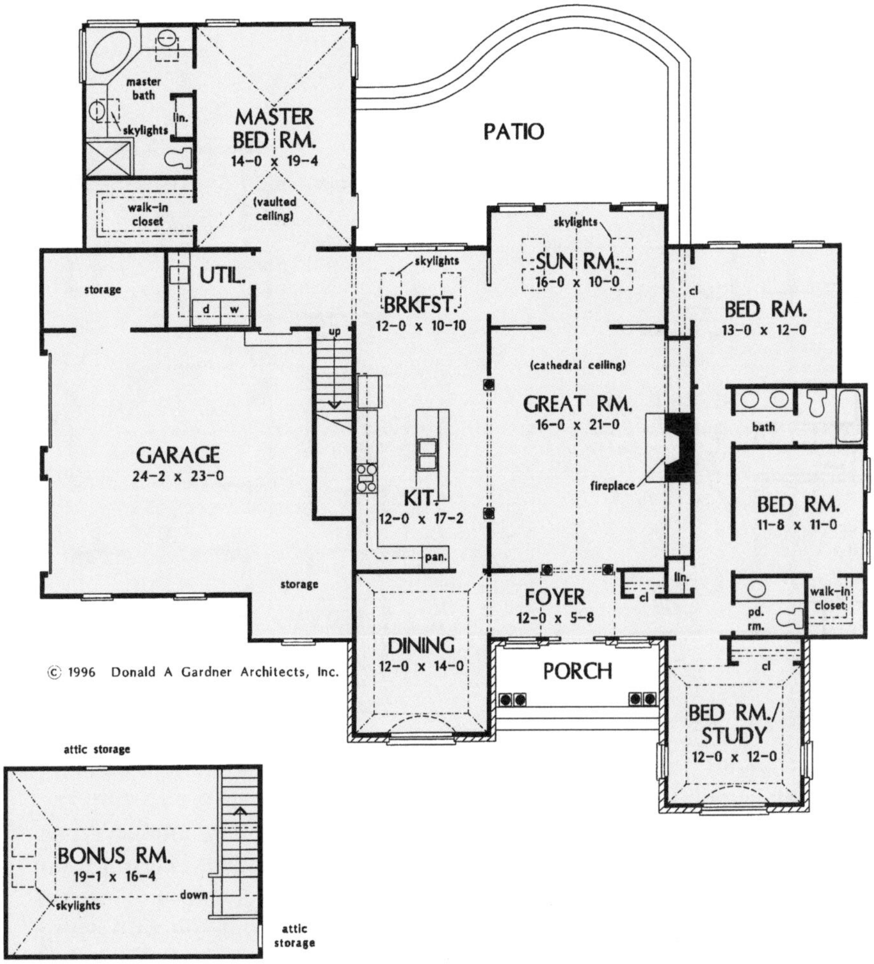
master bath
skylights
lin.
MASTER BED RM. 14-0 x 19-4
(vaulted ceiling)
walk-in closet
PATIO
skylights
SUN RM. 16-0 x 10-0
skylights
BRKFST. 12-0 x 10-10
storage
UTIL.
d w
cl
BED RM. 13-0 x 12-0
up
(cathedral ceiling)
GREAT RM. 16-0 x 21-0
bath
GARAGE 24-2 x 23-0
KIT. 12-0 x 17-2
fireplace
BED RM. 11-8 x 11-0
pan.
storage
lin.
FOYER 12-0 x 5-8
cl
walk-in closet
pd. rm.
DINING 12-0 x 14-0
PORCH
cl
BED RM./ STUDY 12-0 x 12-0
© 1996 Donald A Gardner Architects, Inc.
attic storage
BONUS RM. 19-1 x 16-4
skylights
down
attic storage

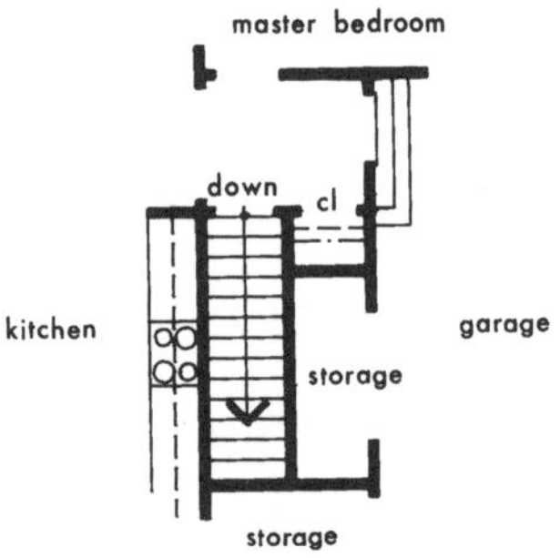
master bedroom
down
cl
kitchen
garage
storage
storage

ALTERNATE PLAN
FOR BASEMENT

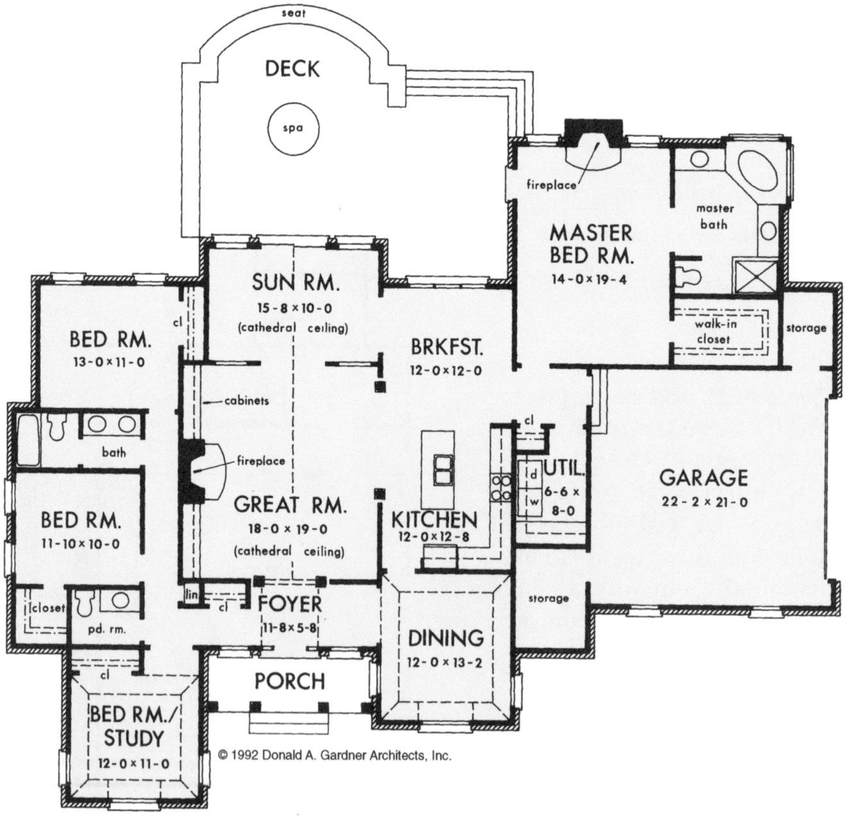
seat
DECK
spa
fireplace
MASTER
BED RM.
14-0×19-4
master
bath
walk-in
closet
storage
SUN RM.
15-8×10-0
(cathedral ceiling)
cl
BED RM.
13-0×11-0
BRKFST.
12-0×12-0
cabinets
cl
bath
fireplace
UTIL.
6-6×
8-0
GARAGE
22-2×21-0
BED RM.
11-10×10-0
GREAT RM.
18-0×19-0
(cathedral ceiling)
KITCHEN
12-0×12-8
lin
cl
FOYER
11-8×5-8
closet
pd. rm.
storage
DINING
12-0×13-2
cl
PORCH
BED RM./
STUDY
12-0×11-0

A covered front porch, an arched-window dormer and brick detailing all combine to give this home plenty of curb appeal. A cozy fireplace and built-in cabinets accent the great room. The island kitchen is partially open to the great room, maintaining a spacious feeling. The sun room and breakfast area will surely brighten each day. The lovely master suite has a romantic fireplace and a pampering bath. Three bedrooms—or two with a study—one full bath and a powder room complete the plan.

Design
HPT830116

Square Footage: 2,526
Width 76'-11" Depth 71'-7"

Graceful arches and columns delicately complement the brick facade of this country house. An extended foyer introduces an exciting interior plan—ten-foot ceilings throughout give a spacious feeling. A cozy fireplace will be appreciated in the great room, as will the nearby screened porch. An efficient kitchen, with a cooktop-island counter and an angled sink, serves both the breakfast room and the formal dining room. The master suite, located at the rear of the plan for privacy, offers many amenities. Two family bedrooms clustered nearby share a full bath. Please specify crawlspace or slab foundation when ordering.

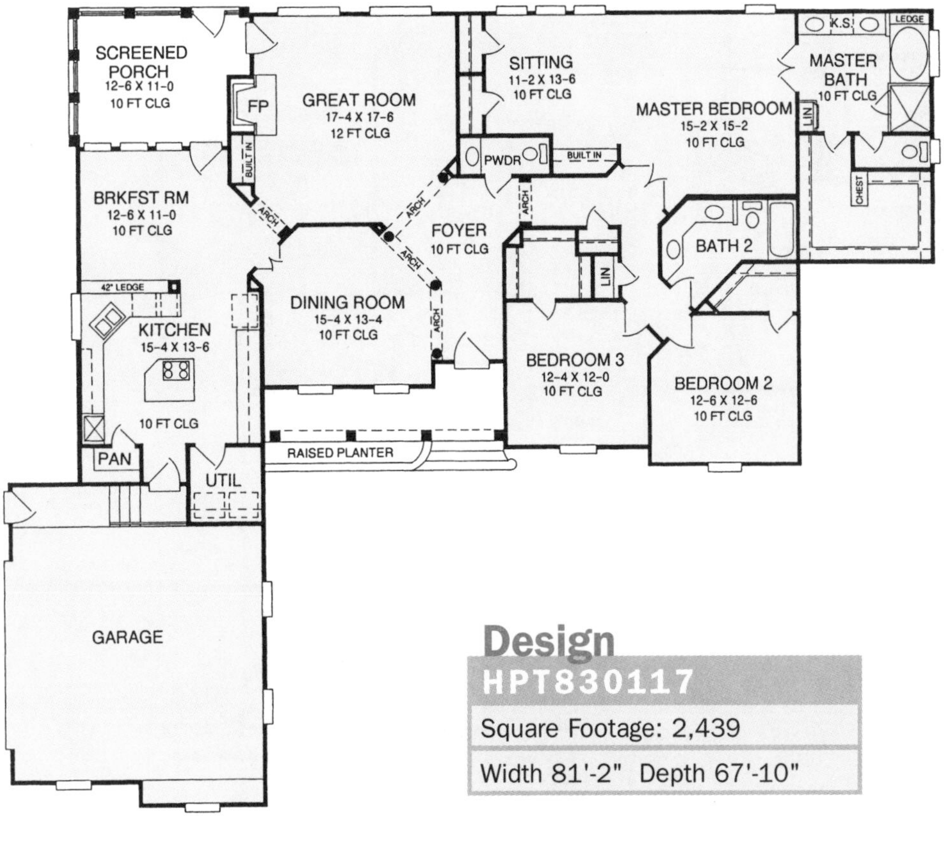

Design
HPT830117

Square Footage: 2,439

Width 81'-2" Depth 67'-10"

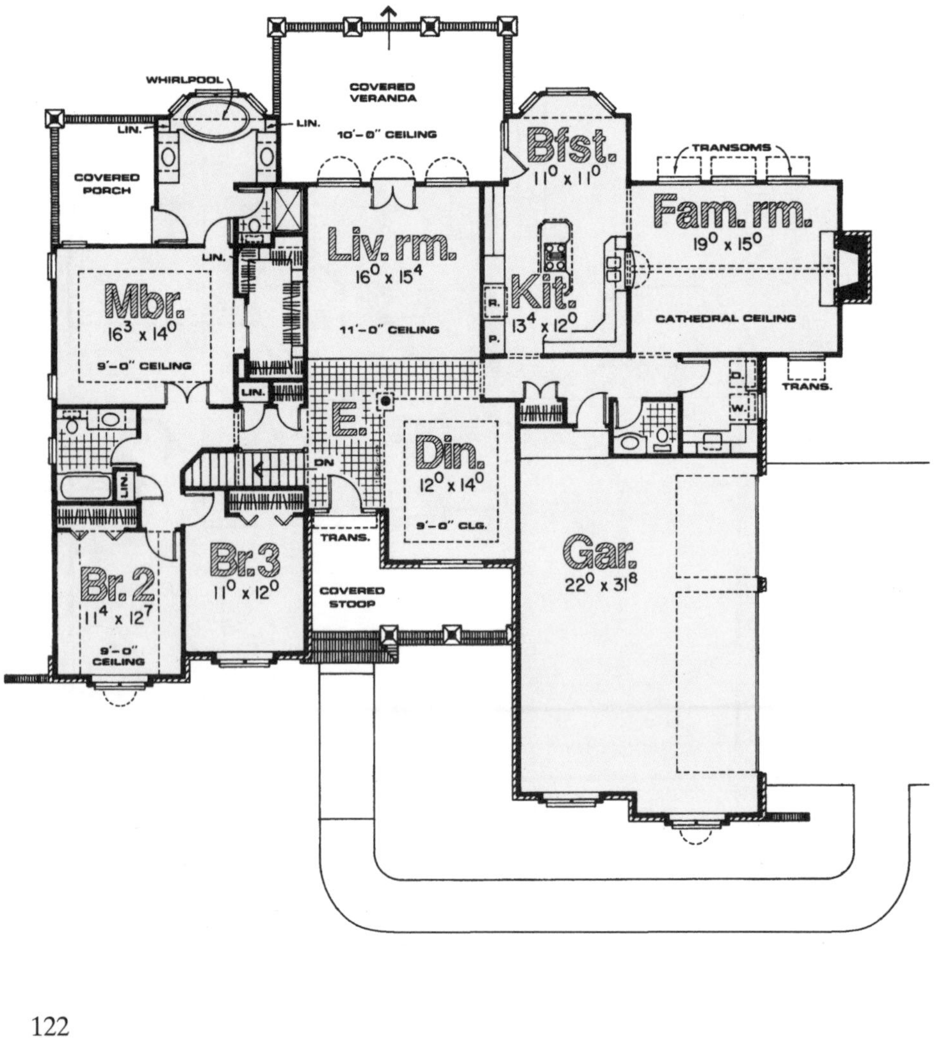

Design HPT830118

Square Footage: 2,399

Width 72'-8" Depth 64'-6"

Interesting window treatments and a charming porch extend the attention-getting nature of this brick ranch home. Beyond the covered porch, the formal dining room is to the right and the multi-windowed living room straight ahead. The L-shaped kitchen features an island cooktop. Located for privacy, the master suite includes a huge walk-in closet. The amenity-filled master bath contains twin vanities and an oval whirlpool tub. Two secondary bedrooms share a full bath.

Design HPT830119

Square Footage: 2,559

Width 65'-6" Depth 63'-10"

Traditional in character, this efficiently designed one-story comes with all the amenities. Ten-foot ceilings in all major living areas give the plan a big-home feel. The kitchen, breakfast room and keeping room are adjacent and open to one another for family gatherings. The kitchen features a large walk-in pantry, desk and snack bar. Family bedrooms are located away from the master suite. A private study is situated off the foyer and could be used for an in-home office or nursery. Please specify crawlspace or slab foundation when ordering.

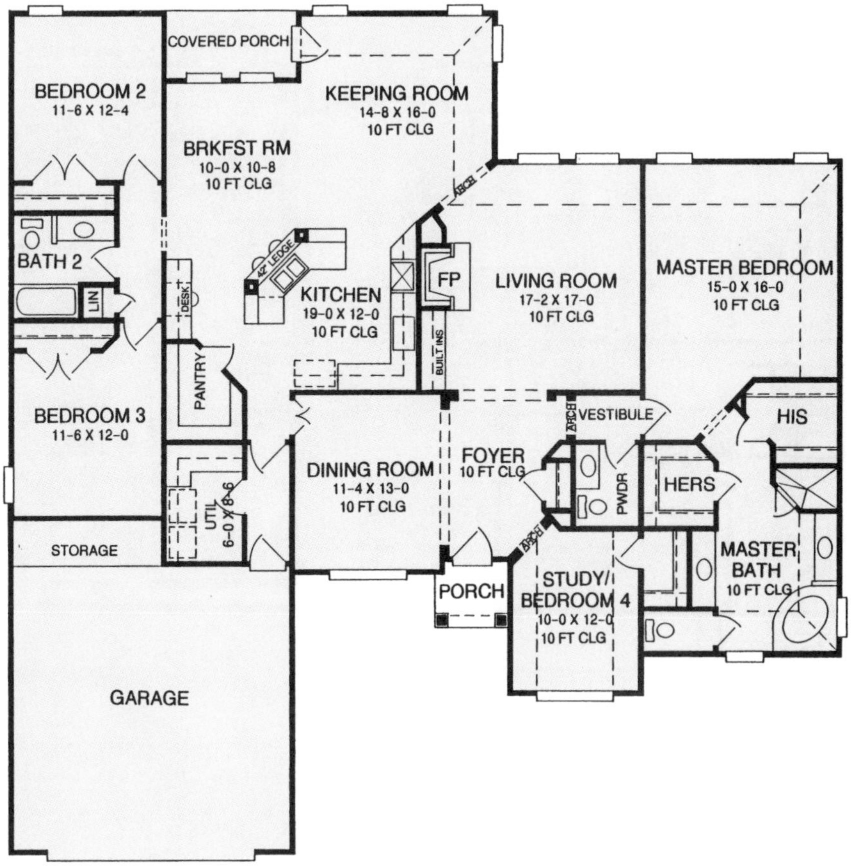

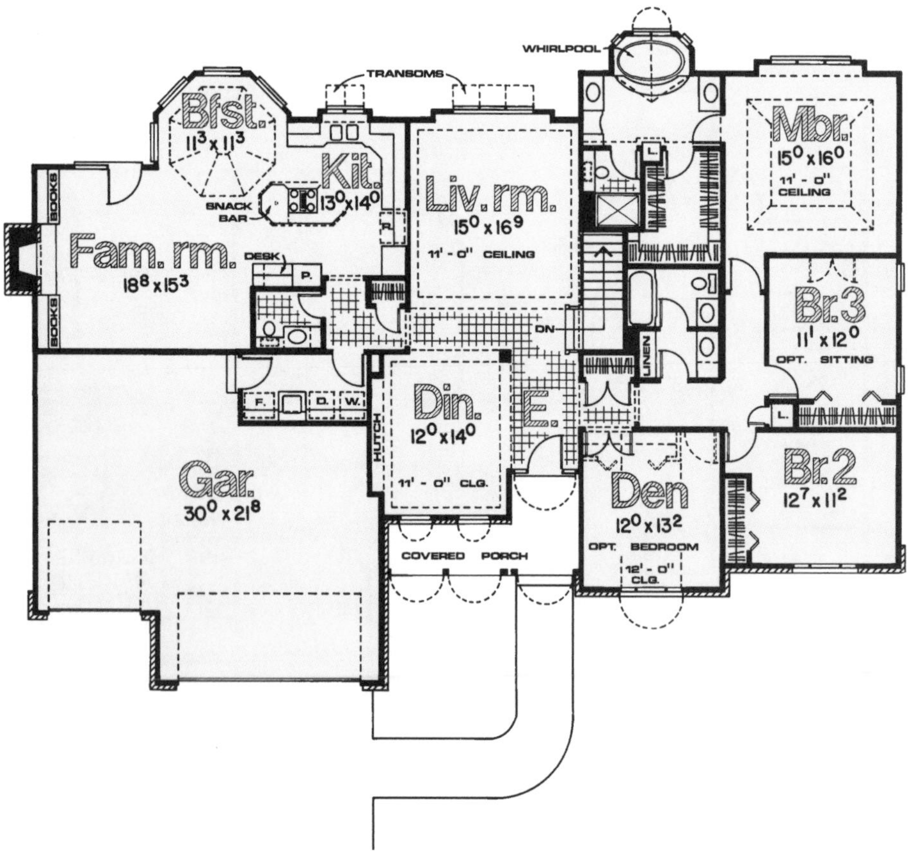

Design

HPT830120

Square Footage: 2,498	
Width 76'-0" Depth 55'-4"	

Elegant arches at the covered entry of this home announce an exquisite floor plan. The tiled entry opens to the formal living and dining rooms, which enjoy open, soaring space defined by arches and a decorative column. A gourmet kitchen offers an island cooktop counter and serves a bayed breakfast nook and a convenient snack bar. The sleeping wing includes a master suite with a whirlpool bath, a sizable walk-in closet, two vanities and a box-bay window. Two family bedrooms share a full bath nearby, while a secluded den offers the possibility of a fourth bedroom.

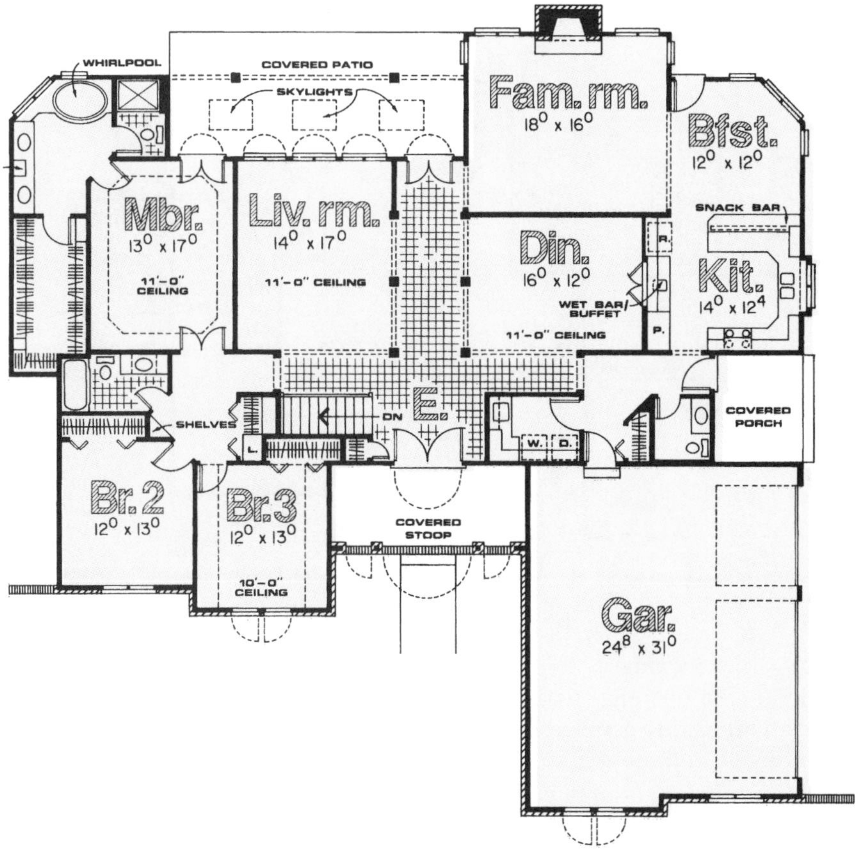

Design HPT830121

Square Footage: 2,598
Width 72'-0" Depth 70'-8"

A grand double-door entry leads to a stunning interior. Columns define the formal living areas: living room to the left and dining room to the right. The adjacent kitchen has a pass-through to the dining room and a snack bar that separates it from the breakfast room. A fireplace flanked by windows warms the family room. The luxurious trend continues in the master suite, which invites relaxation. Two secondary bedrooms share a hall bath.

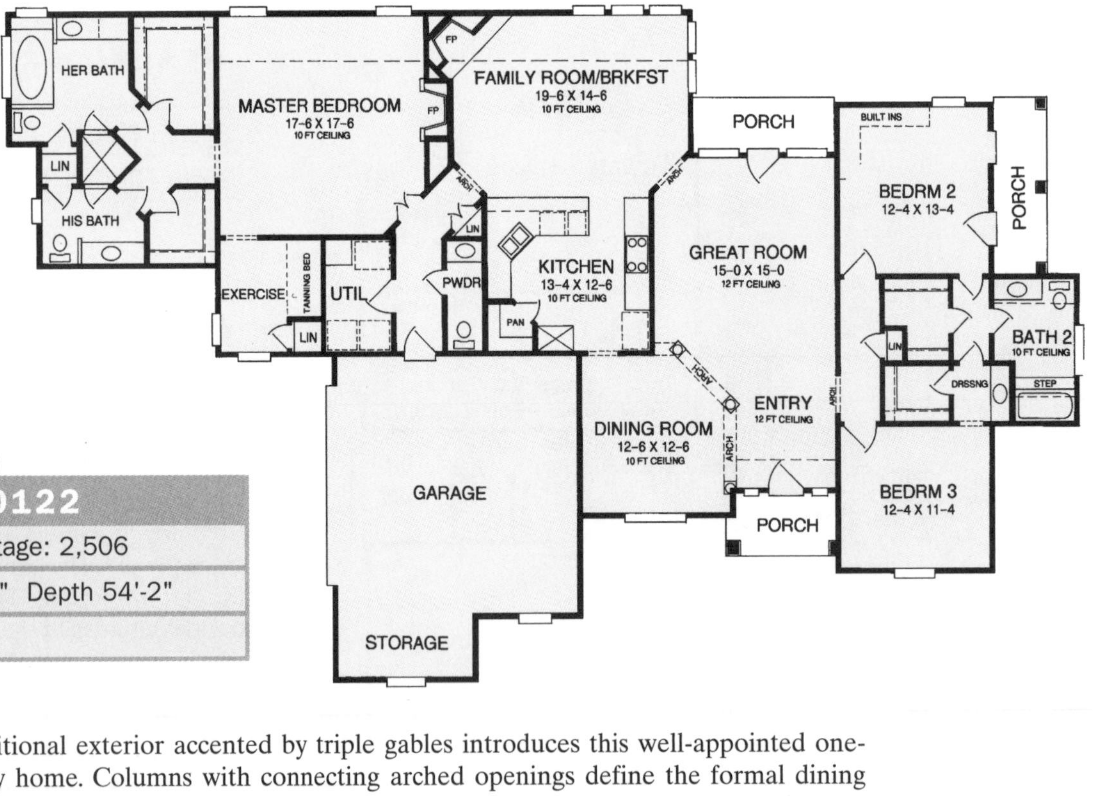

Design HPT830122

Square Footage: 2,506

Width 89'-6" Depth 54'-2"

L

A traditional exterior accented by triple gables introduces this well-appointed one-story home. Columns with connecting arched openings define the formal dining room and create a dramatic entrance. An efficiently planned kitchen faces the spacious family room and breakfast room. The corner fireplace with a raised hearth bids a warm welcome, making this a splendid area for informal entertaining. The romantic master suite is designed with a fireplace and an exercise room. The master bath has large His and Hers walk-in closets as well as His and Hers baths with separate entrances to a shared shower. Two additional bedrooms featuring walk-in closets are located on the opposite side of the home. Please specify crawlspace or slab foundation when ordering.

A bold entrance leads to a two-story foyer and living room, giving the home an elegant, open feel. The kitchen and breakfast room are open to the large family room—a perfect backdrop for everyday living. The master suite has a compartmented bath and a nearby study or nursery. Upstairs, three comfortable bedrooms each has a walk-in closet. Two of the bedrooms share a private bath, another full bath is located in the hall. Please specify basement, crawlspace or slab foundation when ordering.

Design HPT830123

First Floor: 2,547 square feet
Second Floor: 1,128 square feet
Total: 3,675 square feet
Width 67'-8" Depth 77'-2"

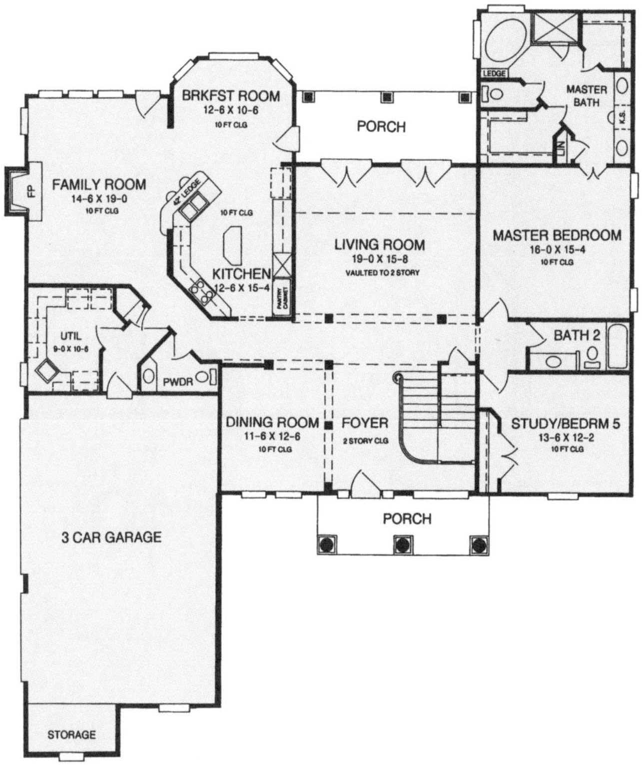

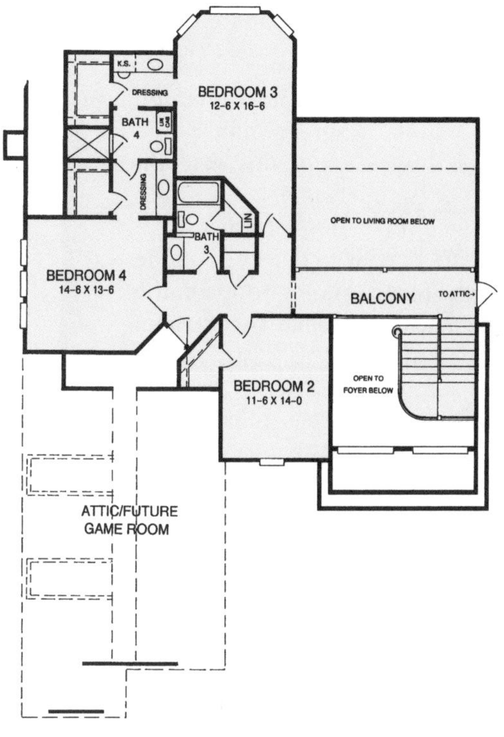

Design

HPT830124

First Floor: 2,894 square feet
Second Floor: 568 square feet
Total: 3,462 square feet
Width 67'-0" Depth 102'-0"

Two guest suites—one on each floor—enhance the floor plan of this magnificent stucco home. A grand entrance provides passage to a foyer that opens to the study on the left, the formal dining room on the right, and the formal living room straight ahead. The casual living area combines a kitchen with an island cooktop, a sun-filled breakfast nook and a spacious leisure room. Arched openings lead into the master bedroom and a lavish master bath that enjoys a private garden. The second-floor guest suite includes a loft and a large observation deck.

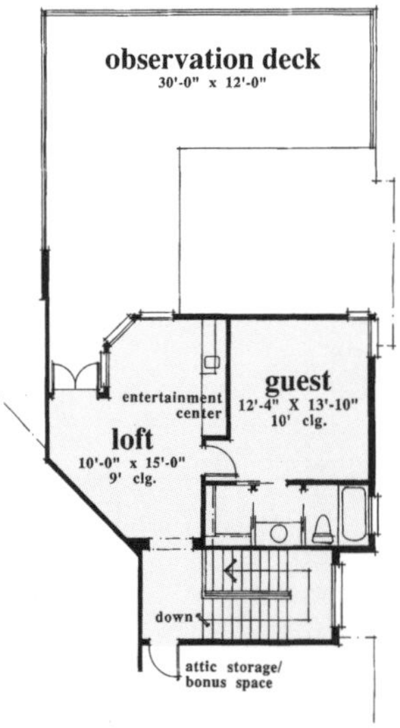

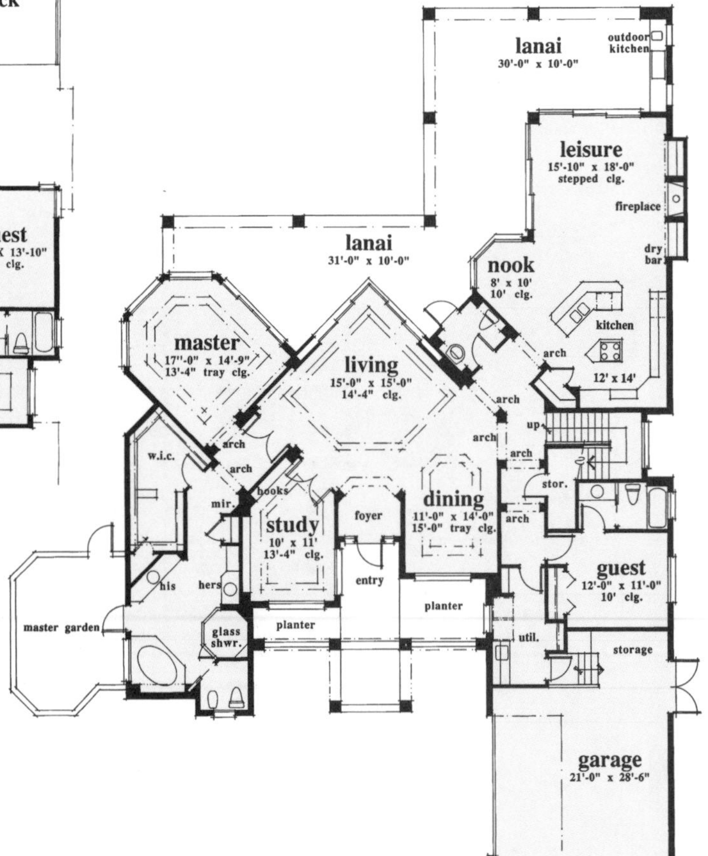

This beautiful home has many attributes, including a bowed dining room and a living room with a fireplace and outdoor access. For family gatherings, the kitchen remains open to the living areas. A study off the foyer will be much appreciated. The master suite enjoys its own personal luxury bath. Upstairs, two bedrooms share a full bath. A loft with a wet bar accommodates playtime.

Design HPT830125

First Floor: 2,551 square feet
Second Floor: 1,037 square feet
Total: 3,588 square feet
Width 76'-0" Depth 90'-0
L

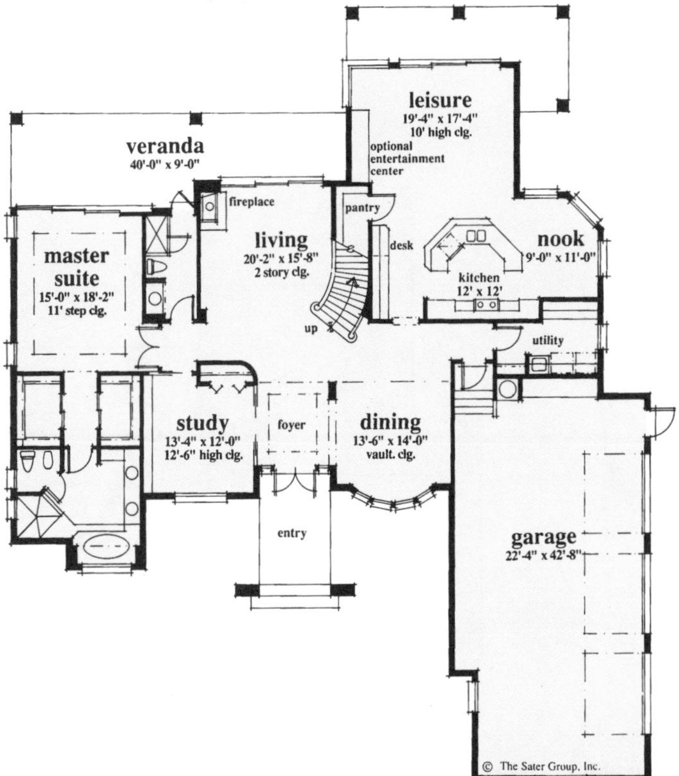

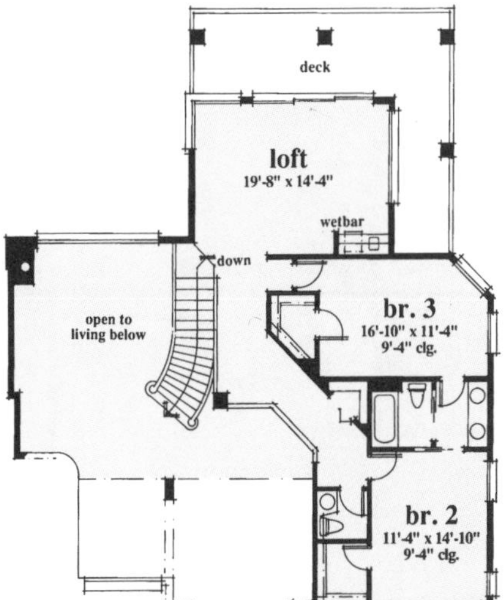

Family living takes on a casually elegant look in this classic 1½-story home. The large foyer opens to the formal dining room, stylishly open to the great room through arches. The two-story great room has French doors to the rear, with a fireplace and wet bar dividing it from casual family living areas. The kitchen has a cooktop island, wrapping counters, a breakfast nook and a cozy keeping room. The luxurious master suite joins a study/sitting room. Upstairs, three bedrooms are fashioned with private bath access and plenty of closet space. Please specify basement, crawlspace or slab foundation when ordering.

Design HPT830126

First Floor: 2,130 square feet

Second Floor: 897 square feet

Total: 3,027 square feet

Width 62'-4" Depth 54'-6"

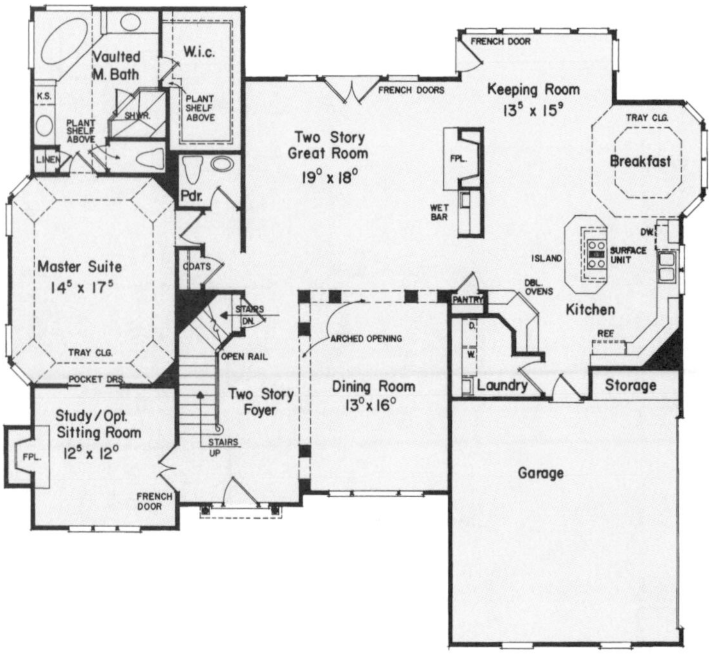

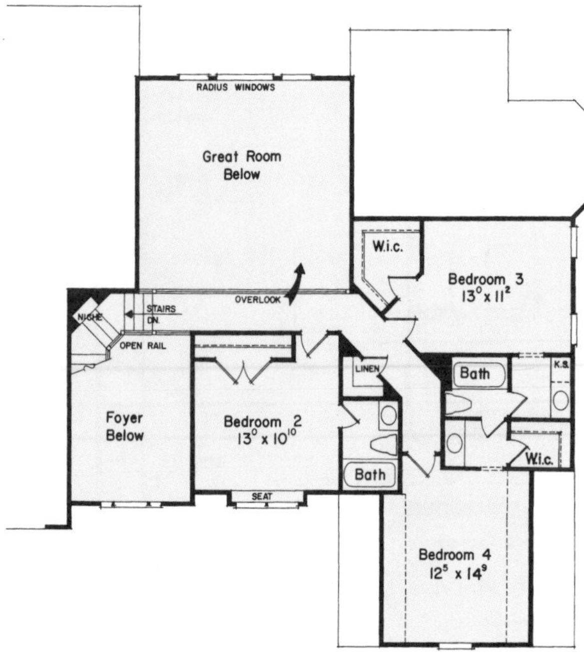

Custom features abound in this traditional home, including plant shelves, built-in shelves and niches, a romantic second-floor balcony and vaulted ceilings in the foyer and the formal living, family and breakfast rooms. The kitchen has ample counter and cabinet space. The master suite has an elegant tray ceiling and an oversized bath with a whirlpool and walk-in closet. Upstairs, two family bedrooms and a bonus room share a compartmented hall bath. Please specify basement, crawlspace or slab foundation when ordering.

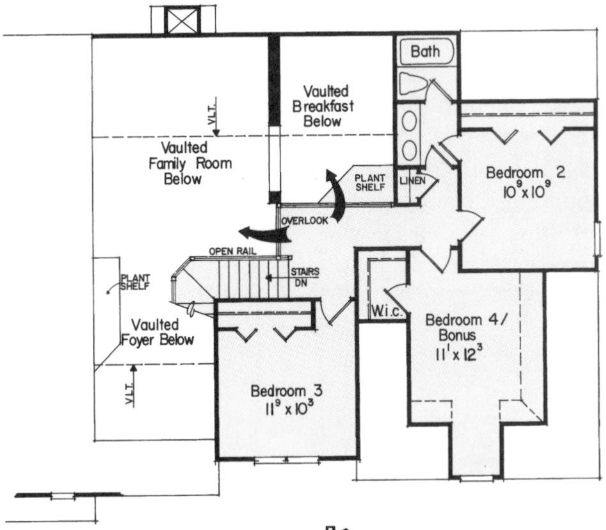

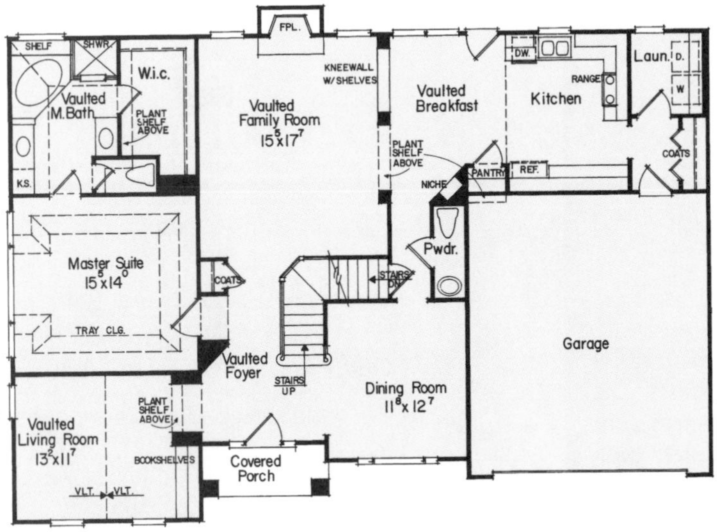

QUOTE ONE®

Cost to build? See page 516 to order complete cost estimate to build this house in your area!

Design HPT830127

First Floor: 1,637 square feet
Second Floor: 671 square feet
Total: 2,308 square feet
Width 58'-0" Depth 41'-4"

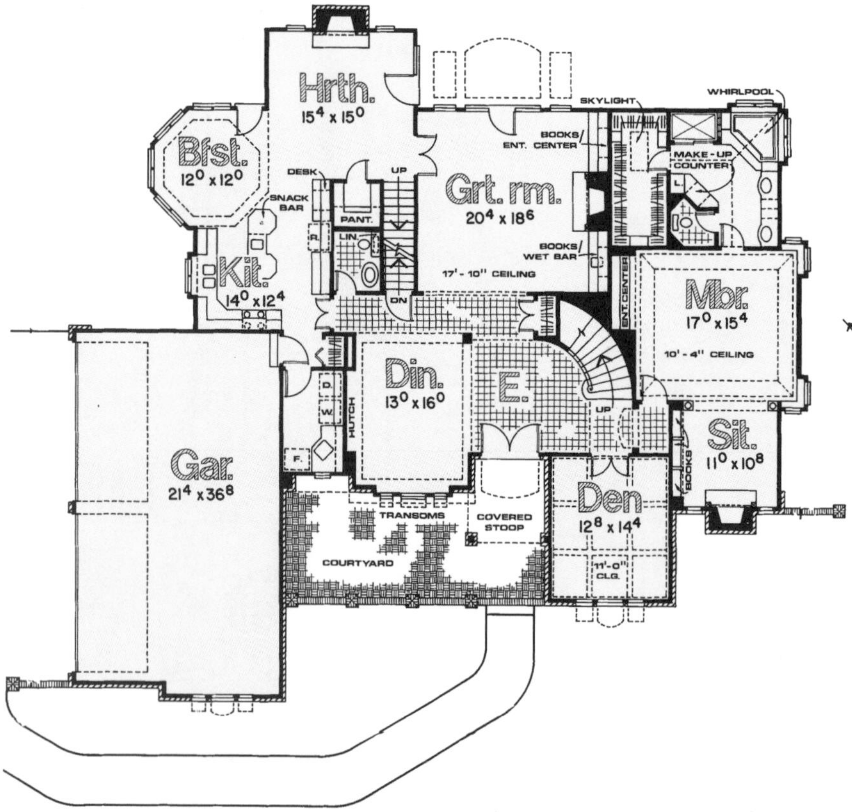

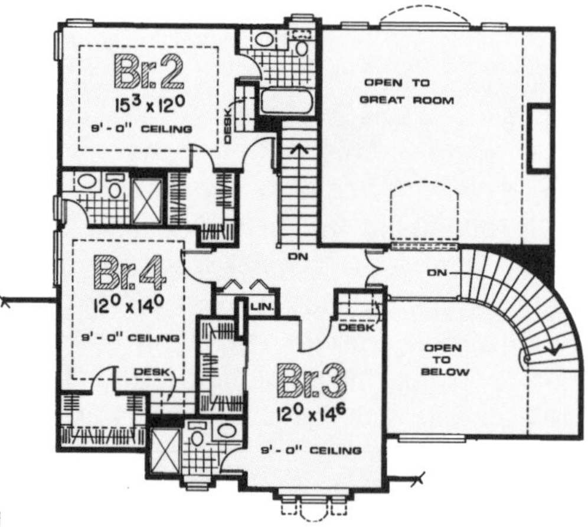

QUOTE ONE®

Cost to build? See page 516 to order complete cost estimate to build this house in your area!

The stone facade of this traditional design evokes images of a quieter life, a life of harmony and comfortable luxury. The master suite offers privacy on the first floor and features a sitting room with bookshelves, two walk-in closets and a private bath with a corner whirlpool tub. Three family bedrooms, each with a walk-in closet, and two baths make up the second floor.

Design HPT830128

First Floor: 2,603 square feet
Second Floor: 1,020 square feet
Total: 3,623 square feet
Width 76'-8" Depth 68'-0"

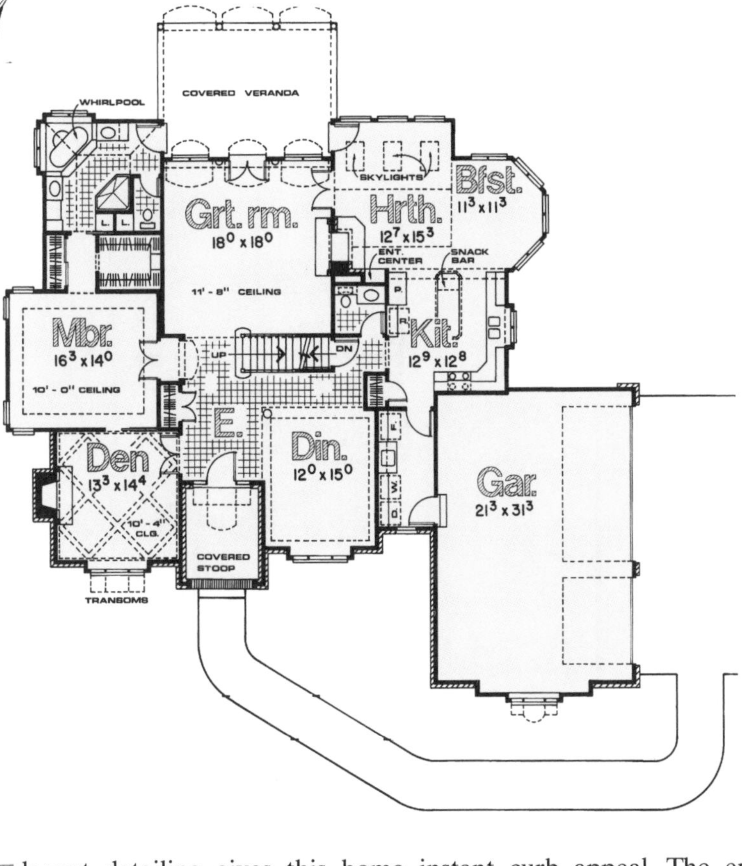

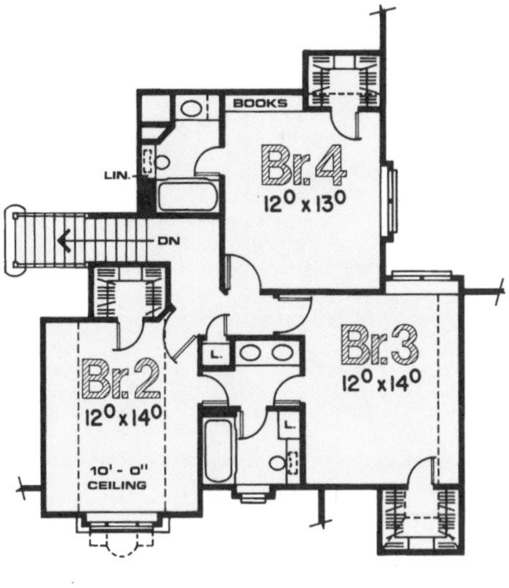

Elegant detailing gives this home instant curb appeal. The entry is flanked by the dining room and the den, with its fireplace and an intriguing ceiling. The great room shares a through-fireplace with the hearth room. A sunny breakfast room and kitchen feature an island with a snack bar, wrapping counters and a pantry. The master suite is luxurious with two closets, a whirlpool tub, His and Hers vanities and access to the veranda. Three family bedrooms offer walk-in closets and private bathroom access.

Design HPT830129

First Floor: 2,084 square feet
Second Floor: 848 square feet
Total: 2,932 square feet
Width 68'-8" Depth 60'-0"

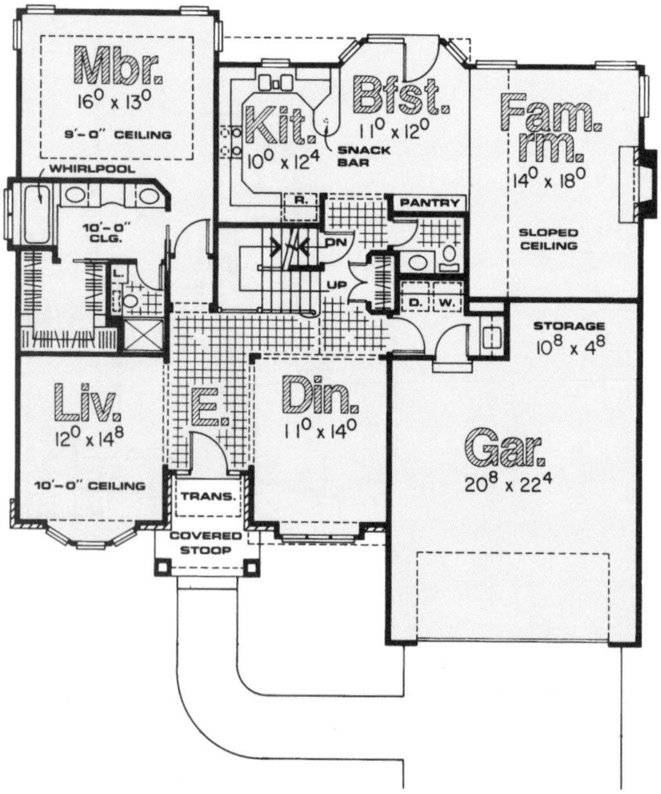

Mbr.
16⁰ x 13⁰
9'-0" CEILING
WHIRLPOOL
10'-0" CLG.
Kit.
10⁰ x 12⁴
Bfst.
11⁰ x 12⁰
SNACK BAR
Fam. rm.
14⁰ x 18⁰
SLOPED CEILING
PANTRY
DN
UP
D.
W.
STORAGE
10⁸ x 4⁸
Liv.
12⁰ x 14⁸
10'-0" CEILING
E.
Din.
11⁰ x 14⁰
Gar.
20⁸ x 22⁴
TRANS.
COVERED STOOP

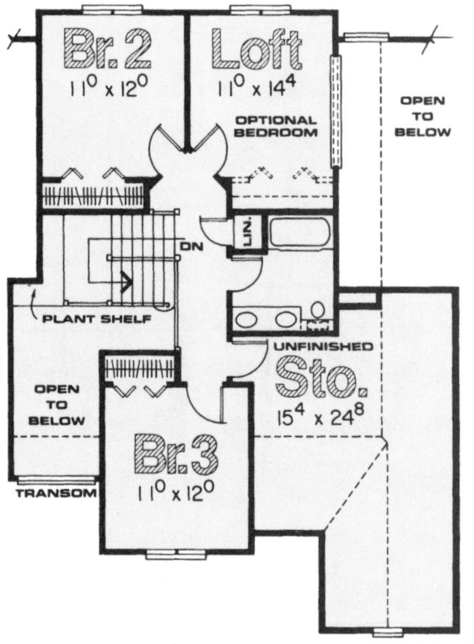

Br. 2
11⁰ x 12⁰
Loft
11⁰ x 14⁴
OPTIONAL BEDROOM
OPEN TO BELOW
DN
PLANT SHELF
UNFINISHED
Sto.
15⁴ x 24⁸
OPEN TO BELOW
Br. 3
11⁰ x 12⁰
TRANSOM

Soft curves under repeating gables form an inviting elevation. The bayed living room and the formal dining room surround a beautiful two-story entry. The master bedroom is finished with a whirlpool tub, twin vanities and a walk-in closet. The upstairs drooms share a hall bath with a dual vanity.

Design
HPT830130

First Floor: 1,651 square feet

Second Floor: 634 square feet

Total: 2,285 square feet

Width 52'-0" Depth 50'-0"

Design HPT830131

First Floor: 1,777 square feet
Second Floor: 719 square feet
Total: 2,496 square feet
Width 58'-0" Depth 59'-4"

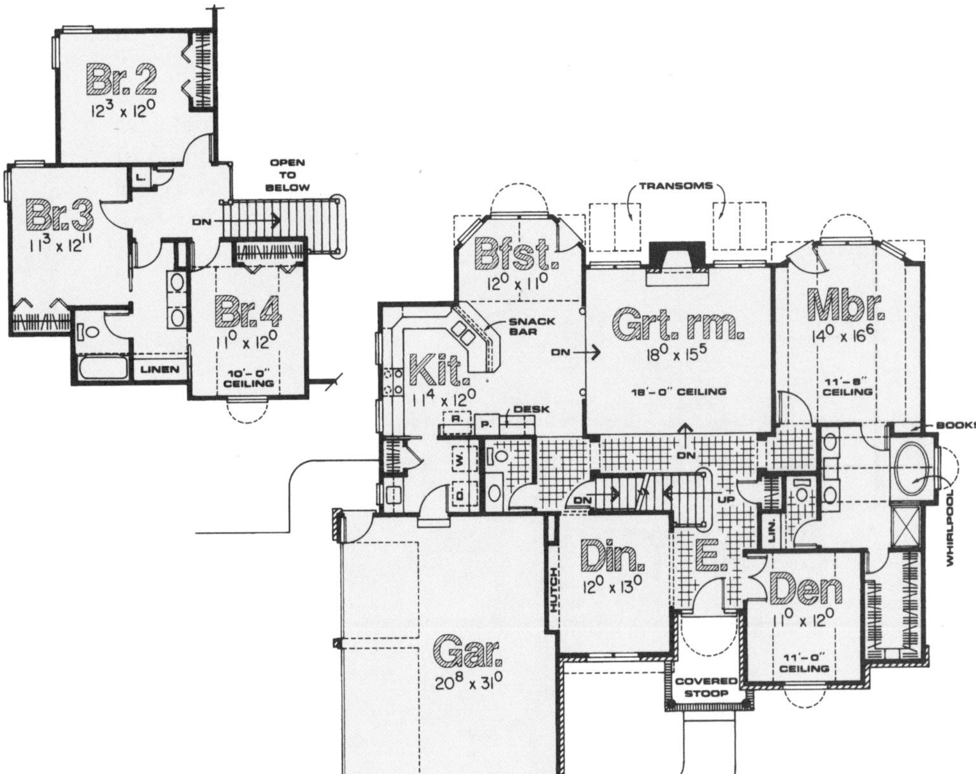

Dramatic rooflines complement an arched pediment and columns, set off by a stunning, glass-paneled entry that highlights this traditional exterior. The tiled entry overlooks the formal dining room and opens to the den through French doors. The great room is down one step from the well-appointed kitchen and bayed breakfast area. A volume ceiling and a bay window highlight the master suite, and a central hall connects three family bedrooms upstairs.

From the curbside of this 1½-story home, brick and stucco accents command attention. Ten-foot ceilings enhance both the living room and the comfortable great room, which are separated by French doors. Family-oriented features in the great room include a through-fireplace and bookcases. The gourmet kitchen and hearth room contain a breakfast nook, snack bar and generous counter space. The main-floor master suite offers a tiered ceiling, huge walk-in closet, corner whirlpool tub and His and Hers vanities. Upstairs, three generous secondary bedrooms share a compartmented bath.

Design HPT830132

First Floor: 2,073 square feet
Second Floor: 741 square feet
Total: 2,814 square feet
Width 64'-0" Depth 58'-0"

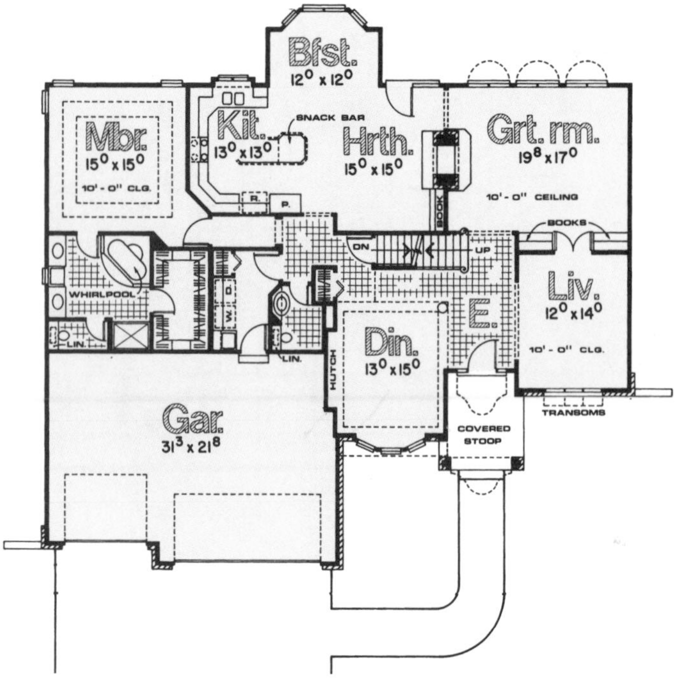

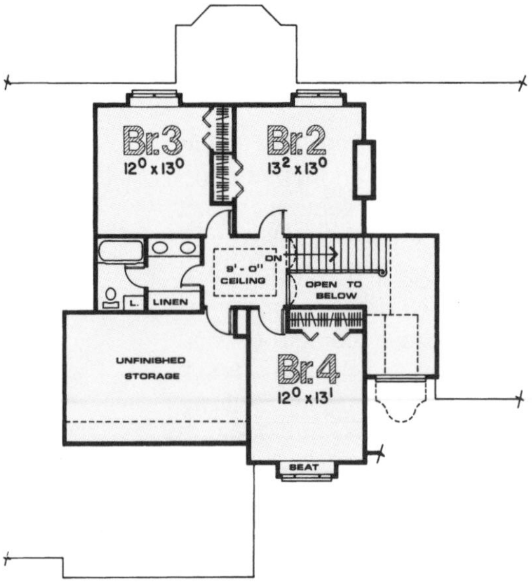

This home, as shown in the photograph, may differ from the actual blueprints. For more detailed information, please check the floor plans carefully.
Photo by Design Basics, Inc.

The gorgeous entry of this traditional home opens to a formal dining room, which offers hutch space, and to a volume living room with a see-through fireplace to the spacious family room. Look for a tall ceiling and dual entertainment centers here. Adjacent is the bayed breakfast area and island kitchen with a wraparound counter and a walk-in pantry. The master suite is highlighted with a formal ceiling in the bedroom and a bath with a two-person whirlpool tub, bayed windows and a double vanity. Upstairs, two bedrooms share private access to a compartmented bath; another bedroom has a private bath.

Design HPT830133

First Floor: 1,860 square feet

Second Floor: 848 square feet

Total: 2,708 square feet

Width 56'-0" Depth 59'-4"

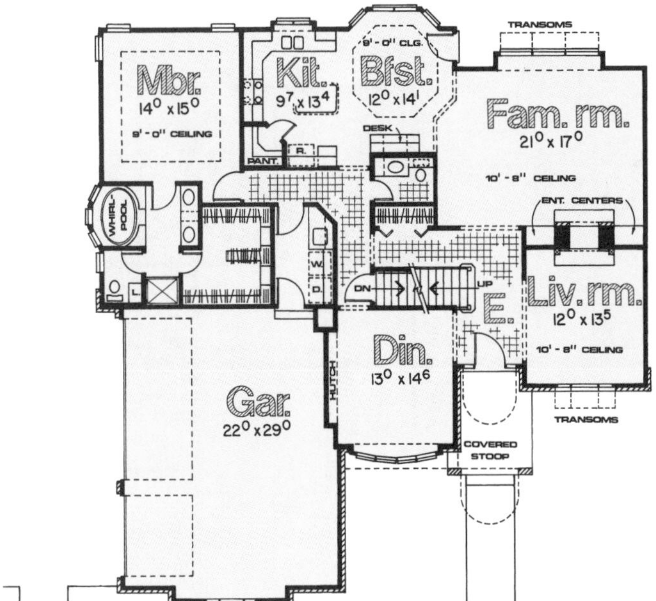

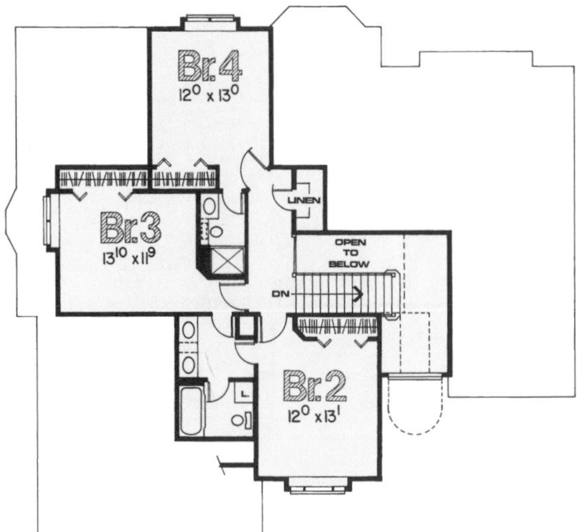

This home, as shown in the photograph, may differ from the actual blueprints. For more detailed information, please check the floor plans carefully.
Photo courtesy of Design Basics, Inc.

This narrow-lot plan features a wraparound porch at the two-story entry, which opens to the formal dining room with beautiful bay windows. The great room features a handsome fireplace and a ten-and-a-half-foot ceiling. A well-equipped island kitchen with a pantry and built-in desk is designed for the serious cook. The large master bedroom enjoys a tray ceiling and a luxury master bath. Upstairs, three secondary bedrooms with ample closet space share a compartmented bath.

Design HPT830134

First Floor: 1,551 square feet

Second Floor: 725 square feet

Total: 2,276 square feet

Width 54'-0" Depth 50'-0"

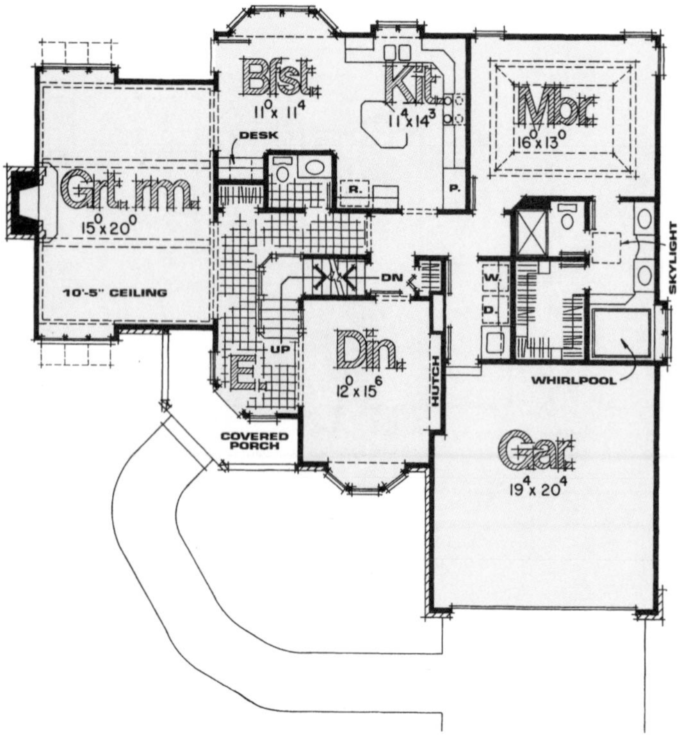

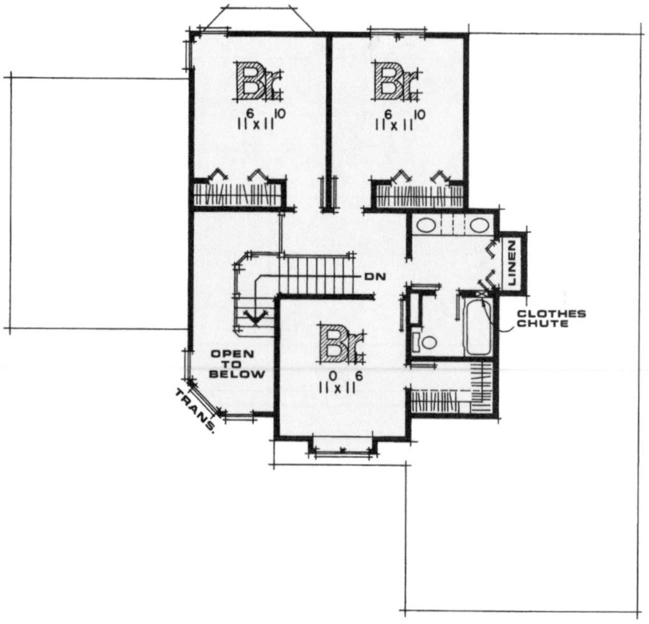

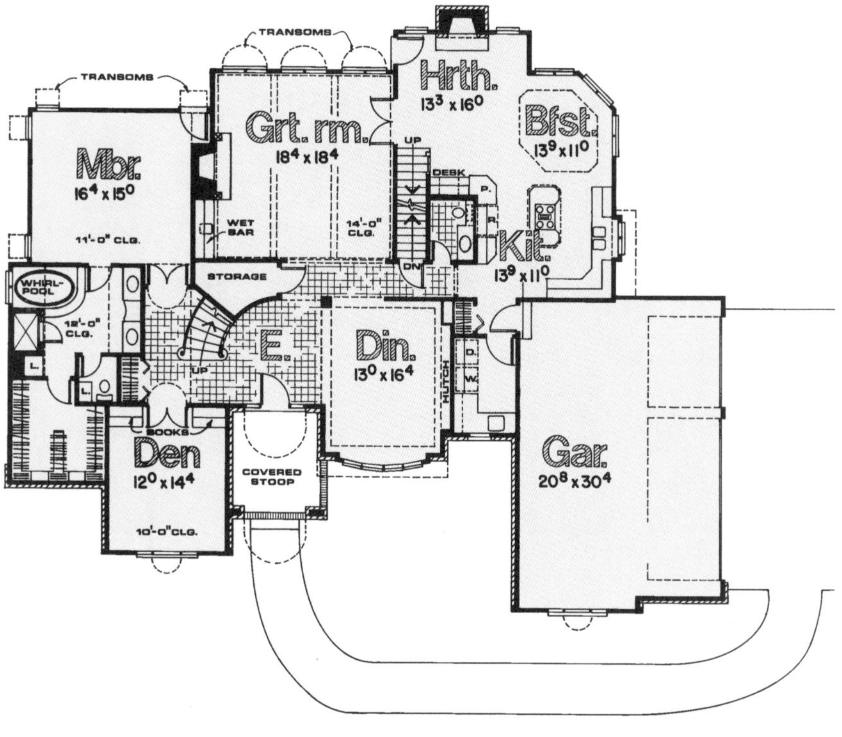

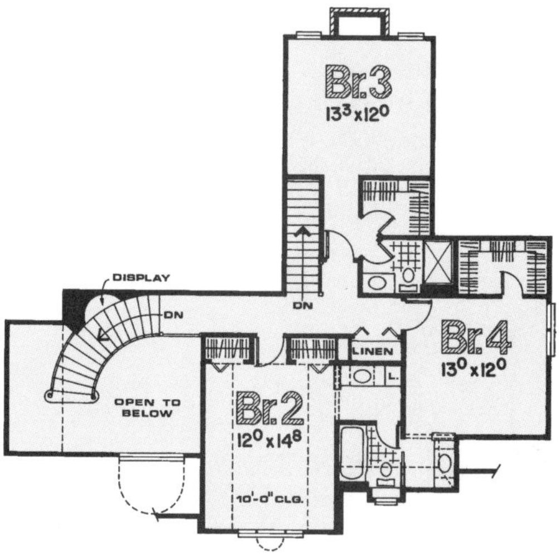

A curving staircase graces the entry to this beautiful home and hints at the wealth of amenities found in the floor plan. Besides an oversized great room with fireplace and arched windows, there's a cozy hearth room with its own fireplace. A secluded den contains bookcases and an arched transom above double doors. The master suite is on the first floor, thoughtfully separated from three family bedrooms upstairs.

Design
HPT830135

First Floor: 2,252 square feet
Second Floor: 920 square feet
Total: 3,172 square feet
Width 73'-4" Depth 57'-4"

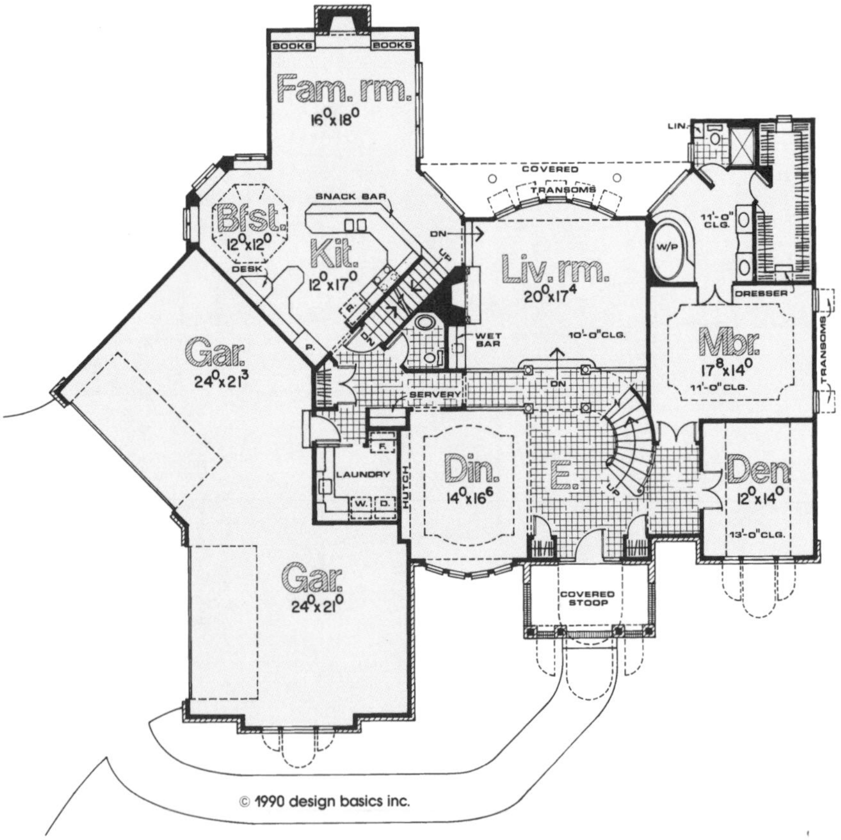

Design

HPT830136

First Floor: 2,617 square feet
Second Floor: 1,072 square feet
Total: 3,689 square feet
Width 83'-5" Depth 73'-4"

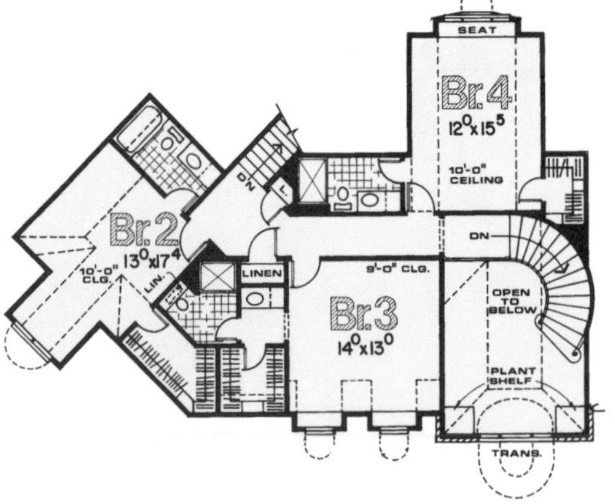

A spectacular volume entry with curving staircase features columns that announce the living room. The living room contains a fireplace, bowed window and wet bar. The formal dining room contains hutch space and nearby servery. All main-level rooms have nine-foot ceilings. To the rear of the plan is the family room. It has bookcases surrounding a fireplace. French doors lead into the den with a stunning window. The master suite is located on the first floor and has a most elegant bath and huge walk-in closet. Second-floor bedrooms also have walk-in closets and private baths.

Design

HPT830137
First Floor: 2,804 square feet
Second Floor: 961 square feet
Total: 3,765 square feet
Width 70'-8" Depth 73'-4"

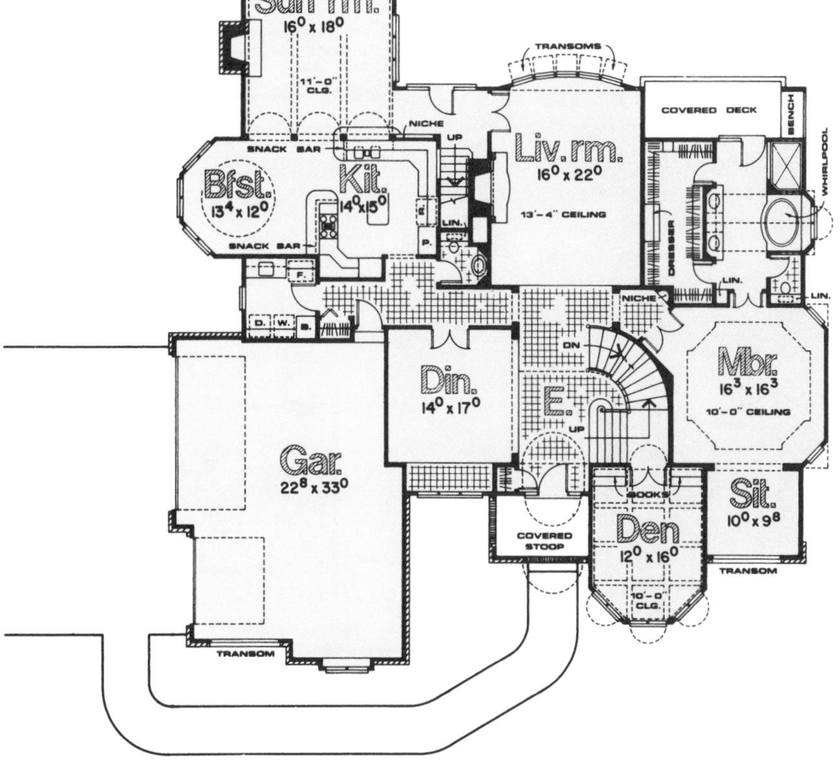

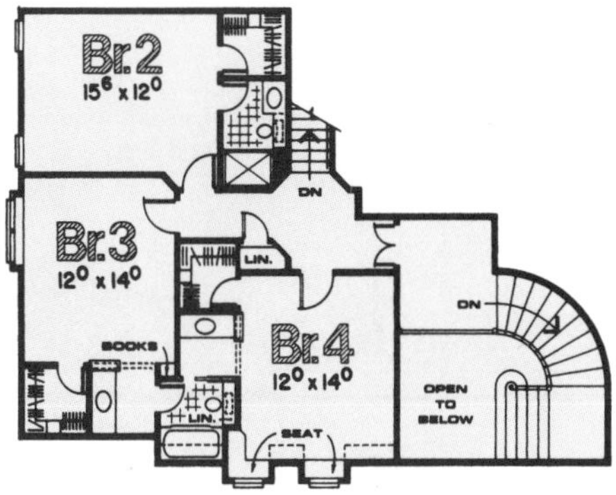

This captivating exterior is accentuated by handsome stone columns and a dramatic cantilevered bay. Inside, formal elegance is captured in the living room, which has a volume ceiling, bowed windows and a fireplace. The kitchen is enhanced with a prep island, snack bar and pantry. Informal gatherings will be enjoyed in the breakfast nook or the sun room. The master suite has an adjoining sitting room and a luxury bath. Upstairs, at the landing level, is a den with a spider-beam ceiling. The second floor houses three bedrooms—two share a bath and one has a private bath.

Design
HPT830138

First Floor: 1,421 square feet
Second Floor: 448 square feet
Total: 1,869 square feet
Width 52'-0" Depth 47'-4"

Always a welcome sight, the covered front porch of this home invites investigation of its delightful floor plan. Living areas to the back of the house include the great room with a see-through fireplace to the bayed dinette and kitchen with a large corner walk-in pantry. A split-bedroom sleeping plan puts the master suite, with a whirlpool tub, on the first floor away from two second-floor bedrooms and a shared full bath.

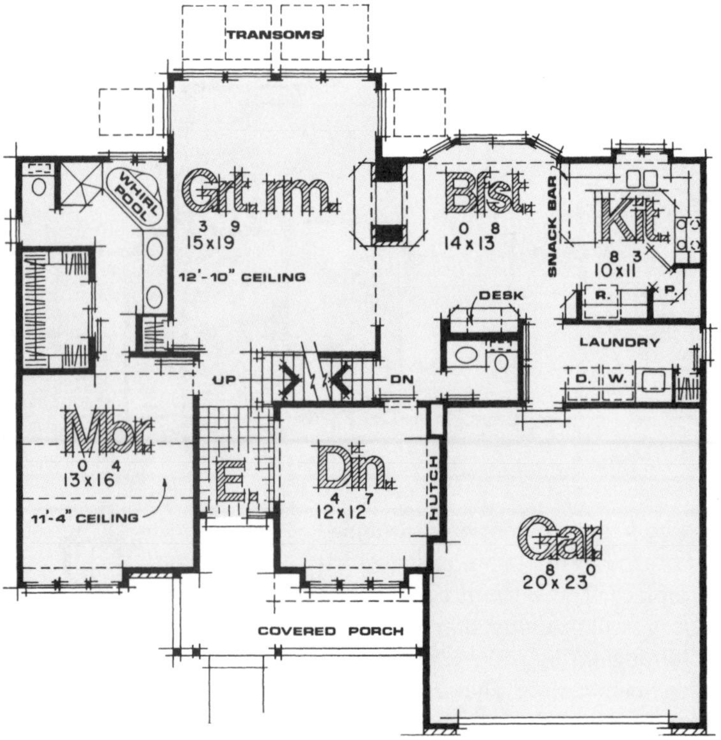

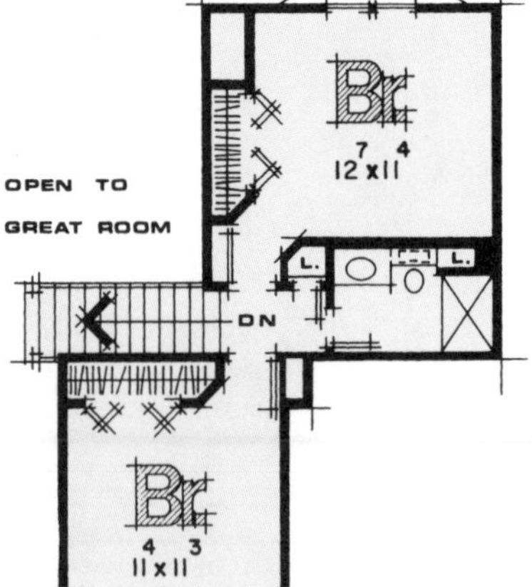

QUOTE ONE®

Cost to build? See page 516 to order complete cost estimate to build this house in your area!

Design HPT830139

First Floor: 1,297 square feet
Second Floor: 388 square feet
Total: 1,685 square feet
Width 52'-0" Depth 45'-4"

A lovely covered porch welcomes family and guests to this delightful 1½-story home. The formal dining room with boxed windows and the great room with fireplace are visible from the entry. A powder room for guests is located just beyond the dining room. An open kitchen/dinette features a pantry, planning desk and a snack-bar counter. The elegant master suite is appointed with a formal ceiling and a window seat. A skylight above the whirlpool tub, a decorator plant shelf and double sinks dress up the master bath. Two family bedrooms on the second floor share a centrally located bath.

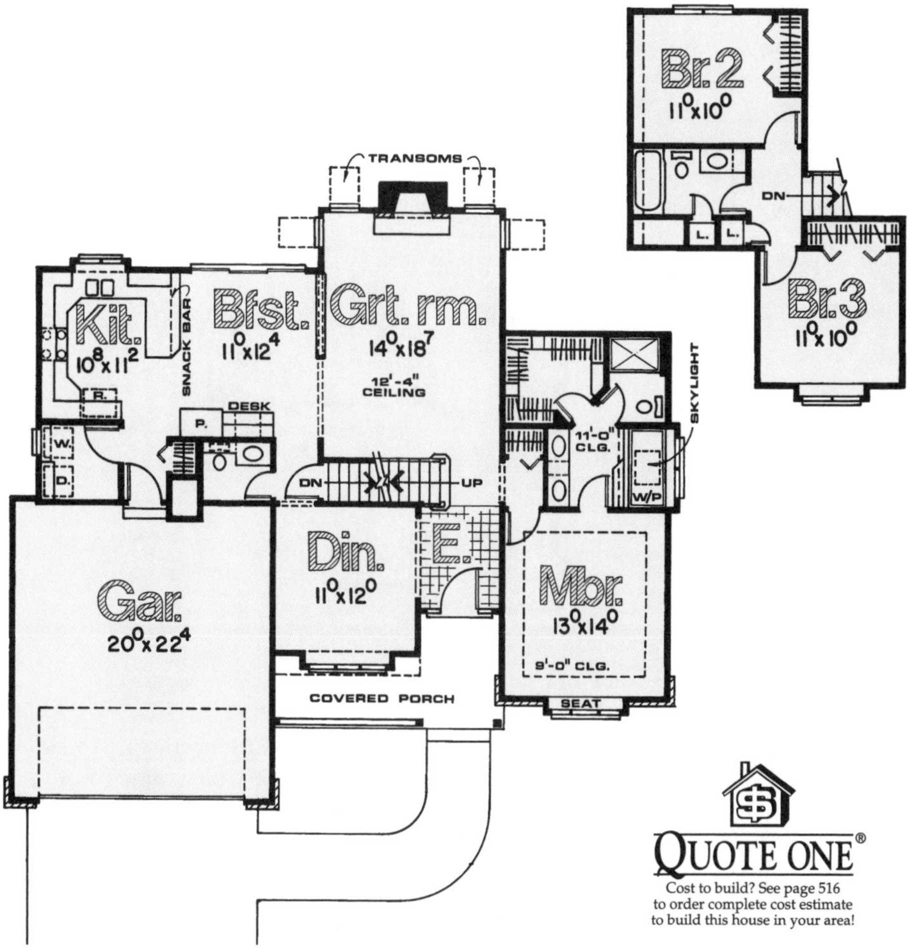

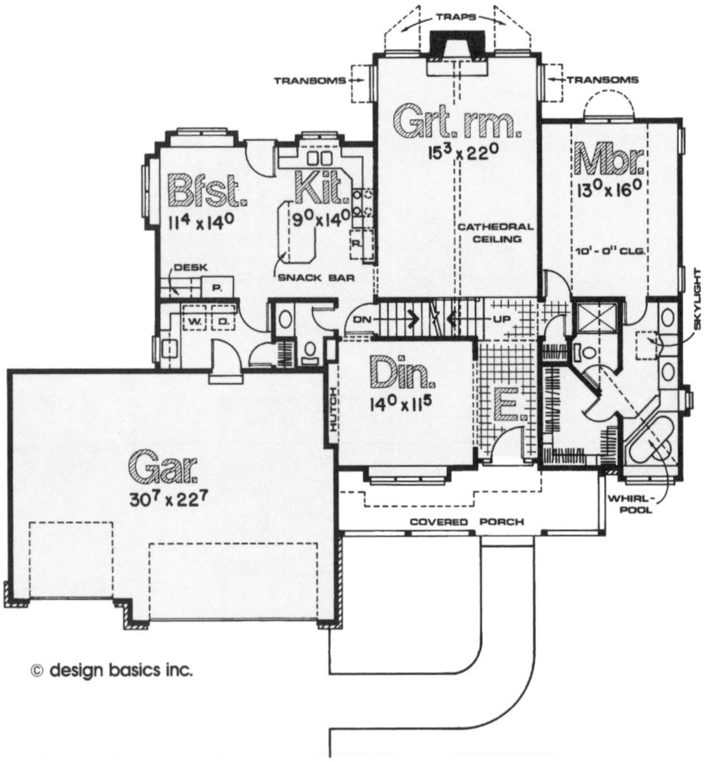

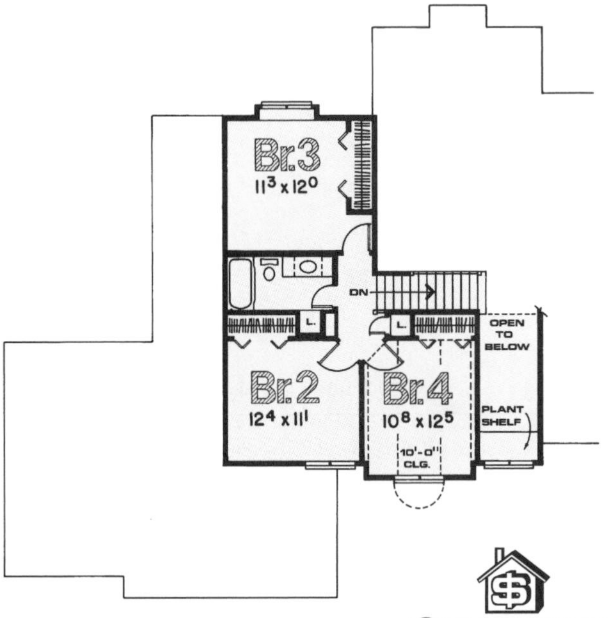

QUOTE ONE®

Cost to build? See page 516 to order complete cost estimate to build this house in your area!

Design HPT830140

First Floor: 1,505 square feet
Second Floor: 610 square feet
Total: 2,115 square feet
Width 64'-0" Depth 52'-0"

Many windows, lap siding and a covered porch give this elevation a welcoming country flair. The formal dining room with hutch space is conveniently located near the island kitchen. Highlighting the spacious great room are a raised-hearth fireplace, a cathedral ceiling and trapezoid windows. Special features in the master suite include a large dressing area with a double vanity, skylight, step-up corner whirlpool tub and generous walk-in closet. Upstairs, three family bedrooms are well separated from the master bedroom and share a hall bath.

A covered porch highlights the elevation of this four-bedroom family home. Upon entering, a spacious great room gains attention. Cooks will enjoy the thoughtfully designed kitchen, with a snack bar, a pantry and a window above the sink. A sunny breakfast room opens to this area. In the master suite, a tiered ceiling, double vanities, corner whirlpool tub and large walk-in closet are sure to please. Upstairs, three secondary bedrooms share a hall bath.

Design
HPT830141

First Floor: 1,348 square feet
Second Floor: 603 square feet
Total: 1,951 square feet
Width 54'-0" Depth 48'-8"

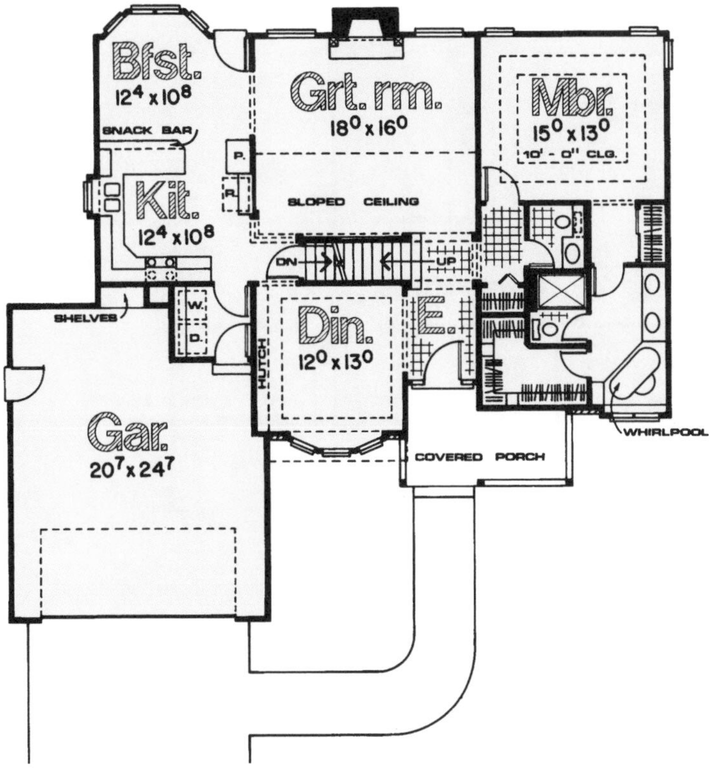

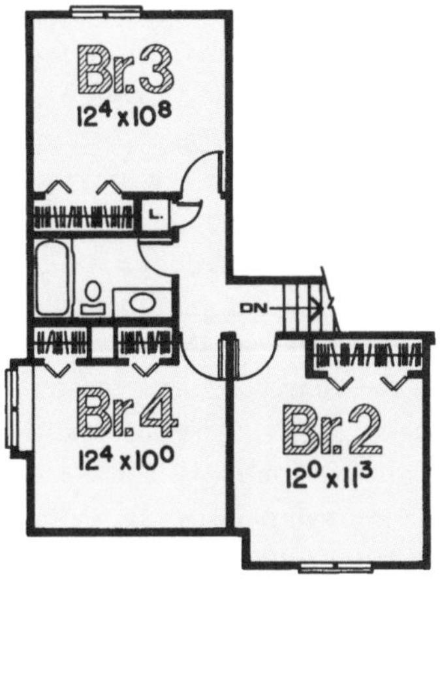

Design HPT830142

First Floor: 1,297 square feet
Second Floor: 558 square feet
Total: 1,855 square feet
Width 52'-0" Depth 45'-4"

The covered front porch of this home opens to a great floor plan. From the entry, go left to reach the formal dining room with its boxed window. Straight back is the great room with a handsome fireplace and tall windows. A snack bar, pantry and planning desk in the kitchen make it convenient and appealing. The breakfast room has sliding glass doors to the rear yard. The master bedroom is on the first floor and has a luxurious bath with a skylit whirlpool tub. Upstairs are three more bedrooms and a full bath.

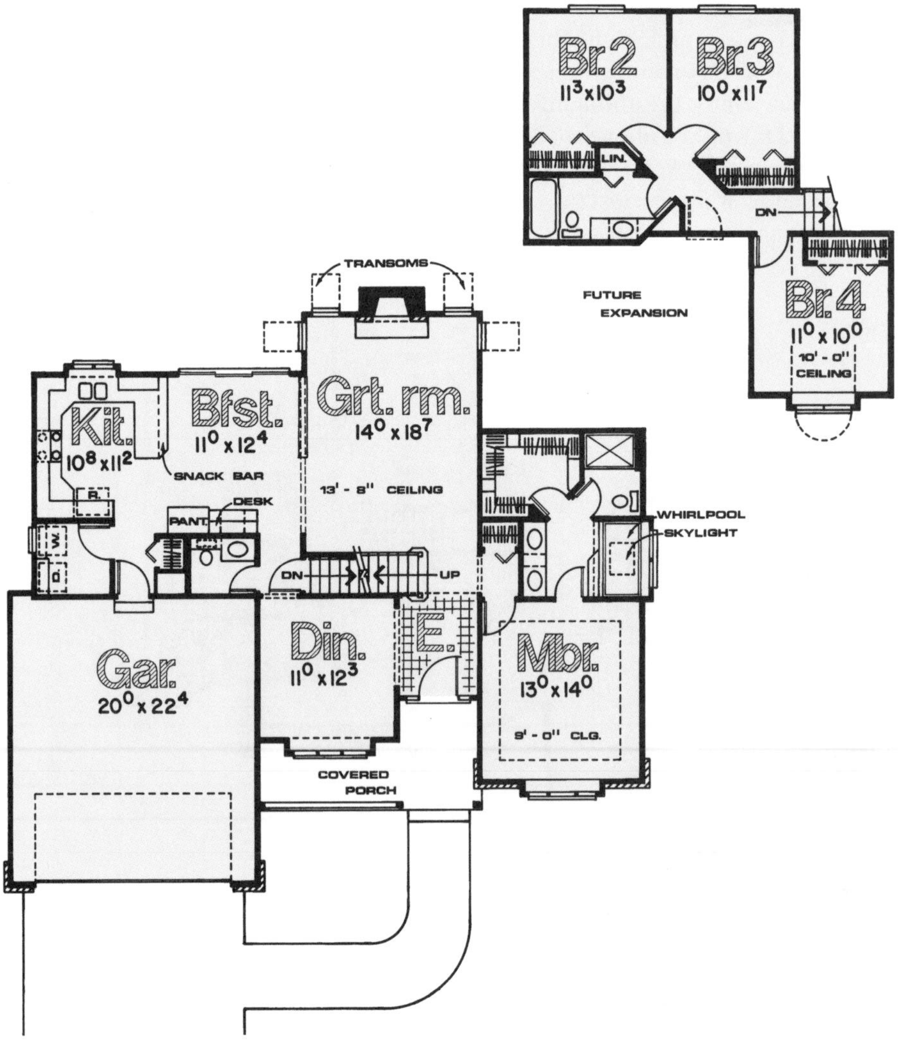

The livability present in this design will delight even the most discerning homeowner. Upon entry, an elegant dining room with built-in hutch space commands attention. A two-story great room provides the perfect setting for entertaining. For quieter pursuits, a den is located at the front of the house. Family time is easily spent in the open kitchen, breakfast room and gathering room. Four bedrooms include a first-floor master suite with a private bath and a large, walk-in closet. Upstairs, two of the secondary bedrooms share a compartmented bath; Bedroom 2 has its own bath.

Design HPT830143

First Floor: 2,158 square feet
Second Floor: 821 square feet
Total: 2,979 square feet
Width 64'-0" Depth 65'-4"

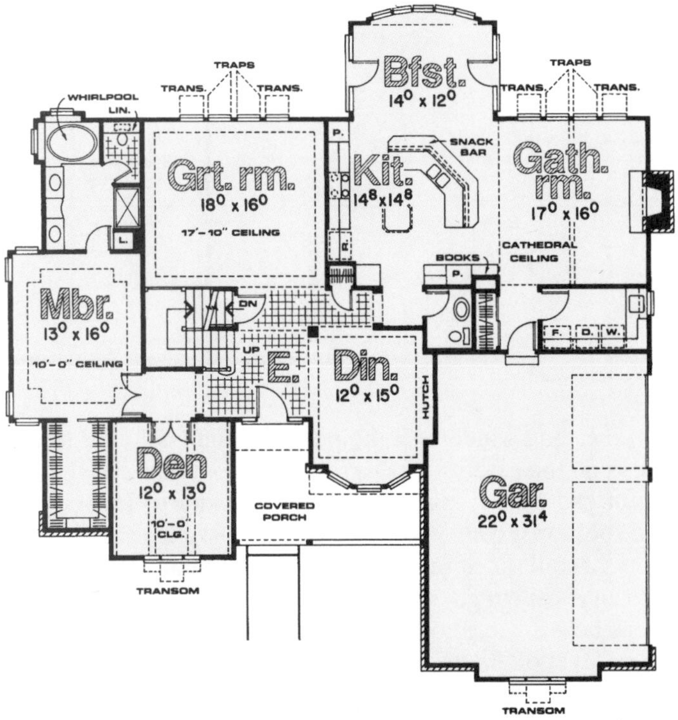

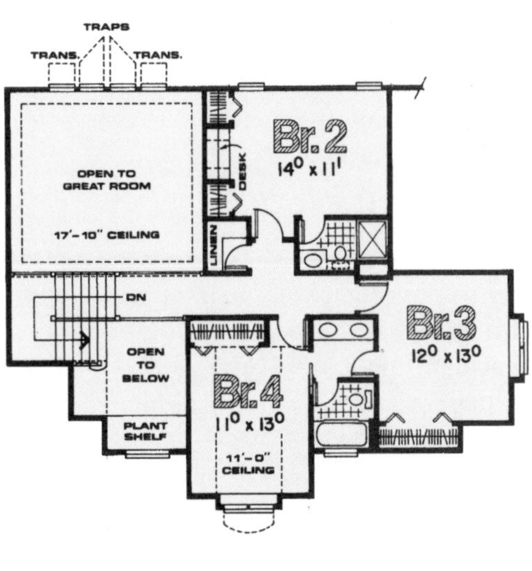

DECK
spa
arched window above door
(cathedral ceiling)
GREAT RM.
17-4 x 19-0
fireplace
walk-in closet
MASTER BED RM.
15-4 x 14-0
master bath
bath
BRKFST.
11-0 x 14-0
KIT.
17-0 x 11-6
up
sto
cl
w d
UTILITY
12-10 x 6-4
BED RM./ STUDY
11-8 x 10-10
FOYER
11-4 x 8-0
DINING RM.
12-4 x 14-0
up
storage
PORCH
GARAGE
20-8 x 21-8
© 1993 Donald A. Gardner Architects, Inc.

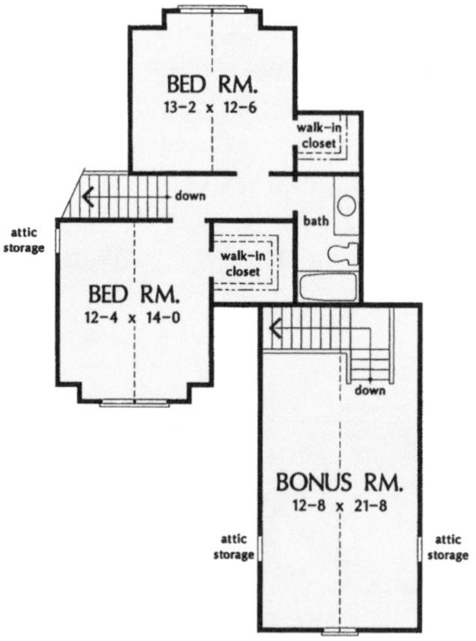
BED RM.
13-2 x 12-6
walk-in closet
down
bath
attic storage
walk-in closet
BED RM.
12-4 x 14-0
down
BONUS RM.
12-8 x 21-8
attic storage
attic storage

Design HPT830144

First Floor: 1,839 square feet

Second Floor: 527 square feet

Total: 2,366 square feet

Bonus Space: 344 square feet

Width 70'-0" Depth 67'-8"

An arched entrance and windows combine with round columns to develop a touch of class on the exterior of this four-bedroom plan. The foyer leads to all areas of the house, minimizing corridor space. The large, open kitchen with an island cooktop is convenient to the breakfast and dining rooms. The master suite has plenty of walk-in closet space and a well-planned bath. A nearby bedroom would make an excellent guest room or study, with an adjacent full bath. An expansive rear deck boasts a location for a spa tub and generous space for outdoor living. The second level offers two bedrooms, with sloped ceilings and walk-in closets, and a full bath. A bonus room is available over the garage.

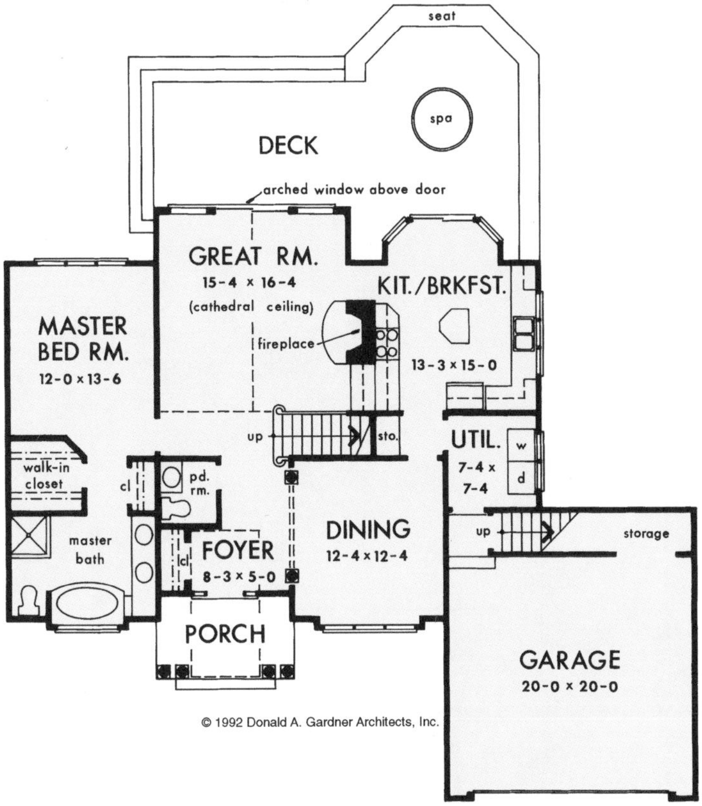

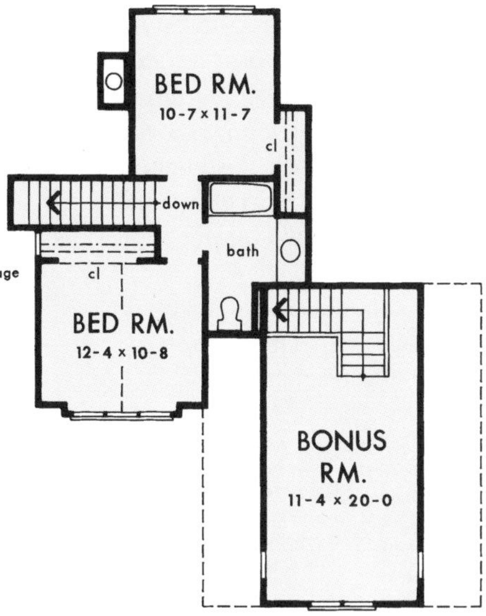

Design HPT830145

First Floor: 1,288 square feet
Second Floor: 410 square feet
Total: 1,698 square feet
Bonus Space: 289 square feet
Width 56'-7" Depth 64'-0"

An arched entrance and windows combine with the round columns of this home for an eye-catching exterior. The dining room features round columns at the entrance, while the great room boasts a cathedral ceiling, fireplace and doors to the deck. A large open kitchen has an island and separate entrance to the deck. A master bedroom with plenty of walk-in closet space includes a bath with a double-bowl vanity, shower and whirlpool tub. On the second level two bedrooms share a full bath.

This home, as shown in the photograph, may differ from the actual blueprints. For more detailed information, please check the floor plans carefully.

This attractive, four-bedroom home projects a refined image with its hipped roof, wood veneer and arched windows. The entrance foyer, flanked by the dining room and a bedroom/study, leads to the spacious great room. The dining room and breakfast room enjoy cathedral ceilings with the kitchen nestled cleverly between. The master suite boasts a cathedral ceiling and a bath with a whirlpool tub. The second floor contains two family bedrooms and a bonus room.

Design
HPT830146

First Floor: 1,675 square feet

Second Floor: 448 square feet

Total: 2,123 square feet

Bonus Space: 345 square feet

Width 53'-8" Depth 69'-8"

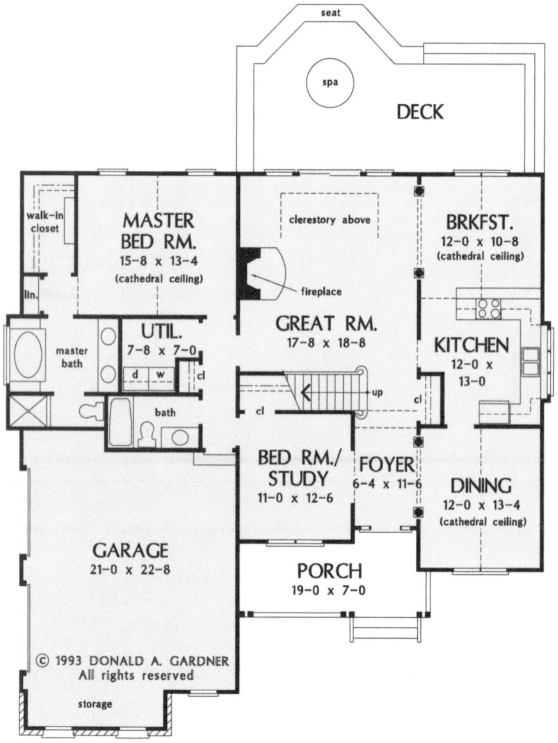

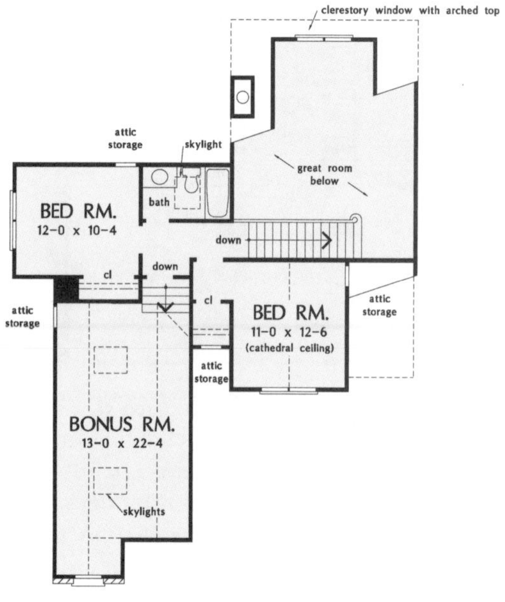

This home, as shown in the photograph, may differ from the actual blueprints. For more detailed information, please check the floor plans carefully. ©1991 Donald A. Gardner Architects, Inc., photography courtesy of Donald A. Gardner Architects, Inc.

Design HPT830147

First Floor: 1,416 square feet
Second Floor: 445 square feet
Total: 1,861 square feet
Bonus Space: 284 square feet
Width 58'-3" Depth 68'-6"

An arched entrance and windows provide a touch of class to the exterior of this plan. The dining room displays decorative columns at the entrance, while the great room boasts a cathedral ceiling and a fireplace. In the master suite, two walk-in closets announce a lavish bath. On the second level are two bedrooms and a bath. Bonus space over the garage can be developed later.

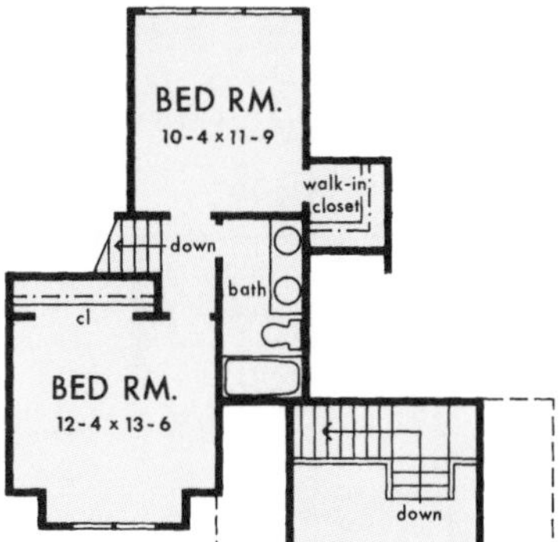

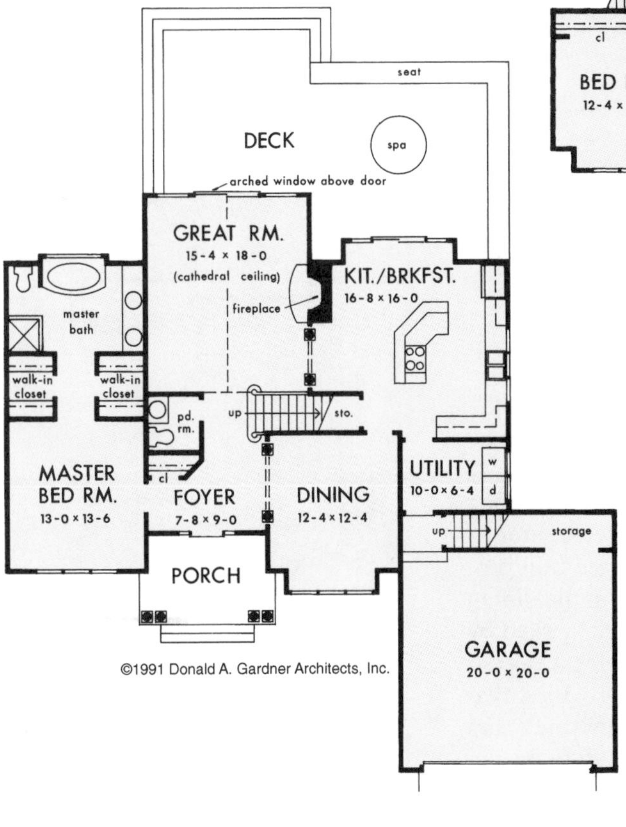

QUOTE ONE®

Cost to build? See page 516 to order complete cost estimate to build this house in your area!

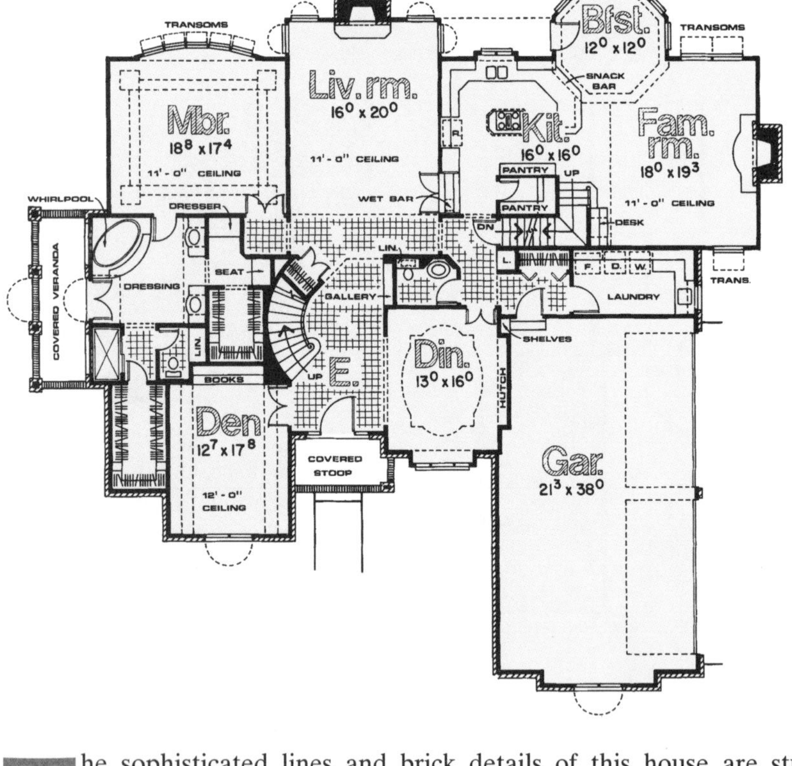

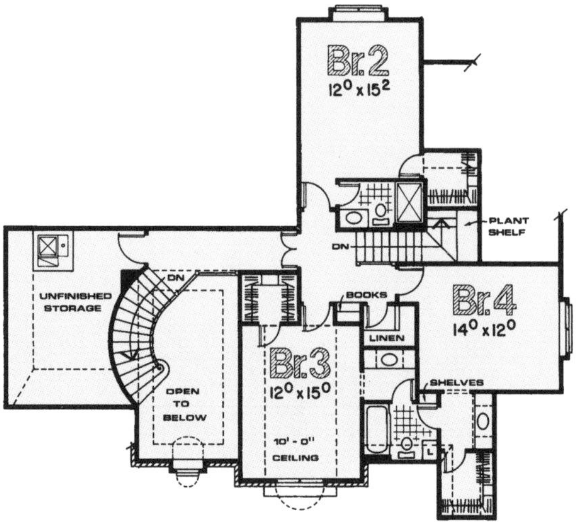

The sophisticated lines and brick details of this house are stunning enhancements. The entry surveys a dramatic, curved staircase. French doors open to the den, where a tiered ceiling and a bookcase wall provide a lofty ambiance. Large gatherings are easily accommodated in the dining room. The living room enjoys an eleven-foot ceiling and a fireplace flanked by transom windows. For more casual living, the family room includes a raised-hearth fireplace and a built-in desk. The gourmet kitchen provides two pantries, an island cooktop, a wrapping counter, a snack bar and private stairs to the second level. Four bedrooms include a pampering master suite on the first floor and three family bedrooms upstairs.

Design
HPT830148

First Floor: 2,789 square feet

Second Floor: 1,038 square feet

Total: 3,827 square feet

Width 78'-0" Depth 73'-8"

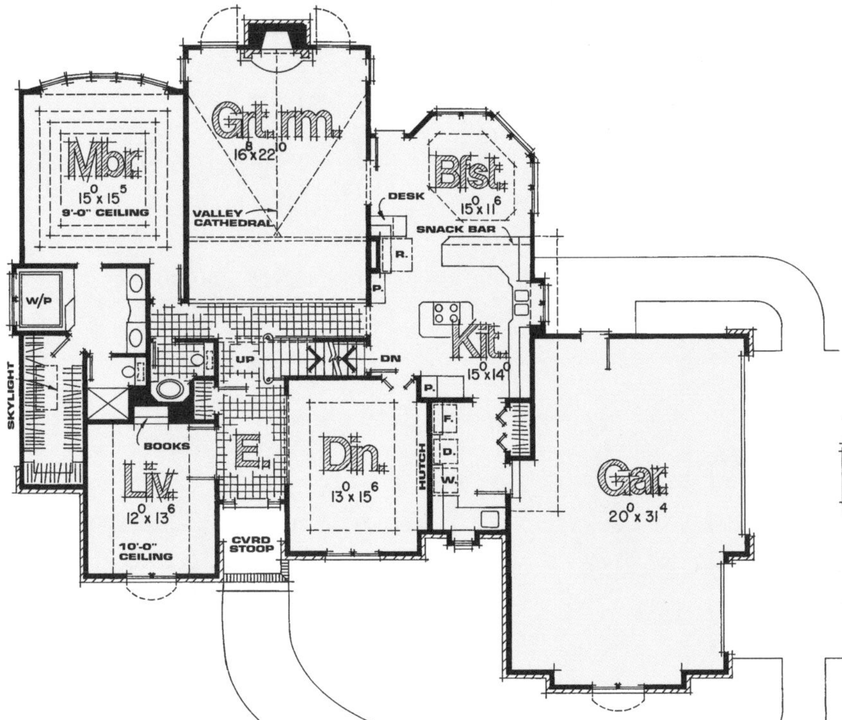

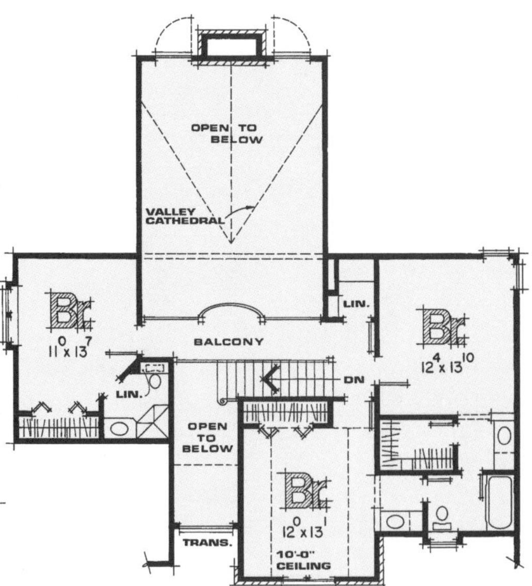

Natural light from transom windows floods the entry of this home, traditionally flanked by the formal living room and dining room. The large great room to the rear of the plan has a cathedral ceiling and a fireplace framed by windows. An island kitchen offers two pantries and a gazebo dinette. The sumptuous master suite has a bow window and tiered ceiling, plus a lush bath. Upstairs bedrooms include two that share a Hollywood bath and one with its own full bath.

Design
HPT830149

First Floor: 1,972 square feet
Second Floor: 893 square feet
Total: 2,865 square feet
Width 68'-0" Depth 58'-0"

This lovely home's foyer opens to the formal dining room, defined by decorative columns, and leads to a two-story great room. The breakfast room joins the great room to create a casual family area. The master suite boasts a coffered ceiling and a sumptuous bath. This home is designed with a walkout basement foundation.

Design HPT830150

First Floor: 2,076 square feet

Second Floor: 843 square feet

Total: 2,919 square feet

Width 57'-6" Depth 51'-6"

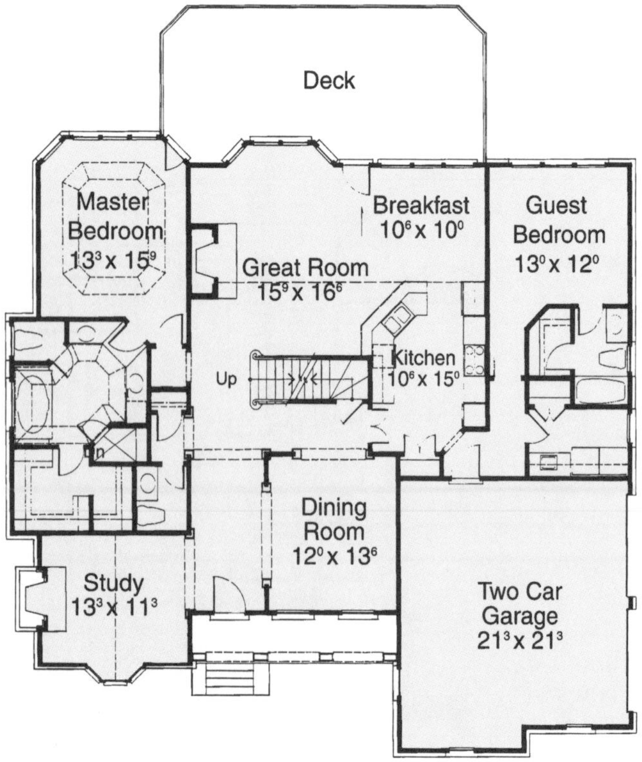

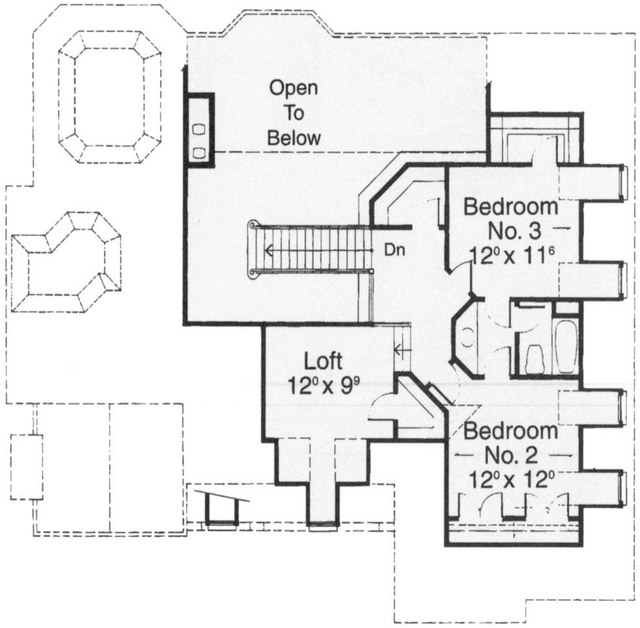

The striking combination of wood framing, shingles and glass creates the exterior of this classic cottage. The foyer opens to the main-level layout. To the left of the foyer is a study with a warming hearth and vaulted ceiling, while to the right is a formal dining room. A great room with an attached breakfast area sits to the rear near the kitchen. A guest room is nestled in the rear of the plan for privacy. The master suite provides an expansive tray ceiling, a glass sitting area and easy passage to the outside deck. Upstairs, two bedrooms are accompanied by a loft for a quiet getaway. This home is designed with a walkout basement foundation.

Design HPT830151

First Floor: 2,070 square feet
Second Floor: 790 square feet
Total: 2,860 square feet
Width 58'-4" Depth 54'-10"

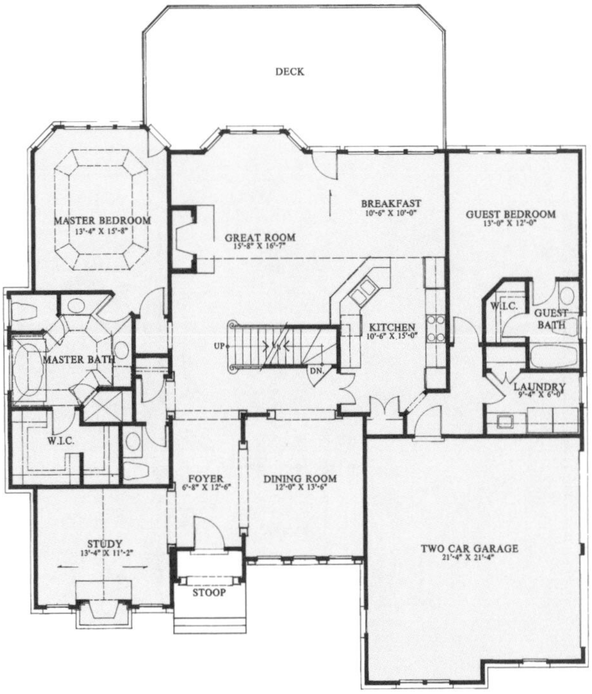

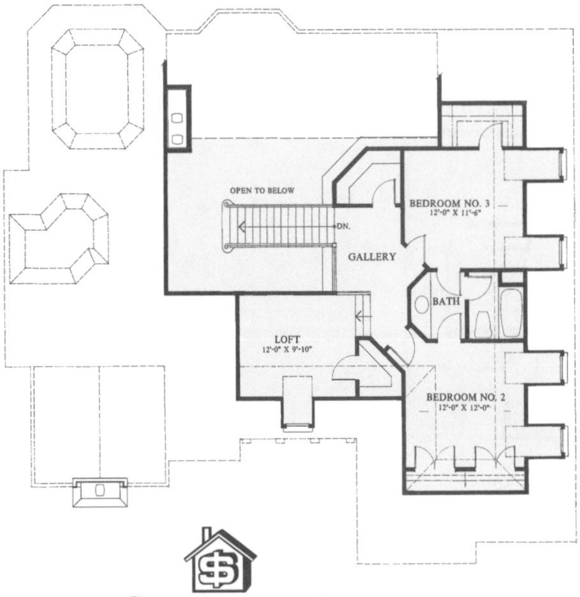

Double columns and an arch-top clerestory window create an inviting entry to this fresh interpretation of traditional style. The two-story foyer features a decorative ledge perfect for displaying a tapestry. Decorative columns and arches open to the formal dining room and to the octagonal great room, which has a ten-foot tray ceiling. The U-shaped kitchen looks over an angled counter to a breakfast bay that brings in the outdoors and shares a through-fireplace with the great room. A sitting area and a lavish bath set off the secluded master suite. A nearby secondary bedroom with its own bath could be used as a guest suite, while upstairs two family bedrooms share a full bath and a hall that leads to an expandable area. Please specify basement, crawlspace or slab foundation when ordering.

Design HPT830152

First Floor: 2,028 square feet
Second Floor: 558 square feet
Total: 2,586 square feet
Bonus Space: 272 square feet
Width 64'-10" Depth 61'-0"

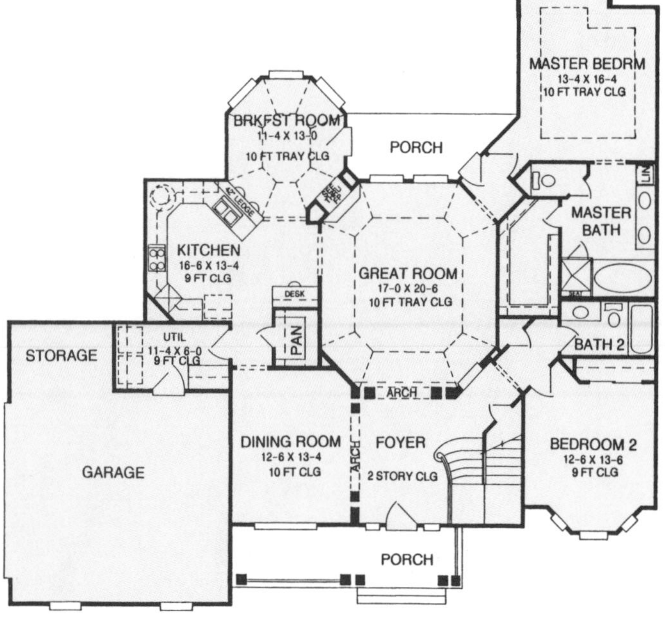

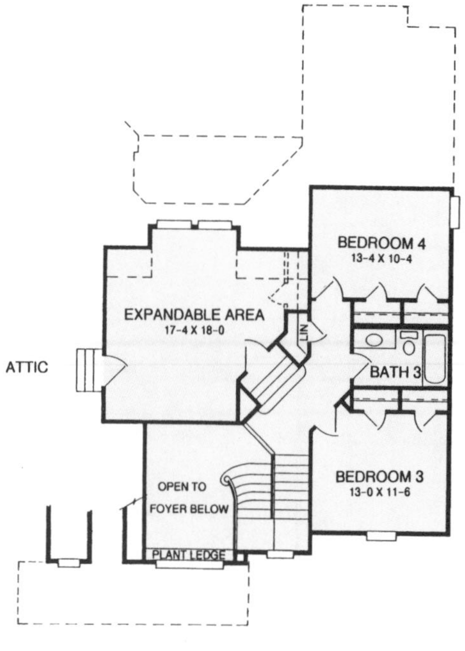

This home, as shown in the photograph, may differ from the actual blueprints. For more detailed information, please check the floor plans carefully.
Photo by Dave Dawson

Multi-pane windows and ink-black shutters stand out against the rich brick-and-horizontal-clapboard backdrop. Inside, the spacious foyer leads directly to a large vaulted great room with its handsome fireplace. The dining room to the right of the foyer features a dramatic vaulted ceiling. In the privacy and quiet of the rear of the home is the master suite with its luxury bath and walk-in closet. This home is designed with a walkout basement foundation.

Design HPT830153

First Floor: 1,580 square feet
Second Floor: 595 square feet
Total: 2,175 square feet
Width 50'-2" Depth 70'-11"

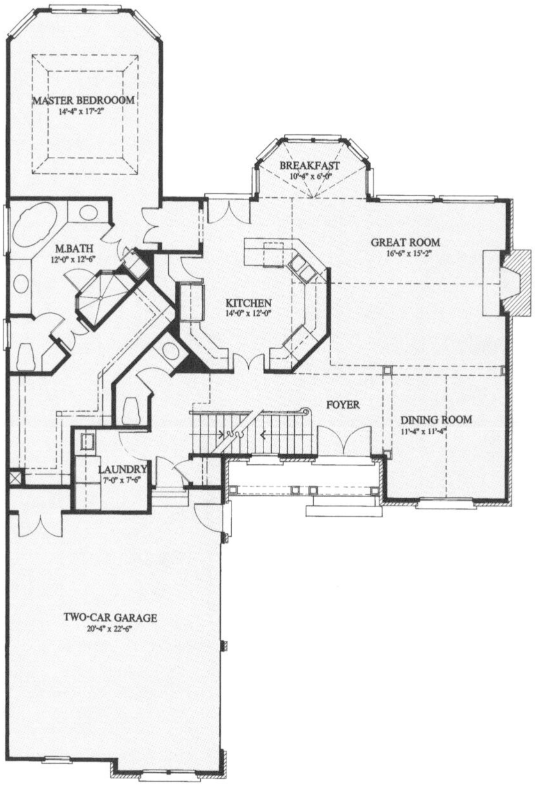

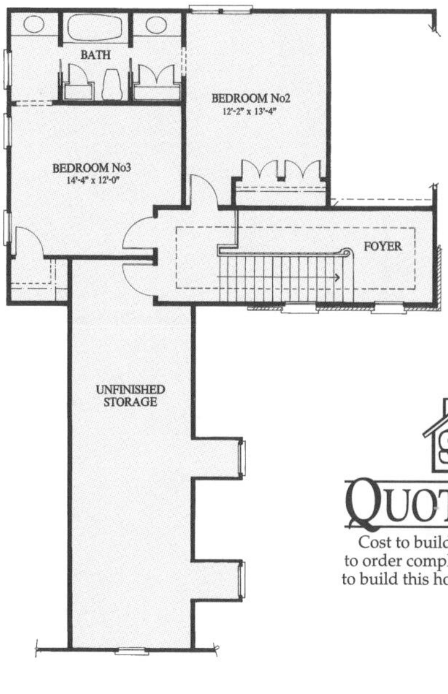

QUOTE ONE®
Cost to build? See page 516 to order complete cost estimate to build this house in your area!

This plan combines a traditional, stately exterior with an updated floor plan to create a house that will please the entire family. The heart of the plan is surely the wide-open living space consisting of the vaulted family room, breakfast area and gourmet kitchen. Highlights here are a full-length fireplace, a French door to the rear yard and an island cooktop. The master suite has a tray ceiling and a vaulted master bath with a garden tub and walk-in closet. The family sleeping area on the upper level gives the option of two bedrooms and a loft overlooking the family room or three bedrooms. Please specify basement or crawlspace foundation when ordering.

Design
HPT830154

First Floor: 1,320 square feet
Second Floor: 554 square feet
Total: 1,874 square feet
Bonus Space: 155 square feet
Width 54'-6" Depth 42'-4"

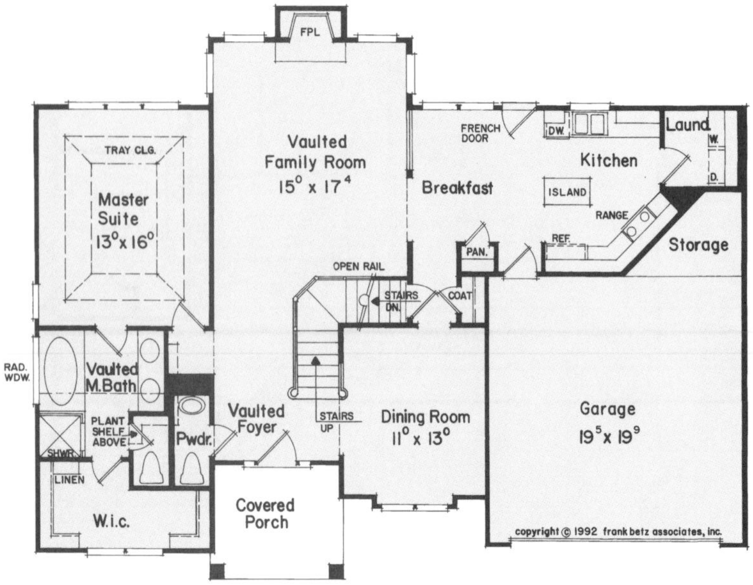

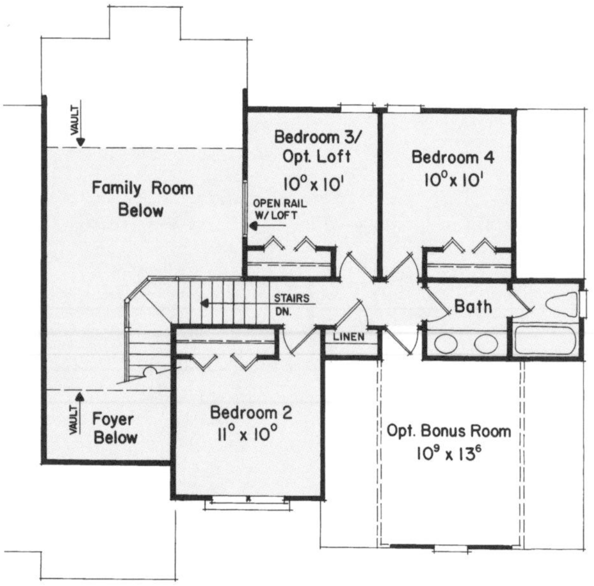

Stucco and stone provide a pleasing contrast to the large-pane windows on the exterior of this two-story family home. Open planning joins the great room and the breakfast room under a dramatic vaulted ceiling. The modified galley kitchen features a serving bar to the breakfast room and has easy access to the formal dining room. The master suite has a tray ceiling, a compartmented bath and a walk-in closet. Stairs lead up to a balcony overlooking the great room and to two family bedrooms. An optional loft can be converted to a fourth bedroom, if desired. Please specify basement or crawlspace foundation when ordering.

Design HPT830155

First Floor: 1,144 square feet
Second Floor: 620 square feet
Total: 1,764 square feet
Loft: 134 square feet
Width 41'-0" Depth 46'-4"

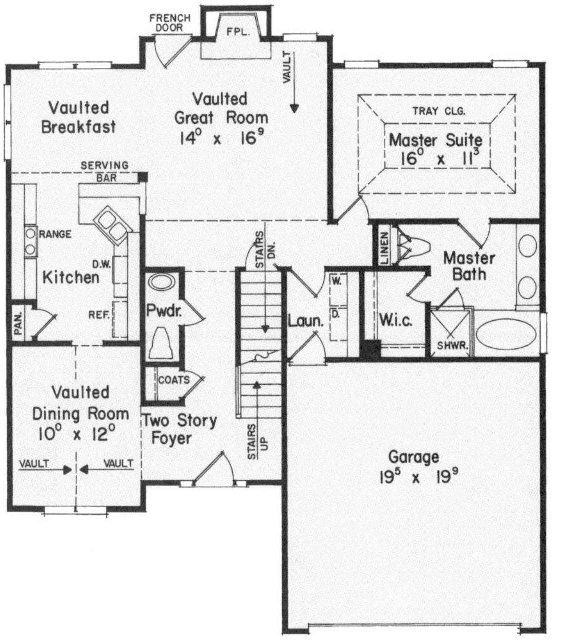

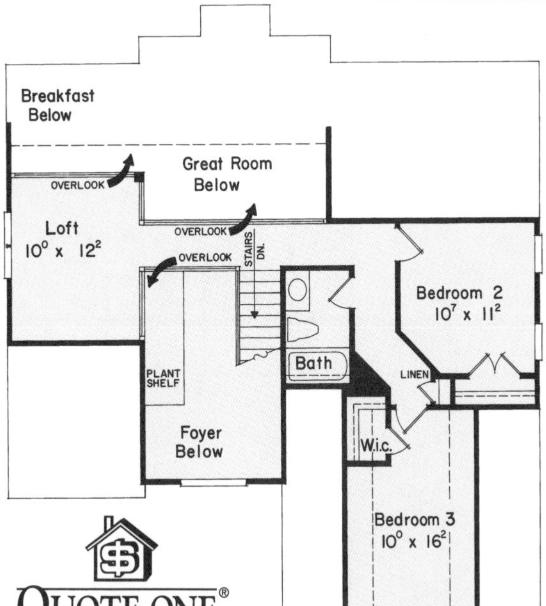

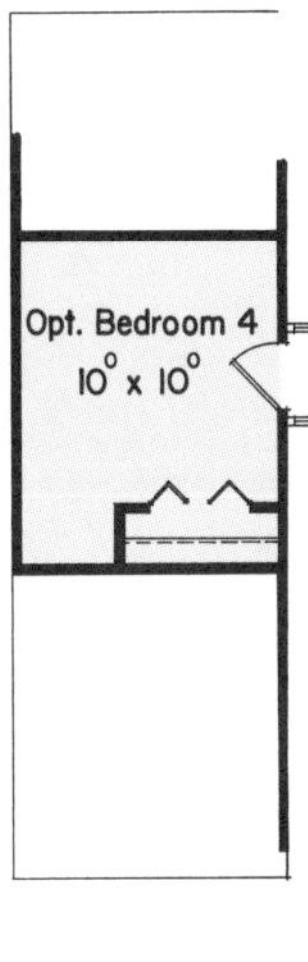

QUOTE ONE®

Cost to build? See page 516 to order complete cost estimate to build this house in your area!

With a delightful flavor, this two-story home features family living at its best. The foyer opens to a study or living room on the left. The dining room on the right offers large proportions and full windows. The family room remains open to the kitchen and the breakfast room. Here, sunny meals are guaranteed with a bay window overlooking the rear yard. In the master suite, a bayed sitting area, a walk-in closet and a pampering bath are sure to please. Upstairs, two family bedrooms flank a loft or study area.

Design HPT830156

First Floor: 1,715 square feet
Second Floor: 620 square feet
Total: 2,335 square feet
Bonus Space: 265 square feet
Width 58'-6" Depth 50'-3"

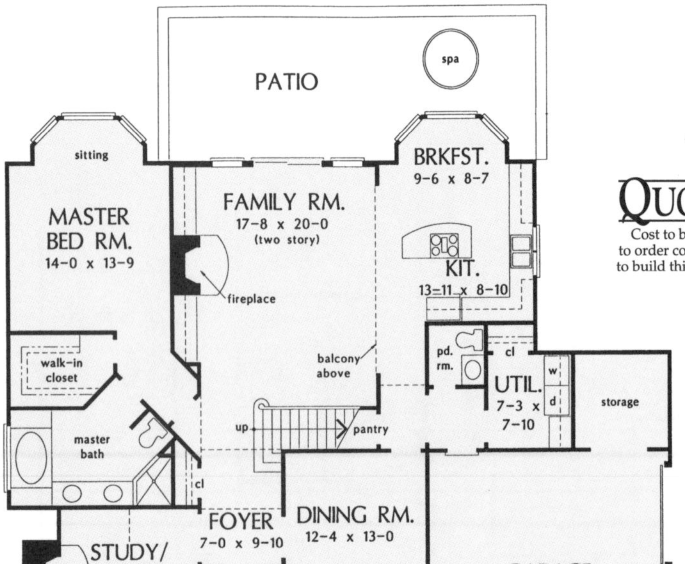

QUOTE ONE®
Cost to build? See page 516
to order complete cost estimate
to build this house in your area!

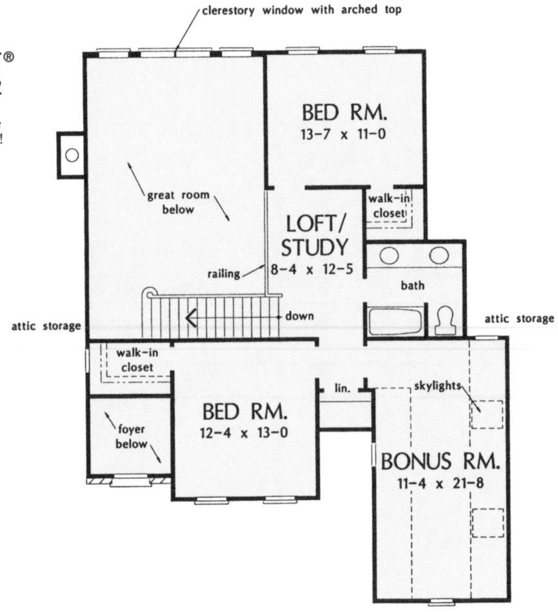

This lovely home with mixed exterior materials is hard to beat. Both casual and formal occasions are accommodated from the great room with a fireplace to the formal dining room with front window views. An informal breakfast room complements the gourmet kitchen; its bay window makes family dining a treat. The first-floor master suite features a huge walk-in closet, corner tub, separate shower and compartmented toilet. There are two family bedrooms upstairs. Unfinished space on the second floor can function as storage or be developed into a fourth bedroom if needed. This home is designed with a walkout basement foundation.

Design HPT830157

First Floor: 1,225 square feet
Second Floor: 565 square feet
Total: 1,790 square feet
Bonus Space: 189 square feet
Width 42'-0" Depth 49'-0"

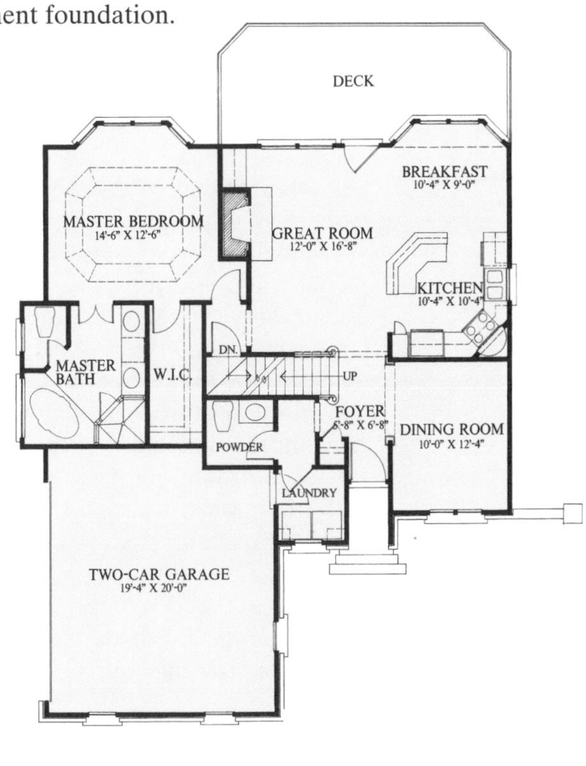

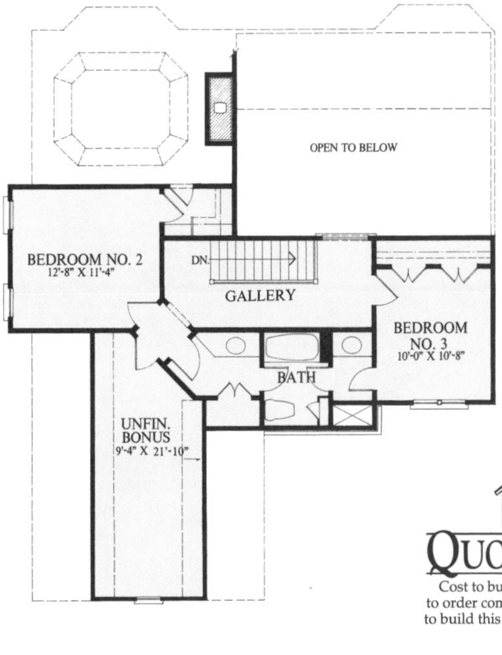

QUOTE ONE®
Cost to build? See page 516 to order complete cost estimate to build this house in your area!

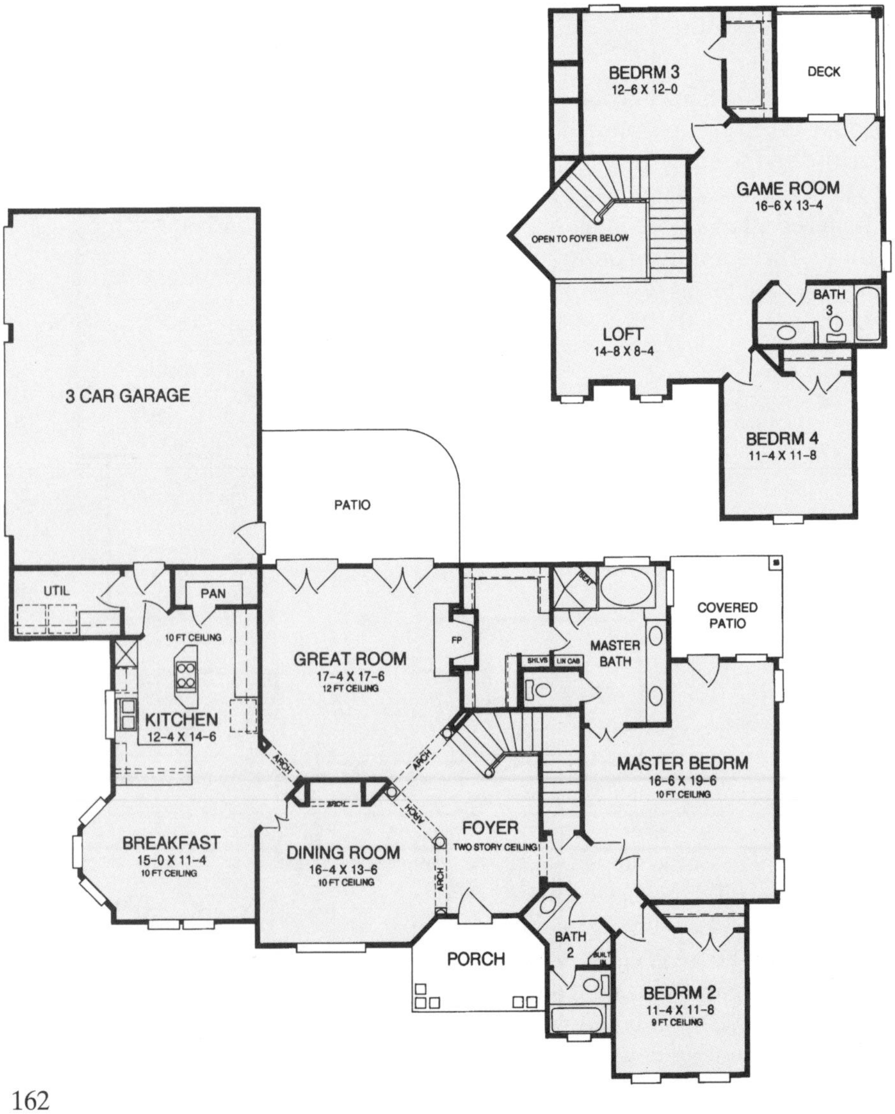

BEDRM 3
12-6 X 12-0
DECK
GAME ROOM
16-6 X 13-4
OPEN TO FOYER BELOW
BATH
3
LOFT
14-8 X 8-4
BEDRM 4
11-4 X 11-8
3 CAR GARAGE
PATIO
UTIL
PAN
10 FT CEILING
KITCHEN
12-4 X 14-6
GREAT ROOM
17-4 X 17-6
12 FT CEILING
FP
SHLVS
LIN CAB
MASTER
BATH
COVERED
PATIO
MASTER BEDRM
16-6 X 19-6
10 FT CEILING
ARCH
BREAKFAST
15-0 X 11-4
10 FT CEILING
DINING ROOM
16-4 X 13-6
10 FT CEILING
FOYER
TWO STORY CEILING
PORCH
BATH
2
BEDRM 2
11-4 X 11-8
9 FT CEILING

Design HPT830158

First Floor: 2,012 square feet
Second Floor: 832 square feet
Total: 2,844 square feet
Width 67'-8" Depth 73'-0"
L

A large arched window, twin dormers and an entry accented by a swoop roof add charm to this two-story home. A grand foyer opens to the formal dining room and the great room. The roomy kitchen features a large pantry, a cooktop island and a snack bar. Lots of natural sunlight streams in from the bay window in the breakfast area. The master bedroom enjoys a private bath with a walk-in closet. The second floor contains two family bedrooms, a full bath, a large game room, a loft and a deck. Please specify crawlspace or slab foundation when ordering.

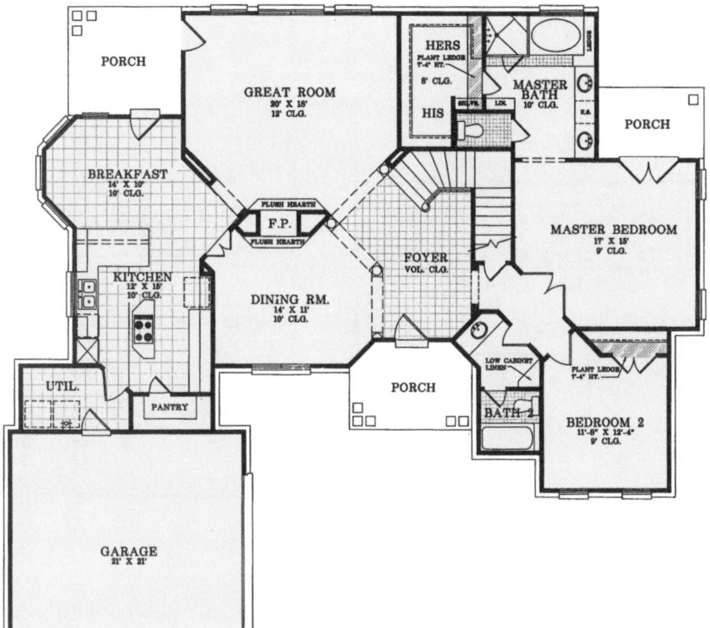

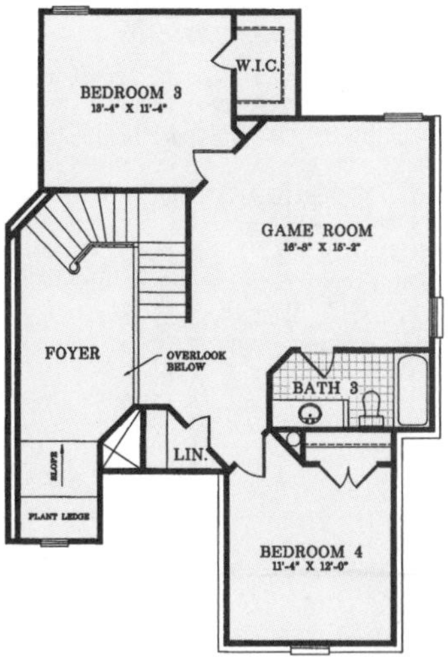

The combination of stacked stone, brick and siding add warmth to this eye-catching elevation. Inside, the large, angled foyer provides unobstructed views into the great room and dining room. A see-through fireplace between the great room and dining room adds elegance and completes the stunning dining room, which is separated from the foyer by large arches supported by round columns. The kitchen includes a bay window and continues with the ten-foot ceilings found throughout the kitchen area. This home is designed with two bedrooms on the first floor. The second bedroom is multi-functional and can be used as a nursery or office/study. The second floor features two bedrooms and a large game room. Please specify crawlspace or slab foundation when ordering.

Design HPT830159

First Floor: 1,961 square feet

Second Floor: 791 square feet

Total: 2,752 square feet

Width 64'-4" Depth 62'-0"

L

Design HPT830160

First Floor: 1,099 square feet
Second Floor: 647 square feet
Total: 1,746 square feet
Bonus Space: 377 square feet
Width 61'-6" Depth 36'-4"

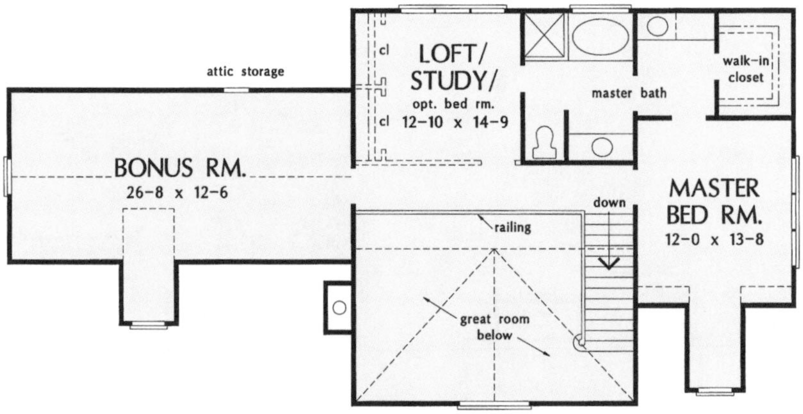

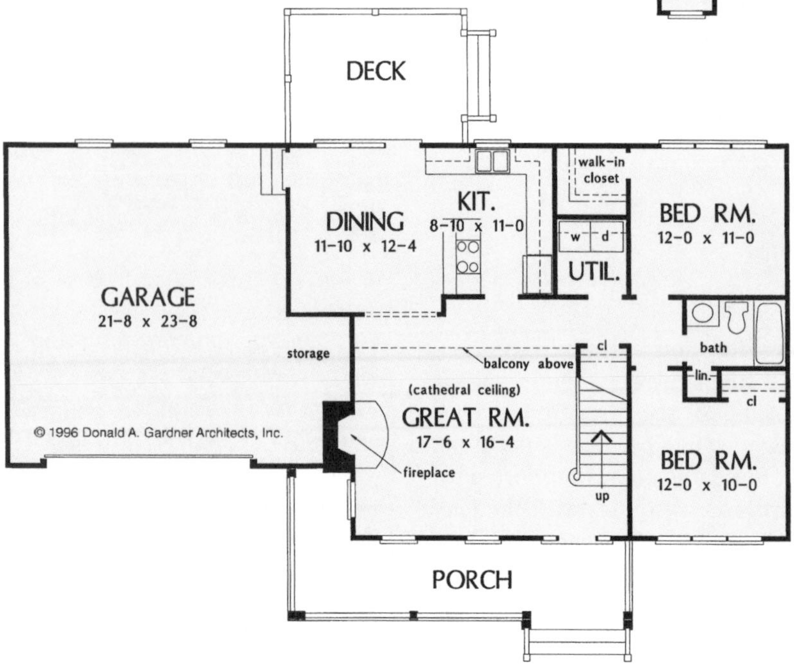

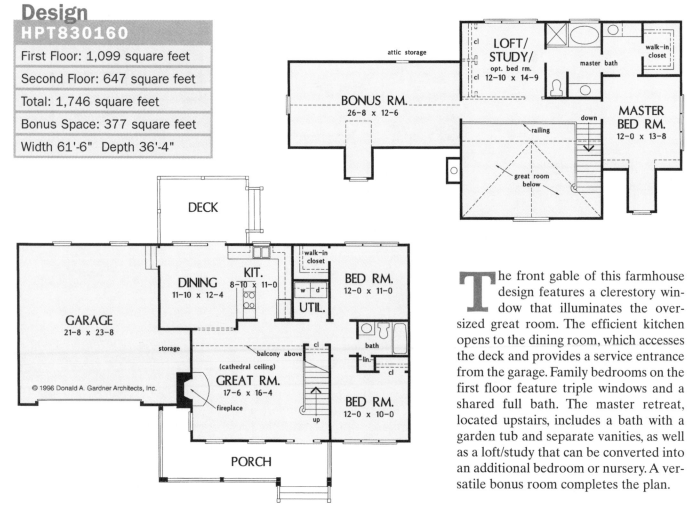

The front gable of this farmhouse design features a clerestory window that illuminates the oversized great room. The efficient kitchen opens to the dining room, which accesses the deck and provides a service entrance from the garage. Family bedrooms on the first floor feature triple windows and a shared full bath. The master retreat, located upstairs, includes a bath with a garden tub and separate vanities, as well as a loft/study that can be converted into an additional bedroom or nursery. A versatile bonus room completes the plan.

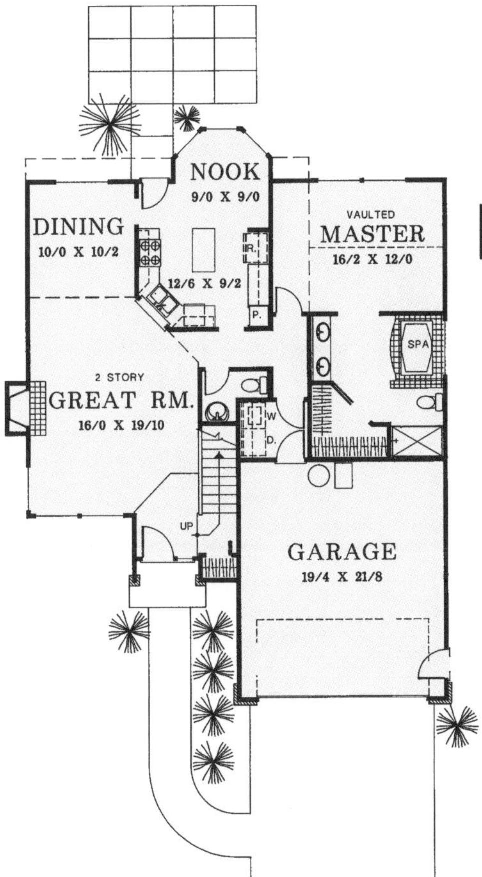
NOOK
9/0 X 9/0
DINING
10/0 X 10/2
12/6 X 9/2
VAULTED
MASTER
16/2 X 12/0
SPA
2 STORY
GREAT RM.
16/0 X 19/10
UP
GARAGE
19/4 X 21/8

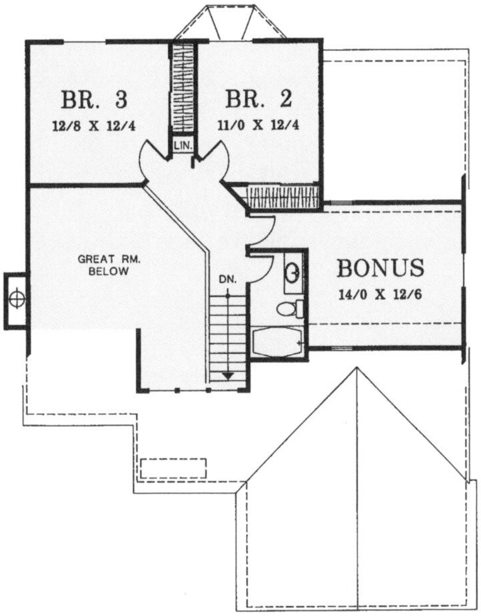
BR. 3
12/8 X 12/4
BR. 2
11/0 X 12/4
LIN.
GREAT RM.
BELOW
DN.
BONUS
14/0 X 12/6

Design HPT830161

First Floor: 1,230 square feet
Second Floor: 477 square feet
Total: 1,707 square feet
Bonus Space: 195 square feet
Width 40'-0" Depth 53'-0"
L

With sunny windows throughout and a wonderfully open living space, this plan appears larger than its modest square footage. The great room is highlighted with a corner window, a fireplace and a soaring ceiling. The dining room continues the open feeling and is easily served from the kitchen. A bayed nook complements the island kitchen that also has a stylish wraparound counter. The master bedroom suite has a lofty vaulted ceiling. Upstairs, there are two family bedrooms that share a full hall bath—plus a bonus room that can be developed as needed.

Stately columns and pitched-roof dormers enhance the exterior of this roomy four-bedroom traditional home designed to grow with your family. The covered porch leads to a T-shaped entry foyer and gallery reaching all family activity areas. The spacious great room features a fireplace with fieldstone hearth and a wide expanse of windows. The tiled island kitchen has convenient access to the formal dining room and the breakfast area. The large master bedroom features a walk-in closet nearly half its size and a well-appointed bath with corner tub. An optional loft with half bath on the second floor can become a playroom for the children or a convenient home office.

Design HPT830162

Square Footage: 2,642

Loft: 697 square feet

Width 86'-10" Depth 55'-1"

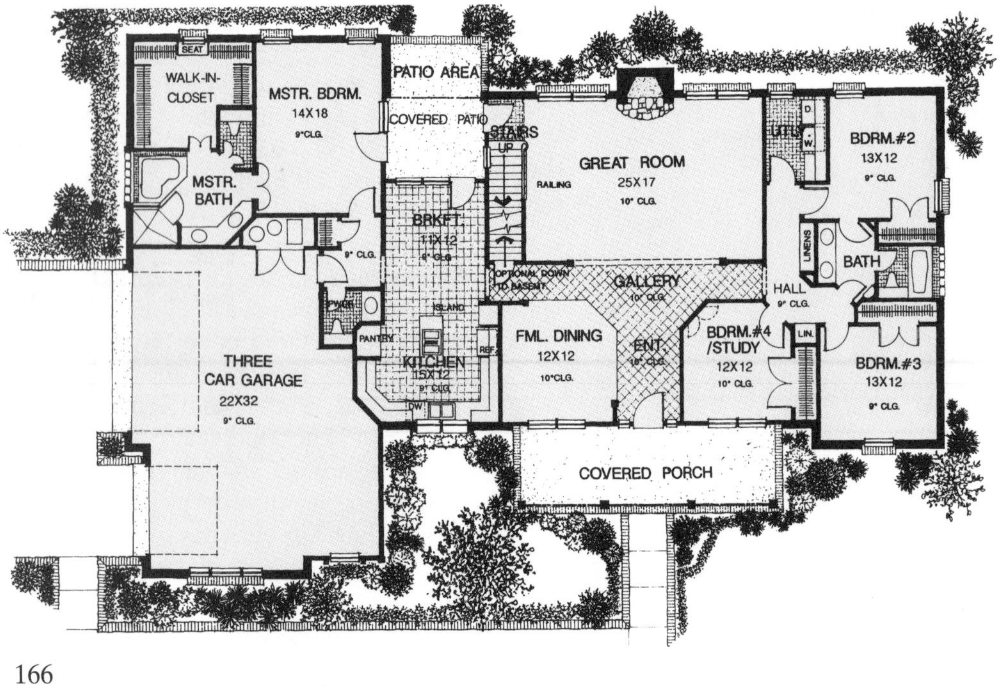

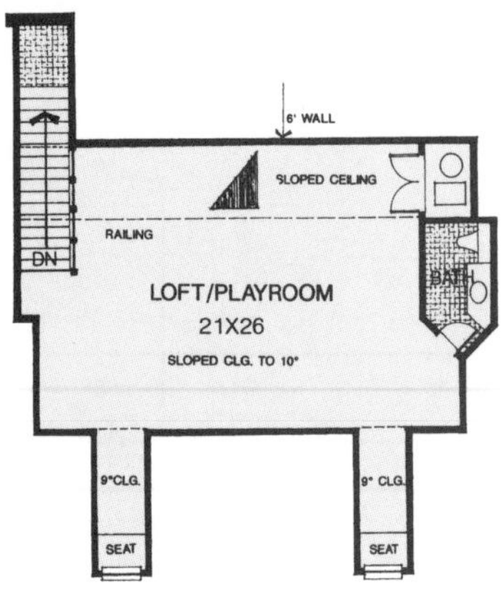

Design HPT830163

First Floor: 1,676 square feet	
Second Floor: 851 square feet	
Total: 2,527 square feet	
Width 55'-0"	Depth 50'-0"

Muntin windows and gentle arches decorate the exterior of this traditional home. A private study or guest suite in the top-left corner of the plan offers its own door to the veranda. The master suite enjoys a spacious bath with twin lavatories, a dressing area and two walk-in closets. A gallery hall on the second floor leads to a computer loft with built-ins for books and software.

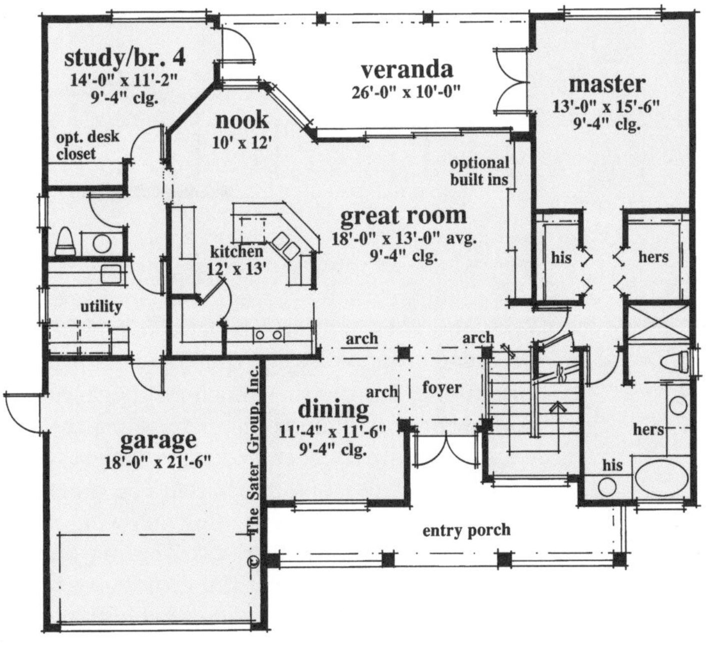

study/br. 4
14'-0" x 11'-2"
9'-4" clg.
veranda
26'-0" x 10'-0"
master
13'-0" x 15'-6"
9'-4" clg.
nook
10' x 12'
opt. desk closet
optional built ins
great room
18'-0" x 13'-0" avg.
9'-4" clg.
kitchen
12' x 13'
his
hers
utility
arch
arch
arch
foyer
dining
11'-4" x 11'-6"
9'-4" clg.
hers
his
garage
18'-0" x 21'-6"
entry porch
© The Sater Group, Inc.

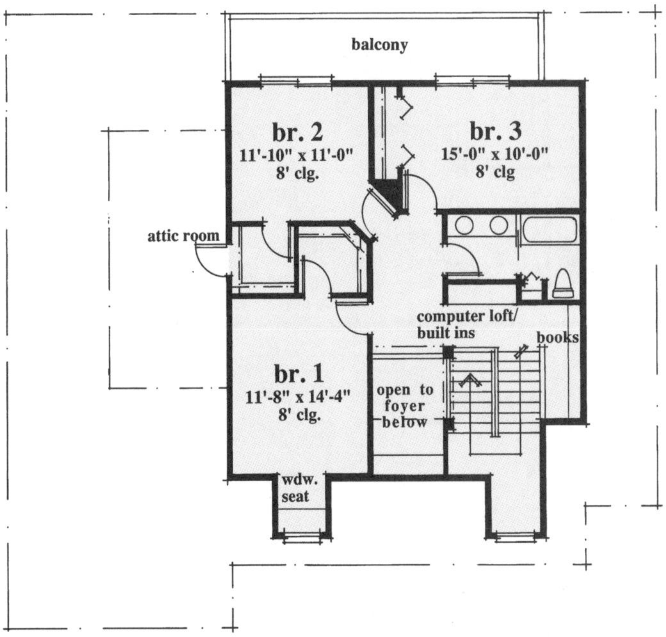

balcony
br. 2
11'-10" x 11'-0"
8' clg.
br. 3
15'-0" x 10'-0"
8' clg
attic room
computer loft/ built ins
books
br. 1
11'-8" x 14'-4"
8' clg.
open to foyer below
wdw. seat

Design HPT830164

First Floor: 2,156 square feet
Second Floor: 707 square feet
Total: 2,863 square feet
Width 65'-4" Depth 81'-4"

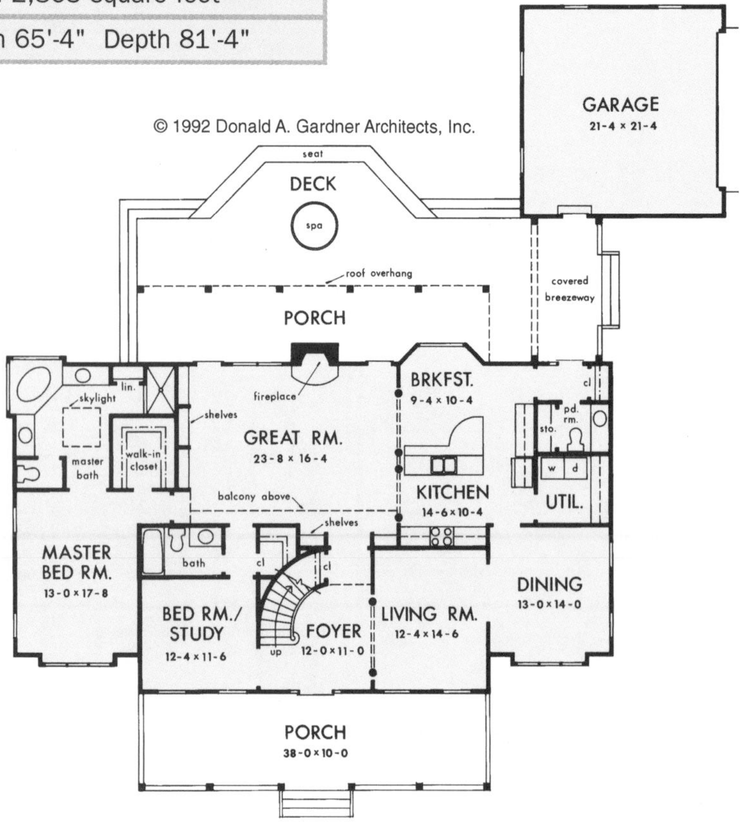
GARAGE
21-4 × 21-4
seat
DECK
spa
roof overhang
covered breezeway
PORCH
BRKFST.
9-4 × 10-4
fireplace
shelves
GREAT RM.
23-8 × 16-4
skylight
lin.
master bath
walk-in closet
pd. rm.
sto.
cl
w
d
KITCHEN
14-6 × 10-4
UTIL.
balcony above
shelves
MASTER BED RM.
13-0 × 17-8
bath
cl
BED RM./ STUDY
12-4 × 11-6
up
FOYER
12-0 × 11-0
LIVING RM.
12-4 × 14-6
DINING
13-0 × 14-0
PORCH
38-0 × 10-0

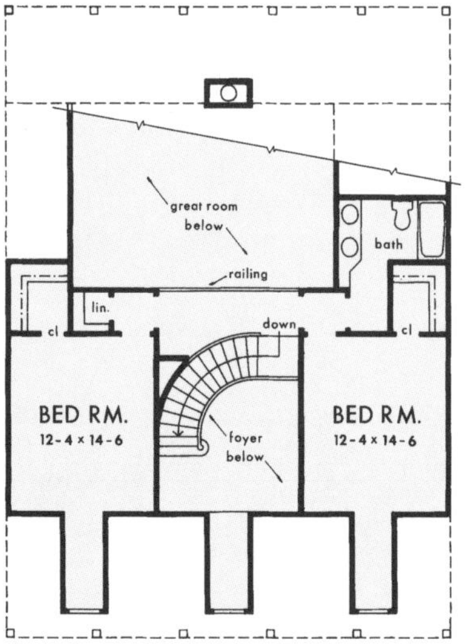
great room below
bath
railing
lin.
cl
down
cl
BED RM.
12-4 × 14-6
foyer below
BED RM.
12-4 × 14-6

This striking country home is enhanced by large front and rear porches and an expansive rear deck for great outdoor living. The foyer with a curved staircase adds a touch of elegance along with the round columns between the foyer and living room and between the great room and kitchen/breakfast area. The great room boasts a cathedral ceiling, allowing a second-level balcony overlook. The master suite is located on the first floor for convenience. A second bedroom with a full bath on the first floor can double as a study.

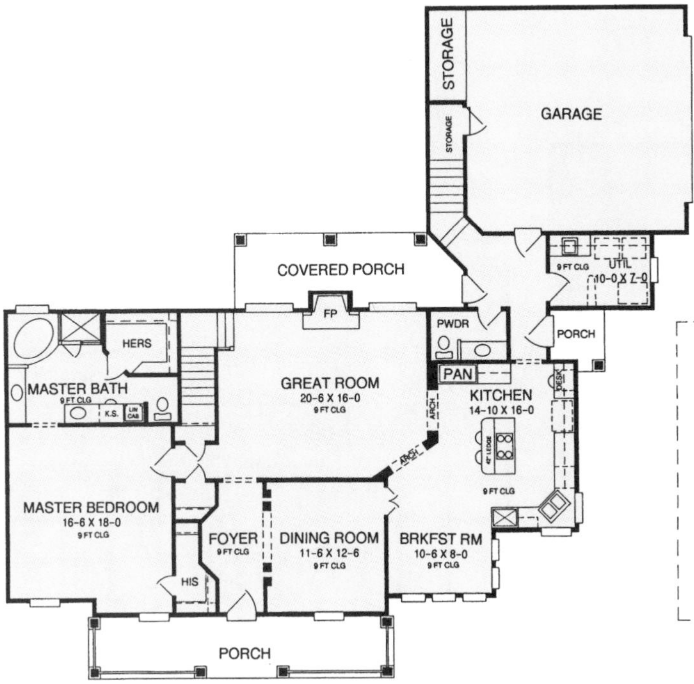
STORAGE
GARAGE
STORAGE
COVERED PORCH
UTIL
10-0 X 7-0
9 FT CLG
FP
PWDR
PORCH
HERS
MASTER BATH
9 FT CLG
K.S.
GREAT ROOM
20-6 X 16-0
9 FT CLG
PAN
KITCHEN
14-10 X 16-0
ARCH
9 FT CLG
MASTER BEDROOM
16-6 X 18-0
9 FT CLG
FOYER
9 FT CLG
DINING ROOM
11-6 X 12-6
9 FT CLG
BRKFST RM
10-6 X 8-0
9 FT CLG
HIS
PORCH

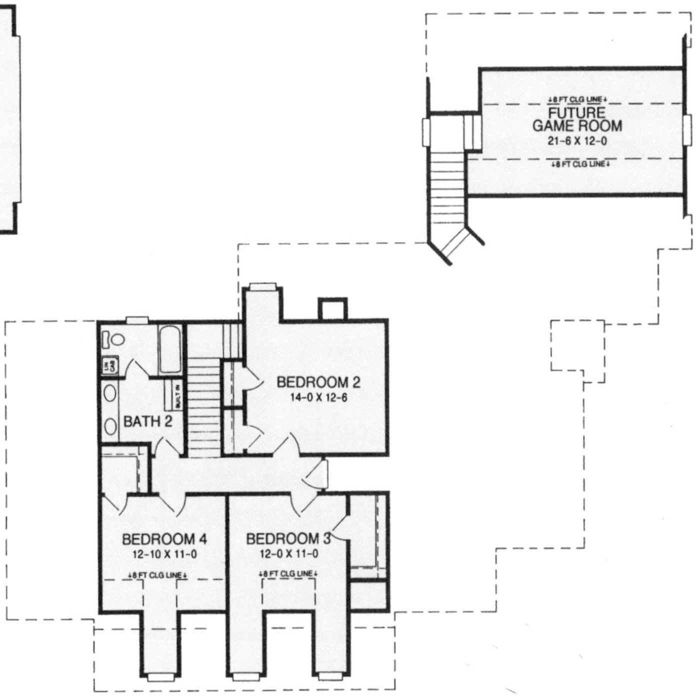

Looking to the past for style, the character of this winning plan is vintage Americana. A huge great room opens through classic arches to the island kitchen and the breakfast room. A corner sink in the kitchen gives the cook a view to the outside and brings in sunlight. Nearby, a small side porch provides a charming entry. The master suite is found on the first floor for privacy. The three bedrooms upstairs share a full bath. Please specify crawlspace or slab foundation when ordering.

Design HPT830165

First Floor: 1,785 square feet
Second Floor: 830 square feet
Total: 2,615 square feet
Width 68'-10" Depth 65'-3"

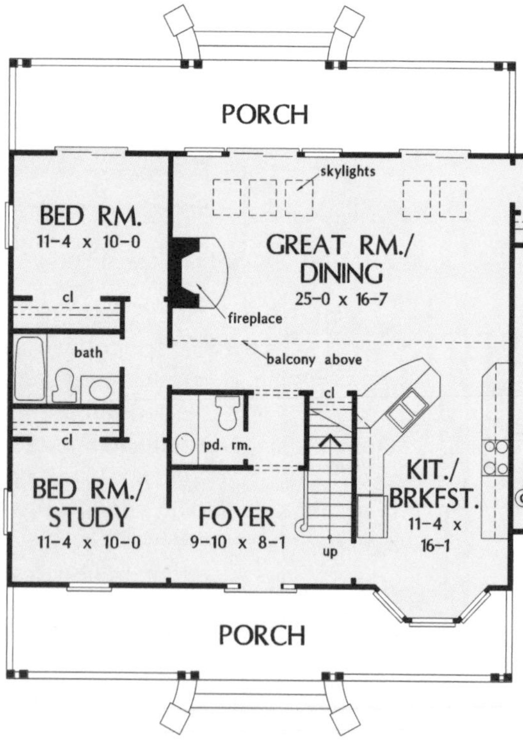
PORCH
BED RM.
11-4 x 10-0
skylights
GREAT RM./
DINING
25-0 x 16-7
fireplace
UTIL.
w
d
storage
cl
bath
balcony above
pd. rm.
GARAGE
20-4 x 20-0
KIT./
BRKFST.
11-4 x
16-1
BED RM./
STUDY
11-4 x 10-0
FOYER
9-10 x 8-1
up
© 1994 DONALD A. GARDNER
All rights reserved
PORCH

QUOTE ONE®

Cost to build? See page 516 to order complete cost estimate to build this house in your area!

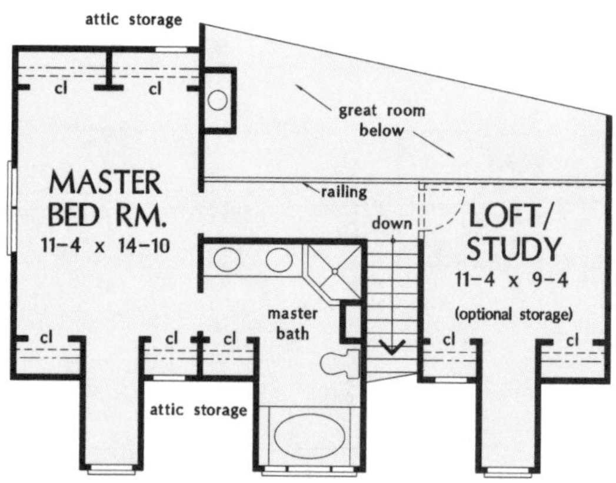
attic storage
cl
great room
below
railing
MASTER
BED RM.
11-4 x 14-10
down
LOFT/
STUDY
11-4 x 9-4
(optional storage)
master
bath
attic storage

Interesting room arrangements make this home unique and inviting. Family bedrooms and a shared bath are on the left and a small hallway on the right leads to the sunny kitchen. Beyond the kitchen is a combination great room and dining area that features a fireplace, access to the large back porch and plenty of windows and skylights. The second floor is reserved for a grand master suite that features plenty of closet space, a separate loft or study area and a wonderful master bath with a bumped-out whirlpool tub.

Design HPT830166

First Floor: 1,234 square feet
Second Floor: 609 square feet
Total: 1,843 square feet
Width 58'-0" Depth 44'-0"

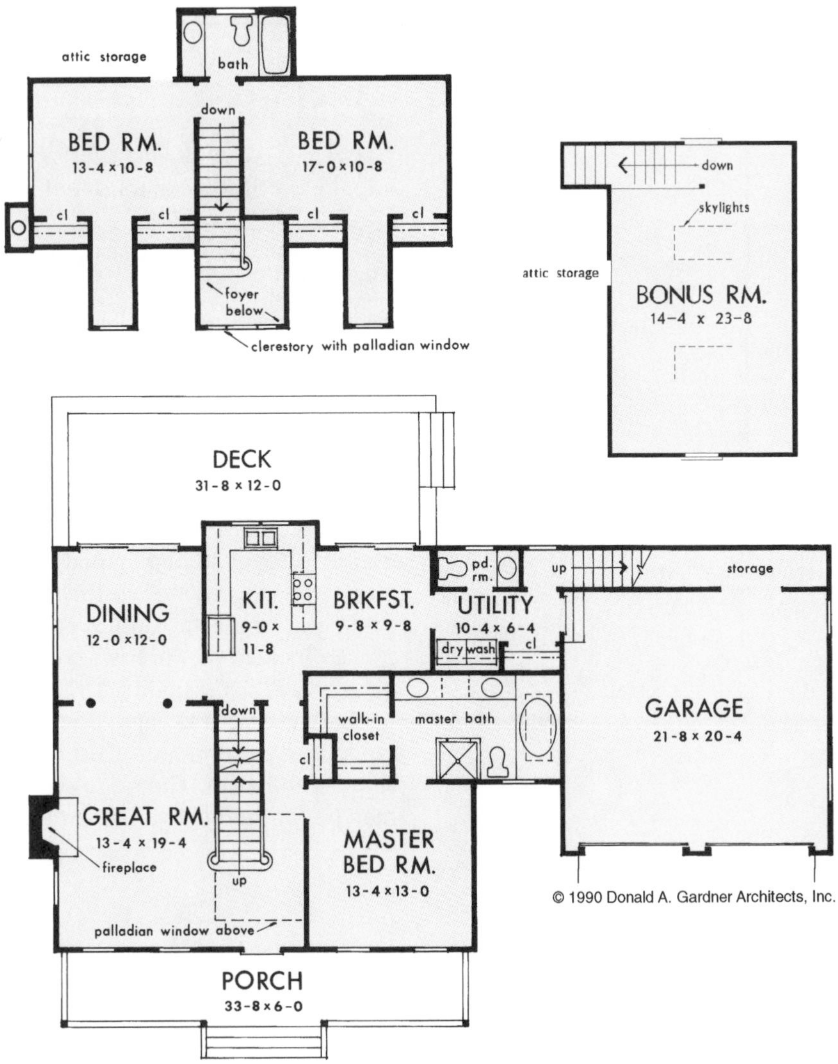
attic storage
bath
down
BED RM.
13-4 x 10-8
BED RM.
17-0 x 10-8
cl
cl
cl
cl
foyer below
clerestory with palladian window
down
skylights
attic storage
BONUS RM.
14-4 x 23-8
DECK
31-8 x 12-0
pd. rm.
up
storage
DINING
12-0 x 12-0
KIT.
9-0 x 11-8
BRKFST.
9-8 x 9-8
UTILITY
10-4 x 6-4
dry
wash
cl
down
walk-in closet
master bath
GARAGE
21-8 x 20-4
cl
GREAT RM.
13-4 x 19-4
fireplace
up
MASTER BED RM.
13-4 x 13-0
palladian window above
PORCH
33-8 x 6-0

Design HPT830167

First Floor: 1,289 square feet
Second Floor: 542 square feet
Total: 1,831 square feet
Bonus Space: 393 square feet
Width 66'-4" Depth 40'-4"

This cozy country cottage is perfect for the growing family—offering both an unfinished basement option and a bonus room. Enter through the two-story foyer with a Palladian window in a clerestory dormer above. The master suite is on the first floor for privacy and accessibility. Its accompanying bath boasts a whirlpool tub with a skylight above and a double-bowl vanity. The second floor contains two bedrooms, a full bath and plenty of storage.

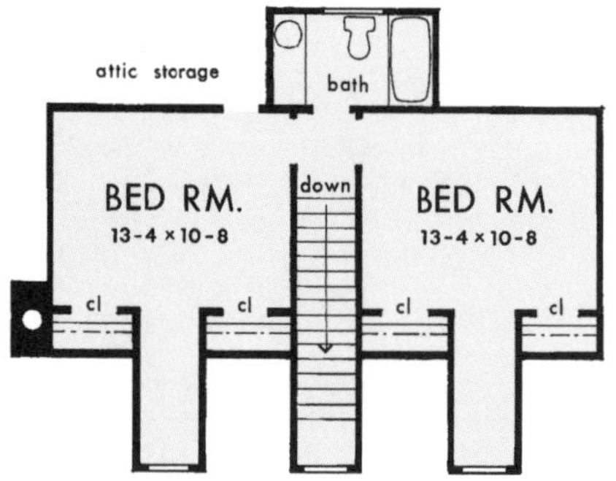
attic storage
bath
BED RM.
13-4 × 10-8
down
BED RM.
13-4 × 10-8
cl
cl
cl
cl

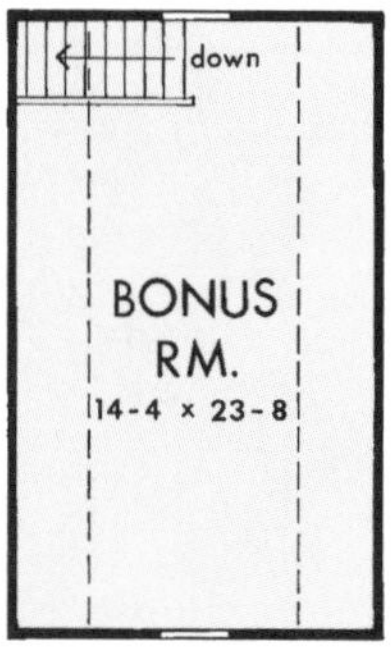
down
BONUS
RM.
14-4 × 23-8

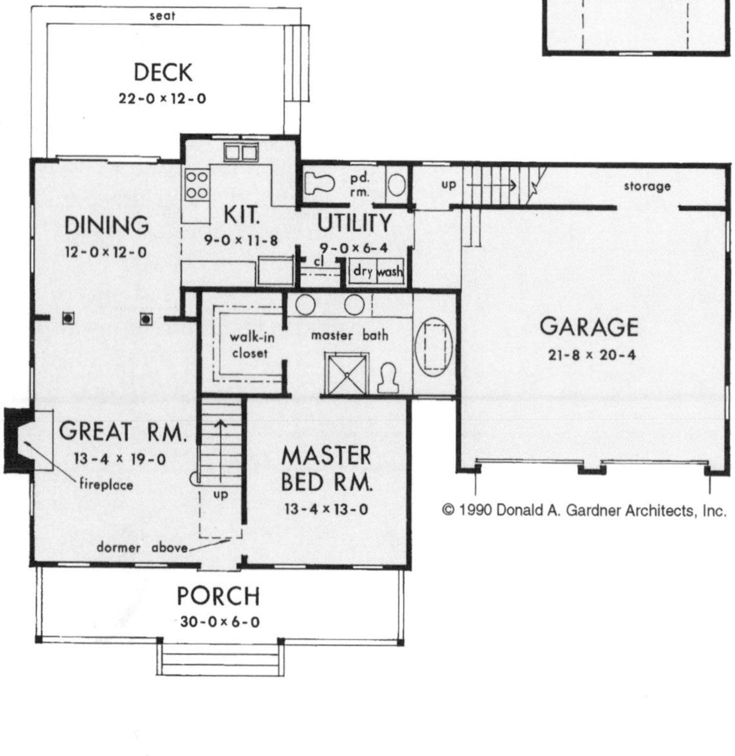
seat
DECK
22-0 × 12-0
DINING
12-0 × 12-0
KIT.
9-0 × 11-8
pd. rm.
UTILITY
9-0 × 6-4
cl
dry
wash
up
storage
walk-in closet
master bath
GARAGE
21-8 × 20-4
GREAT RM.
13-4 × 19-0
fireplace
up
MASTER
BED RM.
13-4 × 13-0
dormer above
PORCH
30-0 × 6-0

Design HPT830168

First Floor: 1,057 square feet
Second Floor: 500 square feet
Total: 1,557 square feet
Bonus Space: 342 square feet
Width 59'-4" Depth 50'-0"

This cozy country cottage is perfect for the economically conscious family. Its entrance foyer is highlighted by a clerestory dormer above for natural light. The master suite is conveniently located on the first level for privacy and accessibility. The master bath boasts a skylight and lush amenities. Second-level bedrooms share a full bath. The bonus room may be finished above the garage.

QUOTE ONE®

Cost to build? See page 516 to order complete cost estimate to build this house in your area!

© 1986 Donald A. Gardner Architects, Inc.

Design HPT830169

First Floor: 1,434 square feet
Second Floor: 604 square feet
Total: 2,038 square feet
Width 47'-4" Depth 69'-0"

One of the first floor's attractions, the sun room will delight all with its spiral staircase leading to a balcony and the master suite. The great room enjoys a fireplace and two sets of sliding glass doors leading to the deck. In the kitchen, a U shape lends itself to outstanding convenience. Three bedrooms include two secondary bedrooms and a glorious master suite. Located on the second floor, the private bedroom has a fireplace, a generous dressing area with a skylight and a lavish bath.

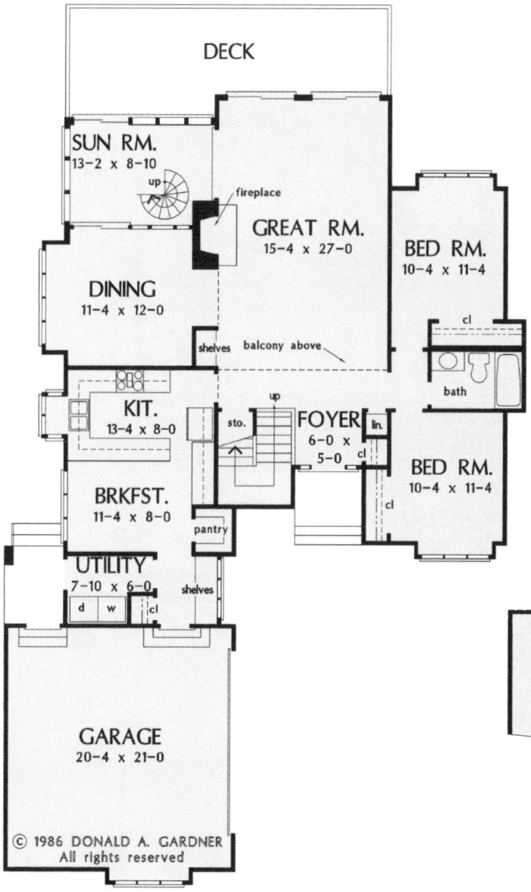
DECK
SUN RM.
13-2 x 8-10
up
fireplace
GREAT RM.
15-4 x 27-0
BED RM.
10-4 x 11-4
DINING
11-4 x 12-0
shelves
balcony above
cl
bath
KIT.
13-4 x 8-0
up
sto.
FOYER
6-0 x 5-0
lin.
cl
BED RM.
10-4 x 11-4
cl
BRKFST.
11-4 x 8-0
pantry
UTILITY
7-10 x 6-0
shelves
d
w
cl
GARAGE
20-4 x 21-0
© 1986 DONALD A. GARDNER
All rights reserved

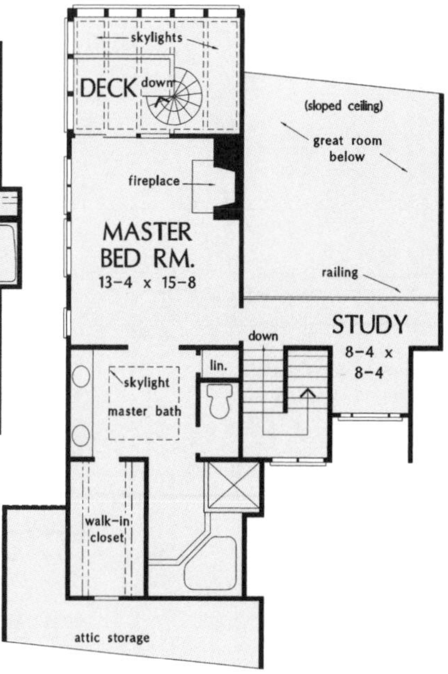
skylights
DECK
down
(sloped ceiling)
great room below
fireplace
MASTER BED RM.
13-4 x 15-8
railing
STUDY
8-4 x 8-4
down
lin.
skylight
master bath
walk-in closet
attic storage

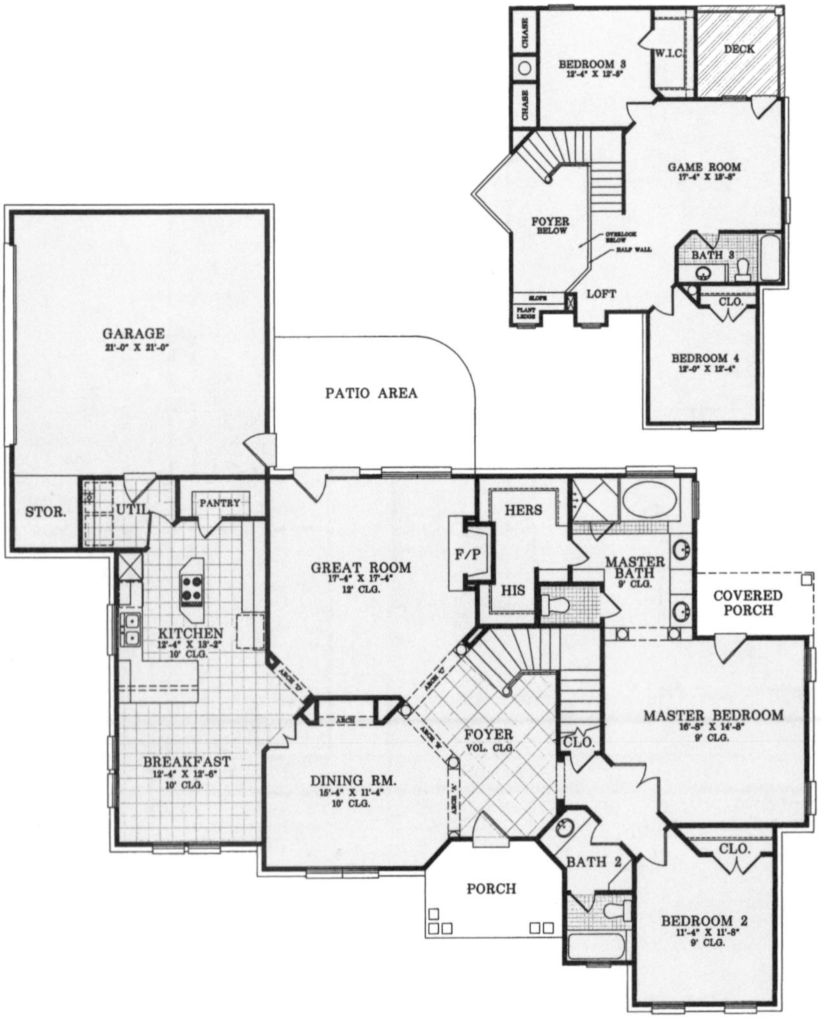
CHASE
BEDROOM 3
12'-4" X 12'-8"
W.I.C.
DECK
CHASE
GAME ROOM
17'-4" X 15'-8"
FOYER
BELOW
OVERLOOK BELOW
HALF WALL
BATH 3
LOFT
CLO.
SLOPE
PLANT LEDGE
BEDROOM 4
12'-0" X 12'-4"
GARAGE
21'-0" X 21'-0"
PATIO AREA
STOR.
UTIL
PANTRY
HERS
GREAT ROOM
17'-4" X 17'-4"
12' CLG.
F/P
MASTER BATH
9' CLG.
HIS
COVERED PORCH
KITCHEN
12'-4" X 13'-2"
10' CLG.
ARCH
MASTER BEDROOM
16'-8" X 14'-8"
9' CLG.
BREAKFAST
12'-4" X 12'-6"
10' CLG.
FOYER
VOL. CLG.
CLO.
DINING RM.
15'-4" X 11'-4"
10' CLG.
BATH 2
CLO.
PORCH
BEDROOM 2
11'-4" X 11'-8"
9' CLG.

Design

HPT830170

First Floor: 1,904 square feet
Second Floor: 792 square feet
Total: 2,696 square feet
Width 67'-8" Depth 64'-10"
L

This charming cottage has all the accoutrements of an English manor. Inside, the angled foyer directs the eye to the arched entrances of the formal dining room and the great room with its fireplace and patio access. The master bedroom and a guest bedroom are located on the opposite side of the house for privacy. Please specify basement, crawlspace or slab foundation when ordering.

The front of this traditional home is characterized by the arch pattern evident in the windows, doorway and above the columned front porch. The master suite includes a vaulted study that also opens from the foyer. The study's two-sided fireplace also warms the bedroom. Through the master suite and beyond two walk-in closets is a bath with dual vanities. Upstairs, there are three more bedrooms and two full baths. This home is designed with a walkout basement foundation.

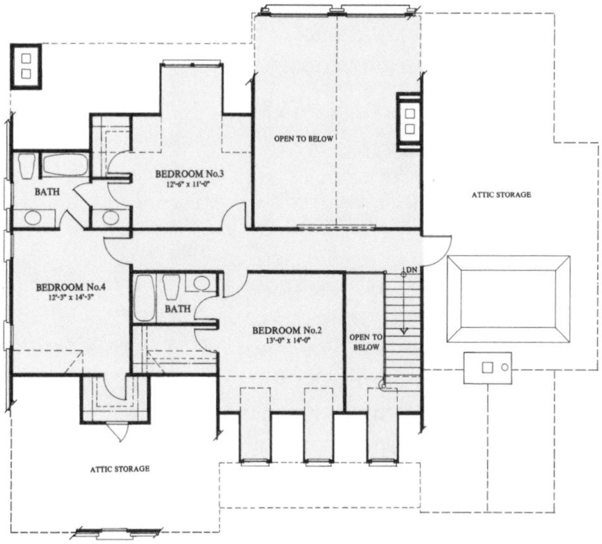

QUOTE ONE®
Cost to build? See page 516 to order complete cost estimate to build this house in your area!

Design
HPT830171

First Floor: 2,355 square feet
Second Floor: 987 square feet
Total: 3,342 square feet
Width 61'-6" Depth 52'-6"

Design

HPT830172

First Floor: 1,810 square feet
Second Floor: 922 square feet
Total: 2,732 square feet
Width 54'-8" Depth 67'-8"

A lovely radius window crowns this impressive entry and brings you into the foyer, which separates the formal living and dining rooms. Efficient planning keeps the casual living area to the rear where the breakfast nook, great room and huge kitchen share views of the deck and backyard beyond. A fireplace flanked by sliding glass doors is the focal point of the great room, as is the bay window in the breakfast nook. The master suite features a large bedroom and a deluxe bath containing a spacious walk-in closet, a soaking tub and a through-fireplace. Upstairs, Bedroom 2 has a private bath and a walk-in closet, while two other bedrooms share a full bath.

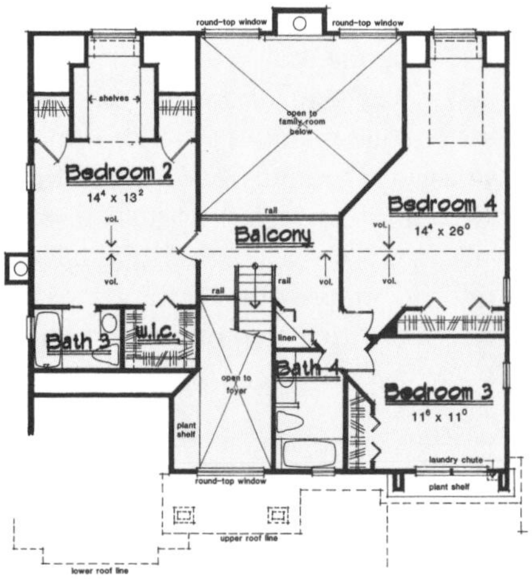

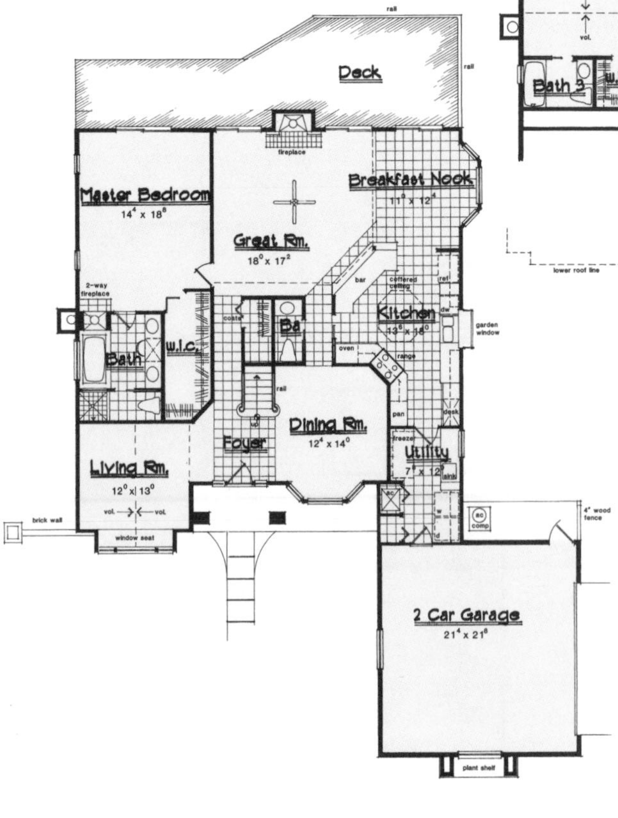

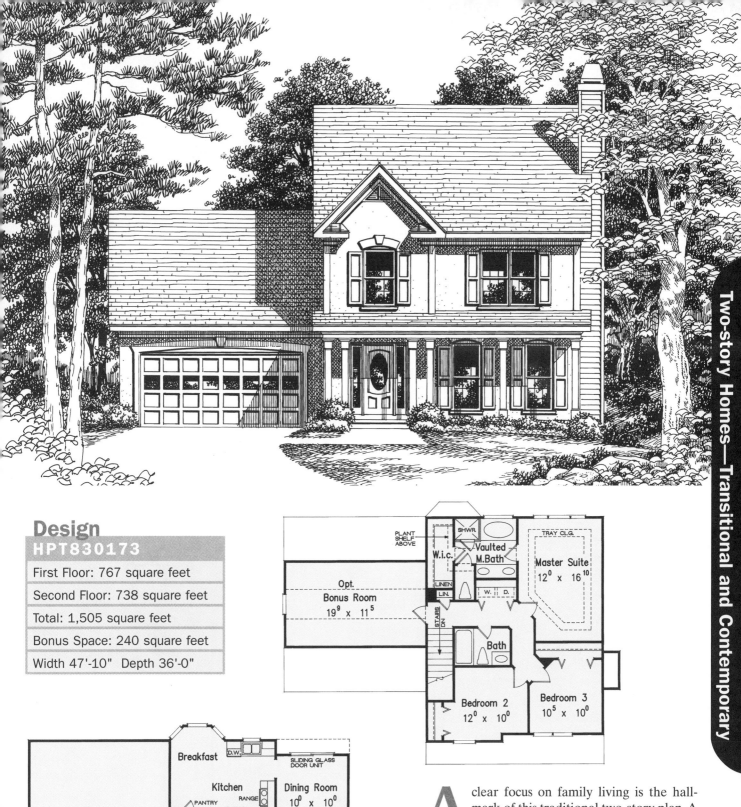

Design HPT830173

First Floor: 767 square feet
Second Floor: 738 square feet
Total: 1,505 square feet
Bonus Space: 240 square feet
Width 47'-10" Depth 36'-0"

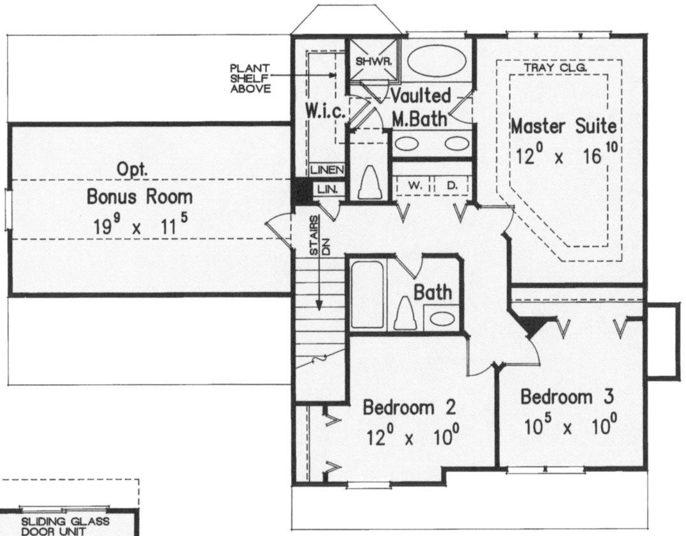
PLANT SHELF ABOVE
SHWR.
W.i.c.
Vaulted M.Bath
TRAY CLG.
Master Suite
12⁰ x 16¹⁰
LINEN
LIN.
W. D.
Opt. Bonus Room
19⁹ x 11⁵
STAIRS DN
Bath
Bedroom 2
12⁰ x 10⁰
Bedroom 3
10⁵ x 10⁰

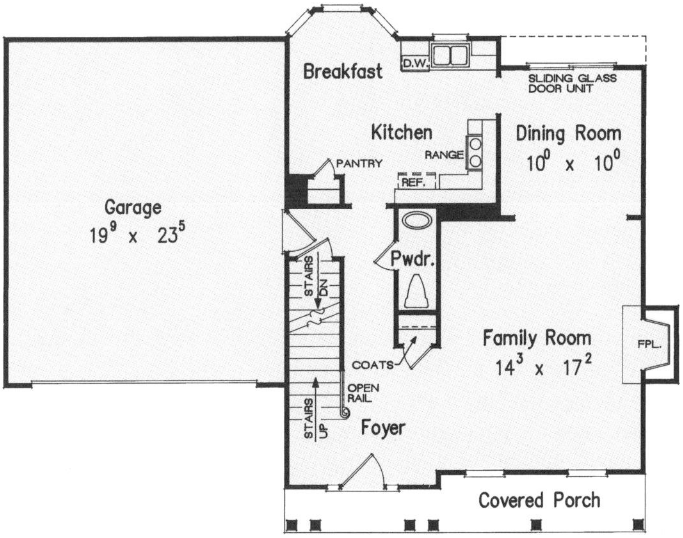
Breakfast
D.W.
SLIDING GLASS DOOR UNIT
Kitchen
Dining Room
10⁰ x 10⁰
PANTRY
RANGE
REF.
Garage
19⁹ x 23⁵
Pwdr.
STAIRS DN
Family Room
14³ x 17²
FPL.
COATS
OPEN RAIL
STAIRS UP
Foyer
Covered Porch

A clear focus on family living is the hallmark of this traditional two-story plan. A columned porch leads to an open foyer and family room complete with a fireplace. A dining room with a sliding glass door is thoughtfully placed between the family room and kitchen. A bayed breakfast nook works well with the roomy kitchen. On the second level a large master suite features a tray ceiling, detailed bath and a space-efficient, walk-in closet. Two family bedrooms, a hall bath and convenient laundry center round out the plan. Please specify basement or crawl-space foundation when ordering.

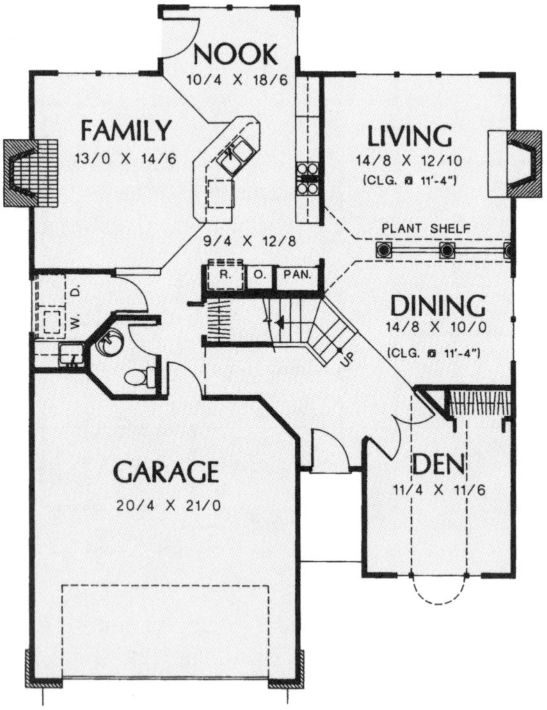

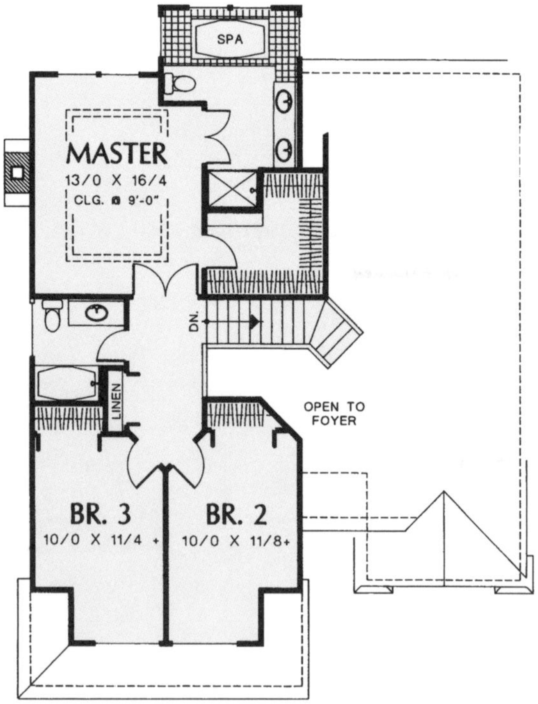

Design HPT830174

First Floor: 1,175 square feet

Second Floor: 891 square feet

Total: 2,066 square feet

Width 38'-0" Depth 51'-0"

L

This charming two-story home is enhanced by horizontal siding on its exterior and a Palladian window at the den. Inside are formal dining and living rooms, both with transom windows, and a family room with fireplace. The island kitchen has an attached nook with outdoor access. A private den with angled double doors opens off the foyer. Upstairs is a master bedroom with a nine-foot tray ceiling and two secondary bedrooms sharing a full bath.

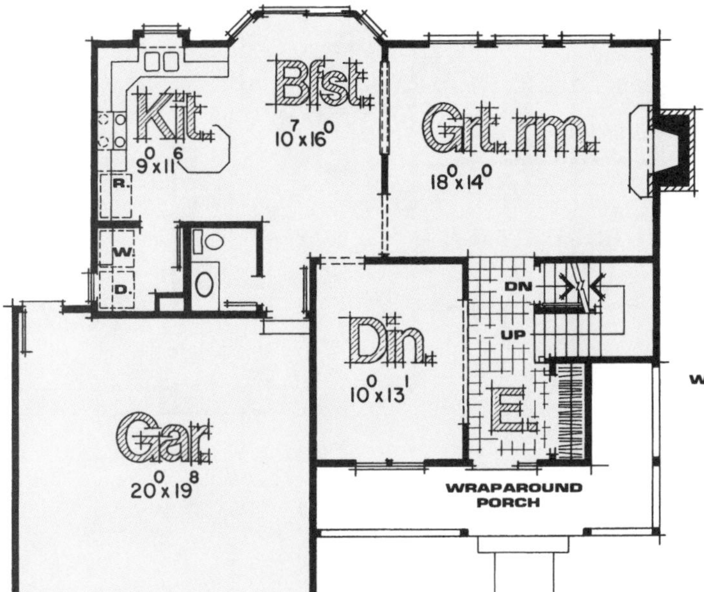

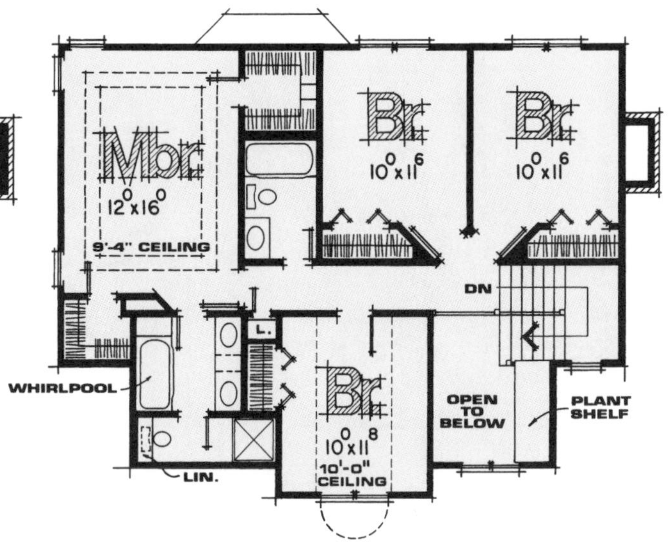

Design HPT830175

First Floor: 919 square feet
Second Floor: 927 square feet
Total: 1,846 square feet
Width 44'-0" Depth 40'-0"

This wonderful country design begins with the wraparound porch of this plan. The island kitchen with a boxed window over the sink is adjacent to a large bayed dinette. The great room includes a fireplace. Upstairs, the large master suite contains His and Hers walk-in closets, corner windows and a private bath area. Three family bedrooms share a full hall bath nearby.

QUOTE ONE®

Cost to build? See page 516 to order complete cost estimate to build this house in your area!

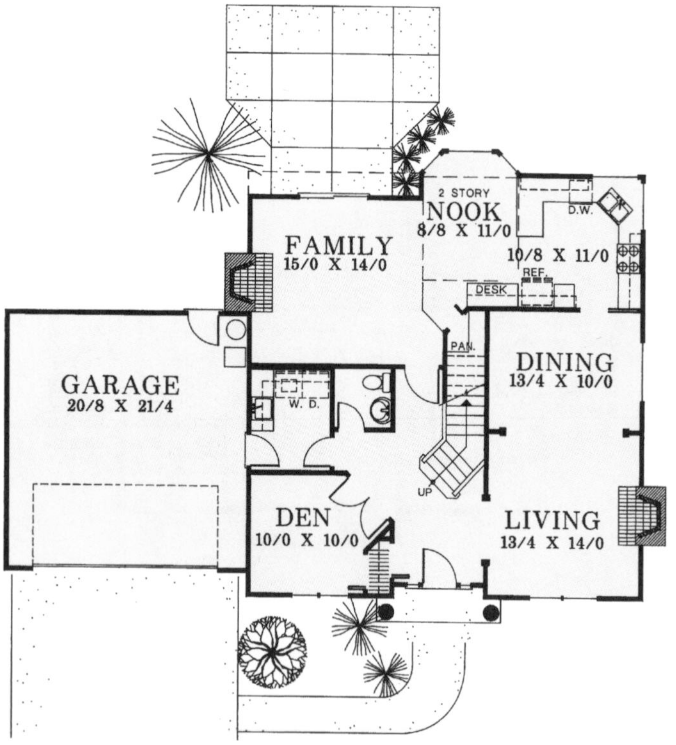

2 STORY
NOOK
8/8 X 11/0
FAMILY
15/0 X 14/0
10/8 X 11/0
D.W.
REF.
DESK
PAN.
DINING
13/4 X 10/0
GARAGE
20/8 X 21/4
W. D.
UP
DEN
10/0 X 10/0
LIVING
13/4 X 14/0

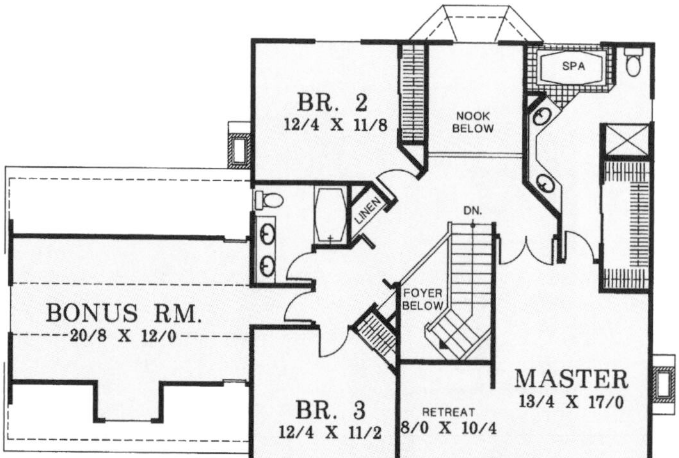

BR. 2
12/4 X 11/8
NOOK BELOW
SPA
LINEN
DN.
BONUS RM.
20/8 X 12/0
FOYER BELOW
MASTER
13/4 X 17/0
BR. 3
12/4 X 11/2
RETREAT
8/0 X 10/4

This gracious home integrates timeless traditional styling with a functional, cost-effective plan. An interesting feature is the two-story nook area with a bay window set between the gourmet kitchen and the large family room. A conveniently located door in the upper hallway opens to the large bonus room over the two-car garage. Rounding out the upper floor are a sumptuous master suite, with its own private retreat out over the entry, and two family bedrooms.

Design
HPT830176

First Floor: 1,236 square feet

Second Floor: 1,120 square feet

Total: 2,356 square feet

Bonus Space: 270 square feet

Width 56'-0" Depth 38'-0"

L

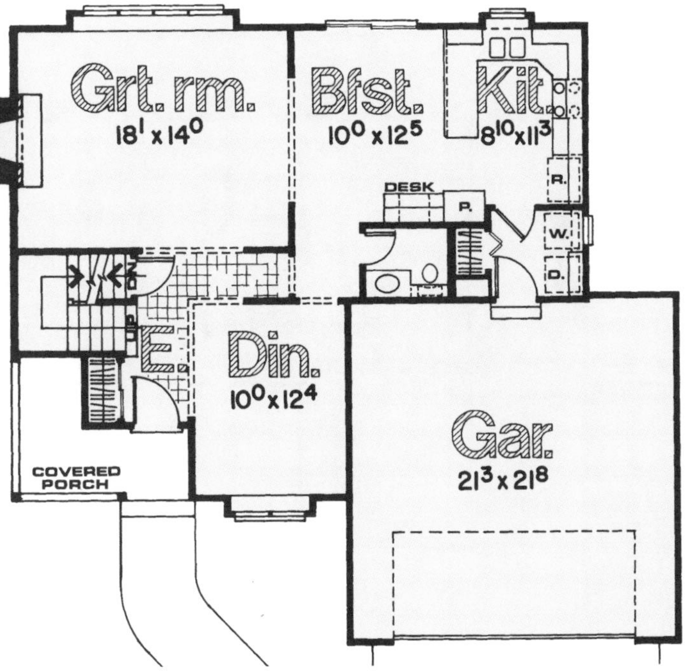

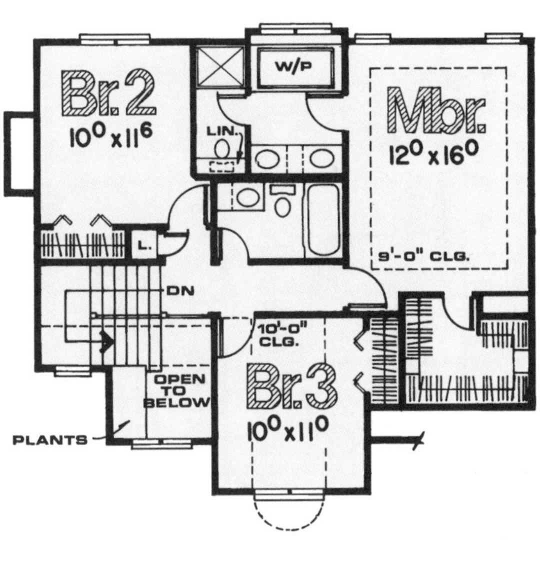

This modestly sized home provides a quaint covered front porch that opens to a two-story foyer. The formal dining room features a boxed window that can be seen from the entry. A fireplace in the great room adds warmth and coziness to the attached breakfast room and the well-planned kitchen. Sliding glass doors lead from the breakfast room to the rear yard. A washer and dryer reside in a nearby utility room, and a closet provides ample storage. A powder room is provided nearby for guests. Three bedrooms occupy the second floor; one of these includes an arched window under a vaulted ceiling. The deluxe master suite provides a large walk-in closet and a dressing area with a double vanity and a whirlpool tub.

Design
HPT830177

First Floor: 891 square feet
Second Floor: 759 square feet
Total: 1,650 square feet
Width 44'-0" Depth 40'-0"

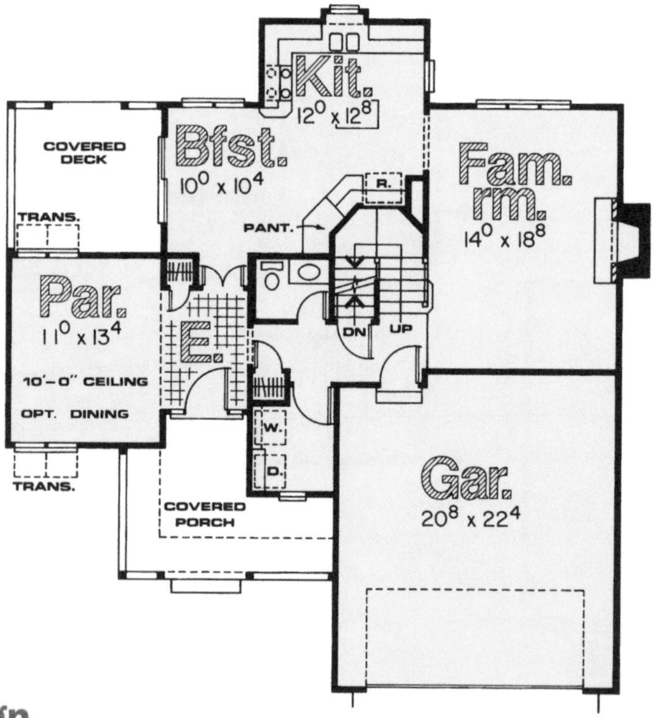

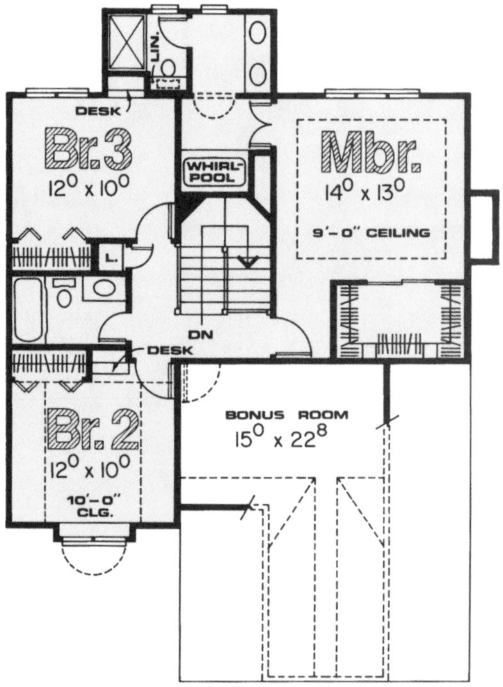

Design HPT830178

First Floor: 976 square feet
Second Floor: 823 square feet
Total: 1,799 square feet
Bonus Space: 345 square feet
Width 45'-4" Depth 48'-0"

Exterior detailing is the first attraction to this home: a gabled roof, an arched window and a rustic covered porch. The floor plan inside offers its own delights, such as a formal parlor with a ten-foot ceiling, a breakfast area leading to a covered deck and an island kitchen with a wrapping pantry. The family room is spacious and contains a warming hearth. Upstairs, the secondary bedrooms each feature a built-in desk. A bonus room allows space for a playroom. The master bedroom features an oversized closet and a bath fit for royalty.

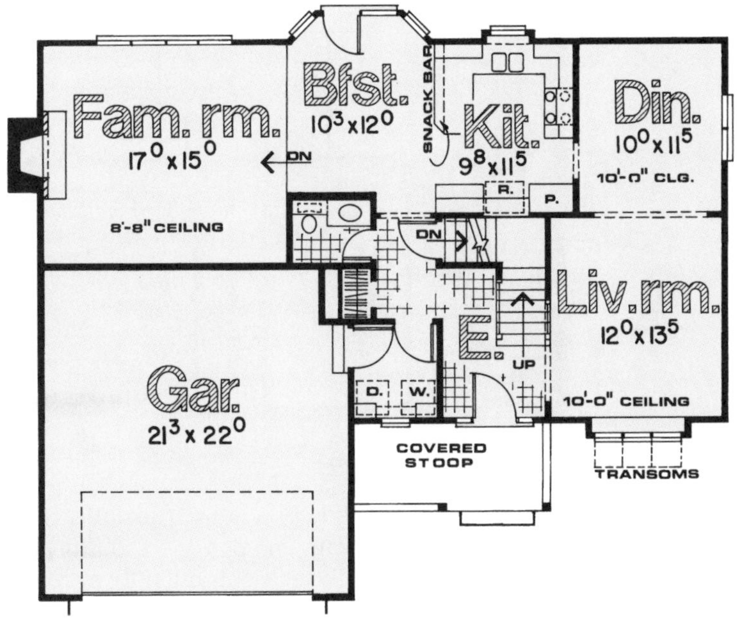

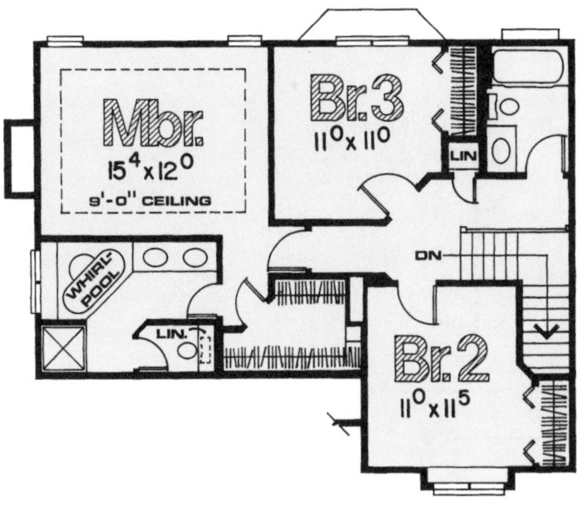

Design HPT830179

First Floor: 1,042 square feet
Second Floor: 803 square feet
Total: 1,845 square feet
Width 48'-0" Depth 40'-0"

At 1,845 square feet, this classic two-story home is perfect for a variety of lifestyles. Upon entry from the covered front porch, the thoughtful floor plan is immediately evident. To the right of the entry is a formal volume living room with ten-foot ceiling. Nearby, the formal dining room enjoys a bright window. Serving the dining room and bright bayed dinette, the kitchen features a pantry, lazy Susan and window sink. Off the breakfast area, step down into the family room with a handsome fireplace and wall of windows. Upstairs, two secondary bedrooms share a hall bath. The private master bedroom contains a boxed ceiling, walk-in closet and a pampering dressing area with double vanity and whirlpool tub.

Design HPT830180

First Floor: 1,156 square feet
Second Floor: 1,239 square feet
Total: 2,395 square feet
Width 57'-3" Depth 39'-0"

This traditional home combines an attractive, classic exterior with an open and sophisticated interior design. To the right of the foyer reside both the living and dining rooms with their individual window treatments. Enter the kitchen from the dining room through a corner butler's pantry for added convenience while entertaining. The open design flows from the breakfast area to the family room with two large bay windows. The open foyer staircase leads to the upper level, beginning with the master suite. The master bath contains a luxurious tub, separate shower and dual vanities, as well as a large linen closet. All three secondary bedrooms share a hall bath that includes a separate vanity and bathing area. This home is designed with a walkout basement foundation.

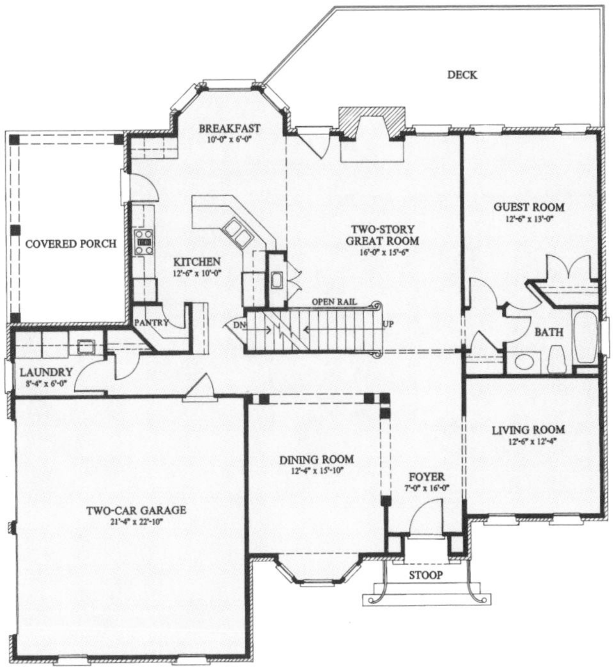

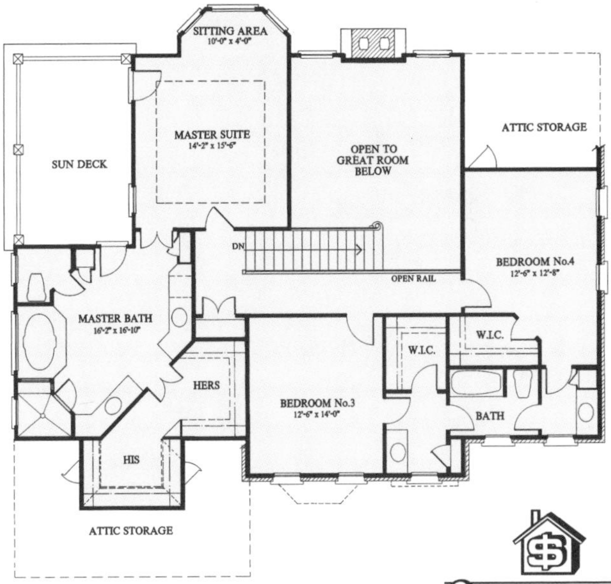

QUOTE ONE®
Cost to build? See page 516
to order complete cost estimate
to build this house in your area!

Classical details and a stately brick exterior accentuate the grace and timeless elegance of this home. Inside, the foyer opens to a large banquet-sized dining room and an adjacent formal living room. Just beyond, the two-story great room awaits, featuring a wet bar and warming fireplace. A large covered porch off the kitchen completes the family center. Upstairs, the master suite features an unusual bay-window design, private sun deck, garden tub, His and Hers vanities and walk-in closets, and a compartmented toilet. Two bedrooms with a connecting bath complete the second floor. This home is designed with a walkout basement foundation.

Design HPT830181

First Floor: 1,581 square feet
Second Floor: 1,415 square feet
Total: 2,996 square feet
Width 55'-0" Depth 52'-0"

Design

HPT830182

First Floor: 1,570 square feet	
Second Floor: 1,630 square feet	
Total: 3,200 square feet	
Width 59'-10"	Depth 43'-4"

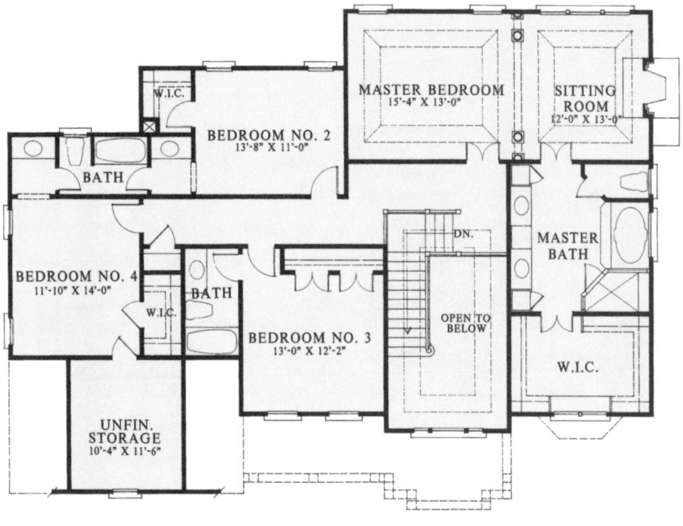

MASTER BEDROOM
15'-4" X 13'-0"
SITTING ROOM
12'-0" X 13'-0"
W.I.C.
BEDROOM NO. 2
13'-8" X 11'-0"
BATH
BEDROOM NO. 4
11'-10" X 14'-0"
W.I.C.
BATH
DN.
MASTER BATH
OPEN TO BELOW
BEDROOM NO. 3
13'-0" X 12'-2"
W.I.C.
UNFIN. STORAGE
10'-4" X 11'-6"

QUOTE ONE®

Cost to build? See page 516 to order complete cost estimate to build this house in your area!

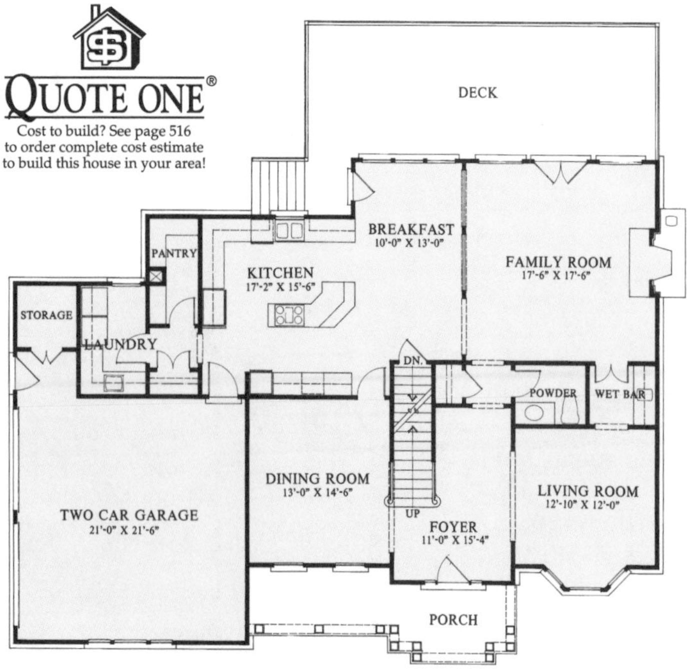

DECK
BREAKFAST
10'-0" X 13'-0"
PANTRY
KITCHEN
17'-2" X 15'-6"
FAMILY ROOM
17'-6" X 17'-6"
STORAGE
LAUNDRY
DN.
POWDER
WET BAR
DINING ROOM
13'-0" X 14'-6"
LIVING ROOM
12'-10" X 12'-0"
TWO CAR GARAGE
21'-0" X 21'-6"
UP
FOYER
11'-0" X 15'-4"
PORCH

This classic Americana design employs wood siding, a variety of window styles and a detailed front porch. Inside, the large two-story foyer flows into the formal dining room with arched window accents and the living room highlighted by a bay window. This home is designed with a walkout basement foundation.

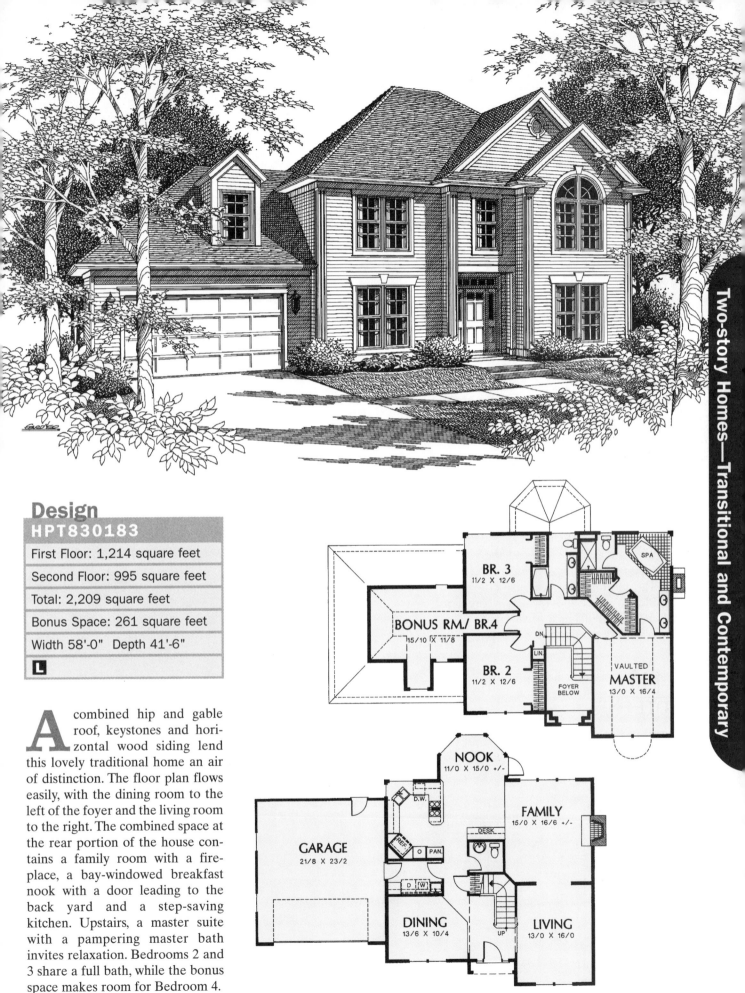

Design HPT830183

First Floor: 1,214 square feet
Second Floor: 995 square feet
Total: 2,209 square feet
Bonus Space: 261 square feet
Width 58'-0" Depth 41'-6"
L

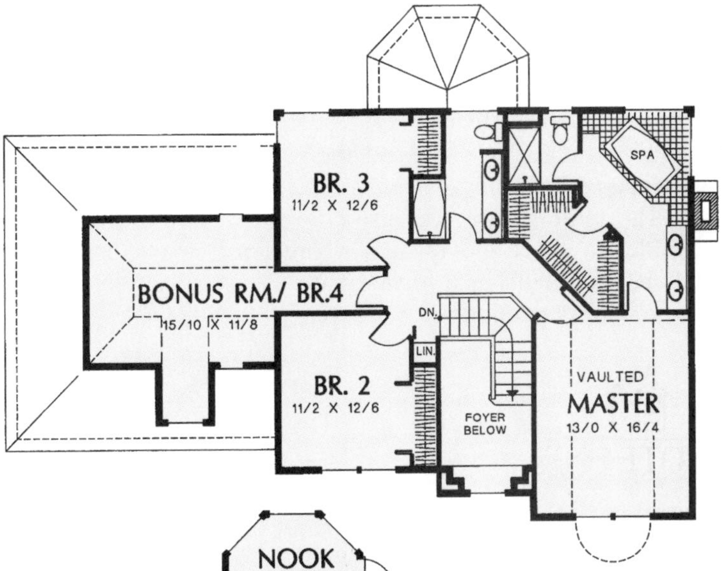

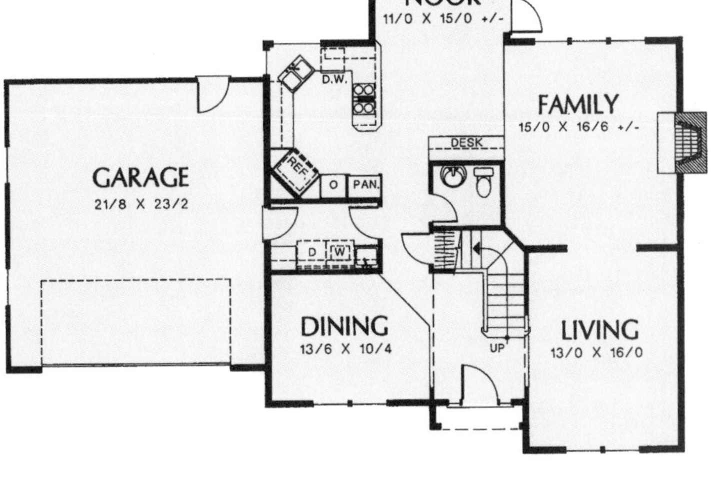

A combined hip and gable roof, keystones and horizontal wood siding lend this lovely traditional home an air of distinction. The floor plan flows easily, with the dining room to the left of the foyer and the living room to the right. The combined space at the rear portion of the house contains a family room with a fireplace, a bay-windowed breakfast nook with a door leading to the back yard and a step-saving kitchen. Upstairs, a master suite with a pampering master bath invites relaxation. Bedrooms 2 and 3 share a full bath, while the bonus space makes room for Bedroom 4.

A chic combination of European style and farmhouse charm gives this two-story home an eclectic appeal. Apart from the private living room, living areas are open and divided by decorative columns at the dining room and the vaulted great room. The spacious kitchen has wraparound counters, a serving bar and a sunny breakfast room. The master suite contains a lovely, vaulted sitting room with a three-sided fireplace and a spa-style bath. Upstairs, two bedrooms share a bath, while another has a private bath. Please specify basement, crawl-space or slab foundation when ordering.

Design HPT830184

First Floor: 2,467 square feet

Second Floor: 928 square feet

Total: 3,395 square feet

Width 64'-6" Depth 62'-10"

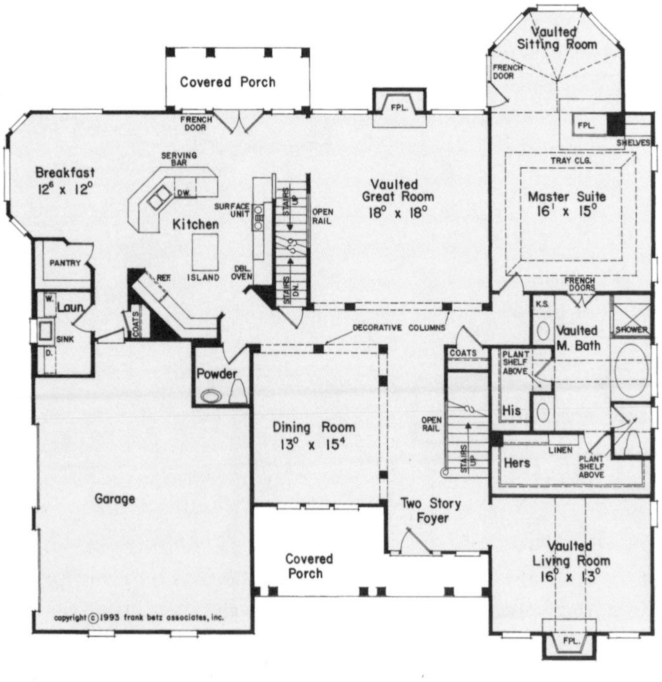

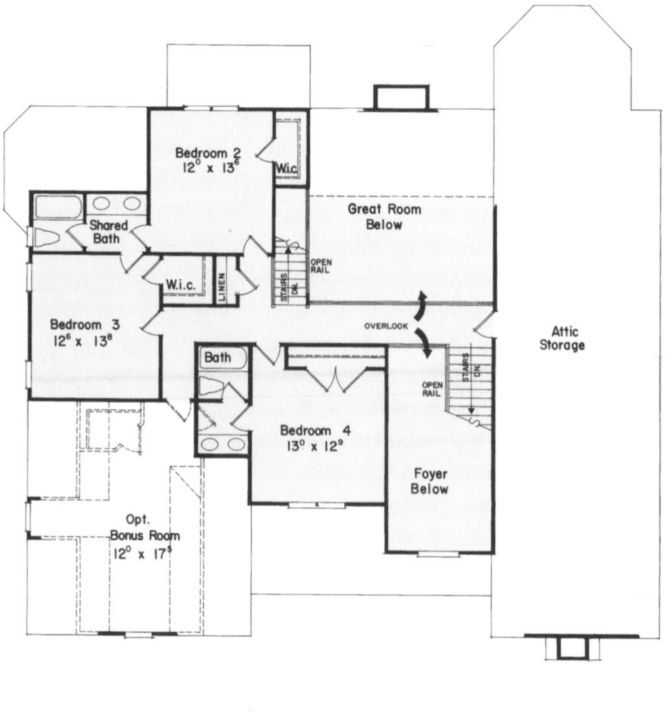

DECK
BREAKFAST
9'-4" X 10'-6"
TWO STORY
GREAT ROOM
16'-8" X 15'-4"
MEDIA ROOM
12'-0" X 12'-0"
KITCHEN
15'-8" X 14'-0"
UP
DN.
POWDER
WET BAR
STORAGE
LAUNDRY
6'-2" X 7'-6"
UP
TWO STORY
FOYER
10'-6" X 13'-0"
LIVING ROOM
12'-0" X 12'-2"
TWO-CAR GARAGE
21'-4" X 21'-4"
DINING ROOM
12'-0" X 13'-0"
PORCH

QUOTE ONE®

Cost to build? See page 516 to order complete cost estimate to build this house in your area!

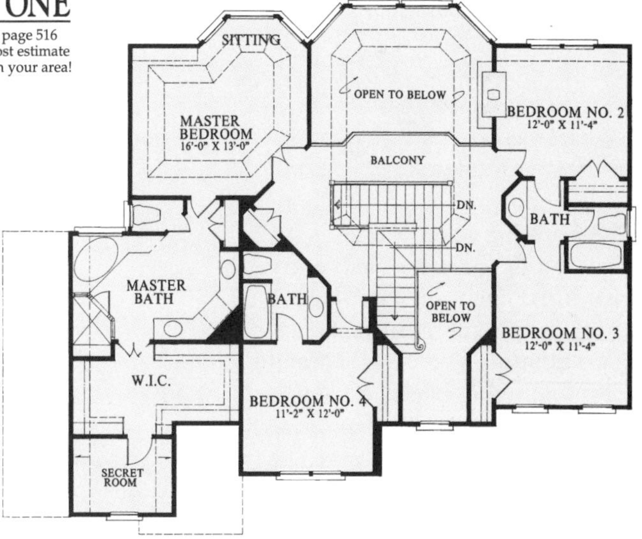
SITTING
OPEN TO BELOW
MASTER
BEDROOM
16'-0" X 13'-0"
BEDROOM NO. 2
12'-0" X 11'-4"
BALCONY
DN.
BATH
DN.
MASTER
BATH
BATH
OPEN TO
BELOW
BEDROOM NO. 3
12'-0" X 11'-4"
W.I.C.
BEDROOM NO. 4
11'-2" X 12'-0"
SECRET
ROOM

Design HPT830185

First Floor: 1,475 square feet
Second Floor: 1,460 square feet
Total: 2,935 square feet
Width 57'-6" Depth 46'-6"

Quaint keystones and shutters offer charming accents to the stucco-and-stone exterior of this stately English country home. The two-story foyer opens through decorative columns to the formal living room. The nearby media room shares a through-fireplace with the two-story great room, which features double doors to the rear deck. A bumped-out bay holds a breakfast area that shares its light with an expansive gourmet kitchen. The left wing of the second floor is dedicated to the rambling master suite, which boasts angled walls, a tray ceiling and a bayed sitting area. This home is designed with a walkout basement foundation.

Design

HPT830186

First Floor: 1,665 square feet

Second Floor: 1,554 square feet

Total: 3,219 square feet

Width 58'-6" Depth 44'-10"

Charming window treatments and a glass-paneled entry introduce interior space that offers just the right combination of comfort and style. Formal rooms flank the two-story foyer, which leads to open casual space defined by decorative columns. The well-appointed kitchen has a cooktop island counter with a snack bar for easy meals. A secluded den or guest bedroom has a nearby full bath, built-in cabinets and an ample closet. Please specify basement or crawlspace foundation when ordering.

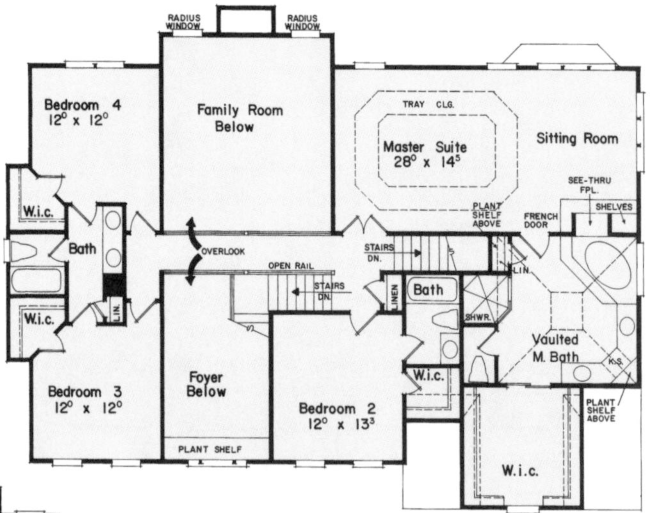

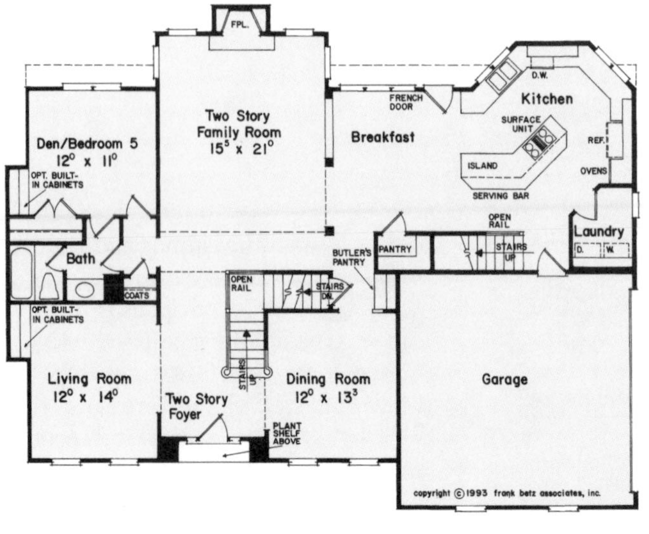

QUOTE ONE®

Cost to build? See page 516 to order complete cost estimate to build this house in your area!

Design HPT830187

First Floor: 1,424 square feet
Second Floor: 1,256 square feet
Total: 2,680 square feet
Width 57'-0" Depth 41'-0"

A grand two-story foyer takes its charm from a bright clerestory window. Just off the foyer lies the formal living area, where the living room joins the dining room with twin boxed columns that are personalized with shelves. The kitchen is placed to easily serve the dining room while remaining open to the breakfast area and vaulted family room. Upstairs, the master suite and bath are nicely balanced with three family bedrooms, a full hall bath and convenient laundry room. Please specify basement, crawlspace or slab foundation when ordering.

QUOTE ONE®
Cost to build? See page 516 to order complete cost estimate to build this house in your area!

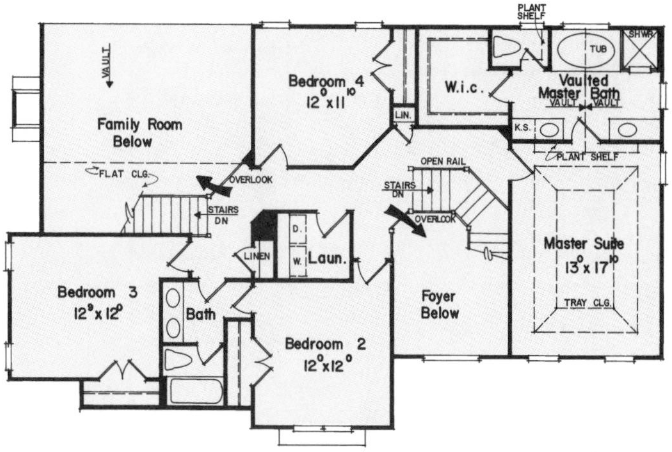

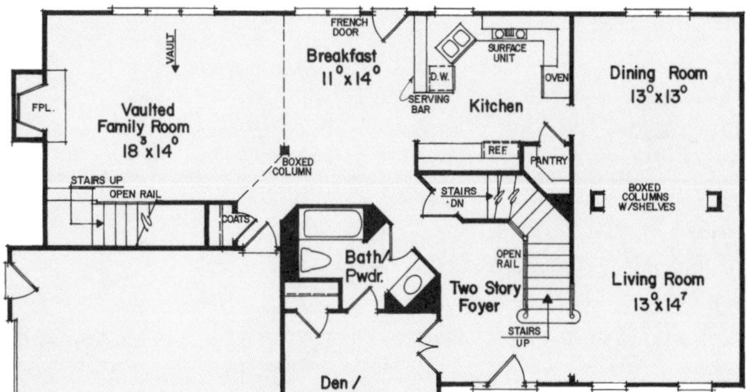

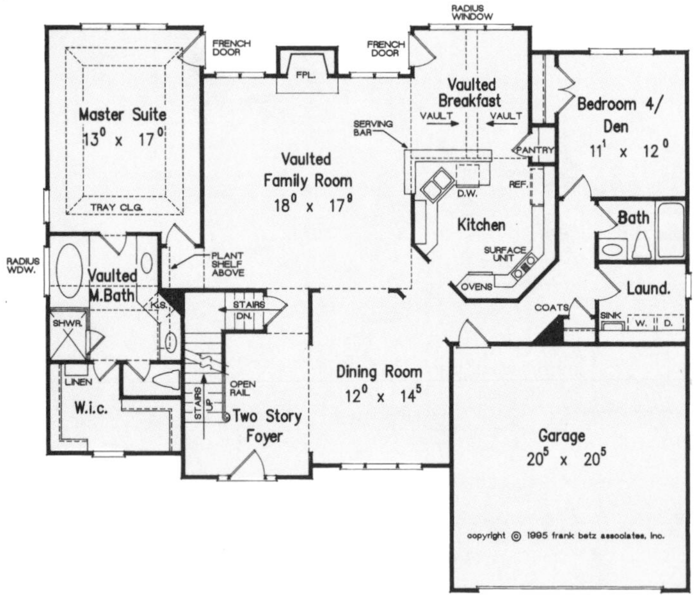

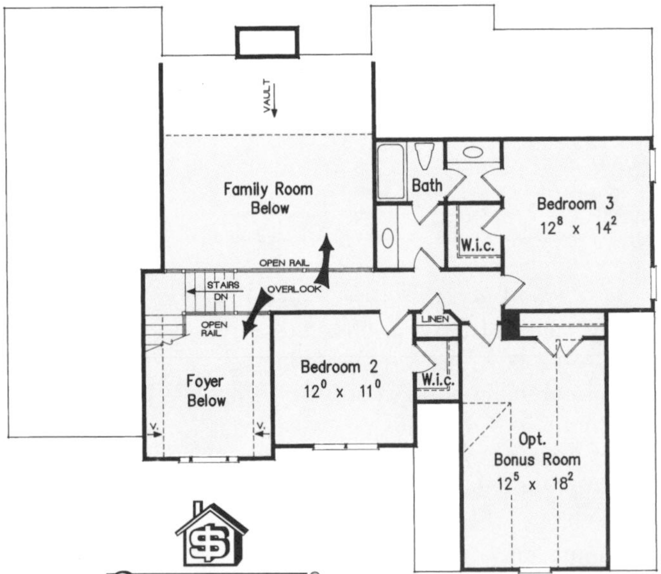

QUOTE ONE®

Cost to build? See page 516 to order complete cost estimate to build this house in your area!

Design HPT830188

First Floor: 1,761 square feet
Second Floor: 580 square feet
Total: 2,341 square feet
Bonus Space: 276 square feet
Width 56'-0" Depth 47'-6"

Stucco accents and flower boxes give this home a cheerful look. Designed for easy living, the formal dining room is placed to the front, with a comfortable family room to the rear. A serving bar extends into the family room from the kitchen. A bedroom and full bath off the kitchen would make a great guest suite. The master suite offers private relaxation. Upstairs, two secondary bedrooms share a full compartmented bath. Please specify basement, crawlspace or slab foundation when ordering.

Design

HPT830189

First Floor: 1,796 square feet
Second Floor: 629 square feet
Total: 2,425 square feet
Bonus Space: 208 square feet
Width 54'-0" Depth 53'-10"

QUOTE ONE®

Cost to build? See page 516 to order complete cost estimate to build this house in your area!

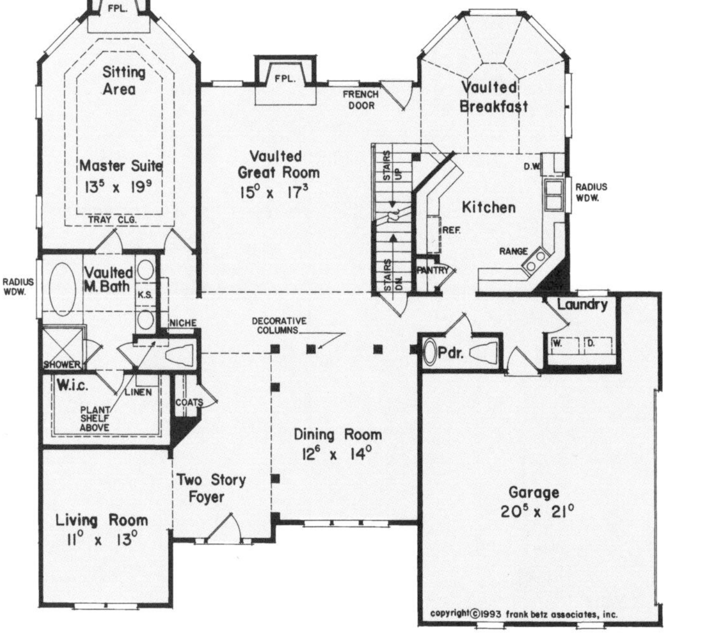

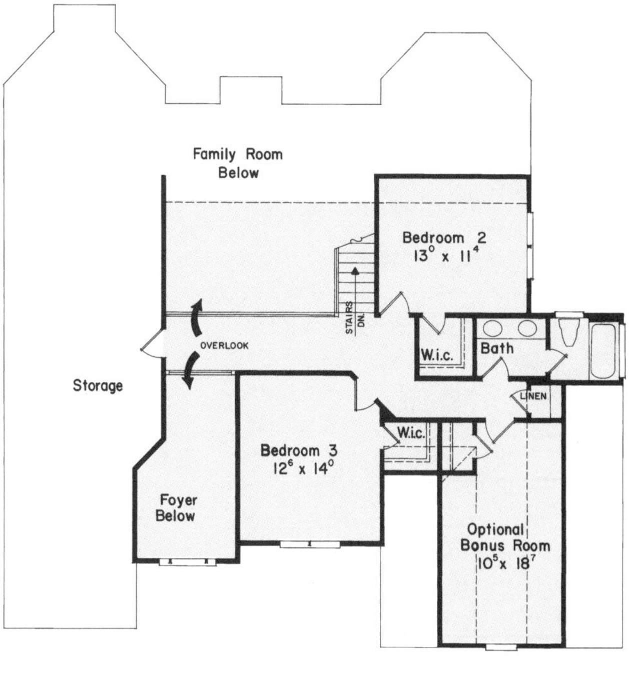

A charming combination of stucco and stone mixed with modern design elements gives this two-story home instant appeal. The vaulted great room continues back, culminating with a fireplace flanked by tall windows. The wraparound kitchen proves efficient with easy service to the vaulted breakfast room. The sumptuous master suite has a sitting area and a vaulted bath. Two family bedrooms are upstairs. Please specify basement, crawlspace or slab foundation when ordering.

Design HPT830190

First Floor: 1,252 square feet
Second Floor: 1,348 square feet
Total: 2,600 square feet
Width 58'-0" Depth 33'-6"

Stately corner quoins and an exterior that's symmetrical in design reflect this home's functional yet elegant floor plan. The two-story foyer is framed by the formal living and dining rooms. The large family room has a fireplace flanked by windows and a French door to the rear yard. The efficient kitchen has a serving bar and an abundance of counter and cabinet space. A stylish twin-entry staircase leads to the three family bedrooms and compartmented bath. The master suite has an oversized bedroom, a sitting room that could double as an exercise area and a spa-syle bath with a walk-in closet. Please specify basement or crawlspace foundation when ordering.

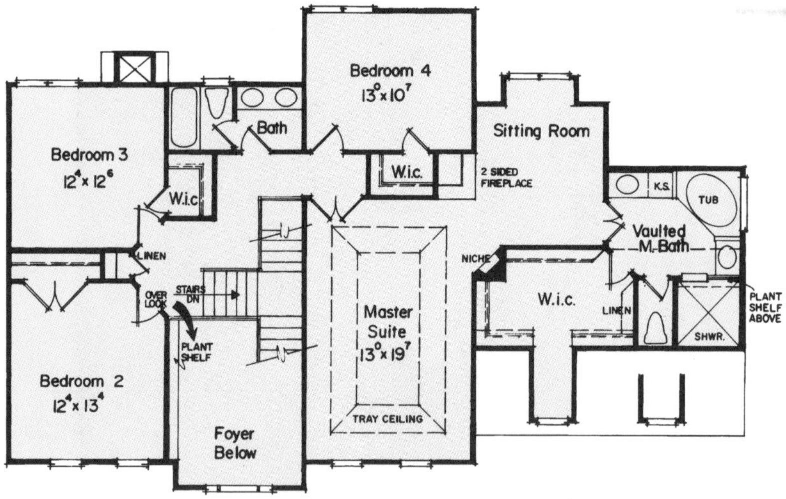

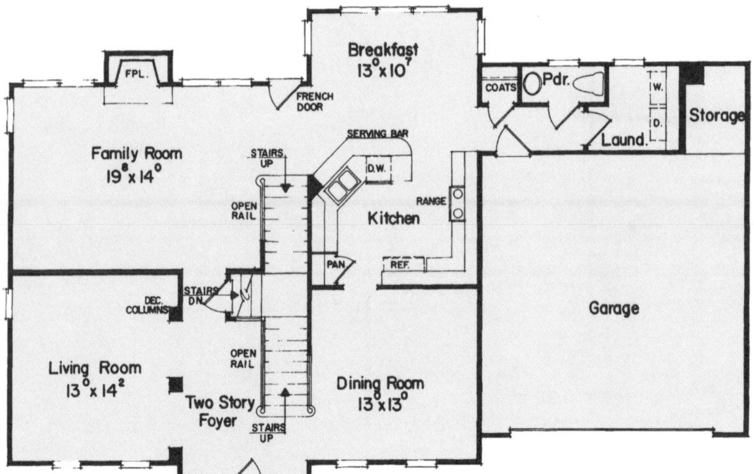

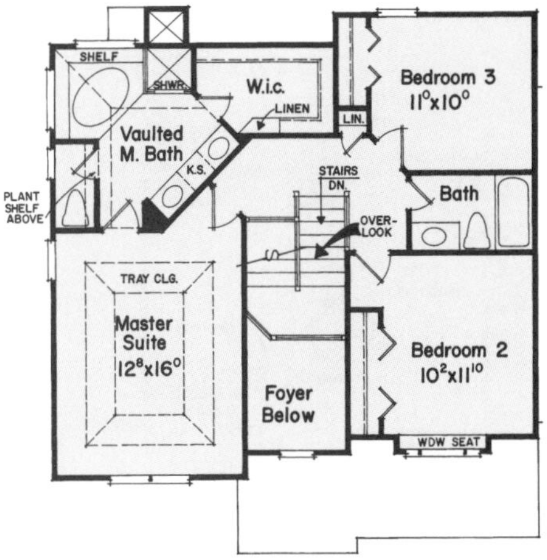

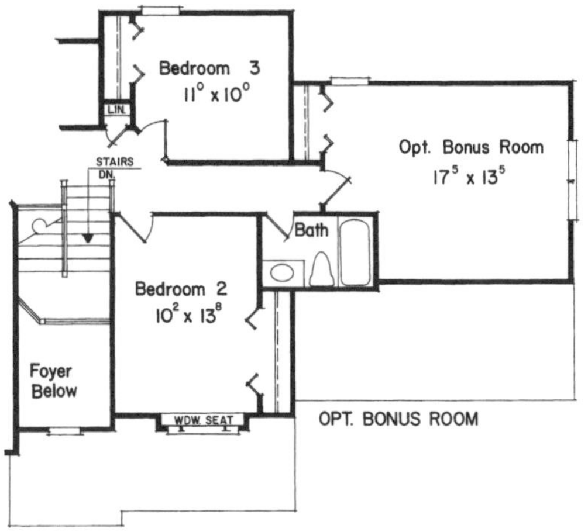

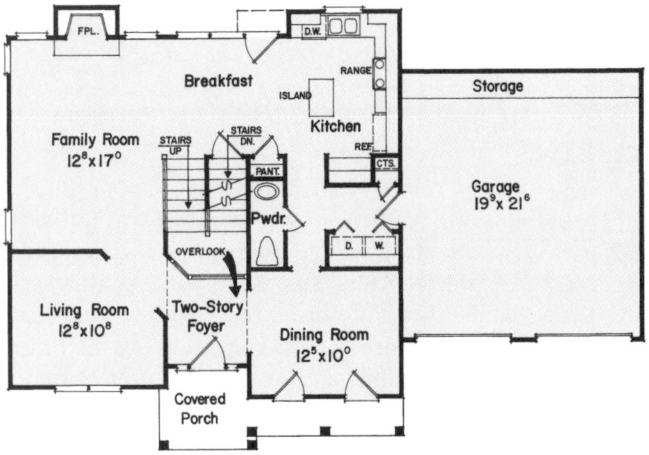

Design

HPT830191
First Floor: 926 square feet
Second Floor: 824 square feet
Total: 1,750 square feet
Width 53'-0" Depth 35'-10"

This charming home goes to great lengths to please the homeowner with a busy family. With formal dining and living rooms traditionally located to the front of the plan, the large family room and kitchen are the focus of casual living. Highlights include a grand fireplace, breakfast nook and a prep island in the kitchen. Upstairs, a lovely master suite with a vaulted bath and large walk-in closet is balanced by two family bedrooms and a full hall bath. Note the optional bonus room layout on this floor. Please specify basement, crawlspace or slab foundation when ordering.

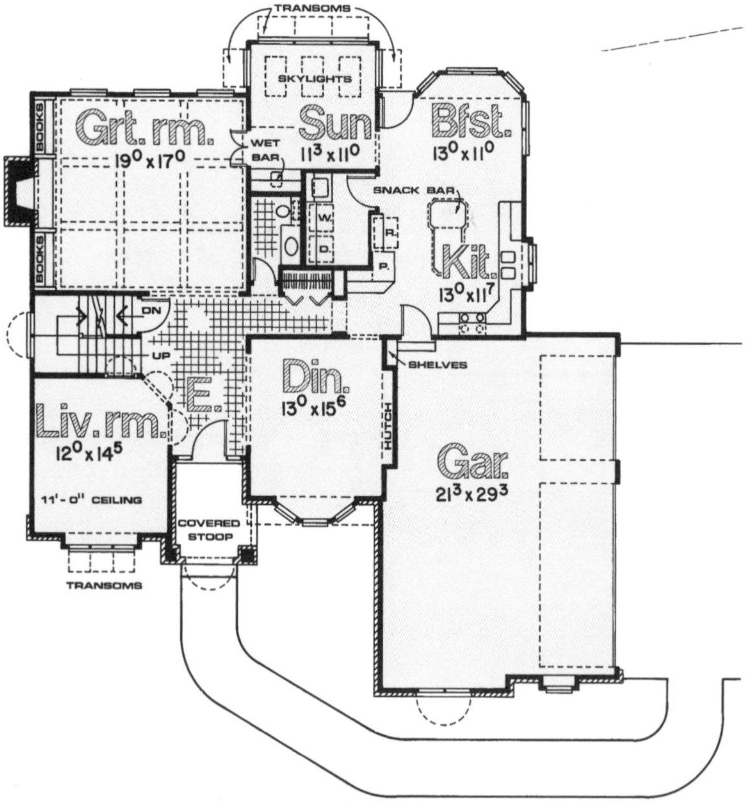

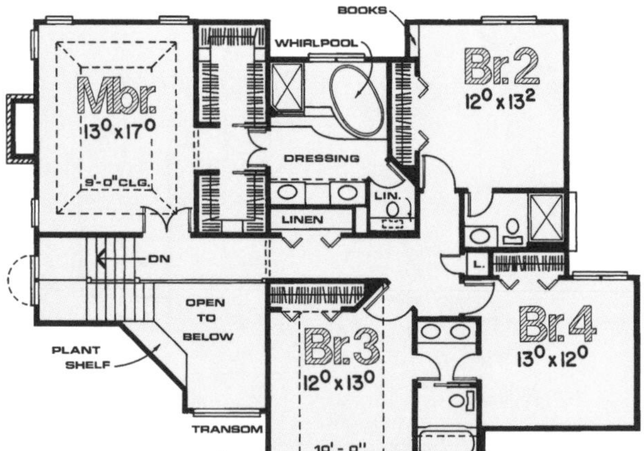

Design
HPT830192

First Floor: 1,520 square feet
Second Floor: 1,334 square feet
Total: 2,854 square feet
Width 53'-4" Depth 56'-8"

This stunning two-story home features an enormous great room with a spider-beam ceiling, built-in bookcases and a fireplace; it connects directly to the sun room with its attached wet bar. This skylit area leads to the breakfast room and island kitchen. Complementing these informal gathering areas are the formal living room and dining room. A luxurious master suite features His and Hers walk-in closets and a dressing area with an angled, oval whirlpool tub. Generous bath arrangements are made for the three secondary bedrooms.

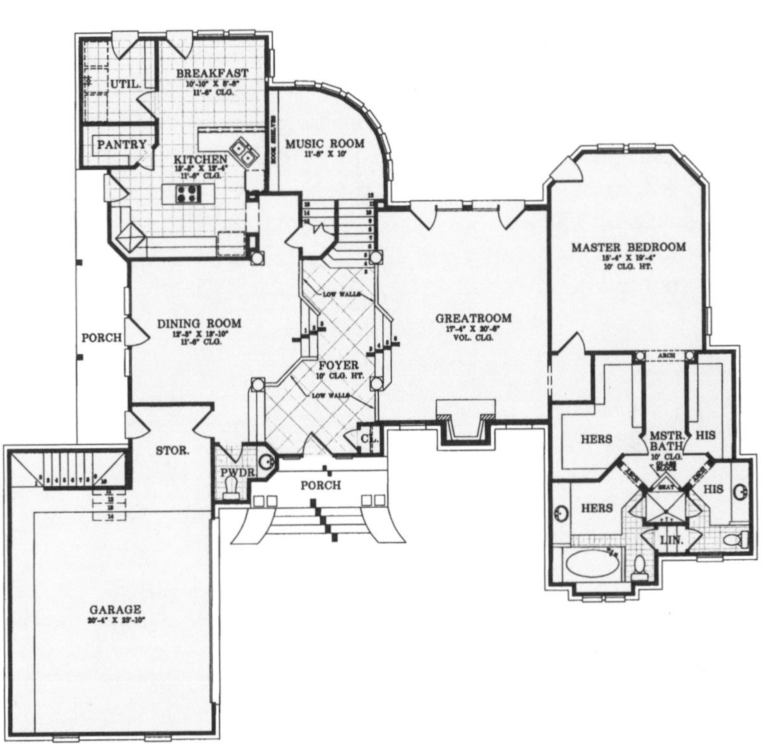

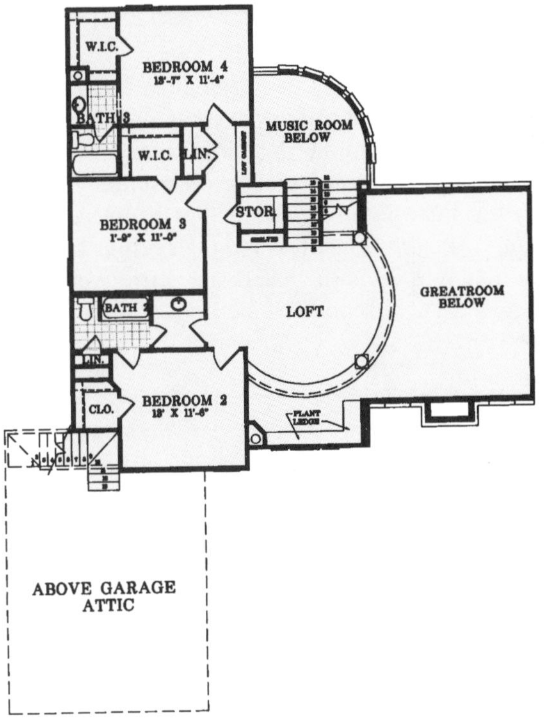

Design HPT830193

First Floor: 2,270 square feet
Second Floor: 1,100 square feet
Total: 3,370 square feet
Width 76'-6" Depth 69'-4"
L

A combination of stacked stone, brick and wood siding makes this home a real beauty from the curb. The foyer steps up to a large great room with a view to the rear grounds. On the other side, steps lead down to the dining room with access to a side porch. The master suite includes a fabulous master bath—really two baths in one—with a His and Hers dressing area and a shared shower. At the half-landing, curved windows frame a traditional music room. Continuing up the stairs, a large circular loft overlooks the great room and leads to three bedrooms and two baths.

From the cozy front porch to the multitude of windows, the enhancements that this home contains are impressive. Formal living and dining areas combine to allow entertainment flexibility. The well-organized kitchen is open to a bayed breakfast area with back yard access and also leads to the huge family room with a fireplace. A private den is located off the entry. The master suite has a high ceiling and a large walk-in closet. The pampering master bath boasts a luxurious sunlit whirlpool tub with separate shower. Three secondary bedrooms share a large, compartmented bath.

Design HPT830194

First Floor: 1,273 square feet
Second Floor: 1,035 square feet
Total: 2,308 square feet
Width 52'-0" Depth 40'-0"

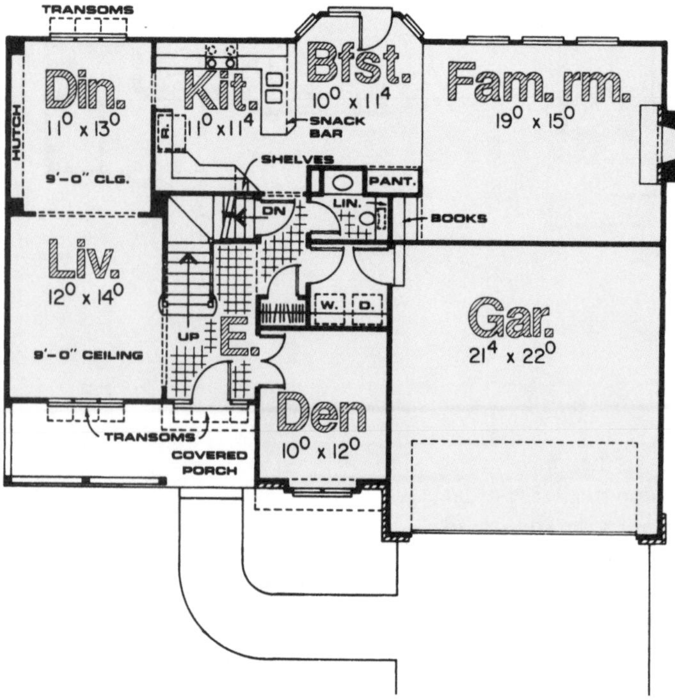

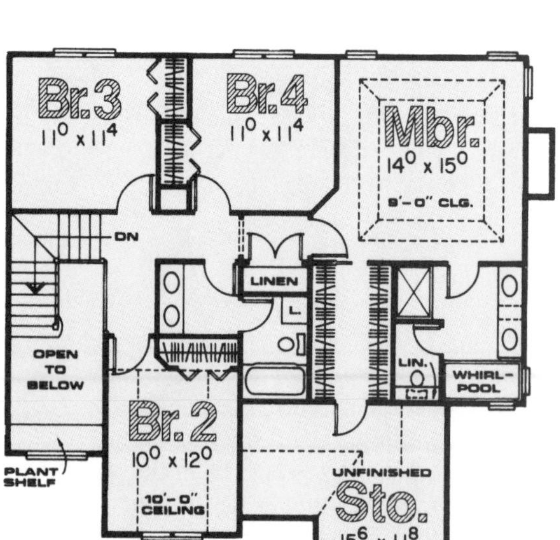

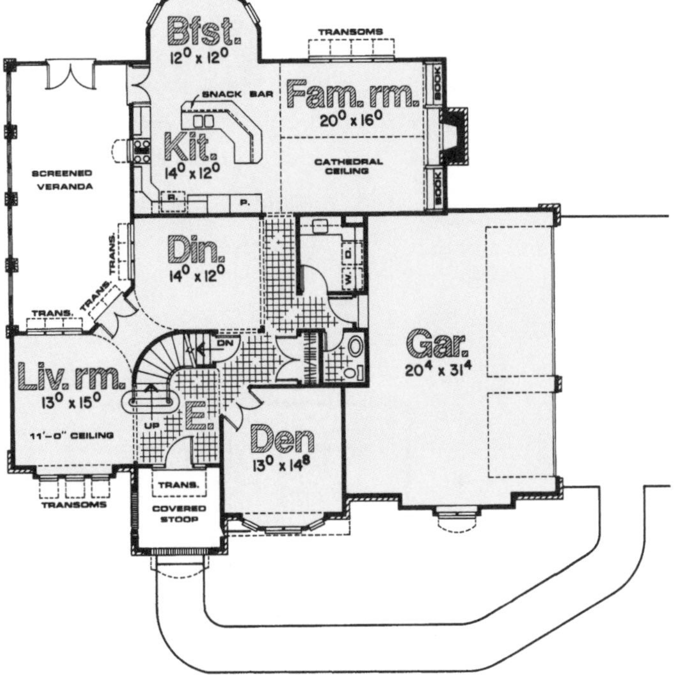

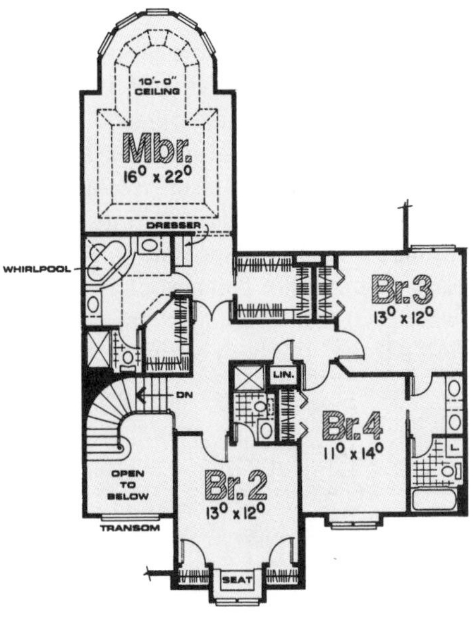

Stucco accents and graceful window treatments enhance the facade of this elegant two-story home. Inside, the two-story foyer is flanked by a formal living room on the left and a bay-windowed den on the right. The large, efficient kitchen easily serves a beautiful breakfast room and a comfortable family room. Note the cathedral ceiling, transom windows, built-in bookcases and warming fireplace in the family room. Upstairs, two secondary bedrooms share a full bath while a third has its own and can be used as a guest suite. The deluxe master suite is sure to please with its detailed ceiling, bayed sitting area, built-in dresser, two walk-in closets and luxurious bath.

Design
HPT830195

First Floor: 1,631 square feet

Second Floor: 1,426 square feet

Total: 3,057 square feet

Width 60'-0" Depth 58'-0"

This delightful plan offers the best in transitional design. Combined dining and living areas provide abundant space for formal entertaining or holiday gatherings. Or if preferred, escape to the den for quiet time with a book—built-in bookshelves fill out one wall of this room. The kitchen makes use of island counter space and the breakfast nook. Take a step down into the large family room and enjoy the ambience of a cozy fireplace and the beam ceiling. A laundry room and powder room round out the first floor. The master suite—with a tiered ceiling and a bath with a whirlpool tub—highlights the second floor. Three additional bedrooms and another full bath complete the design.

Design
HPT830196

First Floor: 1,369 square feet
Second Floor: 1,111 square feet
Total: 2,480 square feet
Width 64'-0" Depth 46'-0"

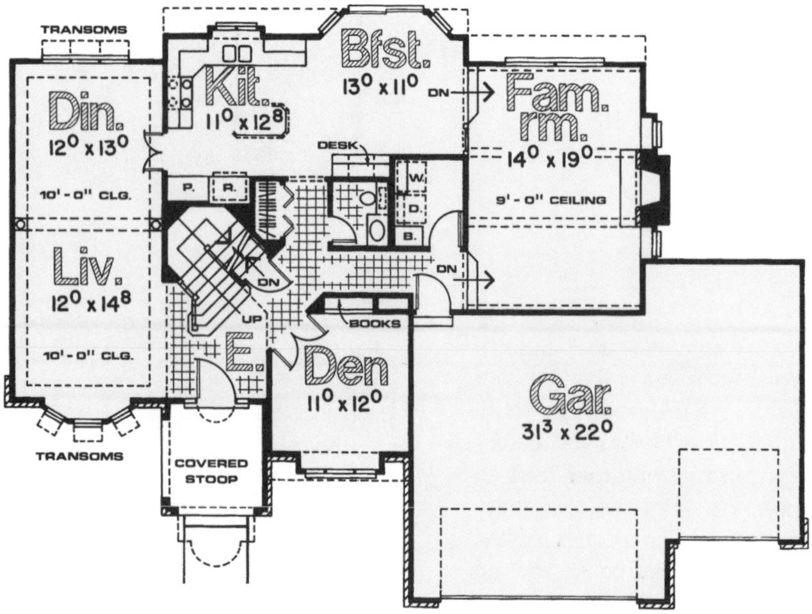

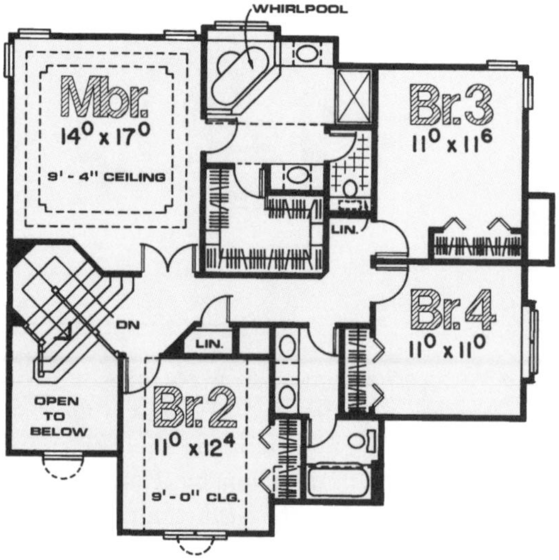

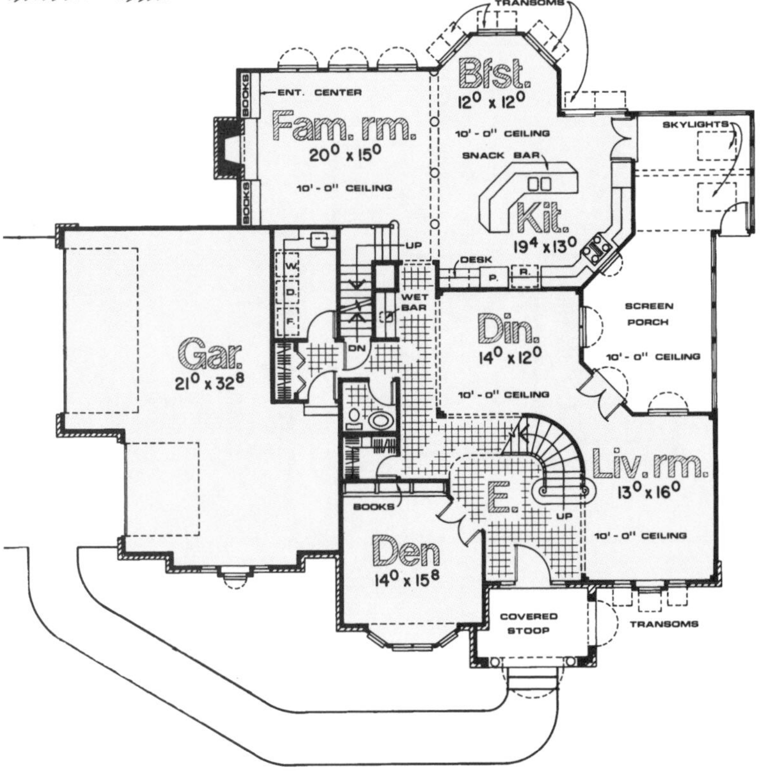

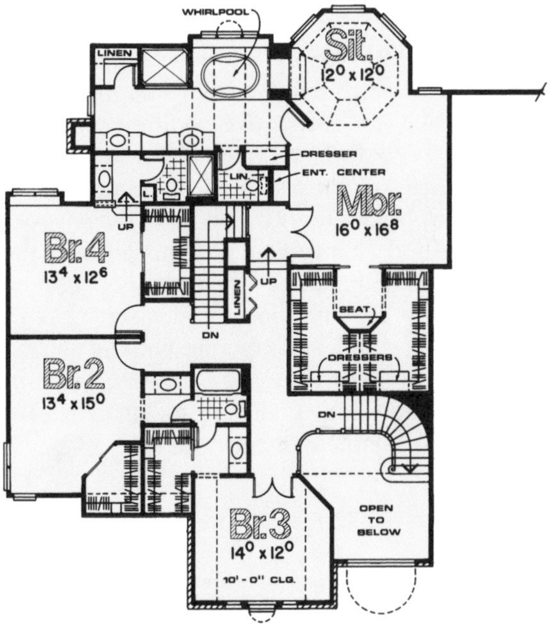

Breathtaking details and bright windows highlight this luxurious two-story home. Just off the spectacular entry is an impressive private den. The curved hall between the living and dining rooms offers many formal entertaining options. In the family room, three arched windows, a built-in entertainment center and a fireplace flanked by bookcases enhance daily comfort. On the second floor, four large bedrooms surround a balcony overlook. The three secondary bedrooms have generous closet space and private access to a bath. A sumptuous master suite awaits the homeowners with its built-in entertainment center and His and Hers walk-in closets.

Design
HPT830197

First Floor: 1,923 square feet
Second Floor: 1,852 square feet
Total: 3,775 square feet
Width 70'-0" Depth 60'-0"

Put a little luxury into your life with this fine brick home. A great room with a fireplace and expansive windows provides the perfect spot for gatherings of all sorts. A large study nearby creates a quiet environment for working at home. The kitchen has a large cooktop island and a convenient walk-in pantry. In the dining room, bumped-out windows shed light on entertaining. The first-floor master suite has its own fireplace and a pampering bath. A second bedroom with a private bath is nearby. Upstairs, two more bedrooms, a full bath and an expansive game room complete the plan.

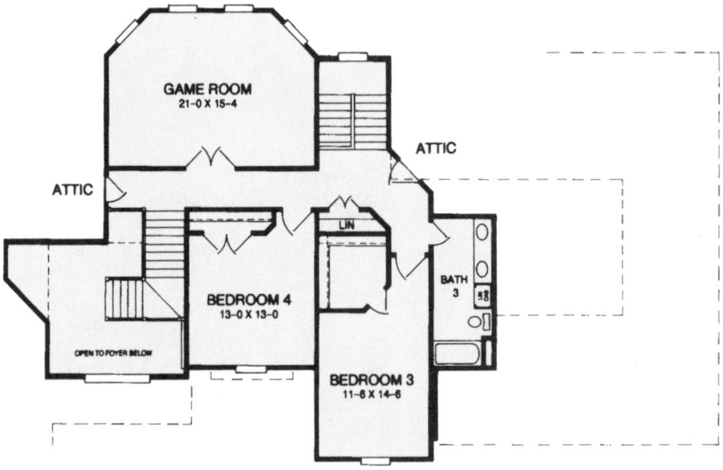

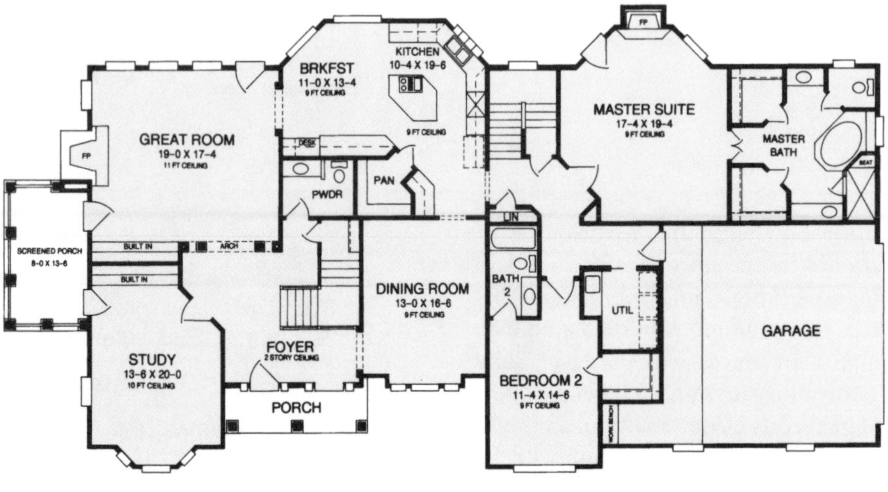

Design HPT830198

First Floor: 2,648 square feet

Second Floor: 1,102 square feet

Total: 3,750 square feet

Width 91'-6" Depth 46'-10"

L

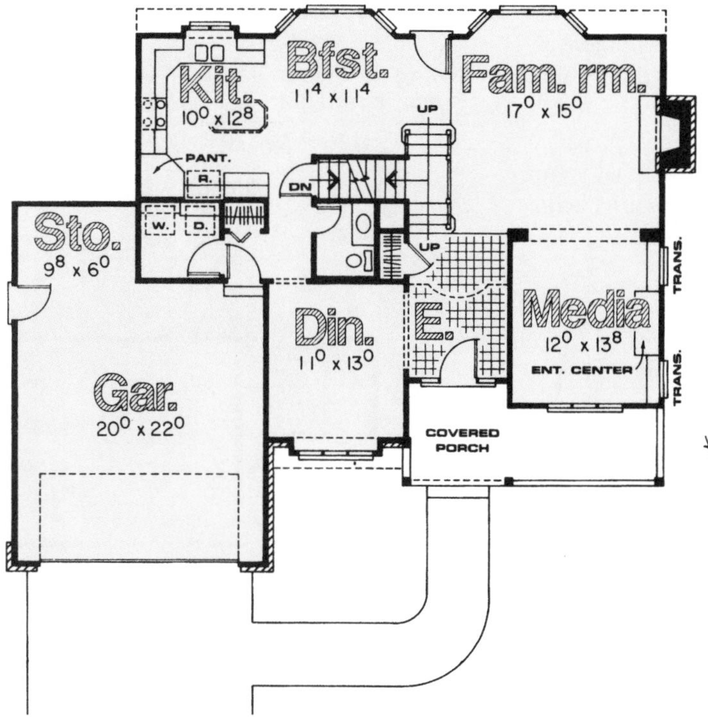

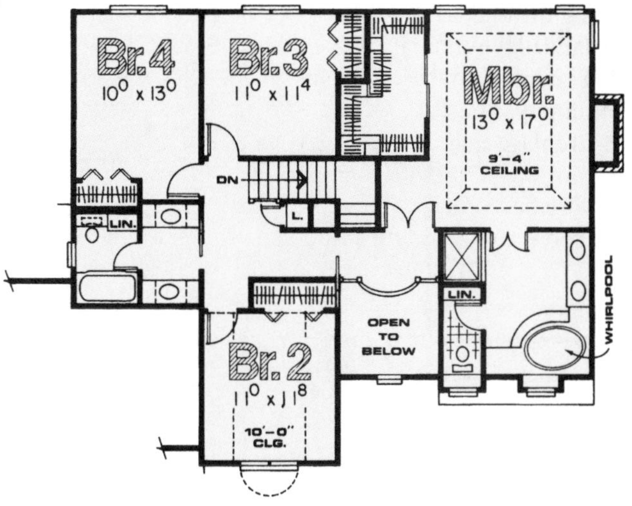

Country charm is found in this home's cozy front porch and bright windows. A media room with a built-in entertainment center is just off the bay-windowed family room. The oversized kitchen has a prep island and spacious breakfast nook. Upstairs, three family bedrooms share a compartmented bath with twin vanities. Elegant French doors lead into the luxurious master suite, which is finished with a corner whirlpool, compartmented toilet and walk-in closet.

Design HPT830199

First Floor: 1,206 square feet
Second Floor: 1,171 square feet
Total: 2,377 square feet
Width 52'-8" Depth 44'-0"

The detailed front porch, attractive chimney, and multiple rooflines all work together to create the pleasing exterior of this home. The floor plan opens with a central foyer flanked by the dining and great rooms. The dining room includes a formal tiered ceiling and hutch space. The great room, with a fireplace and a ten-foot ceiling, provides multi-purpose living space. An ample kitchen includes a breakfast room with a bay window. The highlight of the four-bedroom sleeping area is the master suite with its elegant vaulted ceiling and skylit whirlpool.

Design

HPT830200

First Floor: 1,132 square feet
Second Floor: 1,087 square feet
Total: 2,219 square feet
Width 54'-0" Depth 44'-0"

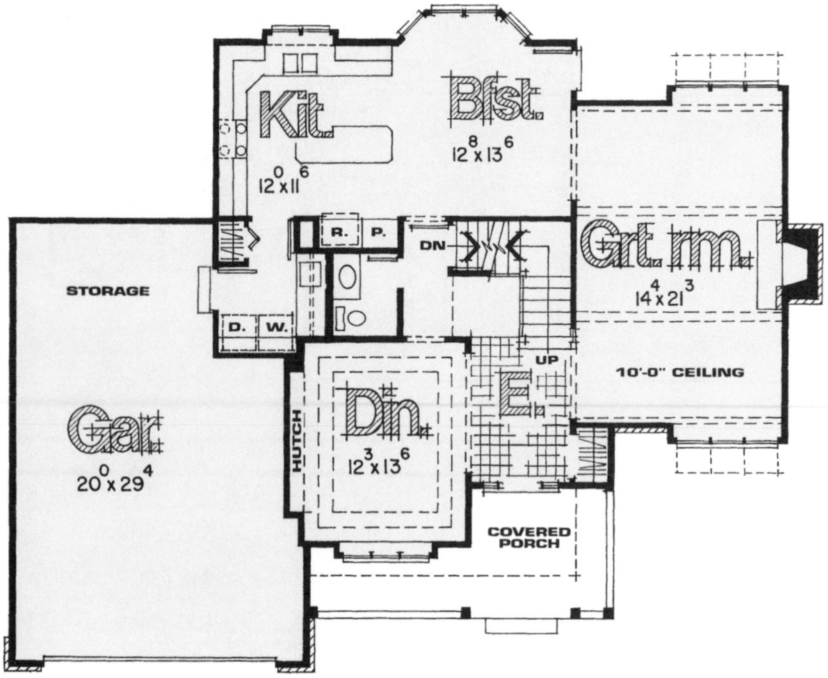

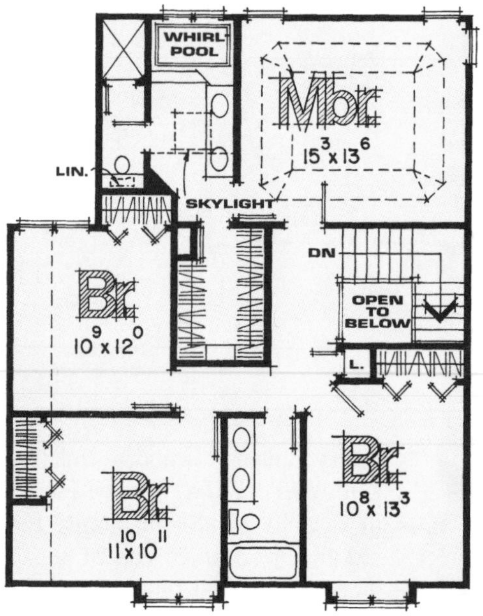

The beautifully proportioned design is complemented by a large covered porch framed with a wood railing. The living room is enhanced by a bay window and French doors leading to the family room. The dining room is accented by a built-in curio cabinet and is convenient to the spacious kitchen with a cooktop island and bayed breakfast nook. Upstairs, the master bedroom contains a distinctive vaulted ceiling plus a luxurious bath with a corner whirlpool tub and a large walk-in closet. Three family bedrooms share a compartmented hall bath.

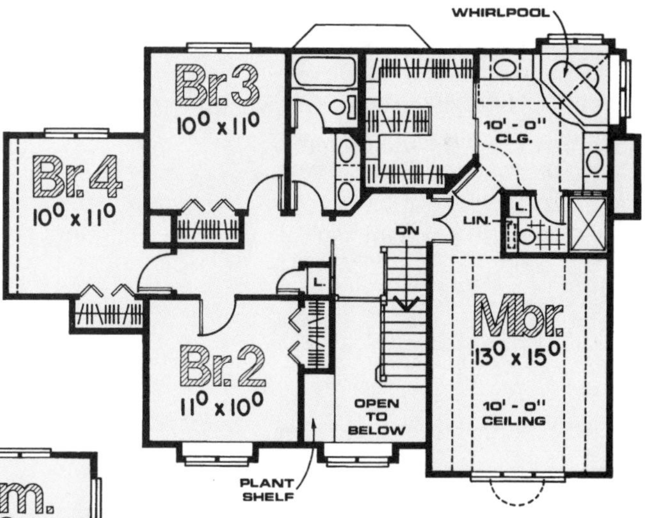

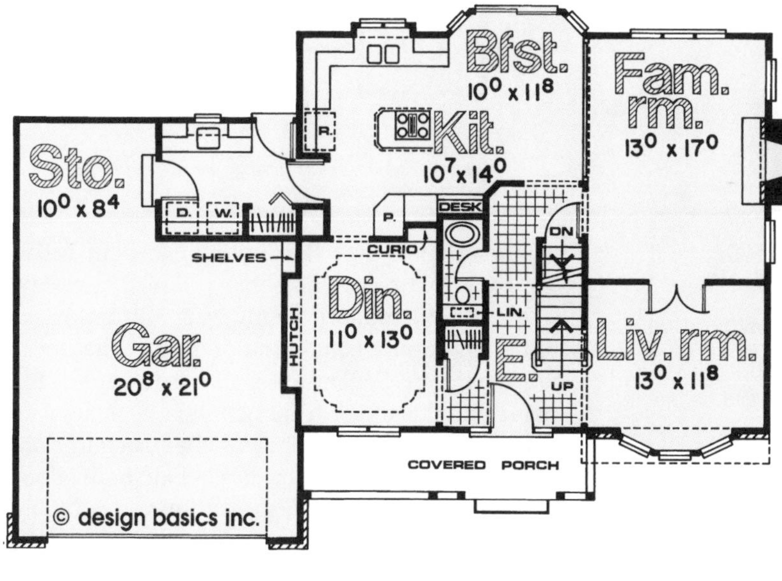

Design HPT830201

First Floor: 1,093 square feet
Second Floor: 1,038 square feet
Total: 2,131 square feet
Width 55'-4" Depth 37'-8"

This home, as shown in the photograph, may differ from the actual blueprints. For more detailed information, please check the floor plans carefully.
Photo by Alan Mascord Design Associates, Inc. ©2003

Design
HPT830202

First Floor: 1,465 square feet
Second Floor: 1,103 square feet
Total: 2,568 square feet
Bonus Space: 303 square feet
Width 63'-0" Depth 48'-0"
L

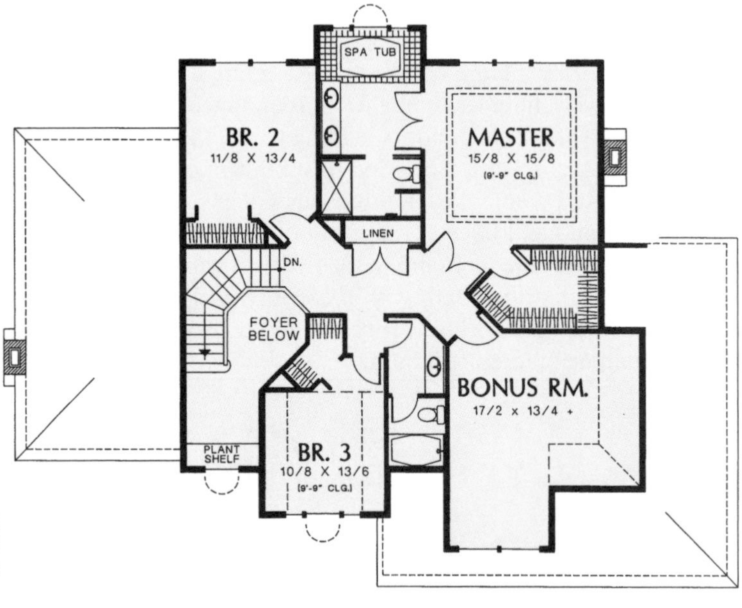

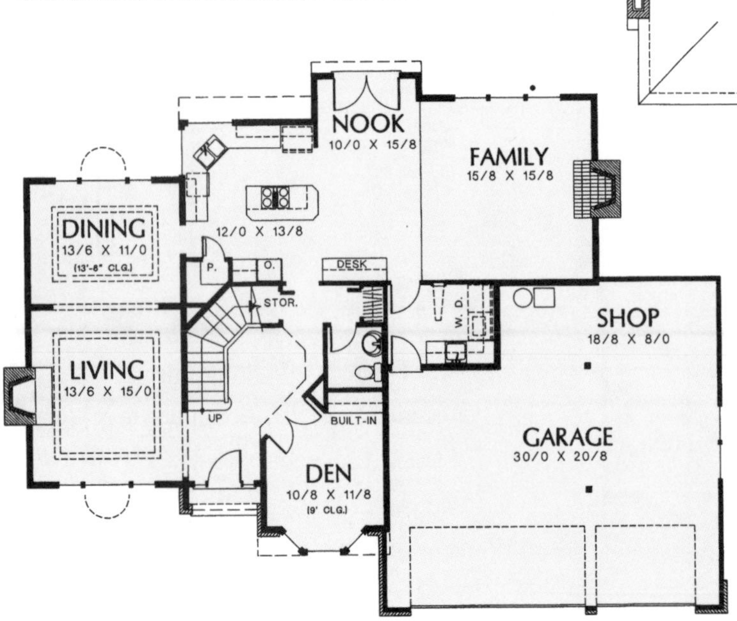

With a plan that boasts excellent traffic patterns, this home will accommodate the modern family well. Formal dining and living rooms remain to one side of the house and create an elegant atmosphere for entertaining. Highlights of the front den include a bay window and built-in bookshelves. Two second-floor family bedrooms share a large hall bath along with a bonus room. The spacious master suite has a walk-in closet and luxurious spa bath.

Design HPT830203

First Floor: 2,764 square feet
Second Floor: 1,598 square feet
Total: 4,362 square feet
Width 74'-6" Depth 65'-10"

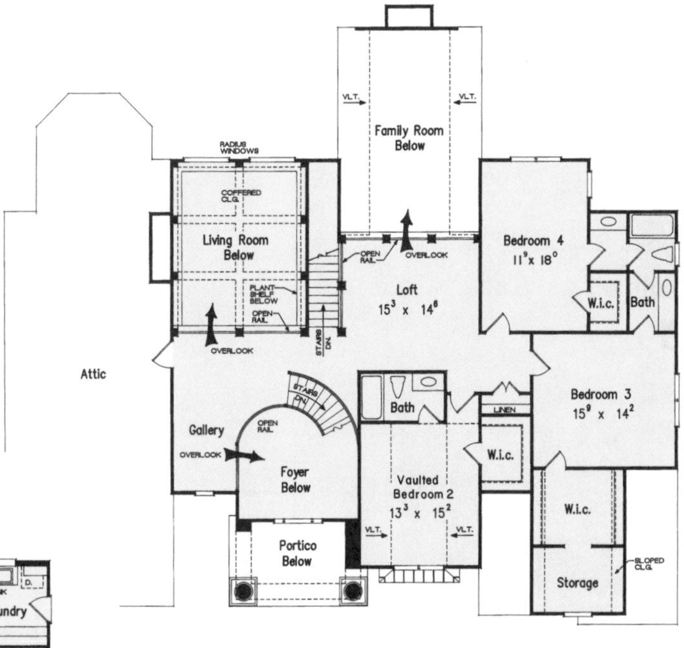

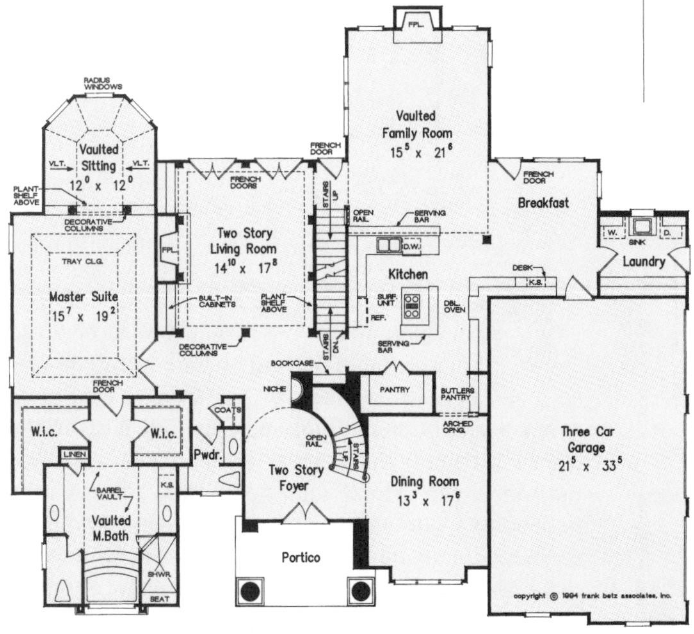

The heart of this magnificent design is the two-story grand room with its fireplace and built-in bookshelves. The private master wing features a secluded study, bayed sitting area and vaulted bath. Upstairs, Bedrooms 3 and 4 each include a built-in desk. Please specify basement or crawlspace foundation when ordering.

Design

HPT830204
First Floor: 1,755 square feet
Second Floor: 2,275 square feet
Total: 4,030 square feet
Width 74'-0" Depth 63'-4"

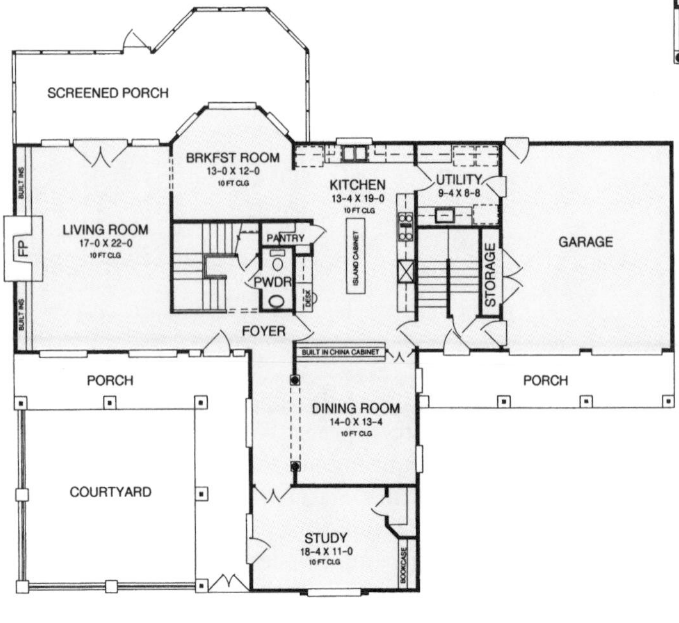

This is classic charming Southern design. The plan opens from a courtyard with covered porch to the main body of the house as well as a self-contained study at the front. The dining room has a built-in china cabinet and is near the island kitchen. The formal living room also has built-ins and a private screened porch. Three family bedrooms—one with a private bath—and the master suite are upstairs. There is also a game room with cathedral ceiling over the garage. Please specify crawlspace or slab foundation when ordering.

The facade of this home is a super prelude to an equally impressive interior. The front porch provides entry to a sleeping level, with the master suite on the right and a secondary bedroom on the left. Upstairs, living areas include a family room with a sitting alcove and a living room with special ceiling treatment. The kitchen serves a breakfast room as well as a barrel-vaulted dining room. A third bedroom and two balconies further the custom nature of this home. On the third floor, an observation room with outdoor access is an extra-special touch. Please specify crawlspace or slab foundation when ordering.

Design HPT830205

First Floor: 1,158 square feet
Second Floor: 1,773 square feet
Total: 2,931 square feet
Observation Room: 173 square feet
Width 39'-10" Depth 58'-11"

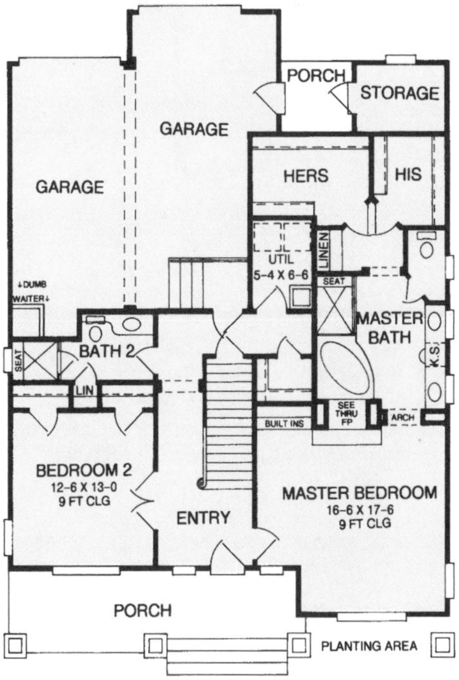

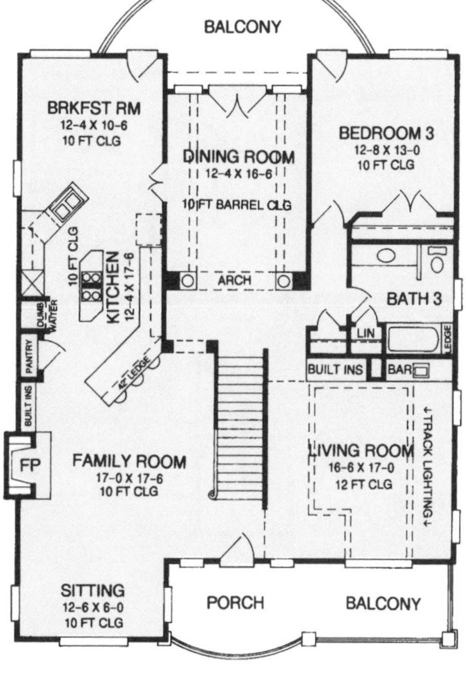

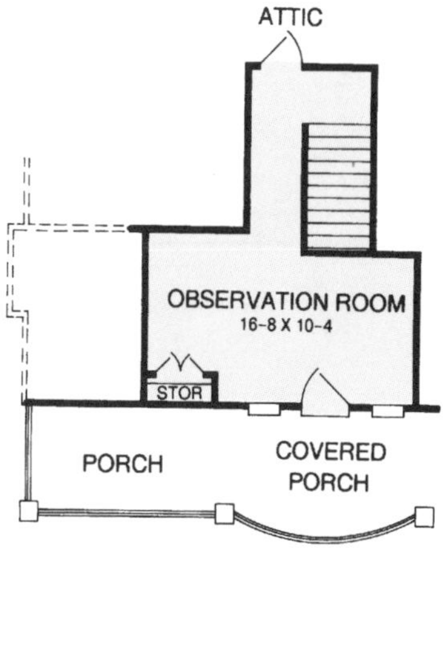

This charming cottage-style home features sweeping rooflines. Inside, a two-story foyer opens through a large arch to the living room with another arch defining the dining room. A see-through fireplace is located between the living room and the breakfast area. The master bedroom, with a sitting area and luxury bath, is located at the right-rear of the house. Bedroom 2 and a full bath are located nearby. Two family bedrooms reside upstairs.

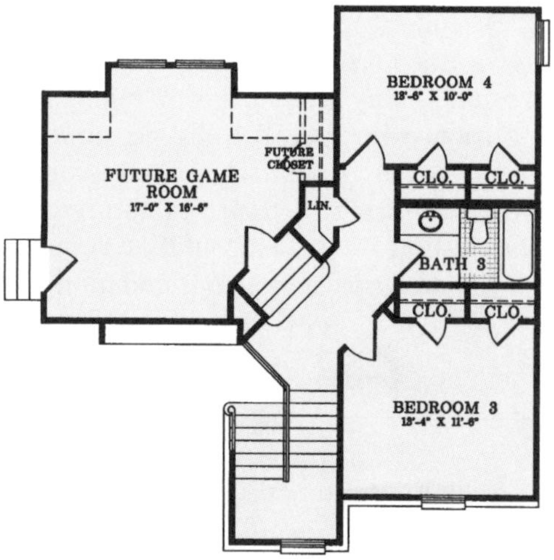

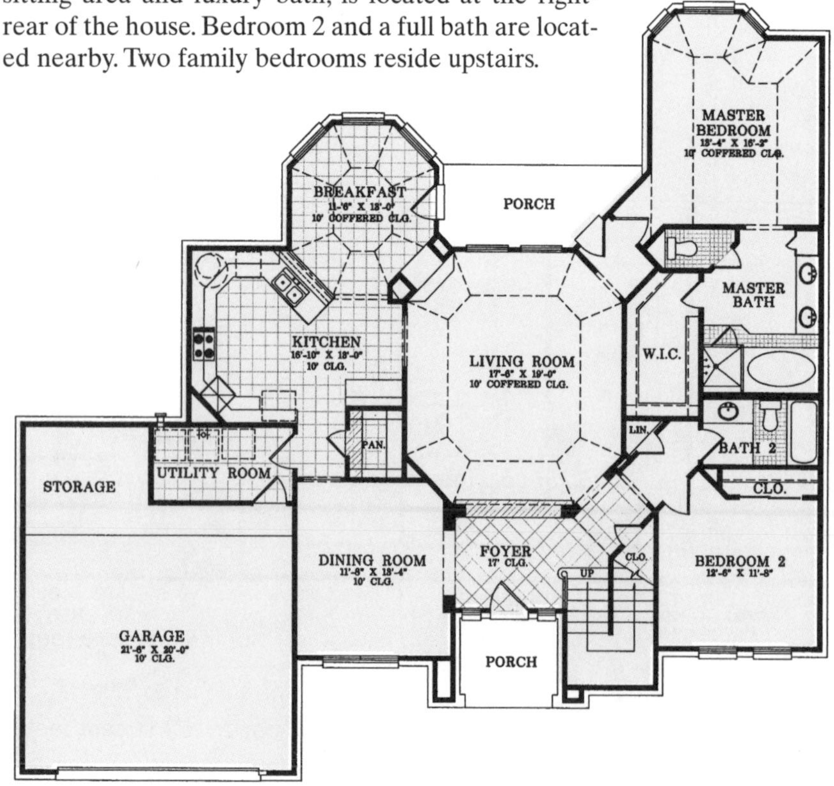

Design HPT830206

First Floor: 1,934 square feet
Second Floor: 528 square feet
Total: 2,462 square feet
Bonus Space: 279 square feet
Width 64'-10" Depth 59'-8"
L

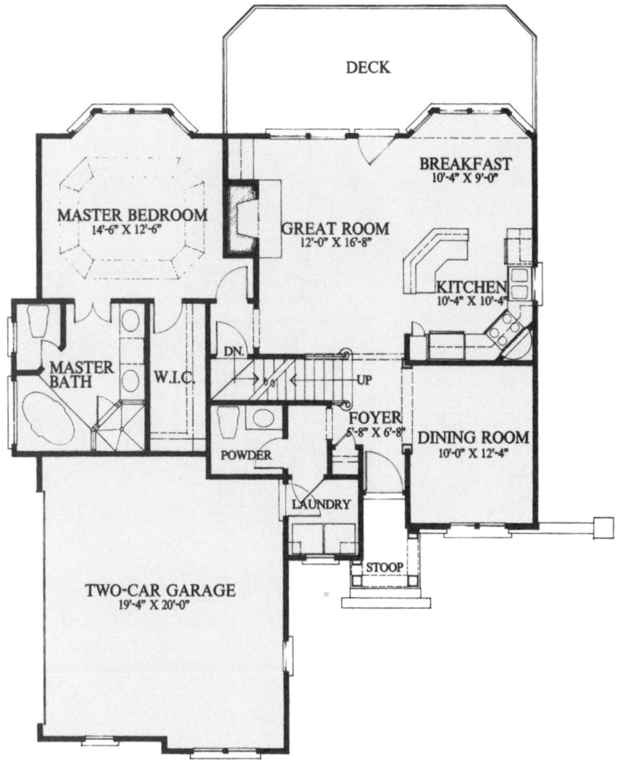
DECK
BREAKFAST
10'-4" X 9'-0"
MASTER BEDROOM
14'-6" X 12'-6"
GREAT ROOM
12'-0" X 16'-8"
KITCHEN
10'-4" X 10'-4"
DN.
UP
MASTER BATH
W.I.C.
FOYER
5'-8" X 6'-8"
DINING ROOM
10'-0" X 12'-4"
POWDER
LAUNDRY
STOOP
TWO-CAR GARAGE
19'-4" X 20'-0"

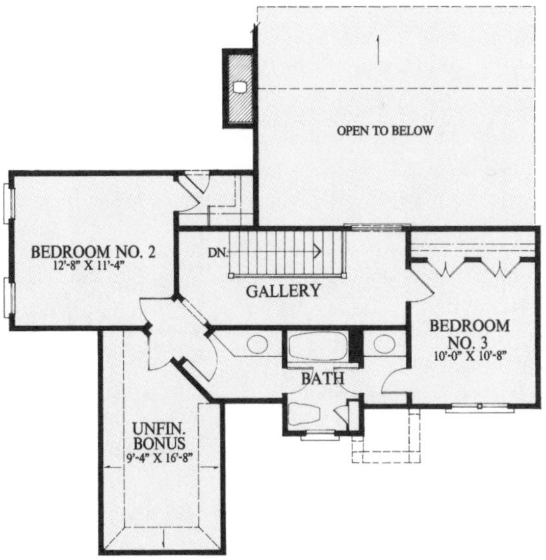
OPEN TO BELOW
BEDROOM NO. 2
12'-8" X 11'-4"
DN.
GALLERY
BEDROOM NO. 3
10'-0" X 10'-8"
BATH
UNFIN. BONUS
9'-4" X 16'-8"

A combination of materials and shapes is reminiscent of an English country home. Beyond the columned entry is a classic raised foyer that leads to a sunken dining room and great room. The openness of the plan is evident in the kitchen and breakfast areas. The master bedroom boasts a tray ceiling, fireplace and bay window. The open gallery staircase overlooks the great room and provides entry to two more bedrooms as well as an unfinished bonus room. This home is designed with a walkout basement foundation.

Design HPT830207

First Floor: 1,225 square feet
Second Floor: 565 square feet
Total: 1,790 square feet
Bonus Space: 158 square feet
Width 42'-0" Depth 50'-0"

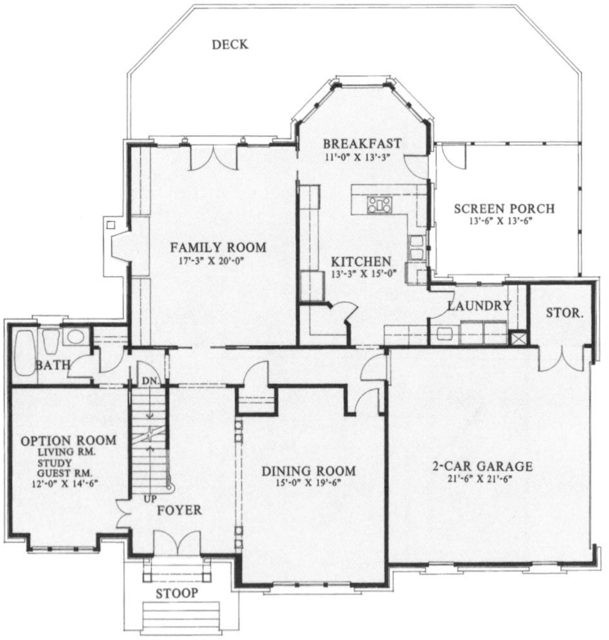
DECK
BREAKFAST
11'-0" X 13'-3"
SCREEN PORCH
13'-6" X 13'-6"
FAMILY ROOM
17'-3" X 20'-0"
KITCHEN
13'-3" X 15'-0"
LAUNDRY
STOR.
BATH
DN.
OPTION ROOM
LIVING RM.
STUDY
GUEST RM.
12'-0" X 14'-6"
DINING ROOM
15'-0" X 19'-6"
2-CAR GARAGE
21'-6" X 21'-6"
UP
FOYER
STOOP

MASTER BATH
MASTER SUITE
17'-3" X 20'-0"
W.I.C.
DN.
OPEN TO BELOW
BATH
BEDROOM NO. 3
12'-0" X 17'-6"
W.I.C.
W.I.C.
BEDROOM NO. 2
13'-6" X 15'-3"

Many generously sized, shuttered windows flood this stunning home with the clear, warming light of outdoors—captivating with its classic styling. The two-story foyer with its tray ceiling makes a dramatic entrance. To the right, a banquet-sized dining room offers space for a buffet, while the large kitchen allows easy access to the bay-windowed breakfast room. To the left is a versatile room that can serve as a living room, study or guest room. Beyond the foyer is the great room, which sports a cheerful fireplace flanked by bookcases. An open-railed stairway leads to three bedrooms on the second floor. The exquisite master suite is truly a room to live in, with its stylish tray ceiling and warming fireplace. Its elegance is intensified right down to the bay window and huge walk-in closet with a built-in dressing table. This home is designed with a walkout basement foundation.

Design

HPT830208

First Floor: 1,710 square feet

Second Floor: 1,470 square feet

Total: 3,180 square feet

Width 61'-6" Depth 50'-6"

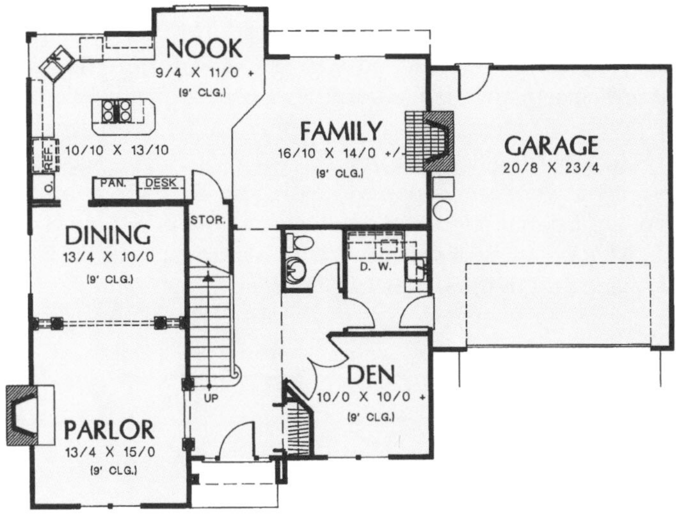
NOOK
9/4 X 11/0 +
(9' CLG.)
10/10 X 13/10
REF.
PAN.
DESK
FAMILY
16/10 X 14/0 +/-
(9' CLG.)
GARAGE
20/8 X 23/4
DINING
13/4 X 10/0
(9' CLG.)
STOR.
D. W.
UP
DEN
10/0 X 10/0 +
(9' CLG.)
PARLOR
13/4 X 15/0
(9' CLG.)

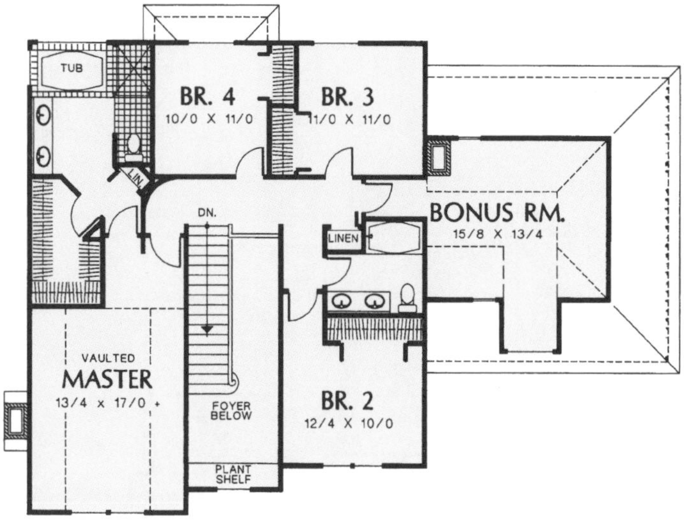
TUB
BR. 4
10/0 X 11/0
BR. 3
11/0 X 11/0
LIN.
DN.
LINEN
BONUS RM.
15/8 X 13/4
VAULTED
MASTER
13/4 x 17/0 +
FOYER
BELOW
BR. 2
12/4 X 10/0
PLANT
SHELF

Design
HPT830209

First Floor: 1,308 square feet

Second Floor: 1,141 square feet

Total: 2,449 square feet

Bonus Space: 266 square feet

Width 56'-0" Depth 42'-0"

L

Quietly stated elegance is the key to this home's attraction. Its floor plan allows plenty of space for formal and informal occasions. The rear of the first floor is devoted to an open area serving as family room, breakfast nook and island kitchen. This area is complemented by a formal parlor and dining room. A private den could function as a guest room with the handy powder room nearby. There are four bedrooms on the second floor. Bonus room over the garage could become an additional bedroom or study.

This home, as shown in the photograph, may differ from the actual blueprints. For more detailed information, please check the floor plans carefully.
Photo by Peter Loppacher

Design
HPT830210

First Floor: 1,966 square feet	
Second Floor: 872 square feet	
Total: 2,838 square feet	
Width 63'-10"	Depth 79'-10"

This elegant two-story brick home, with its corner quoins, varied rooflines and multi-pane windows has so many amenities to offer! Enter the two-story foyer graced by an elegant curved staircase. The formal dining room, defined by columns, sits to the right and accesses the efficient island kitchen through double doors. The large great room is enhanced by direct access to the rear patio and a warming fireplace. The first-floor master suite is secluded for privacy and contains a pampering spa-style bath, His and Her walk-in closets and a private covered porch. Upstairs, a balcony hall overlooking the great room leads to the three family bedrooms, two with walk-in closets. Please specify basement, crawlspace or slab foundation when ordering.

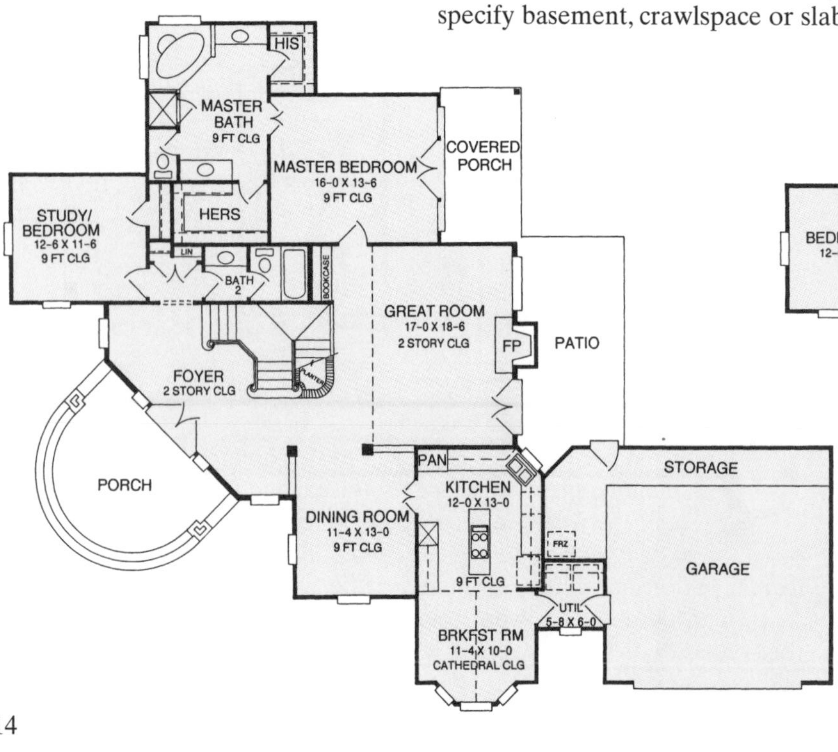

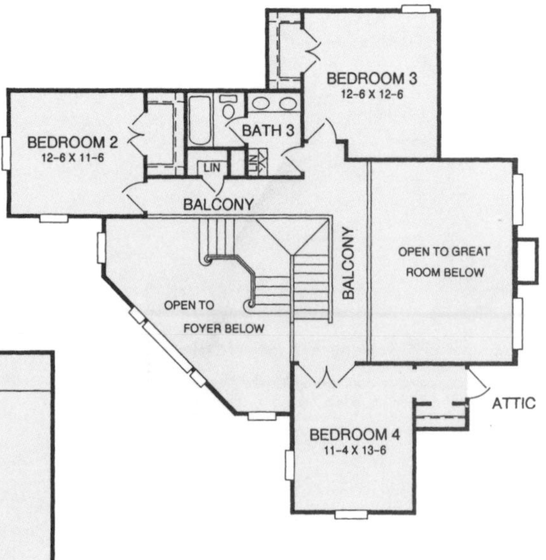

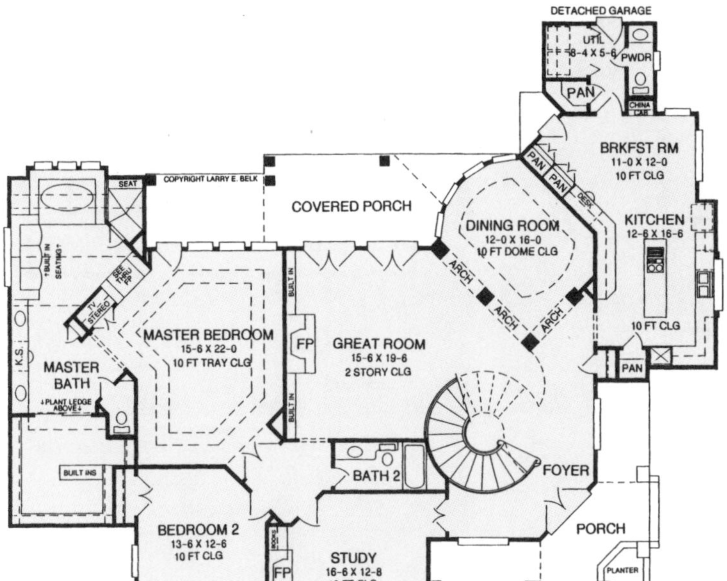

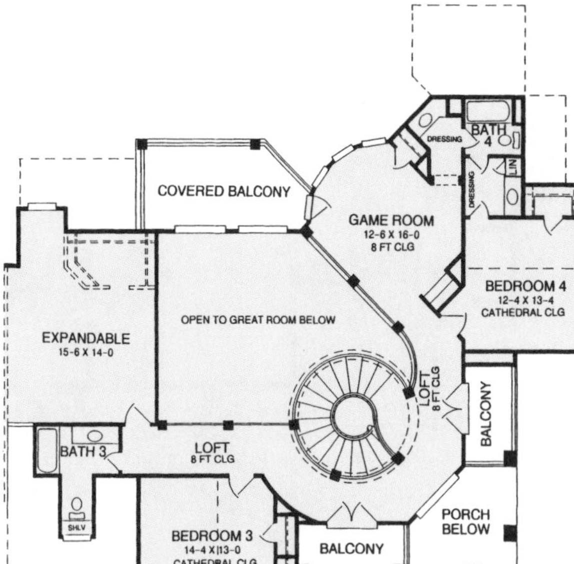

Design HPT830211

First Floor: 2,772 square feet
Second Floor: 933 square feet
Total: 3,705 square feet
Width 74'-8" Depth 61'-10"

A truly grand entry sets the elegant tone of this contemporary home. The foyer opens to a dramatic circular stair, then on to the two-story great room. The dining room is set off by a span of arches. The gourmet kitchen features wrapping counters, a cooktop island and a breakfast room. A huge master bedroom is complemented by a deluxe bath. Upstairs, a loft opens to two balconies and leads to two bedrooms and a game room. Please specify crawlspace or slab foundation when ordering.

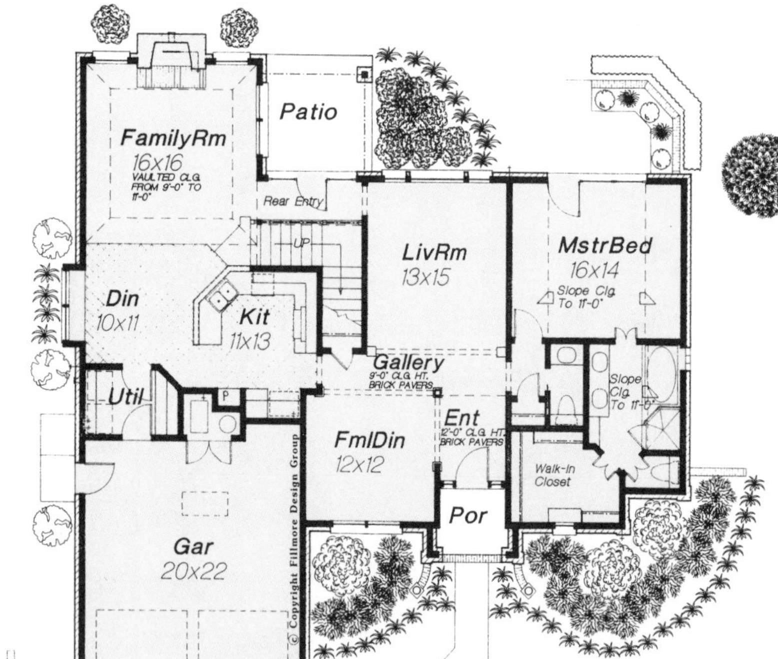

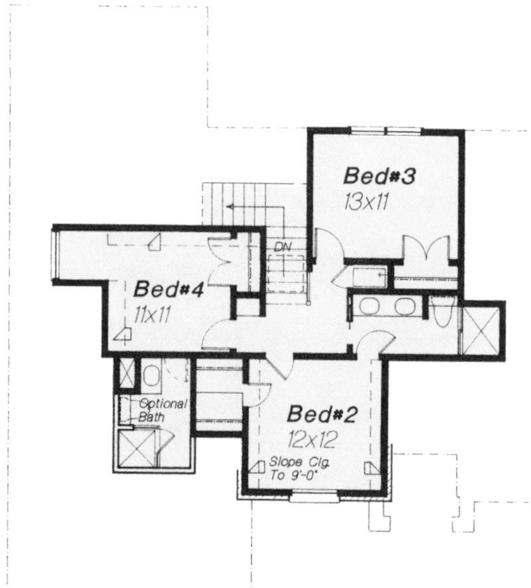

Design HPT830212

First Floor: 1,633 square feet
Second Floor: 629 square feet
Total: 2,262 square feet
Width 55'-0" Depth 55'-7"

High gables, a dramatic entry and corner quoins lend an extra dash of distinction to this fine traditional home. Formal and informal living areas are clearly defined. To the left of the entry you will find the formal dining room graced with columns, and straight ahead, the formal living room. Casual gatherings will be enjoyed in the family room, enhanced with a fireplace and open to the dinette and U-shaped kitchen. A sloped-ceiling master bedroom constitutes the right portion of the plan and accesses the backyard. Highlighting the private bath is a soothing tub, a separate shower and a large walk-in closet. A powder room and a utility room complete the first floor. Upstairs, three family bedrooms share a full bath, with space allocated for an additional bath when needed.

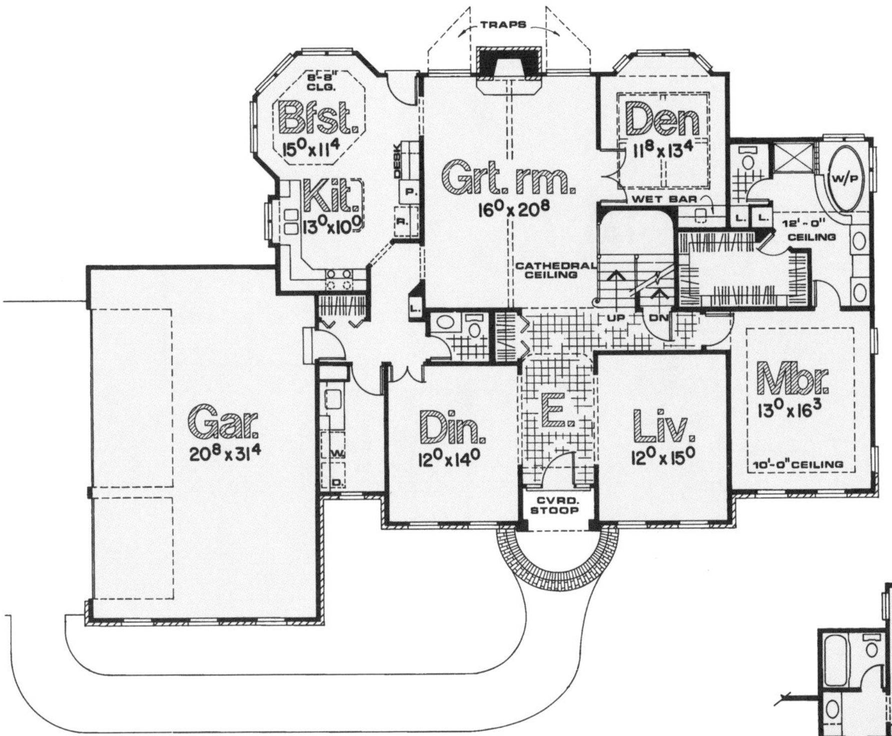

Design
HPT830213

First Floor: 2,063 square feet
Second Floor: 894 square feet
Total: 2,957 square feet
Width 72'-8" Depth 51'-4"

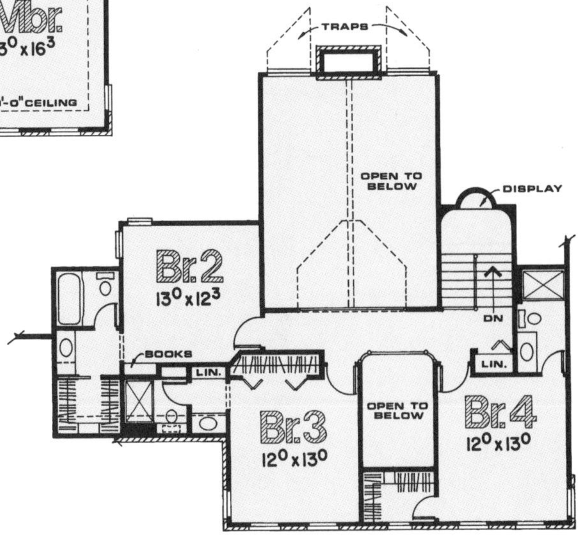

An elegant brick elevation and rows of shuttered windows lend timeless beauty to this two-story Colonial design. The volume entry opens to the formal dining and living rooms and the magnificent great room. Sparkling floor-to-ceiling windows flank the fireplace in the great room, which offers a cathedral ceiling. French doors, bay windows and a decorative ceiling, plus a wet bar, highlight the private den. Special lifestyle amenities in the kitchen and bayed breakfast area include a built-in desk, wrapping counters and an island. A boxed ceiling adds elegance to the master suite. Upstairs, each secondary bedroom contains a roomy closet and private bath.

QUOTE ONE®
Cost to build? See page 516 to order complete cost estimate to build this house in your area!

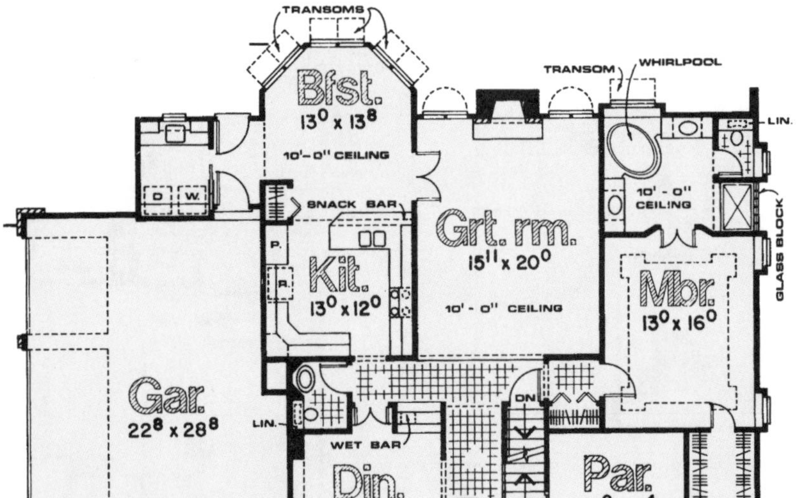

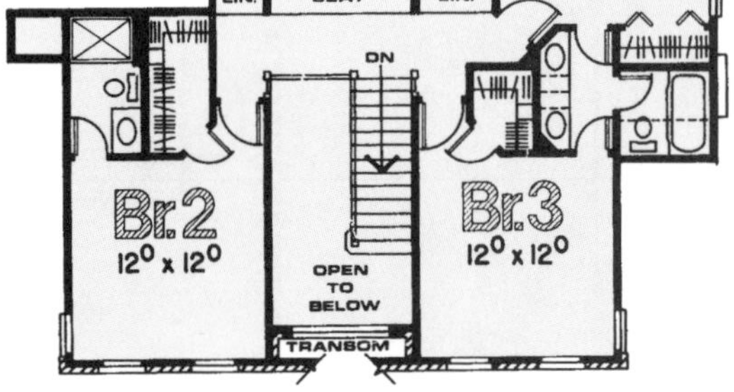

A magnificent brick facade with a three-car, side-loading garage conceals a well-organized floor plan. A tiled foyer leads to the formal dining room, with wet bar and hutch space, on the left and a parlor on the right. Straight ahead is a spacious great room with arched windows flanking a fireplace. The kitchen offers a snack bar and adjoins a bayed breakfast area. The first-floor master bedroom includes a large, walk-in closet and French doors leading to a master bath with angled whirlpool and a glass-block shower. The second floor provides three bedrooms and two full baths. A reading seat flanked by two cabinets overlooks the volume entry.

Design HPT830214

First Floor: 1,865 square feet

Second Floor: 774 square feet

Total: 2,639 square feet

Width 64'-0" Depth 47'-4"

An arched entry and a brick facade highlight the exterior of this two-story Colonial home. The dining room is served by a convenient passageway for quick kitchen service while bright windows and French doors add appeal to the living room. A relaxing family room has a bayed conversation area and a clear view through the dinette into the gourmet kitchen. Upstairs, a U-shaped hall offers separation to all four bedrooms. Homeowners will love the expansive master retreat. This oasis features a private sitting room, two walk-in closets, compartmented bath, separate vanities and a whirlpool tub.

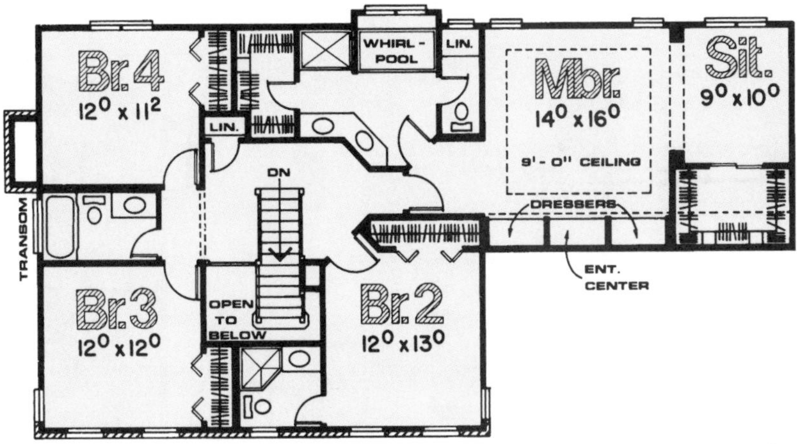

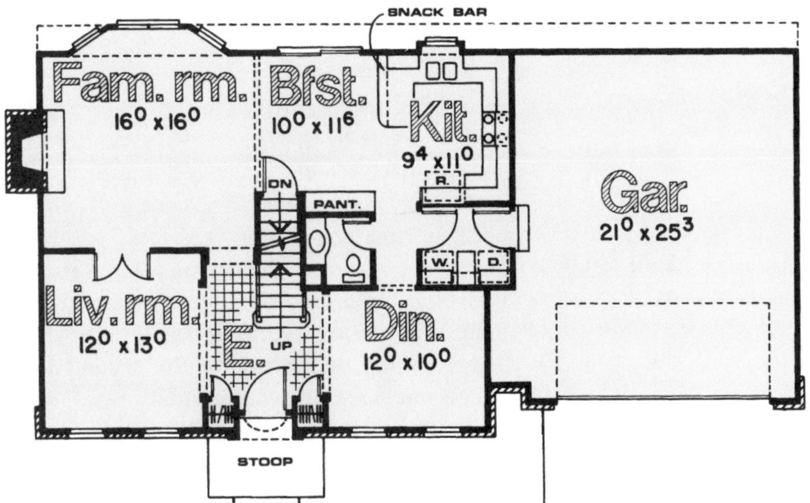

Design

HPT830215
First Floor: 1,000 square feet
Second Floor: 1,345 square feet
Total: 2,345 square feet
Width 57'-4" Depth 30'-0"

Design HPT830216

First Floor: 998 square feet
Second Floor: 1,206 square feet
Total: 2,204 square feet
Width 54'-0" Depth 34'-8"

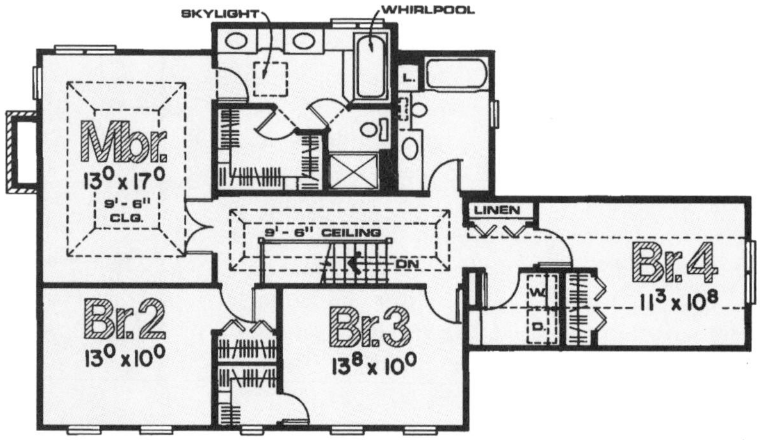

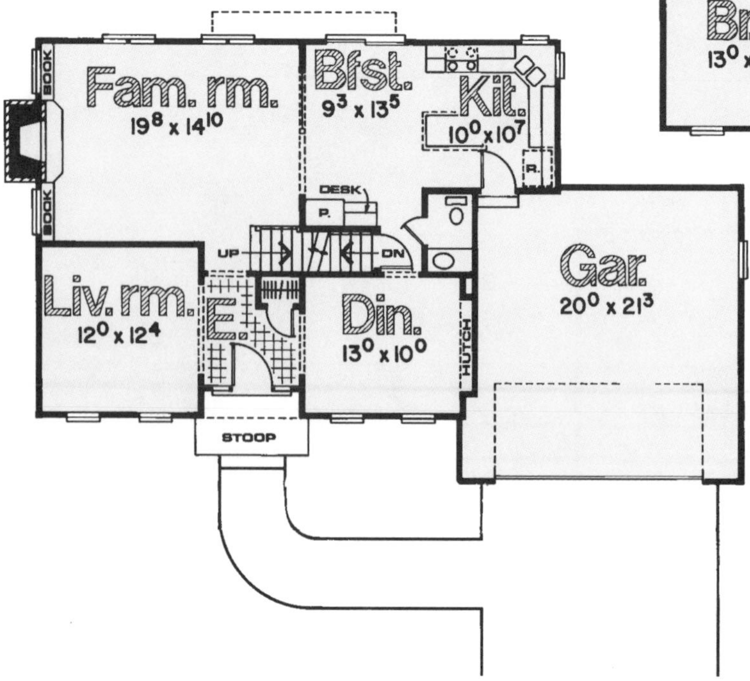

The bright entry of this two-story home opens to the formal living and dining space. To the back is the more informal family room with a fireplace and built-in bookshelves. The kitchen services the breakfast room as well as the dining area. A master bedroom with a deluxe private bath that includes a tub and separate shower is upstairs. Three family bedrooms on the second floor round out sleeping accommodations.

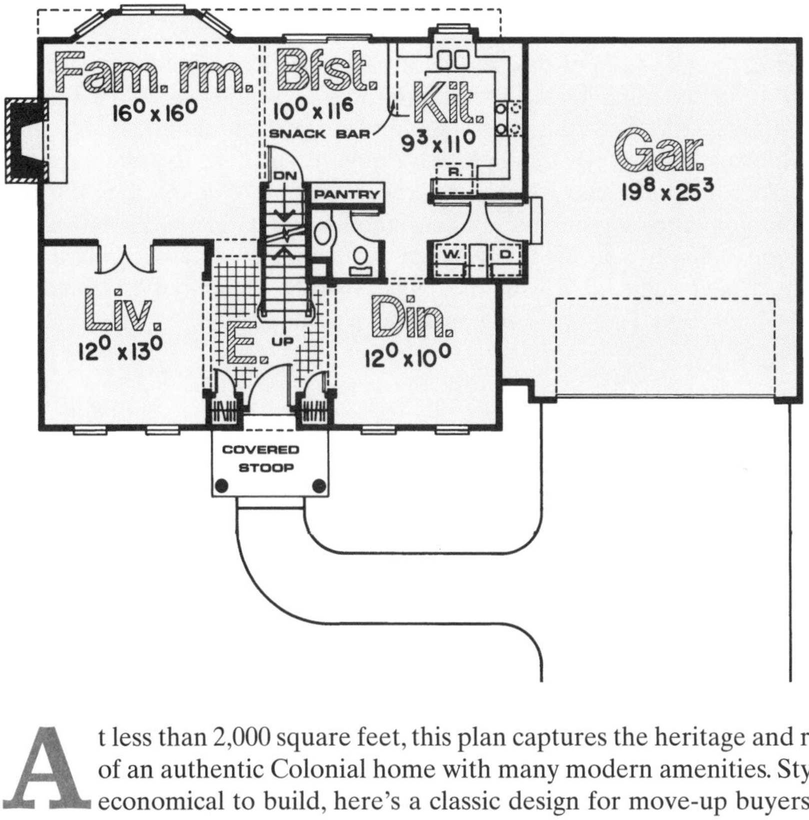
Fam. rm.
16⁰ x 16⁰
Bfst.
10⁰ x 11⁶
SNACK BAR
Kit.
9³ x 11⁰
R.
PANTRY
DN
UP
W.
D.
Gar.
19⁸ x 25³
Liv.
12⁰ x 13⁰
E.
Din.
12⁰ x 10⁰
COVERED
STOOP

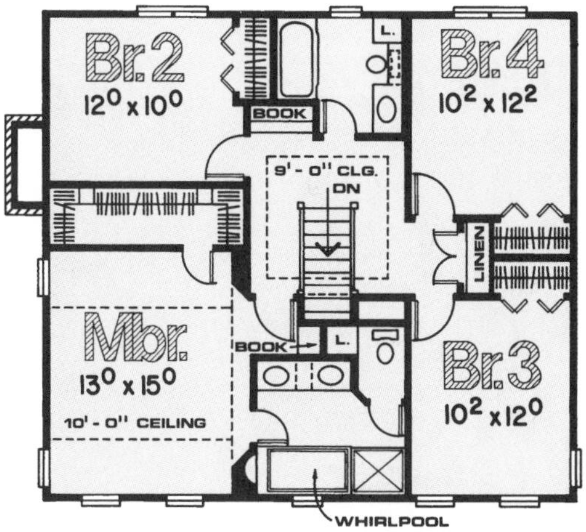
Br. 2
12⁰ x 10⁰
BOOK
L.
Br. 4
10² x 12²
9'-0" CLG.
DN
LINEN
Mbr.
13⁰ x 15⁰
10'-0" CEILING
BOOK
L.
Br. 3
10² x 12⁰
WHIRLPOOL

QUOTE ONE®

Cost to build? See page 516 to order complete cost estimate to build this house in your area!

At less than 2,000 square feet, this plan captures the heritage and romance of an authentic Colonial home with many modern amenities. Stylish, yet economical to build, here's a classic design for move-up buyers. A central hall leads to the formal rooms at the front where the homeowner can display showpiece furnishings. For daily living, the informal rooms can't be beat. A built-in bookcase and large linen cabinet are thoughtful touches upstairs. The master suite shows further evidence of tasteful design. A volume ceiling, large walk-in closet and whirlpool tub await the fortunate homeowner. Each secondary bedroom includes bright windows to add natural lighting and comfort.

Design
HPT830217

First Floor: 1,000 square feet

Second Floor: 993 square feet

Total: 1,993 square feet

Width 56'-0" Depth 30'-0"

Design HPT830218

First Floor: 1,362 square feet
Second Floor: 1,223 square feet
Total: 2,585 square feet
Width 61'-4" Depth 41'-4"

Gracing the elevation of this captivating Colonial are decorative windows and brick detailing. Inside, the dining room is complemented by French doors, a distinctive ceiling treatment and space to accommodate a buffet or hutch. A formal parlor provides a place for quiet relaxation. The family room, with a fireplace, is brightened by an airy bowed window. The spacious kitchen provides a large pantry, a snack bar and an abundant counter space. Half baths are placed conveniently near the family room and laundry. On the second floor, a resplendent master suite filled with the most desirable amenities is joined by three family bedrooms. The side-load garage accommodates three cars.

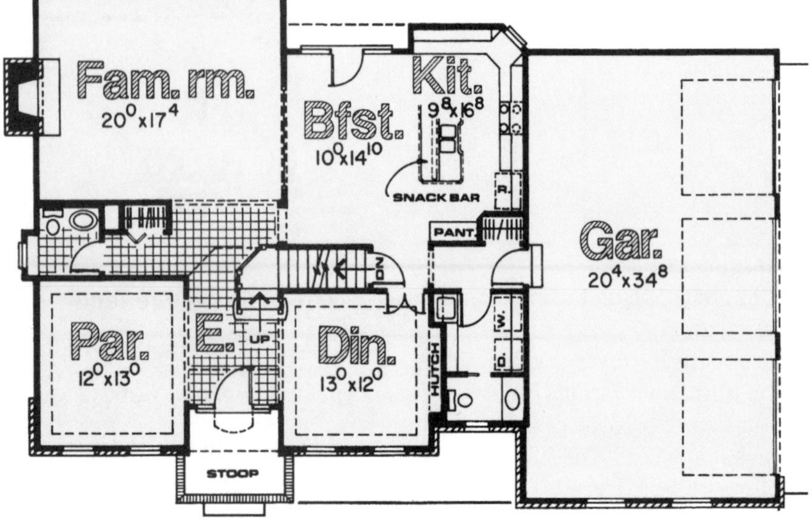

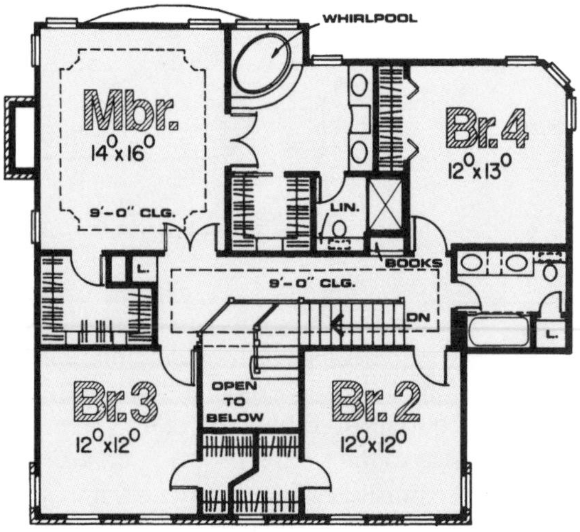

Colonial charm is abundantly displayed in this gracious two-story home. The great room offers views to the covered porch and multi-windowed breakfast area. To the left, a formal dining room provides a special place for dinner parties. An island kitchen with a pantry and plenty of storage has convenient access to all areas. The second floor contains two family bedrooms, a full bath and a master suite. A cathedral ceiling graces the master bedroom. The master bath features a whirlpool bath, an open shower and a generous walk-in closet.

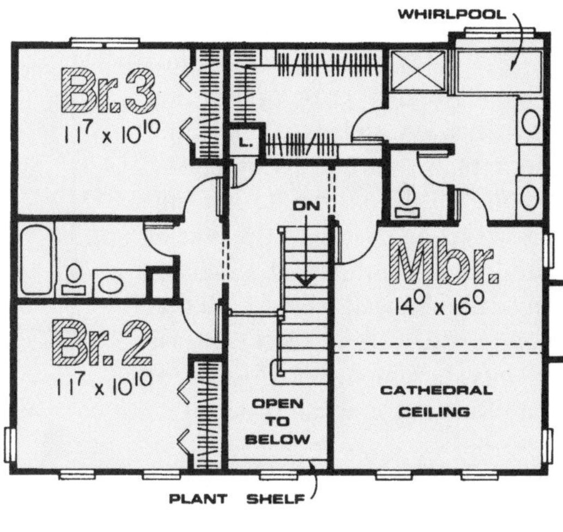

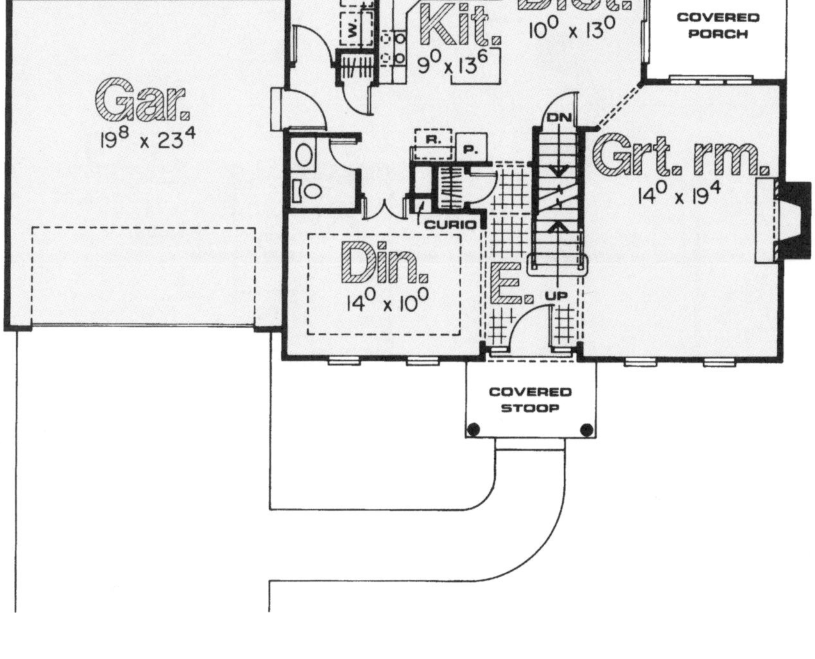

Design HPT830219

First Floor: 941 square feet
Second Floor: 920 square feet
Total: 1,861 square feet
Width 56'-0" Depth 30'-0"

This fetching country home features a second-floor room-to-grow option that is both savvy and stylish. The first floor places formal living spaces to the front of the design and casual living spaces to the rear of the plan. Upstairs, the master suite is enhanced with a bath that contains a walk-in closet. Please specify basement, crawlspace or slab foundation when ordering.

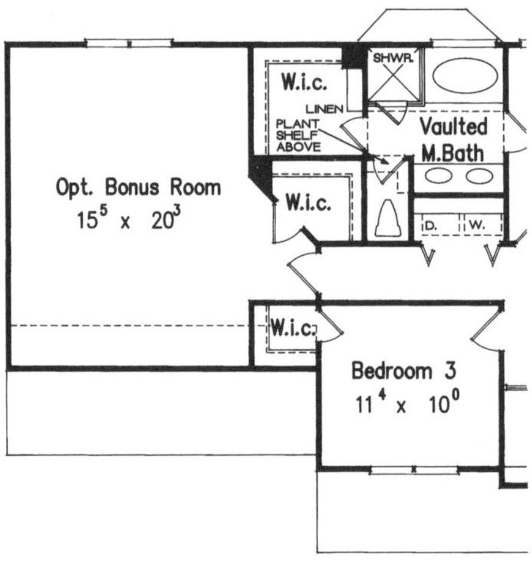

Design
HPT830220

First Floor: 882 square feet

Second Floor: 793 square feet

Total: 1,675 square feet

Bonus Space: 416 square feet

Width 49'-6" Depth 35'-4"

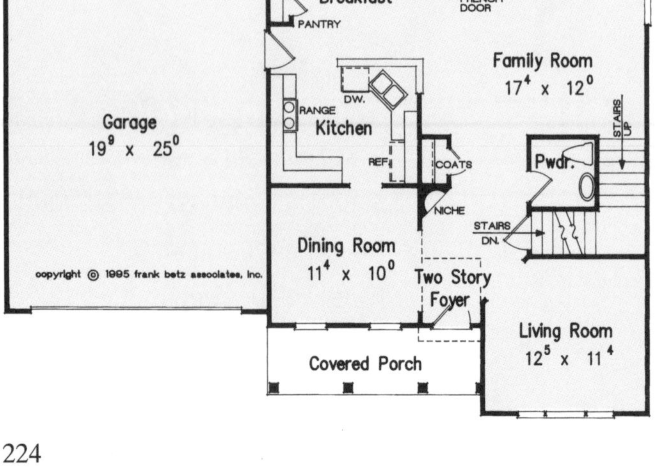

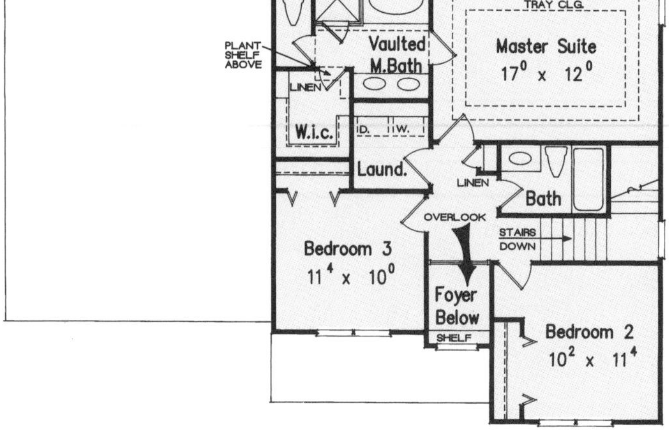

Traditional wood siding gives a look of down-home comfort to this charming two-story home. A brief foyer opens to the family room that is highlighted with a fireplace and pass-through to the kitchen. The efficient kitchen has wrapping counters, a breakfast nook, laundry center and easy service to the dining room. Upstairs, the master suite has elegant ceiling detail, a vaulted bath and roomy walk-in closet. Two family bedrooms share a hall bath. Please specify basement or crawlspace foundation when ordering.

Design HPT830221

First Floor: 719 square feet
Second Floor: 717 square feet
Total: 1,436 square feet
Bonus Space: 290 square feet
Width 45'-10" Depth 35'-6"

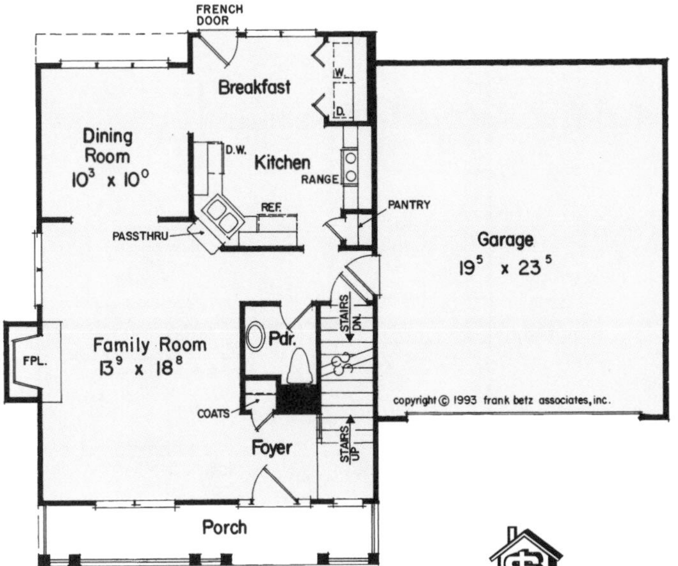

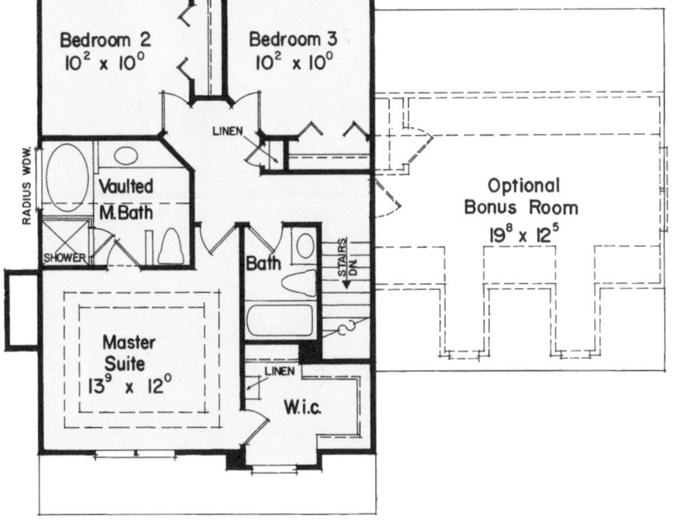

QUOTE ONE®

Cost to build? See page 516 to order complete cost estimate to build this house in your area!

This Colonial farmhouse inspires a sense of history, but is built to be cherished for generations to come. Inside, a two-story foyer opens to a quiet living room with a focal-point fireplace. The L-shaped kitchen overlooks a bright breakfast area with triple-window views and access to the covered rear porch and deck. A cathedral ceiling soars above the great room, which enjoys a warming hearth. The master suite with an oversized private bath nestles to the rear of the plan. A balcony hall on the second floor joins three family bedrooms—Bedroom 2 includes a private bath, while Bedrooms 3 and 4 share a full bath. This home is designed with a walkout basement foundation.

Design HPT830222

First Floor: 2,421 square feet

Second Floor: 1,322 square feet

Total: 3,743 square feet

Width 66'-9" Depth 63'-0"

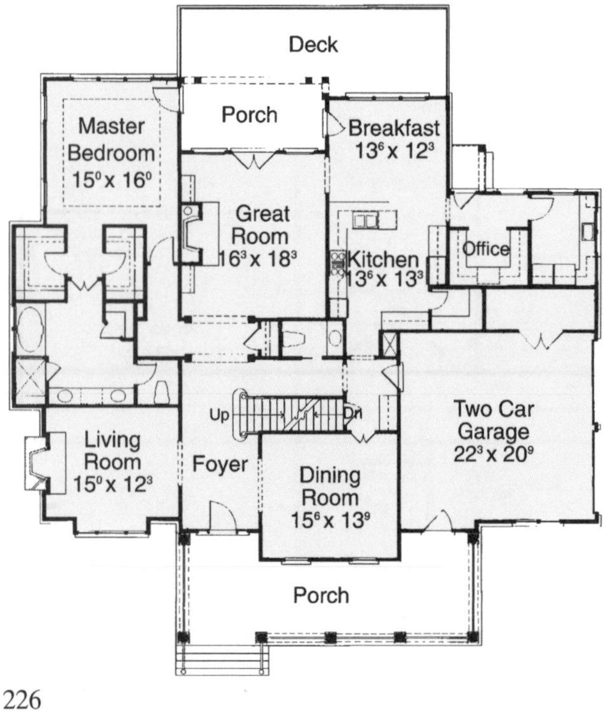

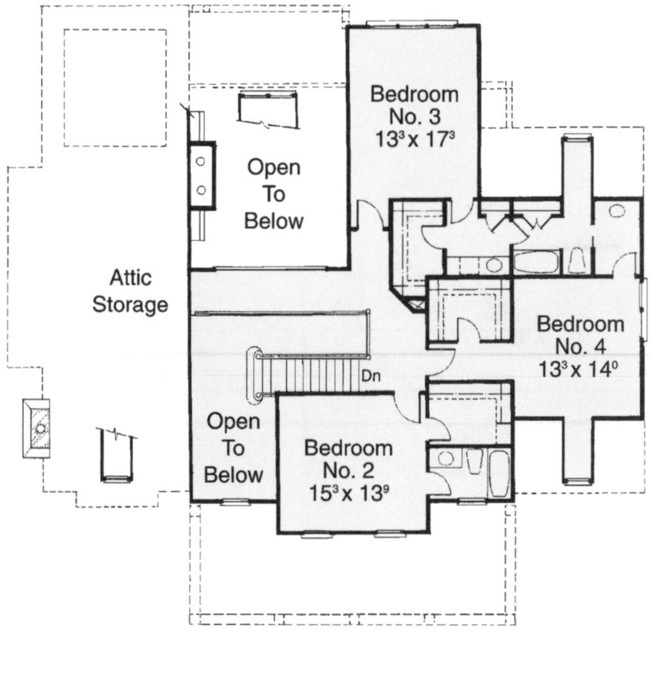

Design HPT830223

First Floor: 1,206 square feet
Second Floor: 1,541 square feet
Total: 2,747 square feet
Width 63'-6" Depth 35'-10"

A perfect design for the busy family, this traditional home includes amenities that focus on family living. The oversized kitchen has a large island with a serving bar and a bay breakfast area. The great room is set apart from the dining room with an elegant arch. The second floor features the handsome master suite, which is complete with a lush, compartmented bath and a walk-in closet. Please specify crawlspace or slab foundation when ordering.

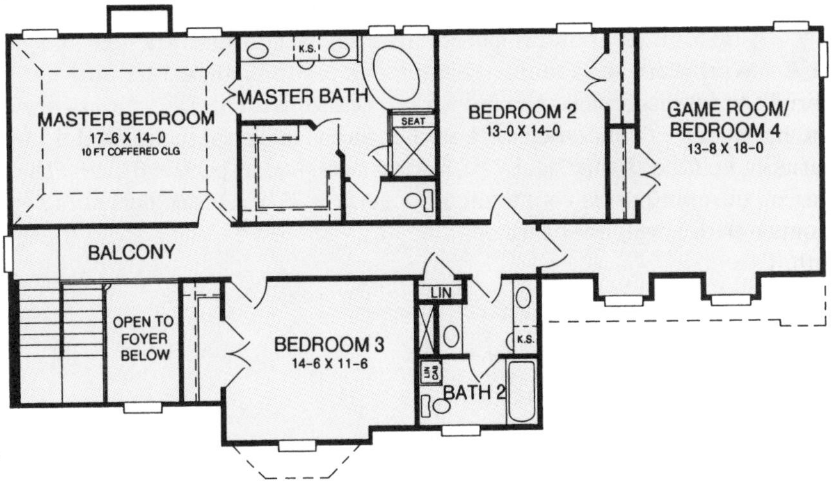
MASTER BEDROOM
17-6 X 14-0
10 FT COFFERED CLG
K.S.
MASTER BATH
SEAT
BEDROOM 2
13-0 X 14-0
GAME ROOM/
BEDROOM 4
13-8 X 18-0
BALCONY
LIN
OPEN TO
FOYER
BELOW
BEDROOM 3
14-6 X 11-6
K.S.
BATH 2

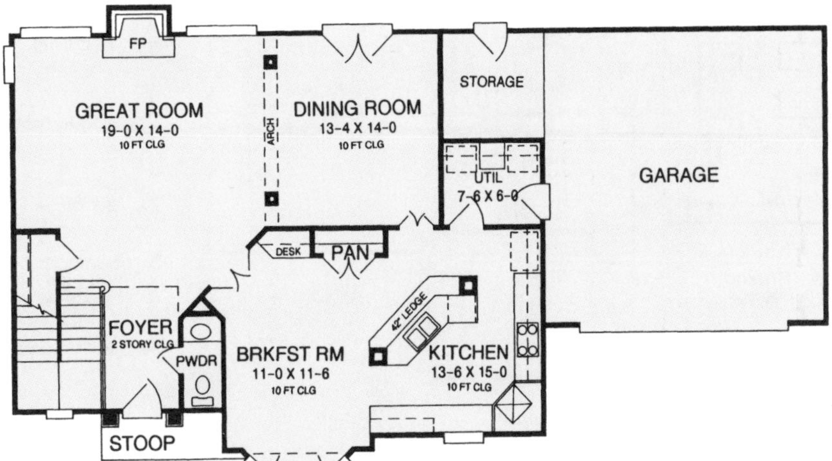
FP
GREAT ROOM
19-0 X 14-0
10 FT CLG
ARCH
DINING ROOM
13-4 X 14-0
10 FT CLG
STORAGE
UTIL
7-6 X 6-0
GARAGE
DESK
PAN
42" LEDGE
FOYER
2 STORY CLG
PWDR
BRKFST RM
11-0 X 11-6
10 FT CLG
KITCHEN
13-6 X 15-0
10 FT CLG
STOOP

Make your mark with this brick traditional. On the first floor, such attributes as informal/formal zones, a gourmet kitchen and a solarium, deck and screened porch are immediate attention getters. In the kitchen, meal preparation is a breeze with an island work station and plenty of counter space. Four bedrooms make up the second floor of this plan. One of the family bedrooms possesses a personal bath. The master bedroom has its own bath and a giant walk-in closet. This home is designed with a walkout basement.

Design HPT830224

First Floor: 1,698 square feet
Second Floor: 1,542 square feet
Total: 3,240 square feet
Width 61'-6" Depth 51'-0"

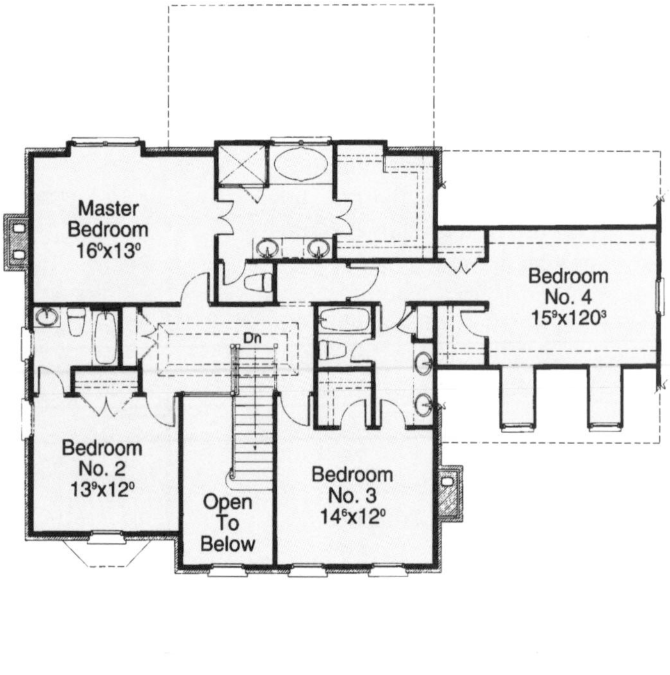

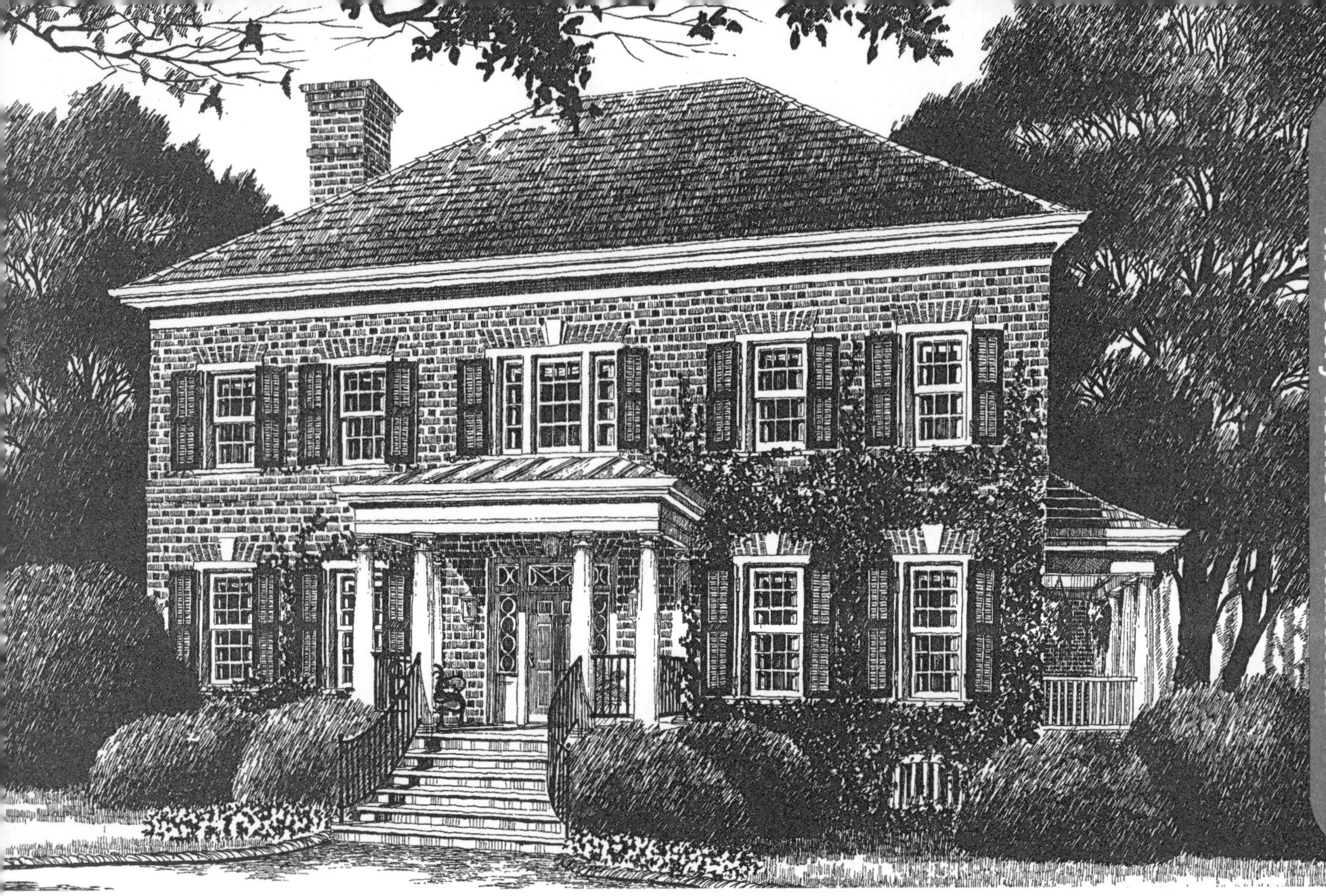

A stately appearance and lots of living space give this home appeal. The foyer introduces formal living and dining rooms. For more casual occasions, a great room opens to the back porch. The breakfast room has convenient proximity to these informal areas. The kitchen has plenty of work space. Four bedrooms on the second floor enjoy complete privacy. In the master bedroom suite, a short hallway flanked by closets leads to a lovely bath with a spa tub, a compartmented toilet, a separate shower and dual lavatories. This home is designed with a walkout basement foundation.

Design

HPT830225

First Floor: 1,828 square feet
Second Floor: 1,552 square feet
Total: 3,380 square feet
Width 54'-3" Depth 70'-3"

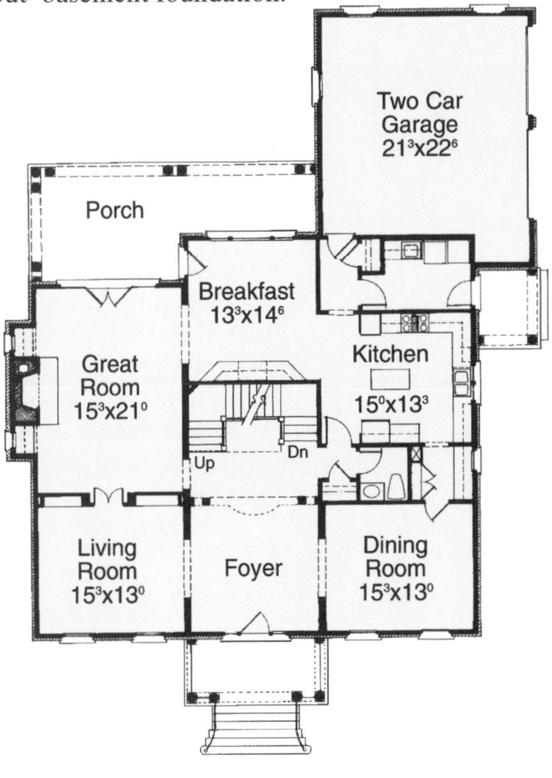

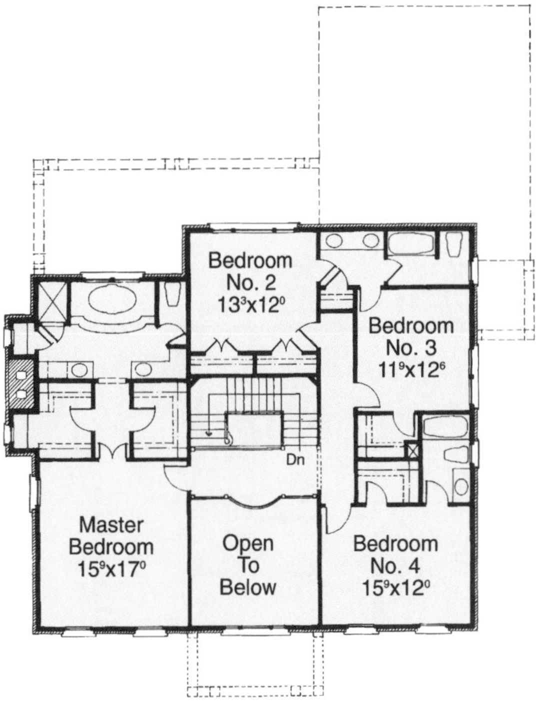

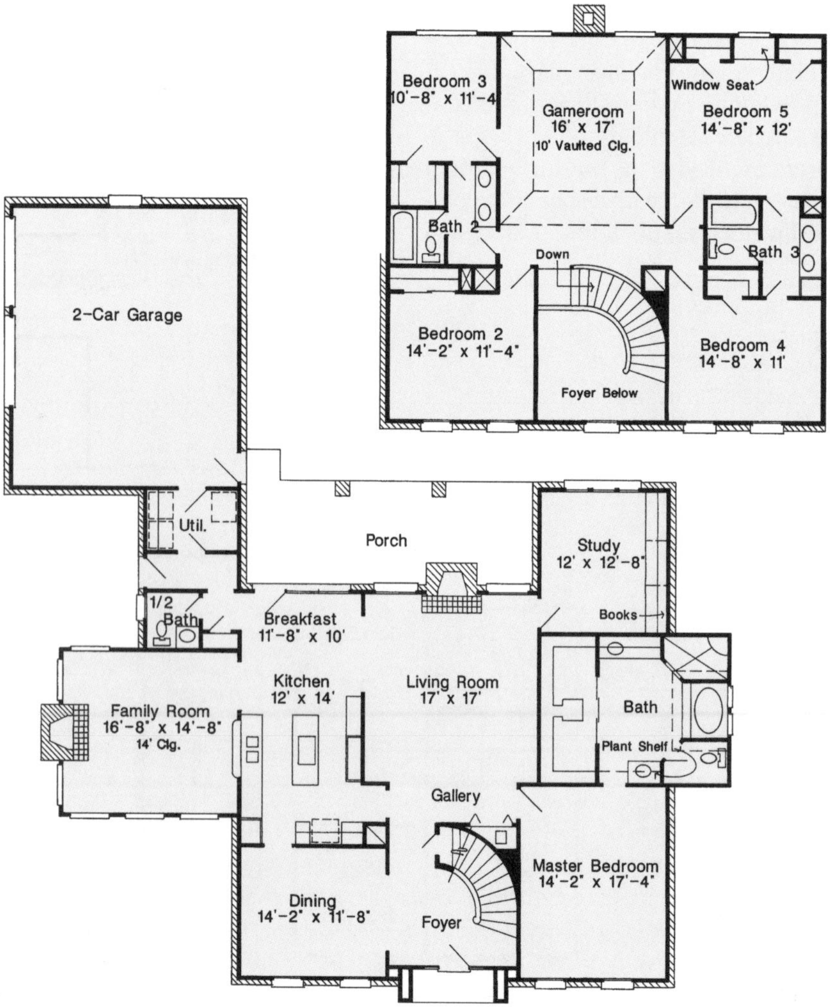

Bedroom 3
10'-8" x 11'-4
Gameroom
16' x 17'
10' Vaulted Clg.
Window Seat
Bedroom 5
14'-8" x 12'
Bath 2
Bath 3
Down
Bedroom 2
14'-2" x 11'-4"
Bedroom 4
14'-8" x 11'
Foyer Below
2-Car Garage
Util.
Porch
Study
12' x 12'-8"
Books
1/2 Bath
Breakfast
11'-8" x 10'
Kitchen
12' x 14'
Living Room
17' x 17'
Bath
Family Room
16'-8" x 14'-8"
14' Clg.
Plant Shelf
Gallery
Master Bedroom
14'-2" x 17'-4"
Dining
14'-2" x 11'-8"
Foyer

Design HPT830226

First Floor: 2,157 square feet
Second Floor: 1,346 square feet
Total: 3,503 square feet
Width 70'-6" Depth 73'-4"

Traditional styling at its best—this plan is a true work of art. The entry foyer contains a curved staircase to the second floor and is open to the formal dining room. The living room has a fireplace as does the family room. A quiet study features built-in shelves and is tucked away to the rear of the plan. Note the master bedroom on the first floor. It boasts a double walk-in closet, corner shower and large tub. Four bedrooms upstairs branch off of game room with vaulted ceiling.

QUOTE ONE®

Cost to build? See page 516 to order complete cost estimate to build this house in your area!

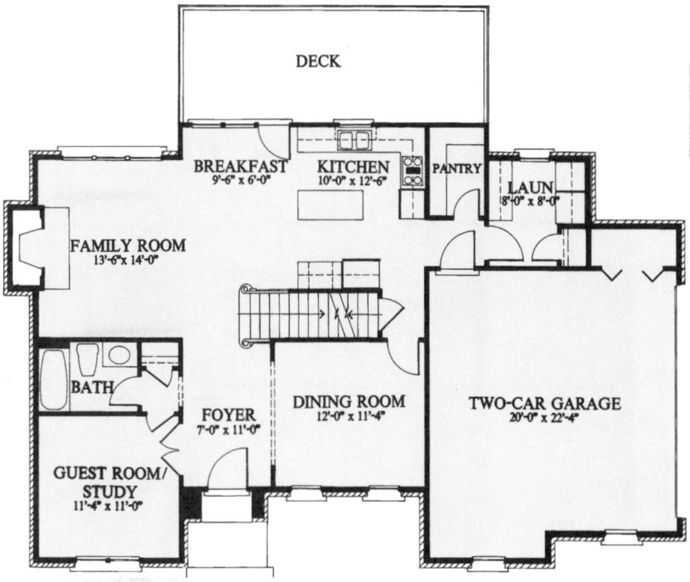

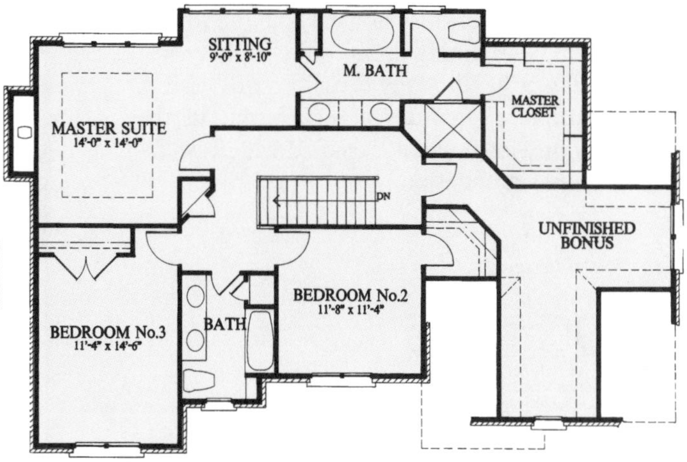

QUOTE ONE®
Cost to build? See page 516 to order complete cost estimate to build this house in your area!

Design HPT830227

First Floor: 1,053 square feet
Second Floor: 1,053 square feet
Total: 2,106 square feet
Bonus Space: 212 square feet
Width 54'-4" Depth 34'-0"

Brick takes a bold stand in grand traditional style in this treasured design. The front study has a nearby full bath, making it a handy guest bedroom. The family room with a fireplace opens to a cozy breakfast area. The kitchen features a prep island and huge pantry. Upstairs, the master bedroom has its own sitting room and a giant-sized closet. Two family bedrooms share a bath. This home is designed with a walkout basement foundation.

Classic design knows no boundaries in this gracious two-story home. From the formal living and dining areas to the more casual family room, it handles any occasion with ease. A central fireplace provides a focal point in the family room. This home is designed with a walk-out basement foundation.

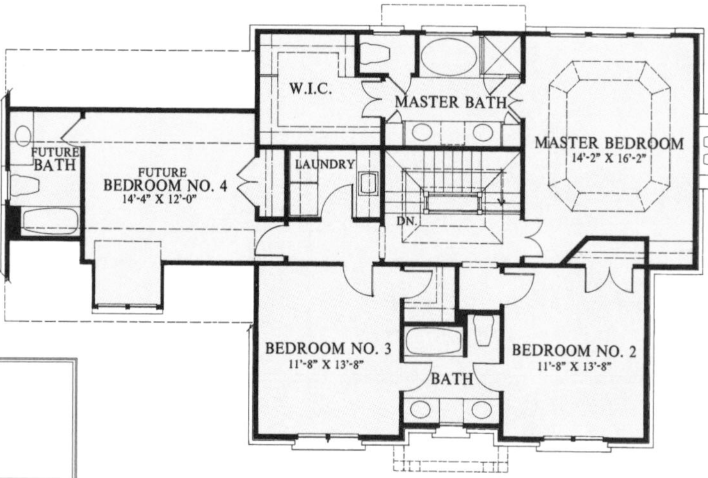

QUOTE ONE®
Cost to build? See page 516 to order complete cost estimate to build this house in your area!

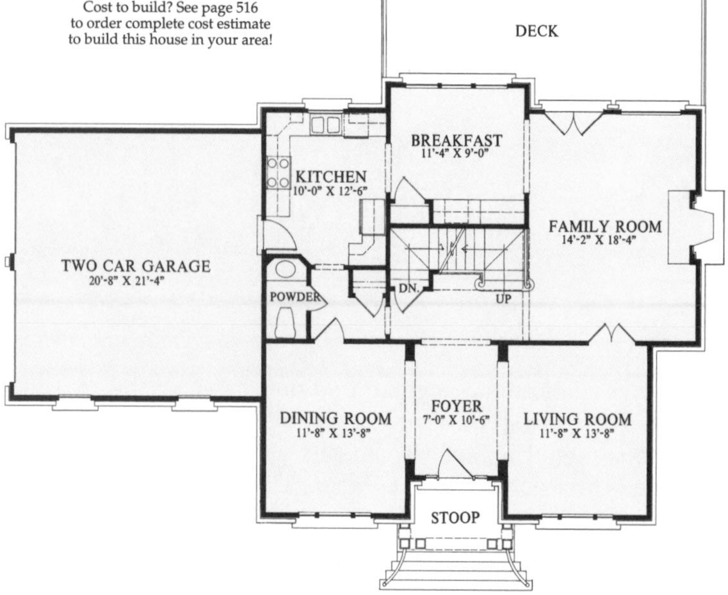

Design HPT830228

First Floor: 1,165 square feet
Second Floor: 1,050 square feet
Total: 2,215 square feet
Bonus Space: 265 square feet
Width 58'-0" Depth 36'-0"

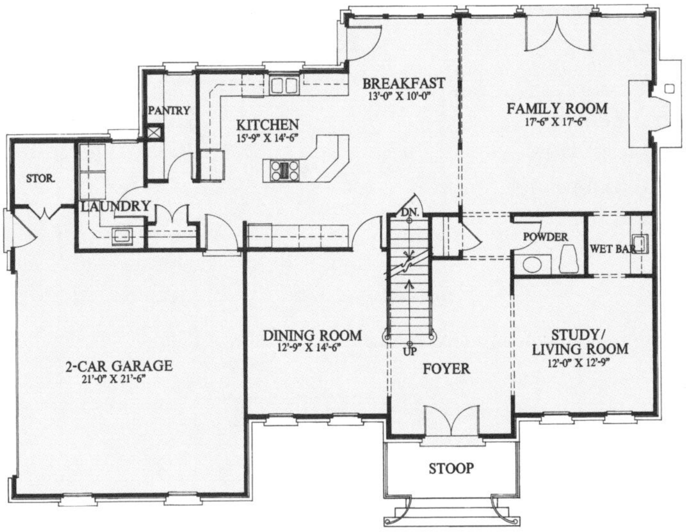

QUOTE ONE®

Cost to build? See page 516 to order complete cost estimate to build this house in your area!

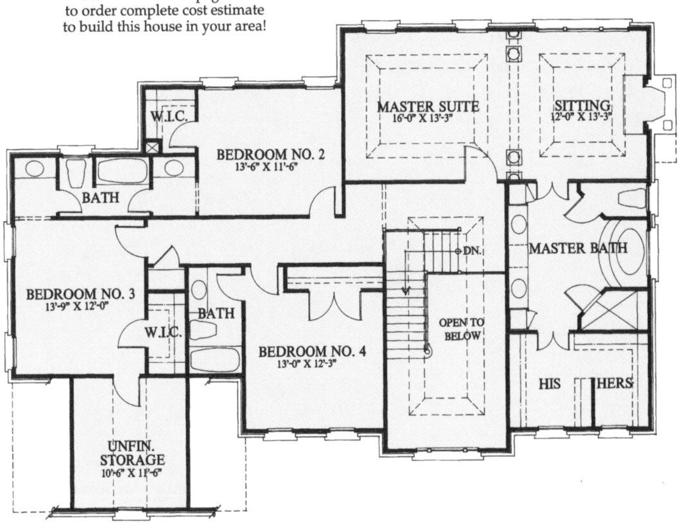

The classic styling of this brick American traditional will be respected for years to come. The formidable double-door entry with a transom and a Palladian window reveals the shining foyer within. It is flanked by the spacious dining room and the formal study or living room. A large family room with a full wall of glass conveniently opens to the breakfast room and kitchen. The master suite features a spacious sitting area with its own fireplace and tray ceiling. Two additional bedrooms share a bath, while a fourth bedroom has its own private bath. This home is designed with a walkout basement foundation.

Design HPT830229

First Floor: 1,554 square feet
Second Floor: 1,648 square feet
Total: 3,202 square feet
Width 60'-0" Depth 43'-0"

The pleasing character of this house does not stop behind its facade. The foyer opens to an encompassing great room with a fireplace and also to the eat-in kitchen. Just beyond the breakfast bay, a door opens to the expansive rear deck. Stairs lead from the great room to the second floor, where a laundry room is conveniently placed near the bedrooms. The master suite spares none of the amenities: a full bath with a double vanity, shower, tub and walk-in closet. Bedrooms 2 and 3 share a full bath. This home is designed with a walkout basement foundation.

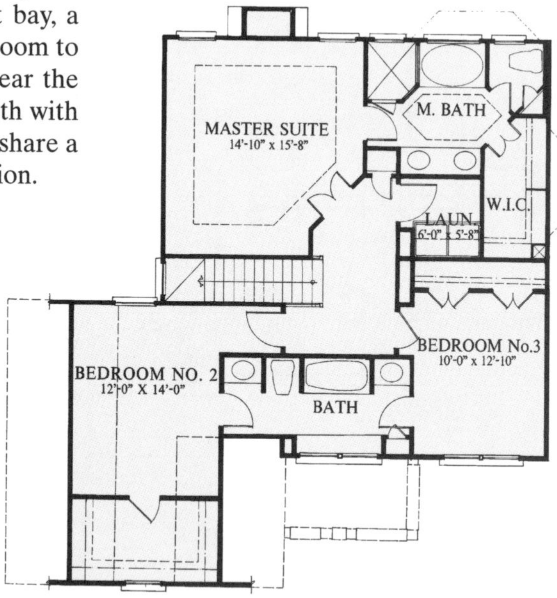

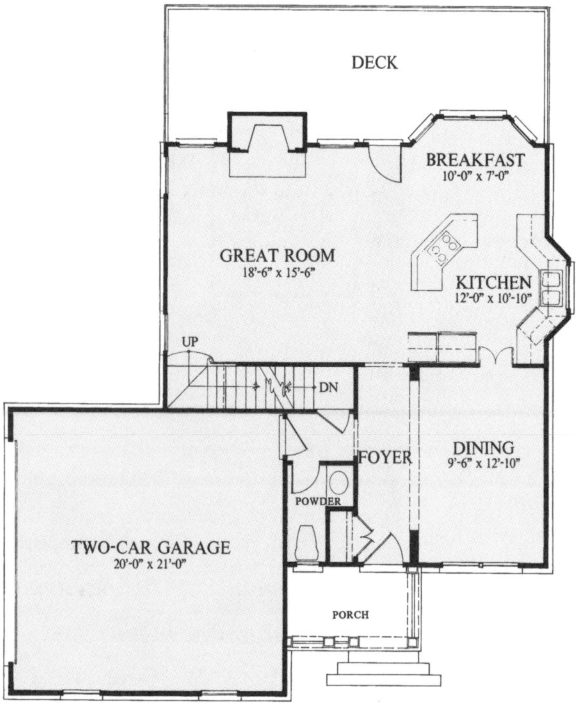

Design

HPT830230

First Floor: 830 square feet
Second Floor: 1,060 square feet
Total: 1,890 square feet
Width 41'-0" Depth 40'-6"

DECK
BREAKFAST
10'-0" x 7'-0"
GREAT ROOM
18'-6" x 15'-6"
KITCHEN
12'-0" x 10'-10"
UP
DN
FOYER
DINING
9'-6" x 12'-10"
PDR
TWO-CAR GARAGE
20'-0" x 21'-0"

QUOTE ONE®
Cost to build? See page 516 to order complete cost estimate to build this house in your area!

MASTER SUITE
14'-10" x 15'-8"
M. BATH
W.I.C.
LAUN.
6'-0" x 5'-8"
W.I.C.
BEDROOM No.2
11'-10" x 9'-6"
BEDROOM No.3
10'-0" x 12'-10"
BATH
W.I.C.

Columns, brickwork and uniquely shaped windows and shutters remind us of the best homes of turn-of-the-century America. The large fireplace, framed by windows, creates a lovely focal point in the great room. Upstairs, double doors lead to the lavish master suite, which features a tray ceiling. Bedrooms 2 and 3 complete this floor, with a shared bath featuring private entrances. This home is designed with a walkout basement foundation.

Design
HPT830231

First Floor: 780 square feet
Second Floor: 915 square feet
Total: 1,695 square feet
Width 41'-0" Depth 41'-0"

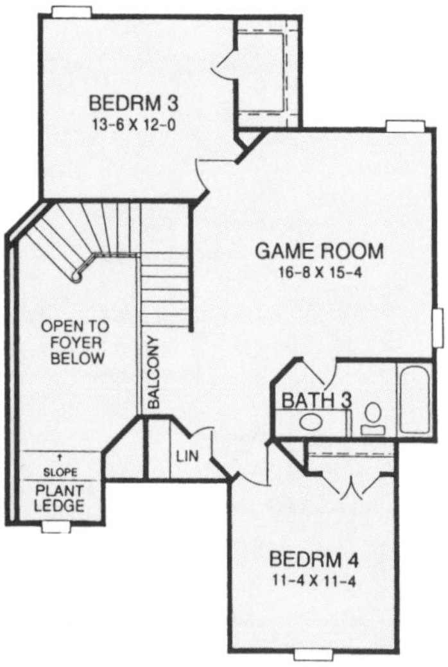
BEDRM 3
13-6 X 12-0
GAME ROOM
16-8 X 15-4
OPEN TO FOYER BELOW
BALCONY
BATH 3
LIN
SLOPE
PLANT LEDGE
BEDRM 4
11-4 X 11-4

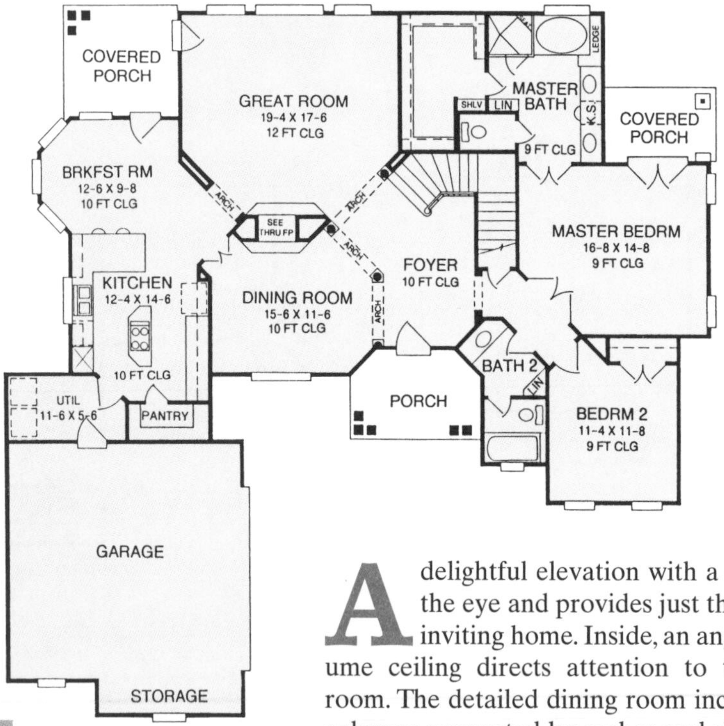
COVERED PORCH
GREAT ROOM
19-4 X 17-6
12 FT CLG
MASTER BATH
SHLV
LIN
K.S.
LEDGE
9 FT CLG
COVERED PORCH
BRKFST RM
12-6 X 9-8
10 FT CLG
ARCH
SEE THRU FP
MASTER BEDRM
16-8 X 14-8
9 FT CLG
FOYER
10 FT CLG
KITCHEN
12-4 X 14-6
DINING ROOM
15-6 X 11-6
10 FT CLG
10 FT CLG
BATH 2
LIN
PORCH
BEDRM 2
11-4 X 11-8
9 FT CLG
UTIL
11-6 X 5-6
PANTRY
GARAGE
STORAGE

QUOTE ONE®

Cost to build? See page 516 to order complete cost estimate to build this house in your area!

Design

HPT830232

First Floor: 1,930 square feet

Second Floor: 791 square feet

Total: 2,721 square feet

Width 64'-4" Depth 62'-0"

L

A delightful elevation with a swoop roof captures the eye and provides just the right touch for this inviting home. Inside, an angled foyer with a volume ceiling directs attention to the enormous great room. The detailed dining room includes massive round columns connected by arches and shares a through-fireplace with the great room. The master suite includes an upscale bath and access to a private covered porch. Nearby, Bedroom 2 is perfect for a nursery or home office/study. The kitchen features a large cooktop island and walk-in pantry. The second floor is dominated by an oversized game room. Two family bedrooms, a bath and a linen closet complete the upstairs. Please specify basement, crawlspace or slab foundation when ordering.

Traditional stylings—pilaster and sidelight accents at the front entry and keystone jack-arched windows with shutters—present a home with class and appeal. The two-story foyer is flanked by the formal dining room and the living room. Beyond the enclosed staircase, the family room, warmed with a fireplace, offers a cozy environment for intimate gatherings. The angled kitchen enjoys a serving bar, and is situated between the dining room and breakfast area for convenience. Note the home office/bedroom, tucked away on the left, with its private entrance to the full bath. The lavish master suite resides on the second floor along with two additional bedrooms, a full bath, laundry and a bonus room.

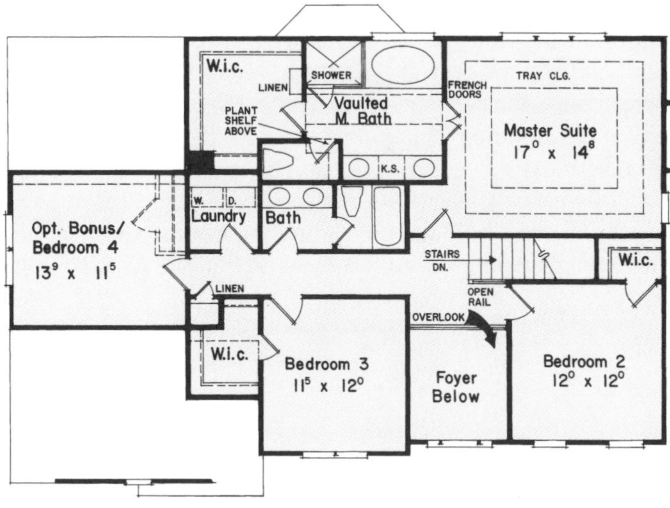

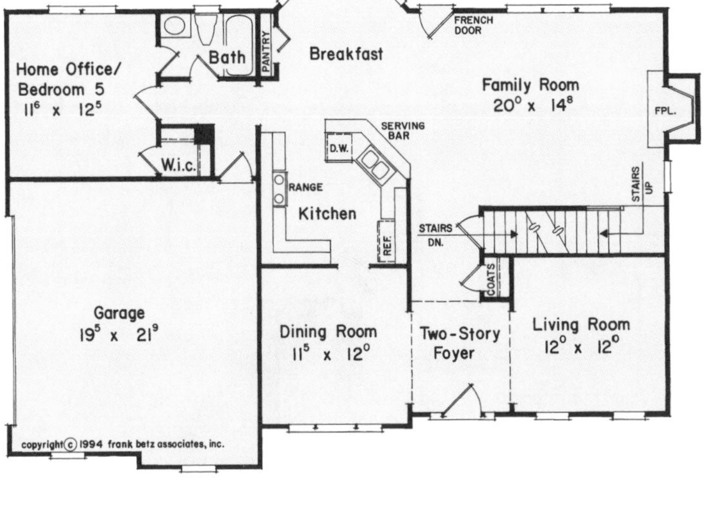

QUOTE ONE®

Cost to build? See page 516 to order complete cost estimate to build this house in your area!

Design HPT830234

First Floor: 2,114 square feet
Second Floor: 1,116 square feet
Total: 3,230 square feet
Width 65'-4" Depth 47'-6"

The best in elegant design is evident in this brick two-story home. From the raised foyer amenities abound: a niche in the dining room, a built-in media center in the living room and built-in bookcases in the study. A two-way fireplace, French doors to a rear covered porch, a huge walk-in closet and a pampering bath all grace the master suite. Even the U-shaped kitchen has built-in hutch space, and its attached breakfast area has French doors to a covered porch. The vaulted living room offers a wall of windows, a central fireplace and a French door to the rear porch. The second floor holds three bedrooms and a game room. Eleven-foot ceilings are the rule in all but one of these rooms.

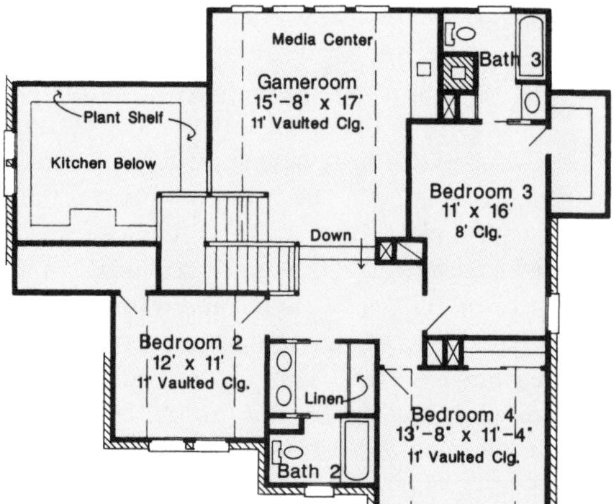

Design
HPT830213

First Floor: 2,063 square feet
Second Floor: 894 square feet
Total: 2,957 square feet
Width 72'-8" Depth 51'-4"

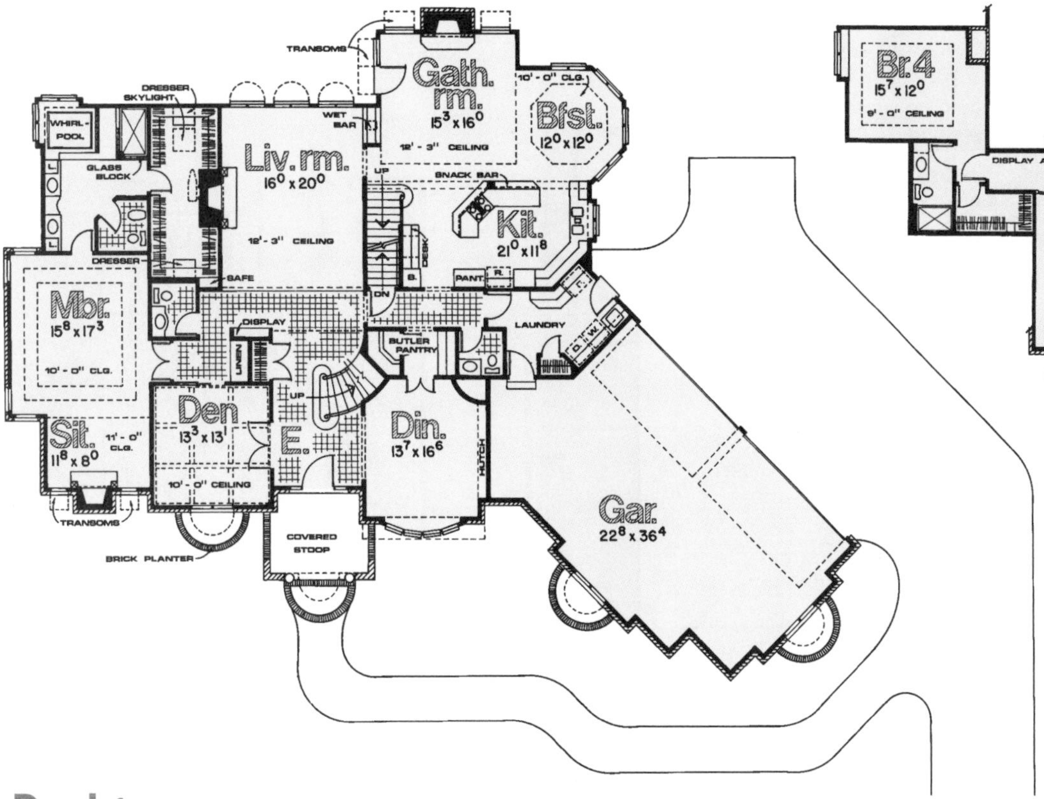

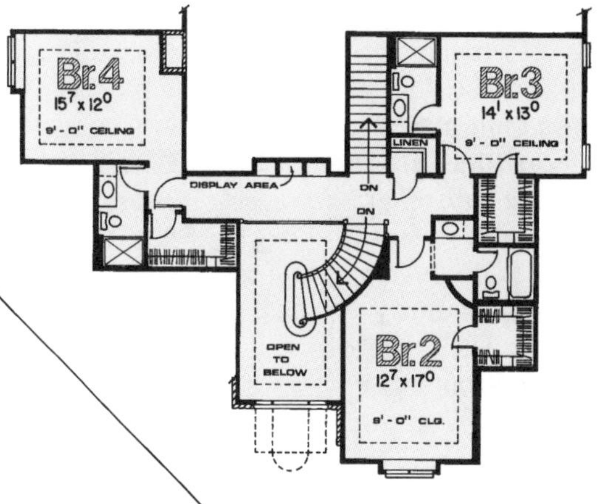

Design HPT830235

First Floor: 2,839 square feet
Second Floor: 1,111 square feet
Total: 3,950 square feet
Width 95'-9" Depth 70'-2"

A two-story foyer introduces the formal living zones of this four-bedroom plan—a den with a ten-foot ceiling, a dining room with an adjoining butler's pantry and a living room with a fireplace and a twelve-foot ceiling. For more casual living, the gathering room shares space with the octagonal breakfast area and the amenity-filled kitchen. The first-floor master bedroom offers a sitting area with a fireplace and a sumptuous bath.

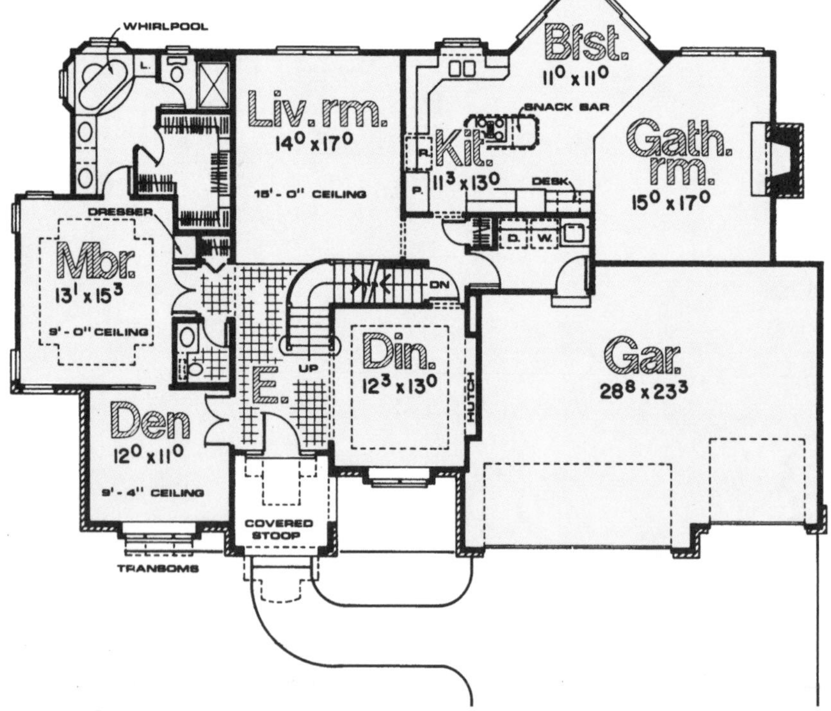

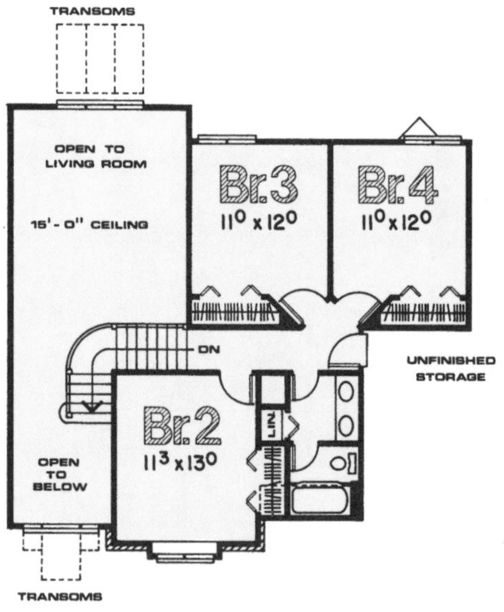

Design HPT830236

First Floor: 1,829 square feet
Second Floor: 657 square feet
Total: 2,486 square feet
Width 68'-8" Depth 47'-8"

Elegant windows and trim details highlight the exterior of this traditional home. In the living room, transom windows let in plenty of light. The formal dining room features hutch space. Casual living is the focus in the heartwarming kitchen and gathering room. Wrapping counters, a cooktop island with snack bar and an angular breakfast nook nicely balance the large gathering room that's accented with a fireplace. The secluded master suite includes a nine-foot ceiling, pocket door to the den, corner whirlpool tub and huge walk-in closet. Three family bedrooms are on the second floor.

Design HPT830237

First Floor: 2,693 square feet
Second Floor: 2,027 square feet
Total: 4,720 square feet
Width 90'-10" Depth 58'-1"

This fantastic home is both a romantic castle retreat and a luxurious custom home. The grand foyer opens to a round study on the left and a formal dining room on the right. The expansive great room has a towering fireplace and is framed by a tiered staircase that opens to a balcony on the second floor. The oversized kitchen has a work island, a wraparound snack bar and a sunny breakfast nook. A thoughtful guest suite with a private bath is tucked behind the great room. Upstairs, the luxurious master suite is accented with a separate sitting room, a fireplace, tiered ceiling and a spa-style bath with two large walk-in closets. One additional family bedroom has a private bath and a walk-in closet. A delightful game room completes this fantasy home. Please specify crawlspace or slab foundation when ordering.

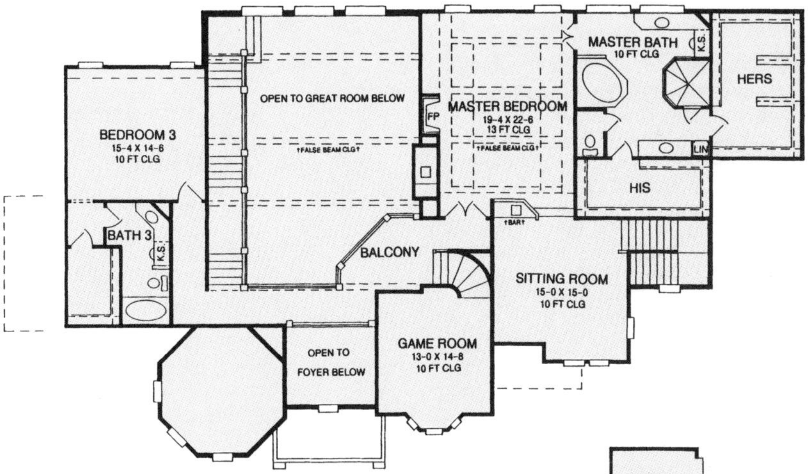

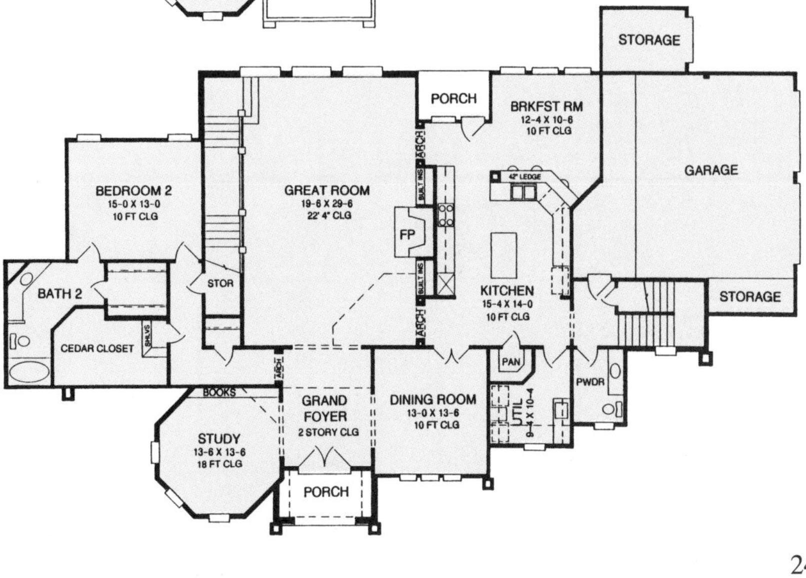

Design
HPT830238

First Floor: 1,165 square feet
Second Floor: 1,050 square feet
Total: 2,215 square feet
Bonus Space: 265 square feet
Width 58'-0" Depth 36'-0"

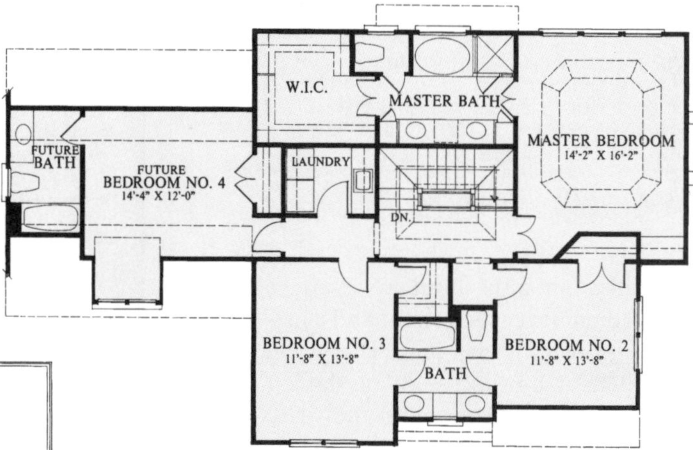
W.I.C.
MASTER BATH
MASTER BEDROOM
14'-2" X 16'-2"
FUTURE BATH
FUTURE BEDROOM NO. 4
14'-4" X 12'-0"
LAUNDRY
DN.
BEDROOM NO. 3
11'-8" X 13'-8"
BEDROOM NO. 2
11'-8" X 13'-8"
BATH

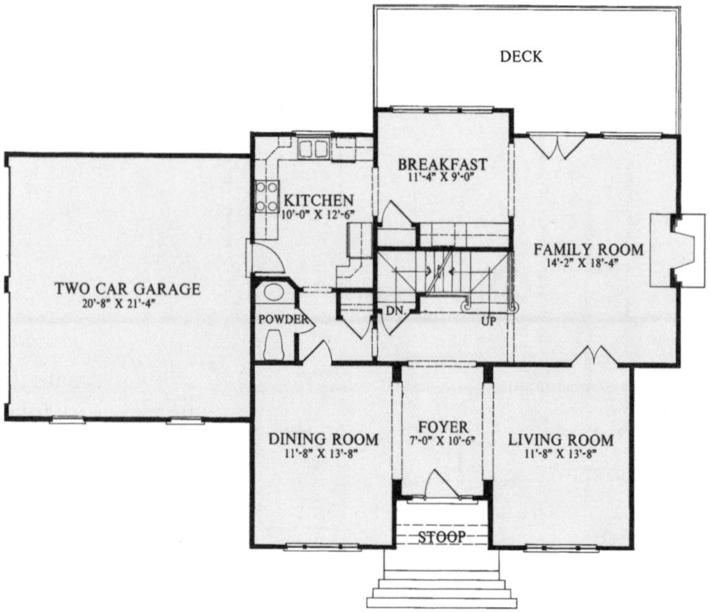
DECK
BREAKFAST
11'-4" X 9'-0"
KITCHEN
10'-0" X 12'-6"
FAMILY ROOM
14'-2" X 18'-4"
TWO CAR GARAGE
20'-8" X 21'-4"
POWDER
DN.
UP
DINING ROOM
11'-8" X 13'-8"
FOYER
7'-0" X 10'-6"
LIVING ROOM
11'-8" X 13'-8"
STOOP

This beautiful European-style stucco home combines contemporary luxury with the convenience of a smaller floor plan. Formal living and dining rooms flank the foyer, while casual living areas reside to the rear of the plan. An L-shaped kitchen opens to a spacious breakfast room with triple views to the rear yard. A central staircase leads to sleeping quarters on the second floor. The master suite promises repose with abundant natural light and a relaxing bath. Bedrooms 2 and 3 share a full bath with a double-bowl vanity. The laundry is also found on the second floor for convenience. Space for a fourth bedroom and an attached bath can be developed later as needs arise. This home is designed with a walkout basement foundation.

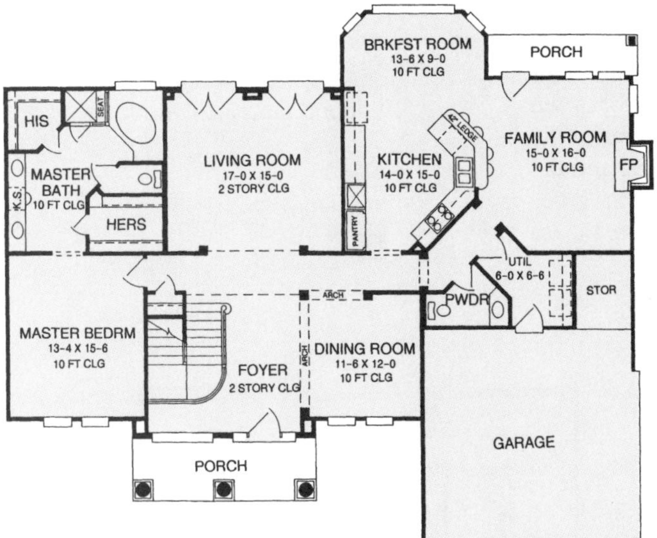

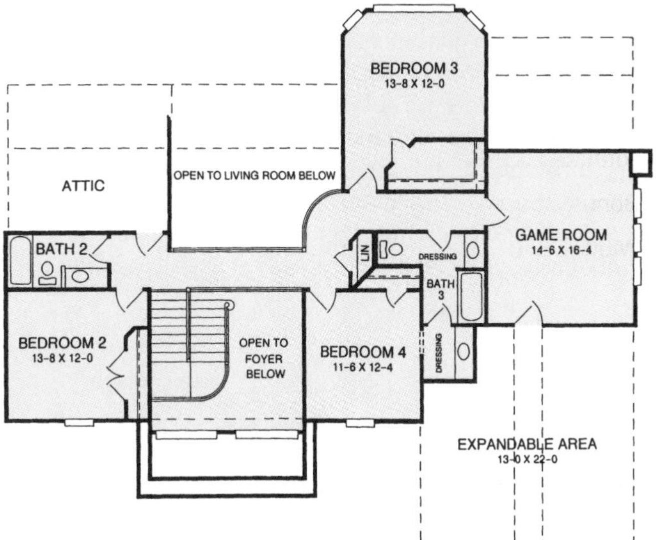

Design HPT830239

First Floor: 1,919 square feet
Second Floor: 1,190 square feet
Total: 3,109 square feet
Bonus Space: 286 square feet
Width 64'-6" Depth 55'-10"

Flower boxes, arches and multi-pane windows all combine to create the elegant facade of this four-bedroom home. Inside, the two-story foyer has a formal dining room to its right and leads to a two-story living room that is filled with light. An efficient kitchen has a bayed breakfast room and shares a snack bar with a cozy family room. Located on the first floor for privacy, the master suite is graced with a luxurious bath. Upstairs, three secondary bedrooms share two full baths and have access to a large game room. Please specify basement, crawlspace or slab foundation when ordering.

This home speaks of luxury and practicality and is abundant in attractive qualities. A study and dining room flank the foyer, while the great room offers a warming fireplace and double French-door access to the rear yard. A butler's pantry acts as a helpful buffer between the kitchen and the columned dining room. Double bays at the rear of the home form the keeping room and the breakfast room on one side and the master bedroom on the other. Three family bedrooms and two baths grace the second floor. A game room is perfect for casual family time. Please specify basement, crawlspace or slab foundation when ordering.

Design HPT830240

First Floor: 2,639 square feet
Second Floor: 1,625 square feet
Total: 4,264 square feet
Width 73'-8" Depth 58'-6"
L

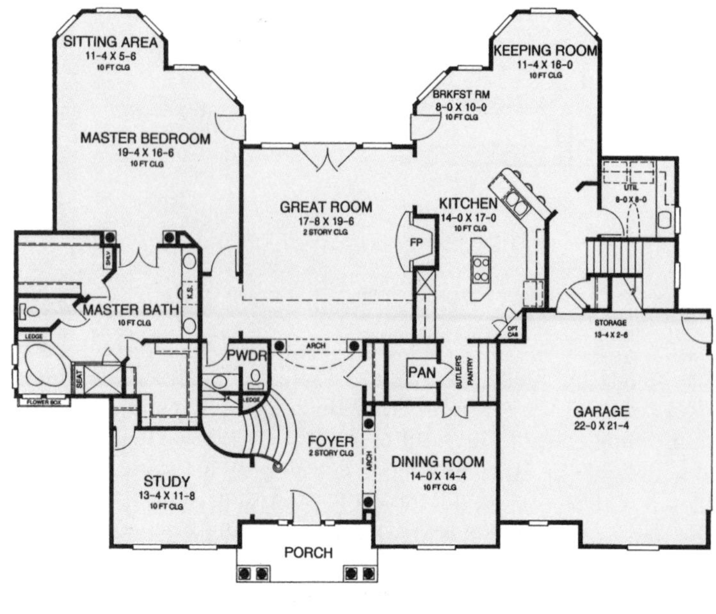

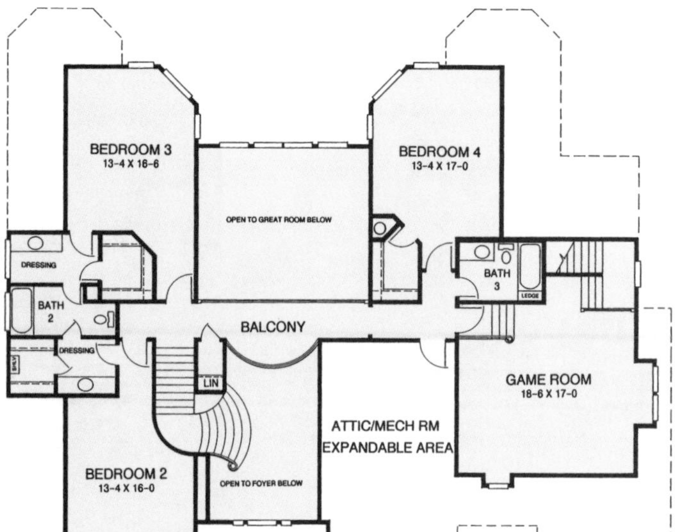

Design HPT830241

First Floor: 2,520 square feet
Second Floor: 1,305 square feet
Total: 3,825 square feet
Width 73'-8" Depth 58'-6"
L

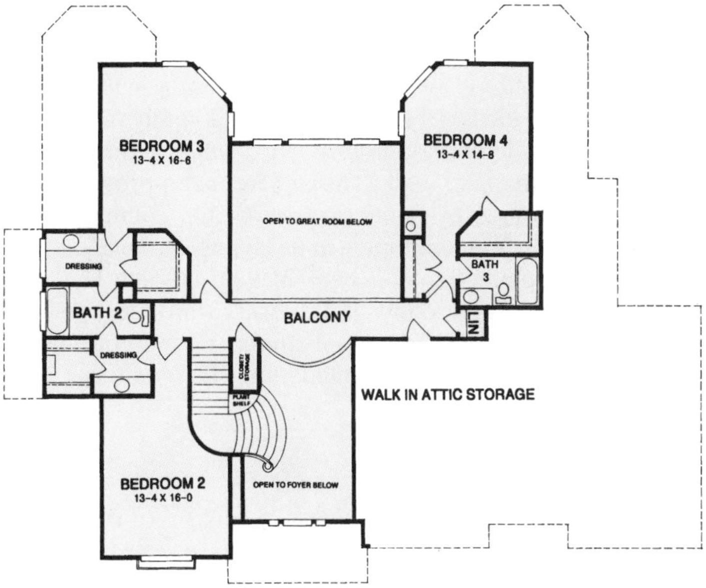

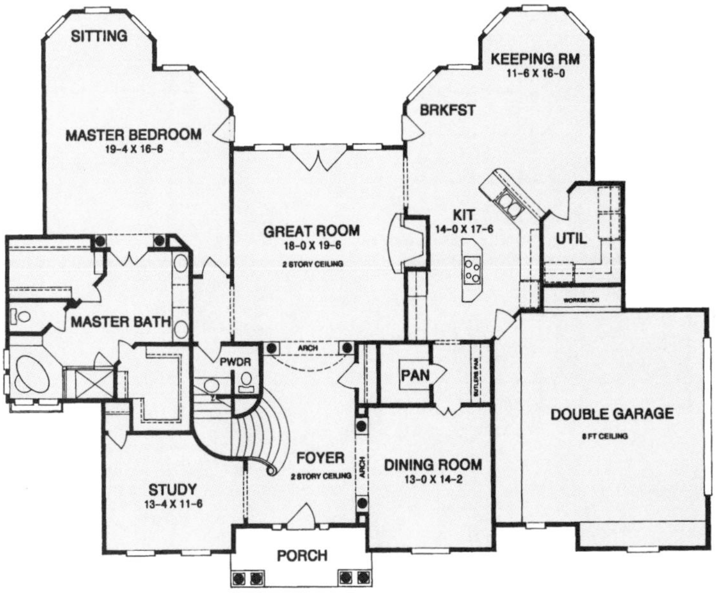

Distinctive touches to this elegant European-style home make an inviting first impression. The two-story foyer is graced by a lovely staircase and a balcony overlook from the upstairs. To the right is the formal dining room; to the left, a study. The great room directly leads to the two-story double bay windows that introduce the kitchen and keeping room. A huge walk-in pantry and adjacent butler's pantry connect the dining room to the kitchen. A marvelous master suite features a sitting room and pampering bath. Upstairs, three bedrooms and two full baths complete the plan.

A stucco finish and front porch with a metal roof dress up a more traditional farmhouse look in this home that's designed for the growing family. A large kitchen, breakfast room and family room are open and adjacent to one another to provide a big area for family gatherings. The family room features a corner fireplace with a raised hearth and provides access to the covered porch in the rear. A two-story living room and a dining room with a ten-foot ceiling are available for more formal entertaining. In the main-floor master suite, the luxuriously appointed master bath includes His and Hers walk-in closets, a seating area at the double vanity and a corner whirlpool tub. Three family bedrooms upstairs share a full bath, a game room and an unfinished expansion area. Please specify crawlspace or slab foundation when ordering.

Design
HPT830242

First Floor: 1,844 square feet

Second Floor: 1,103 square feet

Total: 2,947 square feet

Width 61'-8" Depth 52'-0"

L

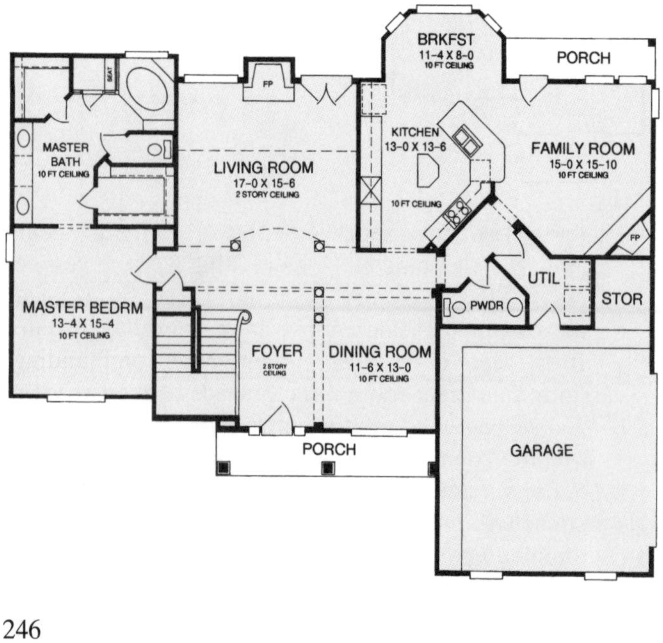

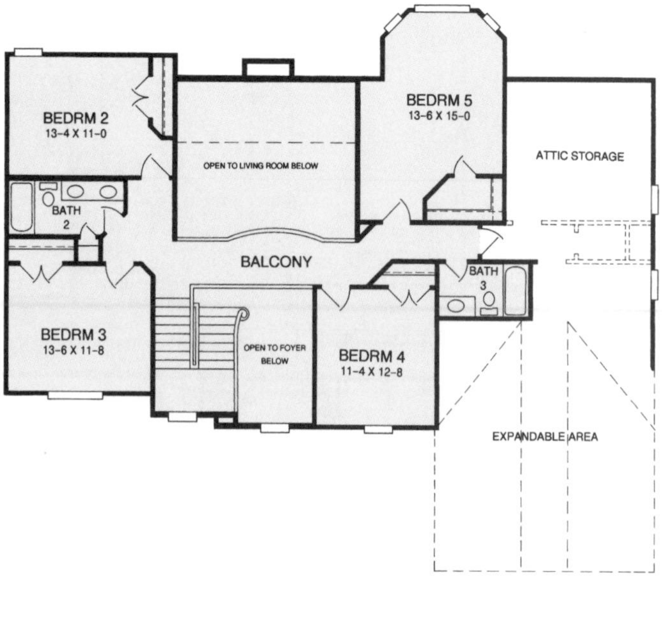

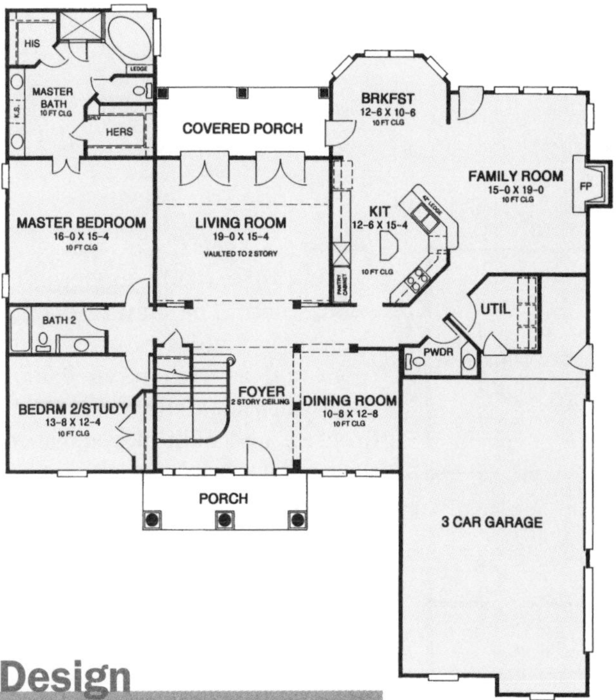
HIS
MASTER BATH 10 FT CLG
HERS
COVERED PORCH
BRKFST 12-6 X 10-6 10 FT CLG
FAMILY ROOM 15-0 X 19-0 10 FT CLG
FP
MASTER BEDROOM 16-0 X 15-4 10 FT CLG
LIVING ROOM 19-0 X 15-4 VAULTED TO 2 STORY
KIT 12-6 X 15-4
UTIL
BATH 2
PWDR
FOYER 2 STORY CEILING
DINING ROOM 10-8 X 12-8 10 FT CLG
BEDRM 2/STUDY 13-8 X 12-4 10 FT CLG
PORCH
3 CAR GARAGE

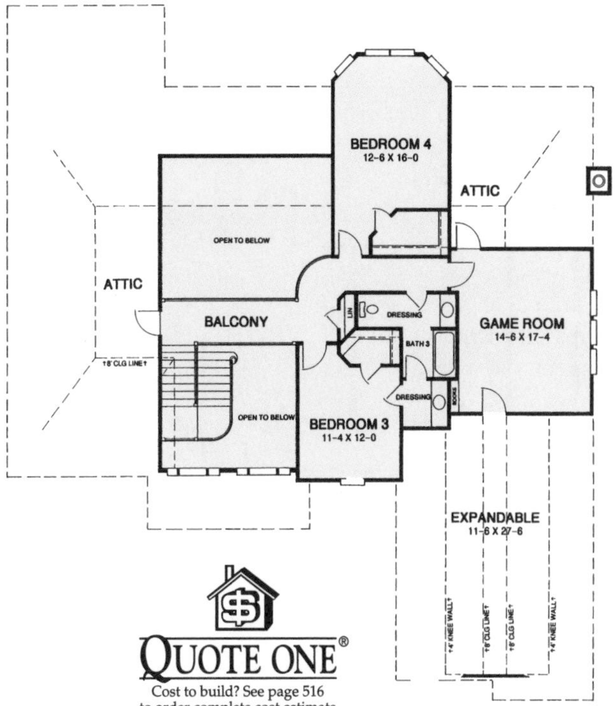
BEDROOM 4 12-6 X 16-0
ATTIC
OPEN TO BELOW
ATTIC
BALCONY
DRESSING
BATH 3
GAME ROOM 14-6 X 17-4
OPEN TO BELOW
BEDROOM 3 11-4 X 12-0
EXPANDABLE 11-6 X 27-6

QUOTE ONE®

Cost to build? See page 516 to order complete cost estimate to build this house in your area!

Design HPT830243

First Floor: 2,469 square feet

Second Floor: 1,025 square feet

Total: 3,494 square feet

Bonus Space: 320 square feet

Width 67'-8" Depth 74'-2"

L

A lovely double arch gives this European-style home a commanding presence. Once inside, a two-story foyer provides an open view directly through the formal living room to the rear grounds beyond. The spacious kitchen with a work island and the bayed breakfast area share space with the family room. The private master suite features dual sinks, twin walk-in closets, a corner garden tub and a separate shower. A large game room completes this wonderful family home. Please specify basement, crawlspace or slab foundation when ordering.

Design

HPT830244

Square Footage: 2,095

Width 65'-0" Depth 55'-6"

This special cottage design carries a fully modern floor plan. The entry leads to open living areas with a dining room and a living room flanking the foyer. The family room—with a fireplace and built-in bookcases—sits near the bright breakfast room with deck access. The efficiently patterned kitchen provides a helpful lead-in to the dining room. Two secondary bedrooms make up the left side of the plan. A full compartmented bath connects them. In the master bedroom suite, a tiered ceiling and a bath with dual vanities, a whirlpool tub, separate shower, compartmented toilet and walk-in closet are sure to please. The two-car, side-load garage opens to the laundry room. This home is designed with a walkout basement foundation.

This French country cottage is a charming example of European architecture. Stucco and stone blend with multiple gables and hipped rooflines to establish the character of the design. A two-story foyer opens to an even more impressive two-story family room with fireplace. To the right, a formal living area opens to a dining room through decorative columns. This room is easily served by a generous kitchen with island cooktop counter. The master suite is also located on the first floor and is well appointed with a coffered ceiling, a walk-in closet and a double-bowl vanity in the bath. The second floor holds two family bedrooms, a full bath, space for an additional bedroom and future bath, and bonus storage space. This home is designed with a walkout basement foundation.

Design HPT830245

First Floor: 1,720 square feet
Second Floor: 545 square feet
Total: 2,265 square feet
Bonus Space: 365 square feet
Width 50'-0" Depth 53'-6"

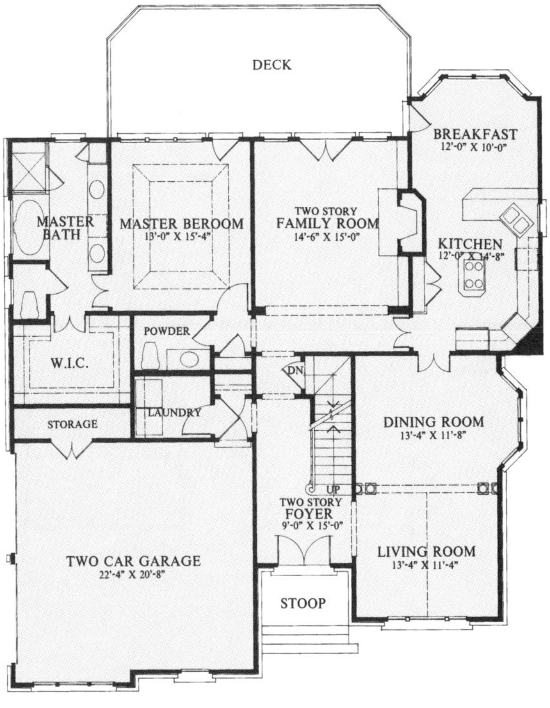

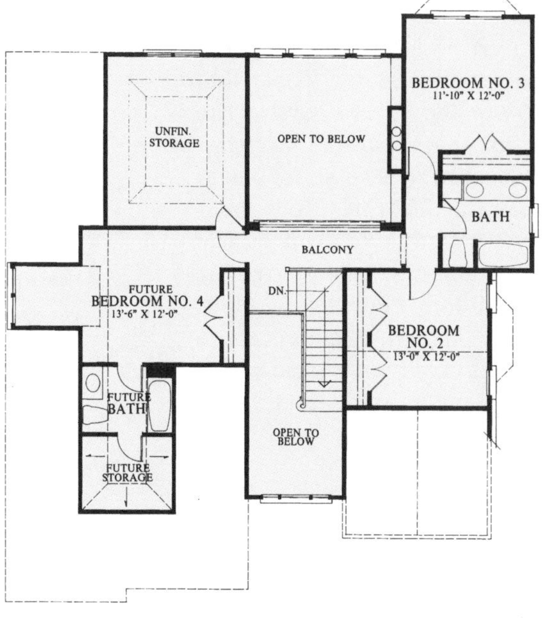

Design

HPT830246

Square Footage: 2,090

Width 61'-0" Depth 72'-0"

This home's European styling will work well in a variety of environments. As for livability, this plan has it all. Begin with the front door, which opens into the dining and great rooms—the latter complete with fireplace and doors that open onto the back porch. The kitchen combines with the breakfast nook to create ample space for meals. This plan incorporates four bedrooms; you may want to use one as an office and another as a study. The master bedroom houses a fabulous bath with twin walk-in closets and a spa tub. This home is designed with a walkout basement foundation.

QUOTE ONE®

Cost to build? See page 516 to order complete cost estimate to build this house in your area!

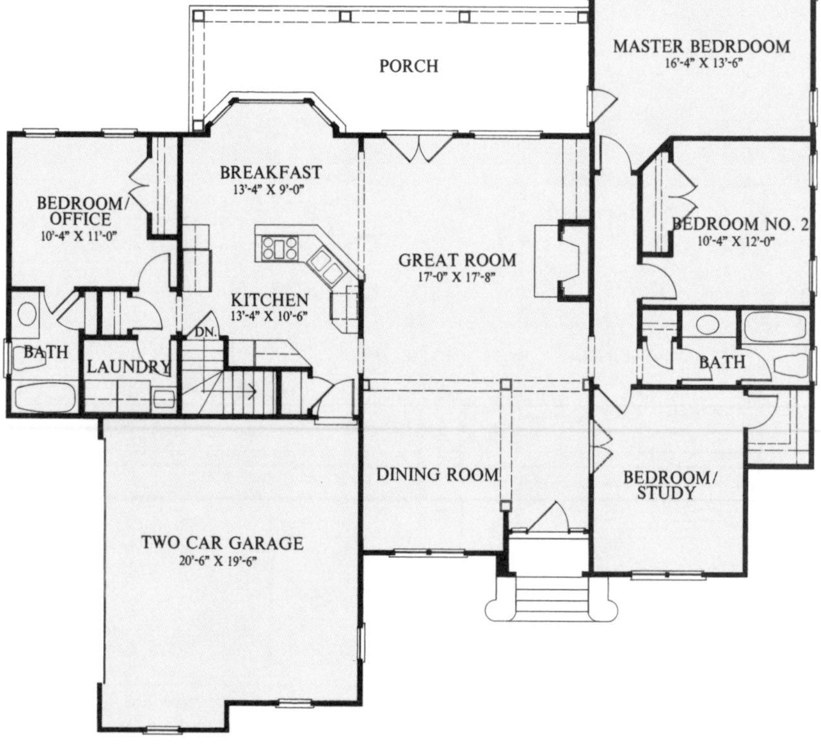

MASTER BATH
PORCH
MASTER BEDRDOOM
16'-4" X 13'-6"
BREAKFAST
13'-4" X 9'-0"
BEDROOM/ OFFICE
10'-4" X 11'-0"
BEDROOM NO. 2
10'-4" X 12'-0"
GREAT ROOM
17'-0" X 17'-8"
KITCHEN
13'-4" X 10'-6"
DN.
BATH
LAUNDRY
BATH
DINING ROOM
BEDROOM/ STUDY
TWO CAR GARAGE
20'-6" X 19'-6"

Inside, the foyer of this lovely European home opens into the great room with a vaulted ceiling and a dining room defined by columns. Kitchen tasks are made easy with this home's step-saving kitchen and breakfast bar. Nestled away at the opposite end of the home, the master suite combines perfect solitude with elegant luxury. Features include a double-door entry, tray ceiling, and niche details. Two family bedrooms share a private bath. This home is designed with a walkout basement foundation.

PORCH
BREAKFAST
10'-0" X 10'-0"
GREAT ROOM
16'-0" X 18'-0"
MASTER BEDROOM
15'-0" X 14'-0"
W.I.C.
MASTER BATH
POWDER
KITCHEN
14'-0" X 11'-4"
DINING ROOM
10'-6" X 13'-0"
FOYER
5'-0" X 9'-0"
BEDROOM
NO. 3
10'-6" X 10'-0"
BEDROOM NO. 2
11'-2" X 11'-0"
BATH
LAUND
5'-2" X
10'-6"
DN.
TWO CAR GARAGE
20'-4" X 19'-4"

Design
HPT830247

Square Footage: 1,815

Width 60'-0" Depth 58'-6"

Design
HPT830248

Square Footage: 4,590

Width 69'-0" Depth 49'-6"

The abundance of details in this plan make it the finest in one-story living. The great room and formal dining room have an open, dramatic sense of space. The kitchen with a preparation island shares the right side of the plan with a bayed breakfast area and a keeping room with a fireplace. Sleeping accommodations to the left of the plan include a master suite and two family bedrooms. This home is designed with a walkout basement foundation.

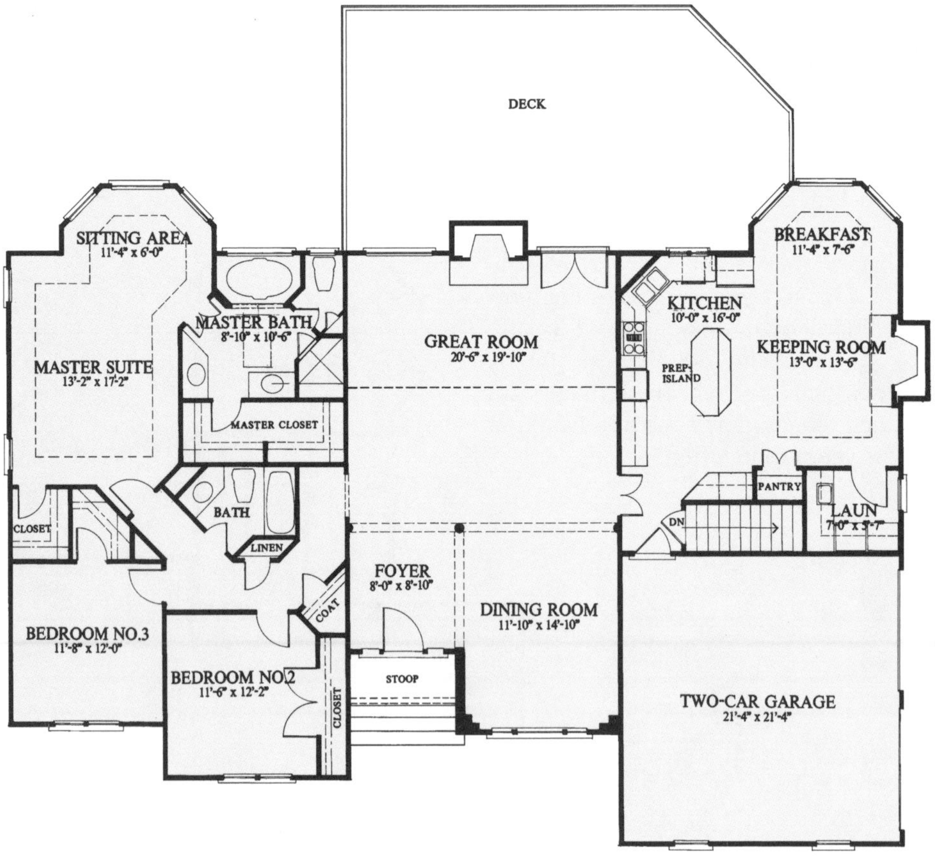
DECK
SITTING AREA 11'-4" x 6'-0"
MASTER BATH 8'-10" x 10'-6"
MASTER SUITE 13'-2" x 17'-2"
MASTER CLOSET
GREAT ROOM 20'-6" x 19'-10"
KITCHEN 10'-0" x 16'-0"
BREAKFAST 11'-4" x 7'-6"
KEEPING ROOM 13'-0" x 13'-6"
PREP-ISLAND
PANTRY
LAUN 7'-0" x 5'-7"
DN
BATH
CLOSET
LINEN
COAT
FOYER 8'-0" x 8'-10"
DINING ROOM 11'-10" x 14'-10"
BEDROOM NO.3 11'-8" x 12'-0"
BEDROOM NO.2 11'-6" x 12'-2"
CLOSET
STOOP
TWO-CAR GARAGE 21'-4" x 21'-4"

QUOTE ONE®

Cost to build? See page 516 to order complete cost estimate to build this house in your area!

Design

HPT830249

Square Footage: 1,684

Width 55'-6" Depth 57'-6"

Charming and compact, this home is as beautiful as it is practical. The impressive arch over the double front door is repeated with an arched window in the formal dining room. This room opens to a spacious great room with a fireplace and is near the kitchen and bayed breakfast area. Split sleeping arrangements put the master suite at the right of the plan and two family bedrooms at the left. This home is designed with a walkout basement foundation.

DECK
BREAKFAST 11'-4" X 8'-6"
BEDROOM NO. 3 11'-6" X 11'-0"
GREAT ROOM 14'-0" X 17'-6"
KITCHEN 11'-4" X 10'-0"
MASTER BEDROOM 12'-4" X 15'-6"
BATH
DN.
HIS
FOYER 6'-6" X 5'-0"
PWDR.
MASTER BATH
BEDROOM NO. 2 11'-0" X 12'-2"
DINING ROOM 11'-4" X 10'-6"
STOOP
LAUNDRY
HERS
TWO-CAR GARAGE 20'-4" X 19'-4"

QUOTE ONE®
Cost to build? See page 516 to order complete cost estimate to build this house in your area!

A grand front window display illuminates the formal dining room and the great room of this country French charmer. Open planning allows for easy access between the formal dining room, great room, vaulted breakfast nook and kitchen. Extra amenities include a decorative column, fireplace and an optional bay window in the breakfast nook. The elegant master suite is fashioned with a tray ceiling in the bedroom, a vaulted master bath and a walk-in closet. Two family bedrooms are designated in a pocket-door hall and share a large hall bath. Please specify basement, crawlspace or slab foundation when ordering.

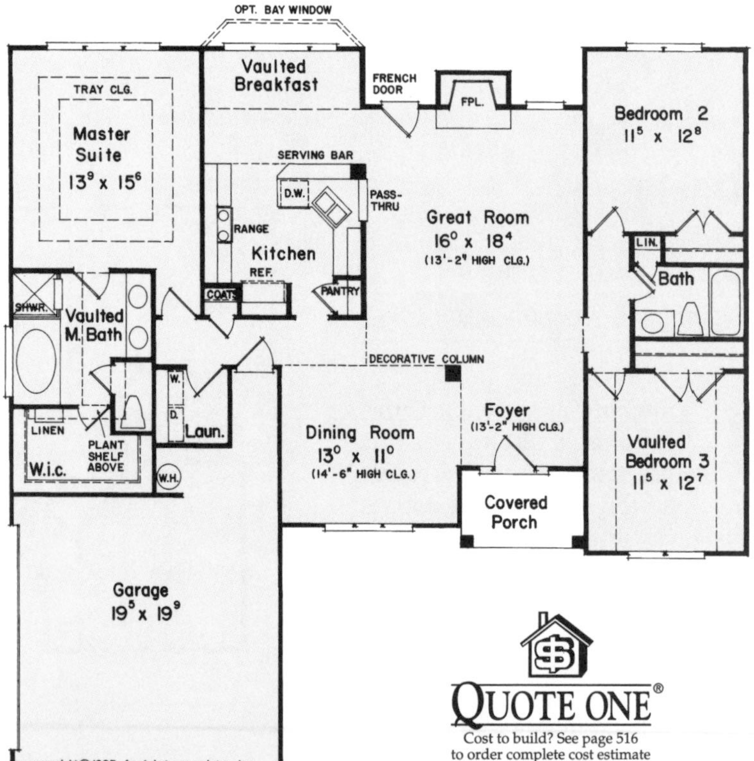

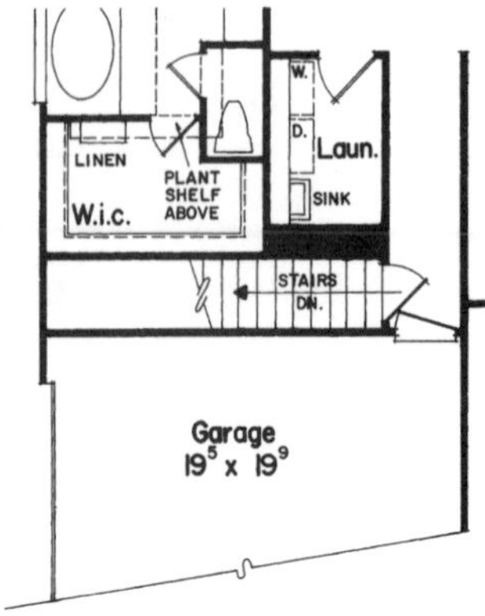

OPTIONAL BASEMENT STAIR LOCATION

Design
HPT830250
Square Footage: 1,670
Width 54'-0" Depth 52'-0"

This home, as shown in the photograph, may differ from the actual blueprints. For more detailed information, please check the floor plans carefully.
Photo by Larry E. Belk Designs

This European-style, brick-and-stucco home showcases an arched entry and presents a commanding presence from the curb. Inside, the living room, the dining room and the family room are located at the rear of the home to provide wide-open views of the rear grounds beyond. A colonnade with connecting arches defines the space for a living room with a fireplace and the dining room. The spacious master suite features a relaxing sitting area, His and Hers closets and an extravagant bath. Take special note of the private His and Hers bathrooms. On the second floor, three bedrooms, two baths and a game room complete the home.

Design HPT830251

First Floor: 2,188 square feet

Second Floor: 1,110 square feet

Total: 3,298 square feet

Width 69'-0" Depth 64'-8"

L

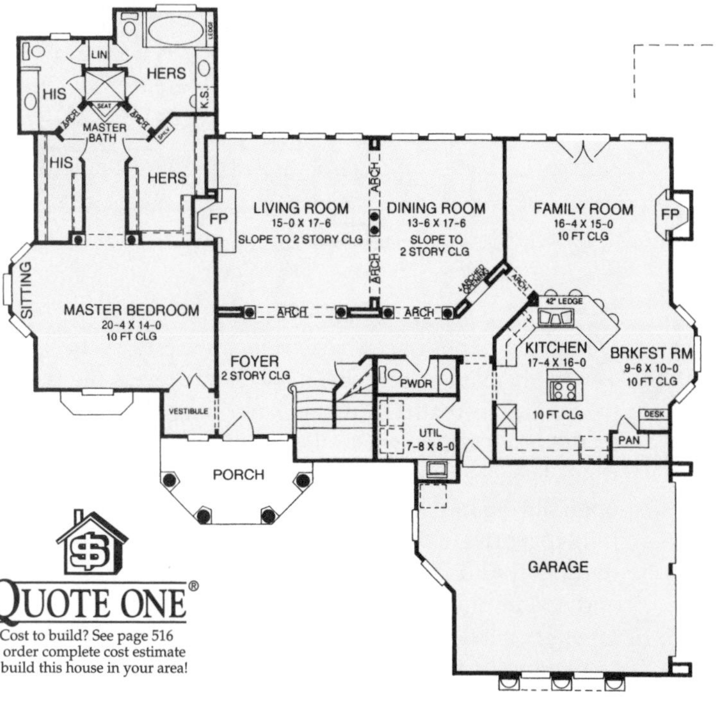

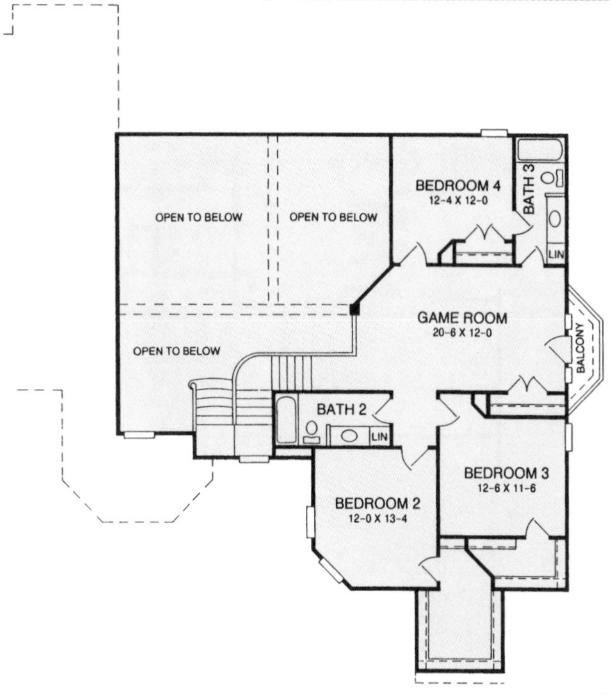

QUOTE ONE®
Cost to build? See page 516 to order complete cost estimate to build this house in your area!

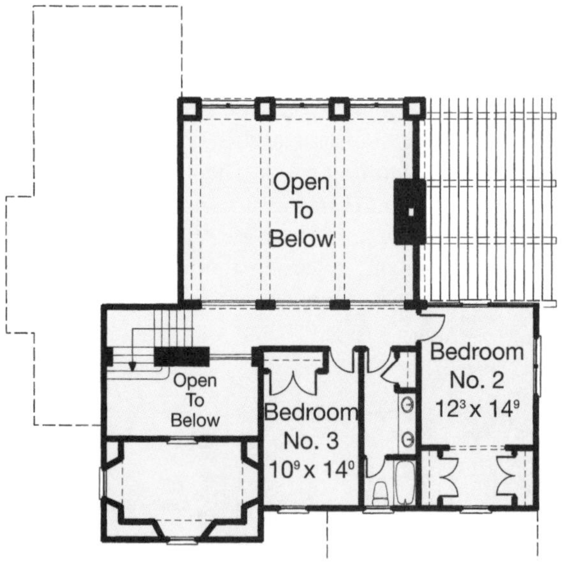

Design
HPT830252

First Floor: 2,058 square feet
Second Floor: 712 square feet
Total: 2,770 square feet
Width 57'-3" Depth 81'-3"

If you've always dreamed of owning a villa, we invite you to experience this European lifestyle—on a perfectly manageable scale. This home offers the best of traditional formality and casual elegance. The foyer leads to the great room, with a bold but stylish fireplace and three French doors to the rear terrace—sure to be left open during fair weather. The large kitchen opens gracefully to a private dining room that has access to a covered outdoor patio. The master suite combines great views and a sumptuous bath to complete this winning design. Upstairs, a balcony hall overlooking the great room leads to two family bedrooms that share a full hall bath.

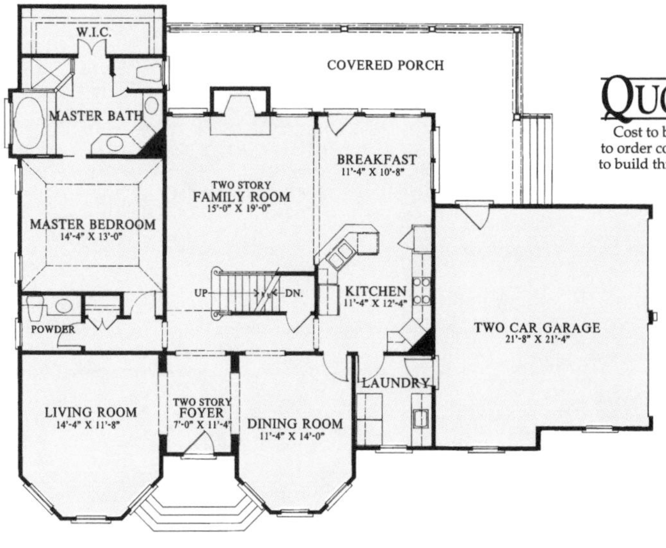
W.I.C.
COVERED PORCH
MASTER BATH
TWO STORY
FAMILY ROOM
15'-0" X 19'-0"
BREAKFAST
11'-4" X 10'-8"
MASTER BEDROOM
14'-4" X 13'-0"
UP
DN.
KITCHEN
11'-4" X 12'-4"
POWDER
TWO CAR GARAGE
21'-8" X 21'-4"
LAUNDRY
LIVING ROOM
14'-4" X 11'-8"
TWO STORY
FOYER
7'-0" X 11'-4"
DINING ROOM
11'-4" X 14'-0"

QUOTE ONE®
Cost to build? See page 516 to order complete cost estimate to build this house in your area!

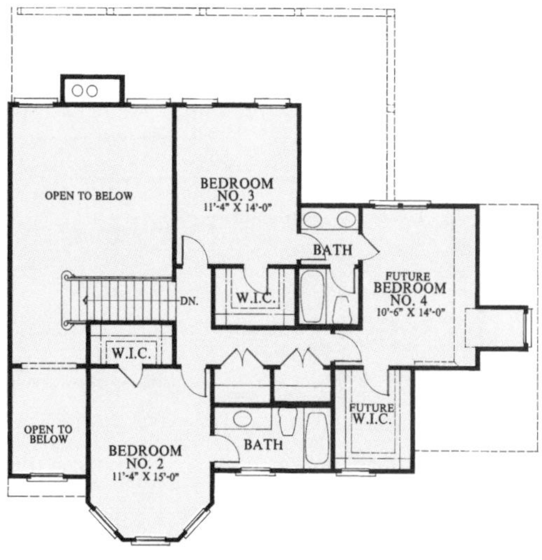
OPEN TO BELOW
BEDROOM
NO. 3
11'-4" X 14'-0"
BATH
FUTURE
BEDROOM
NO. 4
10'-6" X 14'-0"
DN.
W.I.C.
W.I.C.
OPEN TO
BELOW
BEDROOM
NO. 2
11'-4" X 15'-0"
BATH
FUTURE
W.I.C.

This European design is filled with space for formal and informal occasions. Informal areas include an open kitchen, breakfast room and family room with a fireplace. Formal rooms surround the foyer, with the living room on the left and dining room on the right. The master suite is conveniently placed on the first floor, with a gorgeous private bath and a walk-in closet. Each of the family bedrooms upstairs also features a sizable walk-in closet and access to a full bath. Additional storage space is found in the hallway. A fourth bedroom, not included in the square footage, is optional. This home is designed with a walkout basement foundation.

Design HPT830253

First Floor: 1,660 square feet
Second Floor: 665 square feet
Total: 2,325 square feet
Bonus Space: 240 square feet
Width 64'-0" Depth 48'-6"

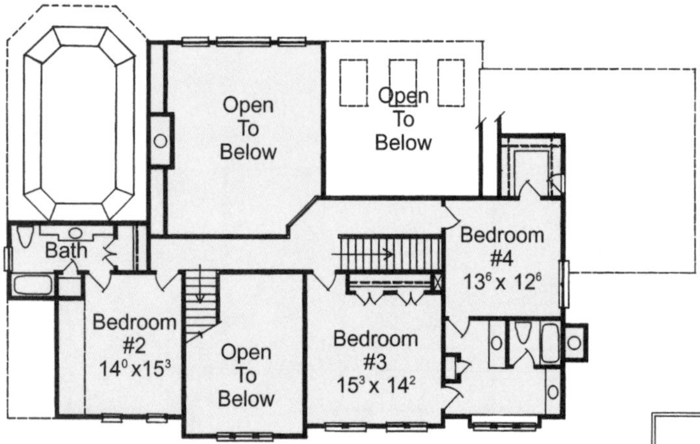

Open
To
Below
Open
To
Below
Bath
Bedroom
#4
13⁶ x 12⁶
Bedroom
#2
14⁰x15³
Open
To
Below
Bedroom
#3
15³ x 14²

Design

HPT830254
First Floor: 2,420 square feet
Second Floor: 1,146 square feet
Total: 3,566 square feet
Width 77'-8" Depth 50'-8"

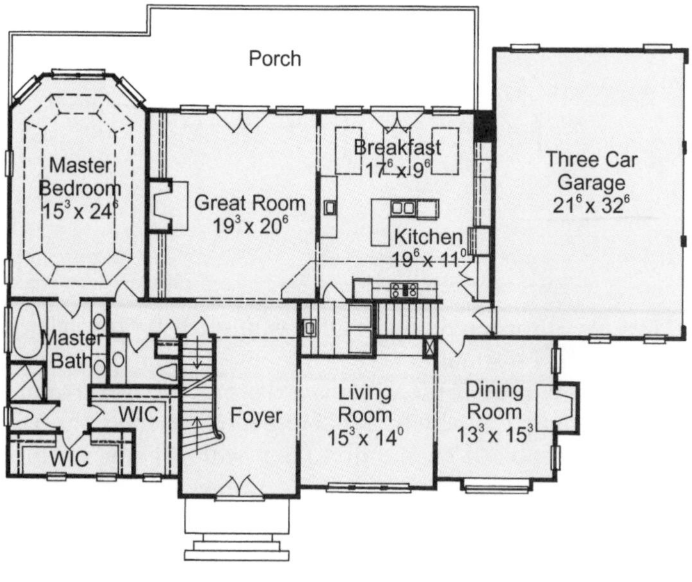

Porch
Master
Bedroom
15³ x 24⁶
Great Room
19³ x 20⁶
Breakfast
17⁶ x 9⁶
Kitchen
19⁶ x 11⁰
Three Car
Garage
21⁶ x 32⁶
Master
Bath
WIC
WIC
Foyer
Living
Room
15³ x 14⁰
Dining
Room
13³ x 15³

Multi-pane glass windows, double French doors and ornamental stucco detailing are complementary elements on the facade of this home. An impressive two-story foyer opens to the formal living and dining rooms. Natural light is available through the attractive windows in each room. The kitchen features a pass-through to the two-story family room and an adjoining skylit breakfast room. The first-floor master suite offers an elegant vaulted bedroom ceiling, a bath with twin vanities, a separate shower and tub, and two spacious walk-in closets. Upstairs, Bedroom 2 has its own bath and can be used as a guest suite. Two other bedrooms share a large bath that includes twin vanities. This home is designed with a walkout basement foundation.

A myriad of glass and ornamental stucco detailing complements the asymmetrical facade of this two-story home. Inside, the striking, two-story foyer provides a dramatic entrance. To the right is the formal dining room. An efficient L-shaped kitchen and bayed breakfast nook are conveniently located near the dining area. The living room, with its welcoming fireplace, opens through double doors to the rear terrace. The private master suite provides access to the rear terrace and adjacent study. The master bath is sure to please with its relaxing garden tub, separate shower, grand His and Hers walk-in closets and a compartmented toilet. The second floor contains three large bedrooms, one with a private bath, while the others share a bath. This home is designed with a walkout basement foundation.

Design HPT830255

First Floor: 2,461 square feet
Second Floor: 1,114 square feet
Total: 3,575 square feet
Width 84'-4" Depth 63'-0"

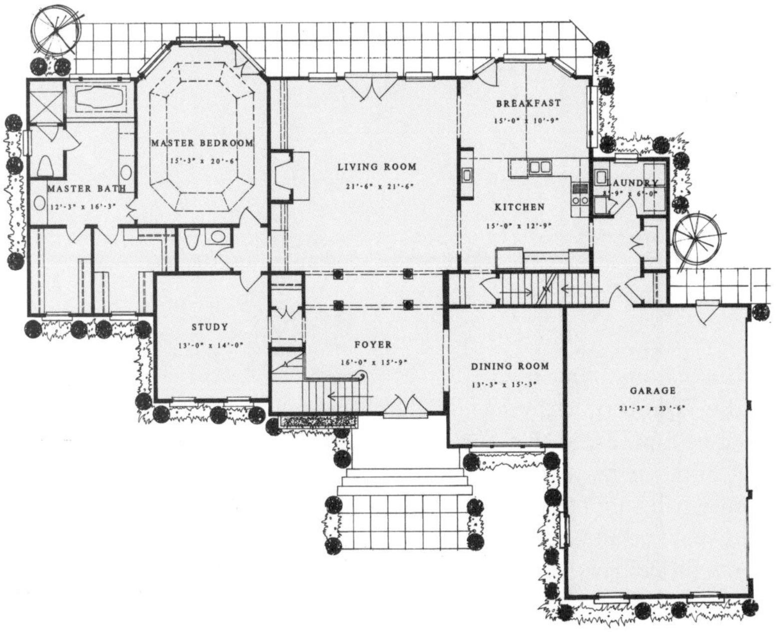

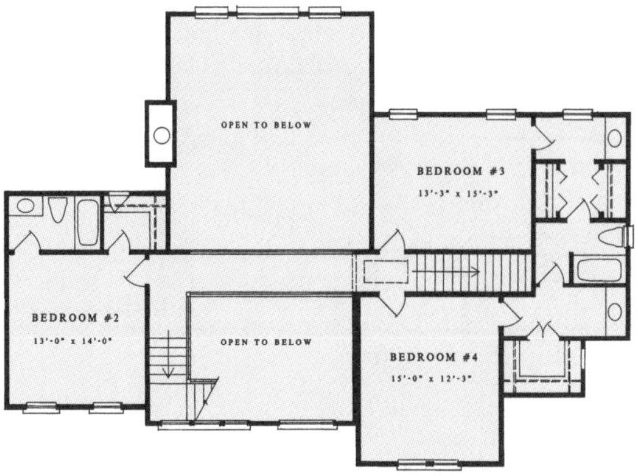

QUOTE ONE®

Cost to build? See page 516 to order complete cost estimate to build this house in your area!

© Design Traditions

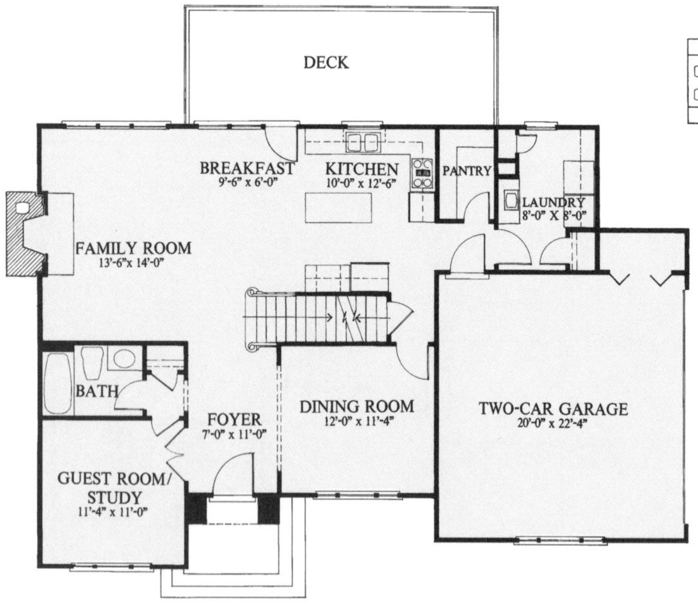
DECK
BREAKFAST
9'-6" x 6'-0"
KITCHEN
10'-0" x 12'-6"
PANTRY
LAUNDRY
8'-0" X 8'-0"
FAMILY ROOM
13'-6"x 14'-0"
BATH
FOYER
7'-0" x 11'-0"
DINING ROOM
12'-0" x 11'-4"
TWO-CAR GARAGE
20'-0" x 22'-4"
GUEST ROOM/
STUDY
11'-4" x 11'-0"

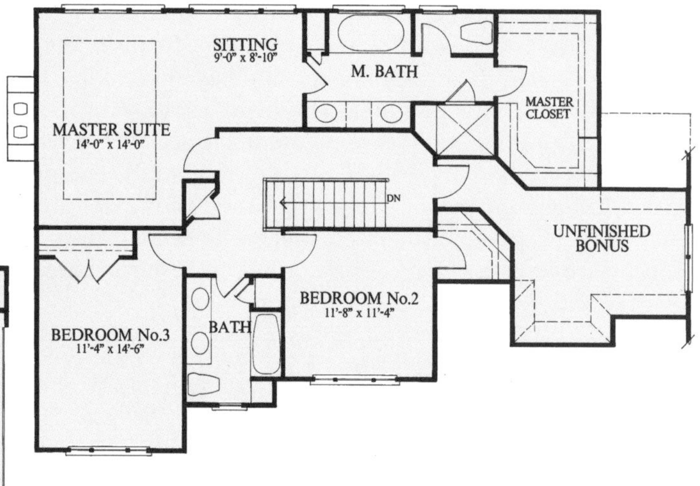
SITTING
9'-0" x 8'-10"
M. BATH
MASTER CLOSET
MASTER SUITE
14'-0" x 14'-0"
DN
UNFINISHED BONUS
BEDROOM No.2
11'-8" x 11'-4"
BEDROOM No.3
11'-4" x 14'-6"
BATH

A stucco exterior gives European appeal to this family home. An expansive family room provides space for entertaining. The formal dining room is just off the foyer. Meal preparation will be a breeze with the work island and large walk-in pantry in the kitchen. Upstairs, the master suite includes a sitting area and enormous bath with dual vanity, whirlpool tub, separate shower and a walk-in closet. Two family bedrooms share a full bath with a dual vanity. The bonus room would make a great home office. This home is designed with a walkout basement foundation.

Design HPT830256

First Floor: 1,103 square feet
Second Floor: 1,103 square feet
Total: 2,206 square feet
Bonus Space: 212 square feet
Width 52'-0" Depth 34'-0"

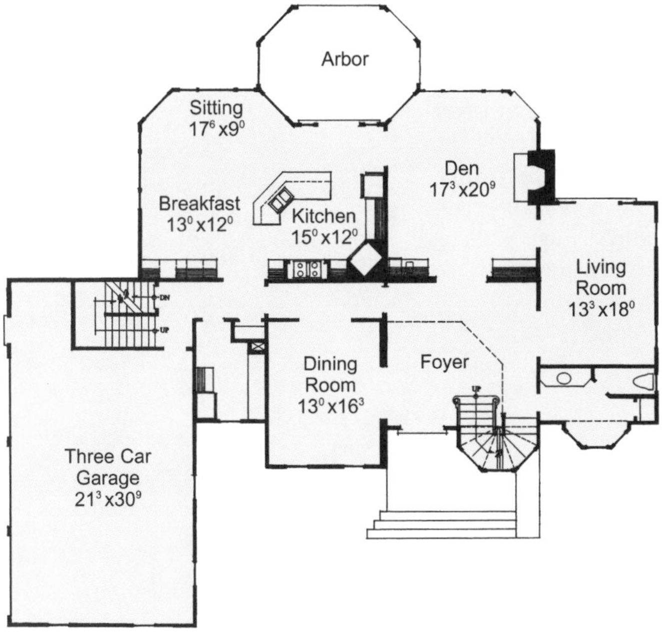

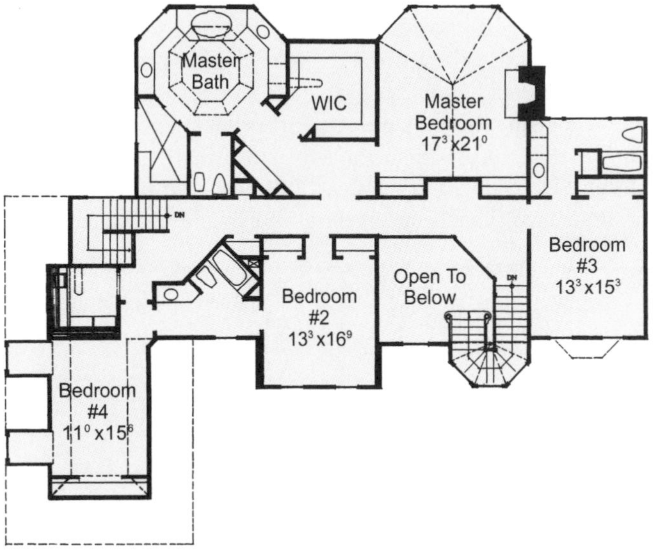

A blend of stucco and stone creates the charm in this French country estate home. The asymmetrical design and arched glass windows add to the European character. Inside, the plan offers a unique arrangement of rooms conducive to today's lifestyles. A living room and a dining room flank the foyer, creating a functional formal area. The large den or family room is positioned at the rear of the home with convenient access to the kitchen, patio and covered arbor. Equally accessible to the arbor and patio are the kitchen and breakfast/sitting area. A large butler's pantry is located near the kitchen and dining room. Upstairs, the vaulted master suite and three large bedrooms provide private retreats. This home is designed with a walkout basement foundation.

Design HPT830257

First Floor: 2,161 square feet
Second Floor: 2,110 square feet
Total: 4,271 square feet
Width 76'-2" Depth 60'-11"

Centuries ago, the center column played a vital role in the support of a double-arched window such as the one that graces this home's exterior. Today's amenities combined with the well-seasoned architecture of Europe offer the best of both worlds. The contemporary floor plan begins with a soaring foyer that opens onto the formal living and dining rooms. Casual living is enjoyed at the rear of the plan in the L-shaped kitchen, the family room and the light-filled breakfast/sun room. A guest bedroom is tucked behind the family room for privacy. Upstairs, an exquisite master suite features a lavish bath and a huge walk-in closet. Two family bedrooms, a full bath and unfinished bonus space complete the second floor. This home is designed with a walkout basement foundation.

Design HPT830258

First Floor: 1,980 square feet
Second Floor: 1,317 square feet
Total: 3,297 square feet
Bonus Space: 255 square feet
Width 58'-9" Depth 66'-9"

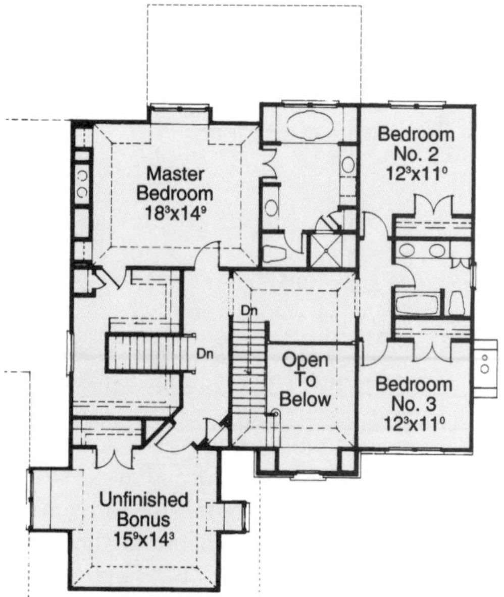

French-entry doors open to a formal dining room on the left with excellent frontal views, and a formal living room on the right that leads to a quiet corner media room. The bayed great room offers access to the rear deck in order to enjoy the full benefits of sun and outdoor activities. A large island kitchen with a bayed breakfast nook completes the first floor of this plan. Upstairs, Bedrooms 2 and 3 share a full bath, while Bedroom 4 includes its own bath. The master bedroom features a bayed sitting area and an exquisite master bath with a wonderful vanity area, massive walk-in closet and unique step-up tub. This home is designed with a walkout basement foundation.

Design HPT830259

First Floor: 1,475 square feet

Second Floor: 1,460 square feet

Total: 2,935 square feet

Width 57'-6" Depth 46'-6"

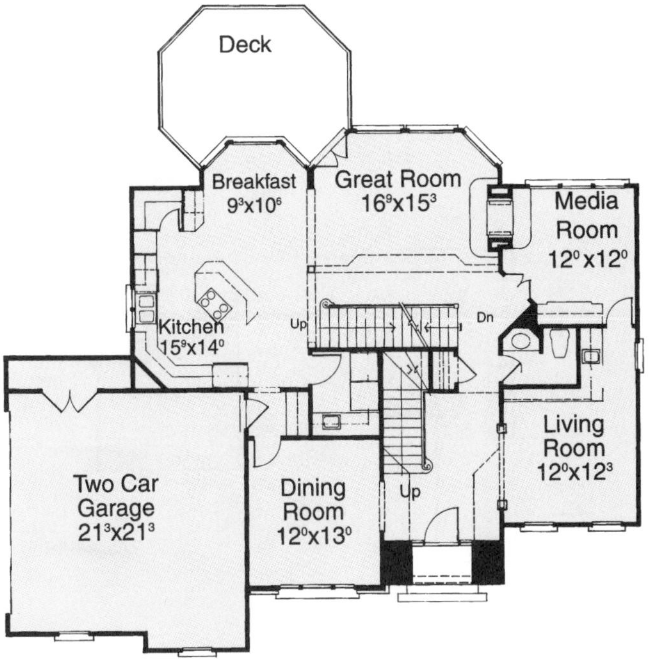

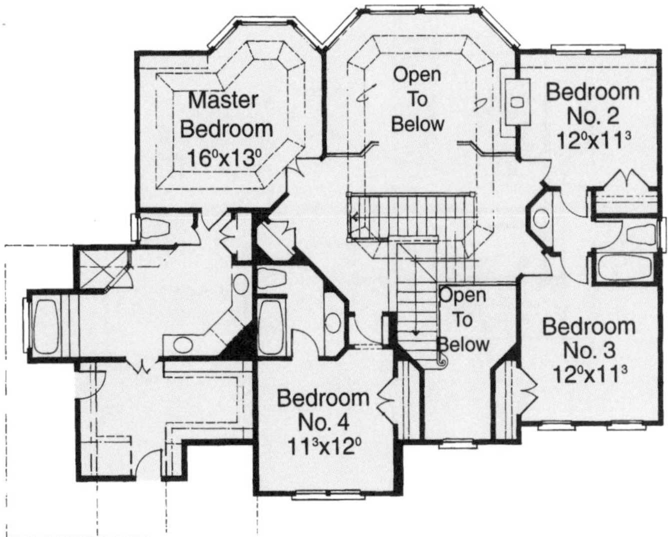

Topping the arched entry is a lovely transom window, which admits sunlight to enhance the magnificence of the two-story foyer. The formal atmosphere of the living and dining rooms is brought together by a through-fireplace. Generously sized windows in these rooms allow views of outside living areas or children's play areas. An additional fireplace can be found in the corner of the keeping room, adjacent to the enormous kitchen and the breakfast area, which is set off by a bay window. The master suite features an expansive master bath with a large walk-in closet. This home is designed with a walkout basement foundation.

Design HPT830260

First Floor: 1,811 square feet
Second Floor: 1,437 square feet
Total: 3,248 square feet
Bonus Space: 286 square feet
Width 53'-6" Depth 60'-6"

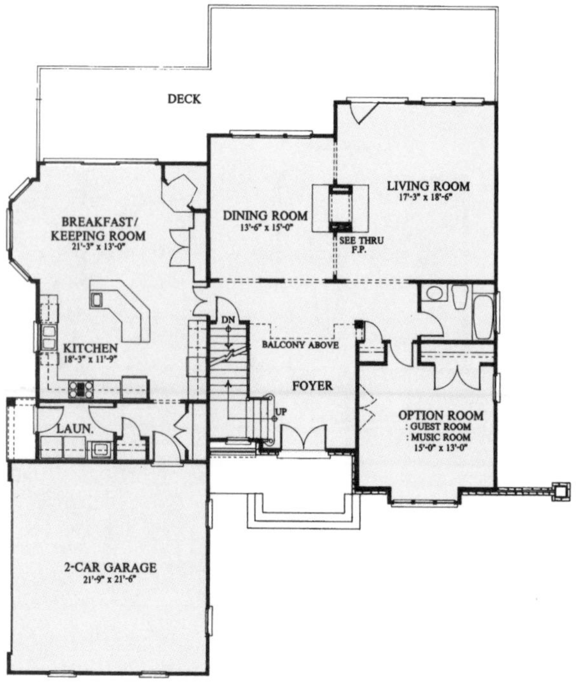

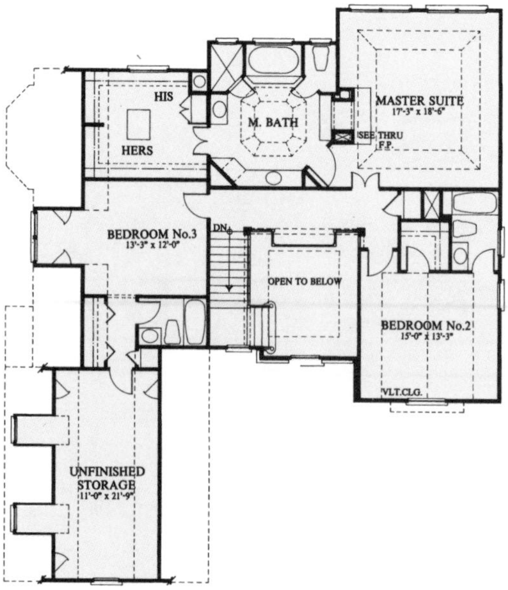

Design HPT830261

First Floor: 1,370 square feet
Second Floor: 1,673 square feet
Total: 3,043 square feet
Width 73'-6" Depth 49'-0"

QUOTE ONE®

Cost to build? See page 516 to order complete cost estimate to build this house in your area!

This English Georgian home features a dramatic brick exterior, with jack-arch detailing that complements a charming porte cochere. A U-shaped staircase and balcony overlook create an elegant foyer. Separated by a classical colonnade detail, the formal living and dining rooms make a perfect area for entertaining. The great room features a centered fireplace and opens to the breakfast room and kitchen, which has plenty of cabinets and counter space. The second floor includes a guest suite, a children's den area, two family bedrooms and the master suite. A cozy fireplace, coffered ceiling and sumptuous bath highlight this lavish suite. This home is designed with a walkout basement foundation.

QUOTE ONE®

Cost to build? See page 516 to order complete cost estimate to build this house in your area!

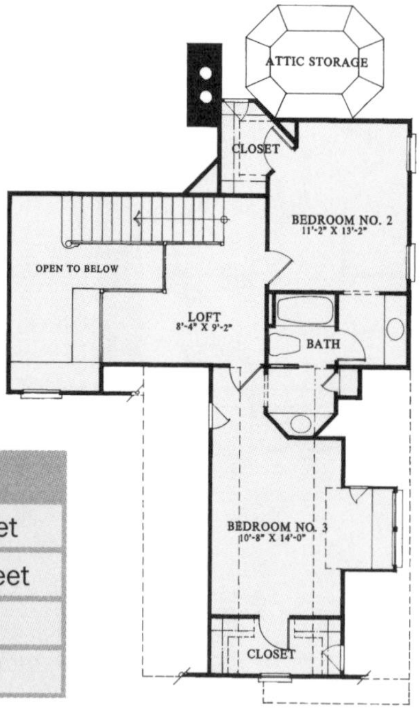

Design HPT830262

First Floor: 1,724 square feet
Second Floor: 700 square feet
Total: 2,424 square feet
Width 47'-10" Depth 63'-8"

All the charm of gables, stonework and multi-level rooflines combine to create this home. To the left of the foyer, you will see the dining room highlighted by a tray ceiling. This room and the living room flow together to form one large entertainment area. The gourmet kitchen holds a work island and adjoining octagonal breakfast room. The great room features a pass-through wet bar, a fireplace and bookcases. The master suite enjoys privacy at the rear of the home. An open-rail loft above the foyer leads to two additional bedrooms with walk-in closets, private vanities and a shared bath. This home is designed with a walkout basement foundation.

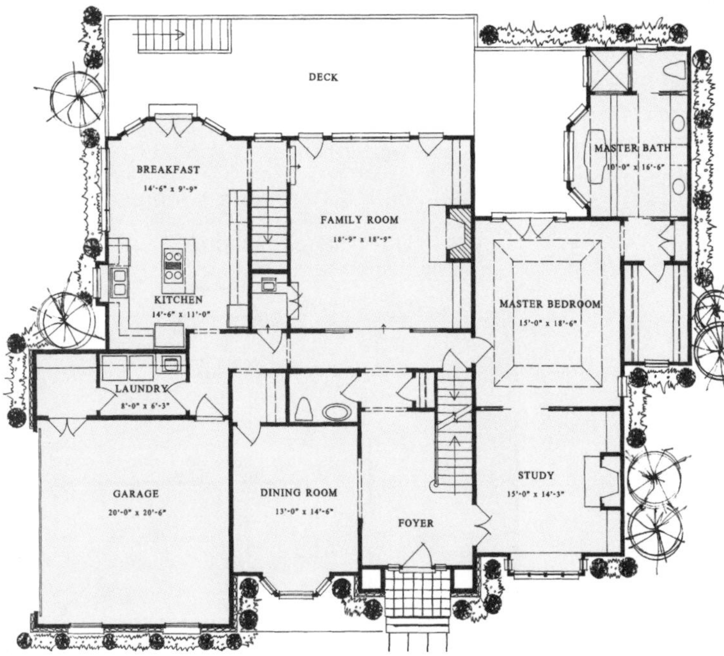

Design

HPT830263

First Floor: 2,346 square feet
Second Floor: 1,260 square feet
Total: 3,606 square feet
Width 68'-11" Depth 58'-9"

The European character of this home is enhanced through the use of stucco and stone on the exterior, giving this French country estate home its charm and beauty. The foyer leads to the dining room and study/living room. The two-story family room is positioned for convenient access to the back staircase, kitchen, wet bar and deck area. The master bedroom is privately located on the right side of the home with an optional entry to the study and a large garden bath. Upstairs are three additional large bedrooms; two have a shared bath and private vanities and one has a full private bath. All bedrooms conveniently access the back staircase and have open-rail views to the family room below. This home is designed with a walkout basement foundation.

A grand facade is a perfect introduction to this stately two-story home that's designed for both formal and casual family living. A two-story foyer that leads to the vaulted living room is punctuated by a dramatic arch with a plant shelf above. Formal entertaining areas are nicely balanced with the vaulted family room and the gourmet kitchen and breakfast nook. The first-floor master suite is designed for luxury and privacy. Upstairs, three family bedrooms each has a walk-in closet and private bath access. Please specify basement or crawlspace foundation when ordering.

Design
HPT830264

First Floor: 1,883 square feet

Second Floor: 803 square feet

Total: 2,686 square feet

Width 58'-6" Depth 59'-4"

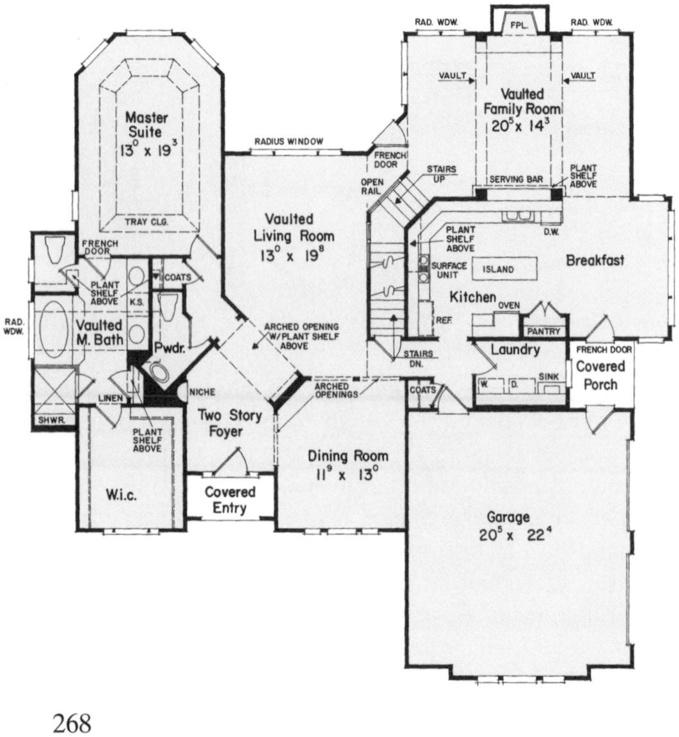

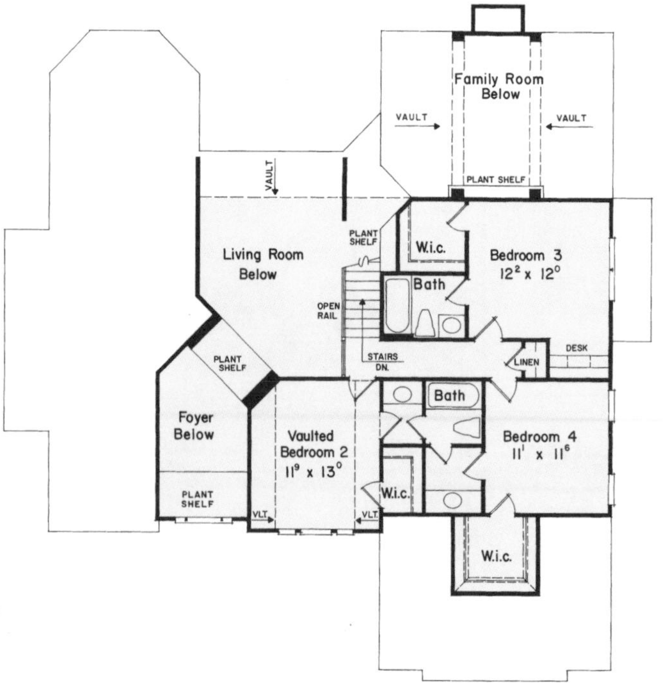

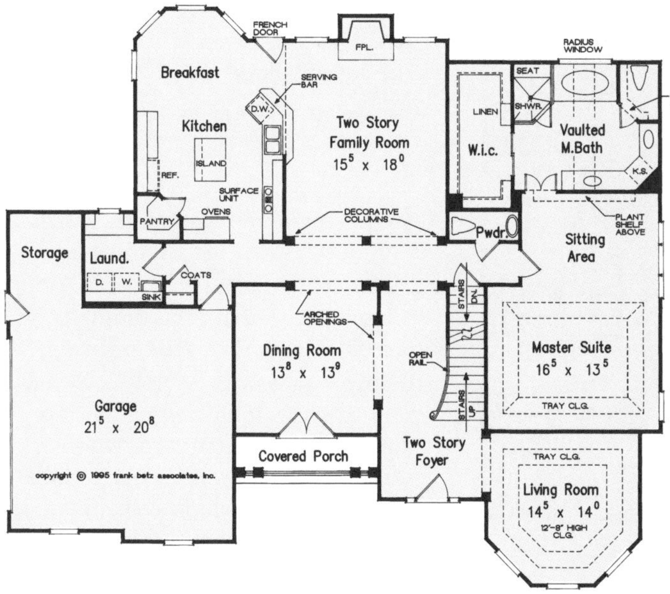

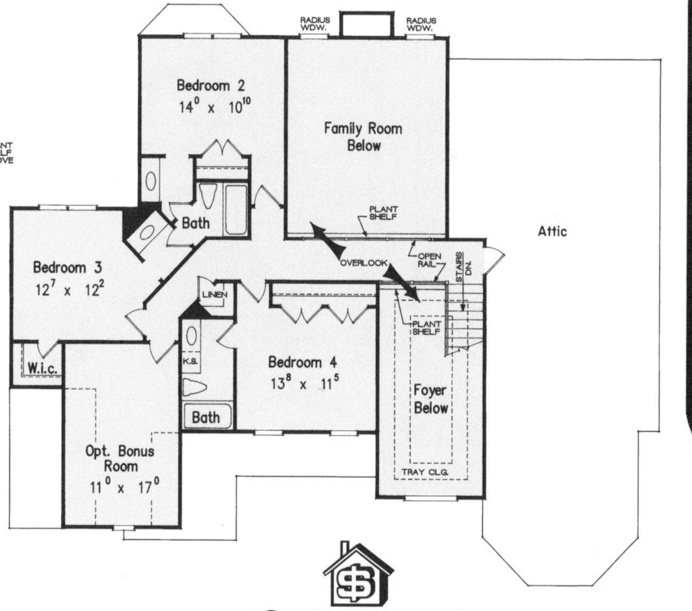

QUOTE ONE®

Cost to build? See page 516 to order complete cost estimate to build this house in your area!

Design

HPT830265
First Floor: 2,044 square feet
Second Floor: 896 square feet
Total: 2,940 square feet
Bonus Space: 197 square feet
Width 63'-0" Depth 54'-0"

A gracious front porch off the formal dining room and a two-story entry set the tone for this elegant home. The living room is set to the front of the plan, thoughtfully separated from casual family areas that radiate from the kitchen. The two-story family room is framed by a balcony hall and accented with a fireplace and serving bar. The first-floor master suite features a sitting area, lush bath and walk-in closet. Upstairs, two family bedrooms share a full bath while a third enjoys a private bath. Please specify basement, crawlspace or slab foundation when ordering.

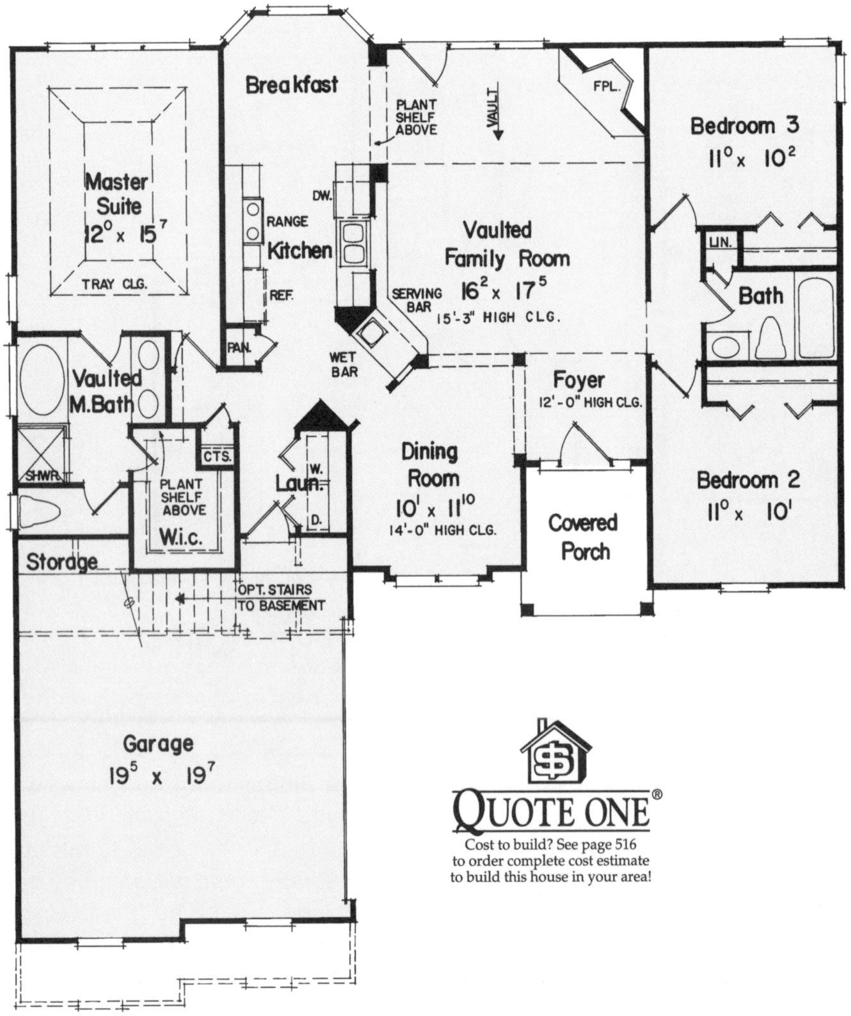

Breakfast
PLANT SHELF ABOVE
VAULT
FPL.
Bedroom 3
11⁰ x 10²
Master Suite
12⁰ x 15⁷
TRAY CLG.
DW.
RANGE
Kitchen
REF.
Vaulted Family Room
16² x 17⁵
SERVING BAR
15'-3" HIGH CLG.
LIN.
Bath
PAN.
WET BAR
Vaulted M.Bath
Foyer
12'-0" HIGH CLG.
CTS.
SHWR.
PLANT SHELF ABOVE
W.i.c.
Laun.
W.
D.
Dining Room
10¹ x 11¹⁰
14'-0" HIGH CLG.
Covered Porch
Bedroom 2
11⁰ x 10¹
Storage
OPT. STAIRS TO BASEMENT
Garage
19⁵ x 19⁷

Design

HPT830266

Square Footage: 1,429

Width 49'-0" Depth 53'-0"

This home's gracious exterior is indicative of the elegant, yet extremely livable floor plan inside. The formal dining room is set off from the foyer and vaulted family room with stately columns. The spacious family room has a corner fireplace, rear-yard door and serving bar from the open galley kitchen. A bay-windowed breakfast nook flanks the kitchen on one end, while a laundry center and wet bar/serving pantry lead to the dining room on the other. The split-bedroom plan allows the amenity-rich master suite maximum privacy. A pocket door off the family room leads to the hall housing the two family bedrooms and a full bath. Please specify basement, crawlspace or slab foundation when ordering.

QUOTE ONE®

Cost to build? See page 516 to order complete cost estimate to build this house in your area!

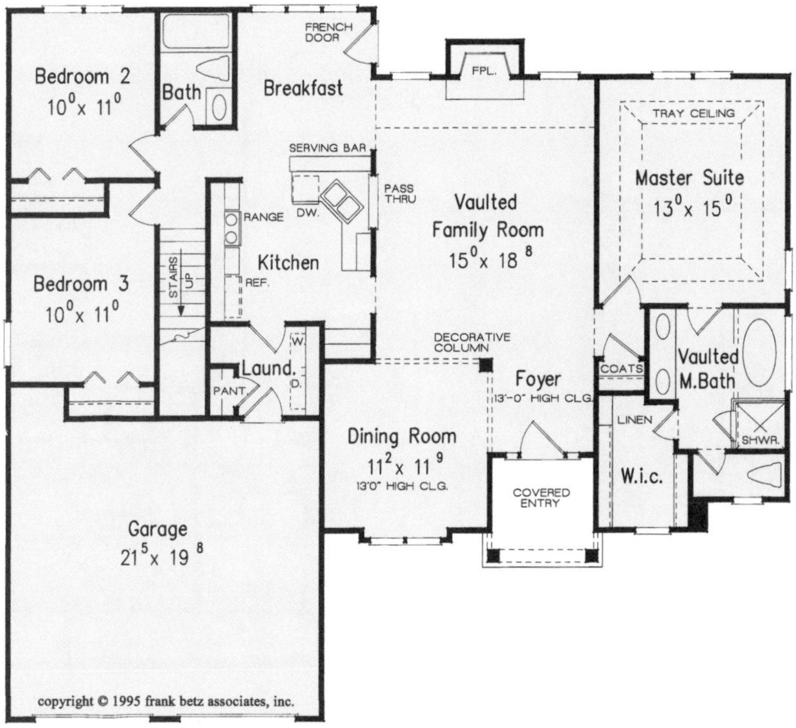
Bedroom 2
10⁰x 11⁰
Bath
Breakfast
FRENCH DOOR
FPL.
TRAY CEILING
Master Suite
13⁰x 15⁰
SERVING BAR
PASS THRU
RANGE
DW.
Vaulted Family Room
15⁰x 18⁸
Kitchen
REF.
STAIRS UP
Bedroom 3
10⁰x 11⁰
DECORATIVE COLUMN
Laund.
W.
D.
PANT.
Foyer
13'-0" HIGH CLG.
COATS
Vaulted M.Bath
LINEN
SHWR.
Dining Room
11²x 11⁹
13'0" HIGH CLG.
COVERED ENTRY
W.i.c.
Garage
21⁵x 19⁸
copyright © 1995 frank betz associates, inc.

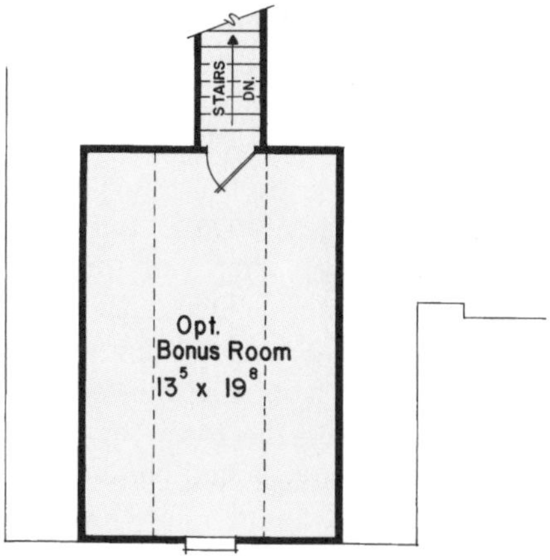
STAIRS DN.
Opt. Bonus Room
13⁵ x 19⁸

A steep front gable and a delightful arch framing the entry porch give this stately European home a distinctive look. Open design describes the spacious family room and formal dining room—tall ceilings and decorative touches like a column and fireplace set them apart. The efficient kitchen has wraparound counters and a cozy breakfast nook. Two family bedrooms and a full bath are separated from the master suite for privacy. The master suite has a vaulted bath, tray ceiling and large walk-in closet. Please specify basement or crawlspace foundation when ordering.

Design
HPT830267

Square Footage: 1,544

Bonus Space: 284 square feet

Width 54'-0" Depth 47'-6"

Design
HPT830268

Square Footage: 2,322

Width 62'-0" Depth 61'-0"

An eclectic mix of building materials—stone, stucco and siding—sings in tune with the European charm of this one-story home. Decorative columns set off the formal dining room and foyer from the vaulted family room, while the formal living room is quietly tucked behind French doors. The master suite has an elegant tray ceiling, bay sitting area and a lush bath. Please specify basement, crawlspace or slab foundation when ordering.

RAD. WDW.
RAD. WDW.
RAD. WDW.
Sitting Area
Breakfast
11'-0" HIGH CLG.
TRAY CEILING
FRENCH DOOR
FRENCH DOOR
ACTIVE DORMER W/ RAD. WDW.
Master Suite
16^6 x 14^0
VAULT
VAULT
DBL. OVEN
W.i.c.
Bedroom 2
11^0 x 13^0
DW.
Kitchen
11'-0" HIGH CLG.
RANGE
ISLAND
Vaulted Family Room
15^8 x 20^2
FPL.
SHWR.
Vaulted M.Bath
RAD. WDW.
COATS
REF.
PANTRY
VAULT
Bath
W.i.c.
LINEN
LINEN
DECORATIVE COLUMNS
W.H.
Bedroom 3
12^{10} x 11^6
ARCHED OPENINGS
SINK
PLANT SHELF ABOVE
Pwdr.
W.i.c.
Foyer
14'-0" HIGH CLG.
Dining Room
12^0 x 14^0
14'-0" HIGH CLG.
W.
D.
Laund.
FRENCH DOORS
OPT. STAIR TO BSMT.
Living Room
13^5 x 14^0
COVERED ENTRY
Garage
20^5 x 20^9
copyright © 1995 frank betz associates, inc.
GARAGE LOCATION WITH BASEMENT

QUOTE ONE®

Cost to build? See page 516 to order complete cost estimate to build this house in your area!

Design

HPT830269

Square Footage: 2,150

Width 64'-0" Depth 60'-4"

From the arched covered entry to the jack-arch window, this house retains the distinction of a much larger home. From the foyer and across the spacious great room, French doors and large side windows give a generous view of the covered rear porch. The dining room is subtly defined by the use of columns and a large triple window. The kitchen has a generous work island and breakfast area and joins the cozy keeping room. Two family bedrooms share a private bath. The home is completed by a quiet master suite located at the rear. It contains a bay window, a garden tub and His and Hers vanities. This home is designed with a walkout basement foundation.

QUOTE ONE®

Cost to build? See page 516 to order complete cost estimate to build this house in your area!

Wood shingles are a cozy touch on the exterior of this home. Interior rooms include a great room with a fireplace, a formal dining room, and a study with another fireplace. A guest room on the first floor contains a full bath and walk-in closet. The master bedroom is also on the first floor for privacy. The second floor holds two additional bedrooms, a loft area and a gallery overlooking the central hall. This home is designed with a walkout basement foundation.

Design

HPT830270
First Floor: 2,070 square feet
Second Floor: 790 square feet
Total: 2,860 square feet
Width 57'-6" Depth 54'-0"

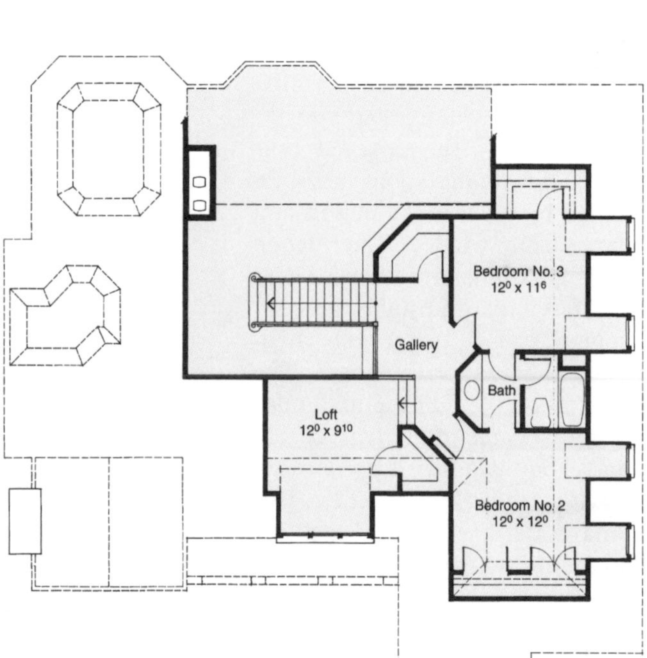

This home, as shown in the photograph, may differ from the actual blueprints. For more detailed information, please check the floor plans carefully.
Photo by Stephen Fuller, Inc.

A perfect blend of stucco and stacked stone sets off keystones, transoms and arches in this French country facade to inspire an elegant spirit. The foyer is flanked by the spacious dining room and the study, accented by a vaulted ceiling and a fireplace. A great room with a full wall of glass connects the interior with the outdoors. A first-floor master suite offers both style and intimacy with a coffered ceiling and a secluded bath. Three additional bedrooms and a hall bath are located upstairs. This home is designed with a walkout basement foundation.

Design HPT830271

First Floor: 1,900 square feet
Second Floor: 800 square feet
Total: 2,700 square feet
Width 63'-0" Depth 51'-0"

QUOTE ONE®
Cost to build? See page 516 to order complete cost estimate to build this house in your area!

Design

HPT830272

Square Footage: 3,352

Width 91'-0" Depth 71'-9"

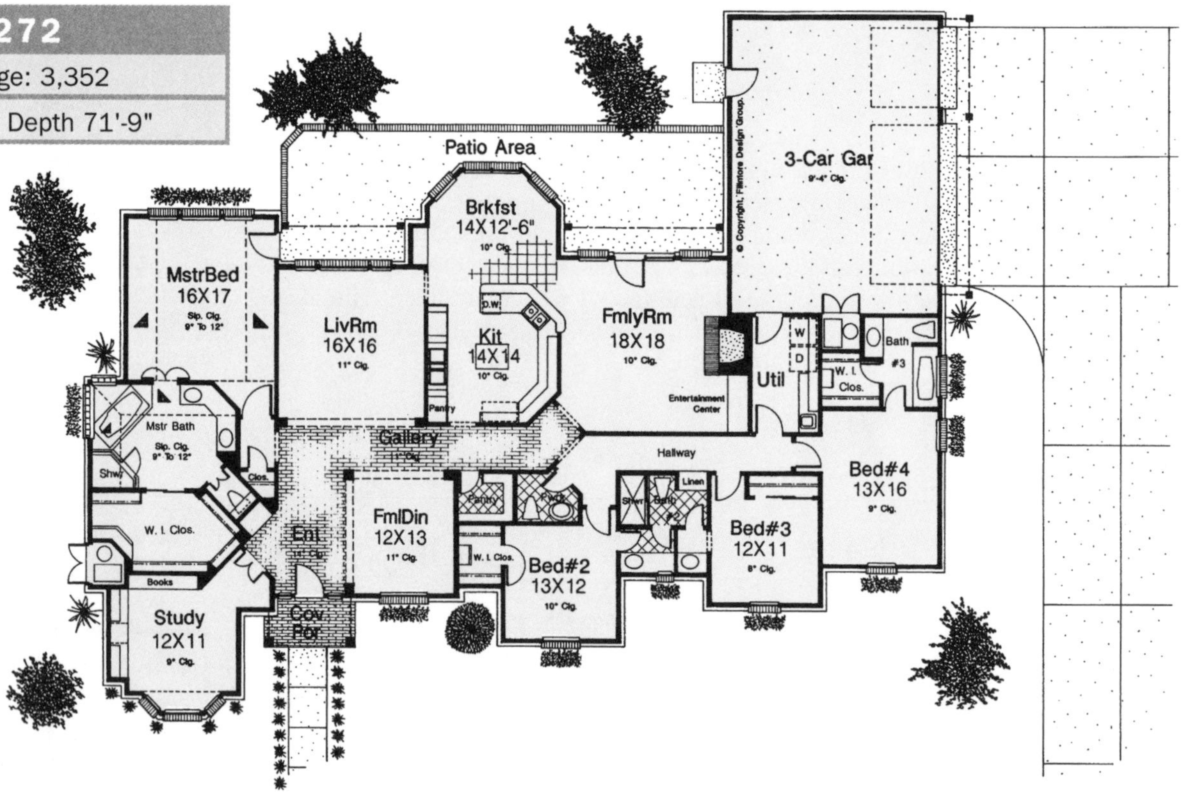
Patio Area
3-Car Gar
Brkfst
14X12'-6"
MstrBed
16X17
LivRm
16X16
Kit
14X14
FmlyRm
18X18
Entertainment Center
Util
Bath
#3
Mstr Bath
Gallery
Hallway
Bed#4
13X16
W. I. Clos.
FmlDin
12X13
Ent
Bed#2
13X12
Bed#3
12X11
Books
Study
12X11
Cov
Por
© Copyright, Fillmore Design Group.

This home combines the rustic charm of shutters and a random stonework wall with the elegance of molded cornices and arched multi-pane windows to create a look all its own. From the nicely detailed covered porch, enter upon the formal dining room to the right and living room to the rear. The arched gallery leads past the kitchen with island and bar to the family room with fireplace and built-in entertainment center. Adjoining the kitchen and family room is the bay-windowed breakfast nook, which looks out onto the rear patio. Three family bedrooms are located to the front. Bedroom 4 offers a private full bath, while Bedrooms 2 and 3 each has its own private vanity in the shared full bath. The left side of the plan comprises the master suite and the double-doored, bay-windowed study with built-ins. The master bedroom offers a triple window overlooking the rear property, a private door to the patio, sloped ceiling, walk-in closet, corner garden tub and compartmented toilet.

Design

HPT830273

Square Footage: 2,888

Width 68'-6" Depth 78'-1"

ALTERNATE ELEVATION

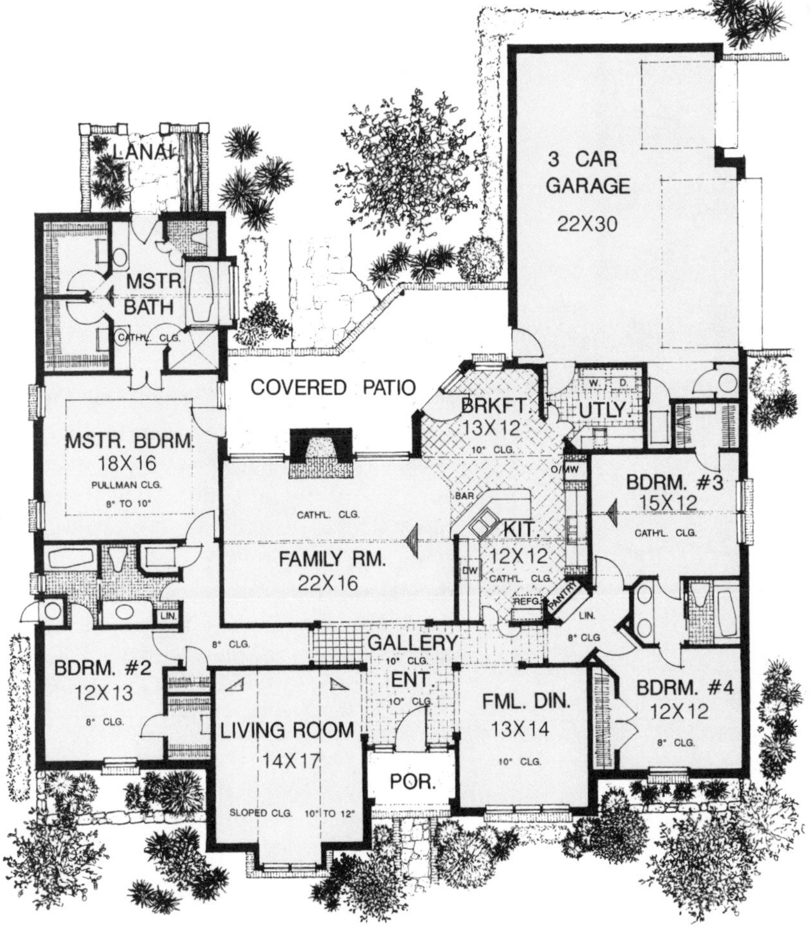
LANAI
MSTR. BATH
CATH'L. CLG.
3 CAR GARAGE
22X30
COVERED PATIO
BRKFT. 13X12
10" CLG.
UTLY.
W. D.
MSTR. BDRM. 18X16
PULLMAN CLG.
8" TO 10"
O/MW
BDRM. #3 15X12
CATH'L. CLG.
CATH'L. CLG.
BAR
KIT. 12X12
CATH'L. CLG.
FAMILY RM. 22X16
DW
REFG.
PANTRY
LIN.
LIN.
8" CLG.
8" CLG.
GALLERY
10" CLG.
ENT.
10" CLG.
BDRM. #2 12X13
8" CLG.
BDRM. #4 12X12
8" CLG.
FML. DIN. 13X14
10" CLG.
LIVING ROOM 14X17
SLOPED CLG. 10" TO 12"
POR.

Choose one of two alternate exteriors—both European style! Stone quoins and shutters give one elevation the appearance of a French country cottage. The other, with keystone window treatment and a copper roof over the bay window creates the impression of a stately French chateau. From the entry, formal living areas are accessed through graceful columned openings. Straight ahead, the comfortable family room awaits with its warming fireplace and cathedral ceiling, offering room to relax and enjoy casual gatherings. The private master suite features a Pullman ceiling, a luxurious bath and twin walk-in closets. Located nearby, Bedroom 2 serves nicely as a guest room or easily converts to a nursery or study. Two family bedrooms with a connecting bath, a handy kitchen and breakfast room, and a utility room complete the floor plan.

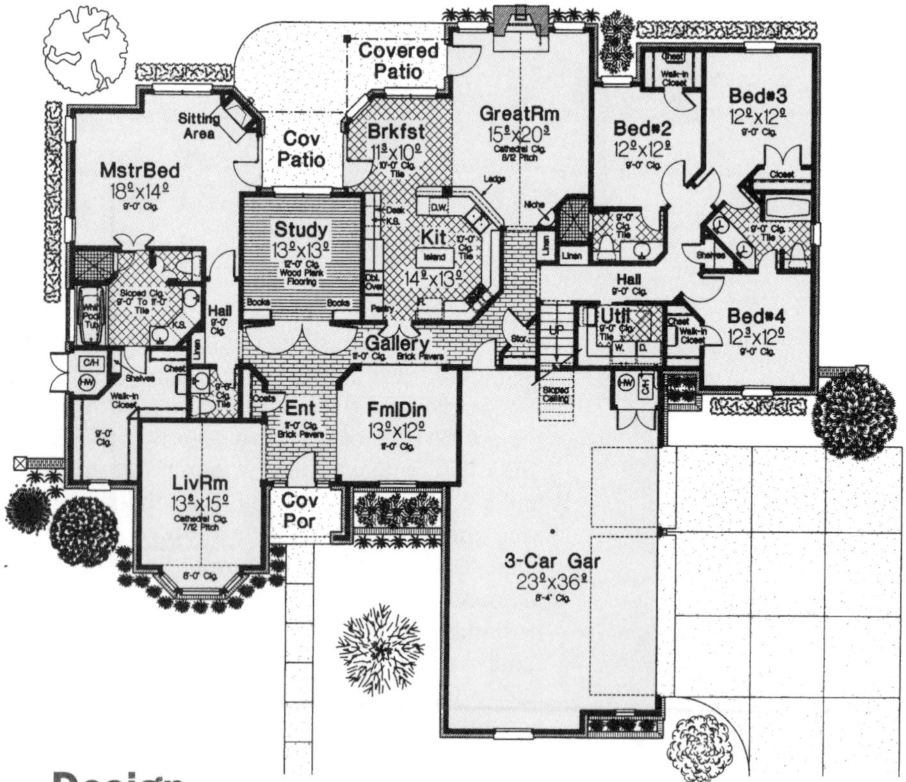

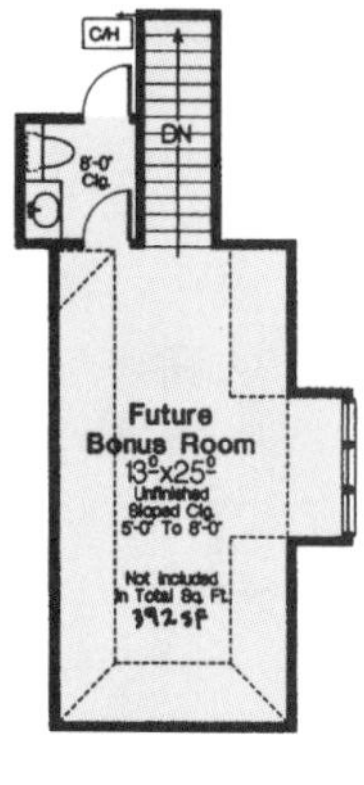

Design HPT830274

Square Footage: 3,012

Bonus Space: 392 square feet

Width 80'-0" Depth 72'-0"

The European appeal of this spacious cottage plan features graceful elegance on the exterior, with abundant amenities found inside. The foyer is flanked by formal living and dining rooms. Straight ahead, double doors open into a study. The master suite features a sitting area with a fireplace and a private bath that extends into an enormous walk-in closet. The island kitchen is central and connects to the breakfast room, which is open to the great room at the rear of the plan. Three family bedrooms are located to the right of the plan. A future bonus room is available for expansion.

Design
HPT830275

Square Footage: 2,361

Bonus Space: 214 square feet

Width 62'-0" Depth 67'-10"

The combination of finely detailed brick and shingle siding recalls some of the distinctive architecture of the East Coast during the early part of this century. The foyer and gallery provide for a functional traffic pattern. The formal dining room to the front of the home is outlined by columns and features a thirteen-foot ceiling. The extensive living area offers a corner fireplace. A screened porch surrounding the breakfast room is an ideal entertainment area. The master suite features two spacious closets and a bath with a garden tub and an oversized shower. Bedroom 4 can serve as a study, nursery, guest room or home office.

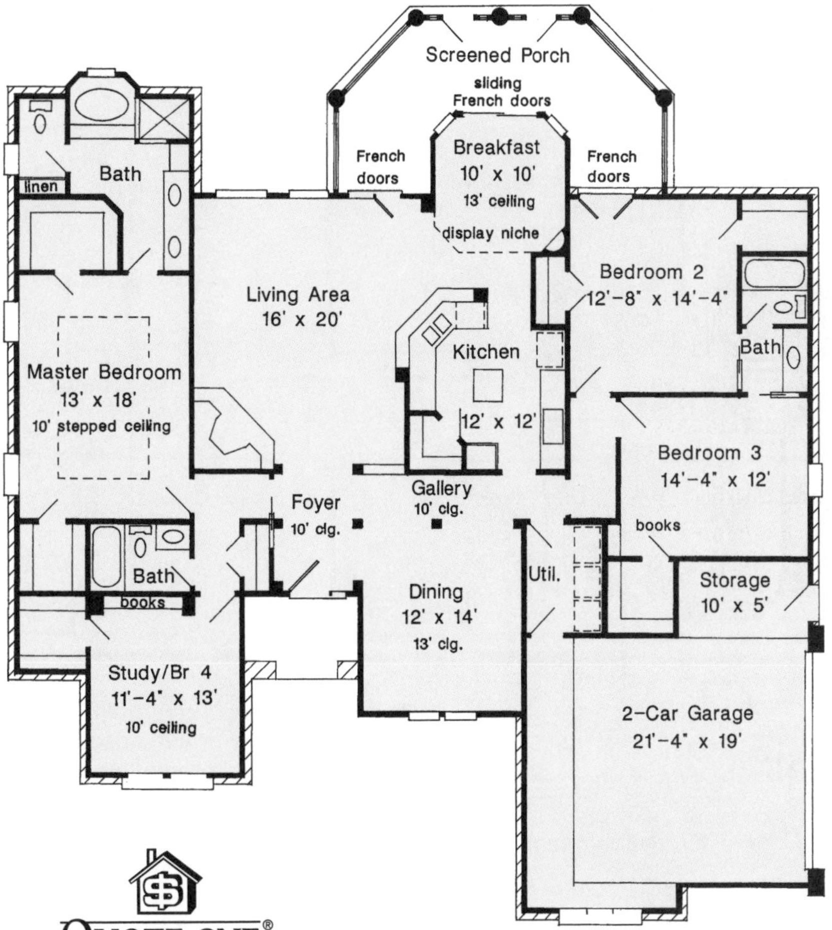

QUOTE ONE®

Cost to build? See page 516 to order complete cost estimate to build this house in your area!

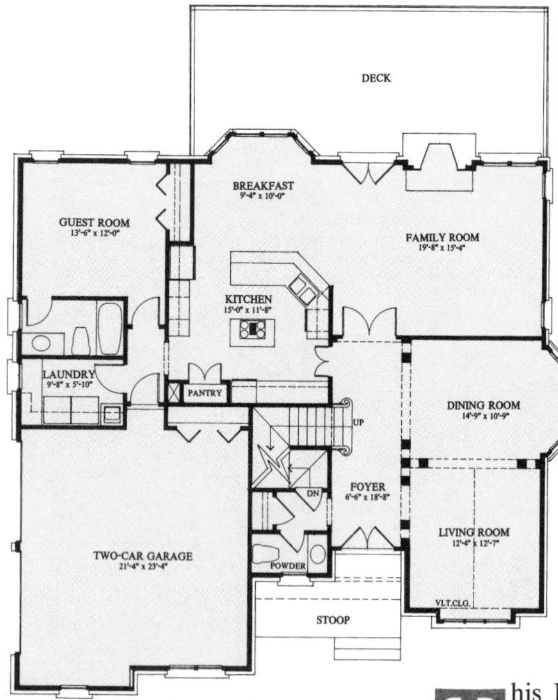
DECK
BREAKFAST
9'-4" x 10'-0"
GUEST ROOM
13'-6" x 12'-0"
FAMILY ROOM
19'-8" x 15'-4"
KITCHEN
15'-0" x 11'-8"
LAUNDRY
9'-8" x 5'-10"
PANTRY
UP
DINING ROOM
14'-9" x 10'-9"
DN
FOYER
6'-6" x 18'-8"
LIVING ROOM
12'-4" x 12'-7"
TWO-CAR GARAGE
21'-4" x 23'-4"
POWDER
VLT.CLG.
STOOP

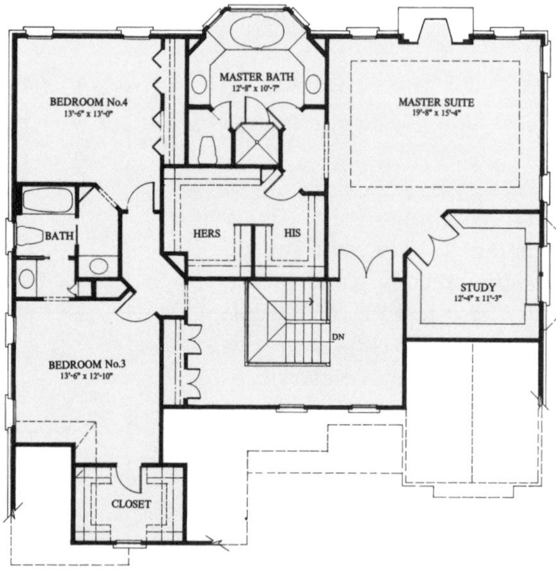
MASTER BATH
12'-8" x 10'-7"
BEDROOM No.4
13'-6" x 13'-0"
MASTER SUITE
19'-8" x 15'-4"
BATH
HERS
HIS
STUDY
12'-4" x 11'-3"
DN
BEDROOM No.3
13'-6" x 12'-10"
CLOSET

Design
HPT830276

First Floor: 1,678 square feet
Second Floor: 1,677 square feet
Total: 3,355 square feet
Width 50'-0" Depth 50'-6"

This English Manor home features a dramatic brick-and-stucco exterior accented by a gabled roofline and artful half-timbering. Inside, the foyer opens to the formal living room with a vaulted ceiling and box-bay window. The dining room flows directly off the living room and features its own angled bay window. Through the double doors lies the center of family activity. An entire wall of glass, accented by a central fireplace, spans from the family room through to the breakfast area and kitchen. For your guests, a bedroom and bath are located on the main level. The second floor provides two additional bedrooms and a bath for children. The master suite—with its tray ceiling, fireplace and private study—is a pleasant retreat. This home is designed with a walkout basement foundation.

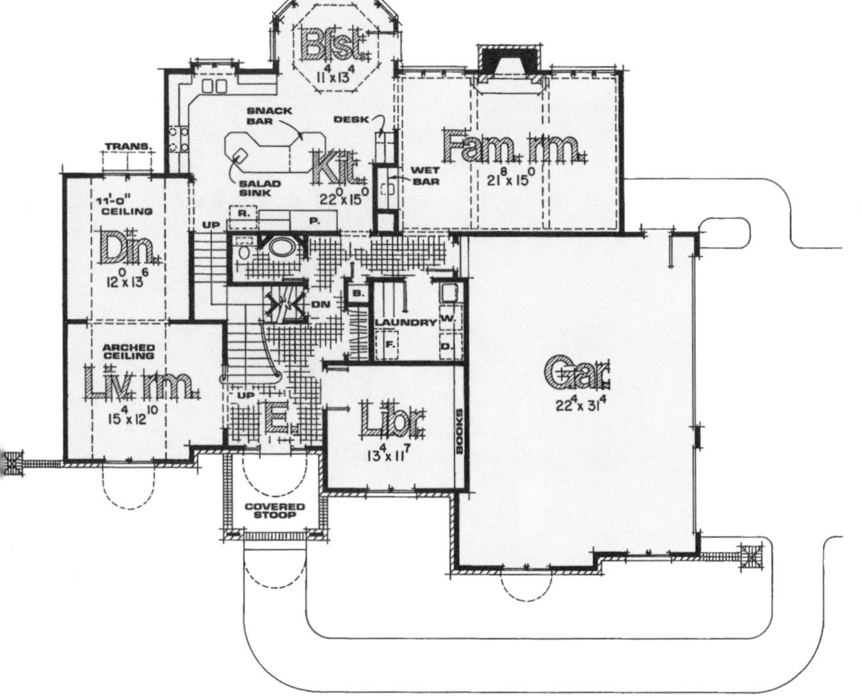

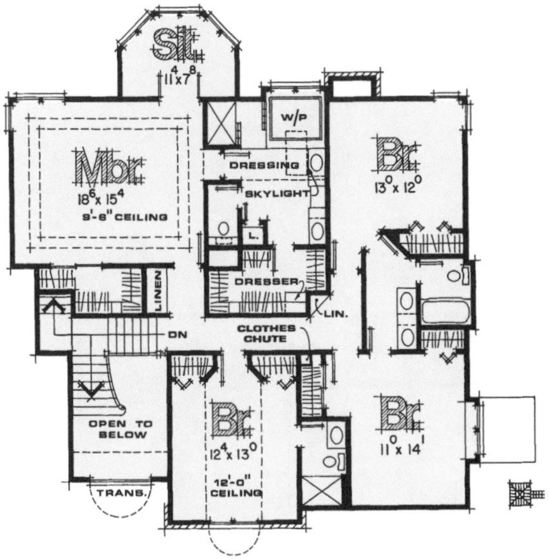

An attractive facade and amenity-filled interior make this home a showplace both outside and in. Immediately off the two-story foyer is the living room and formal dining room, both with interesting ceiling details, and the quiet library with built-in bookcases. The enormous gourmet kitchen features a large island work counter/snack bar, pantry, desk and gazebo breakfast room. Just steps away is the spacious family room with a grand fireplace and windows overlooking the backyard. Upstairs are three family bedrooms served by two baths and a luxurious master suite with a bay-windowed sitting room, detailed ceiling and skylit bath with a whirlpool tub.

Design
HPT830277

First Floor: 1,709 square feet
Second Floor: 1,597 square feet
Total: 3,306 square feet
Width 62'-0" Depth 55'-4"

Design HPT830278

First Floor: 2,733 square feet
Second Floor: 1,003 square feet
Total: 3,736 square feet
Width 74'-8" Depth 76'-3"
L

A stunning octagonal front porch distinguishes this Mediterranean-style villa. The second-story dormer above the porch draws the eye and accents the entry to this lovely home. The home is designed to capture rear views perfect for a golf course or lakeside site. Through arched openings flanked by columns, the adjoining living room and dining room open off the two-story foyer. A see-through fireplace separates the two rooms. The gourmet kitchen, family room and breakfast room flow together. The master suite provides access to a private screened porch. A curved staircase leads to a balcony hall and two bedrooms, each with a private bath. Please specify crawlspace or slab foundation when ordering.

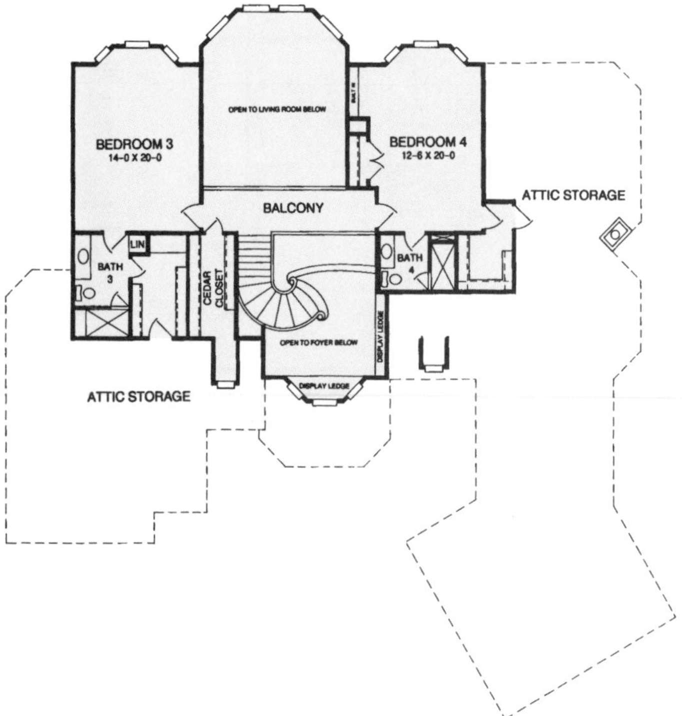

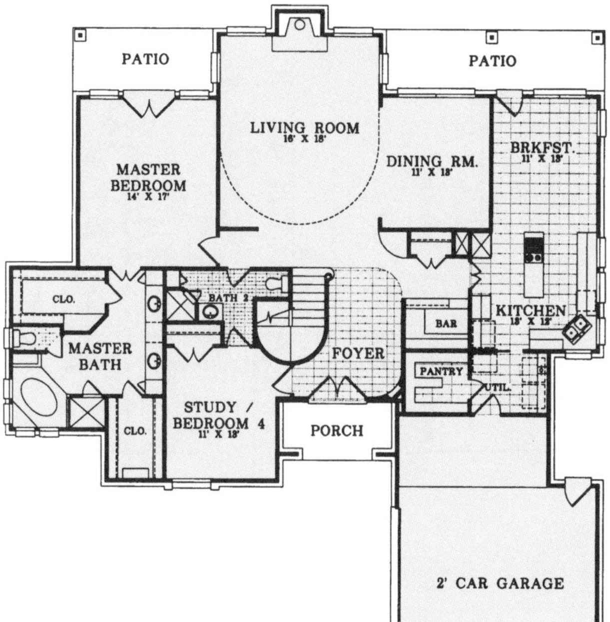

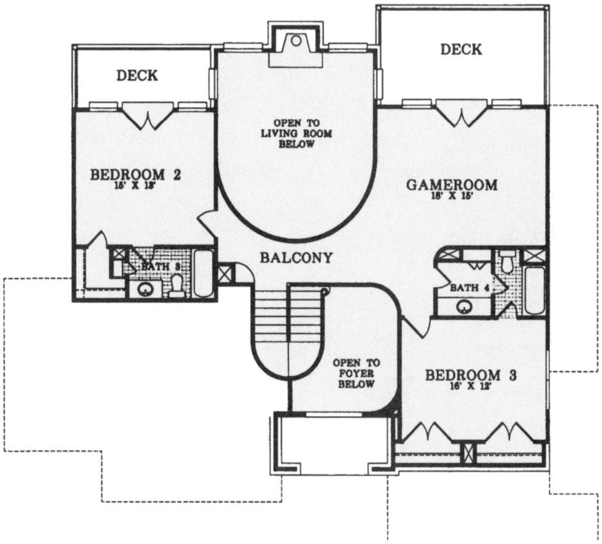

Design HPT830279

First Floor: 2,109 square feet

Second Floor: 1,060 square feet

Total: 3,169 square feet

Width 61'-11" Depth 67'-7"

L

Old World charm blends a warm, inviting exterior with a traditional, efficient floor plan. From the foyer, note the curved wall that rises with the staircase. The kitchen is a delight with its large cooktop island, walk-in pantry and a sunlit sink with a corner grouping of windows. The pampering master suite offers access through French doors to a covered patio and includes a relaxing bath with His and Hers walk-in closets, a corner whirlpool tub surrounded by windows, and dual vanities. Bedroom 4 may be used as a study or an ideal office. Upstairs, a curved balcony overlooks the two-story living room. Bedroom 2 features a full bath, a walk-in closet and access to a private deck. Bedroom 3 has its own full bath. A game room with French doors opening to an upper deck completes the second floor.

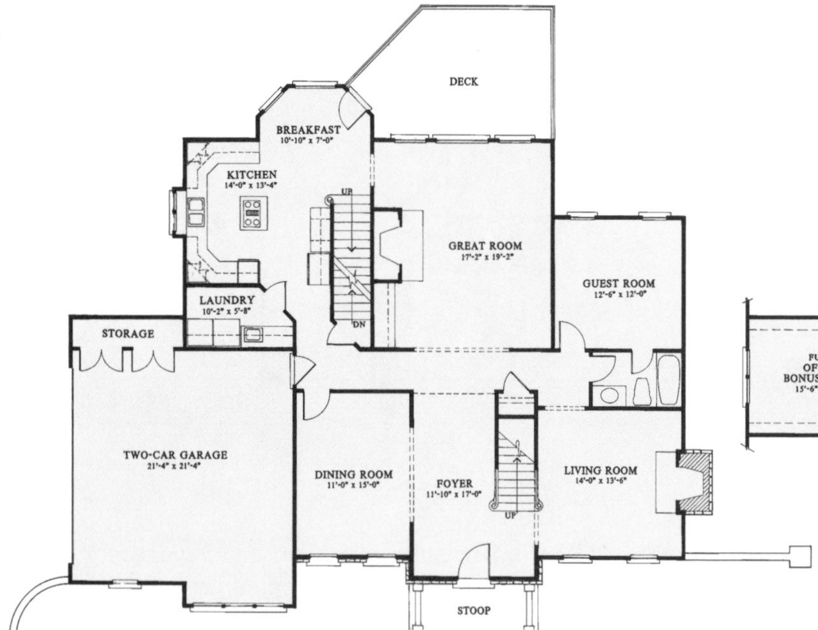

DECK
BREAKFAST
10'-10" x 7'-0"
KITCHEN
14'-0" x 13'-4"
UP
GREAT ROOM
17'-2" x 19'-2"
GUEST ROOM
12'-6" x 12'-0"
LAUNDRY
10'-2" x 5'-8"
DN
STORAGE
TWO-CAR GARAGE
21'-4" x 21'-4"
DINING ROOM
11'-0" x 15'-0"
FOYER
11'-10" x 17'-0"
UP
LIVING ROOM
14'-0" x 13'-6"
STOOP

SITTING AREA
MASTER BATH
UP
TO ATTIC
MASTER SUITE
14'-0" x 19'-2"
BEDROOM No.3
11'-10" x 12'-0"
HERS
HIS
DN
OPEN RAIL
DN
BATH
BATH
FUTURE OFFICE/ BONUS ROOM
15'-6" x 10'-8"
BEDROOM No.2
11'-8" x 12'-10"
OPEN TO BELOW
BEDROOM No.4
11'-10" x 12'-0"

Design HPT830280

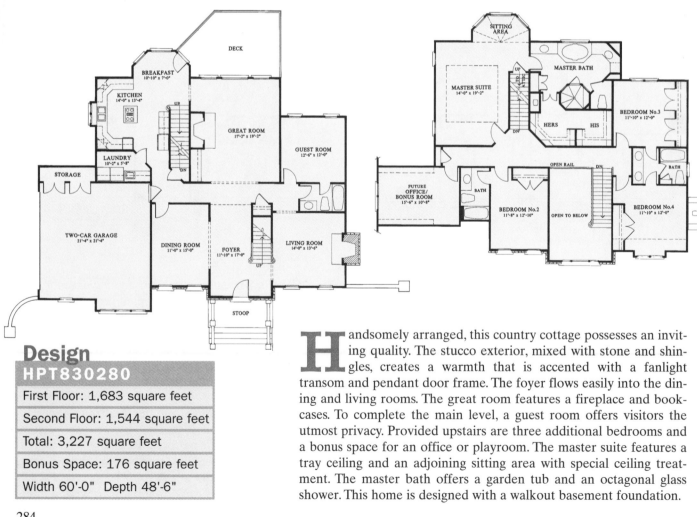

First Floor: 1,683 square feet
Second Floor: 1,544 square feet
Total: 3,227 square feet
Bonus Space: 176 square feet
Width 60'-0" Depth 48'-6"

Handsomely arranged, this country cottage possesses an inviting quality. The stucco exterior, mixed with stone and shingles, creates a warmth that is accented with a fanlight transom and pendant door frame. The foyer flows easily into the dining and living rooms. The great room features a fireplace and bookcases. To complete the main level, a guest room offers visitors the utmost privacy. Provided upstairs are three additional bedrooms and a bonus space for an office or playroom. The master suite features a tray ceiling and an adjoining sitting area with special ceiling treatment. The master bath offers a garden tub and an octagonal glass shower. This home is designed with a walkout basement foundation.

To suit those who favor Classic European styling, this English Manor home features a dramatic brick exterior, which is further emphasized by the varied roofline and the finial atop the uppermost gable. The main level opens to a two-story foyer, with the formal rooms on the right. The living room contains a fireplace set in a bay window. The dining room is separated from the living room by a symmetrical column arrangement. The more casual family room is to the rear. For guests, a bedroom and bath are located on the main level. The second floor provides additional bedrooms and baths for family as well as a magnificent master suite. This home is designed with a walkout basement foundation.

Design HPT830281

First Floor: 1,847 square feet
Second Floor: 1,453 square feet
Total: 3,300 square feet
Width 63'-3" Depth 47'-0"

QUOTE ONE®

Cost to build? See page 516 to order complete cost estimate to build this house in your area!

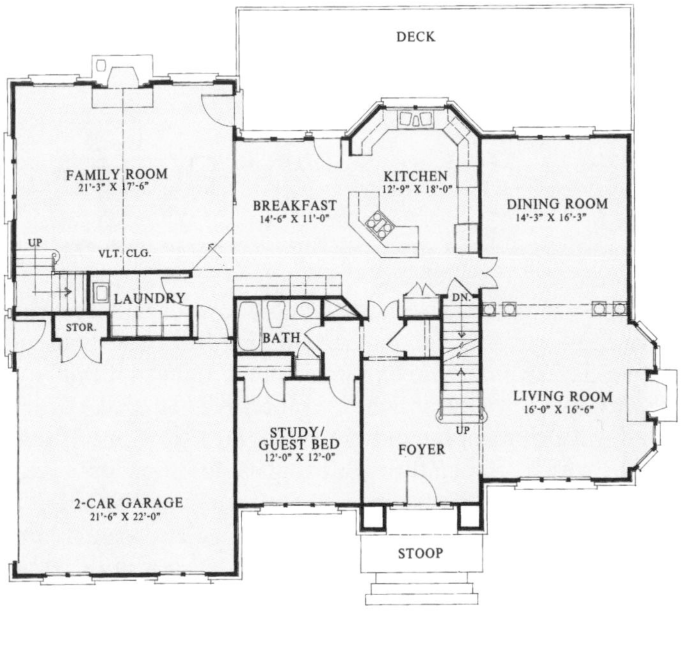

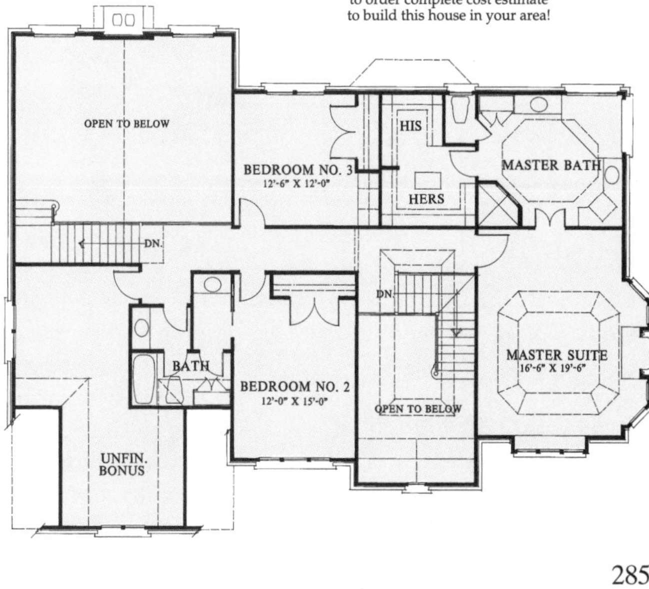

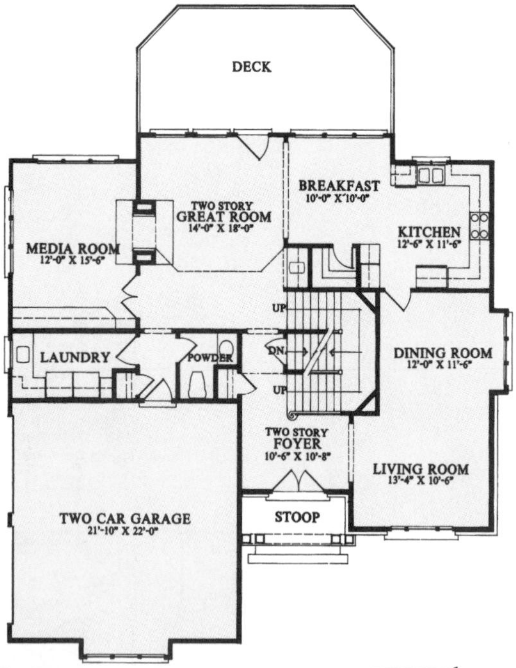
DECK
TWO STORY GREAT ROOM 14'-0" X 18'-0"
BREAKFAST 10'-0" X 10'-0"
KITCHEN 12'-6" X 11'-6"
MEDIA ROOM 12'-0" X 15'-6"
LAUNDRY
POWDER
UP
DN
UP
DINING ROOM 12'-0" X 11'-6"
TWO STORY FOYER 10'-6" X 10'-8"
LIVING ROOM 13'-4" X 10'-6"
STOOP
TWO CAR GARAGE 21'-10" X 22'-0"

SITTING
OPEN TO BELOW
BEDROOM NO. 2 12'-0" X 12'-0"
MASTER BEDROOM 19'-8" X 13'-6"
BALCONY
W.I.C.
W.I.C.
DN
MASTER BATH
BATH
BEDROOM NO. 3 12'-0" X 12'-6"
OPEN TO BELOW
W.I.C.
UNFIN. BONUS 12'-0" X 11'-4"

QUOTE ONE®
Cost to build? See page 516
to order complete cost estimate
to build this house in your area!

Design HPT830282

First Floor: 1,395 square feet
Second Floor: 1,210 square feet
Total: 2,605 square feet
Bonus Space: 225 square feet
Width 47'-0" Depth 49'-6"

The well-balanced use of stucco and stone combined with box-bay window treatments and a covered entry make this English country home especially inviting. The two-story foyer opens on the right to formal living and dining rooms, bright with natural light. A spacious U-shaped kitchen adjoins a breakfast nook with views of the outdoors. This area flows nicely into the two-story great room, which offers a through-fireplace to the media room. A plush retreat awaits the homeowner upstairs with a master suite that offers a quiet, windowed sitting area with views to the rear grounds. Two family bedrooms share a full bath and a balcony hall that has a dramatic view of the great room below. This home is designed with a basement foundation.

Design HPT830283

Square Footage: 2,170

Width 62'-0" Depth 61'-6"

This classic cottage boasts a stone-and-wood exterior with a welcoming arch-top entry that leads to a columned foyer. An extended-hearth fireplace is the focal point of the family room, while a nearby sun room with covered porch access opens up the living area to the outdoors. The gourmet island kitchen opens through double doors from the living area, and the breakfast area looks out to a porch. Sleeping quarters include a master wing with a spacious, angled bath and a sitting room or den that has its own full bath—perfect for a guest suite. On the opposite side of the plan, two family bedrooms share a full bath. This home is designed with a walk-out basement foundation.

QUOTE ONE®

Cost to build? See page 516 to order complete cost estimate to build this house in your area!

Design HPT830284

Square Footage: 2,770

Width 73'-6" Depth 78'-0"

This English cottage with a cedar shake exterior displays the best qualities of a traditional design. The foyer opens to both the dining room and the great room with its fireplace and built-in cabinetry. Surrounded by windows, the breakfast room opens to a gourmet kitchen. Two bedrooms with large closets are joined by a full bath with individual vanities and a window seat. Through double doors at the end of a short hall, the master suite awaits with a tray ceiling and an adjoining sunlit sitting room. This home is designed with a walkout basement foundation.

European Influences

Design HPT830285

Square Footage: 2,935

Width 71'-0" Depth 66'-0"

This spacious one-story home easily accommodates a large family, providing all the luxuries and necessities for gracious living. For formal occasions, a grand dining room sits just off the entry foyer and features a vaulted ceiling. The great room offers a beautiful ceiling treatment and access to the rear deck. For more casual times, the kitchen, breakfast nook and adjoining keeping room with a fireplace fill the bill. The master suite is spacious and filled with amenities that include a sitting room, walk-in closet and access to the rear deck. Two family bedrooms share a full bath. Each of these bedrooms provides its own lavatory. This home is designed with a walkout basement foundation.

MASTER BATH
SITTING RM.
11'-6" X 10'-0"
DECK
KEEPING ROOM
15'-3" X 15'-3"
VLT. CLG.
MASTER SUITE
18'-0" X 16'-0"
W.I.C.
GREAT ROOM
15'-6" X 17'-3"
KITCHEN
14'-0" X 13'-3"
BREAKFAST
14'-0" X 13'-0"
DN.
BEDROOM NO. 3
12'-0" X 12'-0"
W.I.C.
W.I.C.
POWDER
LAUNDRY
FOYER
BATH
BEDROOM NO. 2
13'-3" X 11'-6"
DINING ROOM
13'-3" X 18'-6"
STOOP
VLT. CLG.
2-CAR GARAGE
21'-6" X 21'-6"

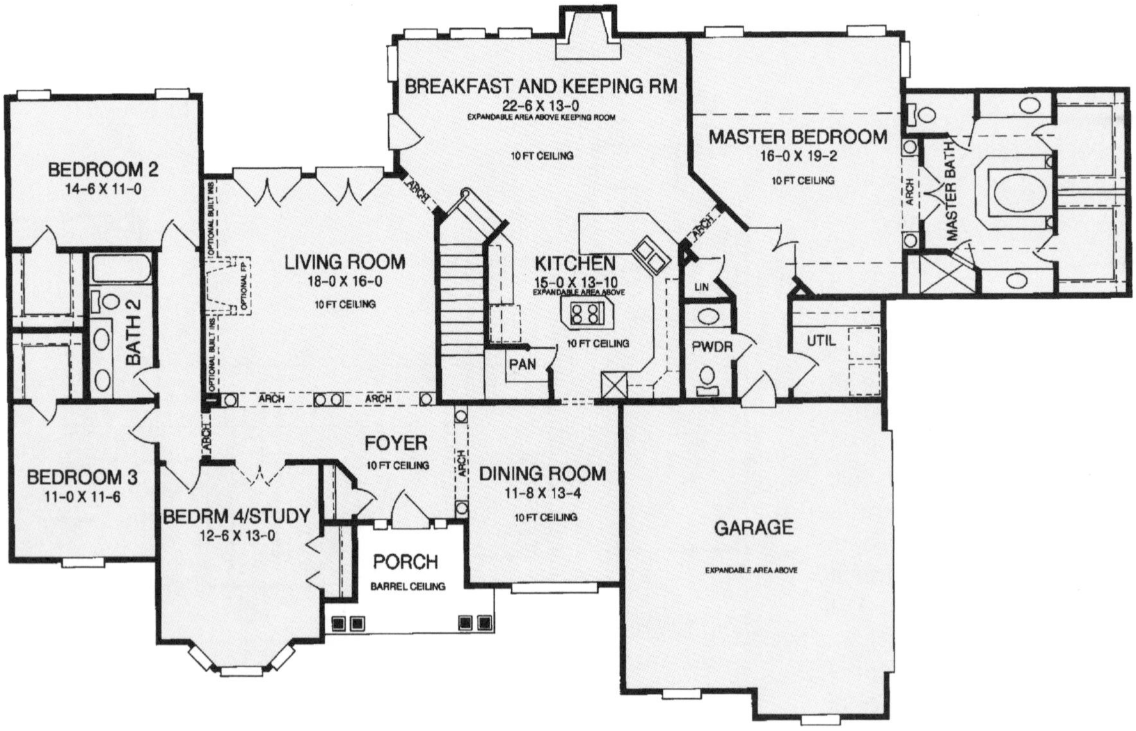

BREAKFAST AND KEEPING RM
22-6 X 13-0
EXPANDABLE AREA ABOVE KEEPING ROOM
10 FT CEILING
MASTER BEDROOM
16-0 X 19-2
10 FT CEILING
MASTER BATH
ARCH
BEDROOM 2
14-6 X 11-0
OPTIONAL BUILT INS
OPTIONAL FP
LIVING ROOM
18-0 X 16-0
10 FT CEILING
ARCH
KITCHEN
15-0 X 13-10
EXPANDABLE AREA ABOVE
10 FT CEILING
ARCH
LIN
PWDR
UTIL
PAN
BATH 2
ARCH
ARCH
ARCH
FOYER
10 FT CEILING
ARCH
BEDROOM 3
11-0 X 11-6
BEDRM 4/STUDY
12-6 X 13-0
DINING ROOM
11-8 X 13-4
10 FT CEILING
GARAGE
EXPANDABLE AREA ABOVE
PORCH
BARREL CEILING

The favorite gathering place of this beautiful home is certain to be its sun-filled breakfast and keeping room complemented by the full kitchen. Thoughtful placement of the kitchen provides easy service to both formal and informal eating areas. A large living room enjoys two sets of double French doors that open to outdoor living areas. French doors also open onto the spacious master suite and its elegant master bath. Here, a soothing whirlpool tub takes center stage. Three other bedrooms, or two bedrooms and a study, are positioned at the opposite end of the house for privacy. Bedrooms 2 and 3 have their own walk-in closets. Please specify slab or crawlspace foundation when ordering.

Design
HPT830286

Square Footage: 2,733

Width 88'-0" Depth 54'-2"

L

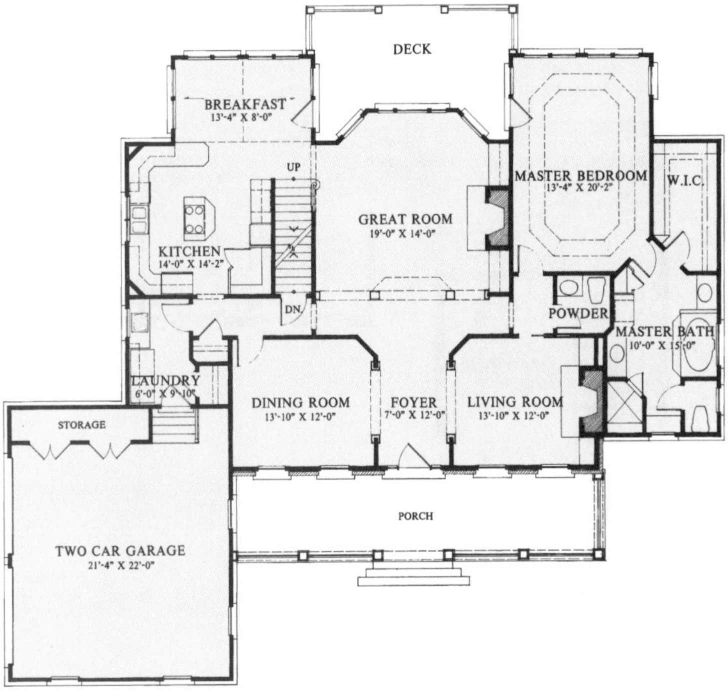

QUOTE ONE®
Cost to build? See page 516
to order complete cost estimate
to build this house in your area!

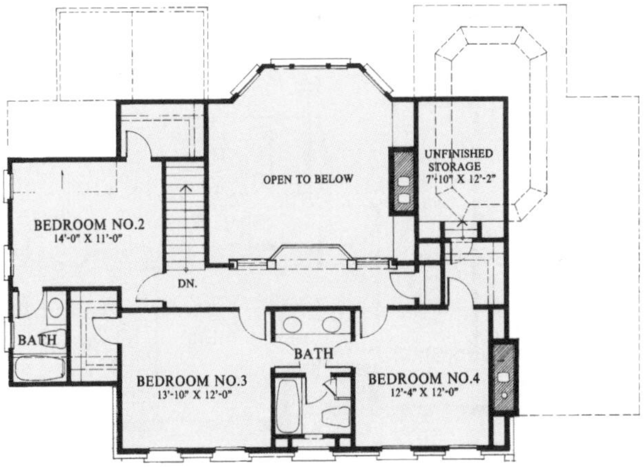

Design HPT830287

First Floor: 2,081 square feet
Second Floor: 940 square feet
Total: 3,021 square feet
Width 69'-9" Depth 65'-0"

This Georgian country-style home displays an impressive appearance. The front porch and columns frame the elegant elliptical entrance. Georgian symmetry balances the living room and dining room off the foyer. The first floor continues into the two-story great room, which offers built-in cabinetry, a fireplace and a large bay window that overlooks the rear deck. A dramatic tray ceiling, a wall of glass and access to the rear deck complete the master bedroom. The master bath features separate vanities and a large walk-in closet. To the left of the great room, a large kitchen opens to a breakfast area with walls of windows. Upstairs, each of three family bedrooms features ample closet space as well as direct access to a bathroom. This home is designed with a walkout basement foundation.

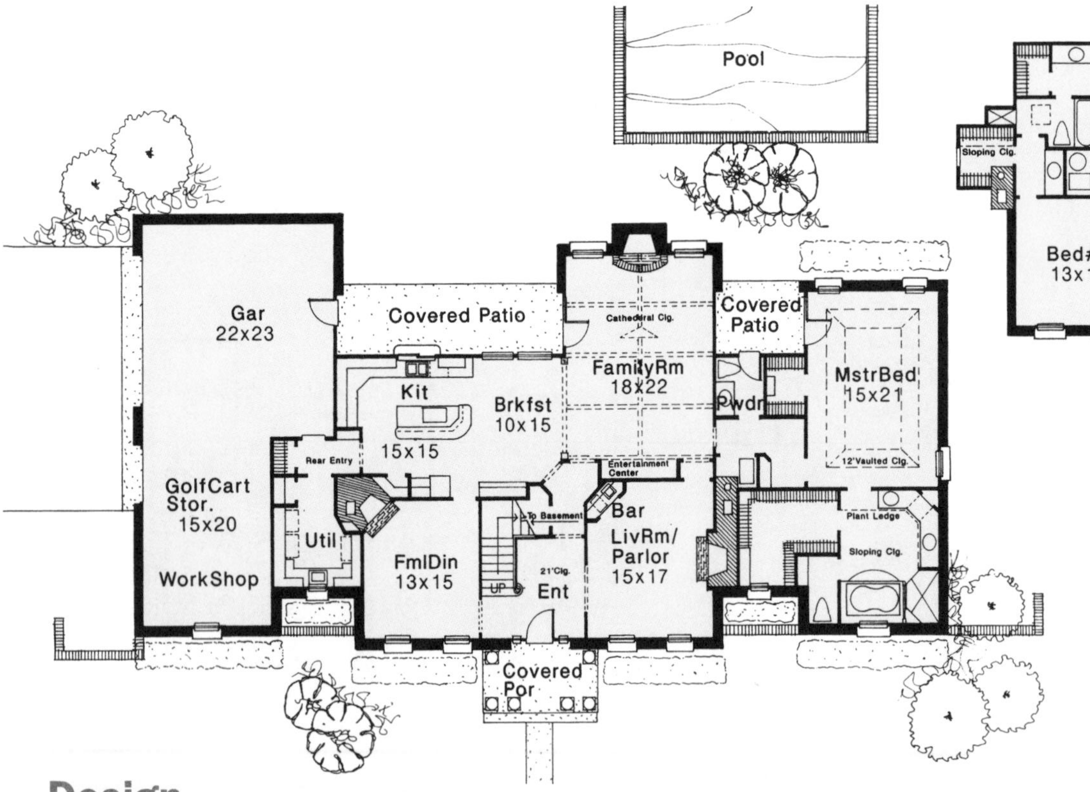

Pool
Gar
22x23
Covered Patio
Cathedral Clg.
FamilyRm
18x22
Covered
Patio
Kit
Brkfst
10x15
15x15
MstrBed
15x21
Pwdr
12'Vaulted Clg.
Rear Entry
Entertainment
Center
GolfCart
Stor.
15x20
To Basement
Bar
Plant Ledge
Util
FmlDin
13x15
LivRm/
Parlor
15x17
Sloping Clg.
21'Clg.
UP
Ent
WorkShop
Covered
Por

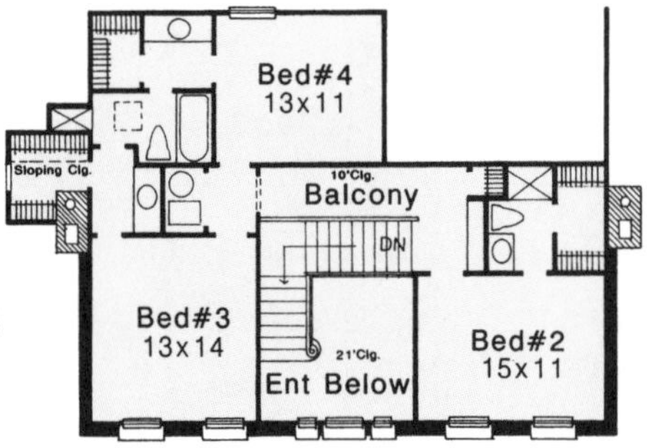

Bed#4
13x11
Sloping Clg.
10'Clg.
Balcony
DN
Bed#3
13x14
21'Clg.
Ent Below
Bed#2
15x11

Design HPT830288

First Floor: 2,432 square feet
Second Floor: 903 square feet
Total: 3,335 square feet
Width 90'-0" Depth 53'-10"

The elegant symmetry of this Southern traditional four-bedroom plan makes it a joy to own. The two-story foyer opens on the right to a formal living room with a built-in wet bar and a fireplace. A massive family room with a cathedral ceiling leads outside to a large covered patio or to the breakfast room and kitchen. A side-entry, three-car garage provides room for a golf cart and separate workshop area. The first-floor master bedroom features a tray ceiling, a secluded covered patio and a plant ledge in the master bath.

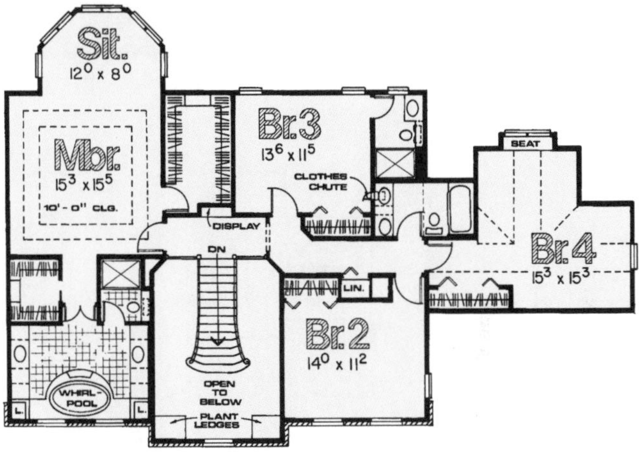

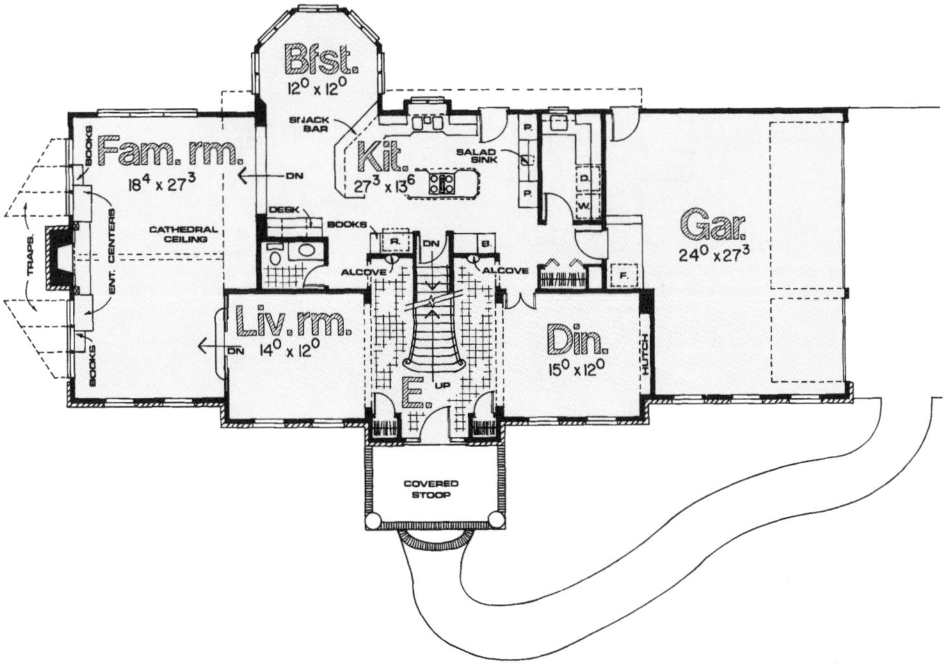

Design

HPT830289

First Floor: 1,717 square feet
Second Floor: 1,518 square feet
Total: 3,235 square feet
Width 78'-0" Depth 42'-0"

Stately columns highlight the facade of this beautiful Southern Colonial home. The open entry allows for views into formal areas and up the tapering staircase. Step down into the huge family room to find large windows, a fireplace, a built-in entertainment center and bookcases. The kitchen features a gazebo breakfast area, serving bar and cooktop island. Upstairs, three family bedrooms share two full baths.

Design
HPT830290

First Floor: 1,960 square feet
Second Floor: 905 square feet
Total: 2,865 square feet
Bonus Space: 297 square feet
Width 61'-0" Depth 70'-6"

Traditionalists will appreciate the classic styling of this Colonial home. The foyer opens to both a banquet-sized dining room and formal living room with a fireplace. Just beyond is the two-story great room. The entire right side of the main level is taken up by the master suite. The other side of the main level includes a large kitchen and a breakfast room just steps away from the detached garage. Upstairs, each bedroom features ample closet space and direct access to a bath. The detached garage features an unfinished office or studio on its second level. This home is designed with a walkout basement foundation.

This new design wears the ageless appeal of classic country style, but gives it a fresh face. A low-pitched roof complements the columns and balusters of the front covered porch and creates a sense of shelter. Formal areas are secluded to one side of the plan, while the family room, gourmet kitchen and sunny breakfast area enjoy open interior space and views to the rear property. A plush master suite on the second floor boasts a windowed whirlpool tub and twin lavatories. Each of two family bedrooms enjoys private access to a shared bath, while a fourth bedroom offers its own full bath. This home is designed with a walkout basement foundation.

Design HPT830291

First Floor: 1,613 square feet	
Second Floor: 1,546 square feet	
Total: 3,159 square feet	
Width 69'-0"	Depth 57'-0"

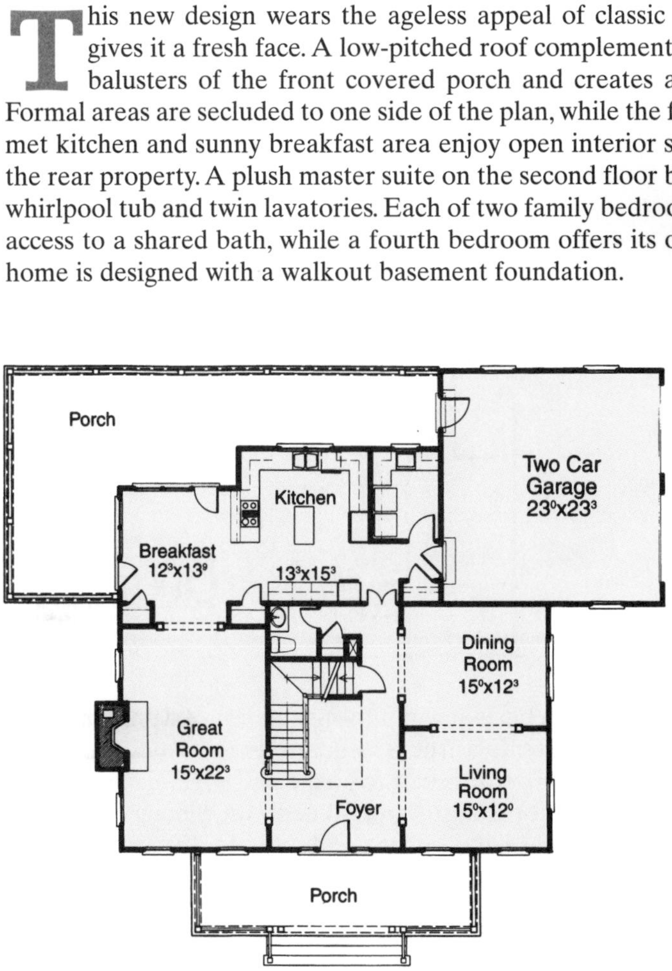

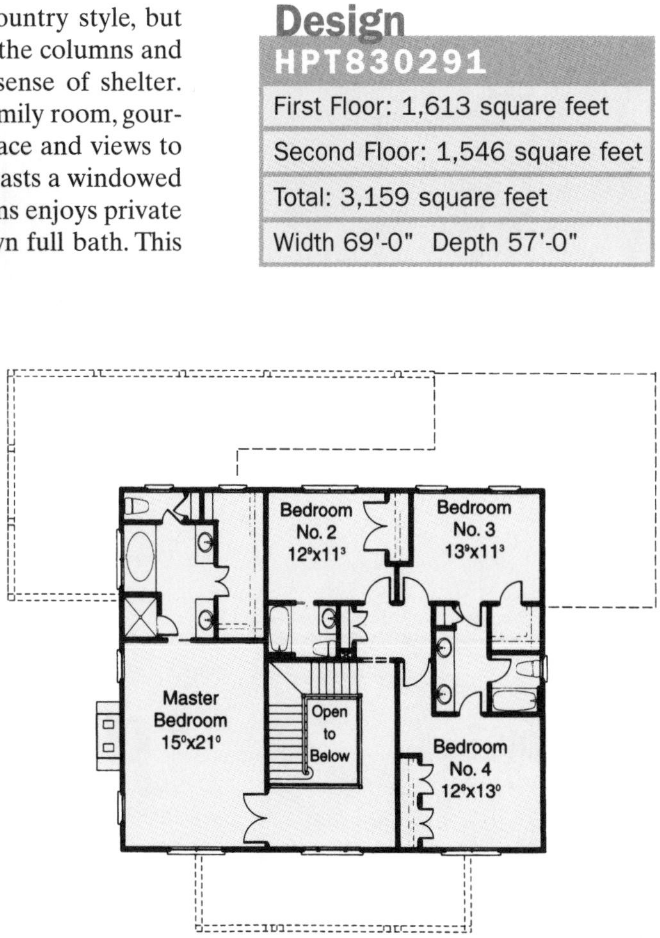

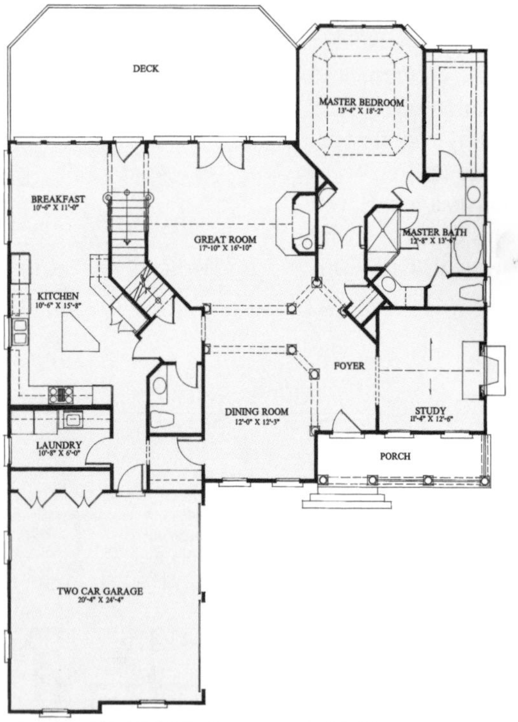

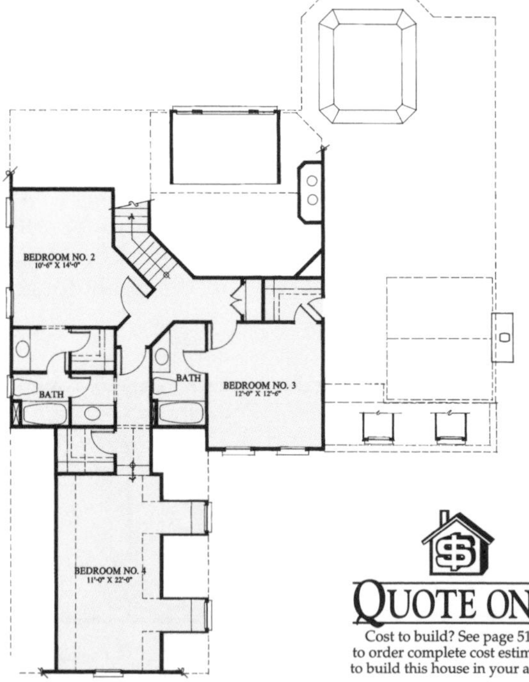

QUOTE ONE®
Cost to build? See page 516 to order complete cost estimate to build this house in your area!

Design
HPT830292

First Floor: 1,944 square feet
Second Floor: 954 square feet
Total: 2,898 square feet
Width 51'-6" Depth 73'-0"

This gracious home combines warm informal materials with a modern, livable floor plan to create a true Southern classic. The dining room, study and great room work together to create one large, exciting space. Just beyond the open rail, the breakfast room is lined with windows. Plenty of counter space and storage make the kitchen truly usable. The master suite, with its tray ceiling and decorative wall niche, is a welcome retreat. Upstairs, two additional bedrooms each has its own vanity within a shared bath, while the third bedroom or guest room includes its own bath and walk-in closet. This home is designed with a walkout basement foundation.

Design HPT830293

Square Footage: 2,846

Width 84'-6" Depth 64'-2"

L

This Southern Colonial home is distinguished by its columned porch and double dormers. Inside, columns and connecting arches define the angled foyer. The master suite is located away from the other bedrooms for privacy and includes a large master bath and a walk-in closet. Three additional bedrooms are located adjacent to the family room. The kitchen, breakfast area and family room are open—perfect for informal entertaining and family gatherings. The foyer, living room and dining room have twelve-foot ceilings. Ten-foot ceilings are used in the family room, kitchen, breakfast area and master suite to give this home an open, spacious feeling. Please specify crawlspace or slab foundation when ordering.

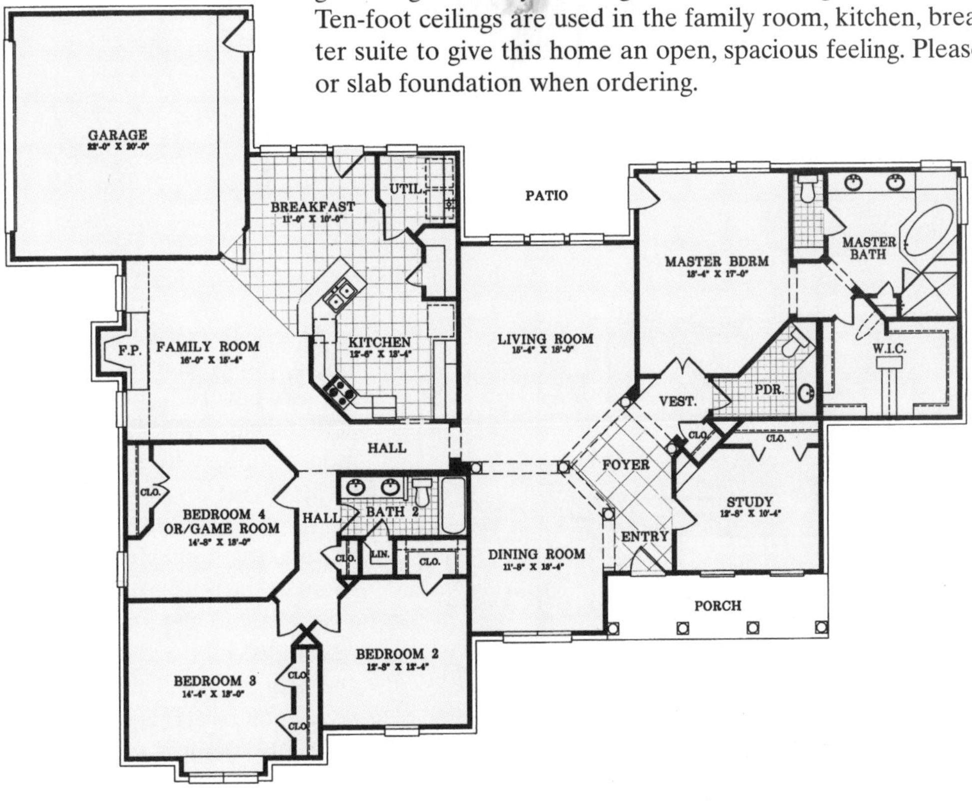

Design HPT830294

First Floor: 2,565 square feet	
Second Floor: 1,375 square feet	
Total: 3,940 square feet	
Width 88'-6"	Depth 58'-6"

QUOTE ONE®
Cost to build? See page 516 to order complete cost estimate to build this house in your area!

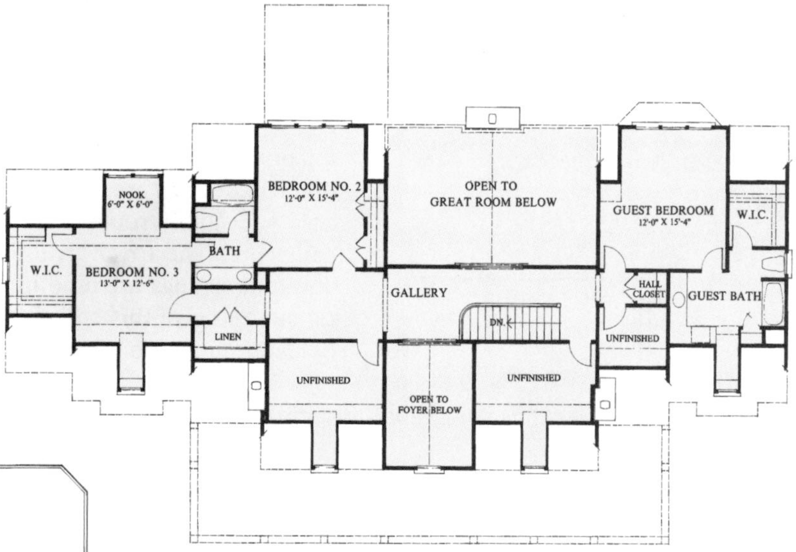

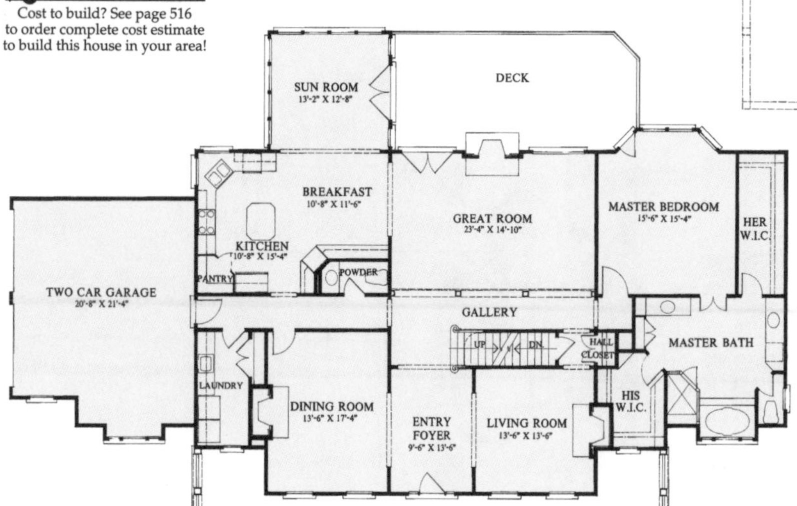

A symmetrical facade with twin chimneys makes a grand statement. A covered porch welcomes visitors and provides a pleasant place to spend a mild evening. The entry foyer is flanked by formal living areas—a dining room and a living room—each with a fireplace. A third fireplace is the highlight of the expansive great room to the rear. An L-shaped kitchen offers a work island and a walk-in pantry as amenities and easily serves the nearby breakfast and sun rooms. The master suite provides lavish luxuries. This home is designed with a walkout basement foundation.

Design HPT830295

Square Footage: 1,856

Width 59'-0" Depth 54'-6"

A covered porch with a recessed entry is crowned with the addition of a front gable. A symmetrical plan of living areas places the living and dining rooms to either side of the foyer, with the family room directly ahead. A graceful arched opening and a fireplace flanked by windows are complemented by extra-high ceilings in the foyer and family room. An efficiently designed kitchen features an abundance of counter and cabinet space along with a serving bar to the breakfast nook. The master suite is separated from the two family bedrooms for privacy. Please specify basement, crawlspace or slab foundation when ordering.

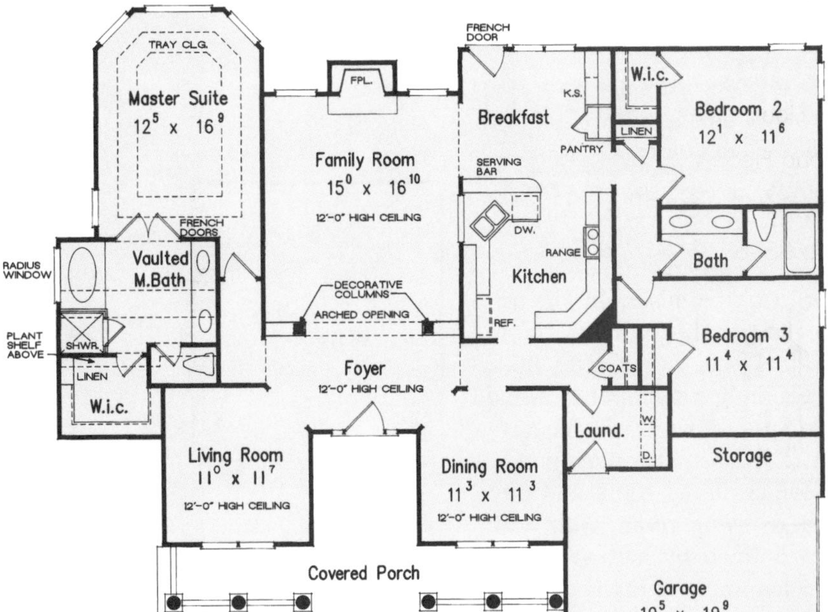

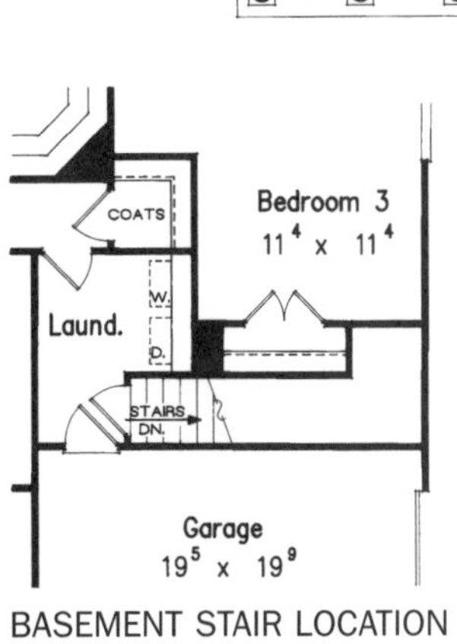

BASEMENT STAIR LOCATION

QUOTE ONE®

Cost to build? See page 516 to order complete cost estimate to build this house in your area!

Design HPT830296

Square Footage: 2,077

Width 50'-4" Depth 69'-10"

Don't be misled by the traditional, Southern charm of this home—the floor plan is simply contemporary while fostering a down-home, country spirit. The open foyer leads past the formal dining room and into the large living room, with both rooms defined by half-walls. The casual living room features built-in cabinets, bookshelves and a media center. From the living room, a large counter borders the country kitchen that's equipped with an island work-top and breakfast nook. The master suite is accessed through a solarium/office and features dual walk-in closets and a grand bath. Two additional bedrooms, one of which can be a study, share a full hall bath.

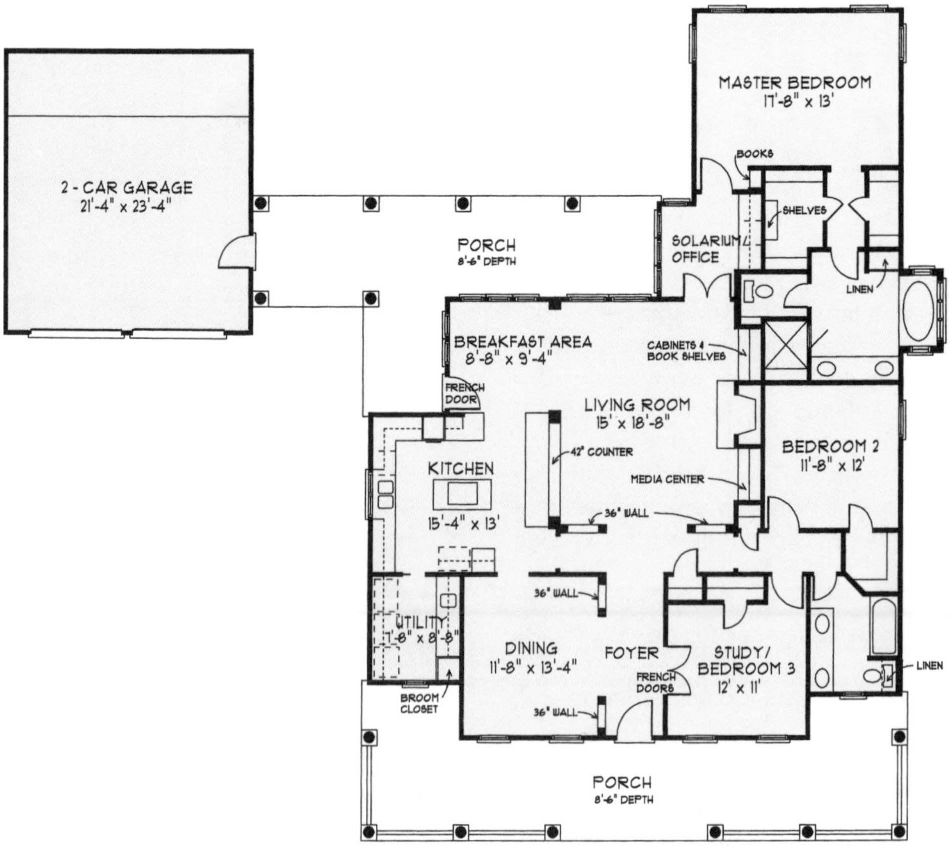

© 1996 Donald A Gardner Architects, Inc.

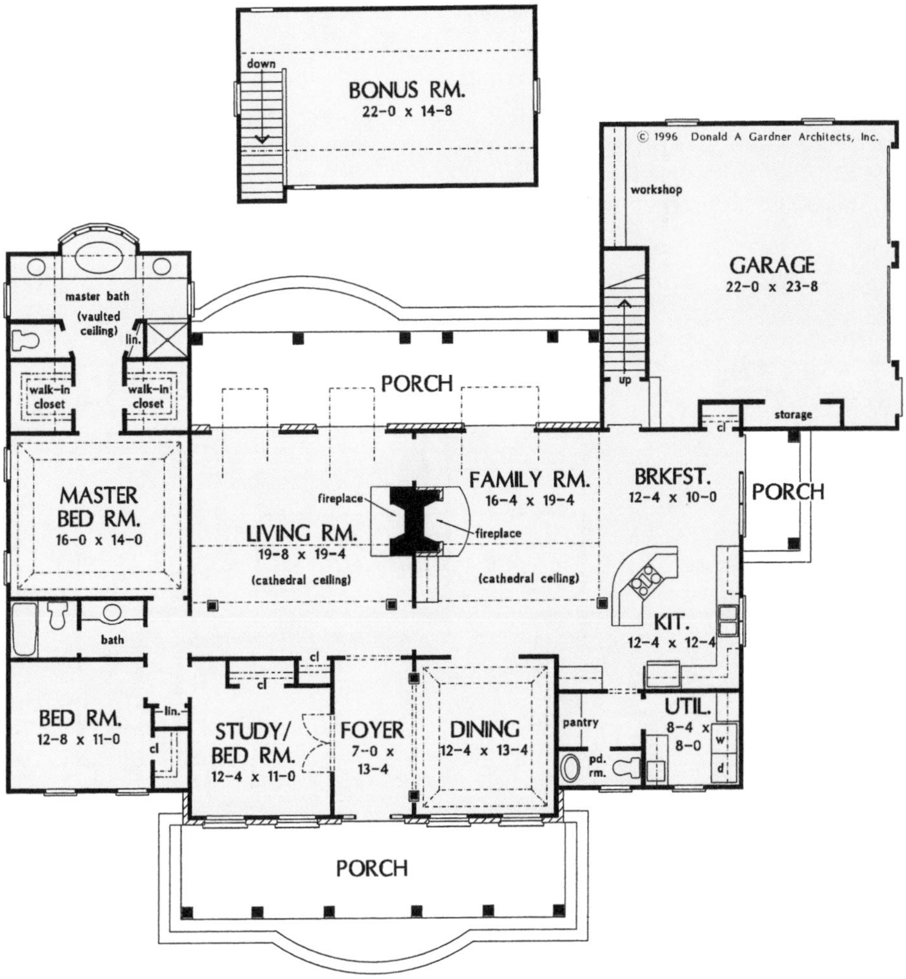
BONUS RM.
22-0 x 14-8
down
© 1996 Donald A Gardner Architects, Inc.
workshop
GARAGE
22-0 x 23-8
up
storage
cl
PORCH
master bath
(vaulted ceiling)
lin.
walk-in closet
walk-in closet
MASTER BED RM.
16-0 x 14-0
fireplace
LIVING RM.
19-8 x 19-4
(cathedral ceiling)
FAMILY RM.
16-4 x 19-4
fireplace
(cathedral ceiling)
BRKFST.
12-4 x 10-0
PORCH
KIT.
12-4 x 12-4
bath
cl
BED RM.
12-8 x 11-0
lin.
cl
STUDY/ BED RM.
12-4 x 11-0
FOYER
7-0 x 13-4
DINING
12-4 x 13-4
pantry
pd. rm.
UTIL.
8-4 x 8-0
w
d
PORCH

Design HPT830297

Square Footage: 2,450
Bonus Space: 423 square feet
Width 79'-8" Depth 68'-8"

A handsome display of columns frames the porch of this gracious Southern home. The foyer opens to the dining room and to a study, which could also be an additional bedroom. The open living room and family room are joined under a dramatic cathedral ceiling, divided with a showpiece fireplace that opens to both rooms. The efficient corner kitchen includes a handy breakfast nook that opens to a morning porch and a work island with a cooktop and curved snack bar. The master suite has a stylish tray ceiling, twin walk-in closets and a compartmented bath with an elegant bumped-out tub.

This home features brick jack arches that frame the arched front door and windows. Inside, the foyer opens directly to the large great room with a fireplace and French doors that lead outside. Just off the foyer, the dining room is defined by columns. Adjacent to the breakfast room is the keeping room, which includes a corner fireplace and more French doors to the large rear porch. The master suite has dual vanities and a spacious walk-in closet. Upstairs, two family bedrooms enjoy separate access to a shared bath while down the hall a fourth bedroom includes a private bath. This home is designed with a walkout basement foundation.

Design HPT830298

First Floor: 1,650 square feet

Second Floor: 1,060 square feet

Total: 2,710 square feet

Width 53'-0" Depth 68'-2"

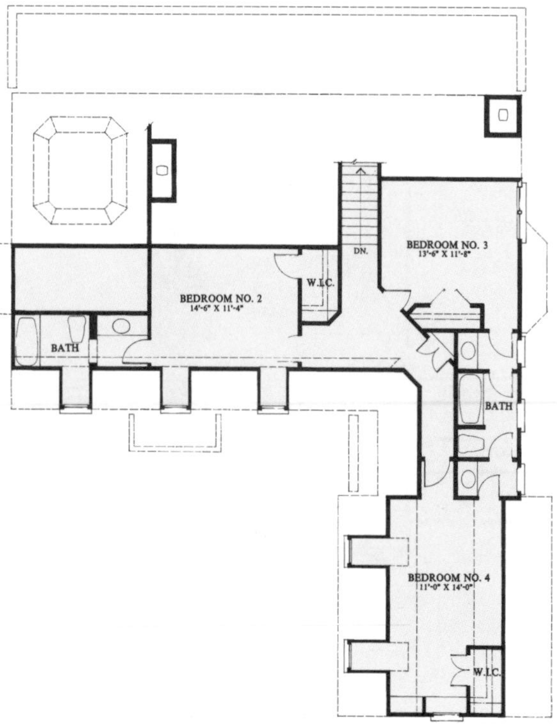

Design
HPT830299

First Floor: 2,380 square feet
Second Floor: 1,295 square feet
Total: 3,675 square feet
Width 77'-4" Depth 58'-4"

QUOTE ONE®
Cost to build? See page 516 to order complete cost estimate to build this house in your area!

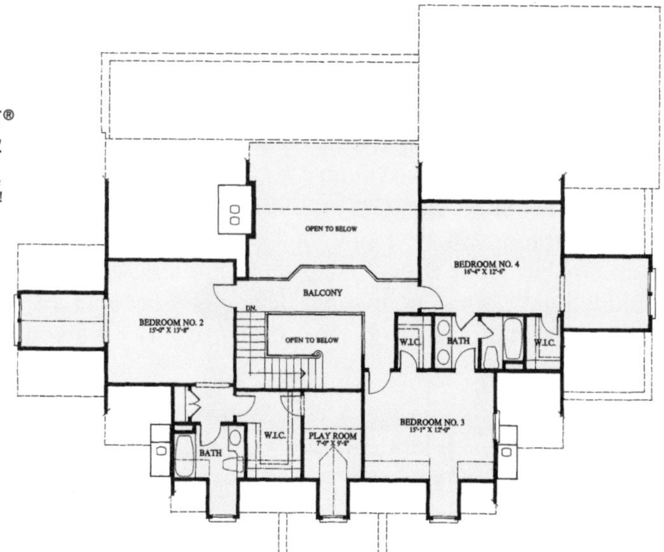

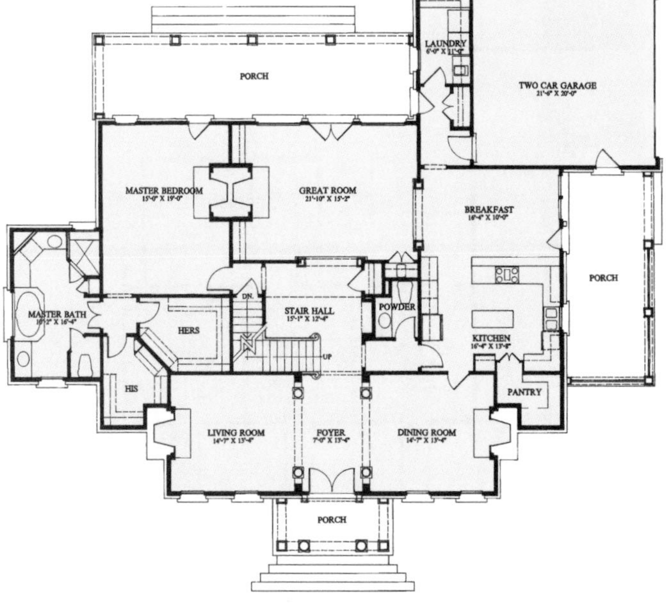

Finely crafted porches—front, side and rear—make this home a classic in traditional Southern living. Past the large French doors, the impressive foyer is flanked by the formal living and dining rooms. Beyond the stair is a vaulted great room with an expanse of windows, a fireplace and built-in bookcases. From here, the breakfast room and kitchen are easily accessible and open to a private side porch. The master suite provides a large bath, two spacious closets, a fireplace and a private entry that opens to the covered rear porch. The second floor contains three bedrooms with private bath access and a playroom. This home is designed with a walkout basement foundation.

A neighborly porch embraces three sides of this comfortable home, extending a hearty welcome from its inviting entrance to its warm country kitchen. Inside, rooms open directly onto one another, preserving an old-fashioned farmhouse atmosphere. A soaring, two-story foyer separates the formal living and dining rooms. Openings on both sides of a warming fireplace in the great room lead to a country kitchen where a range top set into a brick chimney arch recalls cooking on an old-time hearth. A sun drenched breakfast area and an expansive master suite that features a box-bay window and a sumptuous bath bracket the rear porch. Upstairs, dormers accent two family bedrooms and a shared bath, while bonus space can easily become a third bedroom or a convenient home office. This home is designed with a walkout basement foundation.

Design HPT830300

First Floor: 2,236 square feet
Second Floor: 771 square feet
Total: 3,007 square feet
Bonus Space: 275 square feet
Width 76'-0" Depth 62'-3"

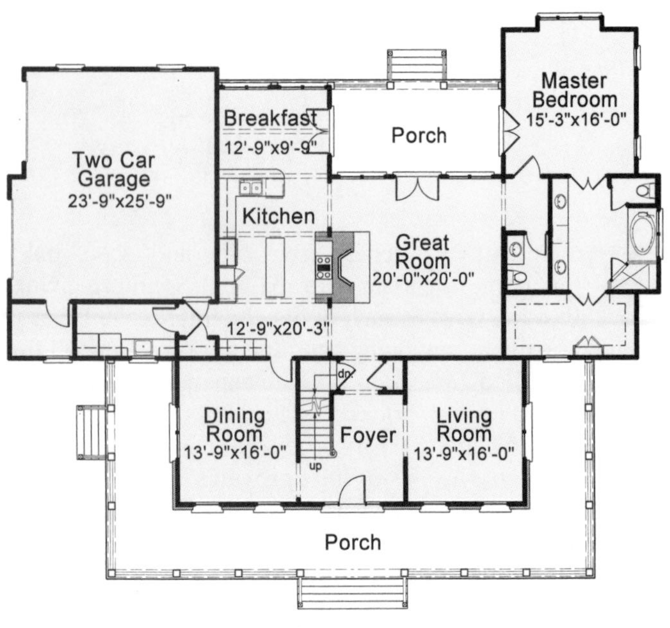

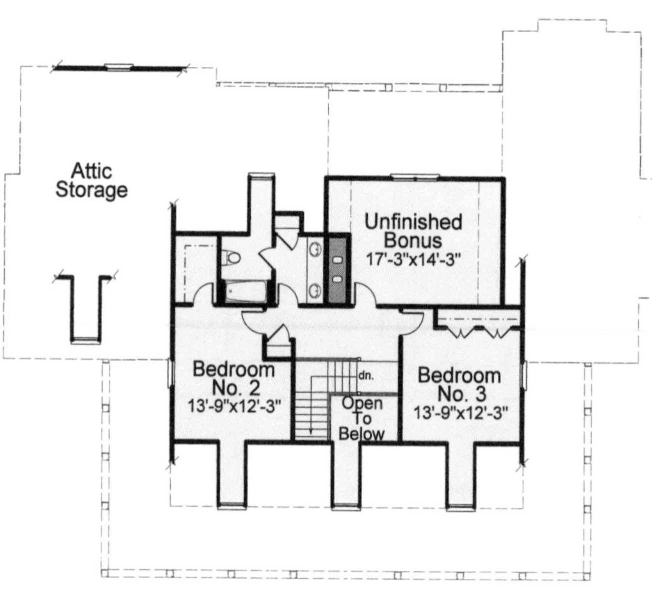

Design HPT830301

Square Footage: 3,066

Width 73'-0" Depth 70'-6"

Descended from the architecture that developed in America's Tidewater country, this updated adaptation retains the insouciant charm of a coastal cottage. At the same time, it offers an elegance that is appropriate for any setting in any climate today. Inside, the family living area is concentrated in the center of the house. Central to the social flow in the house, the great room opens to the kitchen, the breakfast room and the rear porch that runs across the back. The left wing contains a private master suite that includes twin walk-in closets leading into a lavish master bath. Two additional bedrooms share a bath, while Bedroom 4 enjoys a high level of privacy, making it an ideal guest room. This home is designed with a walkout basement foundation.

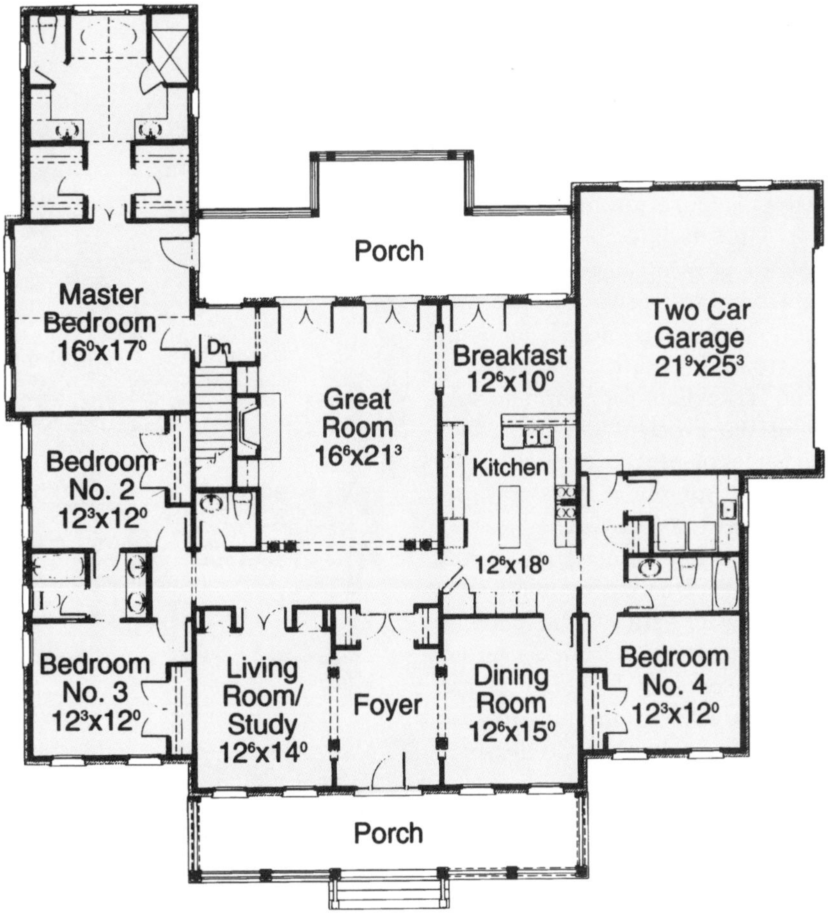

Design
HPT830302

Square Footage: 2,118

Width 73'-4" Depth 49'-1"

This four-bedroom, European-style farmhouse is perfect for a growing family. The great room provides plenty of space for family gatherings—while enjoying the stone fireplace. The cooktop island is excellent for gourmet cooking in the efficient kitchen, which also leaves plenty of extended counter space for meal preparations. Nearby, the breakfast area accesses a covered patio. The master bedroom presents a cathedral ceiling and a deluxe master bath with an immense walk-in closet, two vanities, a garden tub and a separate shower. A full hall bath, a powder room and two storage rooms are available to the three family bedrooms.

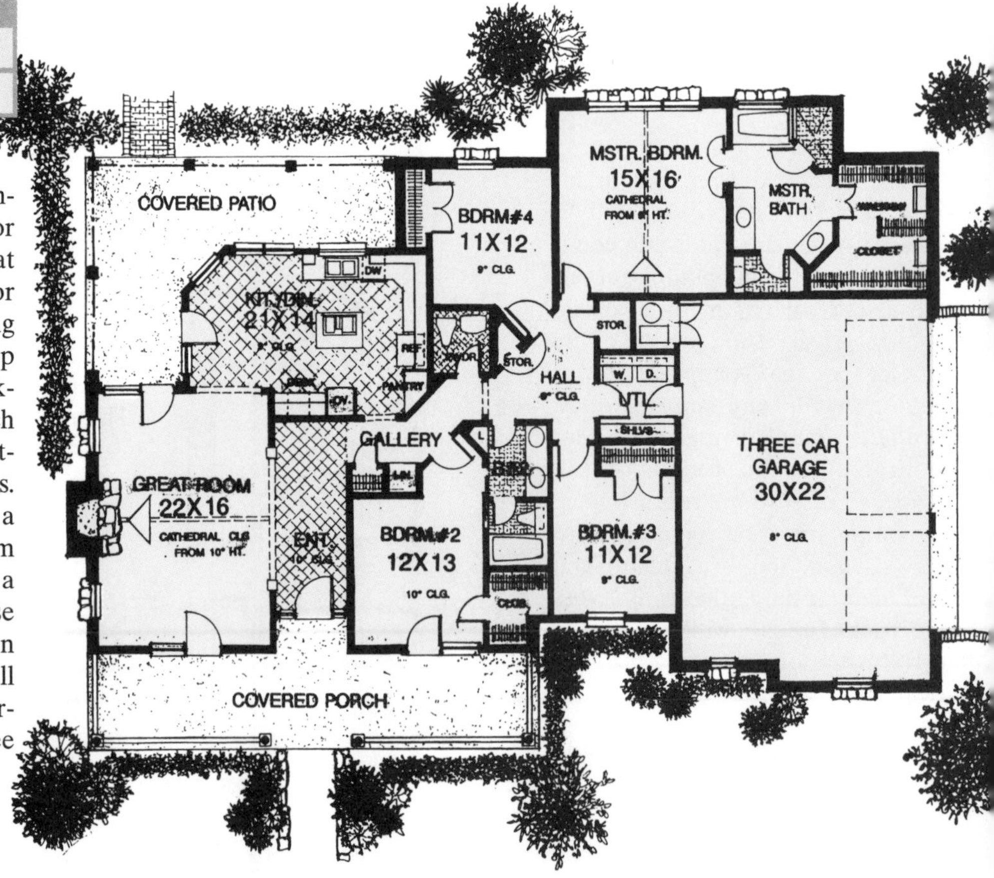

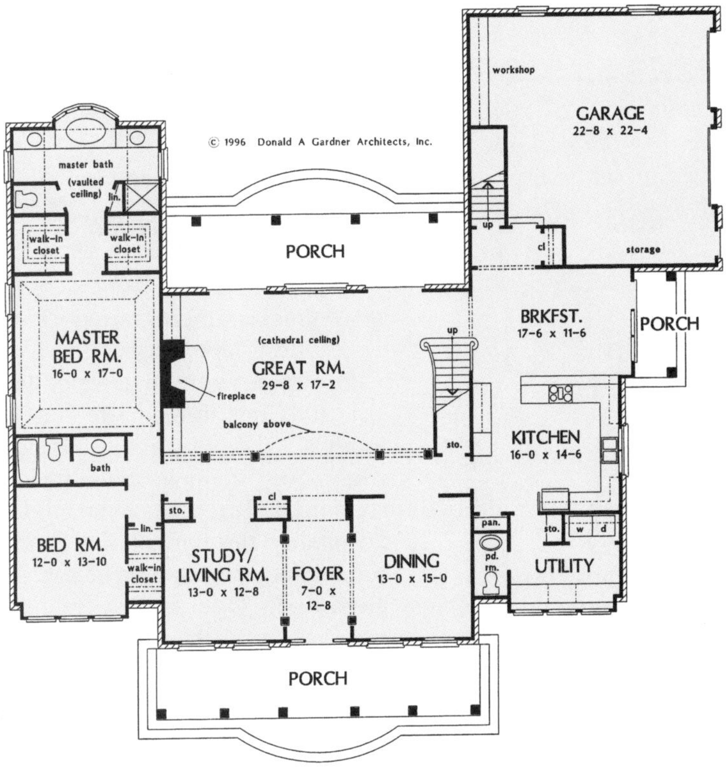

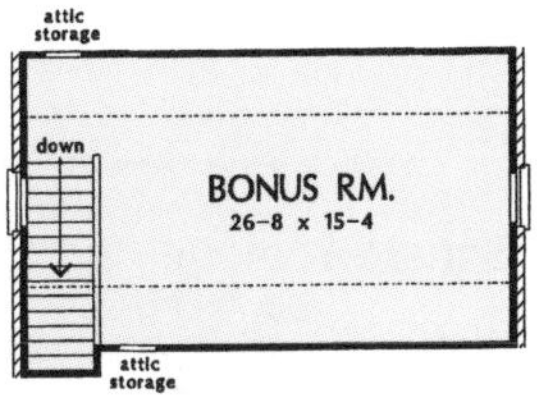

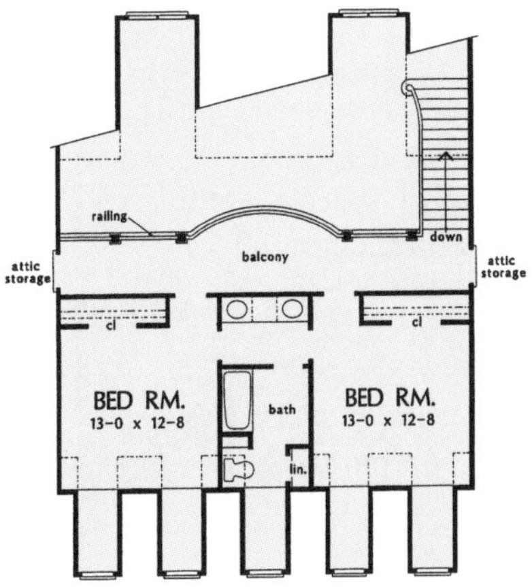

This home has a traditional symmetry in design that is a hallmark of Southern homes. The welcome feel of the front porch is translated throughout the plan with an open arrangement of the formal living and dining rooms and the expansive great room. The kitchen is designed for efficiency with a nearby laundry room and a large breakfast nook. The master bedroom contains an elegant tray ceiling and a posh bath. Upstairs, a balcony hall leads to two family bedrooms that share a compartmented bath.

Design HPT830303

First Floor: 2,920 square feet
Second Floor: 853 square feet
Total: 3,773 square feet
Bonus Space: 458 square feet
Width 78'-7" Depth 75'-7"

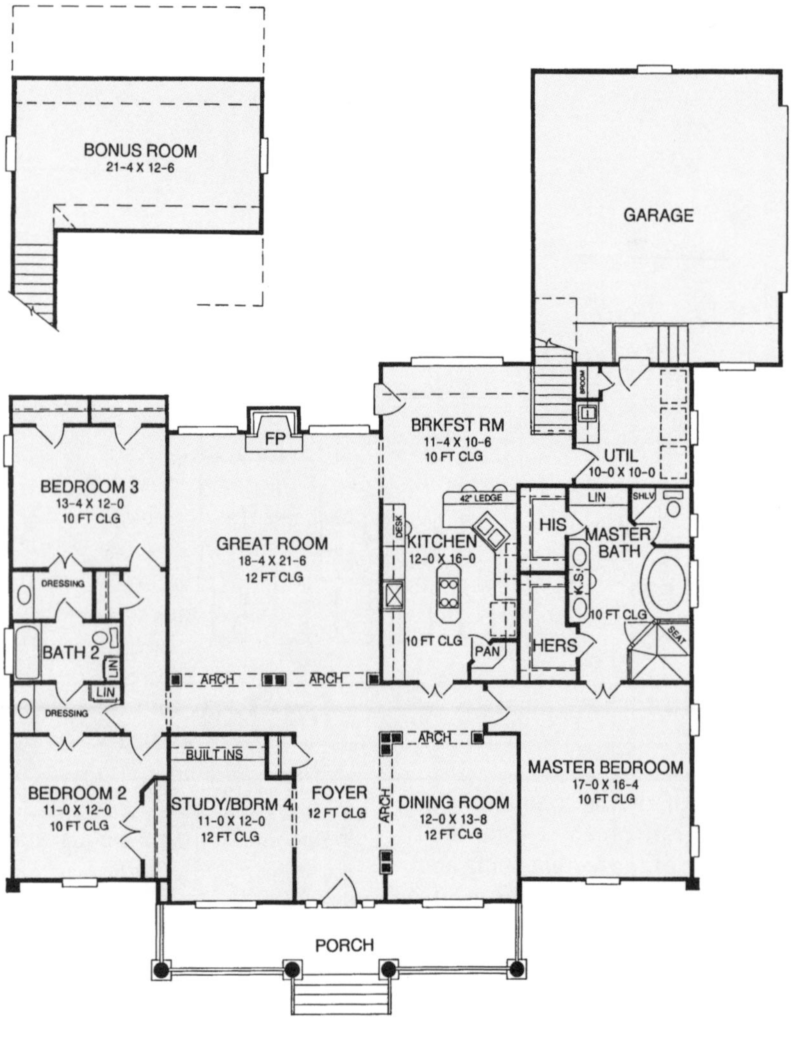
BONUS ROOM
21-4 X 12-6
GARAGE
BRKFST RM
11-4 X 10-6
10 FT CLG
BROOM
UTIL
10-0 X 10-0
FP
BEDROOM 3
13-4 X 12-0
10 FT CLG
GREAT ROOM
18-4 X 21-6
12 FT CLG
42" LEDGE
DESK
KITCHEN
12-0 X 16-0
LIN
SHLV
HIS
MASTER BATH
K.S.
10 FT CLG
SEAT
HERS
DRESSING
BATH 2
LIN
LIN
DRESSING
10 FT CLG
PAN
ARCH
ARCH
ARCH
BUILT INS
BEDROOM 2
11-0 X 12-0
10 FT CLG
STUDY/BDRM 4
11-0 X 12-0
12 FT CLG
FOYER
12 FT CLG
ARCH
DINING ROOM
12-0 X 13-8
12 FT CLG
MASTER BEDROOM
17-0 X 16-4
10 FT CLG
PORCH

Design HPT830304

Square Footage: 2,648
Bonus Space: 266 square feet
Width 68'-10" Depth 77'-10"

This Southern raised elevation looks cozy but lives large, with an interior layout and amenities preferred by today's homeowners. Inside, twelve-foot ceilings and graceful columns and arches lend an aura of hospitality throughout the formal rooms and the living space in the great room. Double doors open to the gourmet kitchen, which offers a built-in desk, a snack counter for easy meals and a breakfast room with a picture window. The secluded master suite features His and Hers walk-in closets, a whirlpool tub and a knee-space vanity. Please specify basement, crawlspace or slab foundation when ordering.

© American Home Gallery, Ltd.

QUOTE ONE®
Cost to build? See page 516
to order complete cost estimate
to build this house in your area!
2-CAR GARAGE
21'-6" X 21'-0"
LAUNDRY
STORAGE
VERANDA
MASTER BATH
MASTER SUITE
15'-9" X 16'-0"
W.I.C.
BREAKFAST
13'-6" X 10'-0"
UP
GREAT ROOM
20'-6" x 17'-6"
KITCHEN
16'-0" X 13'-6"
DN.
BEDROOM NO. 3
12'-0" X 13'-3"
POWDER
PANTRY
DINING ROOM
13'-3" X 14'-9"
FOYER
BEDROOM NO. 2
12'-6" X 13'-3"
BATH
PORTICO

Design HPT830305

Square Footage: 2,697	
Width 65'-3"	Depth 67'-3"

Dual chimneys (one a false chimney created to enhance the aesthetic effect) and a double stairway to the covered entry of this home create a balanced architectural statement. The sunlit foyer leads straight into the spacious great room, where French doors provide a generous view of the covered veranda in back. The great room features a tray ceiling and a fireplace, bordered by twin bookcases. Another great view is offered from the spacious kitchen with a breakfast bar and a roomy work island. The master suite provides a large balanced bath and a spacious closet. This home is designed with a walkout basement foundation.

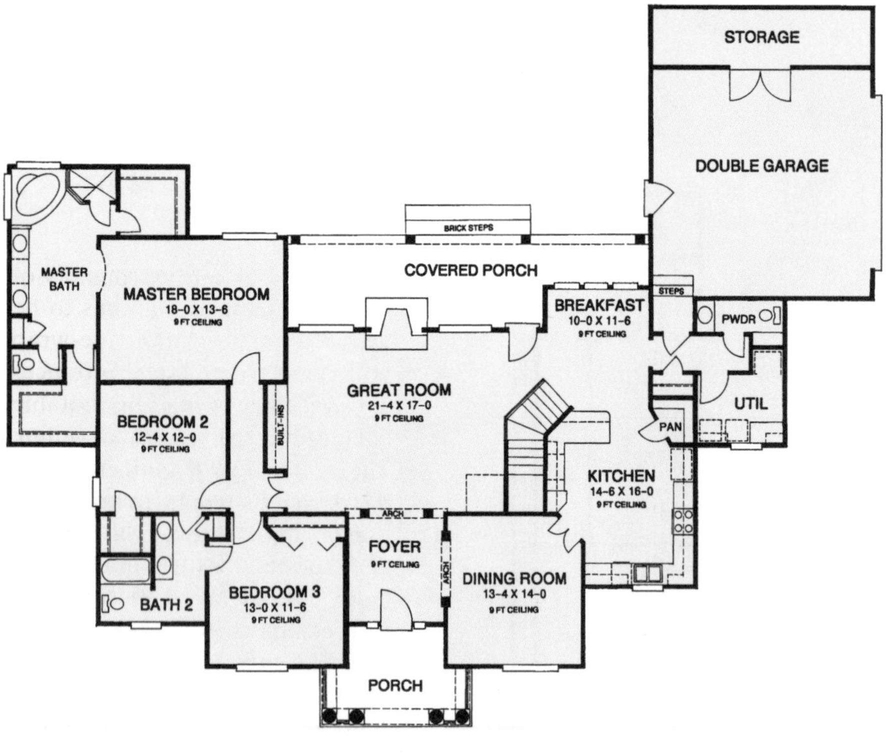

STORAGE
DOUBLE GARAGE
BRICK STEPS
COVERED PORCH
MASTER BATH
MASTER BEDROOM
18-0 X 13-6
9 FT CEILING
BREAKFAST
10-0 X 11-6
9 FT CEILING
STEPS
PWDR
GREAT ROOM
21-4 X 17-0
9 FT CEILING
UTIL
PAN
BUILT-INS
BEDROOM 2
12-4 X 12-0
9 FT CEILING
KITCHEN
14-6 X 16-0
9 FT CEILING
ARCH
FOYER
9 FT CEILING
DINING ROOM
13-4 X 14-0
9 FT CEILING
BATH 2
BEDROOM 3
13-0 X 11-6
9 FT CEILING
PORCH

QUOTE ONE®

Cost to build? See page 516 to order complete cost estimate to build this house in your area!

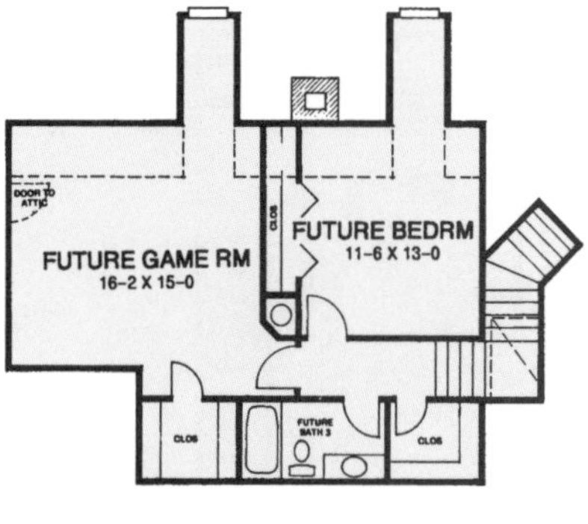

FUTURE GAME RM
16-2 X 15-0
FUTURE BEDRM
11-6 X 13-0

Design HPT830306

Square Footage: 2,409
Bonus Space: 709 square feet
Width 85'-8" Depth 68'-4"

The great room of this home provides a large masonry fireplace. Built-ins are included on one wall for entertainment equipment and books. The master suite is located to the rear of the house and has a luxury bath that includes large walk-in closets. The kitchen, equipped with a snack bar, walk-in pantry and desk, is well designed for the busy cook. From the kitchen area, the staircase rises to an expandable second floor. With a future bedroom, game room and bath upstairs, this home will fit the needs of a growing family. Please specify basement, crawlspace or slab foundation when ordering.

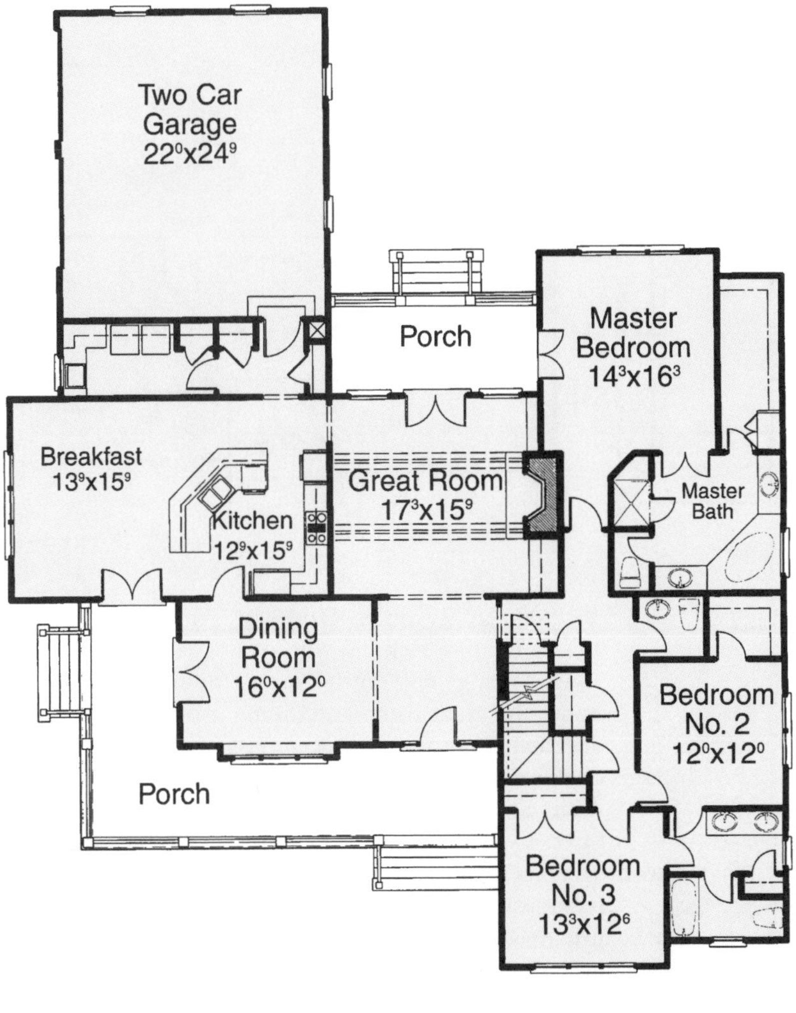

Design HPT830307

Square Footage: 2,485	
Width 64'-9"	Depth 78'-9"

The most inviting amenity of this country plan has to be its extra-wide, side-wrap porch from which three entrances to the home open. The notable great room has a formal ceiling detail, fireplace, built-ins and French doors to the rear porch. Casual entertaining will surely revolve around activity in the open country kitchen. The master bedroom enjoys a lush bath, walk-in closet and private French doors to the rear porch. Two secondary bedrooms share a private bath. A full two-car garage is joined to the rear of the home, out of sight so that the home's curb appeal is not compromised. This house is designed with a walkout basement foundation.

DECK
MASTER BEDROOM
13'-4" X 18'-0"
W.I.C.
BREAKFAST
14'-4" X 10'-6"
MASTER BATH
GREAT ROOM
18'-2" X 16'-6"
KITCHEN
10'-6" X 13'-8"
LIVING ROOM
11'-2" X 12'-6"
FOYER
6'-0" X 10'-0"
DINING ROOM
12'-0" X 12'-0"
POWDER
LAUNDRY
10'-6" X 6'-0"
PORCH
TWO CAR GARAGE
20'-4" X 20'-10"

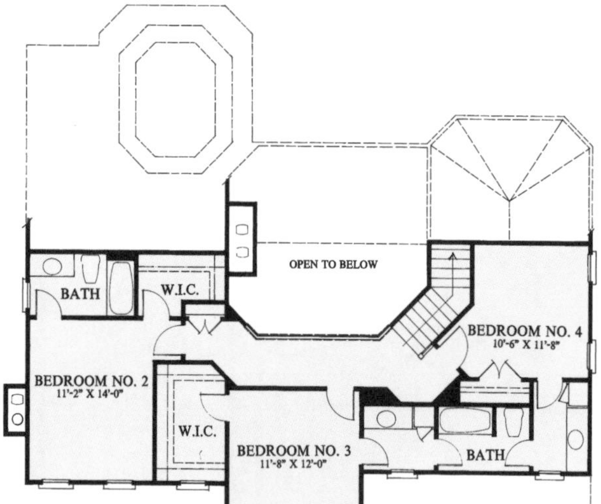

OPEN TO BELOW
BATH
W.I.C.
BEDROOM NO. 4
10'-6" X 11'-8"
BEDROOM NO. 2
11'-2" X 14'-0"
W.I.C.
BEDROOM NO. 3
11'-8" X 12'-0"
BATH

Design HPT830308

First Floor: 1,840 square feet

Second Floor: 950 square feet

Total: 2,790 square feet

Width 58'-6" Depth 62'-0"

The appearance of this early American home brings the past to mind with its wraparound porch, wood siding and flower-box detailing. Inside, columns frame the great room and dining room. Left of the foyer lies the living room with a warming fireplace. The angular kitchen joins a sunny breakfast nook. The master bedroom has a spacious private bath and a walk-in closet. Stairs to the second level lead from the breakfast area to an open landing overlooking the great room. Three family bedrooms—two with walk-in closets and all three with private access to a bath—complete this level. This home is designed with a walkout basement foundation.

Design

HPT830309

First Floor: 1,720 square feet
Second Floor: 545 square feet
Total: 2,265 square feet
Bonus Space: 365 square feet
Width 50'-0" Depth 53'-6"

The foyer opens to the living and dining areas, providing a spectacular entrance to this English country cottage. Just beyond the dining room is a gourmet kitchen with a work island and a food bar opening to the breakfast room. Accented by a fireplace and built-in bookcases, the family room with a ribbon of windows is an excellent setting for family gatherings. Remotely located off the central hallway, the master suite includes rectangular ceiling detail and access to the rear deck, while the master bath features His and Hers vanities, a garden tub and a spacious walk-in closet. The central staircase leads to the balcony overlook and two bedrooms with spacious closets and baths. This home is designed with a walkout basement foundation.

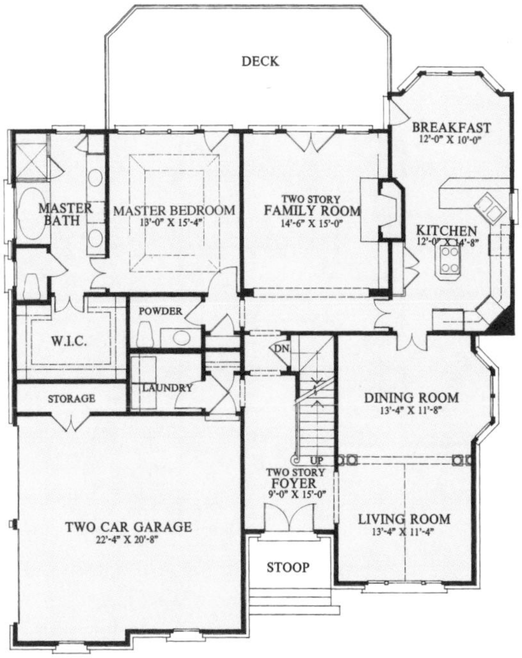

QUOTE ONE®
Cost to build? See page 516
to order complete cost estimate
to build this house in your area!

This grand two-story home proves that tried-and-true traditional style is still the best! Thoughtful planning brings formal living areas to the forefront and places an open, casual living areas to the rear of the plan. Bedroom 4 serves as a multi-purpose room, providing the flexibility desired by today's homeowner. The second floor is devoted to the relaxing master suite, two secondary bedrooms, a full hall bath and a balcony overlook. Please specify basement, crawlspace or slab foundation when ordering.

Design HPT830310

First Floor: 1,135 square feet
Second Floor: 917 square feet
Total: 2,052 square feet
Bonus Space: 216 square feet
Width 52'-4" Depth 37'-6"

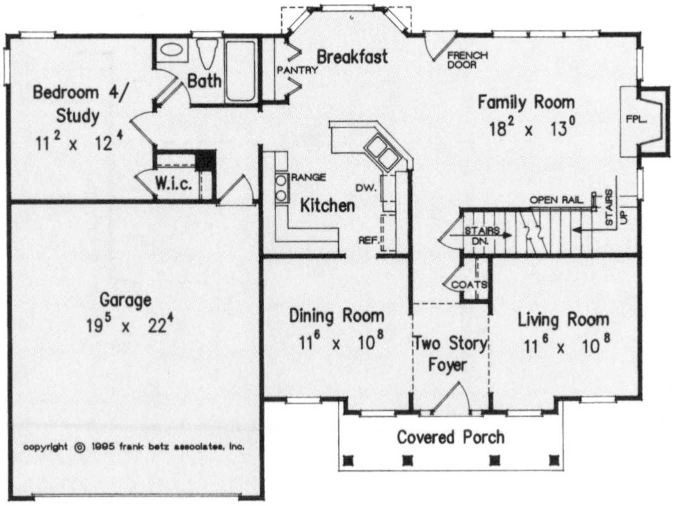

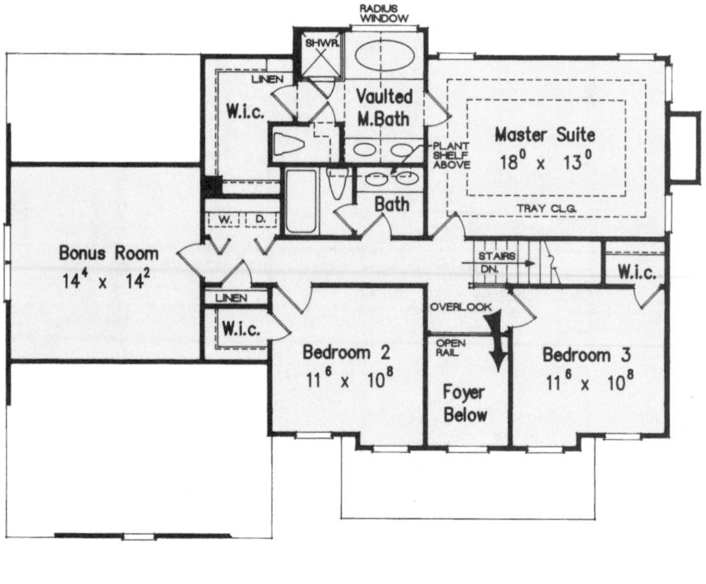

Cost to build? See page 516 to order complete cost estimate to build this house in your area!

Design
HPT830311

First Floor: 1,455 square feet
Second Floor: 1,649 square feet
Total: 3,104 square feet
Width 54'-4" Depth 46'-0"

QUOTE ONE®
Cost to build? See page 516 to order complete cost estimate to build this house in your area!

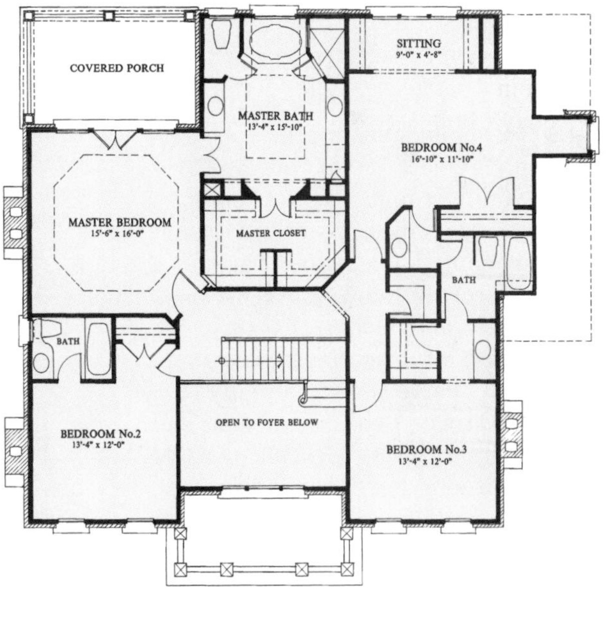

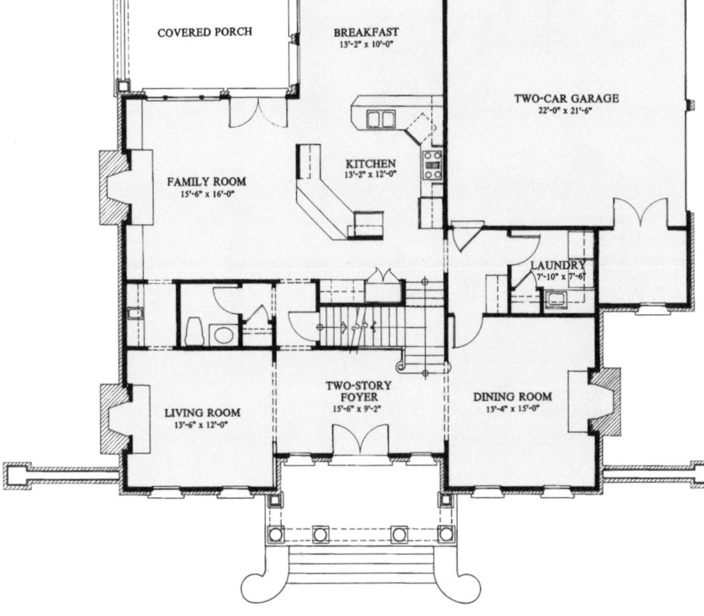

The double wings, twin chimneys and center portico of this home work in concert to create a classic architectural statement. The two-story foyer is flanked by the spacious dining room and formal living room, each containing its own fireplace. This home is designed with a walkout basement foundation.

Traditional Southern ambience distinguishes this stately antebellum home. The dining and living rooms open off the foyer and are defined by a gallery of columns with graceful connecting arches. A see-through fireplace serves both the living and family rooms. The kitchen is designed for efficiency with a corner walk-in pantry, a breakfast bar and a sunny corner window above the sink. The master suite includes a luxury bath with a corner tub accented by columns, as well as a large shower, a vanity area with knee space, two linen cabinets and twin walk-in closets. Upstairs, the two front bedrooms have private balconies; all three bedrooms have private bath access. Please specify crawlspace or slab foundation when ordering.

Design

HPT830312

First Floor: 2,553 square feet
Second Floor: 1,085 square feet
Total: 3,638 square feet
Width 73'-0" Depth 81'-0"Width
L

This home, as shown in the photograph, may differ from the actual blueprints. For more detailed information, please check the floor plans carefully. Photo courtesy of Design Basics, Inc.

Lap siding, special windows and a covered porch enhance the elevation of this popular-style home. The spacious two-story entry surveys the formal dining room, which includes hutch space. An entertainment center, a through-fireplace and bayed windows add appeal to the great room. Families will love the spacious kitchen with its breakfast and hearth rooms. Comfortable secondary bedrooms and a sumptuous master bedroom feature privacy by design. Bedroom 3 is highlighted by a half-round window, volume ceiling and double closets, while Bedroom 4 contains a built-in desk. The master suite possesses a vaulted ceiling, large walk-in closet, His and Hers vanities and an oval whirlpool tub.

Design HPT830313

First Floor: 1,150 square feet
Second Floor: 1,120 square feet
Total: 2,270 square feet
Width 46'-0" Depth 48'-0"

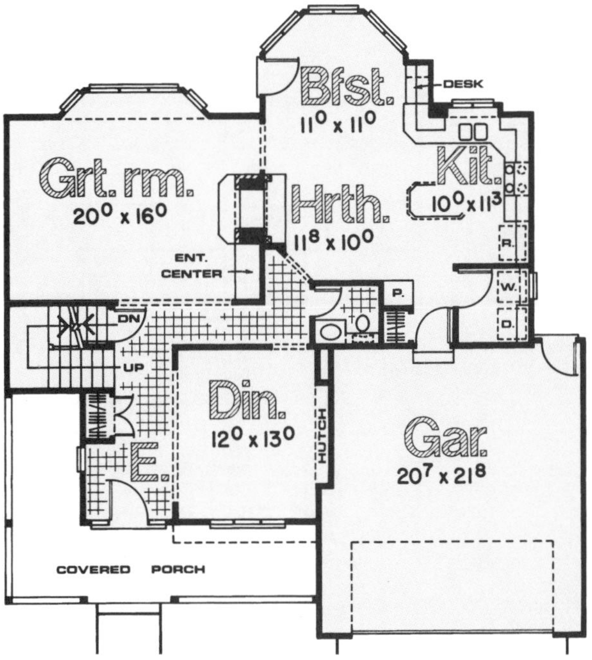

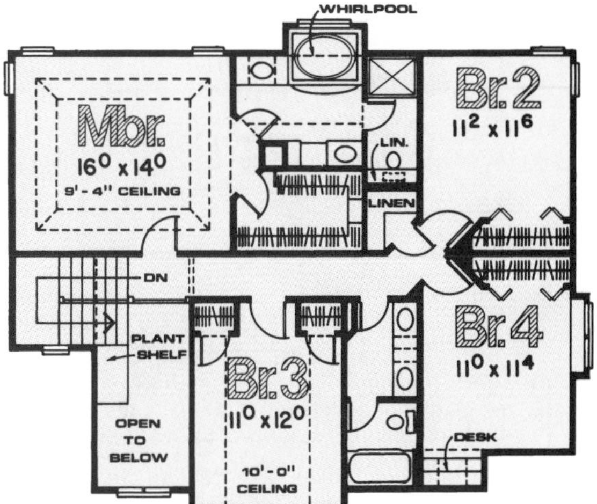

Inside this charming turn-of-the-century design, classical columns separate the foyer and dining room. A French door opens from the living room to a lattice-covered side arbor. Double doors in both the living and family rooms provide access to a bay-windowed study with built-in bookcases and a desk. The large family room contains a fireplace, media cabinet and a serving bar open from the kitchen. A six-foot curved picture window offers a full view of the rear porch from the breakfast and kitchen areas. Upstairs, the master suite features a walk-in closet and an elegant bath with a garden tub inset in a bay window. Bedrooms 3 and 4 share a bath, while Bedroom 2 has a private bath and a bay-windowed alcove.

Design HPT830314

First Floor: 1,354 square feet
Second Floor: 1,418 square feet
Total: 2,772 square feet
Width 46'-6" Depth 65'-8"

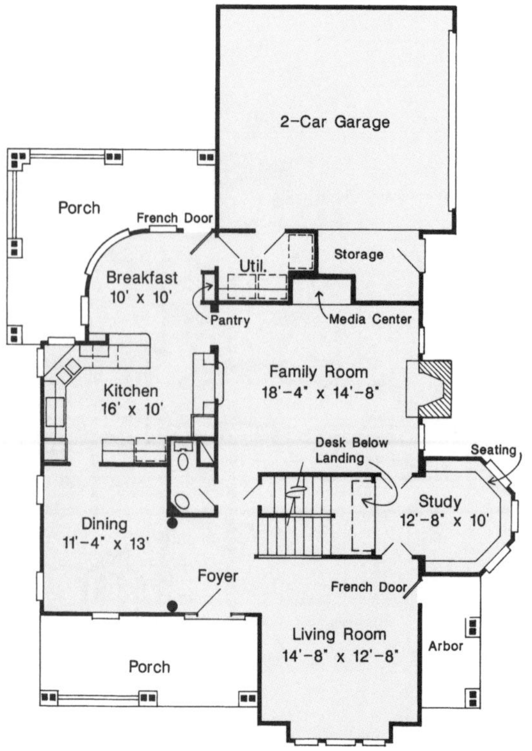

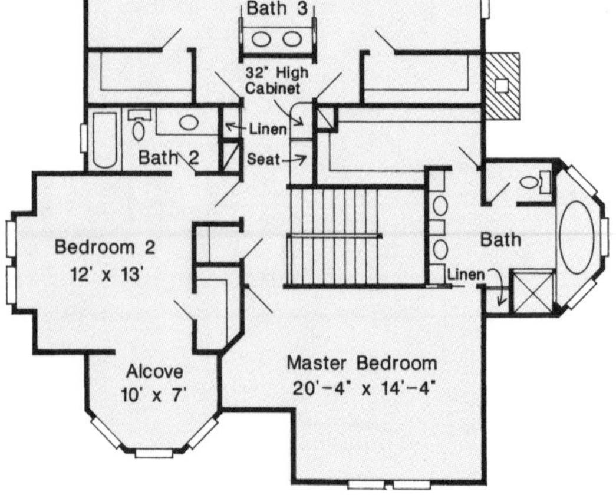

A wraparound veranda with delicate spindlework and a raised turret with leaded-glass windows recall the Queen Anne-style Victorians of the late 1880s. Double doors open from the two-story foyer to a study with built-in bookcases and a bay window. A fireplace adds warmth to the breakfast area and the island kitchen. Above the two-car garage is an optional area that is perfect for a home office or guest quarters. Upstairs, the balcony overlooks the foyer below. An octagonal-shaped ceiling and leaded-glass windows define a cozy sitting area in the master suite. A raised alcove in the master bath contains a garden tub and glass-enclosed shower. An optional exercise loft and plant shelves complete this elegant master bath. Two additional bedrooms—one with a private deck and the other with a cathedral ceiling—share a dressing area and bath.

Design

HPT830315

First Floor: 1,357 square feet
Second Floor: 1,079 square feet
Total: 2,436 square feet
Bonus Space: 228 square feet
Width 42'-8" Depth 75'-0"

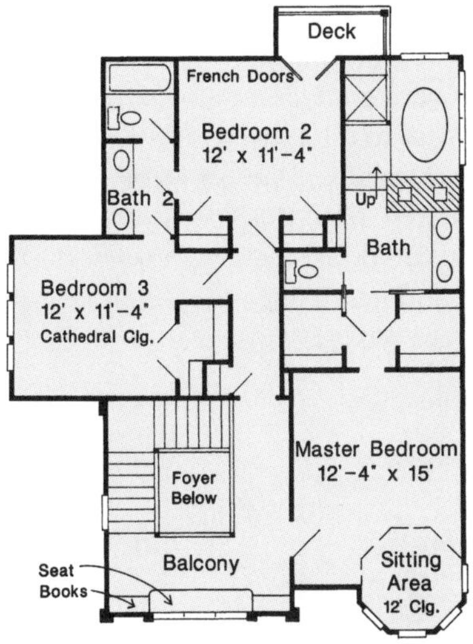

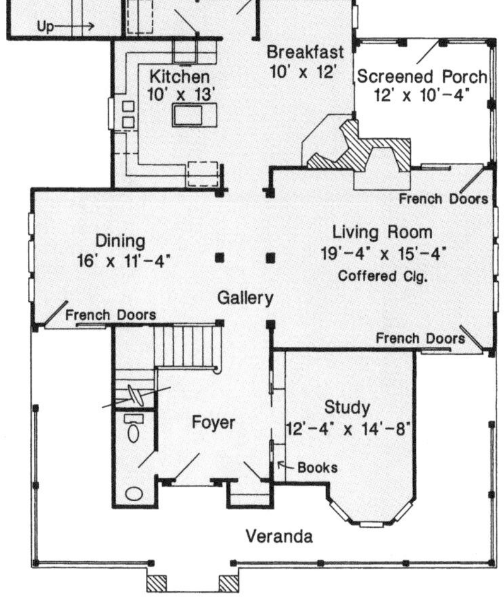

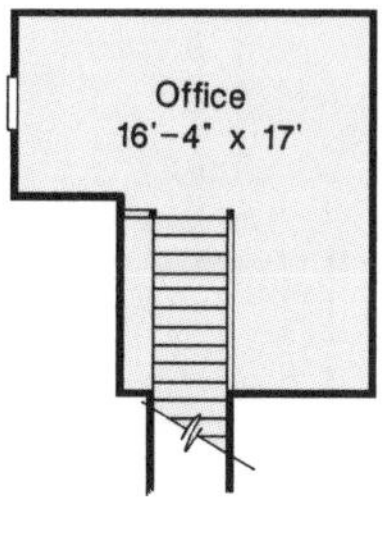

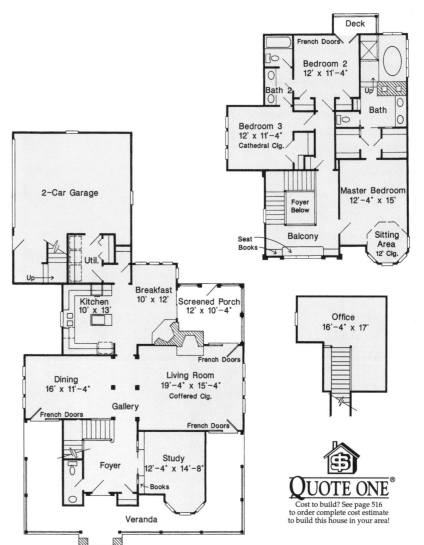

QUOTE ONE®
Cost to build? See page 516 to order complete cost estimate to build this house in your area!

A large covered porch in front and an angled covered veranda out back bring the outdoors into this four-bedroom Victorian design. The traffic flow throughout the main living area is perfect for entertaining large groups—the living room, dining room and study are placed conveniently near each other. The kitchen easily serves these rooms as well as the less formal family room and breakfast nook. Upstairs, a loft and a bonus room separated by a half-wall provide room to grow. A separate shop is adjacent to the three-car garage.

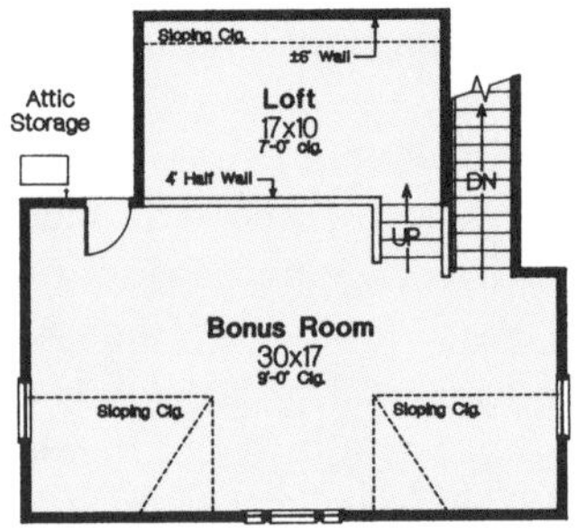

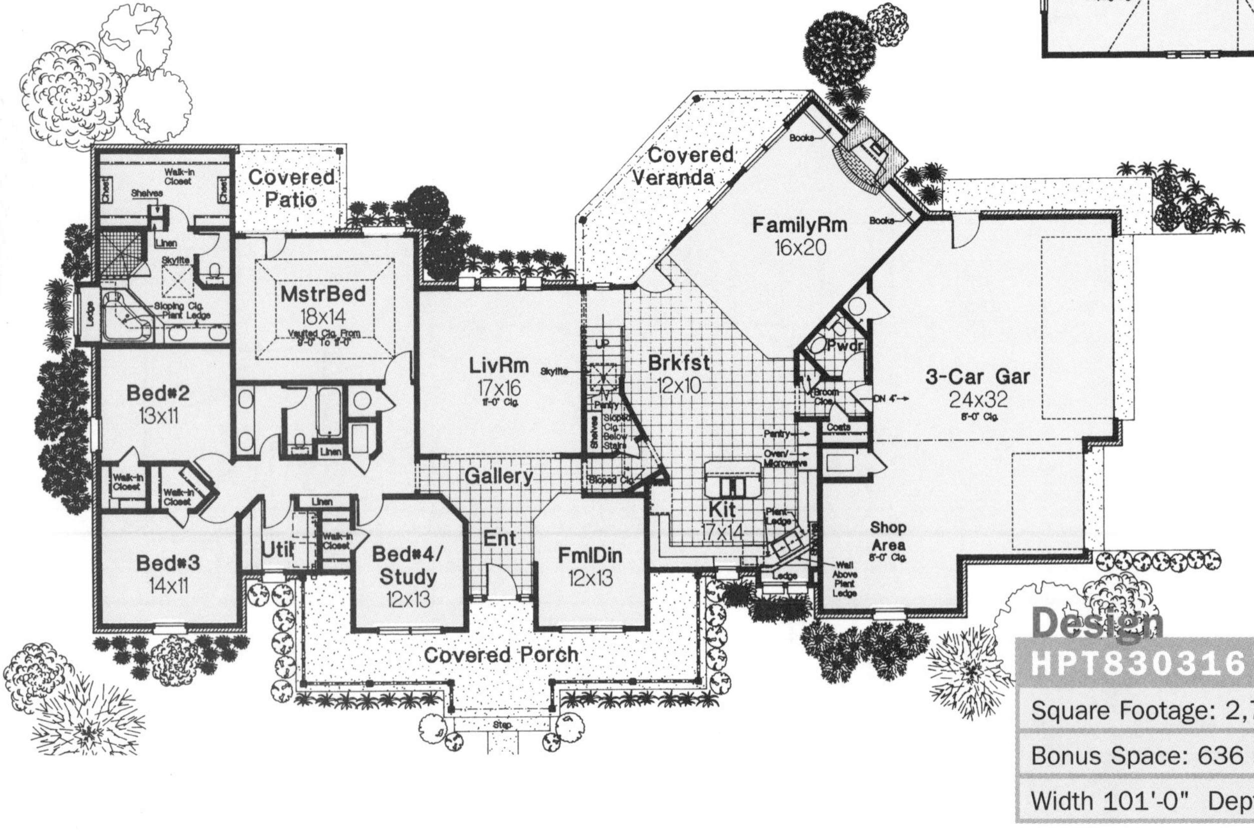

Design

HPT830316

Square Footage: 2,787

Bonus Space: 636 square feet

Width 101'-0" Depth 58'-8"

A wraparound veranda and simple lines give this home an unassuming elegance that is characteristic of its Folk Victorian heritage. Opening directly to the formal dining room, the two-story foyer offers extra space for large dinner parties. Double French doors lead to the study with raised paneling and a cozy fireplace. Built-in bookcases conceal a hidden security vault. The private master suite features a corner garden tub, glass-enclosed shower and a walk-in closet. Overlooking the family room and built-in breakfast nook is the central kitchen. A rear staircase provides convenient access to the second floor from the family room. The balcony provides a view of the foyer below and the Palladian window. Three additional bedrooms complete this exquisite home.

Design HPT830317

First Floor: 1,999 square feet
Second Floor: 933 square feet
Total: 2,932 square feet
Width 80'-0" Depth 59'-0"

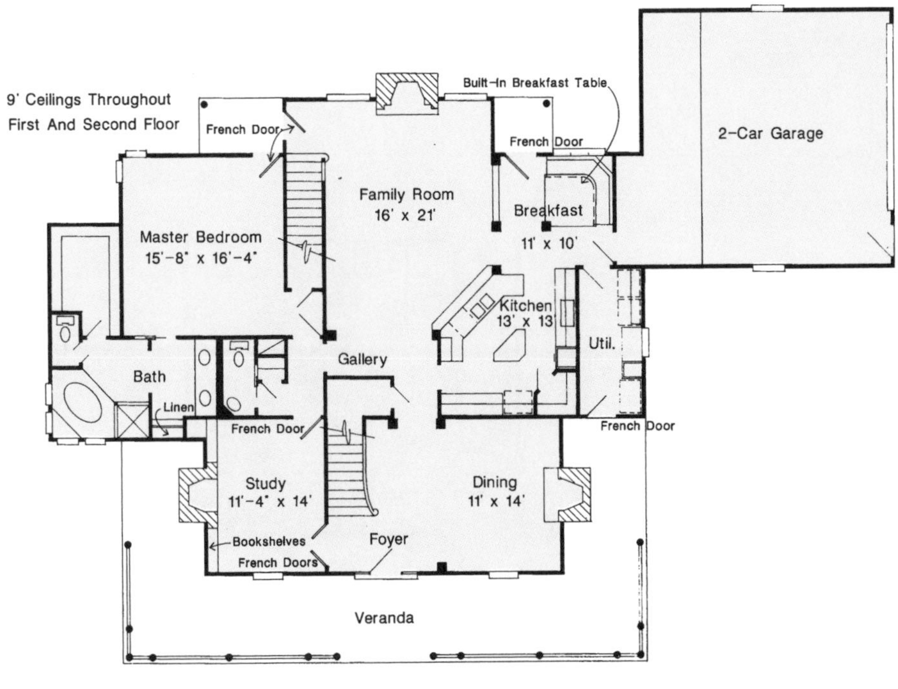

QUOTE ONE®
Cost to build? See page 516 to order complete cost estimate to build this house in your area!

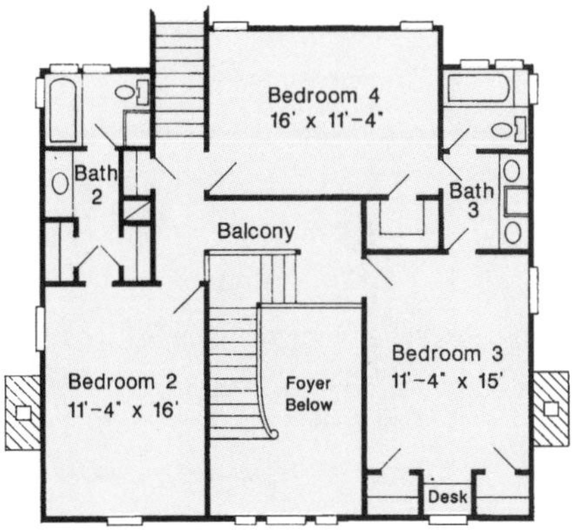

Design

HPT830318

First Floor: 1,337 square feet
Second Floor: 1,025 square feet
Total: 2,362 square feet
Width 50'-6" Depth 72'-6"

This home's covered, angled entry is elegantly echoed by an angled door to a rear covered porch, thus setting the style for this amenity-filled design. Just off the foyer, the formal living and dining rooms create an elegant open space for entertaining, while a focal-point fireplace with an extended hearth warms up a spacious family area. The cooktop-island kitchen and morning nook lead to a powder room and laundry area. Two second-floor bedrooms share a full bath, while the master suite offers a private bath with an oversized whirlpool tub, twin vanities and a walk-in closet.

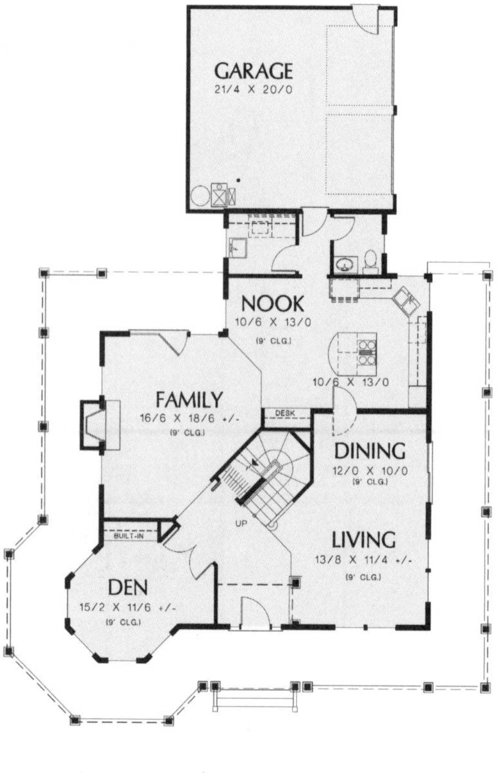

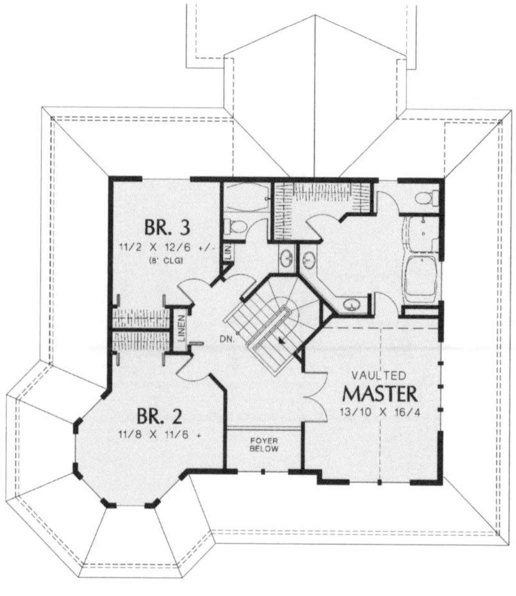

The living area of this spectacular Queen Anne style home features a fireplace and a bay-windowed alcove. The centrally located kitchen overlooks a dining area with full-length windows and a French door. The master bedroom features a large walk-in closet and French doors opening to the rear veranda. The master bath provides additional closet space, along with a glass-enclosed shower and an oval tub in an octagon-shaped alcove. Upstairs, French doors open into a game room. Bedroom 2 offers a walk-in closet and a ten-foot sloped ceiling. Bedroom 3 also provides a walk-in closet and a raised octagon-shaped ceiling. Plans are included for a detached two-car garage and an optional screened porch.

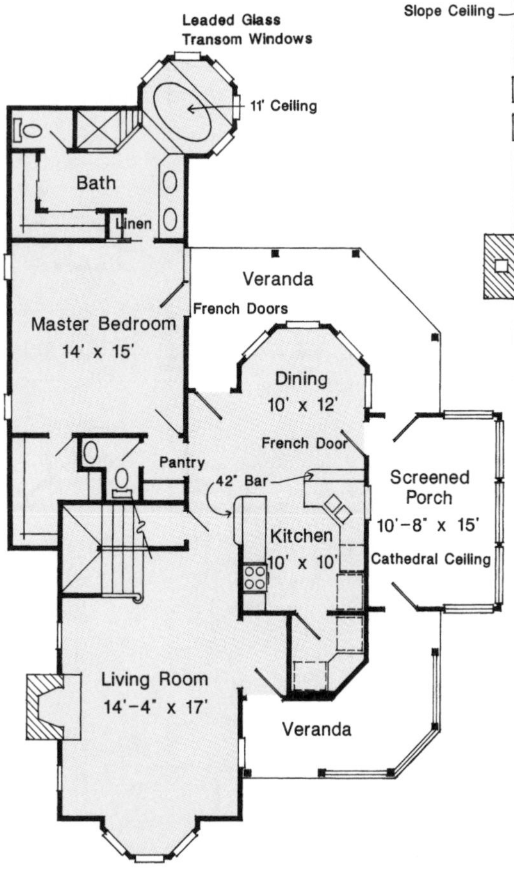
Leaded Glass
Transom Windows
11' Ceiling
Bath
Linen
Veranda
French Doors
Master Bedroom
14' x 15'
Dining
10' x 12'
French Door
Pantry
42" Bar
Screened
Porch
10'-8" x 15'
Cathedral Ceiling
Kitchen
10' x 10'
Living Room
14'-4" x 17'
Veranda

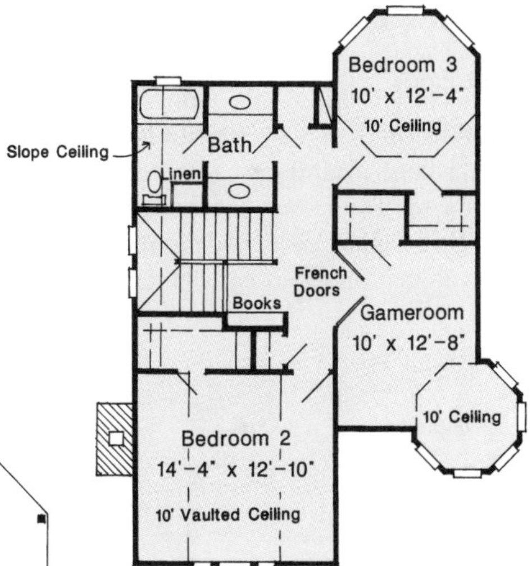
Bedroom 3
10' x 12'-4"
10' Ceiling
Slope Ceiling
Bath
Linen
French
Doors
Books
Gameroom
10' x 12'-8"
10' Ceiling
Bedroom 2
14'-4" x 12'-10"
10' Vaulted Ceiling

Design HPT830319

First Floor: 1,236 square feet
Second Floor: 835 square feet
Total: 2,071 square feet
Width 40'-4" Depth 62'-10"

This Queen Anne Victorian home's angled entry opens to a grand foyer and a formal parlor. French doors open from the foyer to the large study with bookcases and full-length windows. The spacious family room has a fireplace and a wet bar. The kitchen is fashioned with a work island, abundant cabinet space and a sunny breakfast room. Upstairs, the master bedroom contains a private deck and a lush bath with a clawfoot tub. Three additional bedrooms each have walk-in closets and unique features. Plans for a two-car detached garage are included.

Design HPT830320

First Floor: 1,565 square feet
Second Floor: 1,598 square feet
Total: 3,163 square feet
Width 47'-10" Depth 59'-2"

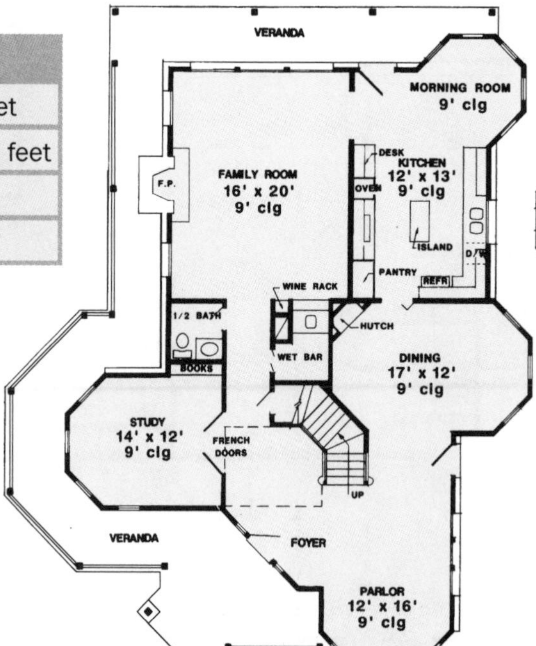

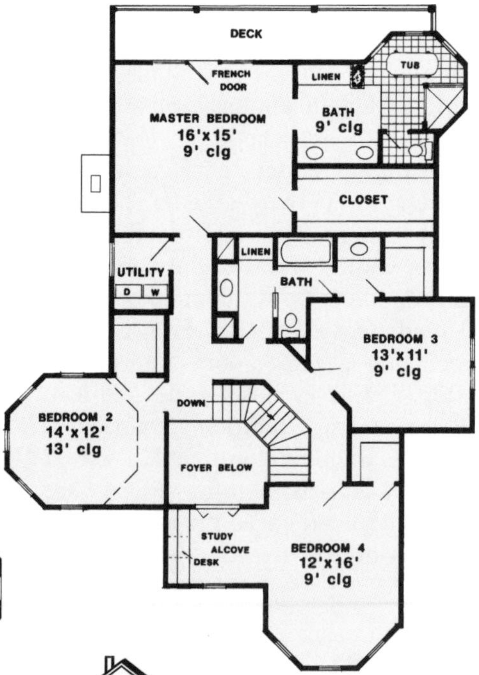

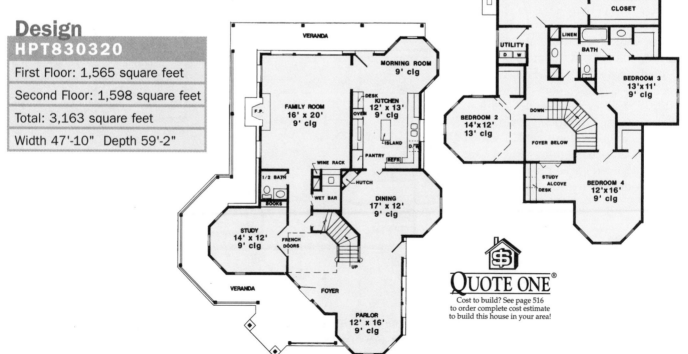

QUOTE ONE®

Cost to build? See page 516 to order complete cost estimate to build this house in your area!

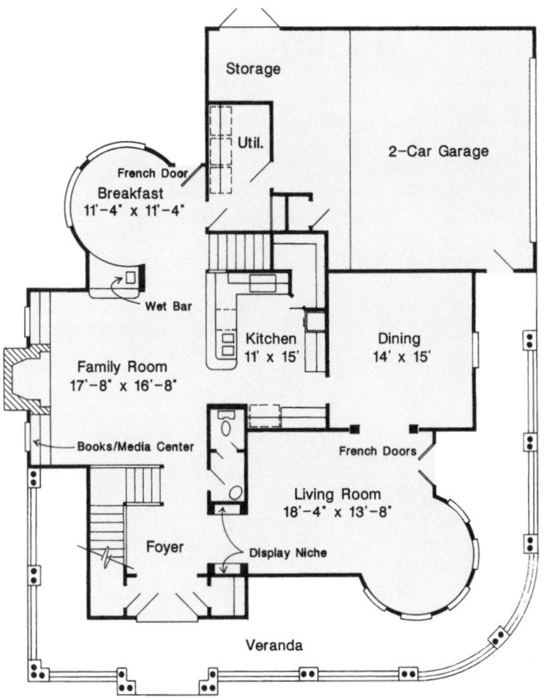
Storage
Util.
2-Car Garage
French Door
Breakfast
11'-4" x 11'-4"
Wet Bar
Family Room
17'-8" x 16'-8"
Kitchen
11' x 15'
Dining
14' x 15'
Books/Media Center
French Doors
Living Room
18'-4" x 13'-8"
Foyer
Display Niche
Veranda

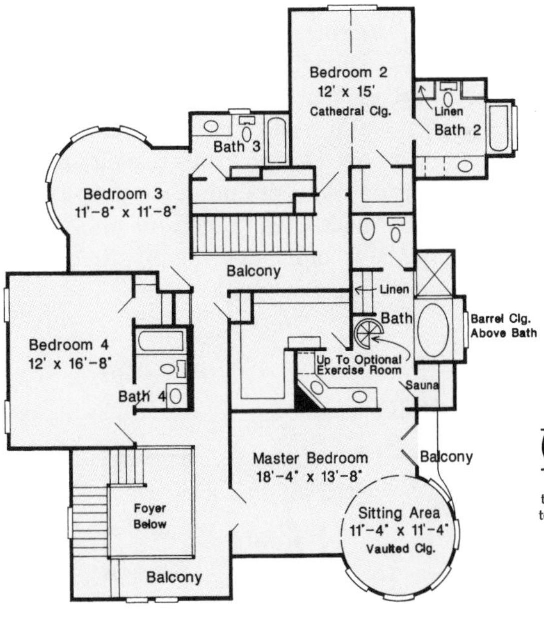
Bedroom 2
12' x 15'
Cathedral Clg.
Linen
Bath 2
Bath 3
Bedroom 3
11'-8" x 11'-8"
Balcony
Linen
Bath
Barrel Clg.
Above Bath
Bedroom 4
12' x 16'-8"
Up To Optional
Exercise Room
Sauna
Bath 4
Master Bedroom
18'-4" x 13'-8"
Balcony
Foyer
Below
Sitting Area
11'-4" x 11'-4"
Vaulted Clg.
Balcony

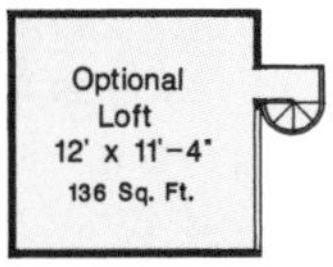
Optional
Loft
12' x 11'-4"
136 Sq. Ft.

Reminiscent of the Queen Anne style, this home offers patterned shingle siding, gable ornaments and turrets. Inside, the living room offers a sunny bay window in the front turret and French doors to a wraparound porch. The efficient U-shaped kitchen is flanked by the formal dining room and the family room. The rear turret holds the breakfast nook. Upstairs is the private master suite with luxurious bath and a sitting area with a vaulted ceiling. Three additional bedrooms, each with a private bath, complete the second floor.

Design HPT830321
First Floor: 1,617 square feet
Second Floor: 1,818 square feet
Total: 3,435 square feet
Bonus Space: 136 square feet
Width 53'-0" Depth 64'-8"

This classy, two-story home with a wraparound covered porch offers a dynamic open floor plan. The entrance foyer and the spacious great room both rise to two stories—a Palladian window at the second level floods these areas with natural light. The kitchen is centrally located for maximum flexibility in layout and, as an added feature, also has a breakfast bar. The large dining room delights with a bay window. The generous master suite has plenty of closet space as well as a bath with a whirlpool tub, a shower and a double-bowl vanity. On the second level, three bedrooms branch off the balcony that overlooks the great room. One large bedroom contains a private bath and a walk-in closet, while the other bedrooms share a full bath.

Design HPT830322

First Floor: 1,346 square feet
Second Floor: 836 square feet
Total: 2,182 square feet
Width 49'-5" Depth 45'-4"

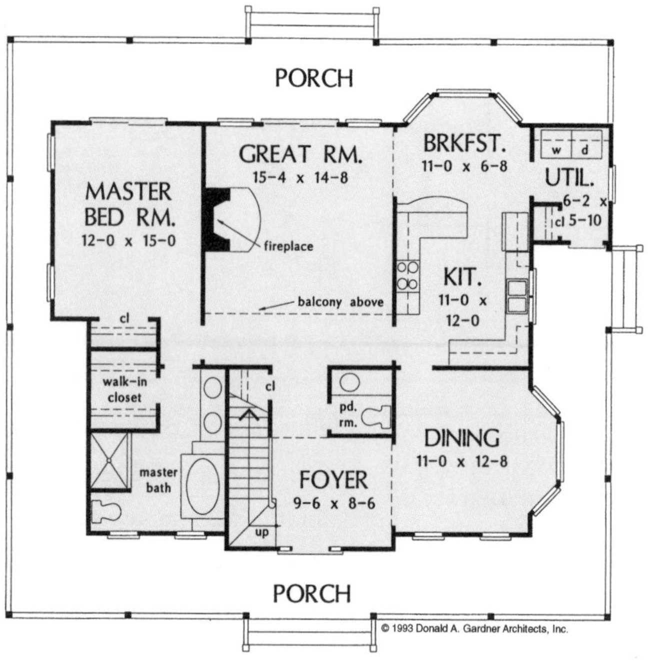

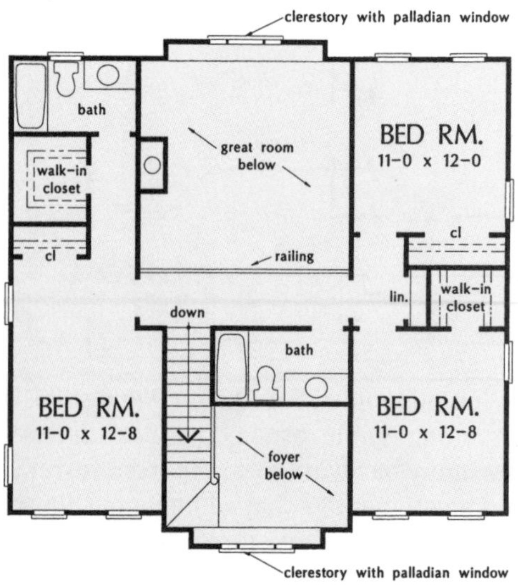

B. NATHAN

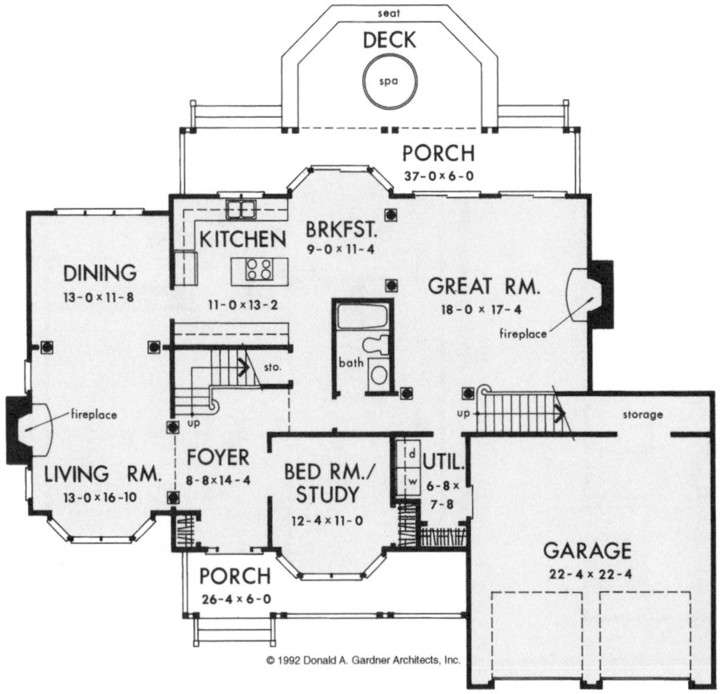
seat
DECK
spa
PORCH
37-0×6-0
KITCHEN
BRKFST.
9-0×11-4
DINING
13-0×11-8
11-0×13-2
GREAT RM.
18-0 × 17-4
fireplace
bath
sto.
fireplace
up
up
storage
FOYER
8-8×14-4
LIVING RM.
13-0×16-10
BED RM./
STUDY
12-4×11-0
UTIL.
6-8×
7-8
d
w
GARAGE
22-4×22-4
PORCH
26-4×6-0
© 1992 Donald A. Gardner Architects, Inc.

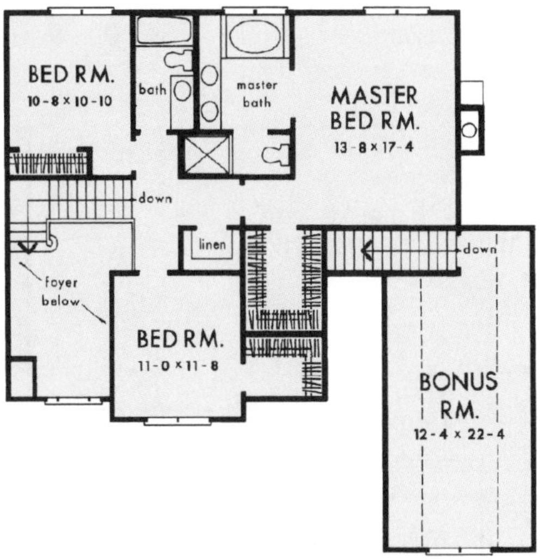
BED RM.
10-8×10-10
bath
master
bath
MASTER
BED RM.
13-8×17-4
down
linen
down
foyer
below
BED RM.
11-0×11-8
BONUS
RM.
12-4×22-4

This home's striking exterior is reinforced by its gables and arched-glass window. The central foyer leads to all spaces in the home's open layout. Both the living room and great room boast fireplaces and round columns. The efficient kitchen offers a cooking island to serve both the dining room and breakfast area. With four bedrooms, the floor plan calls for the master bedroom to be placed on the second level. It holds a large walk-in closet and a generous master bath with a whirlpool tub, separate shower and double-bowl vanity. Two additional bedrooms on this floor share a full bath. A bedroom on the first level can double as a study.

Design
HPT830323

First Floor: 1,569 square feet
Second Floor: 929 square feet
Total: 2,498 square feet
Bonus Space: 320 square feet
Width 65'-8" Depth 61'-4"

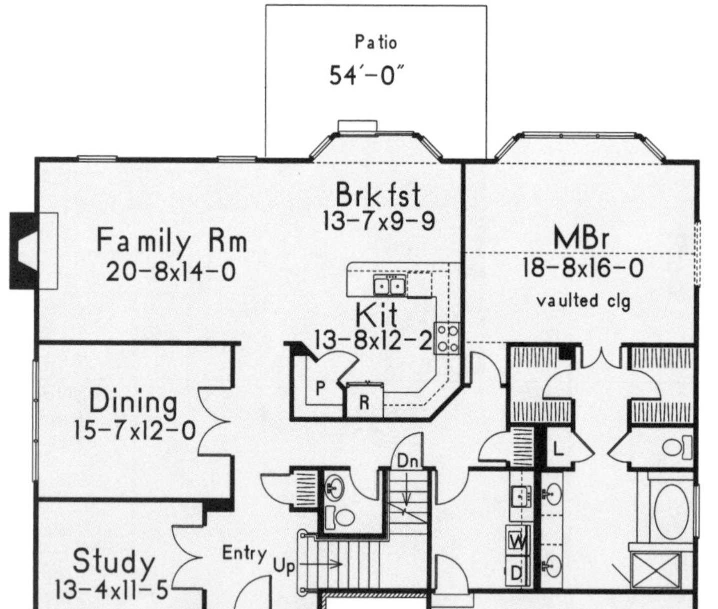

Patio
54'-0"
Brkfst
13-7x9-9
Family Rm
20-8x14-0
MBr
18-8x16-0
vaulted clg
Kit
13-8x12-2
P
R
Dining
15-7x12-0
L
Dn
Study
13-4x11-5
Entry
Up
W
D
Covered Porch
Garage
21-4x21-0

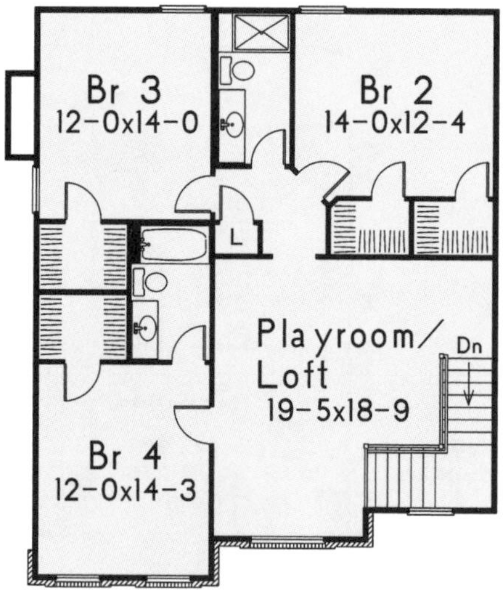

Br 3
12-0x14-0
Br 2
14-0x12-4
L
Playroom/
Loft
19-5x18-9
Dn
Br 4
12-0x14-3

Design HPT830324

First Floor: 1,958 square feet

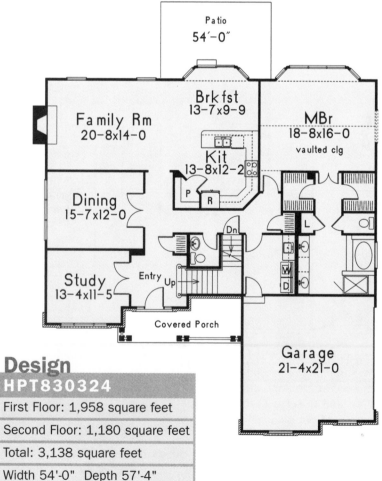

Second Floor: 1,180 square feet

Total: 3,138 square feet

Width 54'-0" Depth 57'-4"

A distinct segmental and keystone design details the windows around this home. An impressive staircase descends into a large entry and study through double doors. The private dining room is spacious and secluded. The family room, master suite and laundry are among the many generously sized rooms. Three large bedrooms, two full baths and four walk-in closets make up the second floor.

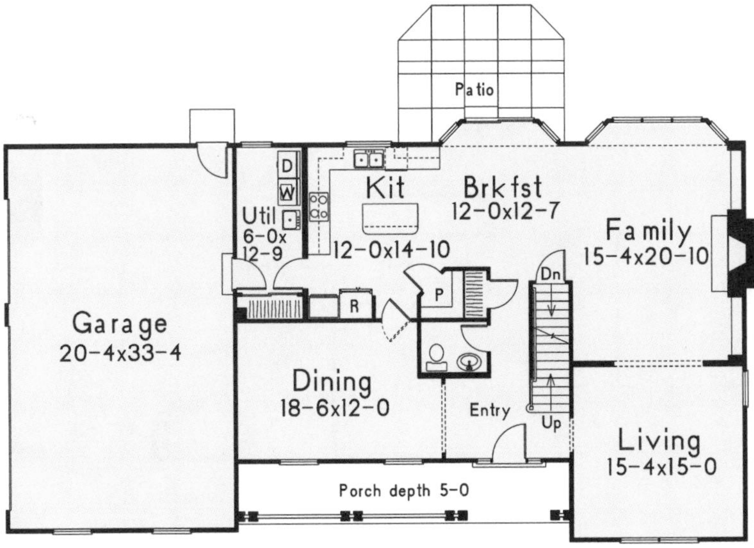
Patio
Kit
12-0x14-10
Brkfst
12-0x12-7
Family
15-4x20-10
Util
6-0x
12-9
D
W
R
P
Dn
Up
Garage
20-4x33-4
Dining
18-6x12-0
Entry
Living
15-4x15-0
Porch depth 5-0

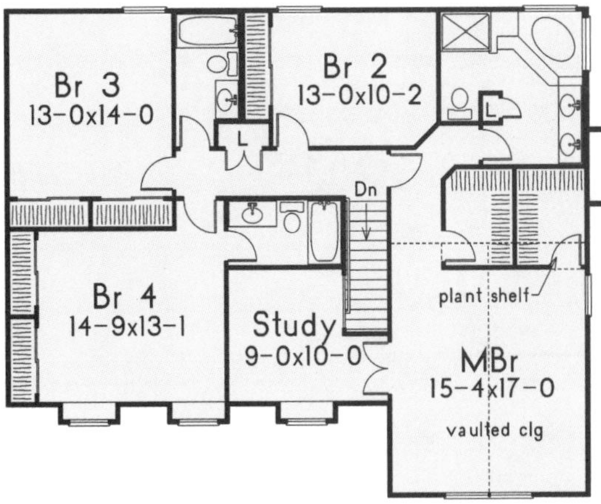
Br 3
13-0x14-0
Br 2
13-0x10-2
L
Dn
Br 4
14-9x13-1
Study
9-0x10-0
plant shelf
MBr
15-4x17-0
vaulted clg

This delightful farmhouse holds two family bedrooms, each with twin closets, and a master suite with a vaulted ceiling and a gorgeous arch-top window. The covered porch announces the entry that presents the stunning staircase. To the left, the spacious formal dining room accommodates large gatherings. A swinging door quiets the distractions of the adjoining island kitchen. A sunny bay, to the right, enlivens the breakfast nook which leads to the family room. To the right of the foyer, the living room opens to the family room via an elegant archway. Upstairs, the master suite includes twin walk-in closets and a study.

Design HPT830325

First Floor: 1,450 square feet
Second Floor: 1,517 square feet
Total: 2,967 square feet
Width 69'-0" Depth 37'-0"

Design

HPT830326

First Floor: 1,484 square feet
Second Floor: 1,061 square feet
Total: 2,545 square feet
Bonus Space: 486 square feet
Width 66'-10" Depth 47'-8"

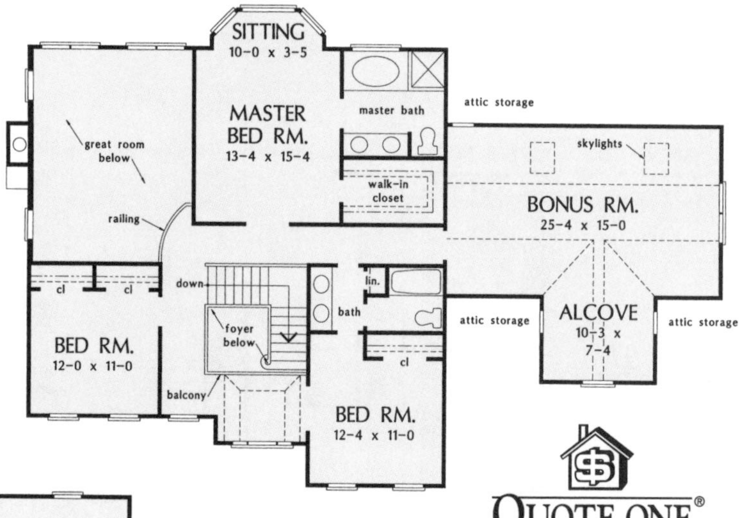

SITTING
10-0 x 3-5
MASTER
BED RM.
13-4 x 15-4
master bath
walk-in
closet
great room
below
railing
attic storage
skylights
BONUS RM.
25-4 x 15-0
down
lin.
bath
cl
cl
cl
BED RM.
12-0 x 11-0
foyer
below
balcony
attic storage
ALCOVE
10-3 x
7-4
attic storage
BED RM.
12-4 x 11-0

QUOTE ONE®

Cost to build? See page 516 to order complete cost estimate to build this house in your area!

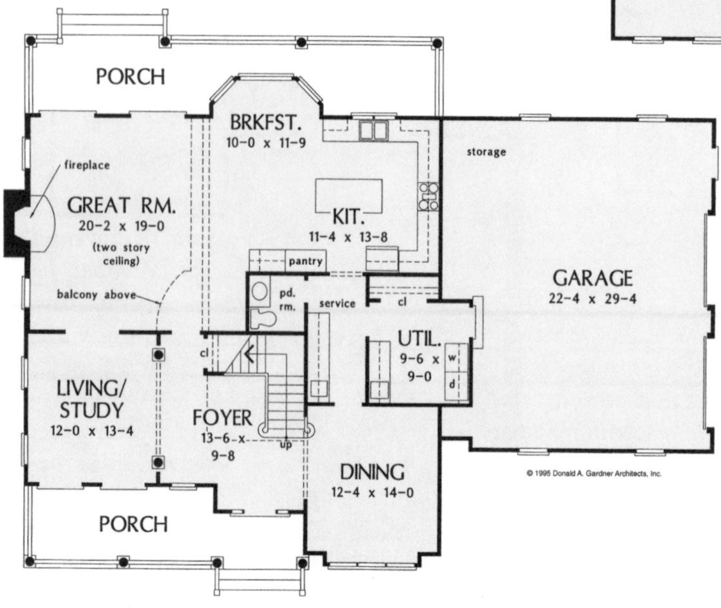

PORCH
BRKFST.
10-0 x 11-9
fireplace
GREAT RM.
20-2 x 19-0
(two story
ceiling)
KIT.
11-4 x 13-8
storage
pantry
balcony above
pd.
rm.
service
cl
GARAGE
22-4 x 29-4
UTIL.
9-6 x
9-0
w
d
cl
LIVING/
STUDY
12-0 x 13-4
FOYER
13-6 x
9-8
up
DINING
12-4 x 14-0
PORCH
© 1995 Donald A. Gardner Architects, Inc.

Here's an upscale country home with down-home comfort. The two-story great room is warmed by a rounded-hearth fireplace. French doors brighten the formal living room, while wide counters, a food-preparation island and a bayed breakfast nook create a dreamy kitchen area. The second floor includes a master suite, two bedrooms that share a full bath, and a skylit bonus room. The master suite boasts a sitting area and a private bath with twin vanities and a whirlpool tub.

Design HPT830327

First Floor: 1,483 square feet
Second Floor: 1,349 square feet
Total: 2,832 square feet
Bonus Space: 486 square feet
Width 66'-10" Depth 47'-8"

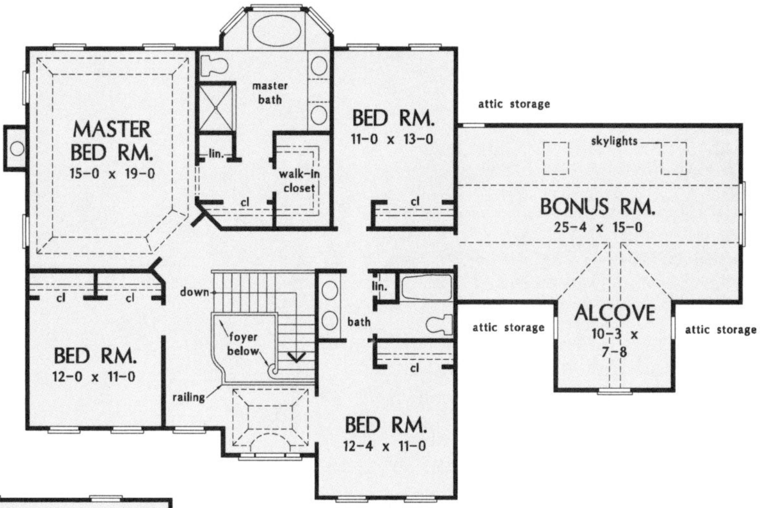
master bath
MASTER BED RM.
15-0 x 19-0
BED RM.
11-0 x 13-0
attic storage
skylights
lin.
walk-in closet
cl
cl
BONUS RM.
25-4 x 15-0
cl
cl
down
lin.
bath
attic storage
ALCOVE
10-3 x 7-8
attic storage
BED RM.
12-0 x 11-0
foyer below
cl
railing
BED RM.
12-4 x 11-0

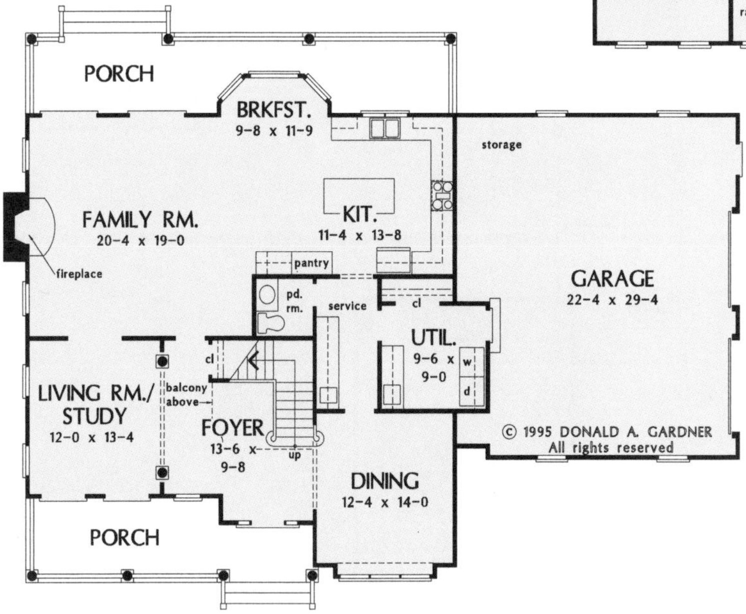
PORCH
BRKFST.
9-8 x 11-9
storage
FAMILY RM.
20-4 x 19-0
fireplace
KIT.
11-4 x 13-8
pantry
pd. rm.
service
cl
GARAGE
22-4 x 29-4
UTIL.
9-6 x 9-0
w
d
cl
balcony above
LIVING RM./ STUDY
12-0 x 13-4
FOYER
13-6 x 9-8
up
© 1995 DONALD A. GARDNER
All rights reserved
DINING
12-4 x 14-0
PORCH

With two covered porches to encourage outdoor living, multi-pane windows and an open layout, this farmhouse has plenty to offer. Columns define the living room/study area. The family room is accented by a fireplace and accesses the rear porch. An adjacent sunny, bayed breakfast room is convenient to the oversized island kitchen. Four bedrooms upstairs include a deluxe master suite with a lush bath and walk-in closet. Three family bedrooms have plenty of storage space and share a full hall bath.

Design HPT830328

First Floor: 943 square feet
Second Floor: 840 square feet
Total: 1,783 square feet
Bonus Space: 323 square feet
Width 53'-4" Depth 64'-4"

Round-top windows and an inviting covered porch offer an irresistible appeal for this three-bedroom plan. A two-story foyer provides a spacious entrance to this well-organized, open layout. Round columns between the great room and kitchen add to the impressive quality of the plan. An expansive deck promotes casual outdoor living to its fullest. The master suite with a walk-in closet and complete master bath is on the second floor, along with two additional bedrooms and a full bath. The bonus room over the garage offers room for expansion.

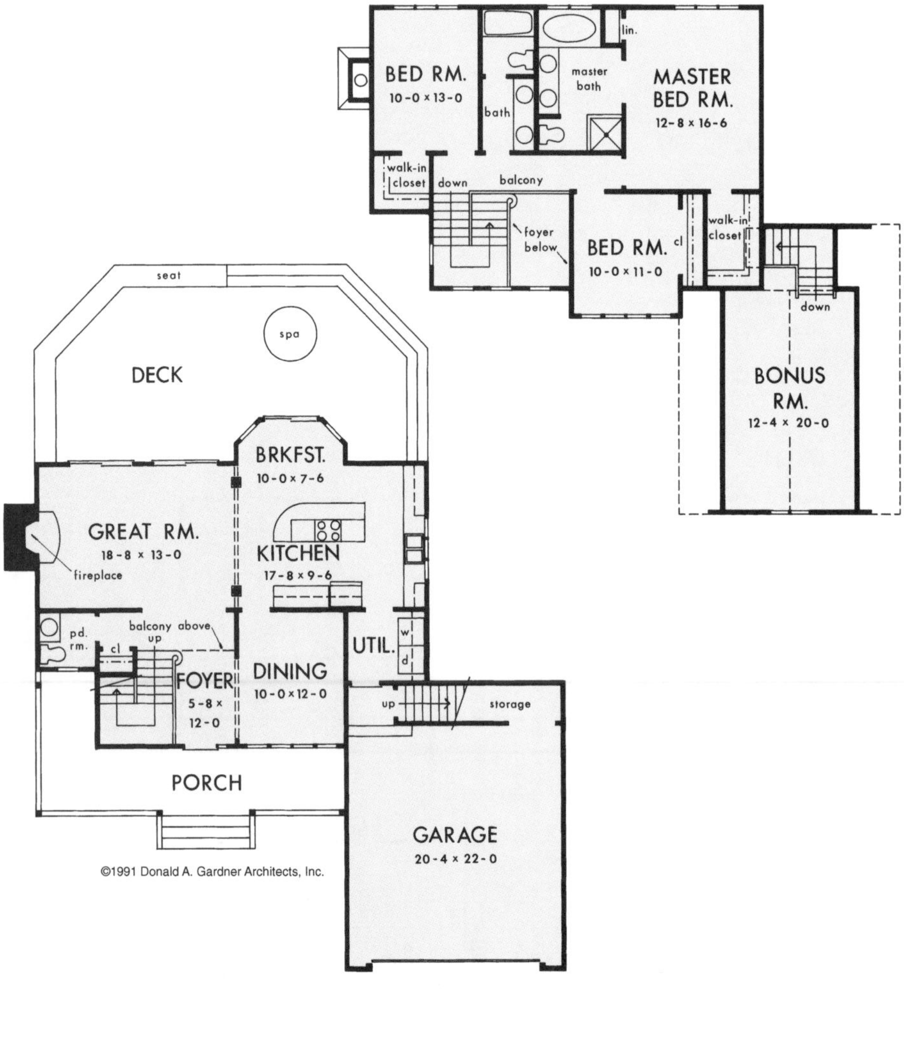

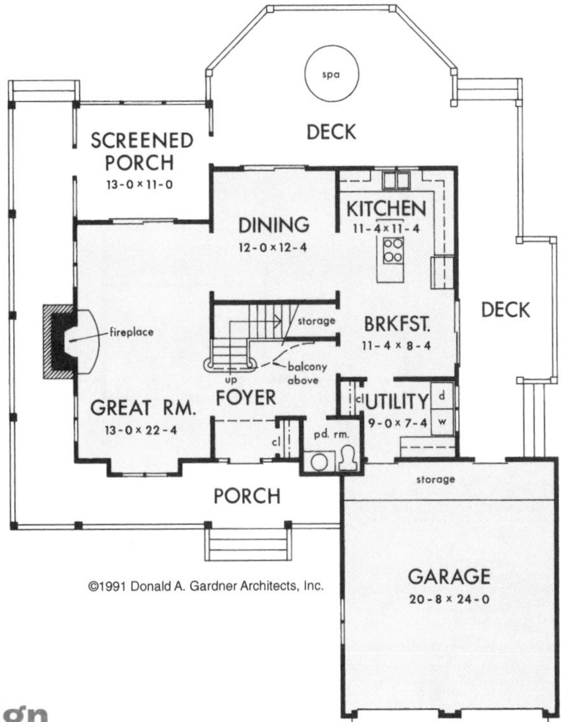
spa
DECK
SCREENED PORCH
13-0 × 11-0
DINING
12-0 × 12-4
KITCHEN
11-4 × 11-4
DECK
fireplace
storage
BRKFST.
11-4 × 8-4
balcony above
up
GREAT RM.
13-0 × 22-4
FOYER
UTILITY
9-0 × 7-4
d
w
cl
pd. rm.
storage
PORCH
GARAGE
20-8 × 24-0

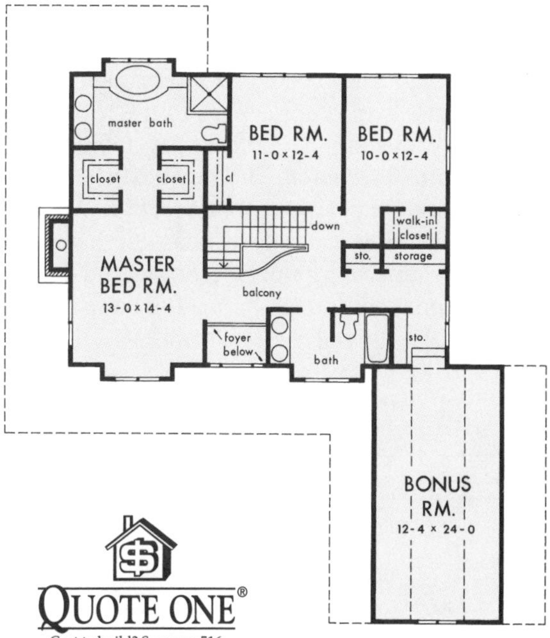
master bath
closet
closet
cl
BED RM.
11-0 × 12-4
BED RM.
10-0 × 12-4
down
walk-in closet
sto.
storage
MASTER BED RM.
13-0 × 14-4
balcony
foyer below
bath
sto.
BONUS RM.
12-4 × 24-0

QUOTE ONE®

Cost to build? See page 516 to order complete cost estimate to build this house in your area!

Design HPT830329

First Floor: 1,025 square feet
Second Floor: 911 square feet
Total: 1,936 square feet
Bonus Space: 410 square feet
Width 53'-8" Depth 67'-8"

The exterior of this three-bedroom home is enhanced by its many gables, arched windows and the wraparound porch. The entry leads to the foyer, which extends to the left into the great room. The great room—with an impressive fireplace—leads to both the dining room and the screened porch, which accesses the deck. An open kitchen offers a country atmosphere. The second-level master suite has two walk-in closets and an impressive bath. Two family bedrooms share a full bath and plenty of storage. There is also bonus space over the garage.

This grand farmhouse features a double-gabled roof, a Palladian window and an intricately detailed brick chimney. The living room opens to the foyer for formal entertaining, while the family room offers a fireplace, wet bar and direct access to the porch. The lavish kitchen boasts a cooking island and serves the dining room, breakfast nook and porch. The master suite on the second level has a large walk-in closet and a master bath with a whirlpool tub, shower and double-bowl vanity. Three additional bedrooms share a full bath.

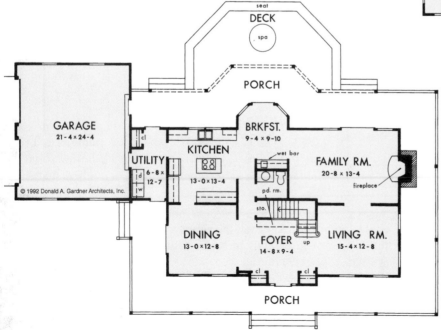

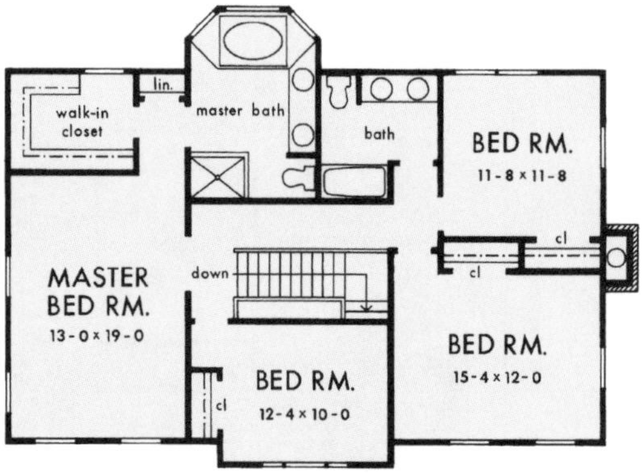

lin.
walk-in closet
master bath
bath
BED RM.
11-8 x 11-8
cl
cl
down
MASTER BED RM.
13-0 x 19-0
BED RM.
15-4 x 12-0
BED RM.
12-4 x 10-0
cl

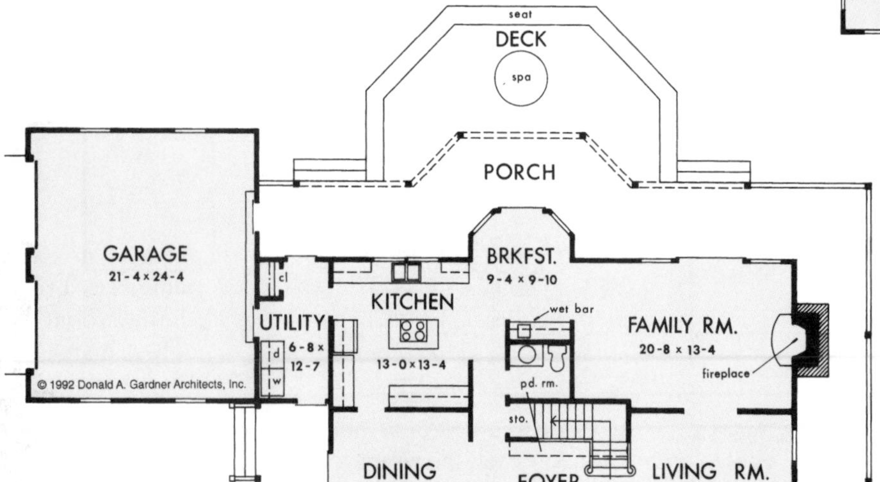

seat
DECK
spa
PORCH
GARAGE
21-4 x 24-4
BRKFST.
9-4 x 9-10
cl
KITCHEN
wet bar
UTILITY
6-8 x 12-7
d
w
13-0 x 13-4
FAMILY RM.
20-8 x 13-4
fireplace
© 1992 Donald A. Gardner Architects, Inc.
pd. rm.
sto.
DINING
13-0 x 12-8
FOYER
14-8 x 9-4
up
LIVING RM.
15-4 x 12-8
cl
cl
PORCH

QUOTE ONE®

Cost to build? See page 516 to order complete cost estimate to build this house in your area!

Design
HPT830330

First Floor: 1,357 square feet

Second Floor: 1,204 square feet

Total: 2,561 square feet

Width 80'-0" Depth 57'-0"

©1995 Donald A. Gardner Architects, Inc.

Design
HPT830331

First Floor: 959 square feet
Second Floor: 833 square feet
Total: 1,792 square feet
Bonus Space: 344 square feet
Width 52'-6" Depth 42'-8"

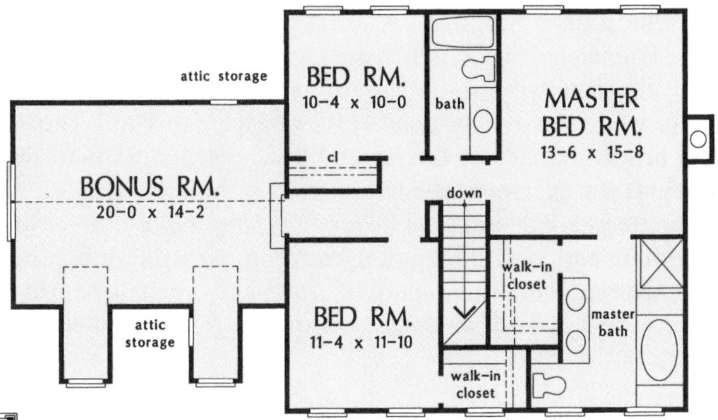
attic storage
BED RM.
10-4 x 10-0
bath
MASTER
BED RM.
13-6 x 15-8
cl
BONUS RM.
20-0 x 14-2
down
walk-in
closet
BED RM.
11-4 x 11-10
master
bath
attic
storage
walk-in
closet

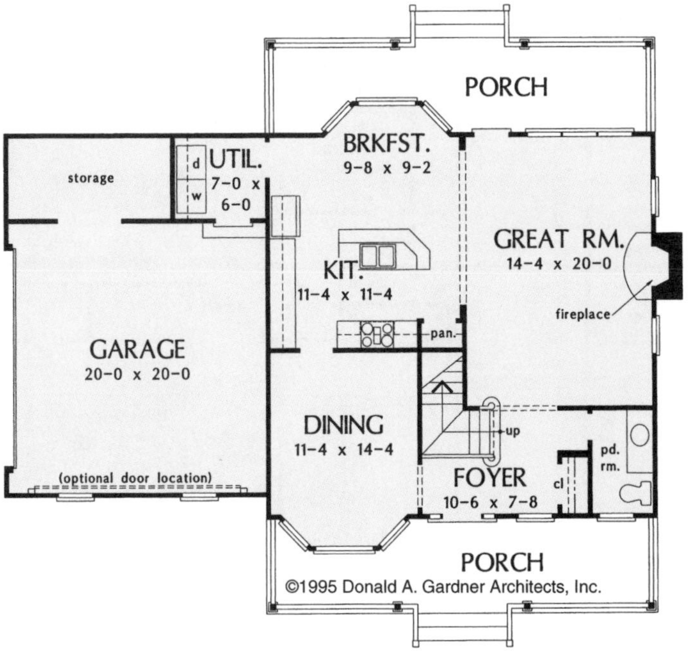
PORCH
BRKFST.
9-8 x 9-2
UTIL.
7-0 x
6-0
d
w
storage
GREAT RM.
14-4 x 20-0
KIT.
11-4 x 11-4
fireplace
pan.
GARAGE
20-0 x 20-0
DINING
11-4 x 14-4
up
pd.
rm.
FOYER
10-6 x 7-8
cl
(optional door location)
PORCH
©1995 Donald A. Gardner Architects, Inc.

From its covered front porch to its covered rear porch, this farmhouse is a real charmer. The formal dining room is filled with light from a bay window. A matching bay is found in the cozy breakfast room. The large great room is graced with a warming fireplace and even more windows. The master suite offers a private bath with an array of luxuries. A bonus room extending over the garage can be developed into a game room, a fourth bedroom or a study at a later date.

Traditional farmhouse symmetry is apparent throughout this family plan. The wide front porch invites relaxation and offers a nice introduction to the two-story foyer. The formal dining and living rooms split off of the foyer; each has two multi-pane windows facing forward. The comfortable family room has a fireplace at the far end and a French door to the rear yard. Most notable is the spacious feeling that comes from the family room being open to the breakfast room and the kitchen. Upstairs, the master suite is detailed with a tray ceiling and a vaulted master bath with a garden tub, compartmented toilet and walk-in closet. Two family bedrooms and a hall bath complete this plan. Please specify basement, slab or crawlspace foundation when ordering.

Design HPT830332

First Floor: 828 square feet

Second Floor: 772 square feet

Total: 1,600 square feet

Width 52'-4" Depth 34'-0"

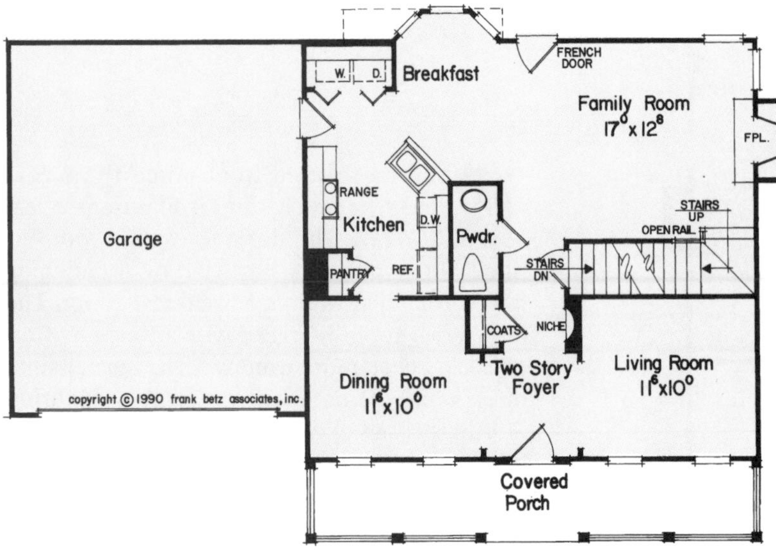

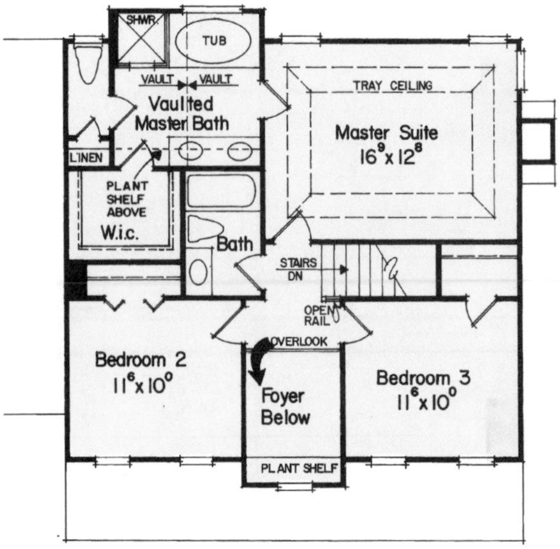

This home, as shown in the photograph, may differ from the actual blueprints. For more detailed information, please check the floor plans carefully. Photo provided by Stephen Fuller, Inc.

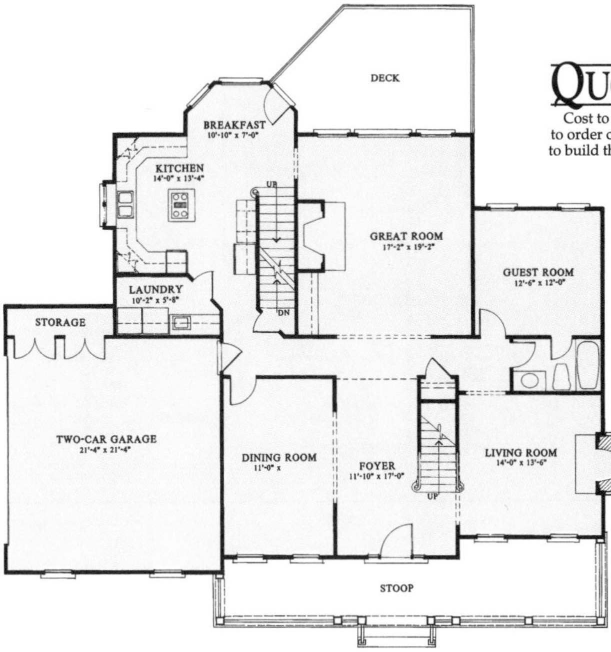

QUOTE ONE®

Cost to build? See page 516 to order complete cost estimate to build this house in your area!

Design HPT830333

First Floor: 1,700 square feet
Second Floor: 1,585 square feet
Total: 3,285 square feet
Bonus Space: 176 square feet
Width 60'-0" Depth 47'-6"

The front porch of this two-story farmhouse opens to a traditional foyer flanked by formal areas. A living room with a fireplace sits on the right and an elongated dining room—perfect for an elegant table—is on the left. For casual family living, a great room—with a fireplace—and a kitchen with a breakfast area will serve the family's needs. A deck off the breakfast room invites outdoor dining. Upstairs, the master suite has a bayed sitting area and a private bath. Two family bedrooms share a compartmented bath while a third has a private bath. A bonus room would make a great office or additional bedroom. This home is designed with a walkout basement foundation.

A wide and welcoming porch is the perfect place to enjoy the out-of-doors on an old-fashioned swing. There is ample space for relaxing indoors, where the parlor, family room and bayed breakfast nook are open to each other. The kitchen is separated from the breakfast nook by a convenient snack bar. Upstairs, the master bedroom features a large walk-in closet and a compartmented bath with a double-bowl vanity. Three family bedrooms share a full hall bath.

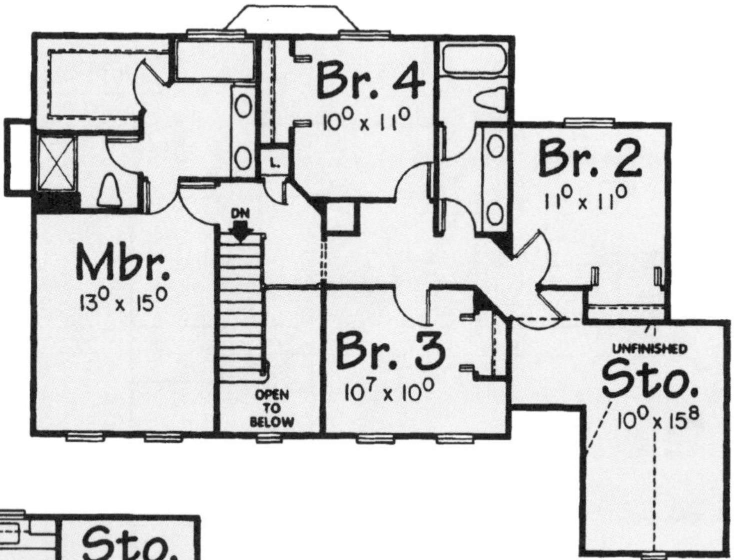

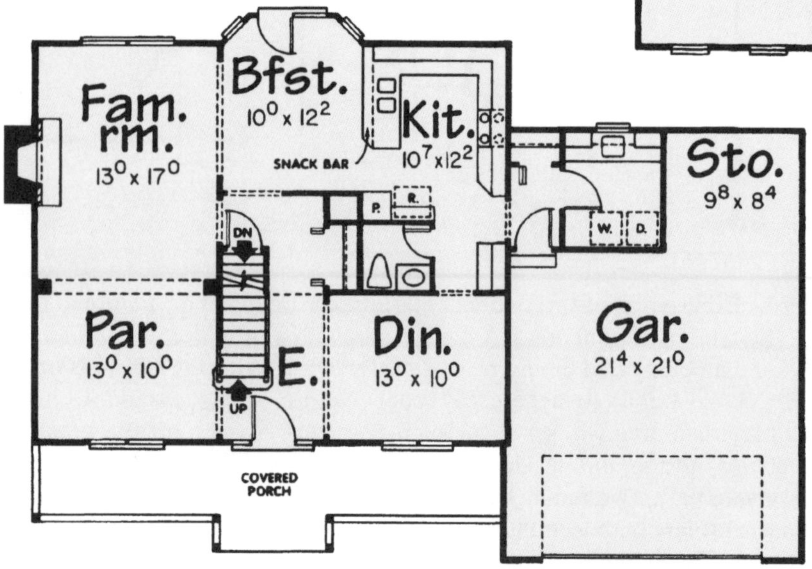

Design
HPT830334

First Floor: 1,086 square feet
Second Floor: 1,033 square feet
Total: 2,119 square feet
Bonus Space: 215 square feet
Width 56'-0" Depth 38'-0"

This home, as shown in the photograph, may differ from the actual blueprints. For more detailed information, please check the floor plans carefully.
Photo courtesy of Design Basics, Inc.

Beginning with the wraparound porch, there's a feeling of country charm in this two-story plan. Formal dining and living rooms, visible from the entry, offer ample space for gracious entertaining. The large family room is truly a place of warmth and welcome with its gorgeous bay window, fireplace and French doors to the living room. The kitchen, with an island counter, pantry and desk, makes cooking a delight. Upstairs, the secondary bedrooms share an efficient compartmented bath. The expansive master bedroom has its own luxury bath with a double vanity, whirlpool tub, walk-in closet and dressing area.

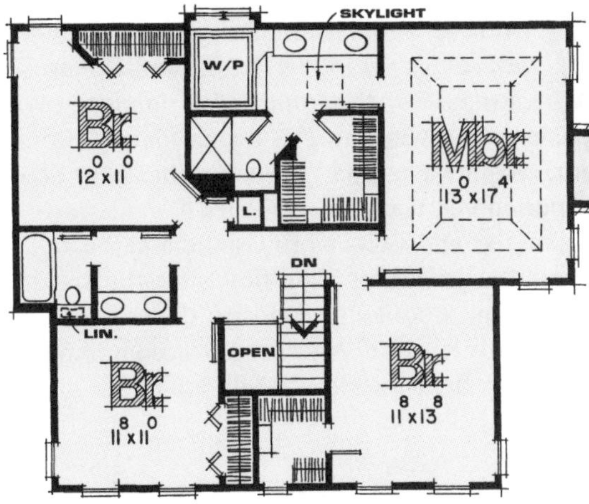

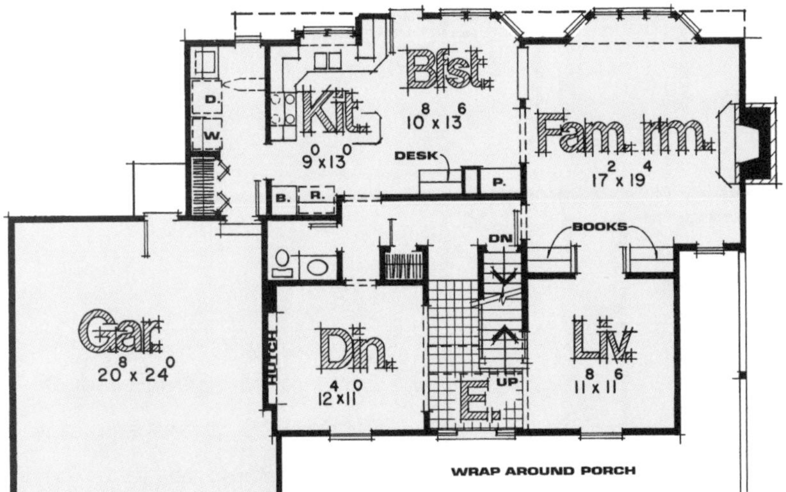

Design

HPT830335
First Floor: 1,188 square feet
Second Floor: 1,172 square feet
Total: 2,360 square feet
Width 58'-0" Depth 40'-0"

Victorian embellishments give a time-honored elegance to this classic family plan. Left of the entry, the front parlor opens to reveal a dramatic bay window. The formal dining room is large enough for a grand party and has easy access to the kitchen. Casual living is sure to center around the corner kitchen with a prep island and the adjoining breakfast room as they flow into the spacious family room. A split stair leads to the second floor, where an oversized master suite is accompanied by three family bedrooms and a full hall bath.

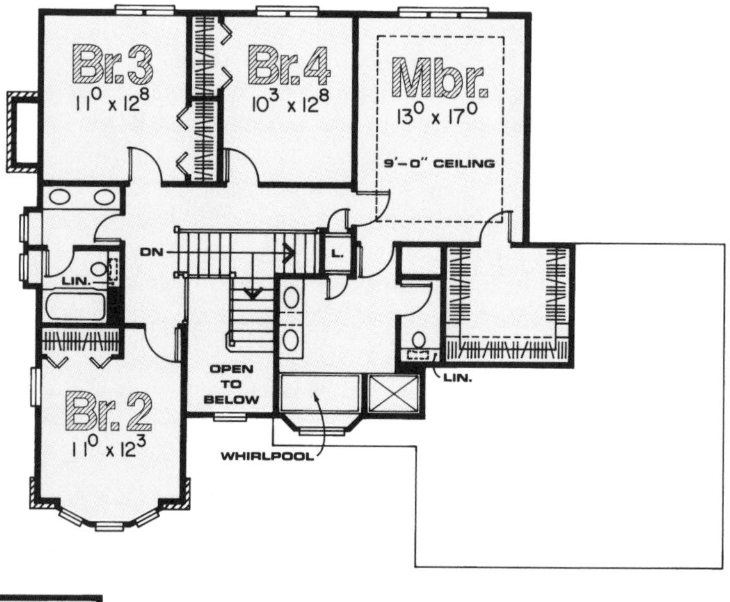

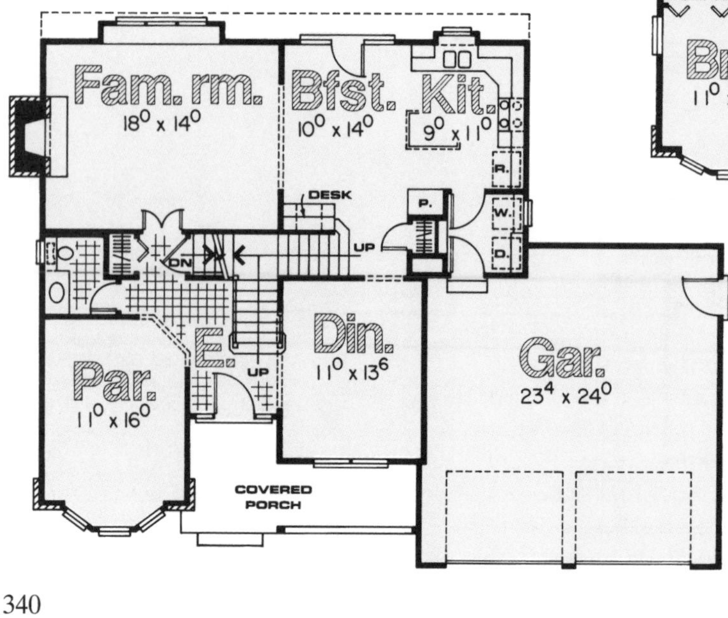

Design
HPT830336

First Floor: 1,134 square feet

Second Floor: 1,149 square feet

Total: 2,283 square feet

Width 53'-4" Depth 42'-0"

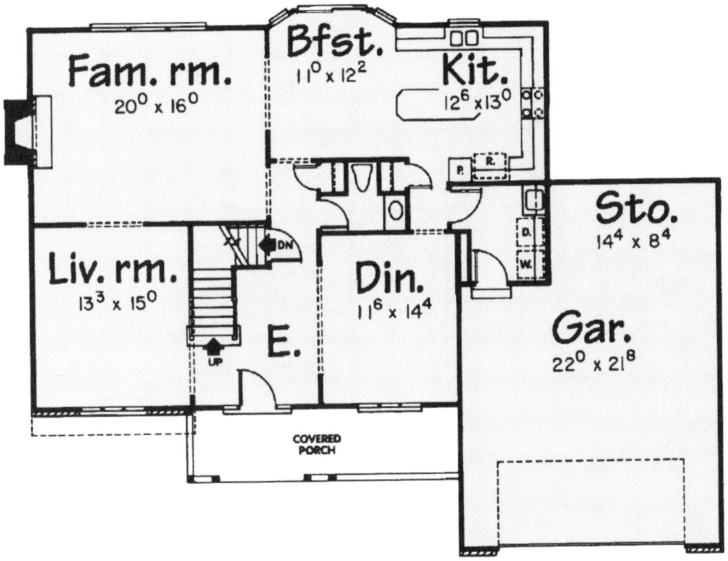
Fam. rm.
20⁰ x 16⁰
Bfst.
11⁰ x 12²
Kit.
12⁶ x 13⁰
Sto.
14⁴ x 8⁴
Liv. rm.
13³ x 15⁰
DN
Din.
11⁶ x 14⁴
E.
UP
Gar.
22⁰ x 21⁸
COVERED PORCH

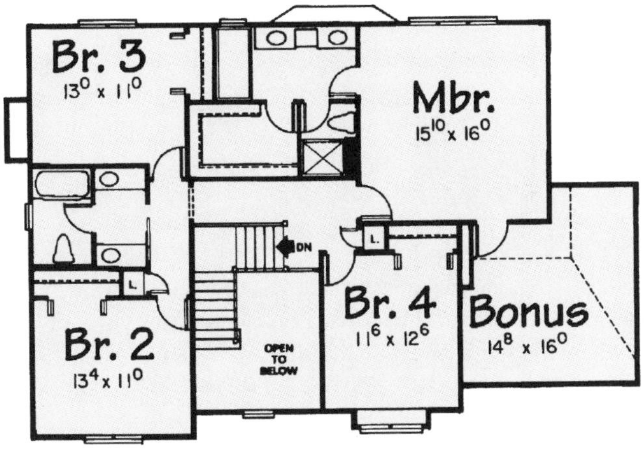
Br. 3
13⁰ x 11⁰
Mbr.
15¹⁰ x 16⁰
DN
Br. 2
13⁴ x 11⁰
OPEN TO BELOW
Br. 4
11⁶ x 12⁶
Bonus
14⁸ x 16⁰

With its brick and siding facade, this farmhouse presents a strong and solid image, while its covered front porch offers a cool place to relax. Inside, flanking the foyer, the formal living room and the formal dining room express elegance in a subtle manner. The family room at the rear of the home is graced by a warming fireplace and has direct access to the bay-windowed breakfast room and island kitchen. The sleeping zone is upstairs and is made up of three secondary bedrooms that share a full hall bath with twin vanities and a master bedroom with a pampering bath and a large walk-in closet. A bonus room is accessible from the master bedroom and can be used for an office, an exercise room or storage.

Design

HPT830337
First Floor: 1,365 square feet
Second Floor: 1,185 square feet
Total: 2,550 square feet
Bonus Space: 240 square feet
Width 59'-4" Depth 45'-4"

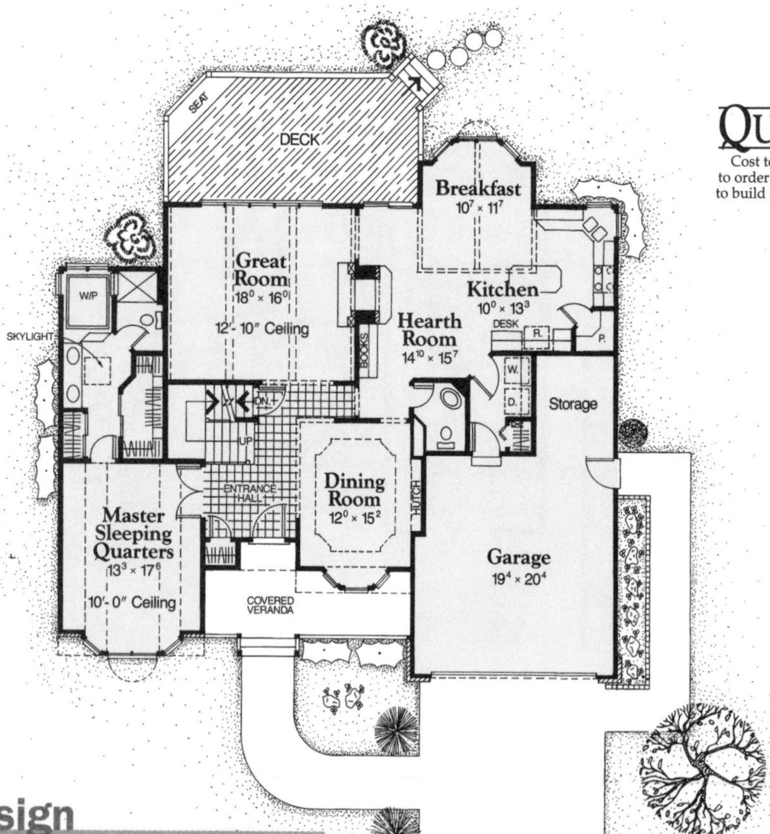

SEAT
DECK
Breakfast
10⁷ × 11⁷
Great Room
18⁰ × 16⁰
12'-10" Ceiling
Kitchen
10⁰ × 13³
Hearth Room
14¹⁰ × 15⁷
BOOKS
DESK
R.
P.
W.
D.
DN.
UP
W/P
SKYLIGHT
Storage
Dining Room
12⁰ × 15²
HUTCH
ENTRANCE HALL
Master Sleeping Quarters
13³ × 17⁶
10'-0" Ceiling
COVERED VERANDA
Garage
19⁴ × 20⁴

QUOTE ONE®

Cost to build? See page 516 to order complete cost estimate to build this house in your area!

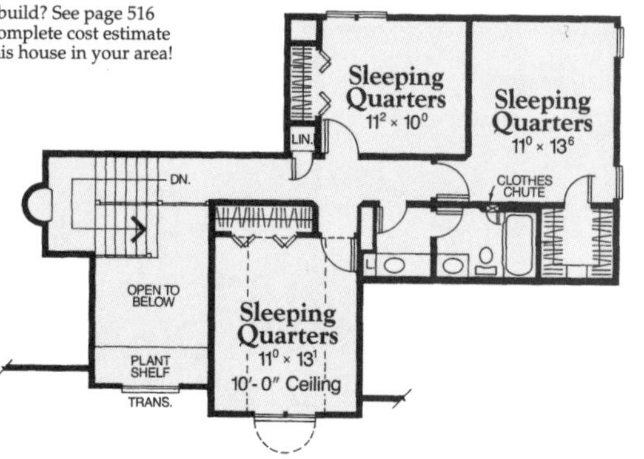

Sleeping Quarters
11² × 10⁰
Sleeping Quarters
11⁰ × 13⁶
LIN.
DN.
CLOTHES CHUTE
OPEN TO BELOW
PLANT SHELF
TRANS.
Sleeping Quarters
11⁰ × 13¹
10'-0" Ceiling

Beautiful arches and elaborate detail give the elevation of this four-bedroom home an unmistakable elegance. Inside, the floor plan is equally appealing. Note the formal dining room with a bay window, visible from the entrance hall. The large great room has a fireplace and a wall of windows with views of the rear property. A hearth room with a built-in bookcase adjoins the kitchen, which boasts a corner walk-in pantry and a spacious breakfast nook with a bay window. The first-floor master suite features His and Hers wardrobes and a large whirlpool tub.

Design

HPT830338

First Floor: 1,653 square feet

Second Floor: 700 square feet

Total: 2,353 square feet

Width 54'-0" Depth 50'-0"

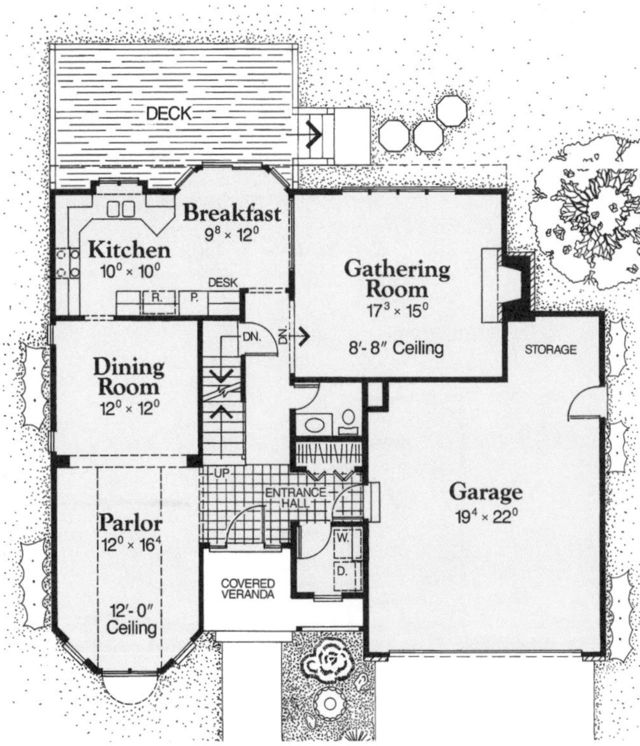
DECK
Breakfast
9⁸ × 12⁰
Kitchen
10⁰ × 10⁰
DESK
R.
P.
Gathering Room
17³ × 15⁰
8'-8" Ceiling
DN.
Dining Room
12⁰ × 12⁰
STORAGE
UP
ENTRANCE HALL
Garage
19⁴ × 22⁰
Parlor
12⁰ × 16⁴
12'-0" Ceiling
W.
D.
COVERED VERANDA

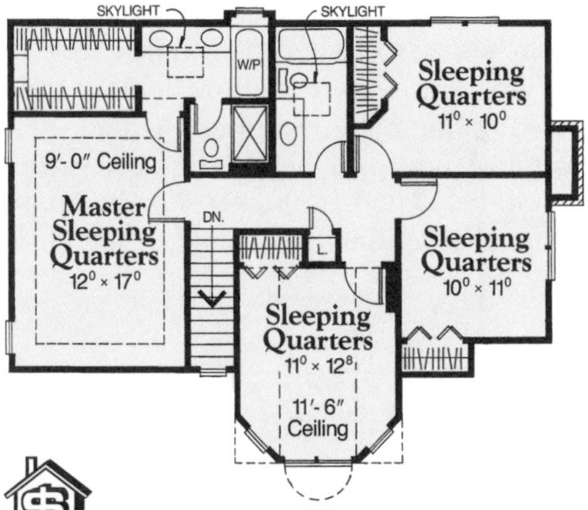
SKYLIGHT
SKYLIGHT
W/P
Sleeping Quarters
11⁰ × 10⁰
9'-0" Ceiling
Master Sleeping Quarters
12⁰ × 17⁰
DN.
L
Sleeping Quarters
10⁰ × 11⁰
Sleeping Quarters
11⁰ × 12⁸
11'-6" Ceiling

QUOTE ONE®
Cost to build? See page 516 to order complete cost estimate to build this house in your area!

Elegant detailing, a charming veranda and a tall brick chimney make a pleasing facade on this four-bedroom, two-story Victorian home. From the large, bayed parlor with a sloped ceiling to the sunken gathering room with a fireplace, there's plenty to appreciate about the floor plan. The formal dining room opens to the parlor for convenient entertaining. An L-shaped kitchen with an attached breakfast room sits nearby. Upstairs quarters include a master suite with a private dressing area and a whirlpool tub, and three family bedrooms.

Design
HPT830339

First Floor: 1,113 square feet
Second Floor: 965 square feet
Total: 2,078 square feet
Width 46'-0" Depth 41'-5"

This home, as shown in the photograph, may differ from the actual blueprints. For more detailed information, please check the floor plans carefully.
Photo courtesy of Larry E. Belk Designs

Clean, contemporary lines, a unique floor plan and a metal roof with a cupola set this farmhouse apart. Remote-control transoms in the cupola open to create an airy and decidedly unique foyer. The great room, sun room, dining room and kitchen flow from one to another for casual entertaining with flair. The rear of the home is fashioned with plenty of windows overlooking the multi-level deck. A front bedroom and bath would make a comfortable guest suite. The master bedroom and bath upstairs are bridged by a pipe-rail balcony that also gives access to a rear deck. An additional bedroom, home office and bath complete this very special plan.

Design HPT830340

Design HPT830340
First Floor: 1,309 square feet
Second Floor: 1,343 square feet
Total: 2,652 square feet
Width 44'-4" Depth 58'-2"
L

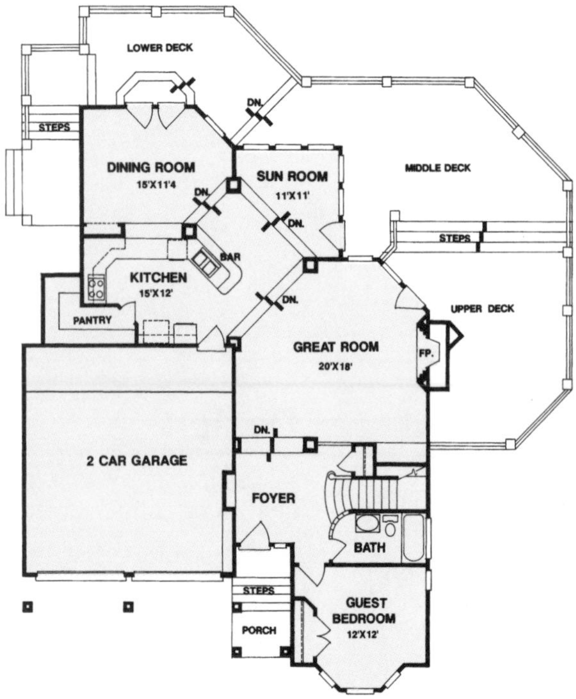

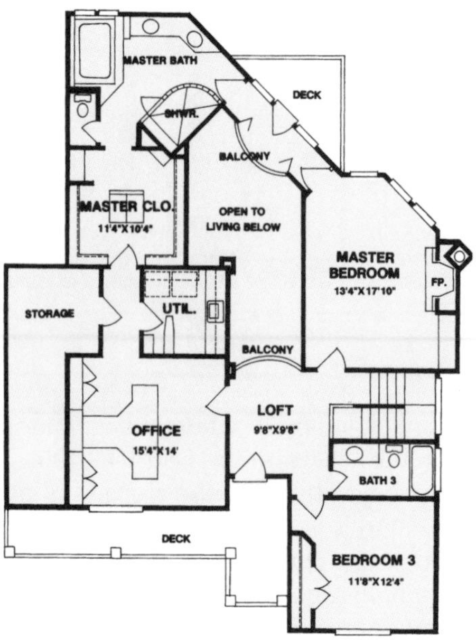

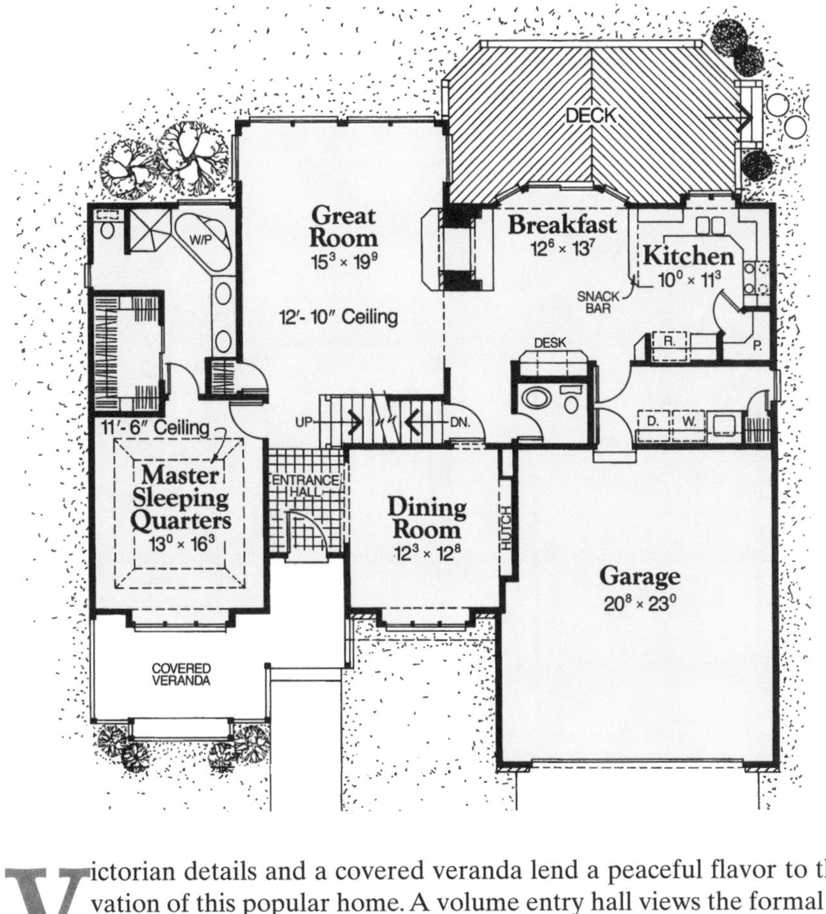

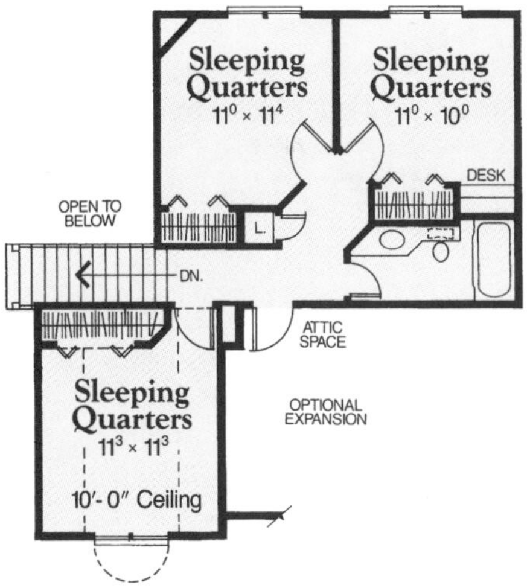

Victorian details and a covered veranda lend a peaceful flavor to the elevation of this popular home. A volume entry hall views the formal dining room and luxurious great room. Imagine the comfort of relaxing in the great room, which features a volume ceiling and abundant windows. The kitchen and breakfast area includes a through-fireplace, snack bar, walk-in pantry and wrapping counters. The secluded master suite features a vaulted ceiling, luxurious dressing/bath area and corner whirlpool tub. Upstairs, the family sleeping quarters contain special amenities unique to each.

Design HPT830341

First Floor: 1,421 square feet
Second Floor: 578 square feet
Total: 1,999 square feet
Width 52'-0" Depth 47'-4"

Design
HPT830342

Square Footage: 1,865

Width 61'-6" Depth 74'-8"

This distinctive Victorian exterior conceals an open, contemporary floor plan. The entrance foyer with round columns offers visual excitement. The octagonal great room has a high tray ceiling and a fireplace. A generous kitchen with an angular island counter is centrally located, providing efficient service to the dining room, breakfast room and deck. The luxurious master bedroom suite has a large walk-in closet and a compartmented bath. Two additional bedrooms—one that would make a lovely study by including an entrance off the foyer—and a full hall bath round out this favorite plan.

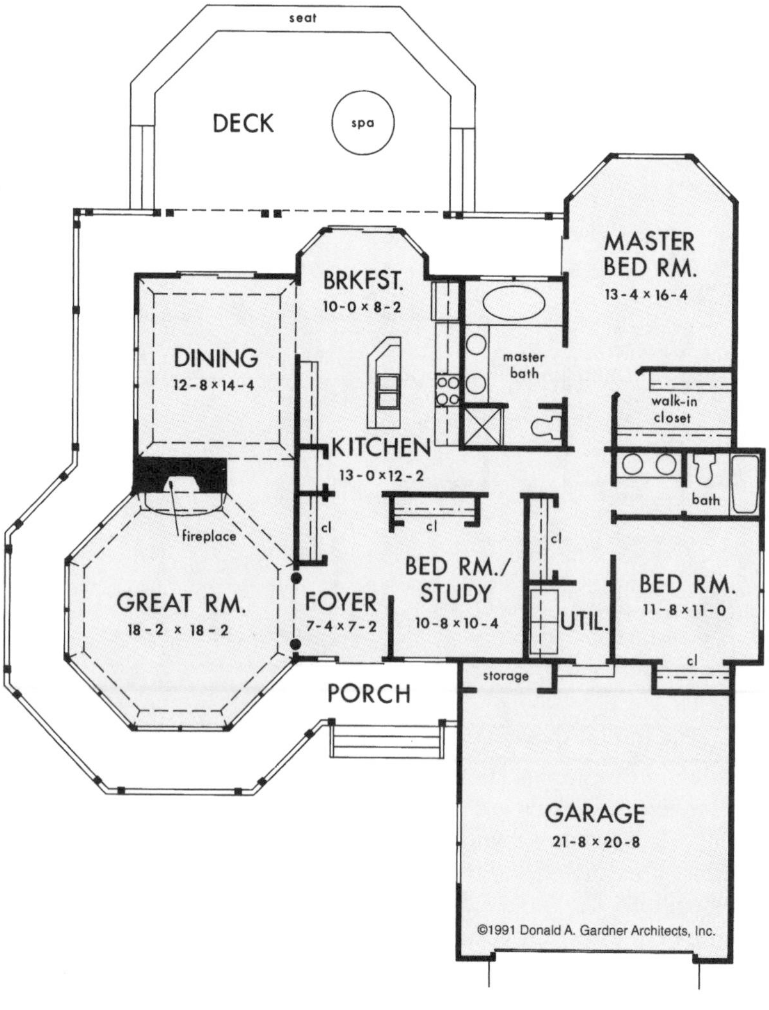

© 1994 Donald A. Gardner Architects, Inc.
B. NATHAN

Design
HPT830343

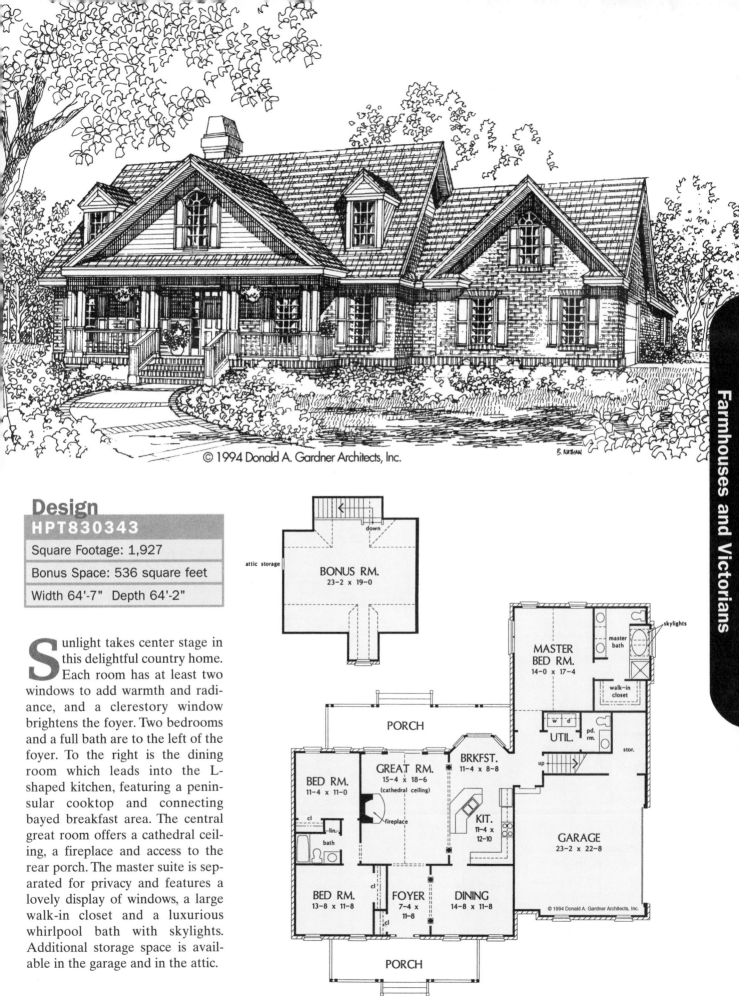

Square Footage: 1,927
Bonus Space: 536 square feet
Width 64'-7" Depth 64'-2"

Sunlight takes center stage in this delightful country home. Each room has at least two windows to add warmth and radiance, and a clerestory window brightens the foyer. Two bedrooms and a full bath are to the left of the foyer. To the right is the dining room which leads into the L-shaped kitchen, featuring a peninsular cooktop and connecting bayed breakfast area. The central great room offers a cathedral ceiling, a fireplace and access to the rear porch. The master suite is separated for privacy and features a lovely display of windows, a large walk-in closet and a luxurious whirlpool bath with skylights. Additional storage space is available in the garage and in the attic.

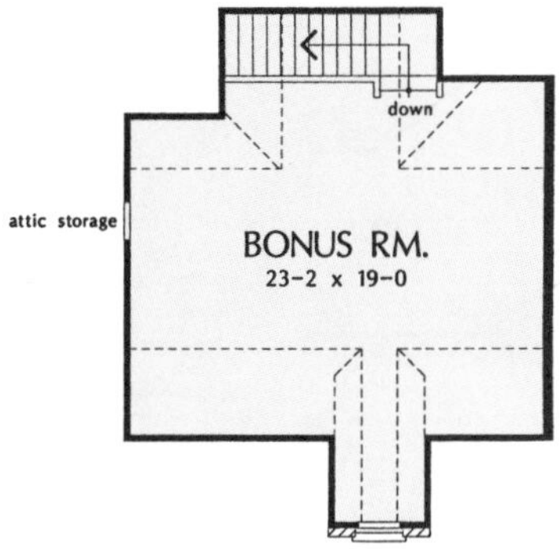
down
attic storage
BONUS RM.
23-2 x 19-0

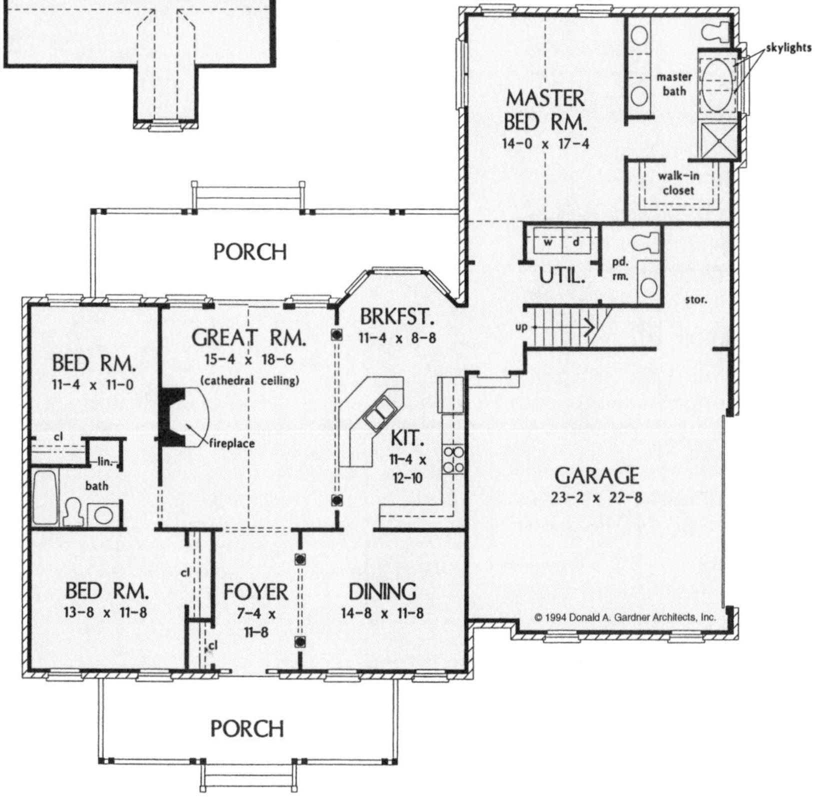
skylights
master bath
MASTER BED RM.
14-0 x 17-4
walk-in closet
PORCH
UTIL.
w d
pd. rm.
stor.
BRKFST.
11-4 x 8-8
up
GREAT RM.
15-4 x 18-6
(cathedral ceiling)
BED RM.
11-4 x 11-0
cl
lin.
bath
fireplace
KIT.
11-4 x 12-10
GARAGE
23-2 x 22-8
BED RM.
13-8 x 11-8
cl
FOYER
7-4 x 11-8
cl
DINING
14-8 x 11-8
© 1994 Donald A. Gardner Architects, Inc.
PORCH

Design HPT830344

First Floor: 1,499 square feet
Second Floor: 665 square feet
Total: 2,164 square feet
Bonus Space: 380 square feet
Width 69'-8" Depth 40'-6"

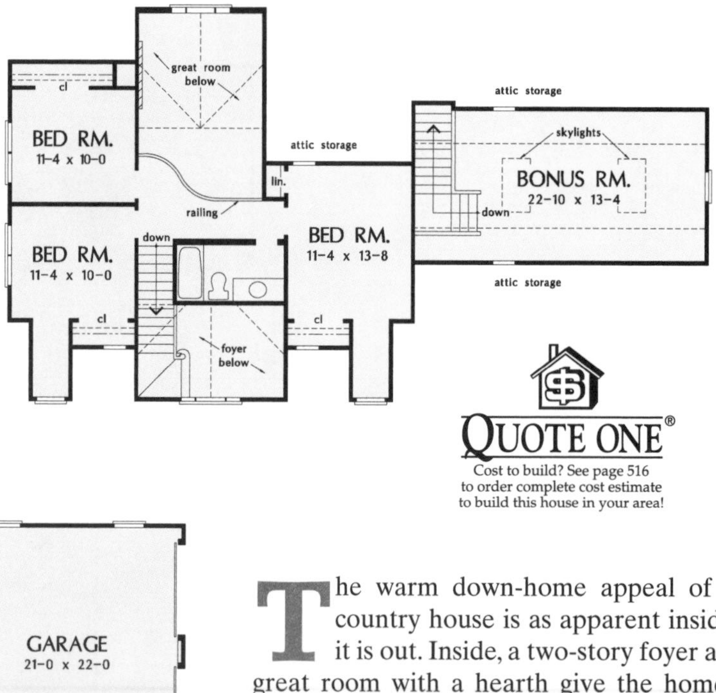

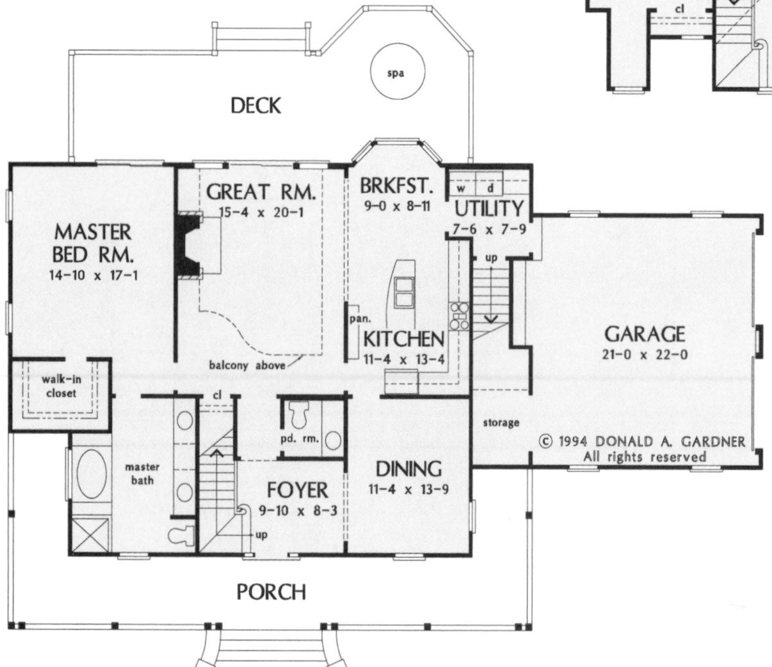

QUOTE ONE®
Cost to build? See page 516 to order complete cost estimate to build this house in your area!

The warm down-home appeal of this country house is as apparent inside as it is out. Inside, a two-story foyer and a great room with a hearth give the home an open feel. The great room leads to the breakfast area and the efficient kitchen with an island work area and a large pantry. The master bedroom is situated on the left side of the house for privacy. It features deck access, a large walk-in closet and a bath that includes dual vanities, a whirlpool tub and a separate shower. Three additional bedrooms, a full bath and bonus space are located upstairs.

B. NATHAN

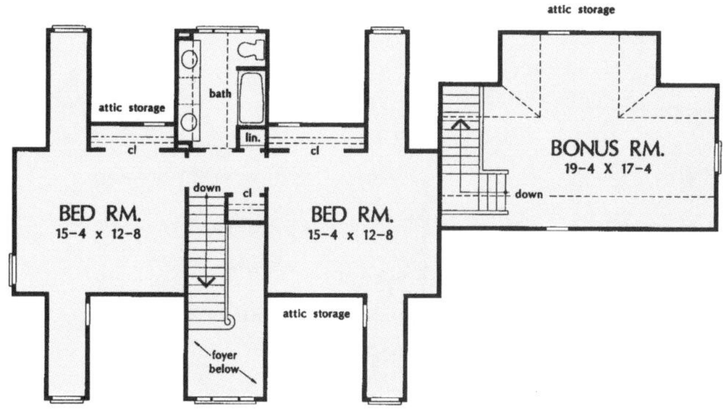

attic storage
BED RM.
15-4 x 12-8
bath
lin.
cl
attic storage
down
BED RM.
15-4 x 12-8
attic storage
foyer below
BONUS RM.
19-4 X 17-4
down

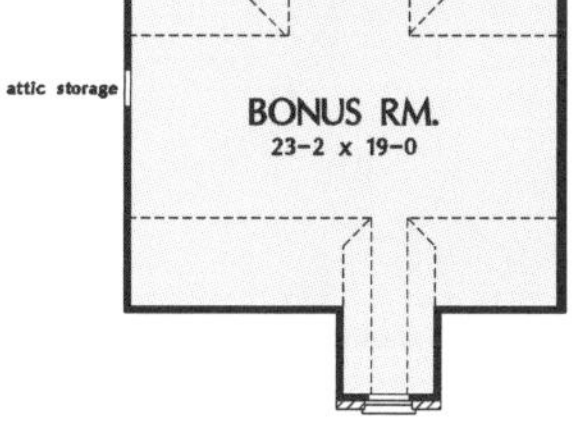

down
attic storage
BONUS RM.
23-2 x 19-0

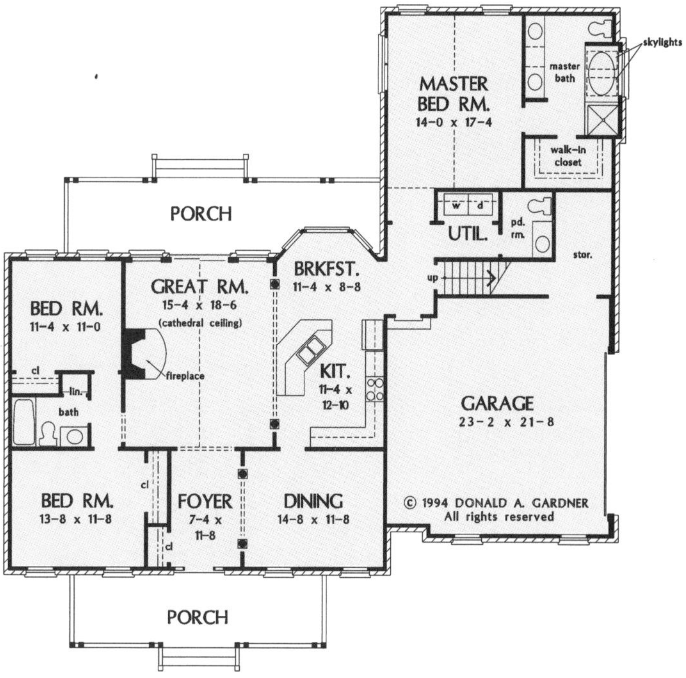

PORCH
MASTER BED RM.
14-0 x 17-4
master bath
skylights
walk-in closet
UTIL.
pd. rm.
stor.
BRKFST.
11-4 x 8-8
GREAT RM.
15-4 x 18-6
(cathedral ceiling)
fireplace
BED RM.
11-4 x 11-0
bath
KIT.
11-4 x 12-10
GARAGE
23-2 x 21-8
BED RM.
13-8 x 11-8
FOYER
7-4 x 11-8
DINING
14-8 x 11-8
© 1994 DONALD A. GARDNER
All rights reserved
PORCH

Design HPT830345

First Floor: 2,087 square feet
Second Floor: 758 square feet
Total: 2,845 square feet
Width 73'-9" Depth 64'-8"

This handsome country exterior will be a pleasure to come home to and it offers both a front covered porch and a rear porch for added outdoor livability. Inside, living areas flow freely. The great room presents lots of windows and a fireplace for added warmth. The breakfast area takes advantage of views out the back while the kitchen serves this area with a large island cooktop. A formal dining room is available for extra-special occasions. The master bedroom suite is privately located at the rear of the plan. It enjoys a luxury bath. Two secondary bedrooms upstairs and a bonus room over the garage finish the plan.

This home, as shown in the photograph, may differ from the actual blueprints. For more detailed information, please check the floor plans carefully.

Design

HPT830346

Square Footage: 1,815
Bonus Space: 336 square feet
Width 70'-8" Depth 70'-2"

Dormers, arched windows and covered porches lend this home its country appeal. Inside, the foyer opens to the dining room on the right and leads through a columned entrance to the great room, which has a fireplace and a cathedral ceiling. The open kitchen easily serves the great room, the breakfast area and the dining room. A cathedral ceiling graces the master bedroom with its walk-in closet and private bath with a dual vanity and a whirlpool tub. Two additional bedrooms share a full bath. A detached garage with a skylit bonus room above is connected to the covered rear porch.

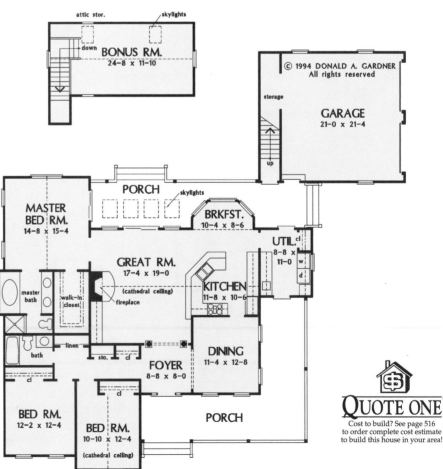

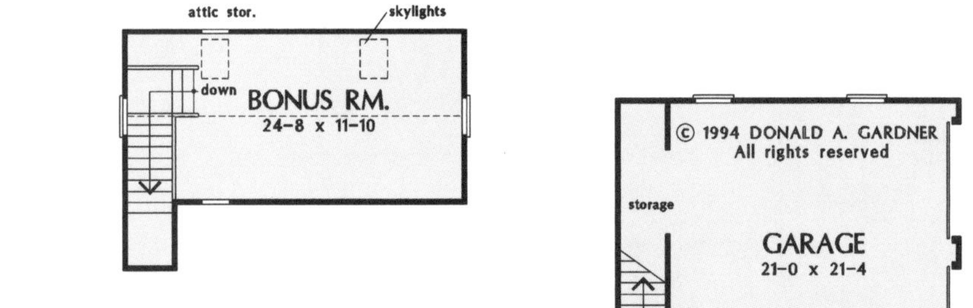

attic stor.
skylights
down
BONUS RM.
24-8 x 11-10
© 1994 DONALD A. GARDNER
All rights reserved
storage
GARAGE
21-0 x 21-4
up
PORCH
skylights
BRKFST.
10-4 x 8-6
MASTER
BED RM.
14-8 x 15-4
UTIL.
8-8 x 11-0
cl
w
d
GREAT RM.
17-4 x 19-0
(cathedral ceiling)
fireplace
KITCHEN
11-8 x 10-6
master bath
walk-in closet
linen
bath
sto.
cl
DINING
11-4 x 12-8
FOYER
8-8 x 8-0
cl
BED RM.
12-2 x 12-4
BED RM.
10-10 x 12-4
(cathedral ceiling)
PORCH

B. NATHAN

Design HPT830347

Square Footage: 1,864
Bonus Space: 420 square feet
Width 70'-4" Depth 56'-4"

Quaint and cozy on the outside with porches front and back, this three-bedroom country home surprises with an open floor plan featuring a large great room with a cathedral ceiling. A central kitchen with an angled counter opens to the breakfast and great rooms for easy entertaining. The privately located master bedroom has a cathedral ceiling and access to the deck. Two secondary bedrooms share a full hall bath. A bonus room makes expanding easy.

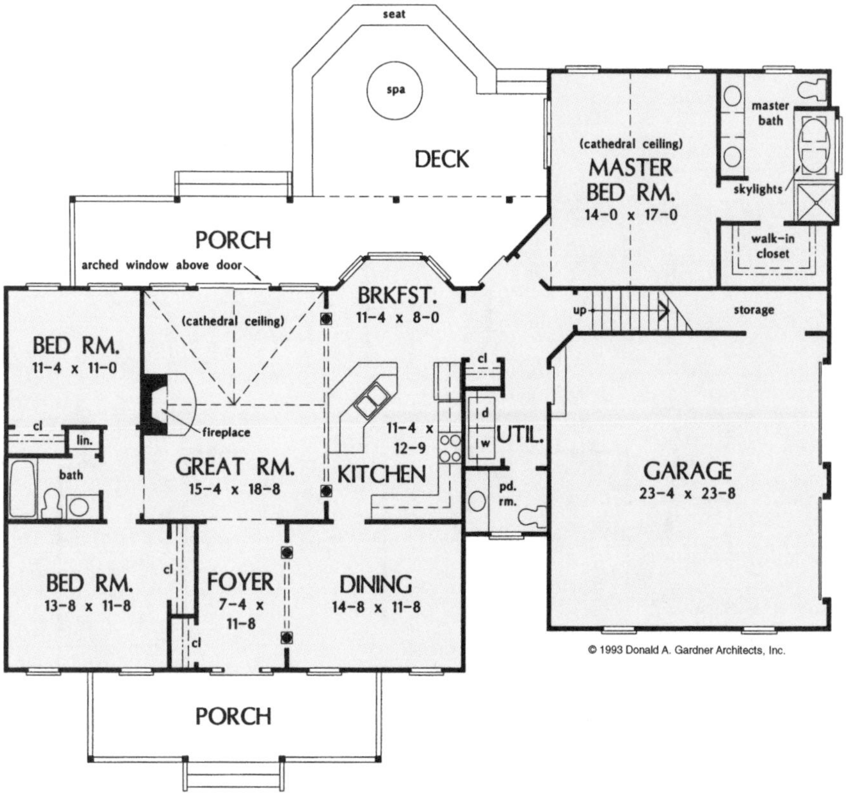
seat
spa
DECK
(cathedral ceiling)
MASTER BED RM.
14-0 x 17-0
master bath
skylights
walk-in closet
PORCH
arched window above door
BRKFST.
11-4 x 8-0
up
storage
BED RM.
11-4 x 11-0
(cathedral ceiling)
cl
lin.
bath
fireplace
GREAT RM.
15-4 x 18-8
KITCHEN
11-4 x 12-9
d
w
UTIL.
pd. rm.
GARAGE
23-4 x 23-8
BED RM.
13-8 x 11-8
cl
FOYER
7-4 x 11-8
DINING
14-8 x 11-8
PORCH

QUOTE ONE®

Cost to build? See page 516 to order complete cost estimate to build this house in your area!

down
skylights
BONUS RM.
14-4 x 23-8

Design HPT830348

First Floor: 1,581 square feet
Second Floor: 549 square feet
Total: 2,130 square feet
Bonus Space: 334 square feet
Width 80'-4" Depth 52'-4"

Great flexibility is available in this plan—the great room/dining room can be reworked into one large great room with the dining room relocated to the family room. A sun room with a cathedral ceiling and sliding glass door to the deck is accessible from both the breakfast and dining rooms. A large kitchen boasts a convenient cooking island. The master bedroom features a fireplace, walk-in closet and spacious private bath. Two second-level bedrooms are equal in size and share a full bath that includes a double-bowl vanity. Both bedrooms have a dormer window and a walk-in closet. A large bonus room over the garage is accessible from the utility room below.

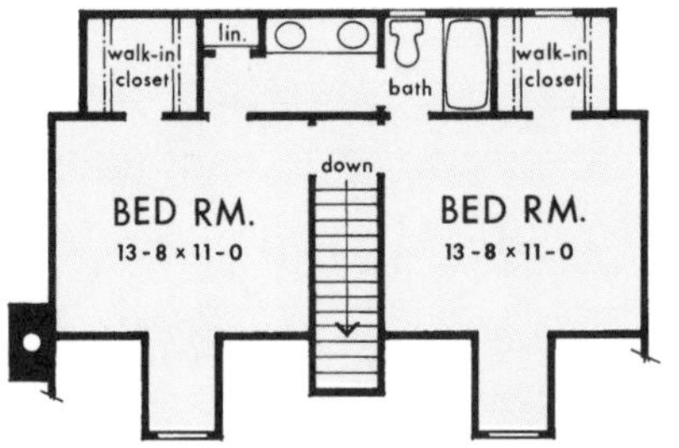

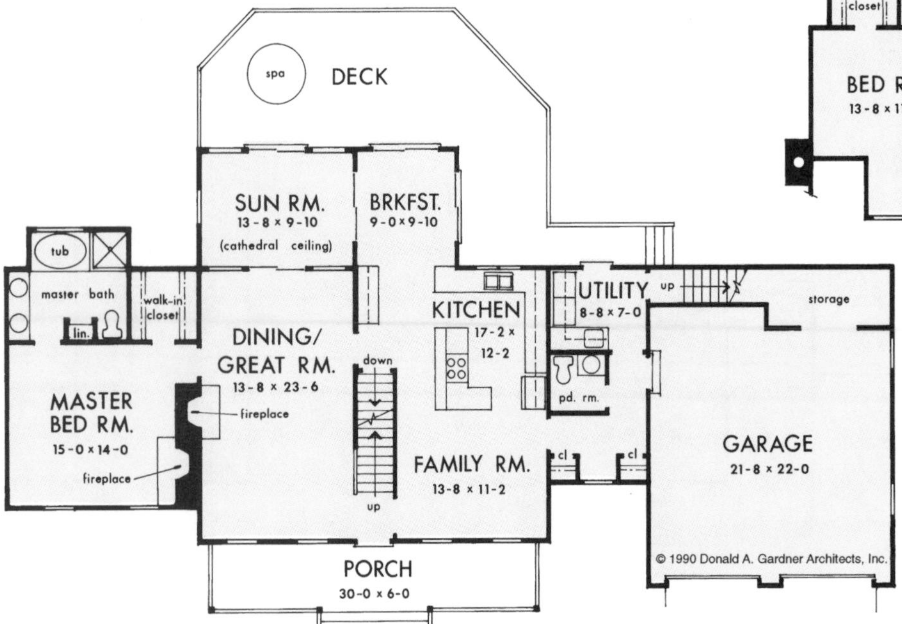

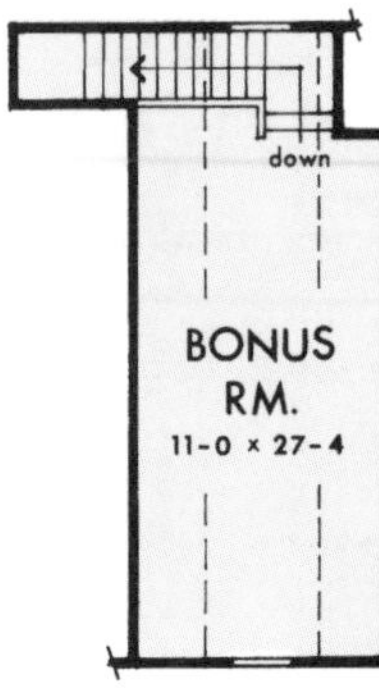

B. NATHAN

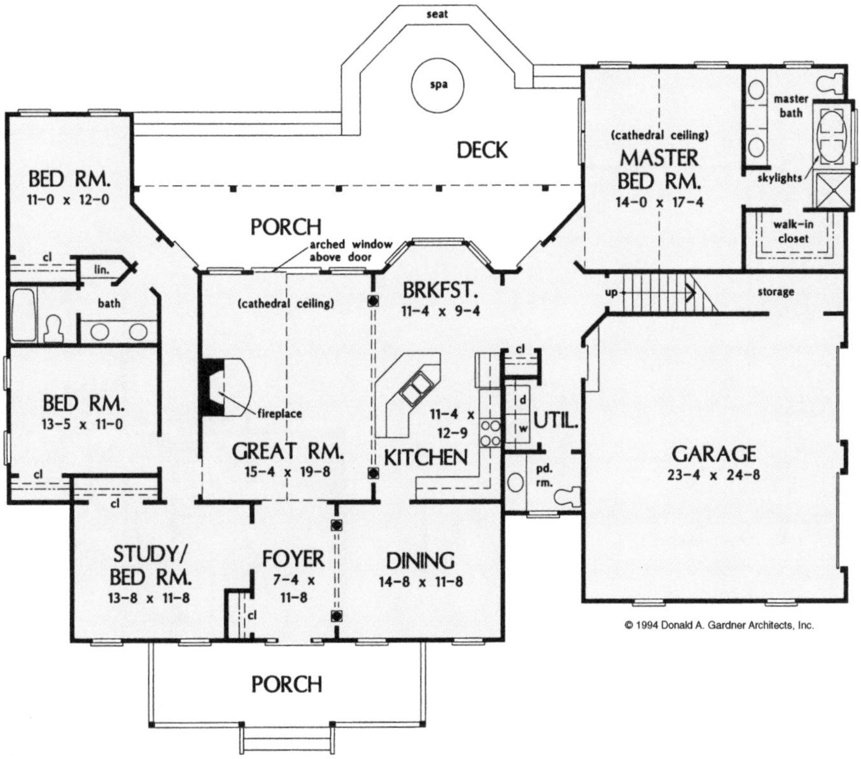
seat
spa
DECK
master bath
(cathedral ceiling)
MASTER BED RM.
14-0 x 17-4
skylights
walk-in closet
BED RM.
11-0 x 12-0
PORCH
arched window above door
cl
lin.
bath
(cathedral ceiling)
BRKFST.
11-4 x 9-4
up
storage
BED RM.
13-5 x 11-0
fireplace
11-4 x 12-9
KITCHEN
cl
d
w
UTIL.
GREAT RM.
15-4 x 19-8
pd. rm.
GARAGE
23-4 x 24-8
cl
cl
STUDY/ BED RM.
13-8 x 11-8
FOYER
7-4 x 11-8
cl
DINING
14-8 x 11-8
PORCH

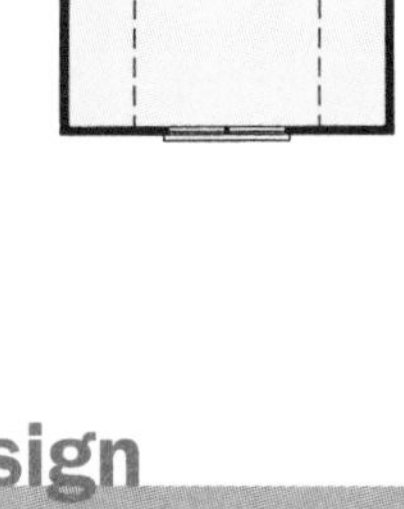
down
BONUS RM.
14-4 x 24-8

QUOTE ONE®

Cost to build? See page 516 to order complete cost estimate to build this house in your area!

This quaint four-bedroom home with front and rear porches reinforces its beauty with arched windows and dormers. The pillared dining room opens on the right, while a study that could double as a guest room is available on the left. Straight ahead lies the massive great room with its cathedral ceiling, enchanting fireplace and access to the private rear porch. Within steps of the dining room is the efficient kitchen and the sunny breakfast nook. The master suite enjoys a cathedral ceiling, rear-deck access and a master bath with a skylit whirlpool tub. Three additional bedrooms located at the opposite end of the house share a full bath.

Design HPT830349

Square Footage: 2,207
Bonus Space: 435 square feet
Width 76'-1" Depth 50'-0"

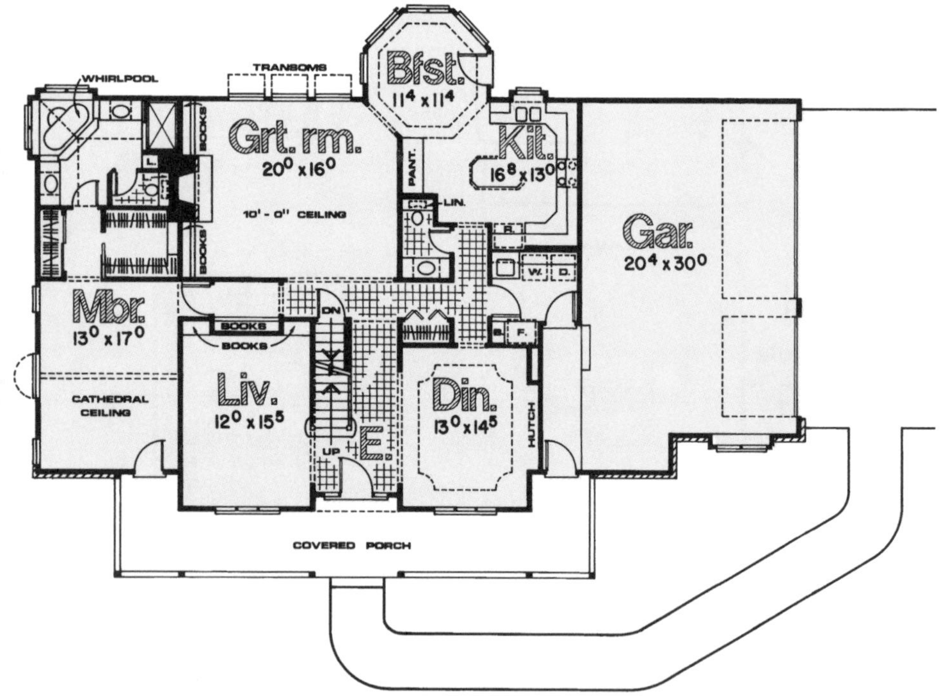

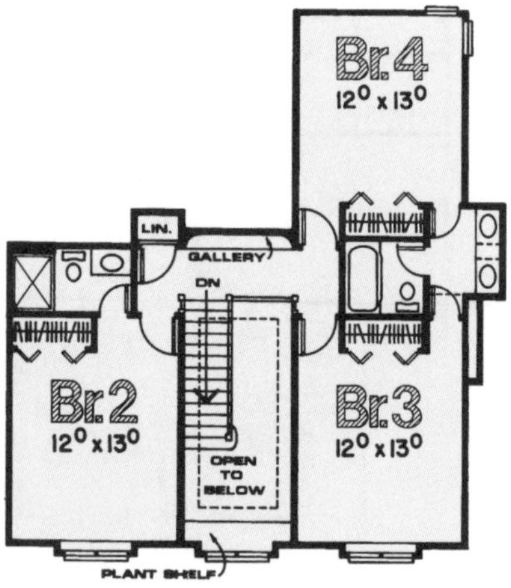

QUOTE ONE®

Cost to build? See page 516 to order complete cost estimate to build this house in your area!

Oval windows and an appealing covered porch lend character to this home. Inside, a volume entry views the formal living and dining rooms. Three large windows and a raised-hearth fireplace flanked by bookcases highlight a volume great room. An island kitchen with a huge pantry serves a captivating gazebo dinette. In the master suite, a cathedral ceiling, corner whirlpool tub and roomy dressing area deserve careful study. A gallery wall for displaying family mementos and prized heirlooms graces the upstairs corridor. Each secondary bedroom offers convenient access to the bathrooms.

Design

HPT830350

First Floor: 1,881 square feet
Second Floor: 814 square feet
Total: 2,695 square feet
Width 72'-0" Depth 45'-4"

Design HPT830351

First Floor: 2,315 square feet

Second Floor: 1,200 square feet

Total: 3,515 square feet

Width 77'-4" Depth 46'-8"

Open to Great Room Below
Bedroom #4 15⁶ x 12⁰
W.I.C.
Gallery
Bath
DN
W.I.C.
Bedroom #2 15⁰ x 12⁰
W.I.C.
Bath
Bedroom #3 15⁰ x 12⁰

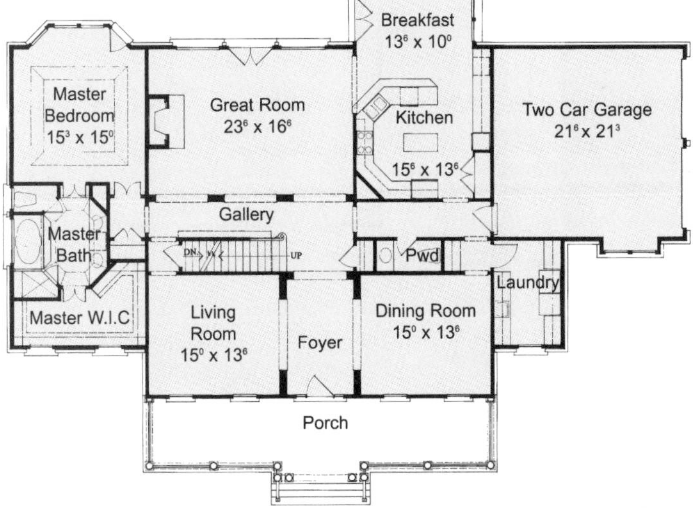
Breakfast 13⁶ x 10⁰
Master Bedroom 15³ x 15⁰
Great Room 23⁶ x 16⁶
Kitchen 15⁶ x 13⁶
Two Car Garage 21⁶ x 21³
Gallery
Master Bath
DN
UP
Pwd
Laundry
Master W.I.C
Living Room 15⁰ x 13⁶
Foyer
Dining Room 15⁰ x 13⁶
Porch

This grand home displays the finest in farmhouse design. Dormer windows and a traditional brick and siding exterior create a welcoming facade. Inside, the entry foyer opens to a formal zone consisting of a living room to the left and a dining room to the right. The kitchen enjoys a pass-through to the breakfast area—the great room is just a step away. Here, a fireplace graces the far end of the room while a wall of glass allows light to penetrate the interior of the room. Double doors grant passage to the backyard. Beyond the first-floor gallery, the master bedroom boasts a tray ceiling, bay window and lavish bath. Upstairs, three family bedrooms all have walk-in closets. This home is designed with a basement foundation.

This home, as shown in the photograph, may differ from the actual blueprints. For more detailed information, please check the floor plans carefully.

Design HPT830352

Square Footage: 1,632

Width 62'-4" Depth 55'-2"

This country home has a big heart in a cozy package. Special touches—interior columns, a bay window and dormers—add elegance. The central great room features a cathedral ceiling and a fireplace. A clerestory window splashes the room with natural light. The open kitchen easily services the breakfast area and the nearby dining room. The private master bedroom, with a tray ceiling and a walk-in closet, boasts amenities found in much larger homes. The bath features a skylight and a whirlpool tub. Two additional bedrooms share a bath. The front bedroom includes a walk-in closet and would make a nice study with an optional foyer entrance.

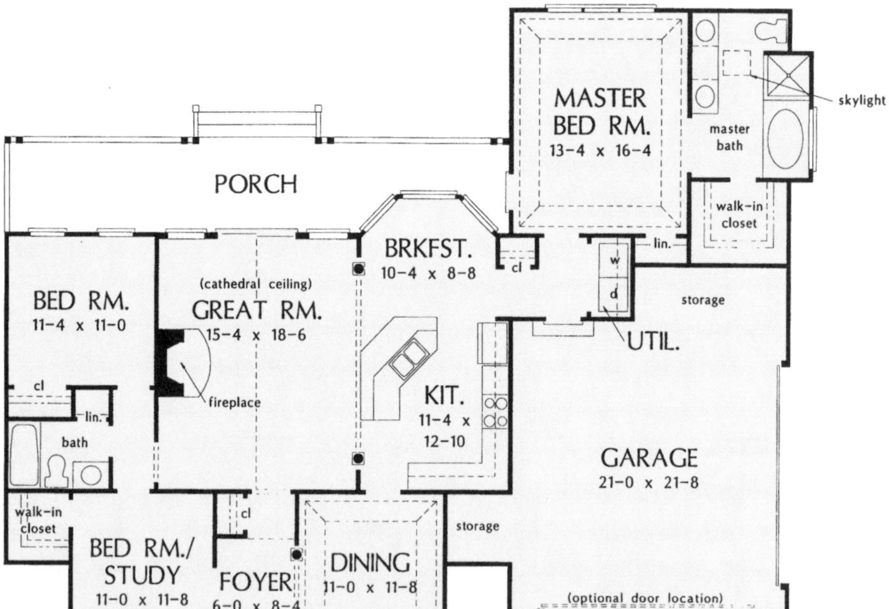

QUOTE ONE®

Cost to build? See page 516 to order complete cost estimate to build this house in your area!

B.NATHAN
© 1994 Donald A. Gardner Architects, Inc.

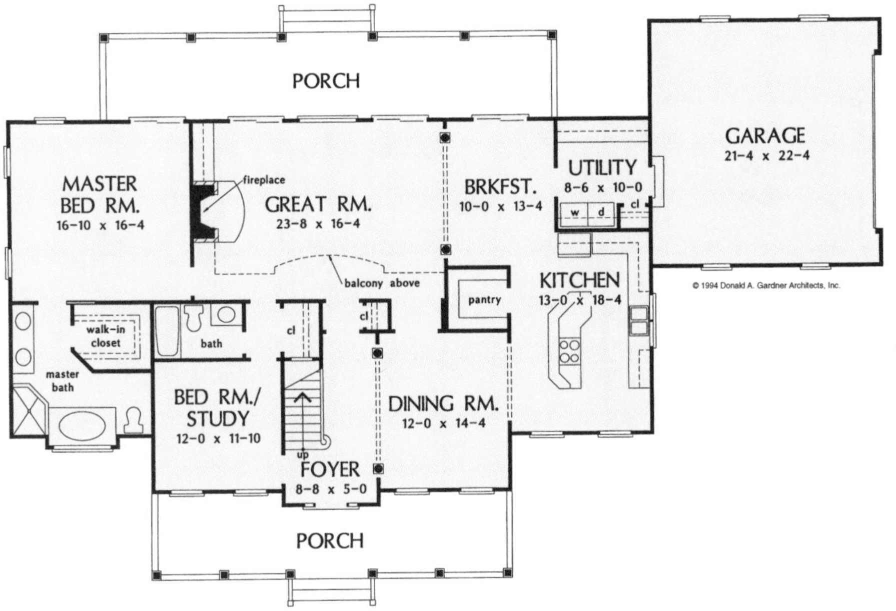
PORCH
GARAGE
21-4 x 22-4
MASTER
BED RM.
16-10 x 16-4
fireplace
GREAT RM.
23-8 x 16-4
BRKFST.
10-0 x 13-4
UTILITY
8-6 x 10-0
w d
cl
balcony above
pantry
KITCHEN
13-0 x 18-4
walk-in
closet
bath
cl
cl
master
bath
BED RM./
STUDY
12-0 x 11-10
DINING RM.
12-0 x 14-4
up
FOYER
8-8 x 5-0
PORCH
© 1994 Donald A. Gardner Architects, Inc.

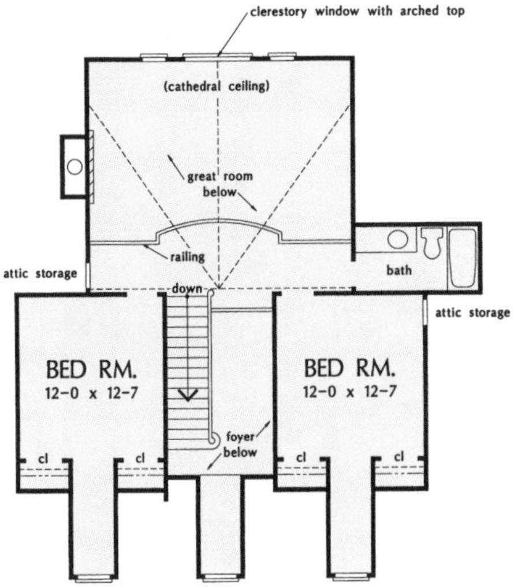
clerestory window with arched top
(cathedral ceiling)
great room
below
railing
attic storage
bath
down
attic storage
BED RM.
12-0 x 12-7
BED RM.
12-0 x 12-7
cl
cl
foyer
below
cl
cl

The two-story great room will soon become the focal point of this exquisite farmhouse. It is easily accessible from all areas of the house and features a cathedral ceiling, interior columns, an inviting fireplace and an overhead balcony. It is readily served by the kitchen with an island cooktop, a large pantry and a nearby utility room. The private master bedroom directly accesses the covered porch and includes a master bath with a double-bowl vanity, whirlpool tub, separate shower and large walk-in closet. The front bedroom, with its separate full bath, can also convert to a study. Two additional bedrooms are located on the second floor and share a full bath. Attic storage areas are easily accessible.

Design

HPT830353
First Floor: 1,975 square feet
Second Floor: 631 square feet
Total: 2,606 square feet
Width 82'-4" Depth 51'-6"

Design HPT830354

Square Footage: 1,832
Bonus Space: 425 square feet
Width 65'-4" Depth 62'-0"

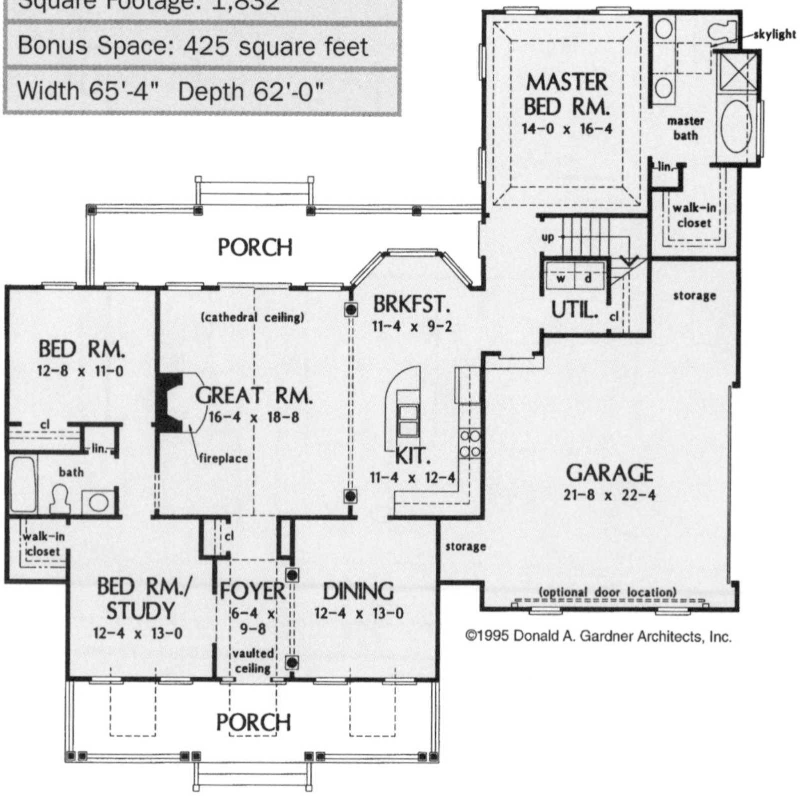
skylight
MASTER BED RM.
14-0 x 16-4
master bath
lin.
walk-in closet
PORCH
up
w d
UTIL.
cl
storage
BRKFST.
11-4 x 9-2
(cathedral ceiling)
BED RM.
12-8 x 11-0
GREAT RM.
16-4 x 18-8
fireplace
cl
lin.
bath
KIT.
11-4 x 12-4
GARAGE
21-8 x 22-4
walk-in closet
cl
storage
BED RM./ STUDY
12-4 x 13-0
FOYER
6-4 x 9-8
vaulted ceiling
DINING
12-4 x 13-0
(optional door location)
PORCH

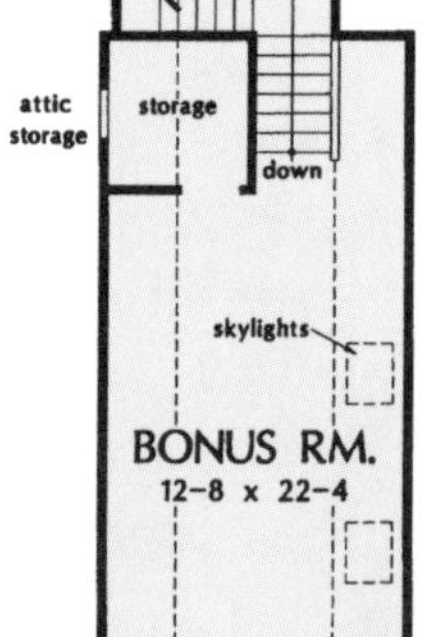
attic storage
storage
down
skylights
BONUS RM.
12-8 x 22-4

QUOTE ONE®
Cost to build? See page 516 to order complete cost estimate to build this house in your area!

This charming country plan boasts a cathedral ceiling in the great room. Dormer windows shed light on the foyer, which opens to a front bedroom/study and to the formal dining room. The kitchen is completely open to the great room and features a stylish snack-bar island and a bay window in the breakfast nook. The master suite offers a tray ceiling and a skylit bath. Two secondary bedrooms share a full bath on the opposite side of the house. Bonus space over the garage may be developed in the future.

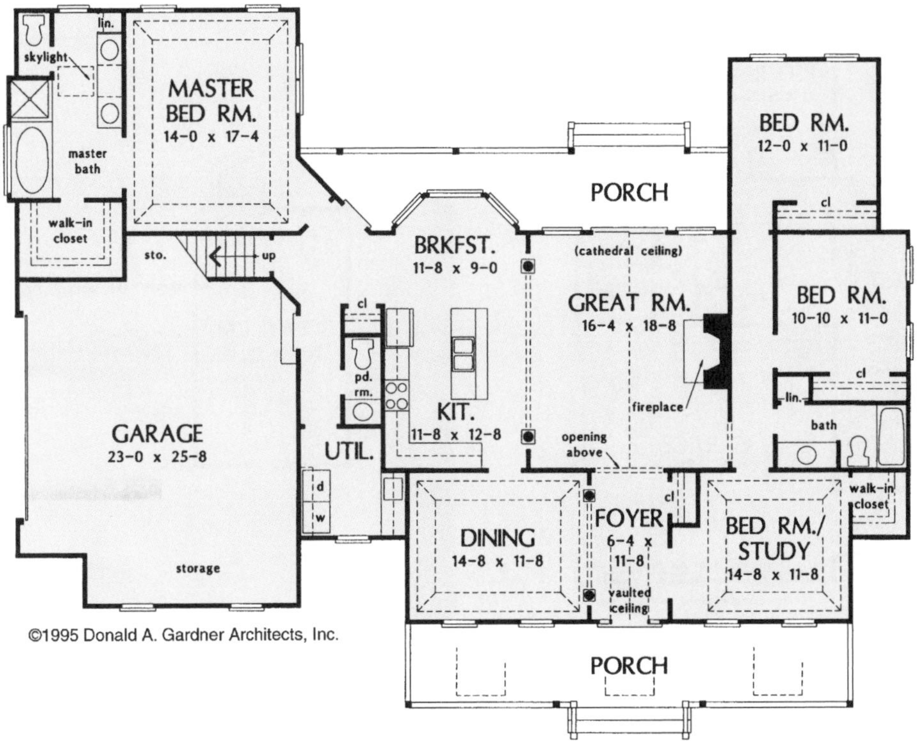
MASTER BED RM.
14-0 x 17-4
lin.
skylight
master bath
walk-in closet
sto.
up
GARAGE
23-0 x 25-8
storage
UTIL.
d
w
cl
pd. rm.
BRKFST.
11-8 x 9-0
KIT.
11-8 x 12-8
PORCH
(cathedral ceiling)
GREAT RM.
16-4 x 18-8
fireplace
opening above
DINING
14-8 x 11-8
FOYER
6-4 x 11-8
vaulted ceiling
cl
BED RM./ STUDY
14-8 x 11-8
BED RM.
12-0 x 11-0
cl
BED RM.
10-10 x 11-0
cl
lin.
bath
walk-in closet
PORCH

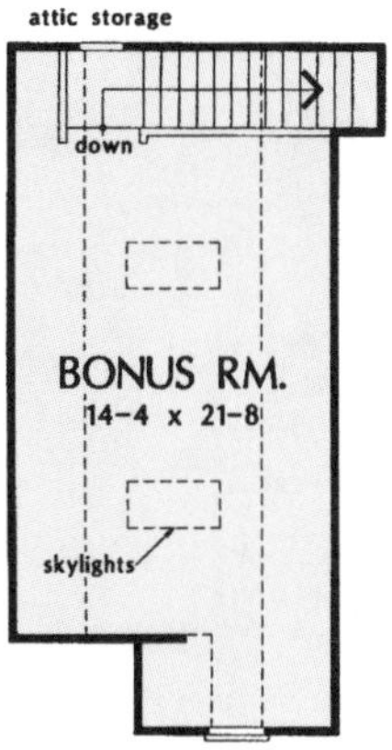
attic storage
down
BONUS RM.
14-4 x 21-8
skylights

Exciting volumes and nine-foot ceilings add elegance to this comfortable, open plan. There's also a tray ceiling in the front bedroom/study. Hosts whose guests always end up in the kitchen will enjoy entertaining here with only columns separating it from the great room. Children's bedrooms share a full bath that's complete with a linen closet. The master suite, located in a quiet wing, is highlighted by a tray ceiling and includes a skylit bath with a garden tub, private toilet, double-bowl vanity and spacious walk-in closet.

Design
HPT830355

Square Footage: 2,192

Bonus Space: 390 square feet

Width 74'-10" Depth 55'-8"

© 1996 Donald A. Gardner Architects, Inc.

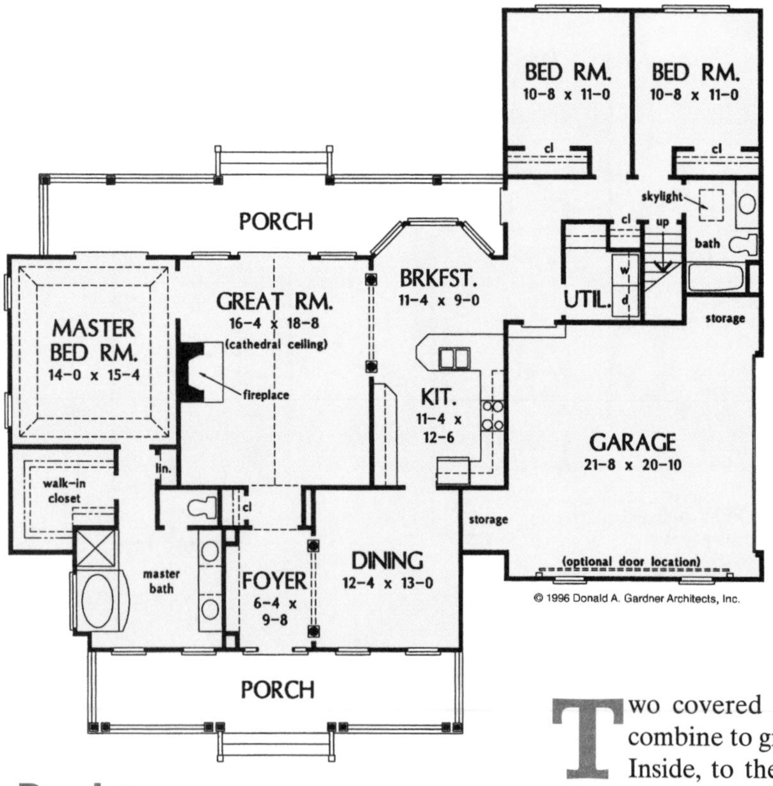
BED RM.
10-8 x 11-0
BED RM.
10-8 x 11-0
cl
cl
skylight
cl
up
bath
PORCH
BRKFST.
11-4 x 9-0
UTIL.
w
d
storage
GREAT RM.
16-4 x 18-8
(cathedral ceiling)
MASTER
BED RM.
14-0 x 15-4
fireplace
KIT.
11-4 x 12-6
GARAGE
21-8 x 20-10
lin.
walk-in
closet
cl
storage
master
bath
FOYER
6-4 x 9-8
DINING
12-4 x 13-0
(optional door location)
© 1996 Donald A. Gardner Architects, Inc.
PORCH

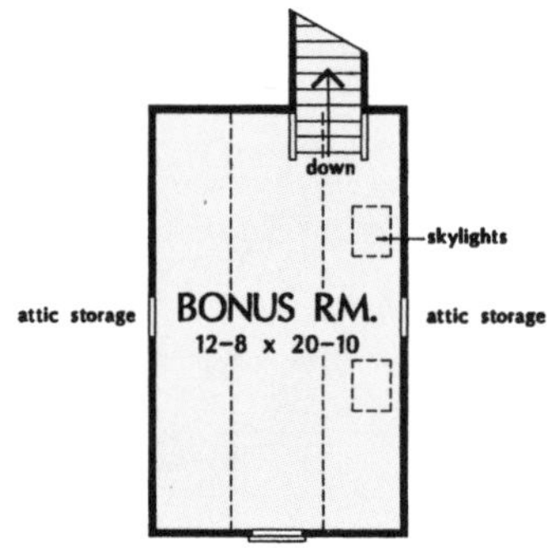
down
skylights
attic storage
BONUS RM.
12-8 x 20-10
attic storage

Two covered porches, three dormers and multi-pane windows combine to give this three-bedroom home plenty of curb appeal. Inside, to the right of the foyer, a formal dining room awaits. Directly ahead, at the rear of the plan, the spacious great room offers a cathedral ceiling, a fireplace and access to the rear porch. The U-shaped kitchen works well with both the dining room and the bayed breakfast room. The sleeping zone is divided for privacy. The two family bedrooms on the right side share a skylit bath and are conveniently close to the laundry room. The deluxe master suite, with its tray ceiling, large walk-in closet and pampering bathroom, is on the left side of the plan.

Design

HPT830356

Square Footage: 1,864
Bonus Space: 319 square feet
Width 65'-0" Depth 59'-8"

© 1994 Donald A. Gardner Architects, Inc.

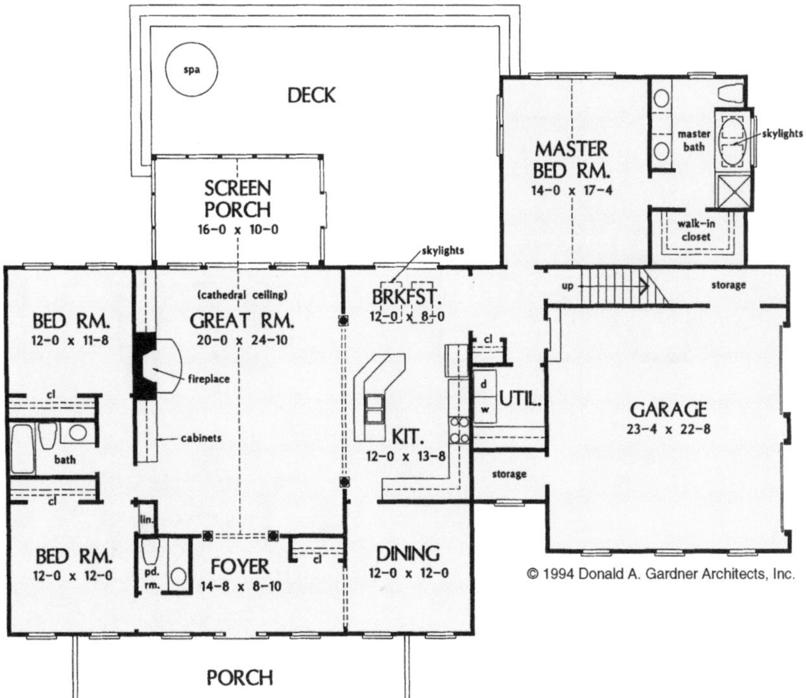

spa
DECK
SCREEN PORCH
16-0 x 10-0
MASTER BED RM.
14-0 x 17-4
master bath
skylights
walk-in closet
skylights
BED RM.
12-0 x 11-8
(cathedral ceiling)
GREAT RM.
20-0 x 24-10
fireplace
cabinets
BRKFST.
12-0 x 8-0
up
storage
cl
cl
bath
cl
d
w
UTIL.
KIT.
12-0 x 13-8
GARAGE
23-4 x 22-8
storage
lin.
BED RM.
12-0 x 12-0
pd. rm.
FOYER
14-8 x 8-10
DINING
12-0 x 12-0
PORCH
© 1994 Donald A. Gardner Architects, Inc.

QUOTE ONE®

Cost to build? See page 516 to order complete cost estimate to build this house in your area!

down
skylights
BONUS RM.
14-4 x 26-4

An expansive front porch, three dormers and a score of windows all add to the charm and character of this country home. The spacious great room features built-in cabinets, a fireplace and a cathedral ceiling that continues into the adjoining screened porch. An island kitchen is conveniently grouped with the great room, the dining room and the skylit breakfast area for the cook who enjoys conversation while preparing meals. The master suite features a cathedral ceiling, a large walk-in closet and a relaxing private bath with a skylit whirlpool tub and separate shower. Two secondary bedrooms share a full bath.

Design
HPT830357

Square Footage: 2,136
Bonus Space: 405 square feet
Width 76'-4" Depth 64'-4"

Design HPT830358

First Floor: 1,783 square feet
Second Floor: 611 square feet
Total: 2,394 square feet
Width 70'-0" Depth 79'-2"

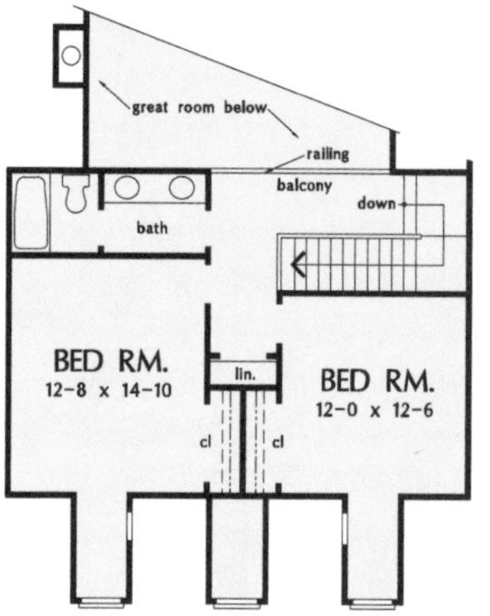
great room below
railing
balcony
down
bath
BED RM.
12-8 x 14-10
lin.
BED RM.
12-0 x 12-6
cl
cl

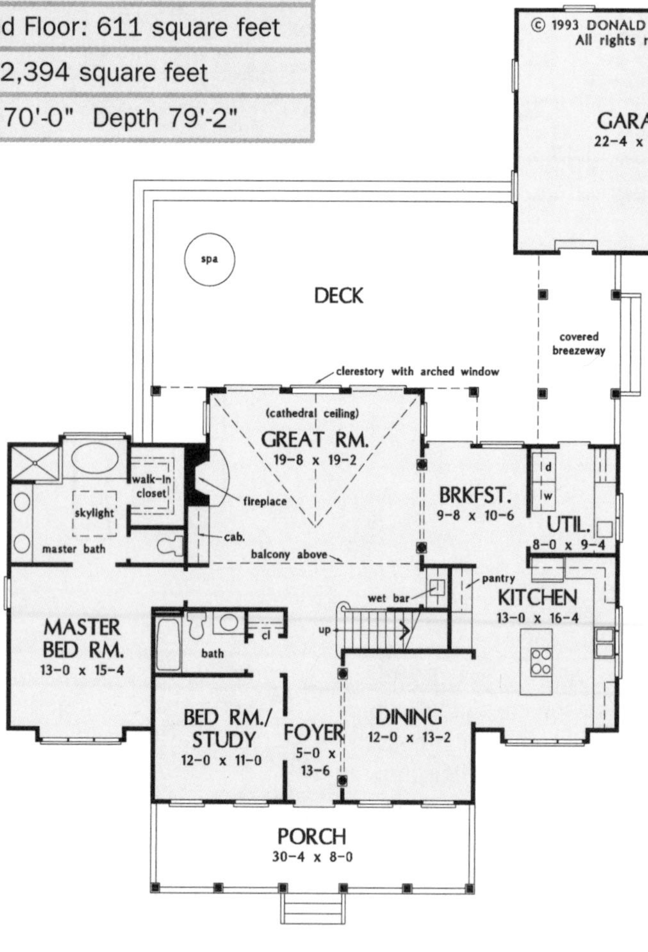
© 1993 DONALD A. GARDNER
All rights reserved
GARAGE
22-4 x 21-4
spa
DECK
covered breezeway
clerestory with arched window
(cathedral ceiling)
GREAT RM.
19-8 x 19-2
walk-in closet
skylight
master bath
fireplace
cab.
balcony above
BRKFST.
9-8 x 10-6
d
w
UTIL.
8-0 x 9-4
pantry
wet bar
KITCHEN
13-0 x 16-4
MASTER BED RM.
13-0 x 15-4
cl
bath
up
BED RM./ STUDY
12-0 x 11-0
FOYER
5-0 x 13-6
DINING
12-0 x 13-2
PORCH
30-4 x 8-0

Onlookers will delight in the symmetry of this facade's arched windows and dormers. The interior offers a great room with a cathedral ceiling. This open plan is packed with the latest design features, including a kitchen with a large island, a wet bar in the great room, a bedroom/study combination on the first floor and a gorgeous master suite with a spa-style bath. Upstairs, two family bedrooms share a compartmented hall bath. An expansive rear deck and generous covered front porch offer maximum outdoor livability.

© 1994 Donald A. Gardner Architects, Inc.
B. NATHAN

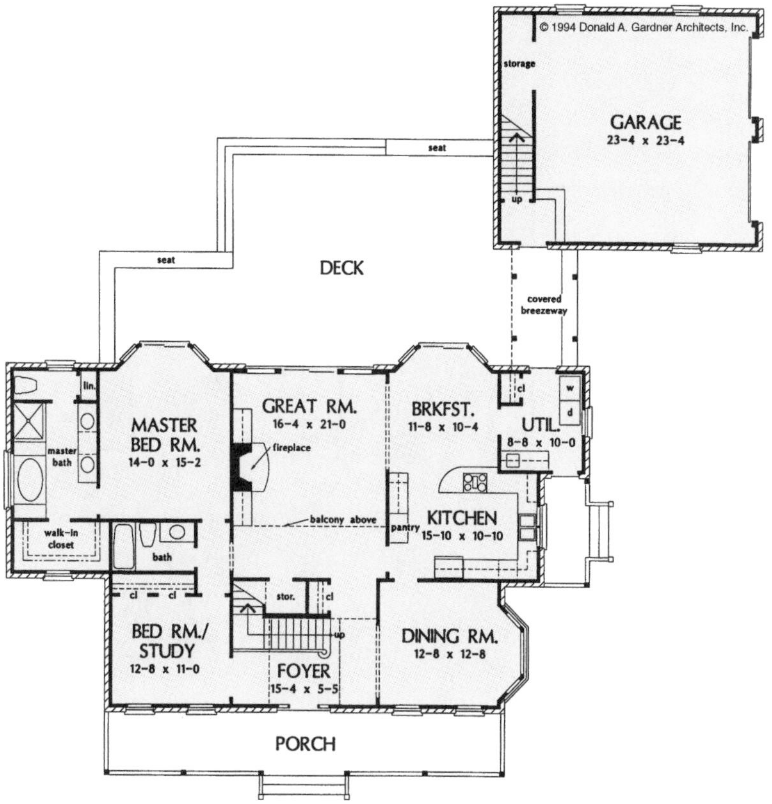
© 1994 Donald A. Gardner Architects, Inc.
storage
GARAGE
23-4 x 23-4
up
seat
DECK
covered breezeway
MASTER BED RM.
14-0 x 15-2
lin.
master bath
walk-in closet
bath
GREAT RM.
16-4 x 21-0
fireplace
balcony above
BRKFST.
11-8 x 10-4
UTIL.
8-8 x 10-0
cl
w
d
KITCHEN
15-10 x 10-10
pantry
stor.
cl
BED RM./ STUDY
12-8 x 11-0
FOYER
15-4 x 5-5
DINING RM.
12-8 x 12-8
PORCH

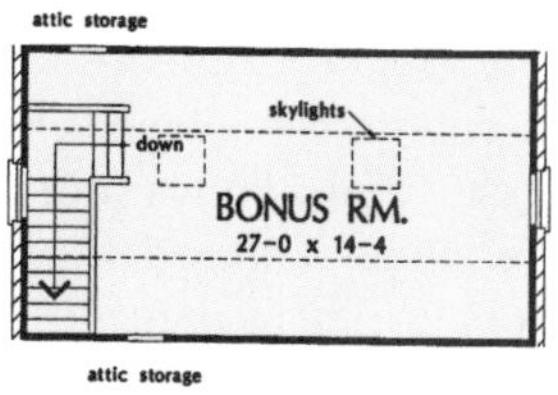
attic storage
skylights
down
BONUS RM.
27-0 x 14-4
attic storage

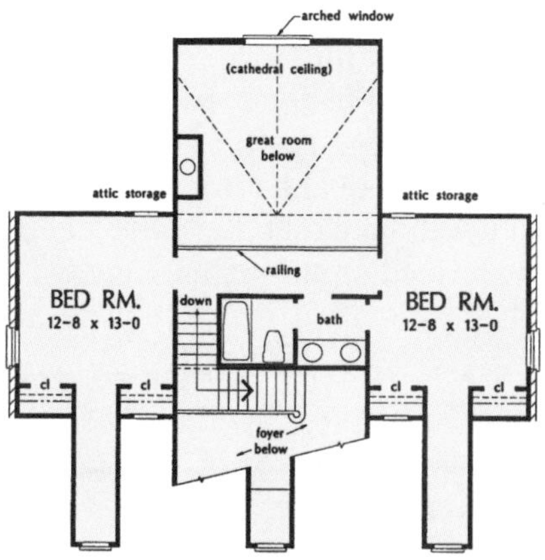
arched window
(cathedral ceiling)
great room below
attic storage
attic storage
railing
BED RM.
12-8 x 13-0
down
bath
BED RM.
12-8 x 13-0
cl
foyer below

Design HPT830359

First Floor: 1,966 square feet
Second Floor: 634 square feet
Total: 2,600 square feet
Bonus Space: 396 square feet
Width 80'-11" Depth 79'-2"

Three bay windows enhance the romance of this country home. Enter from the front porch to the great room with a cathedral ceiling and a fireplace. Enjoy a scenic dinner in the dining room, which is easily accessible from the kitchen. The kitchen has an island cooktop, built-in pantry and sunny breakfast area with a view of the massive deck. The master bedroom completes the picture with a bay window, deck access and a luxurious bath with a whirlpool tub. Two family bedrooms and a full hall bath are located upstairs.

© 1993 Donald A. Gardner Architec

This open country plan boasts front and rear covered porches and a bonus room for future expansion. The slope-ceilinged foyer has a Palladian window clerestory to let in natural light. The spacious great room presents a fireplace, cathedral ceiling and clerestory with arched windows. The second-floor balcony overlooks the great room. A U-shaped kitchen provides the ideal layout for food preparation. For flexibility, access is provided to the bonus room from both the first and second floors. The first-floor master bedroom features a bath with dual lavatories, a separate tub and shower and a walk-in closet. Two large bedrooms and a full bath are located on the second floor.

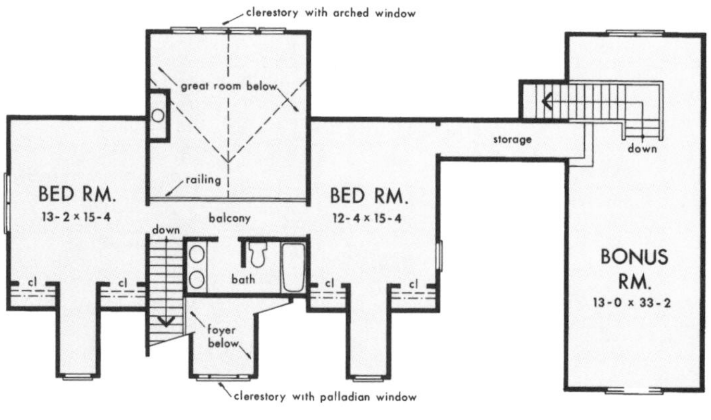

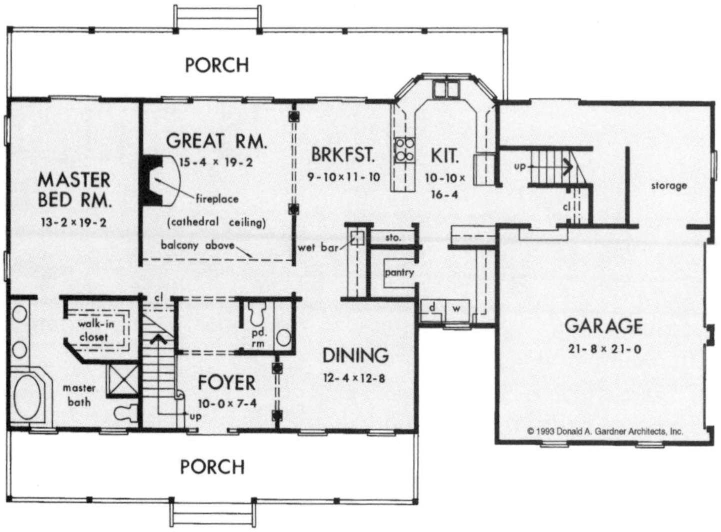

QUOTE ONE®

Cost to build? See page 516 to order complete cost estimate to build this house in your area!

Design HPT830360

First Floor: 1,632 square feet
Second Floor: 669 square feet
Total: 2,301 square feet
Bonus Space: 528 square feet
Width 72'-6" Depth 46'-10"

Design HPT830361

First Floor: 1,484 square feet
Second Floor: 660 square feet
Total: 2,144 square feet
Bonus Space: 389 square feet
Width 72'-8" Depth 54'-4"

Overlooking a covered porch and a deck with a spa, this home's kitchen will be a gourmet's delight. A wraparound counter gives plenty of space, while a snack bar opens to the breakfast nook. In the great room—which delights with a fireplace—quiet gatherings and entertaining will be a pleasure. The master bedroom, complete with a spa-style bath, rests to the right side of the first floor. Upstairs, two bedrooms and a full bath comfortably house family and guests.

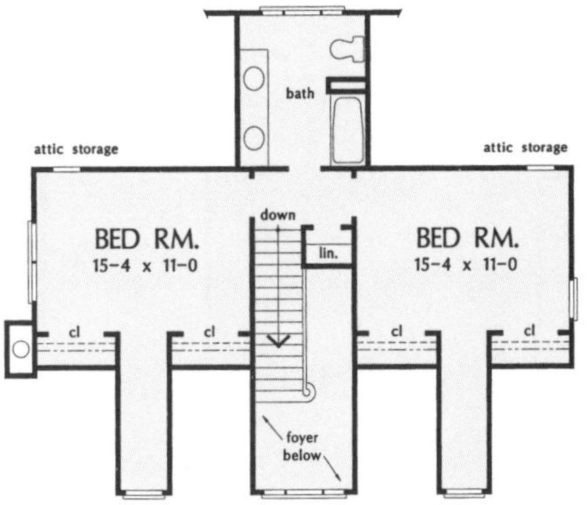

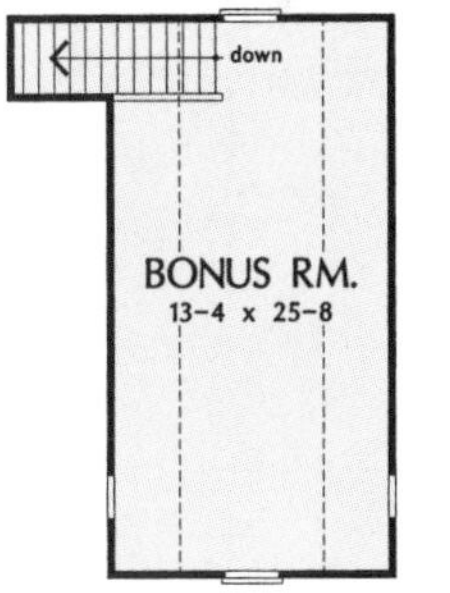

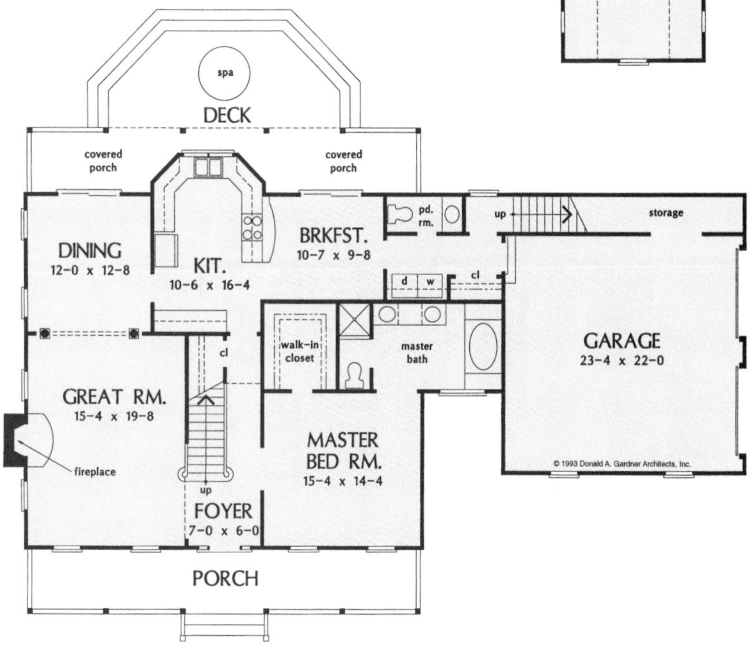

B. NATHAN
© 1990 Donald A. Gardner Architects, Inc.

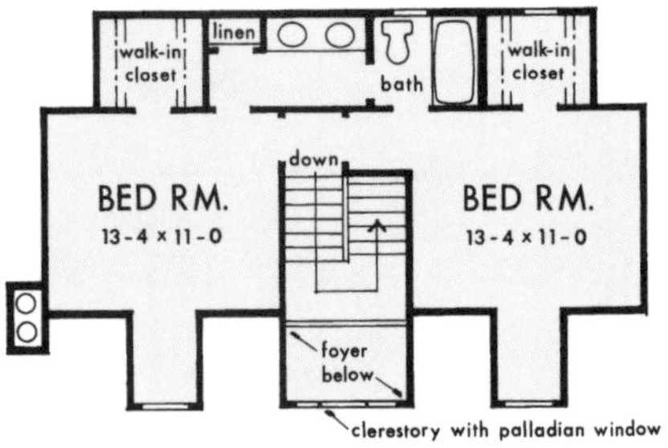

walk-in closet
linen
bath
walk-in closet
down
BED RM.
13-4 × 11-0
BED RM.
13-4 × 11-0
foyer below
clerestory with palladian window

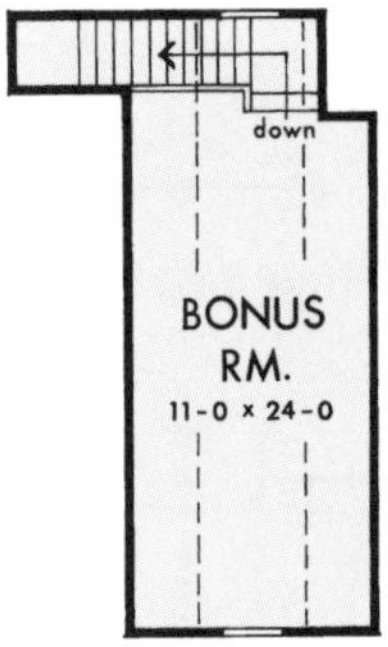

down
BONUS RM.
11-0 × 24-0

Design HPT830362

First Floor: 1,578 square feet
Second Floor: 554 square feet
Total: 2,132 square feet
Width 83'-4" Depth 46'-0"

Enjoy outdoor living with a covered porch at the front of this home and an expansive deck to the rear. The U-shaped kitchen easily serves the breakfast room, the dining room and the nearby family room. A fantastic sun room is accessible from both the dining area and the deluxe master suite. The floor plan allows for great livability and features split bedroom styling with the master suite on the first floor. Two upstairs bedrooms share a full bath. There is also bonus space above the garage for a studio, study or play room.

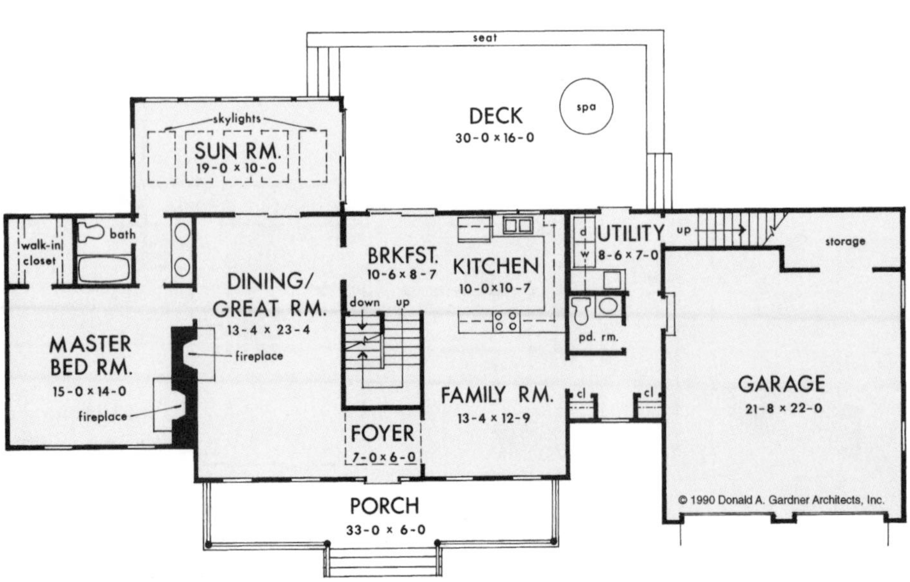

seat
DECK
30-0 × 16-0
spa
skylights
SUN RM.
19-0 × 10-0
walk-in closet
bath
MASTER BED RM.
15-0 × 14-0
fireplace
DINING/ GREAT RM.
13-4 × 23-4
fireplace
BRKFST.
10-6 × 8-7
KITCHEN
10-0 × 10-7
down
up
UTILITY
8-6 × 7-0
up
storage
pd. rm.
FAMILY RM.
13-4 × 12-9
cl
cl
FOYER
7-0 × 6-0
GARAGE
21-8 × 22-0
PORCH
33-0 × 6-0
© 1990 Donald A. Gardner Architects, Inc.

© 1994 Donald A. Gardner Architects, Inc.

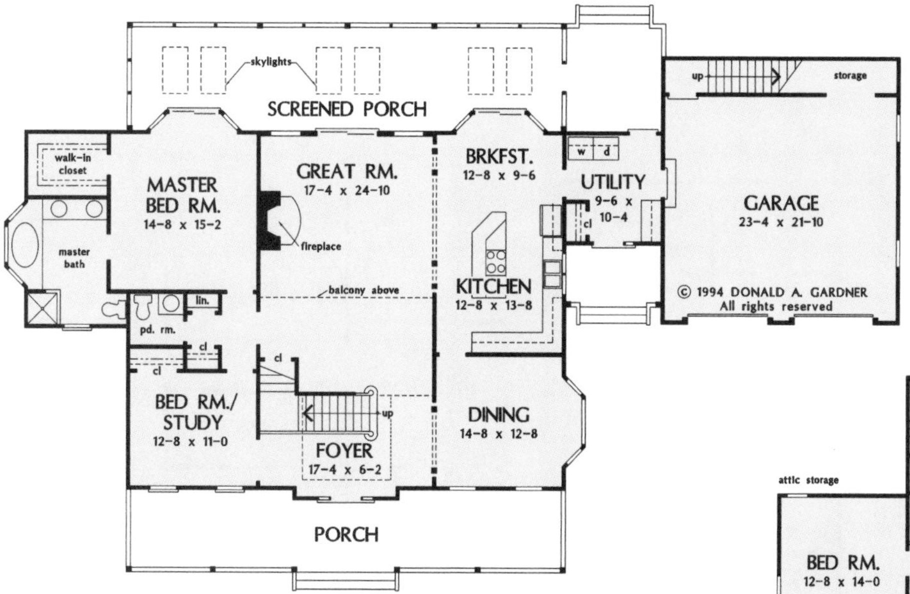
skylights
SCREENED PORCH
walk-in closet
MASTER BED RM. 14-8 x 15-2
master bath
GREAT RM. 17-4 x 24-10
fireplace
balcony above
BRKFST. 12-8 x 9-6
w d
UTILITY 9-6 x 10-4
cl
KITCHEN 12-8 x 13-8
up
storage
GARAGE 23-4 x 21-10
© 1994 DONALD A. GARDNER All rights reserved
lin.
pd. rm.
cl
BED RM./ STUDY 12-8 x 11-0
FOYER 17-4 x 6-2
DINING 14-8 x 12-8
PORCH

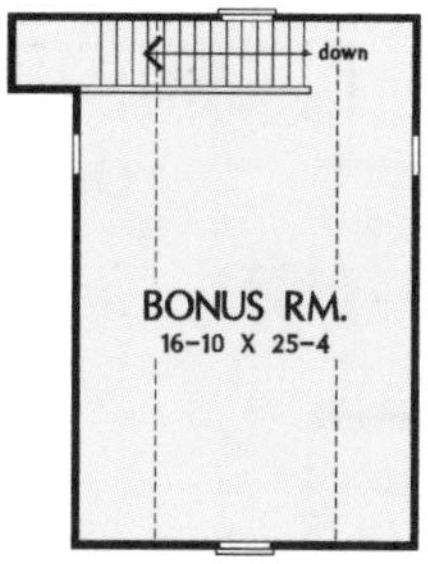
down
BONUS RM. 16-10 X 25-4

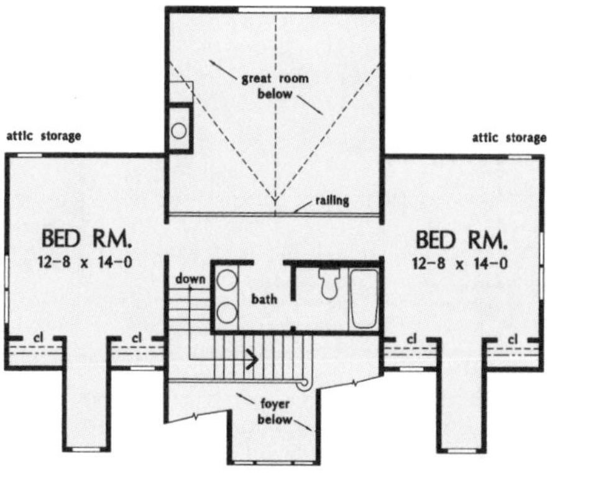
great room below
attic storage
attic storage
railing
BED RM. 12-8 x 14-0
BED RM. 12-8 x 14-0
down
bath
cl
cl
cl
cl
foyer below

Design HPT830363

First Floor: 1,907 square feet
Second Floor: 656 square feet
Total: 2,563 square feet
Bonus Space: 467 square feet
Width 89'-10" Depth 53'-4"

Sunny bay windows splash this favorite farmhouse with style, and create a charming facade that's set off by an old-fashioned country porch. Inside, the two-story foyer opens to a formal dining room and to a study, which could be used as a guest suite. The casual living area enjoys a fireplace with an extended hearth and access to an expansive screened porch. The sensational master suite offers a walk-in closet and a bath with a bumped-out bay tub, twin vanities and a separate shower. The two family bedrooms share a full bath upstairs.

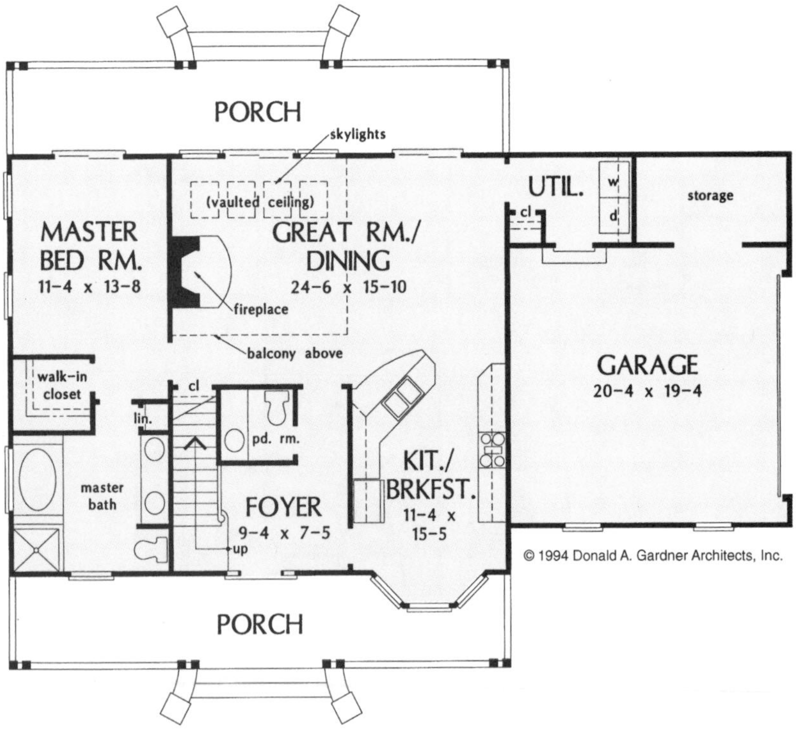
PORCH
skylights
(vaulted ceiling)
MASTER BED RM.
11-4 x 13-8
GREAT RM./ DINING
24-6 x 15-10
fireplace
balcony above
UTIL.
w
d
cl
storage
GARAGE
20-4 x 19-4
walk-in closet
lin.
cl
pd. rm.
master bath
FOYER
9-4 x 7-5
up
KIT./ BRKFST.
11-4 x 15-5
PORCH
© 1994 Donald A. Gardner Architects, Inc.

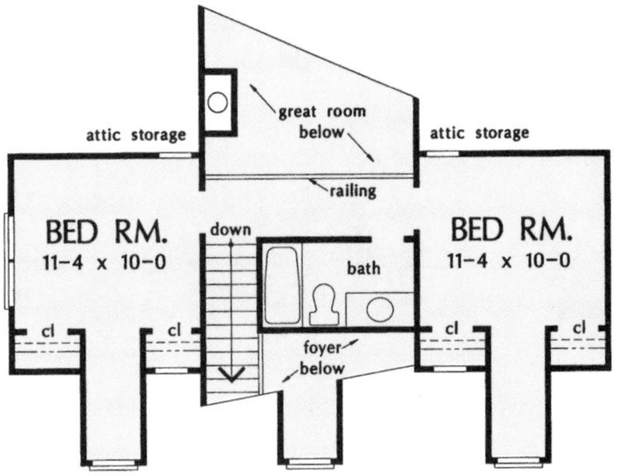
great room below
attic storage
attic storage
railing
BED RM.
11-4 x 10-0
down
bath
BED RM.
11-4 x 10-0
cl
cl
cl
cl
foyer below

Open floor planning gives this efficient three-bedroom home a much larger feeling. The two-story foyer leads to the great room and dining area which sports a vaulted ceiling accented with skylights. The eat-in kitchen has a stylish angled snack bar that opens to the great room. Privacy is assured in the first-floor master suite which features a walk-in closet and a pampering bath. Upstairs, a balcony hall that overlooks the great room leads to two family bedrooms with a full bath shared in between.

Design HPT830364

First Floor: 1,164 square feet
Second Floor: 458 square feet
Total: 1,622 square feet
Width 57'-6" Depth 42'-7"

Design
HPT830365

First Floor: 1,506 square feet
Second Floor: 513 square feet
Total: 2,019 square feet
Bonus Space: 397 square feet
Width 65'-4" Depth 67'-10"

With a casually elegant exterior, this three-bedroom farmhouse celebrates sunlight with a Palladian window dormer and a rear arched window. The clerestory window in the two-story foyer shines natural light into the entry, while the arched window lights the great room with its fireplace and cathedral ceiling. The L-shaped kitchen features an island cooktop and a bayed breakfast area with views of the backyard. The master suite is a calm retreat and includes a walk-in closet and luxurious bath. Two family bedrooms and a bonus room are located upstairs.

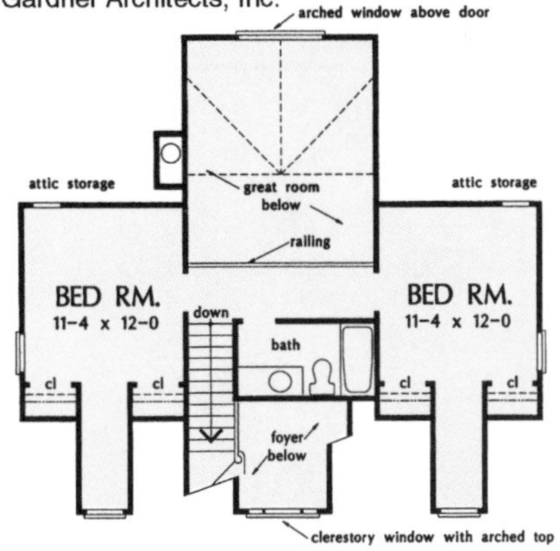
arched window above door
attic storage
great room below
railing
attic storage
BED RM.
11-4 x 12-0
down
bath
BED RM.
11-4 x 12-0
cl
cl
cl
cl
foyer below
clerestory window with arched top

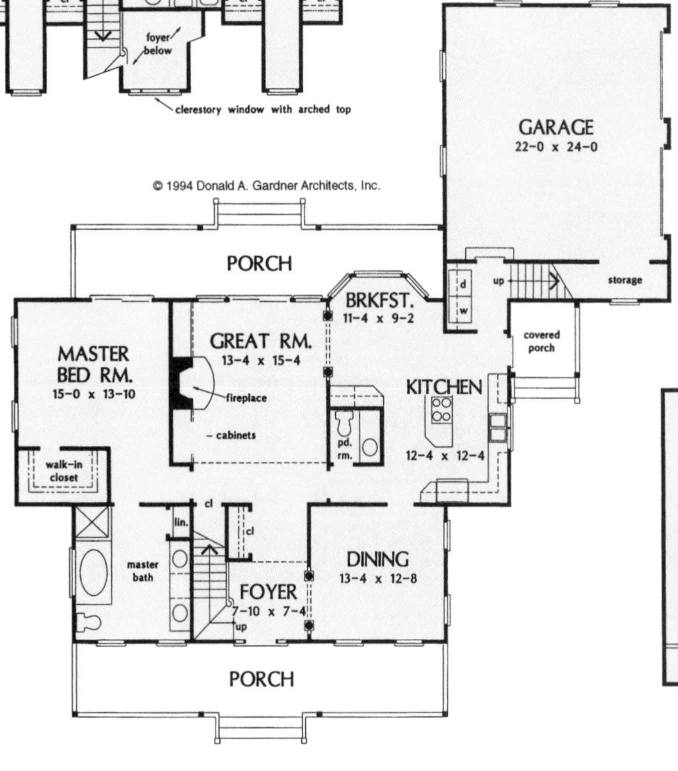
GARAGE
22-0 x 24-0
© 1994 Donald A. Gardner Architects, Inc.
PORCH
up
storage
d
w
BRKFST.
11-4 x 9-2
covered porch
MASTER BED RM.
15-0 x 13-10
GREAT RM.
13-4 x 15-4
fireplace
cabinets
KITCHEN
pd. rm.
12-4 x 12-4
walk-in closet
cl
lin.
cl
master bath
DINING
13-4 x 12-8
FOYER
7-10 x 7-4
up
PORCH

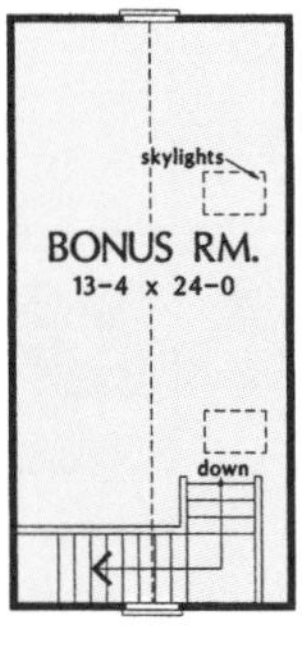
skylights
BONUS RM.
13-4 x 24-0
down

© 1994 Donald A. Gardner Architects, Inc.

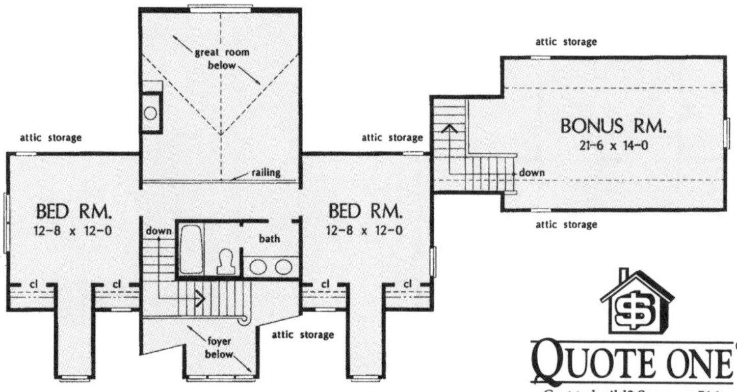

great room below
attic storage
attic storage
BONUS RM.
21-6 x 14-0
attic storage
railing
attic storage
down
BED RM.
12-8 x 12-0
BED RM.
12-8 x 12-0
down
bath
attic storage
cl
cl
cl
cl
foyer below
attic storage

QUOTE ONE®

Cost to build? See page 516 to order complete cost estimate to build this house in your area!

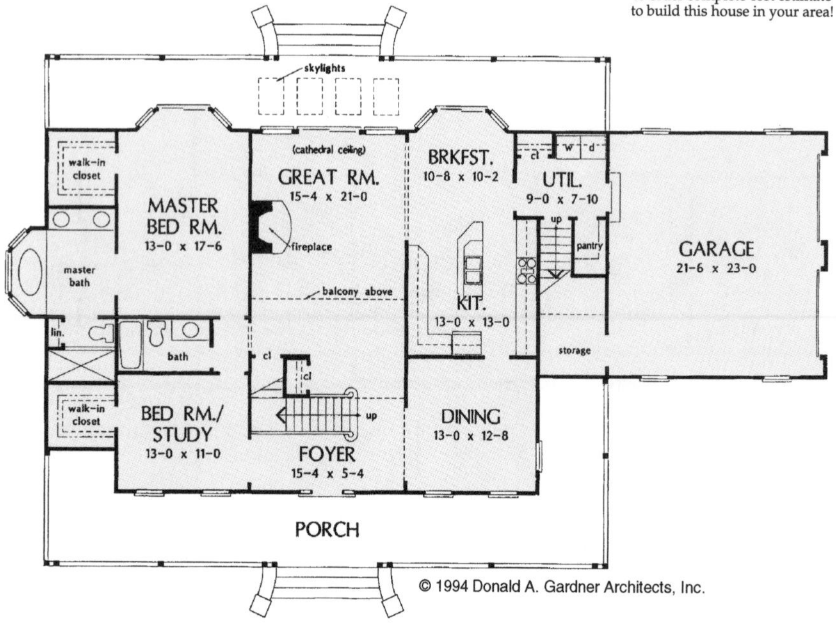

skylights
(cathedral ceiling)
walk-in closet
GREAT RM.
15-4 x 21-0
BRKFST.
10-8 x 10-2
UTIL.
9-0 x 7-10
MASTER BED RM.
13-0 x 17-6
fireplace
pantry
master bath
GARAGE
21-6 x 23-0
balcony above
KIT.
13-0 x 13-0
lin.
bath
storage
cl
walk-in closet
BED RM./ STUDY
13-0 x 11-0
up
DINING
13-0 x 12-8
FOYER
15-4 x 5-4
PORCH

© 1994 Donald A. Gardner Architects, Inc.

Design HPT830366

First Floor: 1,841 square feet
Second Floor: 594 square feet
Total: 2,435 square feet
Bonus Space: 391 square feet
Width 82'-2" Depth 48'-10"

Spaciousness and lots of amenities earmark this design as a family favorite. The front wraparound porch leads to the foyer where a bedroom/study and dining room open. The central great room presents a warming fireplace, a two-story cathedral ceiling and access to the rear porch. The kitchen features an island food-prep counter and opens to a bayed breakfast area, which conveniently accesses the garage through a side utility room. In the master suite, a private bath with a bumped-out tub and a walk-in closet are extra enhancements. Upstairs, two bedrooms flank a full bath. A bonus room over the garage allows for future expansion.

Design HPT830367

First Floor: 2,176 square feet
Second Floor: 861 square feet
Total: 3,037 square feet
Bonus Space: 483 square feet
Width 94'-0" Depth 58'-4"

Country living is at its best in this spacious five-bedroom farmhouse with a wrap-around porch. A front Palladian window dormer and rear clerestory windows add exciting visual elements to the exterior and provide natural light to the interior. The large great room boasts a fireplace, bookshelves and a raised cathedral ceiling, allowing the curved balcony to overlook from above. Special features such as a large cooktop island in the kitchen, a wet bar, a bedroom/study combination and a generous bonus room over the garage set this plan apart from the rest.

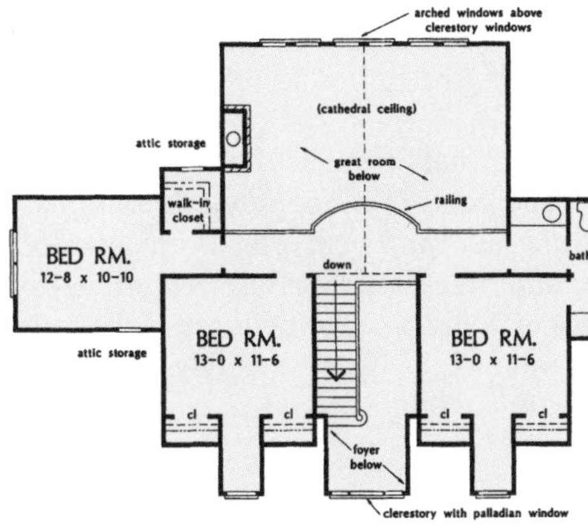

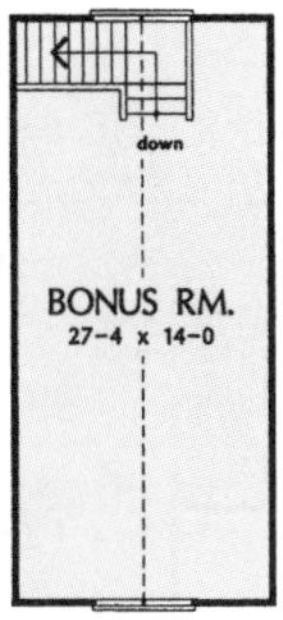

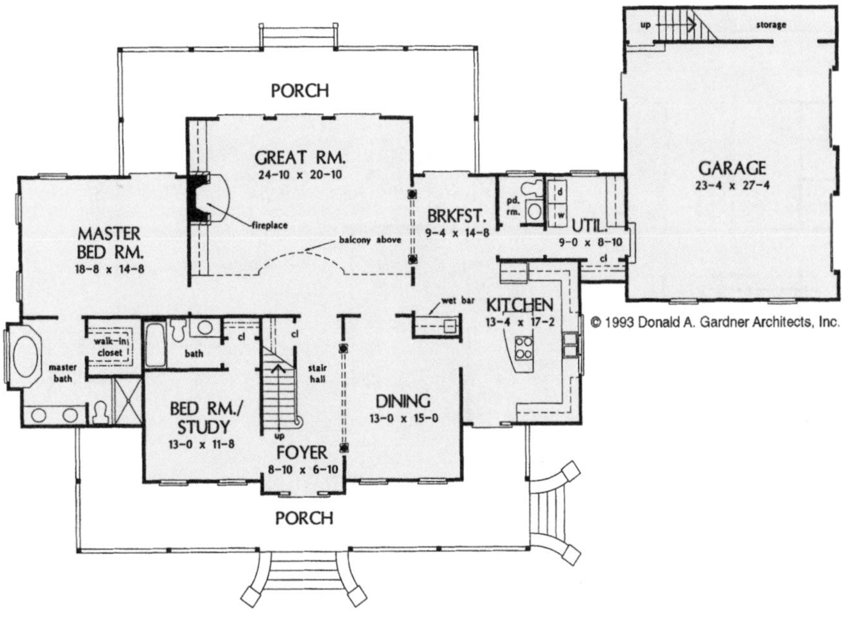

Design HPT830368

First Floor: 2,064 square feet	
Second Floor: 594 square feet	
Total: 2,658 square feet	
Bonus Space: 483 square feet	
Width 92'-0" Depth 57'-8"	

You'll find country living at its best when meandering through this four-bedroom farmhouse with its wraparound porch. A front Palladian dormer window and rear clerestory windows in the great room add exciting visual elements to the exterior while providing natural light to the interior. The large great room boasts a fireplace, bookshelves and a raised cathedral ceiling, allowing a curved balcony overlook above. The great room, master bedroom and breakfast room are accessible to the rear porch for greater circulation and flexibility. Special features such as the large cooktop island in the kitchen, the wet bar, the bedroom/study, the generous bonus room over the garage and ample storage space make this plan a country favorite.

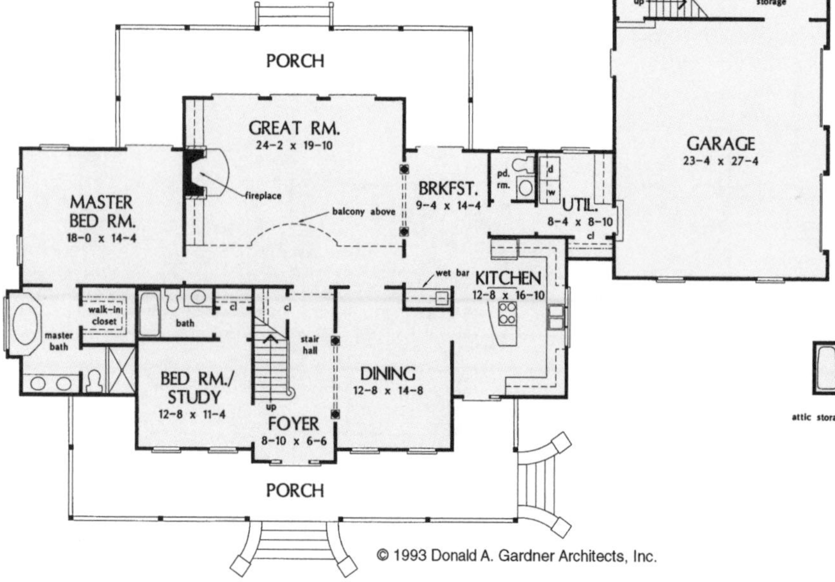

QUOTE ONE®
Cost to build? See page 516
to order complete cost estimate
to build this house in your area!

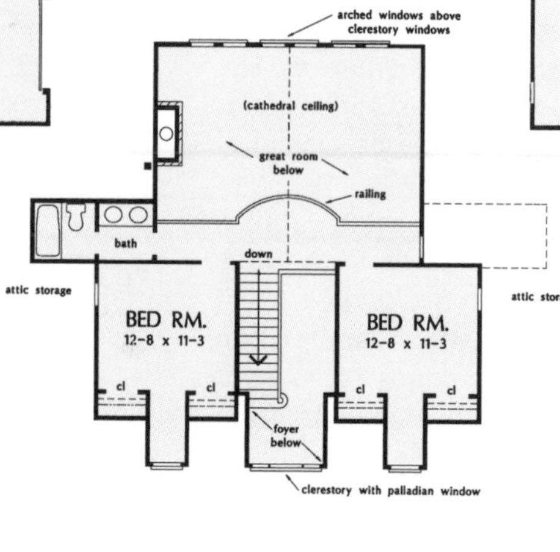

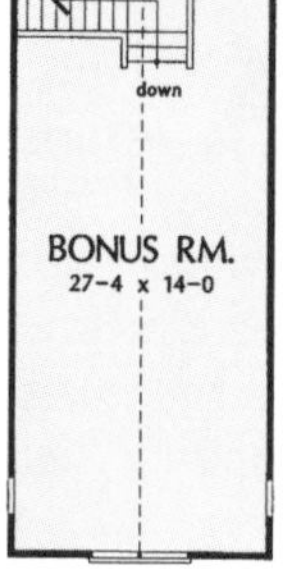

This home, as shown in the photograph, may differ from the actual blueprints. For more detailed information, please check the floor plans carefully.

Design HPT830369

First Floor: 2,316 square feet
Second Floor: 721 square feet
Total: 3,037 square feet
Bonus Space: 545 square feet
Width 95'-4" Depth 54'-10"

This gracious farmhouse with its wraparound porch offers a touch of symmetry in a well-defined, open plan. The entrance foyer has a Palladian clerestory window that gives an abundance of natural light to the interior. The vaulted great room furthers this feeling of airiness with a second-floor balcony above and two sets of sliding glass doors leading to the porch out back. For privacy, the master suite occupies the right side of the first floor. With a sitting room and all the amenities of a spa-style bath, this room won't fail to please. Two more bedrooms and a double-vanity bath are located upstairs.

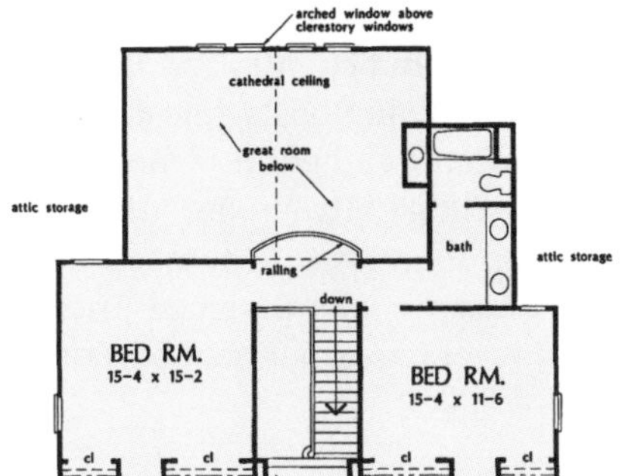

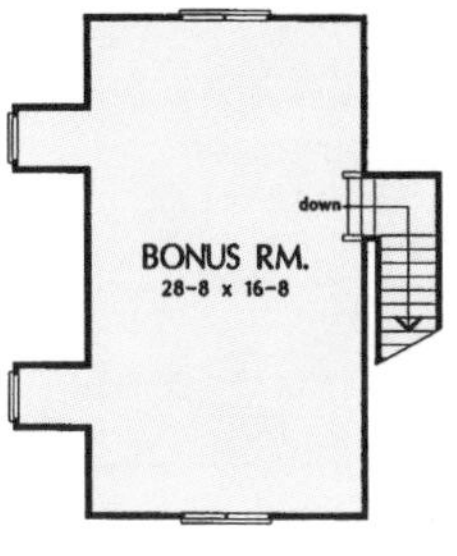

QUOTE ONE®
Cost to build? See page 516 to order complete cost estimate to build this house in your area!

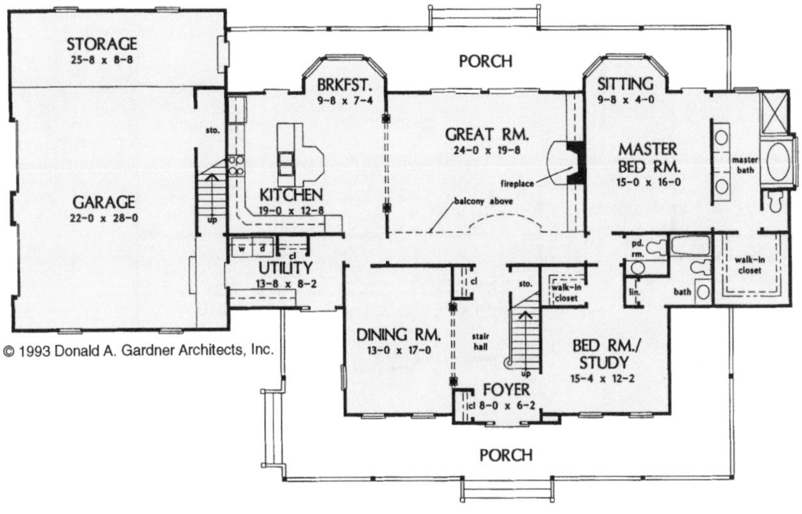

Design

HPT830370
First Floor: 2,238 square feet
Second Floor: 768 square feet
Total: 3,006 square feet
Width 94'-1" Depth 59'-10"

This grand country farmhouse with a wraparound porch offers comfortable living at its finest. The open floor plan is accented by the great room's cathedral ceiling and the entrance foyer with clerestory windows. The large kitchen has lots of counter space, a sunny breakfast nook and a cooktop island with a bumped-out snack bar. The master suite has beautiful bay windows, a well-designed private bath and a spacious walk-in closet. The second level has two large bedrooms, a full bath and plenty of attic storage.

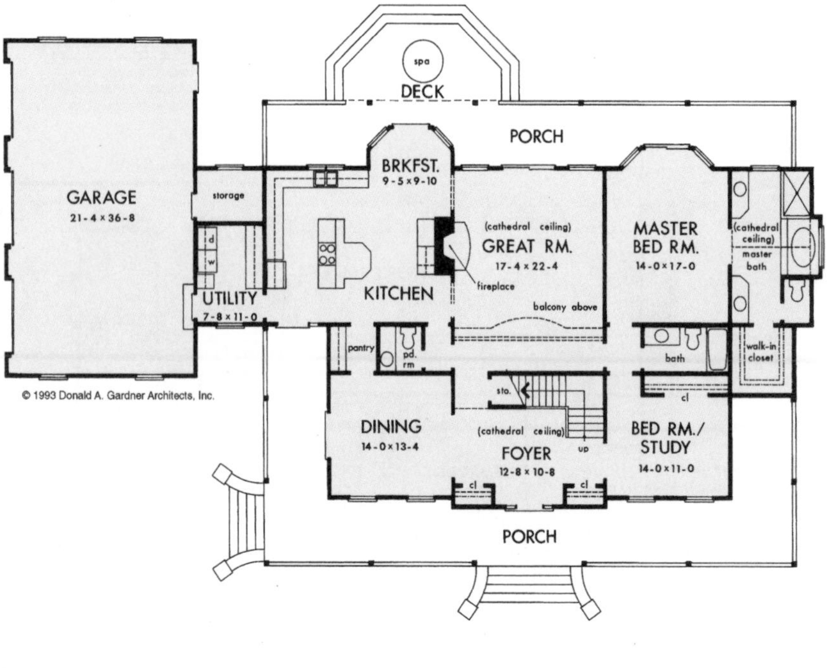

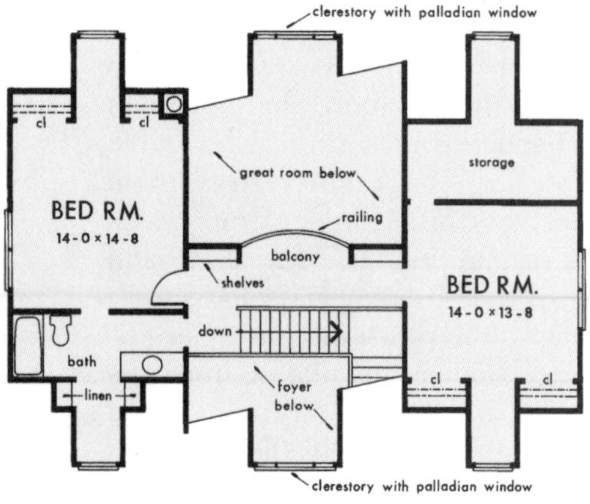

Design
HPT830371

First Floor: 1,766 square feet
Second Floor: 670 square feet
Total: 2,436 square feet
Width 59'-10" Depth 53'-4"

This farmhouse celebrates sunlight with a Palladian window dormer, a skylit screened porch and a rear arched window. The clerestory window in the foyer throws natural light across the loft to a great room with a fireplace and a cathedral ceiling. The central island kitchen and the breakfast area are open to the great room. The master suite is a calm retreat and opens to the screened porch through a bay area. Upstairs, a loft overlooking the great room connects two family bedrooms, each with a private bath.

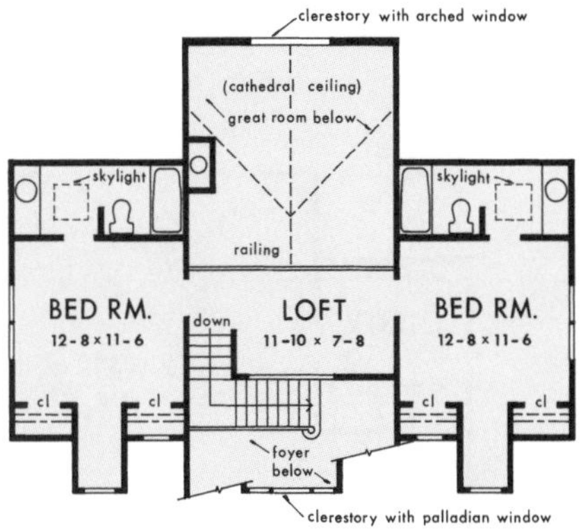
clerestory with arched window
(cathedral ceiling)
great room below
skylight
skylight
railing
BED RM.
12-8 x 11-6
LOFT
11-10 x 7-8
BED RM.
12-8 x 11-6
down
cl
cl
cl
cl
foyer below
clerestory with palladian window

QUOTE ONE®
Cost to build? See page 516 to order complete cost estimate to build this house in your area!

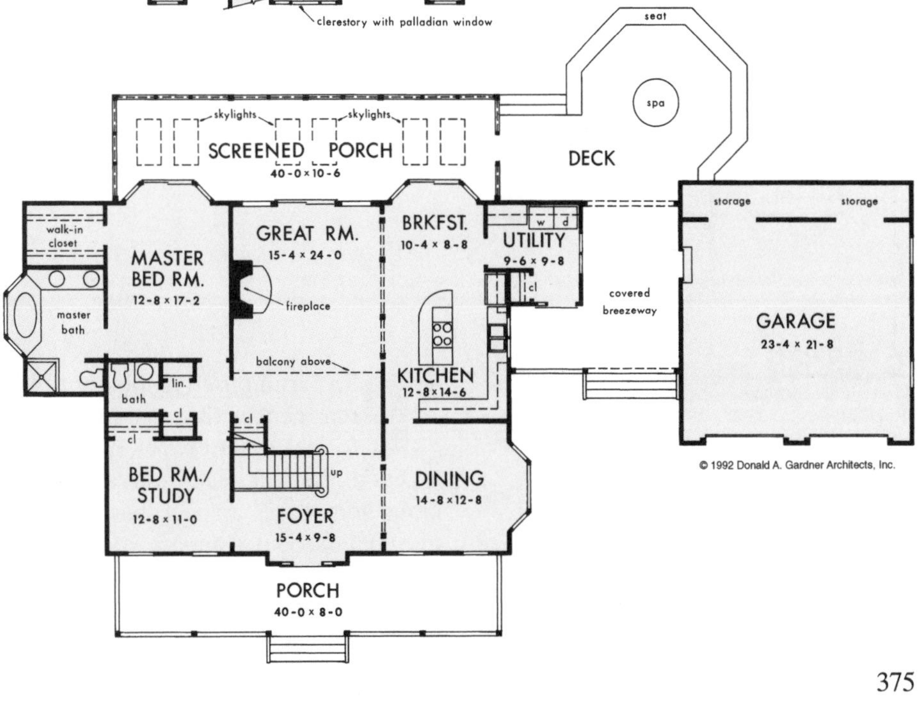
seat
spa
skylights
skylights
SCREENED PORCH
40-0 x 10-6
DECK
walk-in closet
MASTER BED RM.
12-8 x 17-2
master bath
GREAT RM.
15-4 x 24-0
fireplace
balcony above
BRKFST.
10-4 x 8-8
UTILITY
9-6 x 9-8
w d
cl
covered breezeway
storage
storage
GARAGE
23-4 x 21-8
KITCHEN
12-8 x 14-6
bath
lin.
cl
cl
cl
up
BED RM./ STUDY
12-8 x 11-0
FOYER
15-4 x 9-8
DINING
14-8 x 12-8
PORCH
40-0 x 8-0
© 1992 Donald A. Gardner Architects, Inc.

B. NATHAN
© 1995 Donald A. Gardner Architects, Inc.

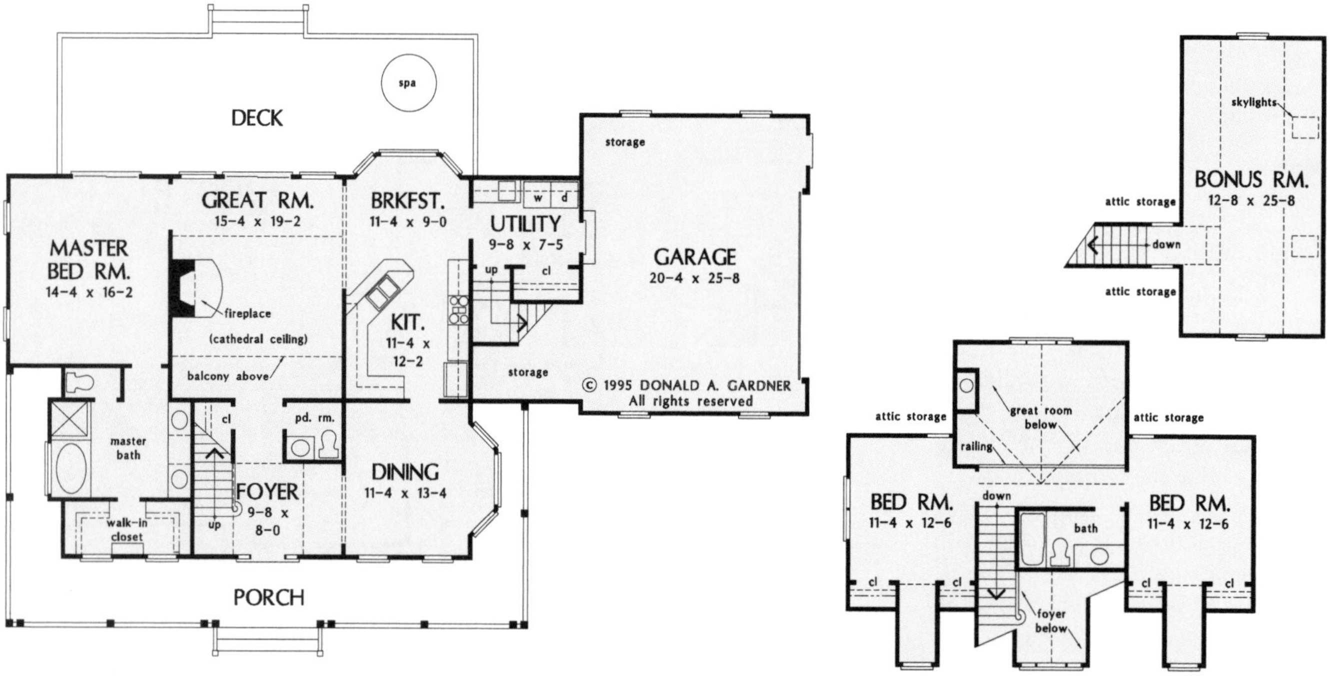
DECK
spa
GREAT RM.
15-4 x 19-2
BRKFST.
11-4 x 9-0
UTILITY
9-8 x 7-5
w
d
storage
GARAGE
20-4 x 25-8
MASTER
BED RM.
14-4 x 16-2
fireplace
(cathedral ceiling)
balcony above
KIT.
11-4 x
12-2
up
cl
storage
© 1995 DONALD A. GARDNER
All rights reserved
master
bath
cl
pd. rm.
FOYER
9-8 x
8-0
up
DINING
11-4 x 13-4
walk-in
closet
PORCH
skylights
BONUS RM.
12-8 x 25-8
attic storage
down
attic storage
attic storage
great room
below
railing
attic storage
BED RM.
11-4 x 12-6
down
bath
BED RM.
11-4 x 12-6
cl
cl
cl
cl
foyer
below

Design HPT830372

First Floor: 1,480 square feet
Second Floor: 511 square feet
Total: 1,991 square feet
Bonus Space: 363 square feet
Width 73'-0" Depth 51'-10"

This farmhouse has plenty to offer, from its covered front porch to its rear deck with a spa. Inside, the amenities continue, including a bayed formal dining room, a great room—with both a fireplace and direct access to the rear deck—and a bayed breakfast nook. A nearby kitchen is spacious and shares a snack bar with the breakfast/great room area. A deluxe master bedroom pampers you with access to the rear deck and a luxurious bath made up of a whirlpool tub, a separate shower, twin vanities and a walk-in closet. Upstairs, away from the master bedroom for privacy, two family bedrooms share a full hall bath and a balcony overlooking the great room.

Design HPT830373

First Floor: 1,871 square feet
Second Floor: 731 square feet
Total: 2,602 square feet
Bonus Space: 402 square feet
Width 77'-6" Depth 70'-0"

This fetching four-bedroom country home has porches and dormers at both front and rear to offer a welcoming touch. The spacious great room enjoys a large fireplace, a cathedral ceiling and an arched clerestory window. An efficient kitchen is centrally located in order to provide service to the dining room and bayed breakfast area and includes a cooktop island. The expansive master suite is located on the first floor with a generous walk-in closet and a luxurious private bath. A front bedroom would make a lovely study or guest room. The second level is highlighted by a balcony hall that leads to two family bedrooms sharing a full bath.

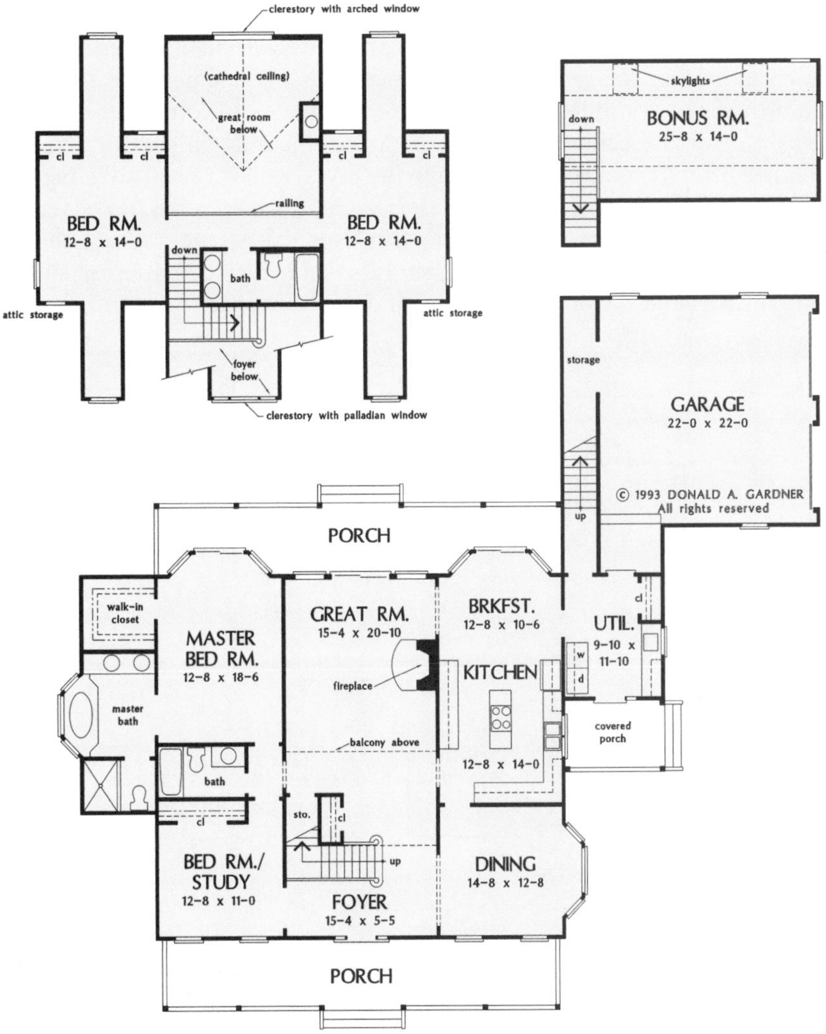

Country living is at its best in this spacious four-bedroom farmhouse with a wraparound porch. A front Palladian window dormer and rear clerestory windows in the great room add exciting visual elements to the exterior, while providing natural light to the interior. In the great room, a fireplace, bookshelves, a cathedral ceiling and a balcony overlook create a comfortable atmosphere. The formal dining room is open to the foyer, while the versatile living room could be used as a study. Special features such as a large cooktop island in the kitchen, a wet bar, a generous bonus room over the garage and ample storage space set this plan apart from others. You'll also love the fact that the master suite, the great room and the breakfast room all directly access the rear porch.

Design HPT830374

First Floor: 2,176 square feet
Second Floor: 861 square feet
Total: 3,037 square feet
Bonus Space: 483 square feet
Width 94'-0" Depth 58'-4"

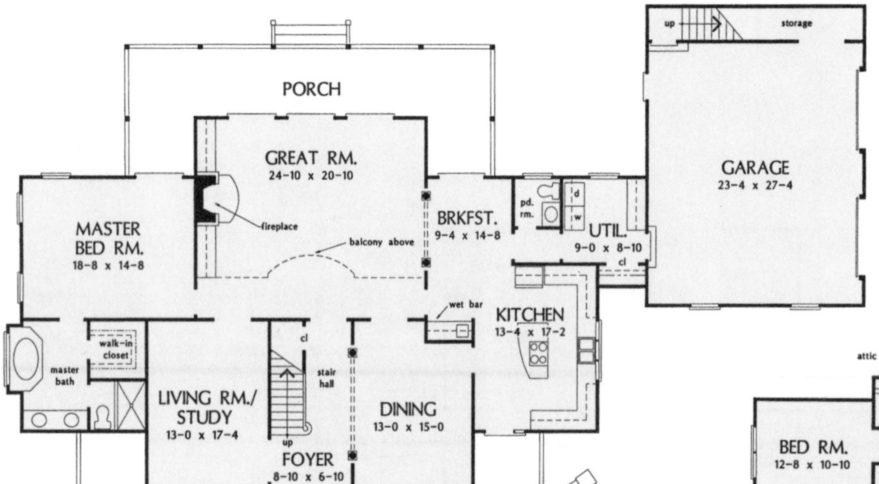

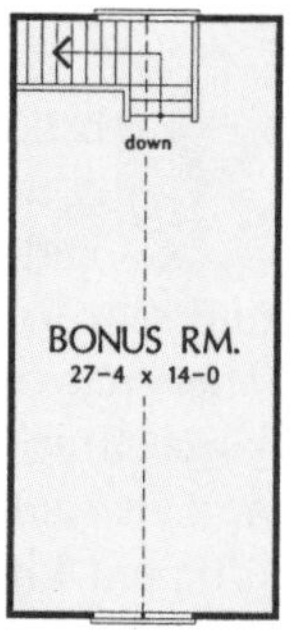

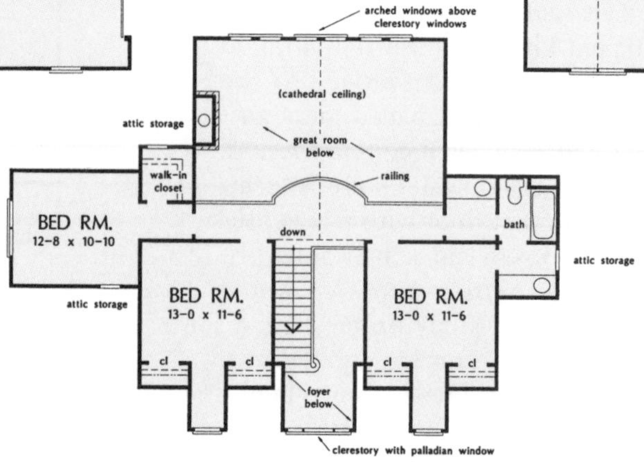

Design
HPT830375

First Floor: 1,576 square feet
Second Floor: 947 square feet
Total: 2,523 square feet
Bonus Space: 405 square feet
Width 71'-4" Depth 66'-0"

Enjoy balmy breezes as you relax on the wraparound porch of this delightful country farmhouse. The foyer introduces a dining room to the right and a bedroom or study to the left. The expansive great room—with its cozy fireplace—has direct access to the rear porch. Columns define the kitchen, with its large island cooktop, and a sunny breakfast area. A built-in pantry and a desk are popular features here. A powder room and a utility room are located nearby. The master bedroom features a tray ceiling and a luxurious bath. Two additional bedrooms share a skylit bath.

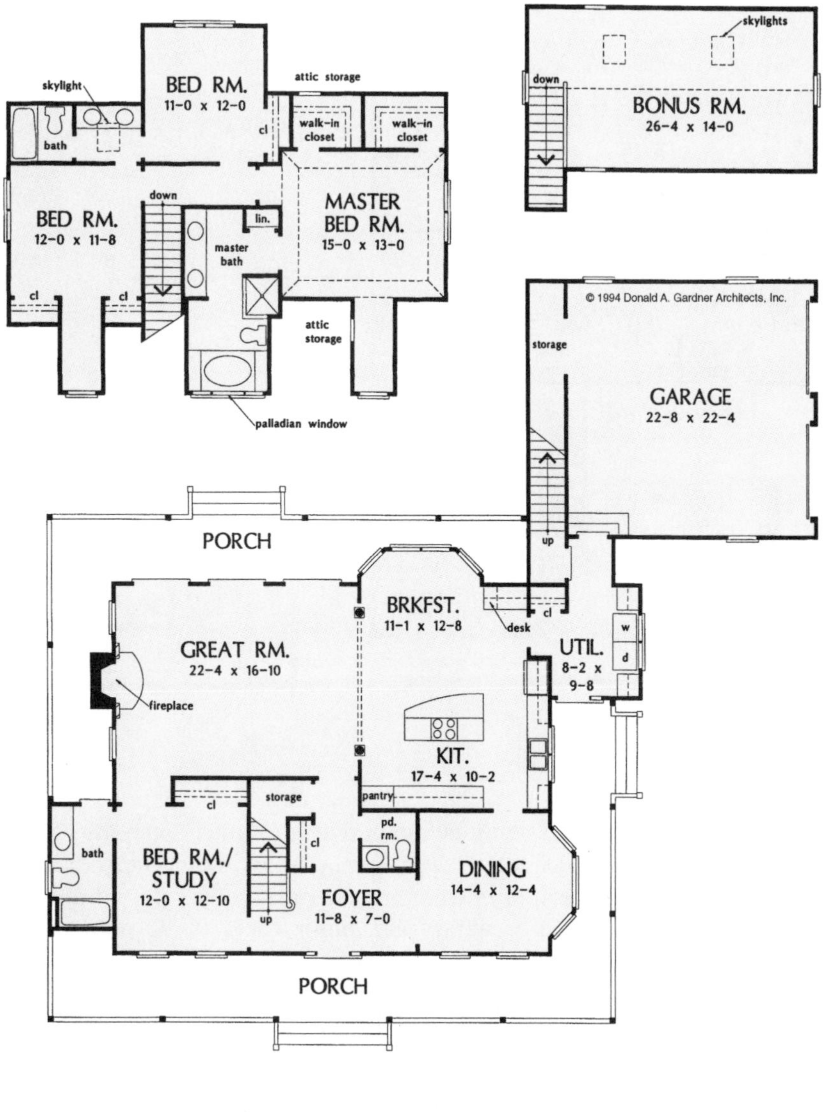

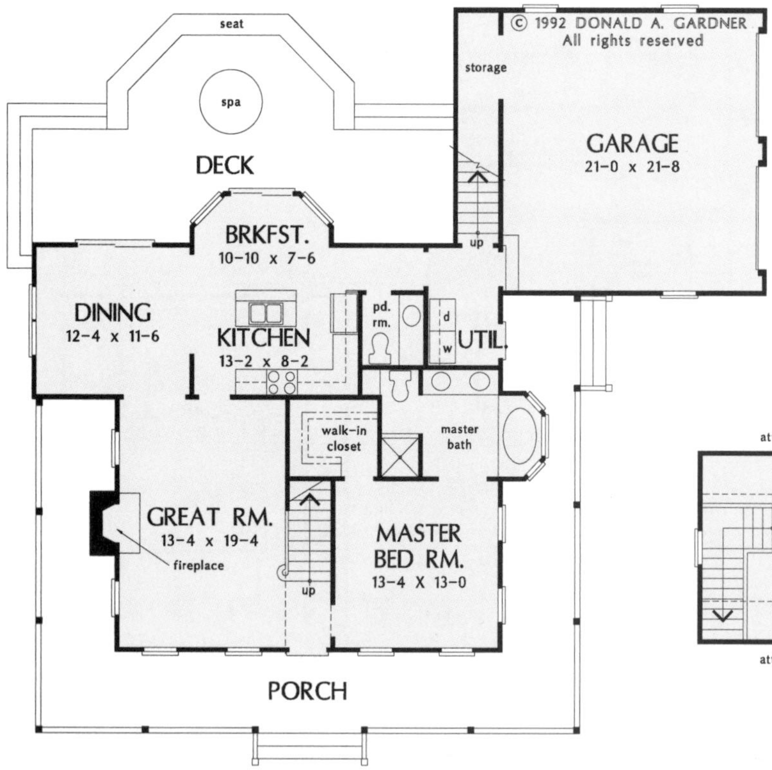
© 1992 DONALD A. GARDNER
All rights reserved
seat
spa
DECK
storage
GARAGE
21-0 x 21-8
BRKFST.
10-10 x 7-6
up
DINING
12-4 x 11-6
KITCHEN
13-2 x 8-2
pd. rm.
d
w
UTIL.
walk-in closet
master bath
GREAT RM.
13-4 x 19-4
fireplace
MASTER
BED RM.
13-4 X 13-0
up
PORCH

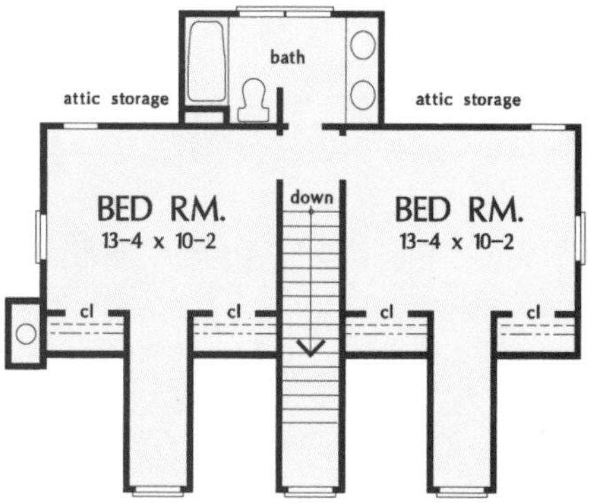
bath
attic storage
attic storage
BED RM.
13-4 x 10-2
down
BED RM.
13-4 x 10-2
cl
cl
cl
cl

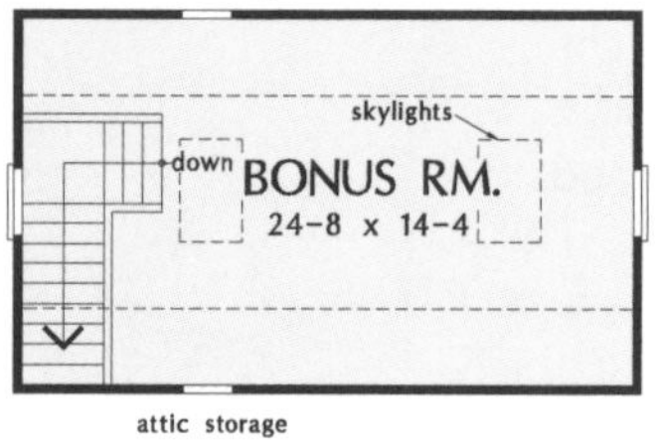
attic storage
skylights
down
BONUS RM.
24-8 x 14-4
attic storage

QUOTE ONE®

Cost to build? See page 516 to order complete cost estimate to build this house in your area!

Look this plan over and you'll be amazed at how much livability can be found in less than 2,000 square feet. A wraparound porch welcomes visitors to the home. Inside lies an enormous great room with a fireplace. To the rear of the home, the breakfast and dining rooms have sliding glass doors to a large deck with room for a spa. The master bedroom contains a walk-in closet and an airy bath with a whirlpool tub. Two bedrooms and a full bath are found on the second floor, as well as a bonus room over the garage.

Design HPT830376

First Floor: 1,145 square feet
Second Floor: 518 square feet
Total: 1,663 square feet
Bonus Space: 380 square feet
Width 59'-4" Depth 56'-6"

Design HPT830377

First Floor: 1,537 square feet	
Second Floor: 641 square feet	
Total: 2,178 square feet	
Bonus Space: 418 square feet	
Width 65'-8" Depth 70'-0"	

This charming farmhouse begins with a two-story entrance foyer with a Palladian window in a clerestory dormer above for natural light. The L-shaped kitchen with its central island serves both the bright bay-windowed breakfast nook and the spacious dining room. Family can gather in the aptly named great room, drawn to the warming hearth fireplace. The master suite, with its large walk-in closet, is on the first level for privacy and accessibility. The master bath includes a whirlpool tub, a shower and a double-bowl vanity. The second level has two bedrooms, a full bath and plenty of storage.

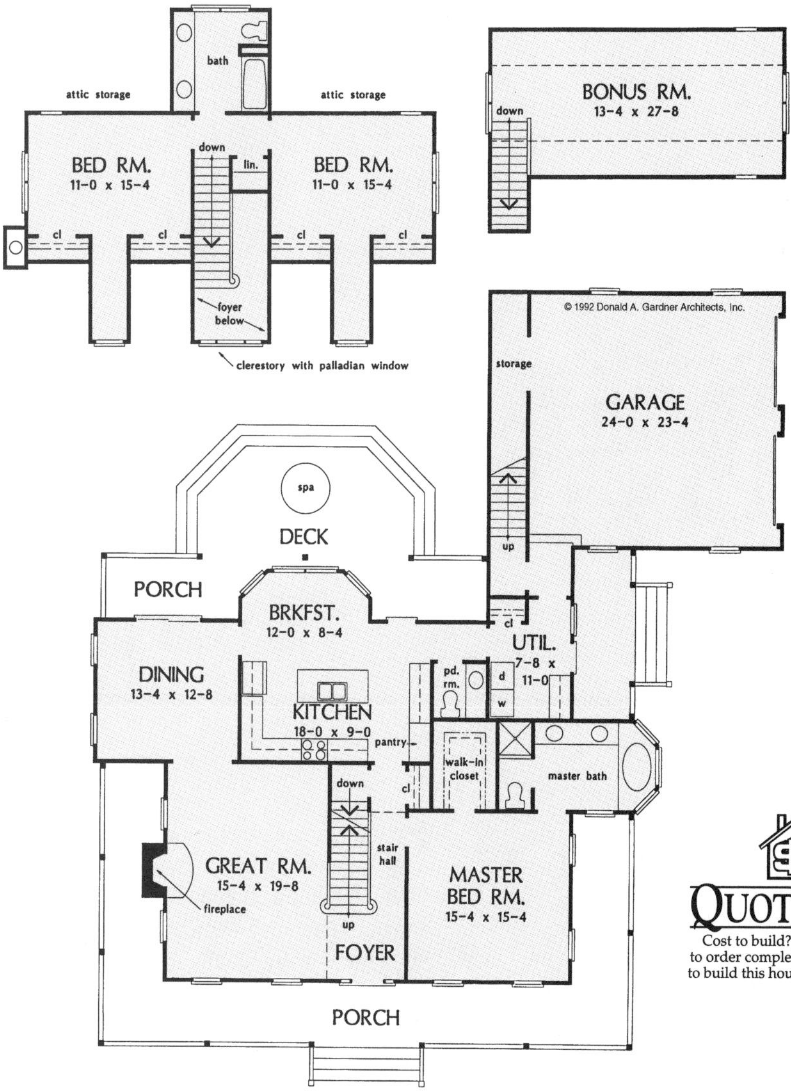

QUOTE ONE®

Cost to build? See page 516 to order complete cost estimate to build this house in your area!

© 1992 Donald A. Gardner Architects, Inc.

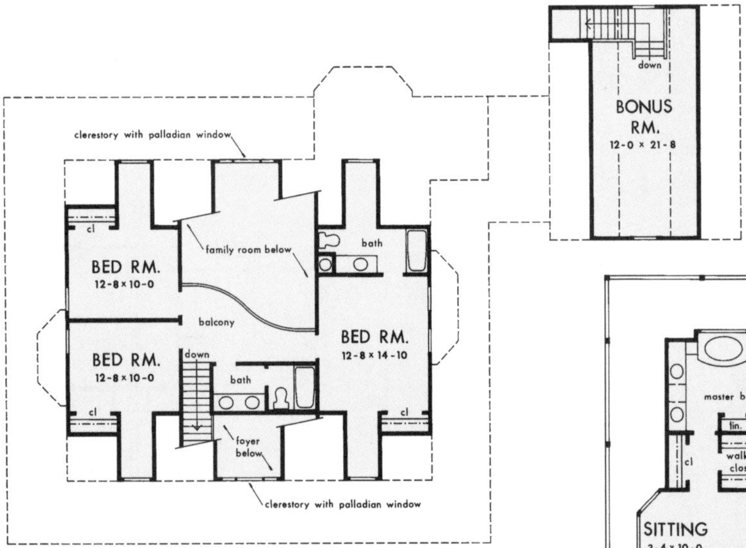

BONUS RM.
12-0 × 21-8
down
clerestory with palladian window
cl
BED RM.
12-8 × 10-0
family room below
bath
balcony
BED RM.
12-8 × 14-10
BED RM.
12-8 × 10-0
down
bath
cl
cl
foyer below
clerestory with palladian window

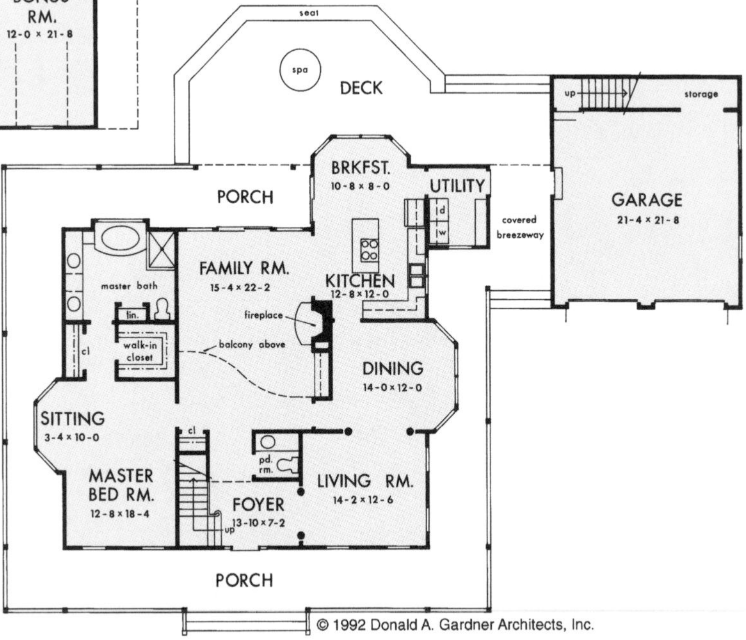

seat
spa
DECK
up
storage
BRKFST.
10-8 × 8-0
UTILITY
PORCH
GARAGE
21-4 × 21-8
covered breezeway
master bath
FAMILY RM.
15-4 × 22-2
KITCHEN
12-8 × 12-0
lin.
fireplace
walk-in closet
cl
balcony above
DINING
14-0 × 12-0
SITTING
3-4 × 10-0
cl
pd. rm.
MASTER BED RM.
12-8 × 18-4
LIVING RM.
14-2 × 12-6
FOYER
13-10 × 7-2
up
PORCH

© 1992 Donald A. Gardner Architects, Inc.

Design HPT830378

First Floor: 1,759 square feet
Second Floor: 888 square feet
Total: 2,647 square feet
Bonus Space: 324 square feet
Width 85'-0" Depth 67'-4"

This four-bedroom country farmhouse invites enjoyment of the outdoors with a true wraparound porch and a spacious deck and spa. Front and rear Palladian window dormers allow natural light to brighten the foyer and family room and lend sparkling accents to the country-style exterior. A gracefully curved balcony overlooks the two-story great room, warmed by a fireplace with an extended hearth. The master suite includes a large walk-in closet, a special sitting area and a master bath with whirlpool tub, separate shower and twin vanities.

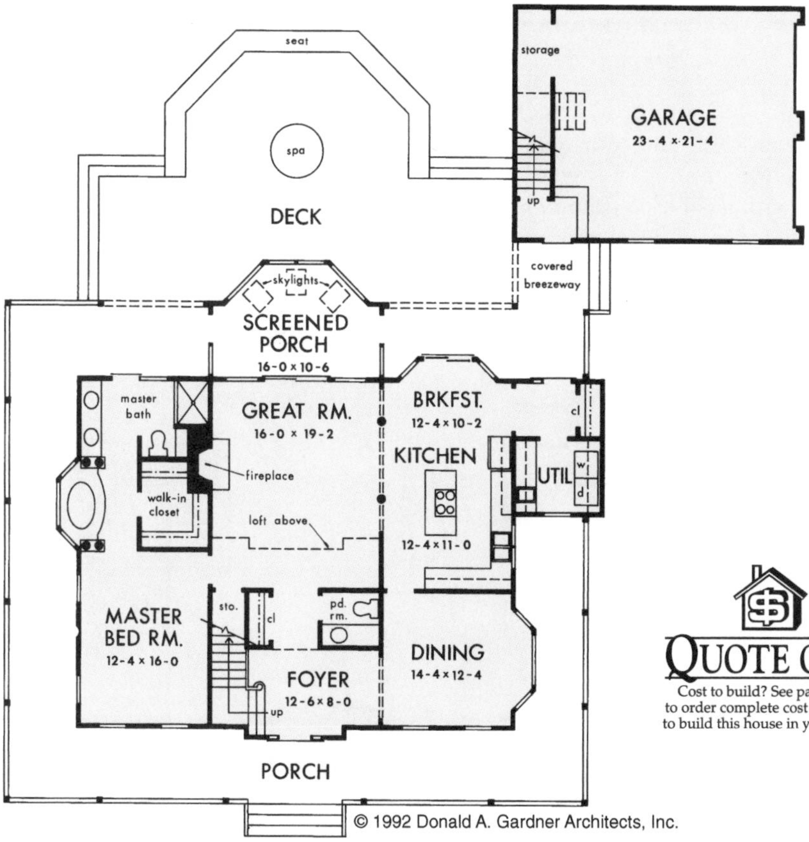

seat
spa
DECK
skylights
SCREENED PORCH
16-0 × 10-6
storage
GARAGE
23-4 × 21-4
up
covered breezeway
master bath
GREAT RM.
16-0 × 19-2
fireplace
walk-in closet
loft above
BRKFST.
12-4 × 10-2
cl
KITCHEN
12-4 × 11-0
UTIL
w
d
MASTER BED RM.
12-4 × 16-0
sto.
cl
pd. rm.
FOYER
12-6 × 8-0
up
DINING
14-4 × 12-4
PORCH

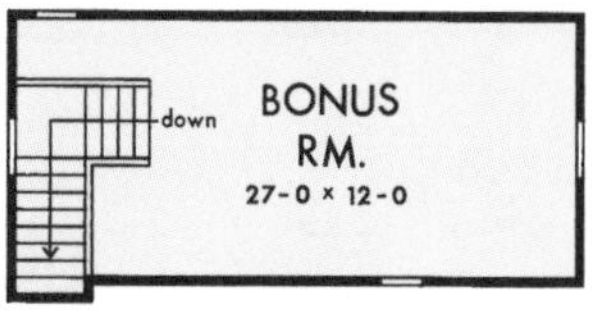

down
BONUS RM.
27-0 × 12-0

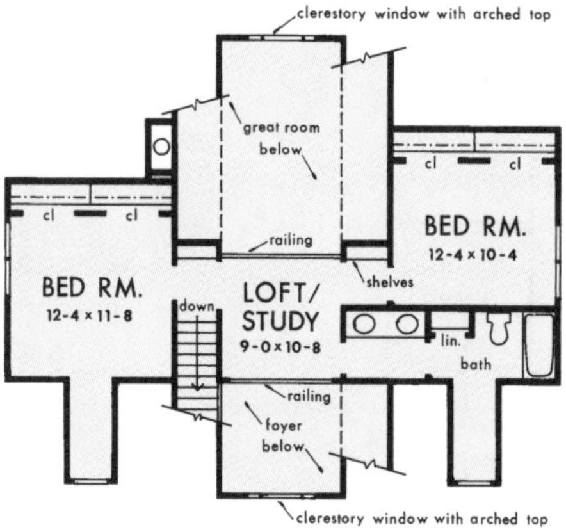

clerestory window with arched top
great room below
cl
cl
cl
cl
BED RM.
12-4 × 11-8
railing
shelves
BED RM.
12-4 × 10-4
down
LOFT/ STUDY
9-0 × 10-8
lin.
bath
railing
foyer below
clerestory window with arched top

QUOTE ONE®

Cost to build? See page 516 to order complete cost estimate to build this house in your area!

Clerestory windows with arched tops enhance the exterior both front and back, as well as allowing natural light to penetrate into the foyer and the great room. A kitchen with an island counter and a breakfast area is open to the great room. The master suite includes a walk-in closet and a lush master bath. The second level contains two bedrooms sharing a full bath and a loft/study area overlooking the great room.

Design HPT830379
First Floor: 1,526 square feet
Second Floor: 635 square feet
Total: 2,161 square feet
Bonus Space: 355 square feet
Width 76'-4" Depth 74'-2"

© 1993 Donald A. Gardner Architects, Inc.

This complete farmhouse projects an exciting and comfortable feeling with its wraparound porch, arched windows and dormers. A Palladian window in the clerestory above the entrance foyer allows an abundance of natural light. The large kitchen with a cooking island easily services the breakfast area and dining room. The generous great room with a fireplace offers access to the spacious screened porch for carefree outdoor living. The master bedroom suite, located on the first level for privacy and convenience, has a luxurious master bath. The second level allows for three bedrooms and a full bath. Don't miss the garage with a bonus room—both meet the main house via a covered breezeway.

Design HPT830380

First Floor: 1,585 square feet
Second Floor: 731 square feet
Total: 2,316 square feet
Bonus Space: 419 square feet
Width 80'-4" Depth 58'-0"

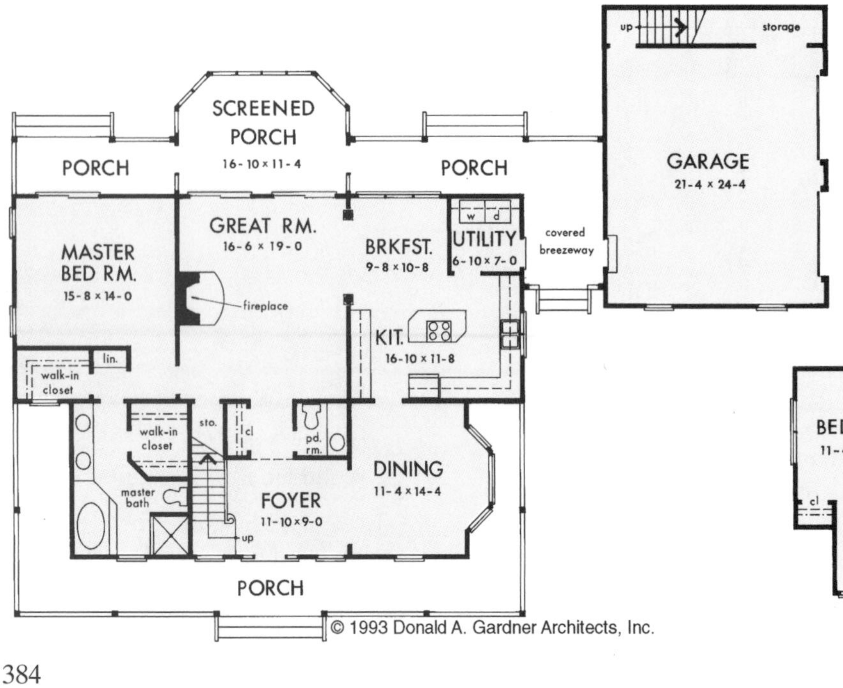

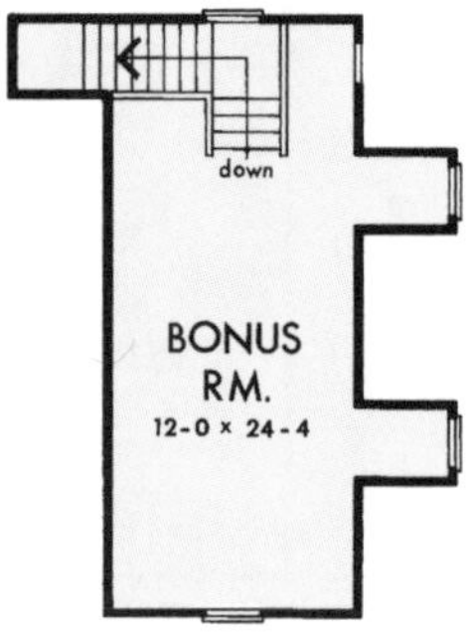

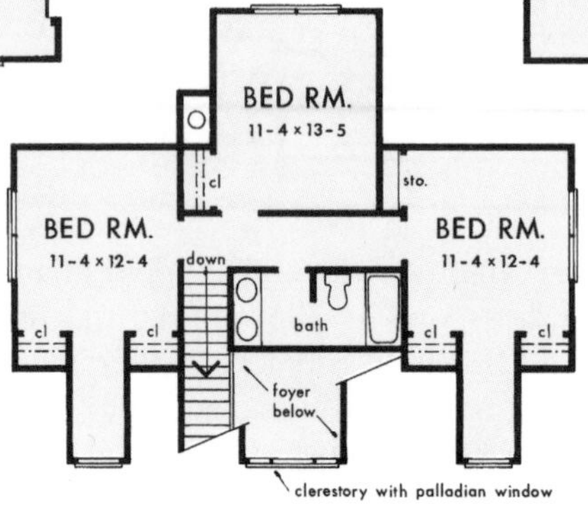

B. NATHAN
©1993 Donald A. Gardner Architects, Inc.

Design HPT830381

First Floor: 1,618 square feet
Second Floor: 570 square feet
Total: 2,188 square feet
Bonus Space: 495 square feet
Width 87'-0" Depth 57'-0"

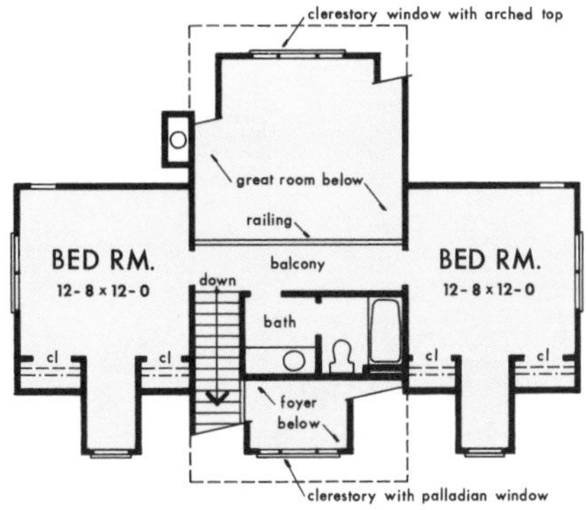
clerestory window with arched top
great room below
railing
balcony
BED RM.
12-8 x 12-0
BED RM.
12-8 x 12-0
down
bath
cl
cl
cl
cl
foyer below
clerestory with palladian window

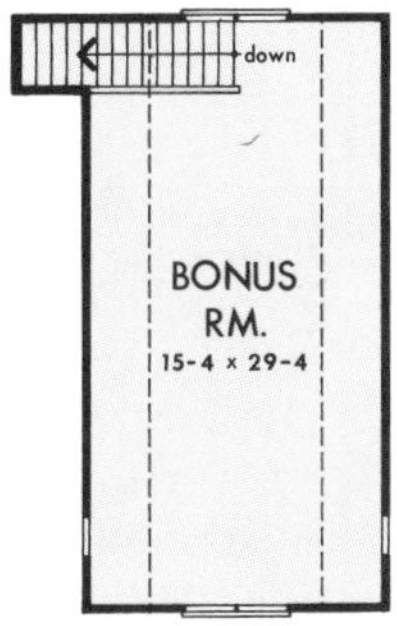
down
BONUS RM.
15-4 x 29-4

The entrance foyer and the great room enjoy Palladian clerestory windows that allow natural light to enter the well-planned interior of this country home. The spacious great room boasts a fireplace, built-in cabinets and an overlook from the second-floor balcony. The kitchen has a cooktop island counter and is placed conveniently between the breakfast room and the formal dining room. A generous first-floor master suite offers plenty of closet space and a lavish bath with a windowed whirlpool tub. Upstairs, two family bedrooms share a full bath. Bonus space over the garage awaits later development.

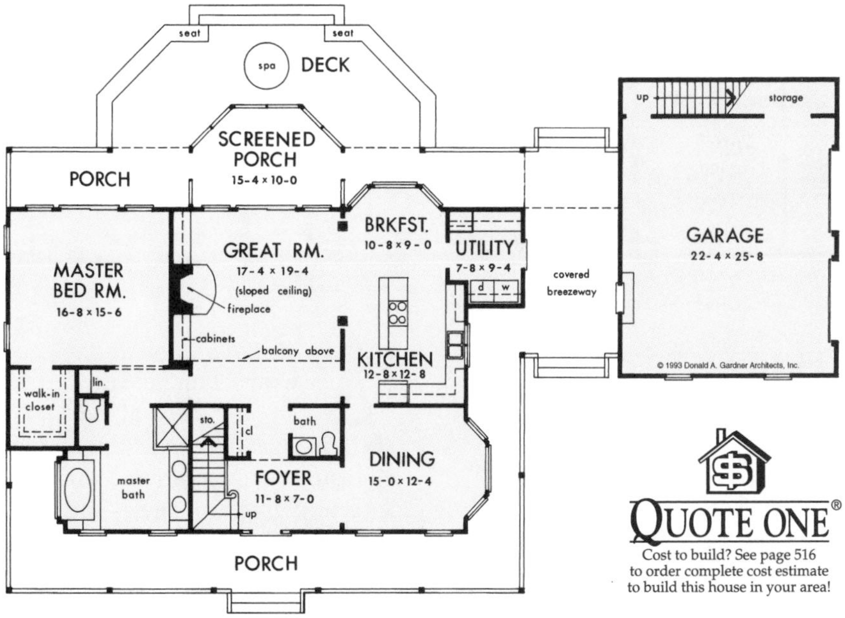
seat
seat
spa
DECK
SCREENED PORCH
15-4 x 10-0
PORCH
MASTER BED RM.
16-8 x 15-6
GREAT RM.
17-4 x 19-4
(sloped ceiling)
fireplace
cabinets
balcony above
BRKFST.
10-8 x 9-0
UTILITY
7-8 x 9-4
d
w
KITCHEN
12-8 x 12-8
covered breezeway
up
storage
GARAGE
22-4 x 25-8
© 1993 Donald A. Gardner Architects, Inc.
walk-in closet
lin.
sto.
cl
bath
master bath
FOYER
11-8 x 7-0
up
DINING
15-0 x 12-4
PORCH

QUOTE ONE®
Cost to build? See page 516 to order complete cost estimate to build this house in your area!

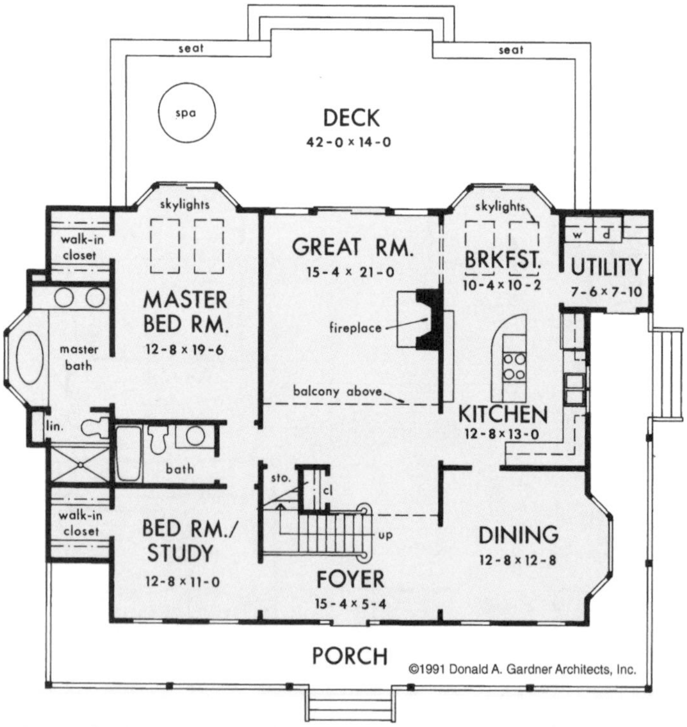
seat
seat
spa
DECK
42-0 x 14-0
skylights
skylights
walk-in closet
GREAT RM.
15-4 x 21-0
BRKFST.
10-4 x 10-2
w d
UTILITY
7-6 x 7-10
MASTER BED RM.
12-8 x 19-6
fireplace
master bath
balcony above
KITCHEN
12-8 x 13-0
lin.
bath
sto.
cl
walk-in closet
BED RM./ STUDY
12-8 x 11-0
up
DINING
12-8 x 12-8
FOYER
15-4 x 5-4
PORCH
©1991 Donald A. Gardner Architects, Inc.

QUOTE ONE®

Cost to build? See page 516 to order complete cost estimate to build this house in your area!

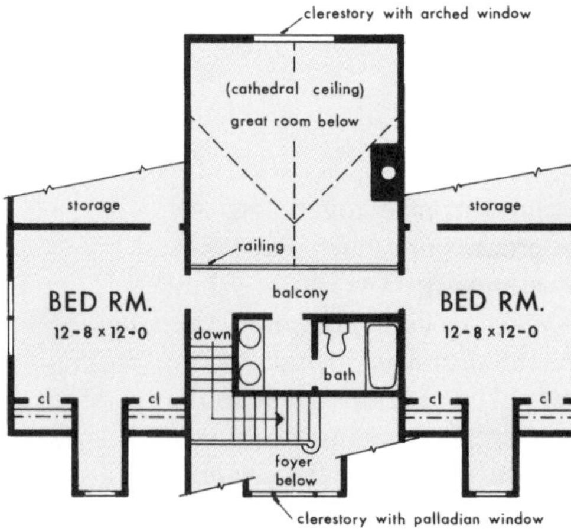
clerestory with arched window
(cathedral ceiling)
great room below
storage
storage
railing
balcony
BED RM.
12-8 x 12-0
BED RM.
12-8 x 12-0
down
bath
cl
cl
cl
cl
foyer below
clerestory with palladian window

Design HPT830382

First Floor: 1,756 square feet

Second Floor: 565 square feet

Total: 2,321 square feet

Width 56'-8" Depth 54'-4"

A wraparound covered porch at the front and sides of this house and an open deck at the back provide plenty of outside living area. The spacious great room features a fireplace, cathedral ceiling and clerestory with an arched window. The kitchen includes a cooktop island—sure to please any chef—and opens to the skylit breakfast nook.The first-floor master bedroom contains a generous closet and a bath with a garden tub, double-bowl vanity and shower. The second floor sports two bedrooms and a full bath with a double-bowl vanity.

Design HPT830383

First Floor: 1,356 square feet
Second Floor: 542 square feet
Total: 1,898 square feet
Bonus Space: 393 square feet
Width 59'-0" Depth 64'-0"

The welcoming charm of this farmhouse is expressed by its many windows and its covered, wraparound porch. A two-story entrance foyer is enhanced by a Palladian window in a clerestory dormer above to allow natural lighting. A first-floor master suite allows privacy and accessibility. The master bath includes a whirlpool tub, separate shower and double-bowl vanity, along with a walk-in closet. The second floor provides two additional bedrooms, a full bath and plenty of storage space.

QUOTE ONE®

Cost to build? See page 516 to order complete cost estimate to build this house in your area!

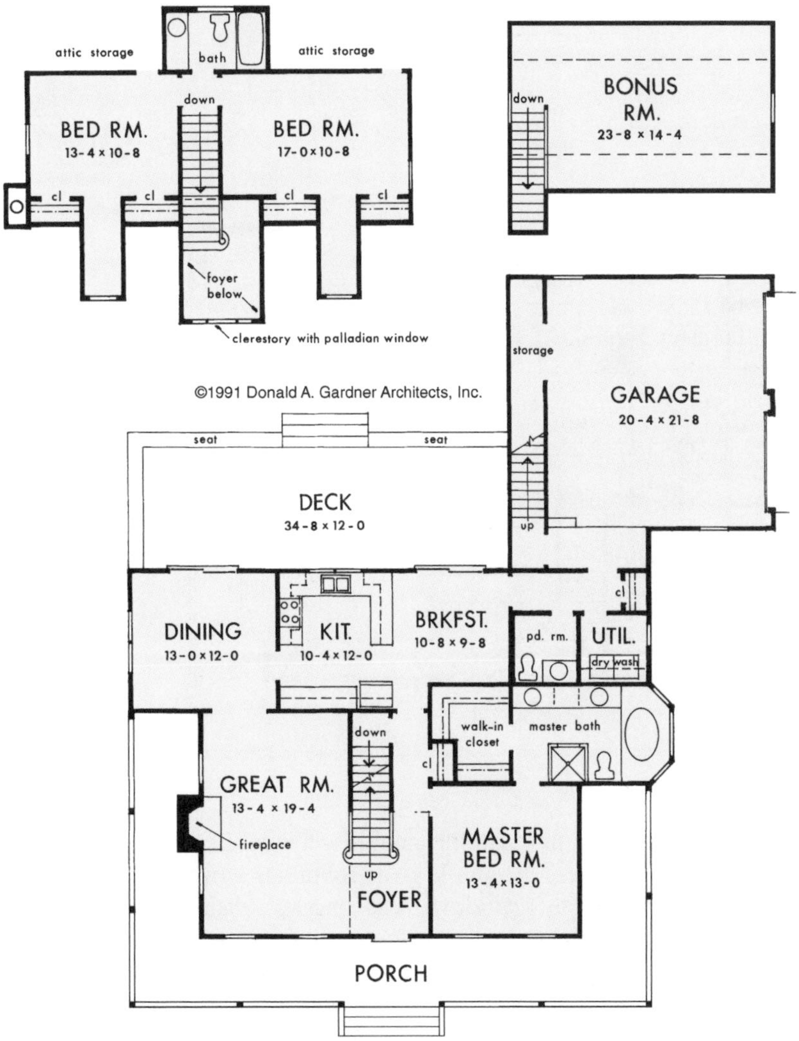
attic storage
bath
attic storage
down
BED RM.
13-4 x 10-8
BED RM.
17-0 x 10-8
cl
cl
cl
cl
foyer below
clerestory with palladian window
down
BONUS RM.
23-8 x 14-4
storage
©1991 Donald A. Gardner Architects, Inc.
GARAGE
20-4 x 21-8
seat
seat
DECK
34-8 x 12-0
up
cl
DINING
13-0 x 12-0
KIT.
10-4 x 12-0
BRKFST.
10-8 x 9-8
pd. rm.
UTIL.
dry wash
walk-in closet
master bath
down
cl
GREAT RM.
13-4 x 19-4
fireplace
up
FOYER
MASTER BED RM.
13-4 x 13-0
PORCH

© 1991 Donald A. Gardner Architects, Inc.
B. NATHAN.

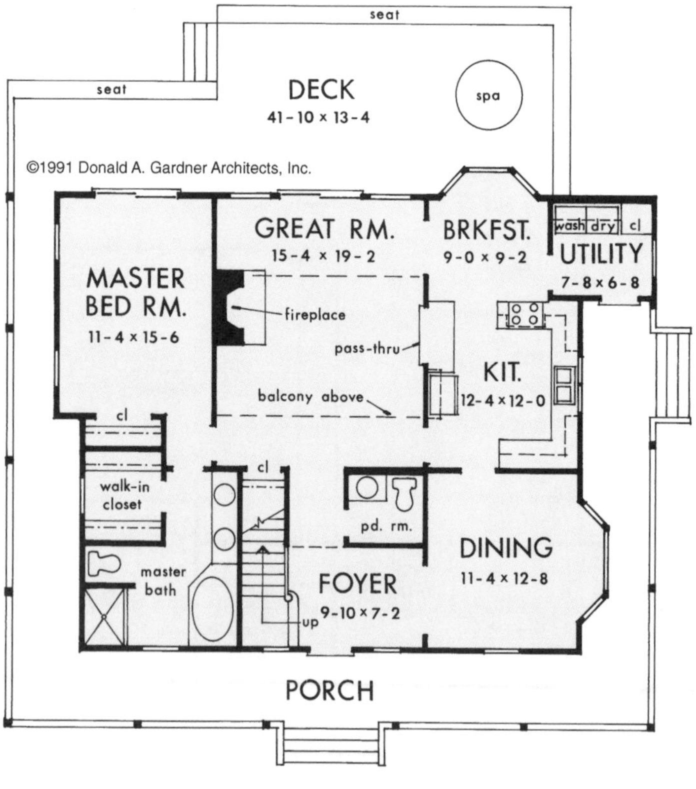
seat
seat
DECK
41-10 × 13-4
spa
©1991 Donald A. Gardner Architects, Inc.
MASTER BED RM.
11-4 × 15-6
GREAT RM.
15-4 × 19-2
BRKFST.
9-0 × 9-2
wash
dry
cl
UTILITY
7-8 × 6-8
fireplace
pass-thru
KIT.
12-4 × 12-0
balcony above
cl
walk-in closet
cl
pd. rm.
master bath
DINING
11-4 × 12-8
FOYER
9-10 × 7-2
up
PORCH

QUOTE ONE®

Cost to build? See page 516 to order complete cost estimate to build this house in your area!

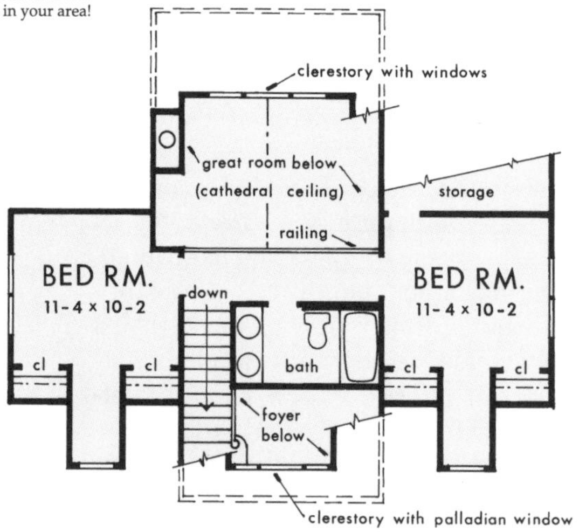
clerestory with windows
great room below
(cathedral ceiling)
railing
storage
BED RM.
11-4 × 10-2
down
BED RM.
11-4 × 10-2
cl
cl
bath
cl
cl
foyer below
clerestory with palladian window

Design HPT830384

First Floor: 1,325 square feet
Second Floor: 453 square feet
Total: 1,778 square feet
Width 48'-4" Depth 51'-10"

This compact design has all the amenities available in larger plans with little wasted space. The ample great room has a fireplace, a cathedral ceiling and clerestory windows. A second-level balcony overlooks this gathering area. The generous master suite pampers with a separate tub and shower and a walk-in closet. Two family bedrooms located on the second level share a full bath that includes a double vanity.

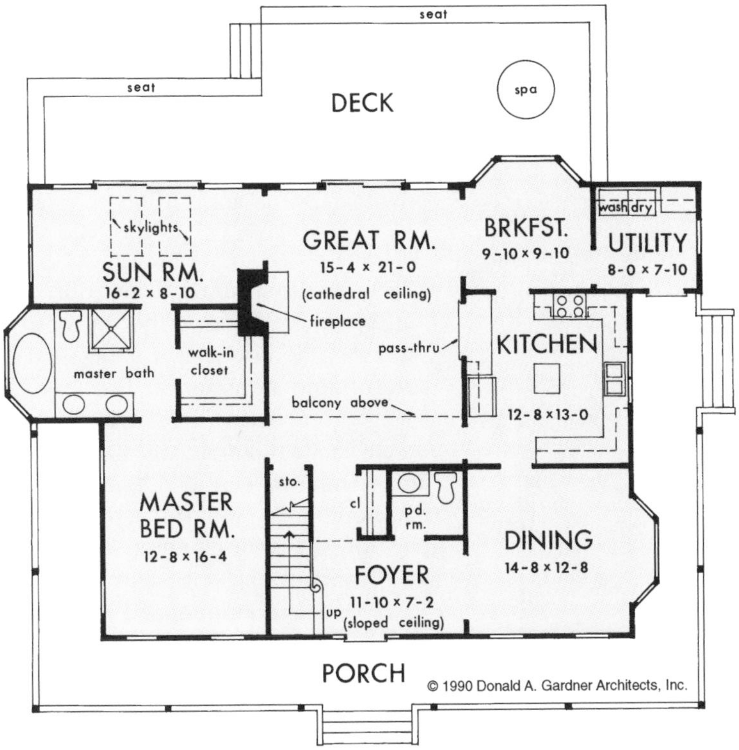
seat
seat
DECK
spa
skylights
SUN RM.
16-2 × 8-10
GREAT RM.
15-4 × 21-0
(cathedral ceiling)
fireplace
BRKFST.
9-10 × 9-10
wash dry
UTILITY
8-0 × 7-10
KITCHEN
12-8 × 13-0
pass-thru
master bath
walk-in closet
balcony above
MASTER BED RM.
12-8 × 16-4
sto.
cl
pd. rm.
FOYER
11-10 × 7-2
(sloped ceiling)
up
DINING
14-8 × 12-8
PORCH
© 1990 Donald A. Gardner Architects, Inc.

QUOTE ONE®
Cost to build? See page 516 to order complete cost estimate to build this house in your area!

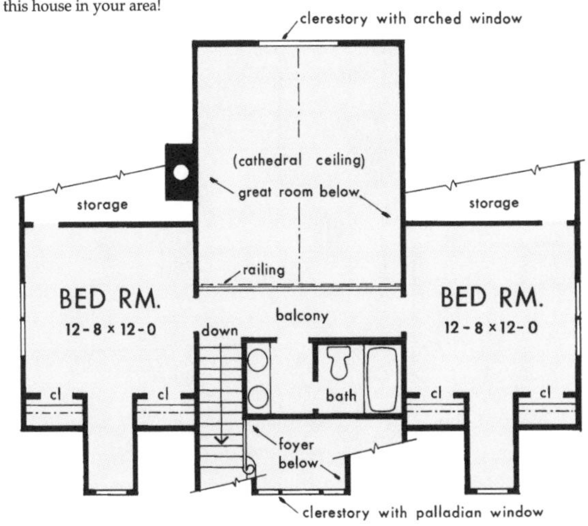
clerestory with arched window
(cathedral ceiling)
great room below
storage
storage
railing
BED RM.
12-8 × 12-0
BED RM.
12-8 × 12-0
balcony
down
cl
cl
bath
cl
cl
foyer below
clerestory with palladian window

A wraparound porch at the front and sides of this house and a deck with a built-in spa provide outside living area. The great room is appointed with a fireplace, cathedral ceiling and clerestory with an arched window. The kitchen is centrally located for maximum flexibility in layout and features a food-preparation island. Besides the first-floor master bedroom, which offers access to the sun room, there are two second-floor bedrooms that share a full bath.

Design HPT830385

First Floor: 1,651 square feet
Second Floor: 567 square feet
Total: 2,218 square feet
Width 55'-0" Depth 53'-10"

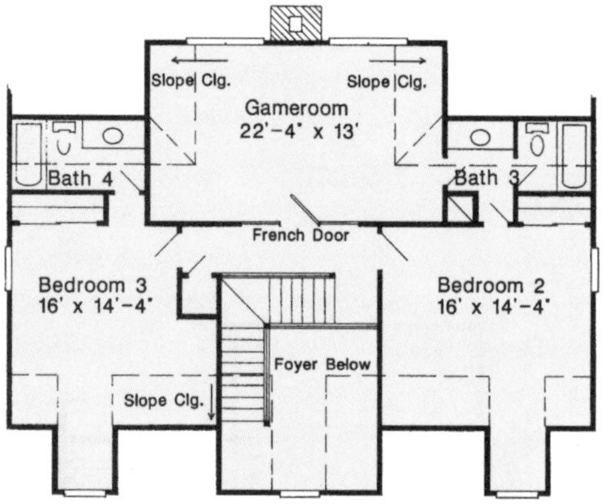

Slope Clg.
Slope Clg.
Gameroom
22'-4" x 13'
Bath 4
Bath 3
French Door
Bedroom 3
16' x 14'-4"
Bedroom 2
16' x 14'-4"
Foyer Below
Slope Clg.

QUOTE ONE®

Cost to build? See page 516 to order complete cost estimate to build this house in your area!

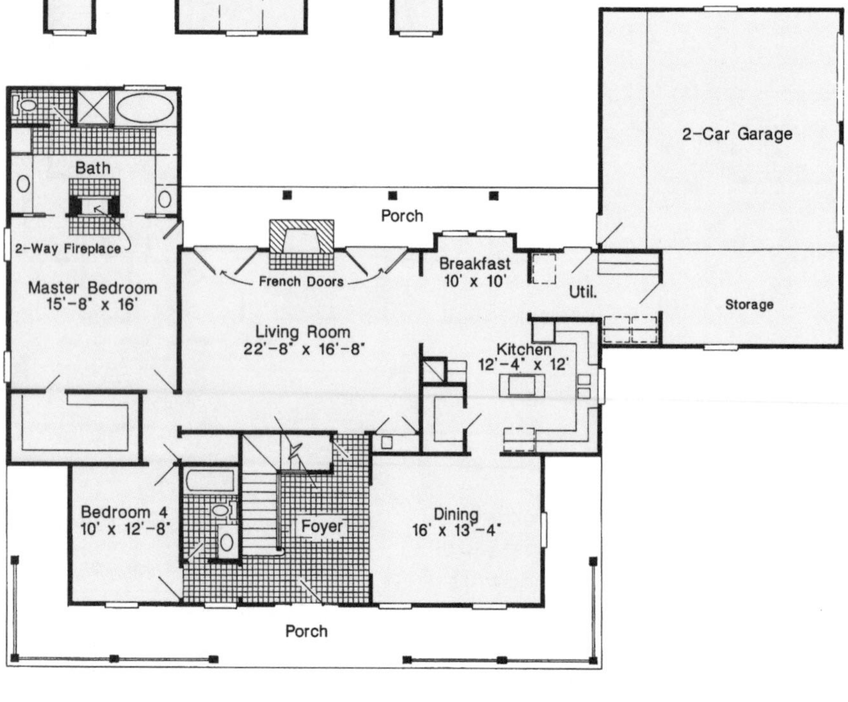

2-Car Garage
Bath
Porch
2-Way Fireplace
Breakfast
10' x 10'
French Doors
Util.
Master Bedroom
15'-8" x 16'
Storage
Living Room
22'-8" x 16'-8"
Kitchen
12'-4" x 12'
Bedroom 4
10' x 12'-8"
Foyer
Dining
16' x 13'-4"
Porch

Design HPT830386

First Floor: 1,995 square feet
Second Floor: 1,077 square feet
Total: 3,072 square feet
Width 79'-0" Depth 60'-6"

A wraparound front porch and dormer windows give this home a casual and comfortable appearance. The large living room features French doors on each side of an elegant fireplace, and a built-in wet bar. An island cooktop, and a walk-in pantry are part of the well-planned kitchen. The utility room, with extra work space, leads to an attached two-car garage and storage area. The master bedroom contains generous closet space and a two-way fireplace opening into the master bath. His and Hers lavatories, an oversized tub and a glass-enclosed shower complete this elegant master bath. The second-floor balcony opens to a large game room. Bedroom 3 has a private bath, while Bedroom 2 shares a bath with the game room.

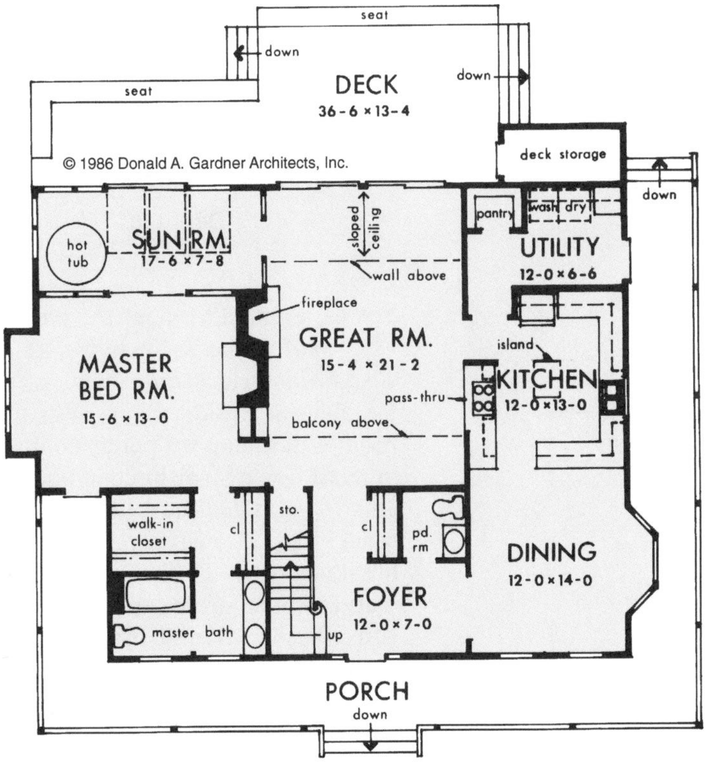
seat
down
DECK
36-6 × 13-4
down
seat
deck storage
© 1986 Donald A. Gardner Architects, Inc.
down
pantry
wash dry
hot tub
SUN RM.
17-6 × 7-8
sloped ceiling
wall above
UTILITY
12-0 × 6-6
fireplace
GREAT RM.
15-4 × 21-2
island
MASTER BED RM.
15-6 × 13-0
pass-thru
KITCHEN
12-0 × 13-0
balcony above
walk-in closet
cl
sto.
cl
pd. rm
DINING
12-0 × 14-0
FOYER
12-0 × 7-0
master bath
up
PORCH
down

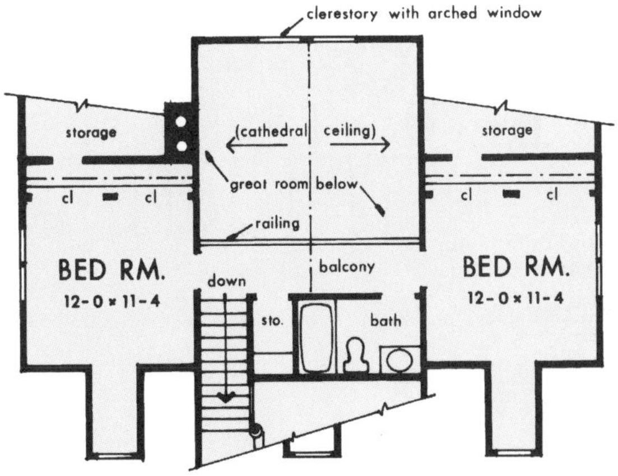
clerestory with arched window
storage
(cathedral ceiling)
storage
great room below
cl
cl
cl
cl
railing
BED RM.
12-0 × 11-4
down
balcony
BED RM.
12-0 × 11-4
sto.
bath

Outdoor living is encouraged in a wraparound covered porch at the front and sides of this house, as well as the open deck with storage to the rear. The country feel is updated with arched rear windows and a sun room. The spacious great room has a fireplace, cathedral ceiling and clerestory windows. The kitchen occupies a central location between the dining room and the great room for equally convenient formal and informal occasions. A generous master suite has a fireplace and access to the sun room and covered porch. The second level features two family bedrooms, a full bath and storage space.

Design
HPT830387

First Floor: 1,562 square feet
Second Floor: 537 square feet
Total: 2,099 square feet
Width 45'-0" Depth 44'-6"

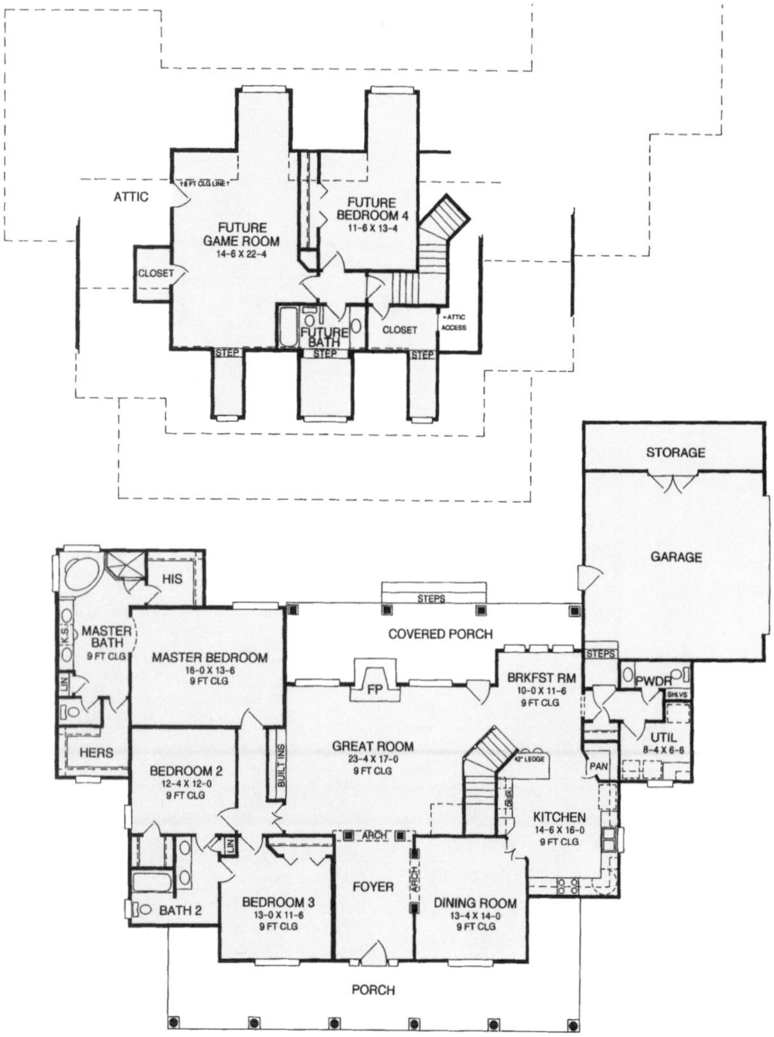

Design HPT830388

Square Footage: 2,465
Bonus Space: 788 square feet
Width 85'-8" Depth 70'-7"

Designed to meet the needs of today's lifestyles, this historical elevation is a familiar one. Inside, the large great room is designed with entertaining in mind. The nearby kitchen boasts all the latest features, including a snack bar, extensive pantry and breakfast room. The bedroom wing features a luxurious master suite with a lush bath and twin walk-in closets. Two additional bedrooms are comfortably sized, and each has its own access to a private bath. The upper level can be finished later and is designed to add a bedroom, a full bath and a large game room with a closet. Please specify crawlspace or slab foundation when ordering.

This home, as shown in the photograph, may differ from the actual blueprints. For more detailed information, please check the floor plans carefully. ©1996 Donald A. Gardner Architects, Inc., Photography courtesy of Donald A. Gardner Architects, Inc.

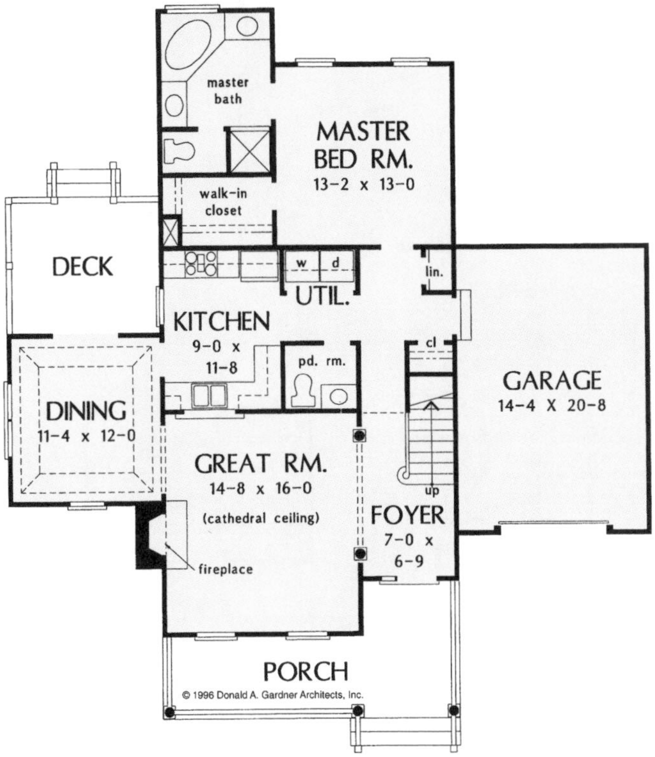

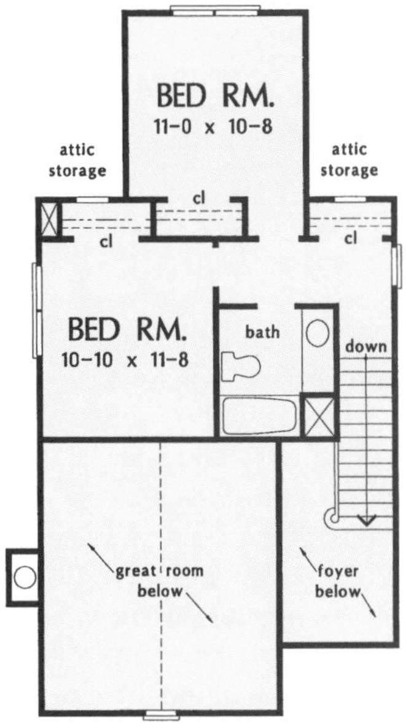

This home is a great starter for a young family with plans to grow or for empty-nesters with a need for guest rooms. On the first floor, the front porch is perfect for relaxing. Inside, the foyer opens through a columned entrance to the large great room with its cathedral ceiling and fireplace. The master bedroom features a walk-in closet and a corner whirlpool tub. The two secondary bedrooms and a shared bath on the second floor could also be used as office space. Additional attic storage is available as family needs expand.

Design HPT830389

First Floor: 1,116 square feet
Second Floor: 442 square feet
Total: 1,558 square feet
Width 49'-0" Depth 52'-0"

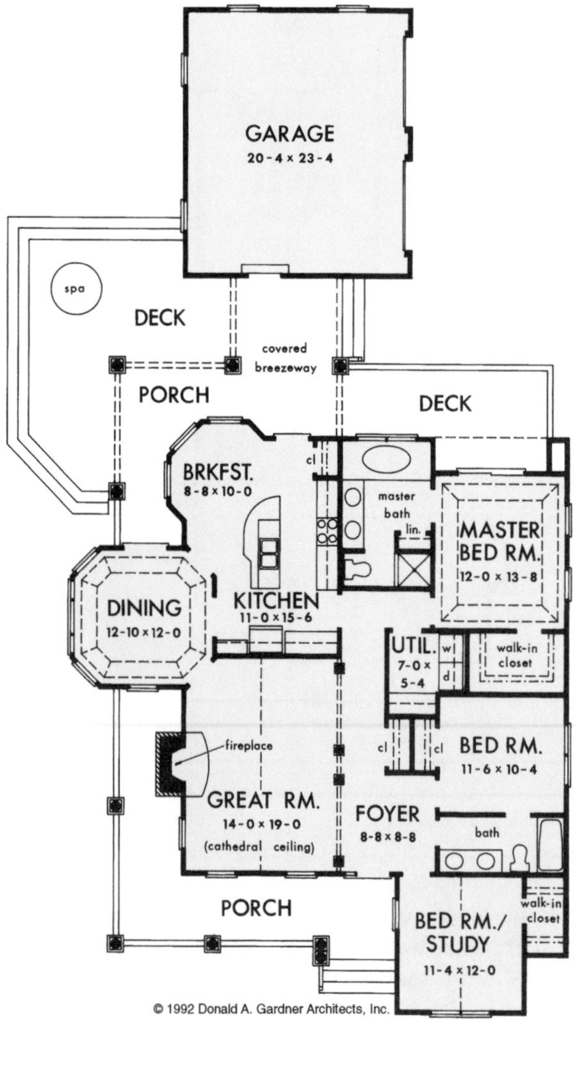

Design HPT830390

Square Footage: 1,677

Width 49'-10" Depth 89'-6"

This cozy, three-bedroom plan with arched windows and a wraparound porch displays a sense of elegance uncommon to a plan this size. Cathedral ceilings grace both the great room and the bedroom/study, while tray ceilings appear in the dining room and master bedroom. The open kitchen design allows for a serving island which is convenient to the breakfast area, dining room and rear porch. The master suite has direct access to the deck and also features a large walk-in closet and master bath with double-bowl vanity, shower and whirlpool tub. A covered breezeway connects the garage to the house.

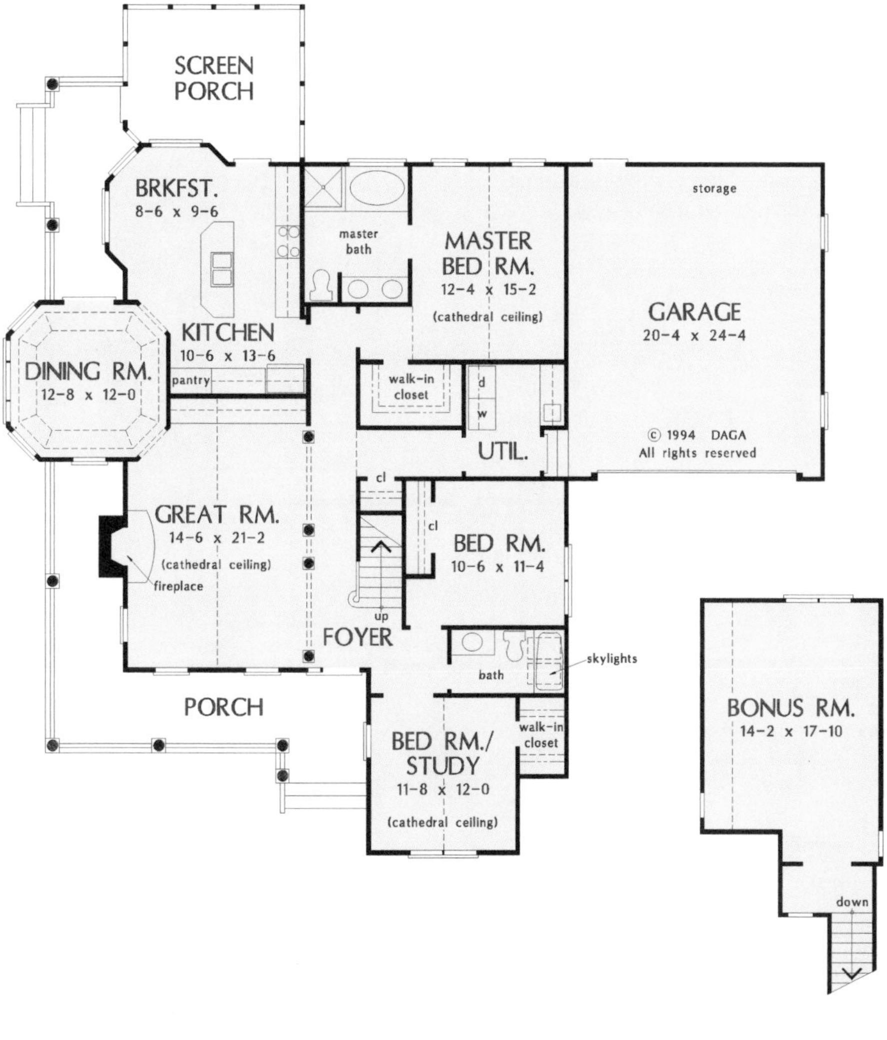
SCREEN PORCH
BRKFST. 8-6 x 9-6
master bath
MASTER BED RM. 12-4 x 15-2 (cathedral ceiling)
storage
GARAGE 20-4 x 24-4
KITCHEN 10-6 x 13-6
DINING RM. 12-8 x 12-0
pantry
walk-in closet
d w
UTIL.
© 1994 DAGA All rights reserved
cl
GREAT RM. 14-6 x 21-2 (cathedral ceiling)
fireplace
BED RM. 10-6 x 11-4
up
FOYER
bath
skylights
PORCH
walk-in closet
BED RM./ STUDY 11-8 x 12-0 (cathedral ceiling)
BONUS RM. 14-2 x 17-10
down

Design HPT830391

Square Footage: 1,787
Bonus Space: 326 square feet
Width 66'-2" Depth 66'-8"

A neighborly porch as friendly as a handshake wraps around this charming country home. Inside, cathedral ceilings promote a feeling of spaciousness. The great room is enhanced with a fireplace and built-in bookshelves. A uniquely shaped formal dining room separates the kitchen and breakfast area. Outdoor pursuits—rain or shine—will be enjoyed from the screened porch. The master suite is located at the rear of the plan for privacy and features a walk-in closet and a luxurious bath. Two additional bedrooms—one with a walk-in closet—share a skylit bath.

This economical plan offers an impressive visual statement with its comfortable and well-proportioned appearance. The entrance foyer leads to all areas of the house. The great room, dining area and kitchen are all open to one another allowing visual interaction. The great room and dining area share a cathedral ceiling. The fireplace is flanked by bookshelves and cabinets. The master suite has a cathedral ceiling, walk-in closet and master bath with double-bowl vanity, whirlpool tub and shower.

Design
HPT830392

Square Footage: 1,287

Width 66'-4" Depth 48'-0"

QUOTE ONE®
Cost to build? See page 516 to order complete cost estimate to build this house in your area!

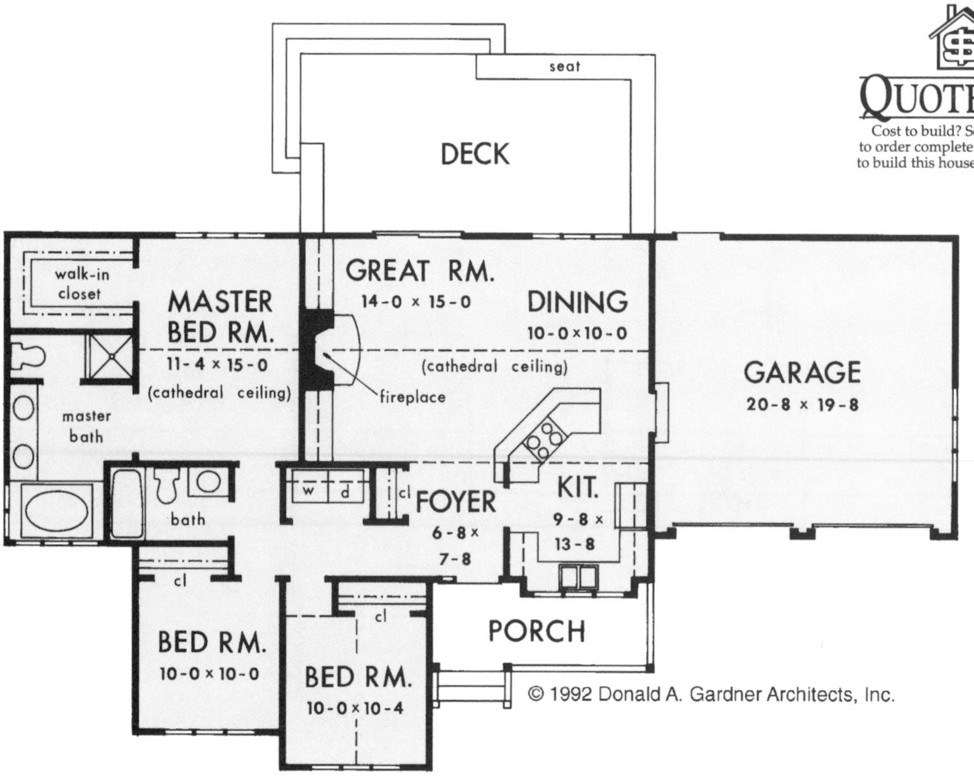

Twin dormers perch above a welcoming covered front porch in this three-bedroom home. Inside, a formal dining room on the right is defined by pillars, while the spacious great room lies directly ahead. This room is enhanced by a fireplace, plenty of windows, access to the rear yard, and a forty-two-inch ledge looking into the angular kitchen. Nearby, a bayed breakfast room awaits casual mealtimes. The sleeping zone consists of two family bedrooms sharing a full hall bath and a luxurious master bedroom suite with a huge walk-in closet and a sumptuous private bath. Please specify crawlspace or slab foundation when ordering.

Design HPT830393

Square Footage: 1,654
Width 54'-10" Depth 69'-10"

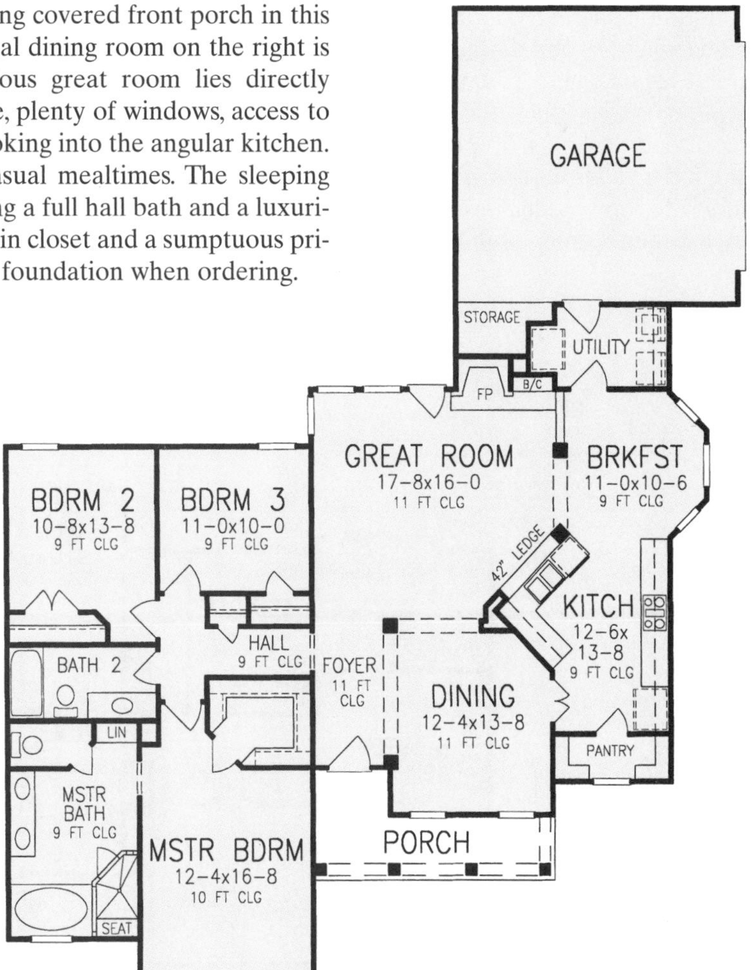
GARAGE
STORAGE
UTILITY
FP
B/C
GREAT ROOM
17-8x16-0
11 FT CLG
BRKFST
11-0x10-6
9 FT CLG
42" LEDGE
KITCH
12-6x
13-8
9 FT CLG
BDRM 2
10-8x13-8
9 FT CLG
BDRM 3
11-0x10-0
9 FT CLG
HALL
9 FT CLG
FOYER
11 FT
CLG
BATH 2
LIN
DINING
12-4x13-8
11 FT CLG
PANTRY
MSTR
BATH
9 FT CLG
SEAT
MSTR BDRM
12-4x16-8
10 FT CLG
PORCH

This traditional country cottage with front and side porches, arched windows and dormers projects a comfortable character. Elegant round columns define the dining room while providing pleasing visuals in this open, modern plan. The great room has a cathedral ceiling, fireplace and sliding glass doors. The master suite has a generous bedroom and a roomy bath consisting of whirlpool tub, shower, double-bowl vanity and walk-in closet. Two family bedrooms share a full bath with double-bowl vanity.

Design
HPT830394

Square Footage: 1,687

Width 77'-4" Depth 62'-10"

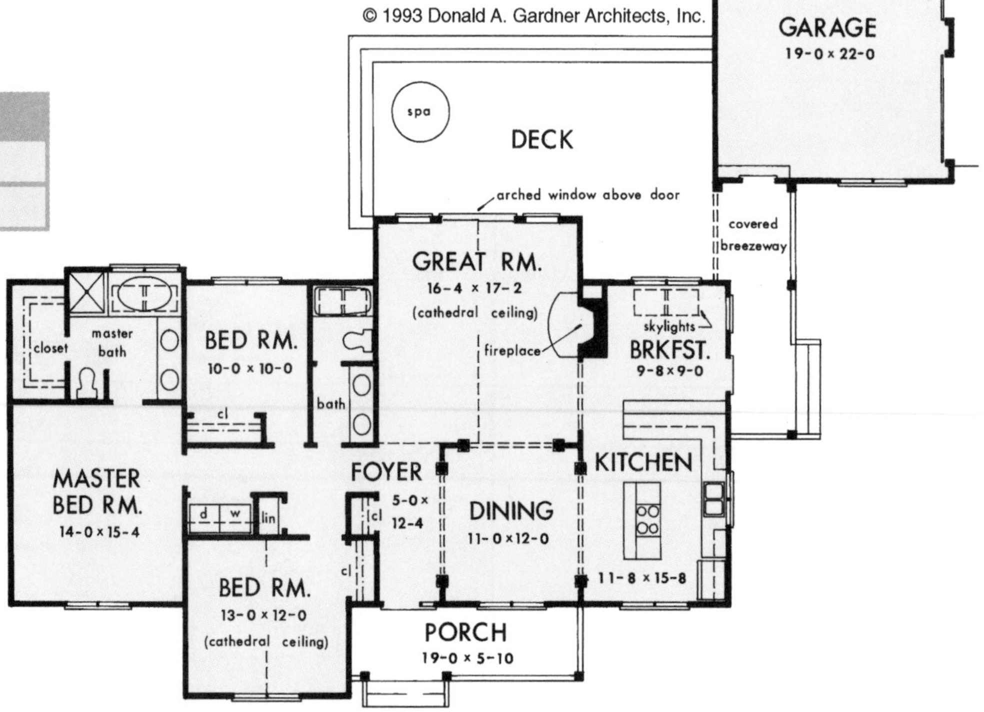

Elegant dormers and arch-topped windows offer a charming facade for this traditional design, with plenty of fabulous amenities to be found within. Lead guests leisurely through the foyer and central hall to a magnificent great room with vaulted ceiling and skylight, centered fireplace, decorative plant shelf and access to the rear deck. Attached to the nearby kitchen, a breakfast nook opens to a screened porch, perfect for informal alfresco dining. The well-appointed kitchen also serves the adjacent dining room for more formal occasions. A secluded main-floor master suite introduces high elegance with a cathedral ceiling and a Palladian-style window. A spacious walk-in closet, a whirlpool tub and a separate shower complete the comforts of this suite. Upstairs, a balcony hall connects two additional bedrooms that share a full bath.

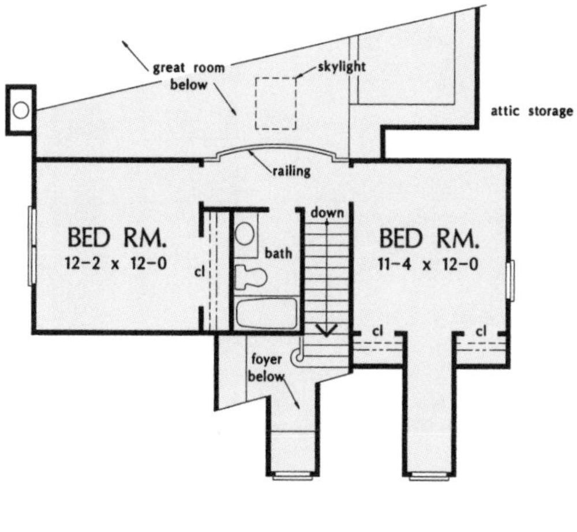

QUOTE ONE®

Cost to build? See page 516 to order complete cost estimate to build this house in your area!

Design HPT830395

First Floor: 1,335 square feet
Second Floor: 488 square feet
Total: 1,823 square feet
Width 61'-6" Depth 54'-0"

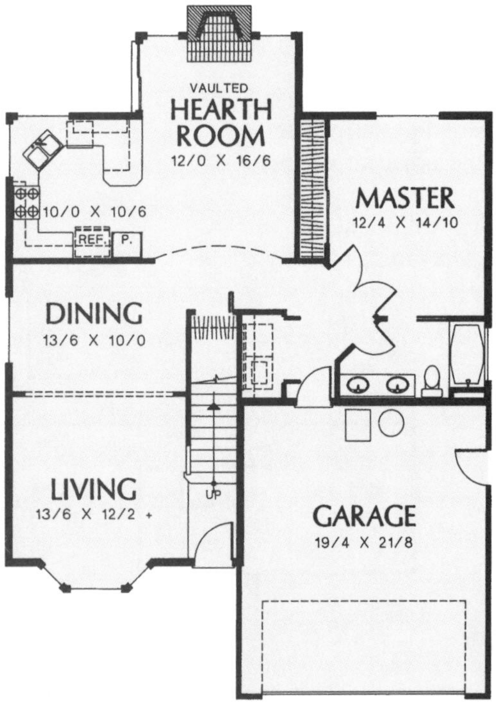

VAULTED
HEARTH ROOM
12/0 X 16/6
10/0 X 10/6
REF.
P.
MASTER
12/4 X 14/10
DINING
13/6 X 10/0
LIVING
13/6 X 12/2 +
UP
GARAGE
19/4 X 21/8

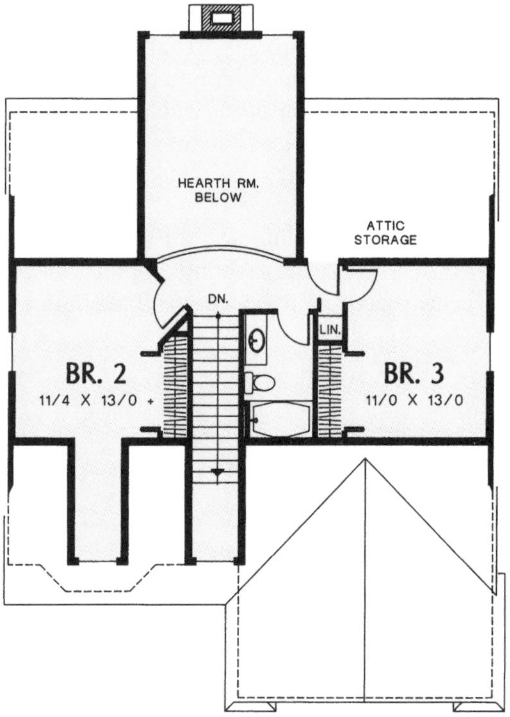

HEARTH RM.
BELOW
ATTIC
STORAGE
DN.
LIN.
BR. 2
11/4 X 13/0 +
BR. 3
11/0 X 13/0

Design HPT830396

First Floor: 1,150 square feet
Second Floor: 543 square feet
Total: 1,693 square feet
Width 38'-0" Depth 50'-0"
L

Perfect for smaller lots, this functional cottage puts every inch of floor space to use with style. Enter into the formal living and dining room that's elegantly accented with a bay window. Casual living takes center stage in the fantastic hearth room with a dramatic, two-story, vaulted ceiling and windows flanking the fireplace. The adjoining kitchen has a sunny corner sink and a snack bar. The first-floor master suite has double-door access, an extra-long closet and a private master bath that also has a hall-access door. At the top of the stairs, a bowed balcony overlooks the hearth room while giving passage to the two secondary bedrooms and a full hall bath.

A multi-pane bay window, dormers, a cupola, a covered porch and a varied facade combine to dress up this intriguing country cottage. The foyer leads to a great room with a cathedral ceiling and a fireplace. An amenity-filled master suite is highlighted by a master bath that includes a separate shower and garden tub. Two additional bedrooms are located at the front of the house for privacy and share a full bath.

Design
HPT830397

Square Footage: 1,512

Width 63'-4" Depth 53'-5"

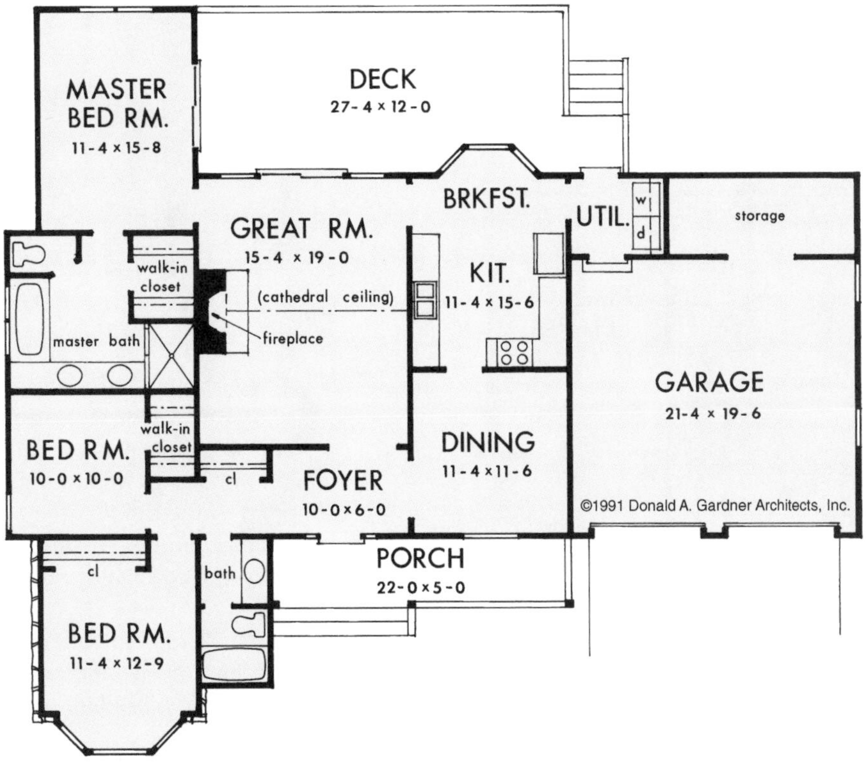

© 1992 Donald A. Gardner Architects, Inc.
B. NATHAN

Design HPT830398

First Floor: 1,039 square feet
Second Floor: 583 square feet
Total: 1,622 square feet
Width 37'-9" Depth 44'-8"

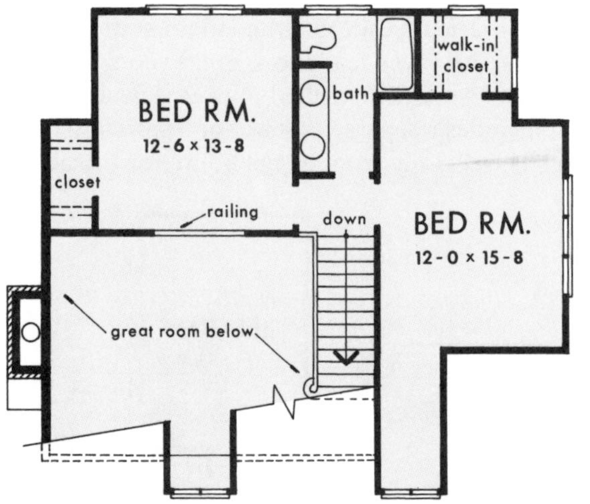
BED RM.
12-6 × 13-8
bath
walk-in closet
closet
railing
down
BED RM.
12-0 × 15-8
great room below

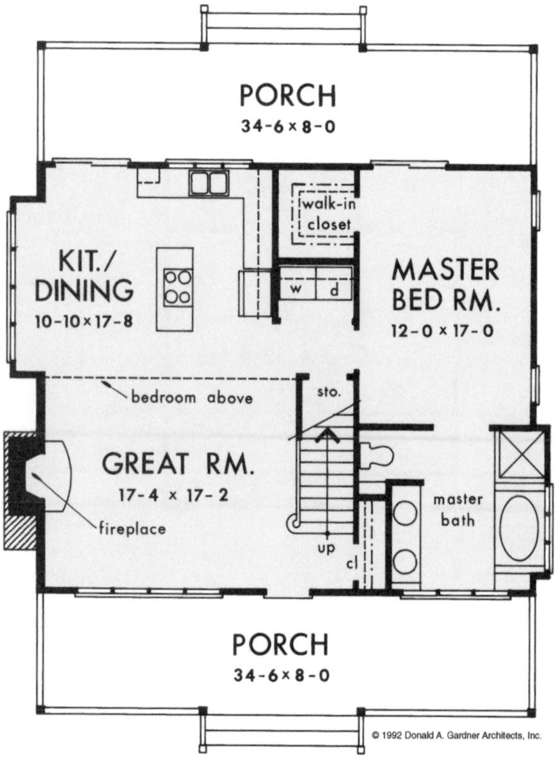
PORCH
34-6 × 8-0
walk-in closet
KIT./ DINING
10-10 × 17-8
w
d
MASTER BED RM.
12-0 × 17-0
bedroom above
sto.
GREAT RM.
17-4 × 17-2
fireplace
up
cl
master bath
PORCH
34-6 × 8-0
© 1992 Donald A. Gardner Architects, Inc.

Charming and compact, this delightful two-story cabin is perfect for the small family or empty-nester. Designed with casual living in mind, the two-story great room is completely open to the dining area and the spacious island kitchen. The master suite is on the first floor for privacy and convenience. It features a roomy bath and a walk-in closet. Upstairs, two comfortable bedrooms—one includes a dormer window, the other features a balcony overlooking the great room—share a full hall bath.

B. NATHAN

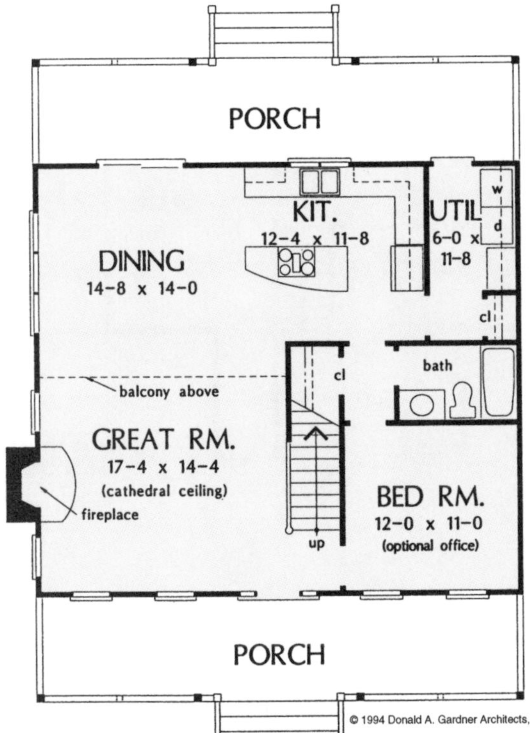
PORCH
KIT.
12-4 x 11-8
UTIL
6-0 x
11-8
w
d
DINING
14-8 x 14-0
cl
bath
cl
balcony above
GREAT RM.
17-4 x 14-4
(cathedral ceiling)
fireplace
BED RM.
12-0 x 11-0
(optional office)
up
PORCH

QUOTE ONE®
Cost to build? See page 516 to order complete cost estimate to build this house in your area!

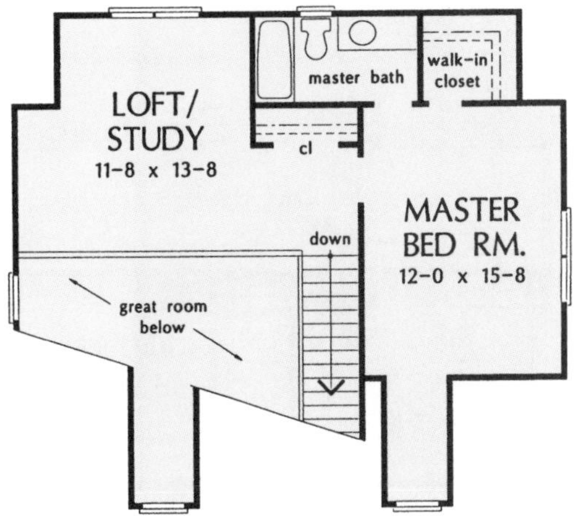
master bath
walk-in
closet
LOFT/
STUDY
11-8 x 13-8
cl
MASTER
BED RM.
12-0 x 15-8
down
great room
below

A country farmhouse exterior combined with an open floor plan creates a comfortable home or vacation getaway. The great room, warmed by a fireplace and opened by a cathedral ceiling, combines well with the dining room and the kitchen. Flexibility is offered in a front bedroom with a full bath that easily doubles as a home office. The second floor contains the master bedroom with a walk-in closet and a private bath. The loft/study overlooks the great room below. Front and rear porches provide plenty of room for outdoor enjoyment.

Design
HPT830399

First Floor: 966 square feet
Second Floor: 584 square feet
Total: 1,550 square feet
Width 35'-9" Depth 43'-0"

© 1992 Donald A. Gardner Architects, Inc.
B·NATHAN·

Design HPT830400

First Floor: 1,027 square feet

Second Floor: 580 square feet

Total: 1,607 square feet

Width 37'-4" Depth 44'-8"

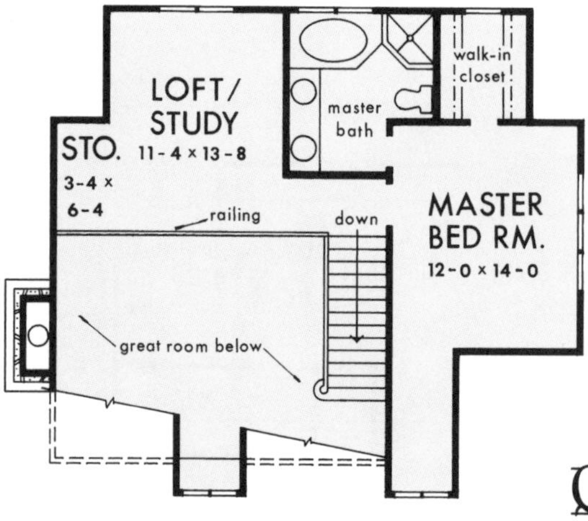

LOFT/
STUDY
11-4 × 13-8
STO.
3-4 ×
6-4
master
bath
walk-in
closet
railing
down
MASTER
BED RM.
12-0 × 14-0
great room below

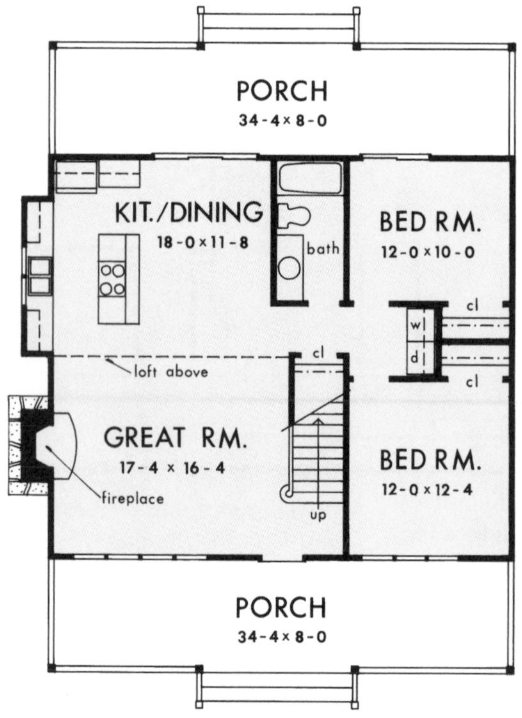

PORCH
34-4 × 8-0
KIT./DINING
18-0 × 11-8
bath
BED RM.
12-0 × 10-0
cl
w
d
cl
cl
loft above
GREAT RM.
17-4 × 16-4
fireplace
up
BED RM.
12-0 × 12-4
PORCH
34-4 × 8-0

QUOTE ONE®

Cost to build? See page 516 to order complete cost estimate to build this house in your area!

This economical and rustic three-bedroom plan sports a relaxing country image with both front and back covered porches. The openness of the great room to the kitchen/dining areas and the loft/study area is reinforced with a shared cathedral ceiling. An abundance of windows in the great room, sliding glass doors in the kitchen and an over-the-sink window fill this open space with natural light and usher in the beauty of the outdoors. The first floor allows for two bedrooms, a full bath and a utility area. The master suite on the second floor has a walk-in closet and a private bath. Completing the second floor, a loft/study overlooks the great room below, providing space for quiet, reflective moments.

Design HPT830401

First Floor: 1,100 square feet
Second Floor: 584 square feet
Total: 1,684 square feet
Width 36'-8" Depth 45'-0"

A relaxing country image projects from the front and rear covered porches of this rustic three-bedroom home. Open planning extends to the great room, the dining room and the efficient kitchen. A shared cathedral ceiling creates an impressive space. Completing the first floor are two family bedrooms, a full bath and a handy utility area. The second floor contains the master suite featuring a spacious walk-in closet and a private bath with a whirlpool tub and separate corner shower. A generous loft/study overlooks the great room below.

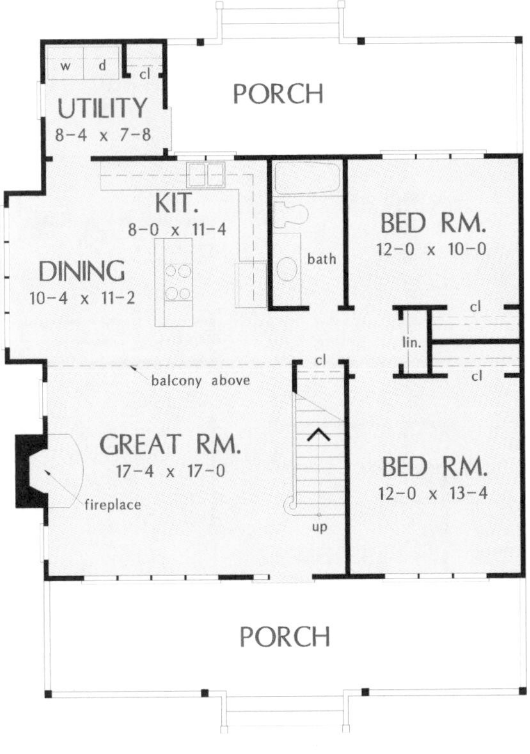

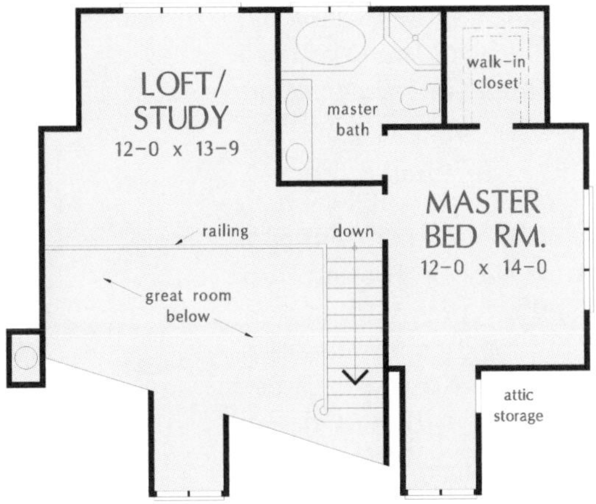

QUOTE ONE®
Cost to build? See page 516
to order complete cost estimate
to build this house in your area!

Design HPT830402

Square Footage: 1,772

Width 45'-8" Depth 50'-2"

A Folk Victorian flair gives this home its curb appeal. Inside, a large living room boasts a centerpiece fireplace and a coffered ceiling. The kitchen offers a breakfast bar and a pantry. The master suite includes a ten-foot coffered ceiling and a luxury bath complete with a corner whirlpool tub, separate shower, His and Hers vanities and a roomy walk-in closet. Two additional bedrooms and a bath are nearby. A two-car garage plan is included with this design and can be connected to the home with a breezeway. Please specify crawlspace or slab foundation when ordering.

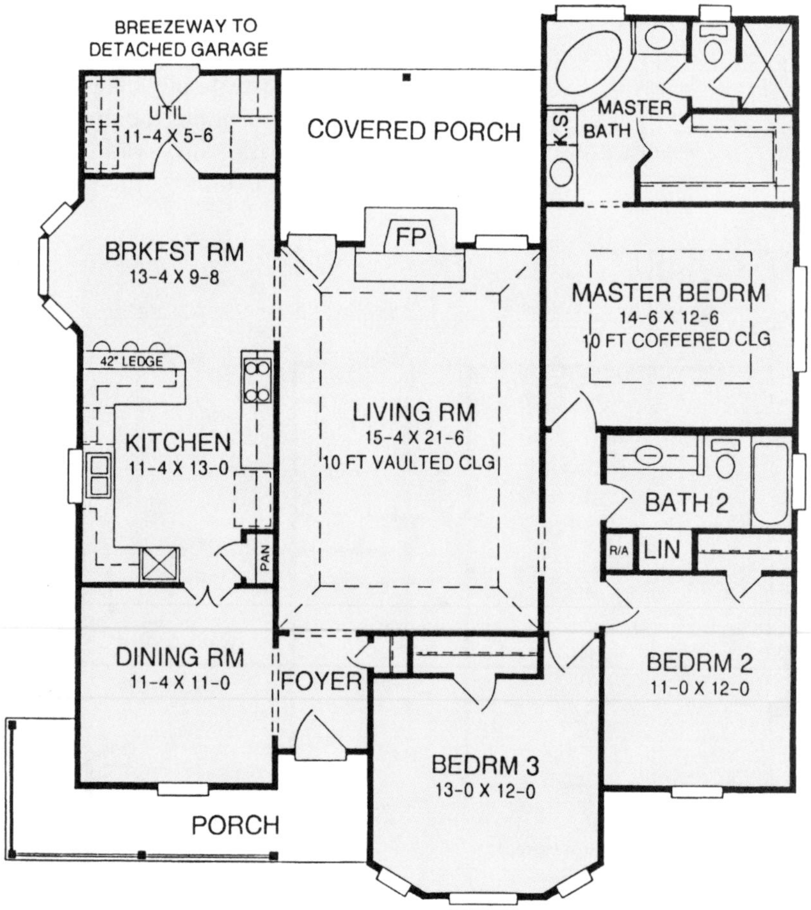

Design HPT830403

Square Footage: 1,565

Width 50'-0" Depth 52'-10"

L

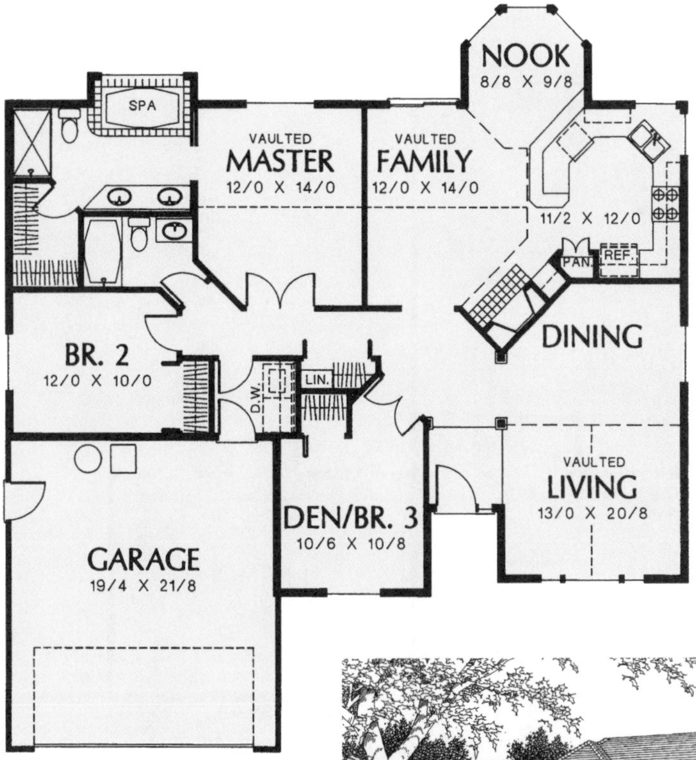
NOOK
8/8 X 9/8
SPA
VAULTED
MASTER
12/0 X 14/0
VAULTED
FAMILY
12/0 X 14/0
11/2 X 12/0
PAN.
REF.
DINING
BR. 2
12/0 X 10/0
D.W.
LIN.
VAULTED
LIVING
13/0 X 20/8
DEN/BR. 3
10/6 X 10/8
GARAGE
19/4 X 21/8

This charming traditional home offers front-facing gables and a comfortable blend of shingles and vertical siding. Inside, a columned foyer opens to a vaulted living room, which offers a Palladian window and adjoins the formal dining room. An angled fireplace with an extended-tile hearth highlights the vaulted family room, which leads to a bayed breakfast nook. The nearby kitchen enjoys a windowed corner double sink and ample counter and pantry space. The master suite boasts a tile-rimmed spa tub as well as a separate shower and sizable walk-in closet. A family bedroom easily accesses a hall bath. A quiet den, third bedroom or guest room opens from the central hall through French doors. An alternate elevation is available for this home.

ALTERNATE ELEVATION

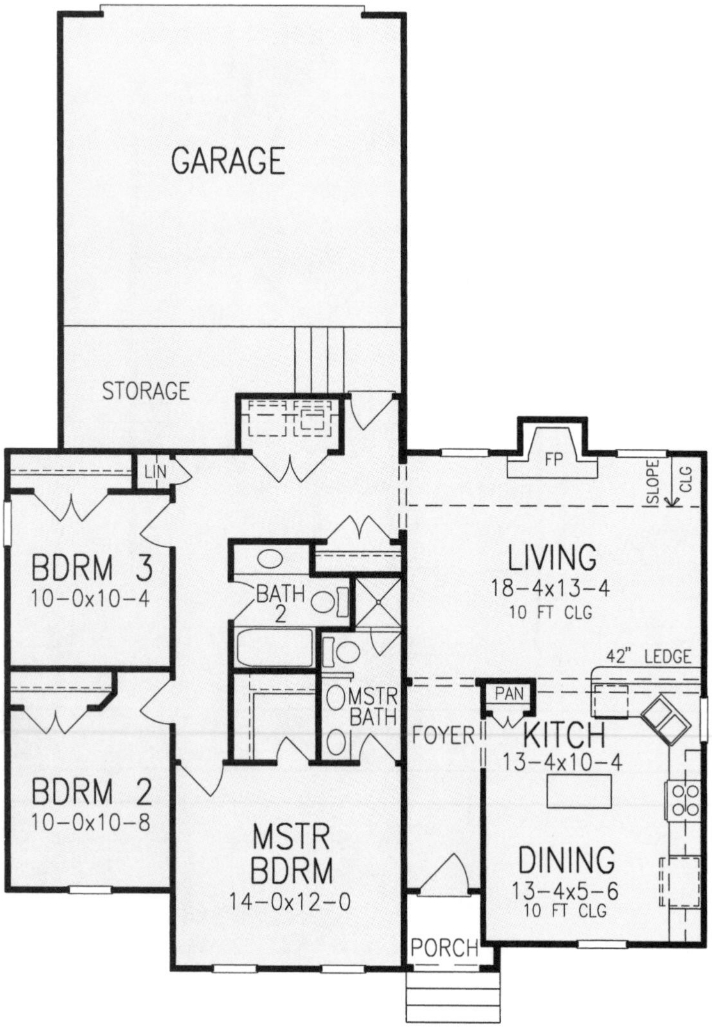
GARAGE
STORAGE
LIN
FP
SLOPE
CLG
BDRM 3
10-0x10-4
BATH
2
LIVING
18-4x13-4
10 FT CLG
42" LEDGE
PAN
MSTR
BATH
FOYER
KITCH
13-4x10-4
BDRM 2
10-0x10-8
MSTR
BDRM
14-0x12-0
DINING
13-4x5-6
10 FT CLG
PORCH

Design HPT830404

Square Footage: 1,322	
Width 44'-6"	Depth 58'-2"

A fine first impression is offered with the delightful chalet roofline on the entry of this efficient country design. A traditional foyer opens to the large living room. Accents include a sloped ten-foot ceiling, a snack bar from the kitchen and windows that frame the fireplace. The kitchen has a corner sink, island prep area and a dining nook. The front-facing master bedroom has a walk-in closet and a twin-sink vanity in the bath. Two family bedrooms share a hall bath. A hallway laundry center and a two-car garage, discreetly set at the rear of the house, complete this plan. Please specify crawlspace or slab foundation when ordering.

Design
HPT830405

Square Footage: 1,087	
Width 35'-10"	Depth 42'-2"

From the multi-pane windows to the corner quoins, this home's facade is enchanting. Inside, attractive arches flank the entryway; one arch leads to the breakfast room and an efficient kitchen, the other to the deluxe master suite. Directly ahead of the foyer is the large great room accessible to the rear yard and the two family bedrooms. In the master suite, a sumptuous bath offers a double-bowl vanity and a large walk-in closet. Two family bedrooms located on the opposite end of the home share a full hall bath. Please specify crawlspace or slab foundation when ordering.

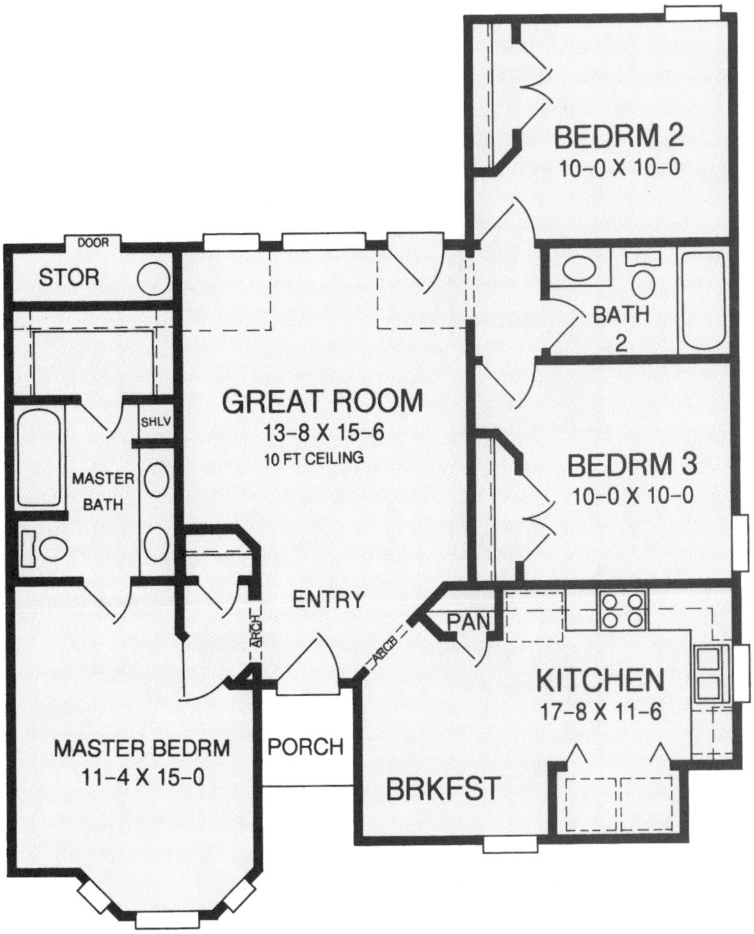
BEDRM 2
10-0 X 10-0
DOOR
STOR
BATH
2
GREAT ROOM
13-8 X 15-6
10 FT CEILING
SHLV
MASTER
BATH
BEDRM 3
10-0 X 10-0
ENTRY
PAN
ARCH
ARCH
KITCHEN
17-8 X 11-6
MASTER BEDRM
11-4 X 15-0
PORCH
BRKFST

Fine detailing and multiple rooflines give this home plenty of curb appeal. A large living room with a fireplace is the focal point for this lovely home. The dining room and sunny breakfast room provide complementary eating areas. The master bedroom features a large walk-in closet and a bath with a combination whirlpool tub and shower. Two additional bedrooms and a full hall bath complete this livable plan. Please specify crawlspace or slab foundation when ordering.

Design
HPT830406

Square Footage: 1,402

Width 59'-10" Depth 40'-10"

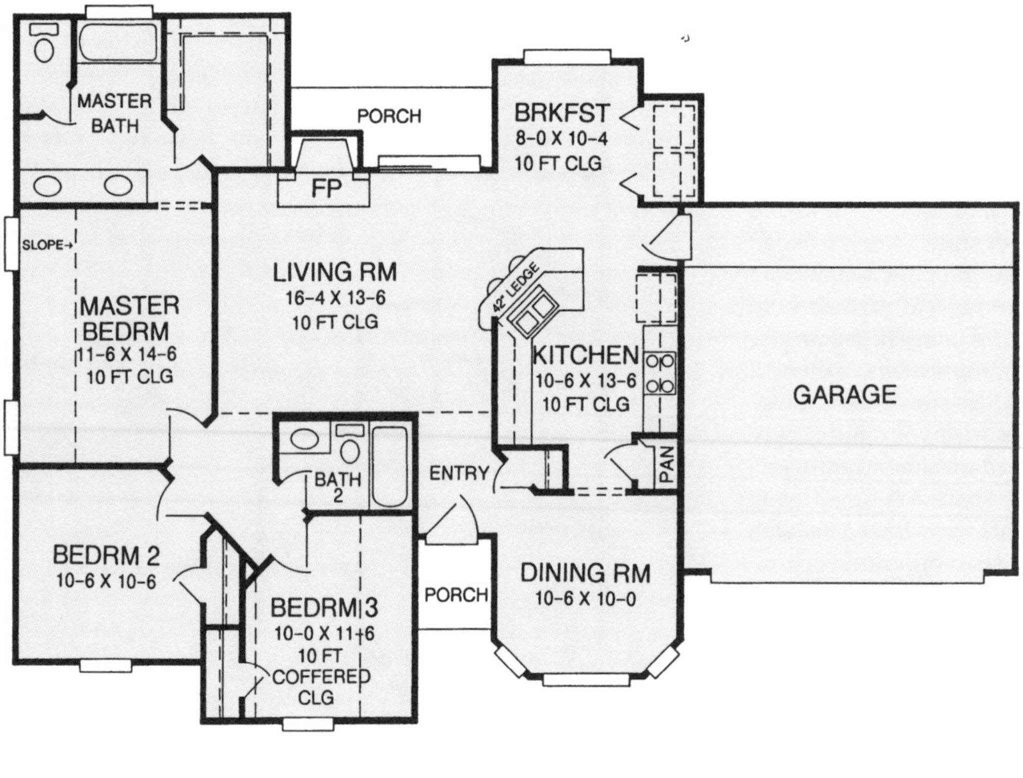

MASTER BATH
PORCH
BRKFST
8-0 X 10-4
10 FT CLG
FP
SLOPE
LIVING RM
16-4 X 13-6
10 FT CLG
MASTER BEDRM
11-6 X 14-6
10 FT CLG
42" LEDGE
KITCHEN
10-6 X 13-6
10 FT CLG
GARAGE
BATH 2
ENTRY
PAN
BEDRM 2
10-6 X 10-6
BEDRM 3
10-0 X 11-6
10 FT COFFERED CLG
PORCH
DINING RM
10-6 X 10-0

Design HPT830407

Square Footage: 1,310

Width 49'-10" Depth 40'-6"

This charming plan is perfect for families just starting out or for the empty-nester looking to pare down. Every room is designed for maximum livability, from the living room with a corner fireplace to the efficient kitchen with a snack bar and hidden washer and dryer. The master bedroom is fashioned with a dual-vanity bath and a walk-in closet equipped with shelves. Two additional bedrooms each have a walk-in closet and share a hall bath. Please specify crawlspace or slab foundation when ordering.

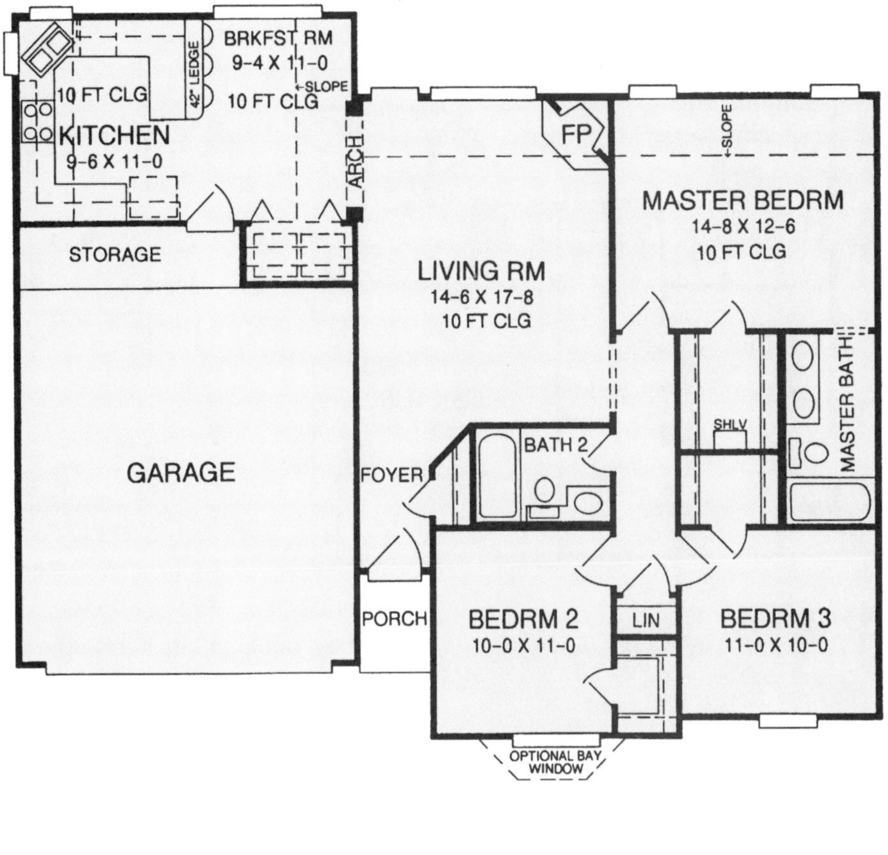

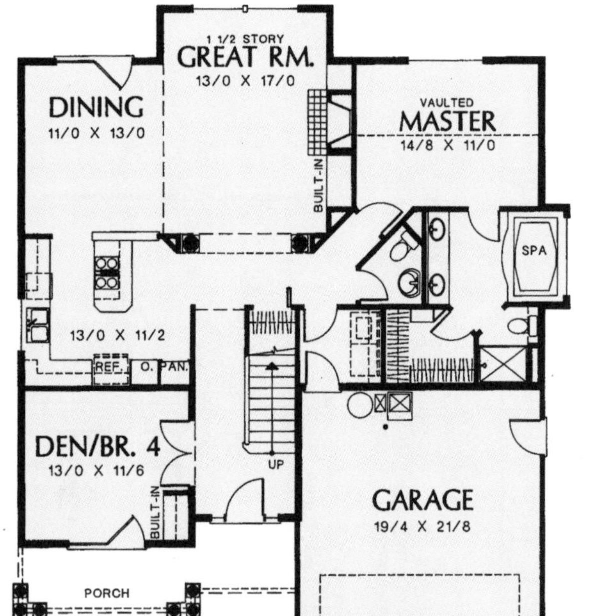
1 1/2 STORY
GREAT RM.
13/0 X 17/0
DINING
11/0 X 13/0
VAULTED
MASTER
14/8 X 11/0
BUILT-IN
SPA
13/0 X 11/2
REF.
O. PAN.
DEN/BR. 4
13/0 X 11/6
BUILT-IN
UP
GARAGE
19/4 X 21/8
PORCH

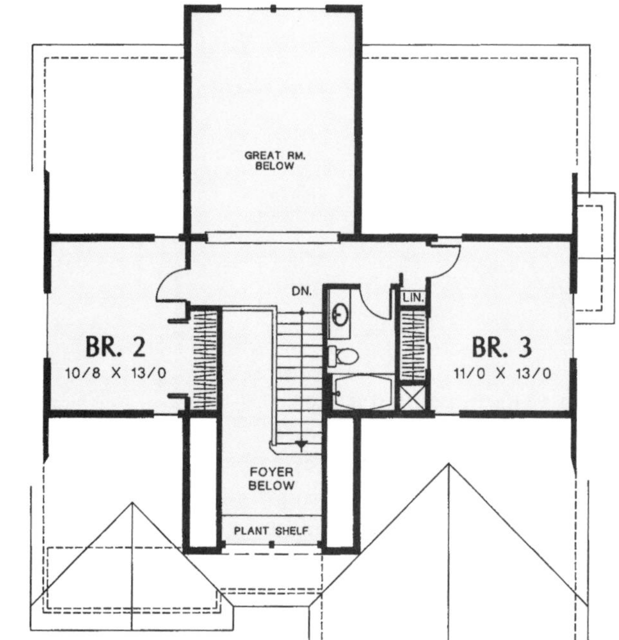
GREAT RM.
BELOW
DN.
LIN.
BR. 2
10/8 X 13/0
BR. 3
11/0 X 13/0
FOYER
BELOW
PLANT SHELF

Design

HPT830408

First Floor: 1,396 square feet

Second Floor: 523 square feet

Total: 1,919 square feet

Width 44'-0" Depth 51'-0"

L

Double pillars herald the entry to this charming design. They are offset from the front door and introduce a porch that leads to the den (or make it a fourth bedroom). Living areas center on the casual life and include a great room, with a fireplace, that opens directly to the dining room. The kitchen is L-shaped for convenience and features an island cooktop. The master suite on the first floor sports a vaulted ceiling and bath with spa tub and separate shower. The upper floor holds two secondary bedrooms and a full bath. The open staircase is decorated with a plant shelf that receives light from double windows over the foyer.

This design takes inspiration from the casual fishing cabins of the Pacific Northwest and interprets it for modern livability. It offers three options for a main entrance. One door opens to a mud porch, where a small hall leads to a galley kitchen and the vaulted great room. Two French doors on the side porch open into a dining room with bay-window seating. Another porch entrance opens directly into the great room, which is centered around a massive stone fireplace and accented with a wall of windows. The secluded master bedroom features a bath with a claw-foot tub and twin pedestal sinks, as well as a separate shower and walk-in closet. Two more bedrooms share a bath. An unfinished loft looks over the great room.

Design HPT830409

Square Footage: 2,019
Loft: 384 square feet
Width 56'-0" Depth 56'-3"

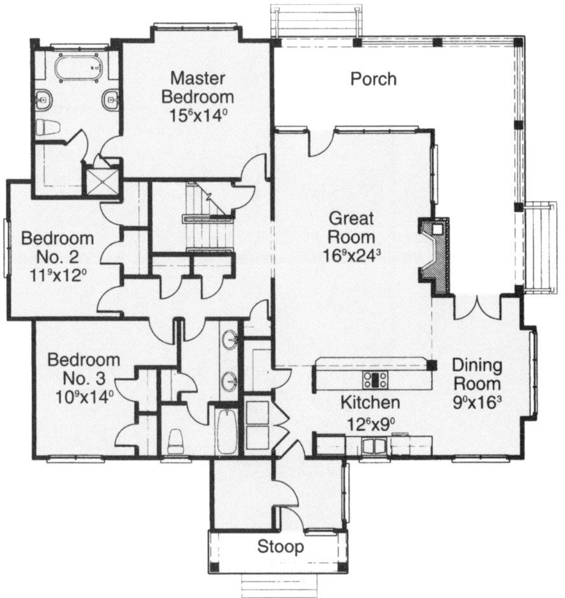

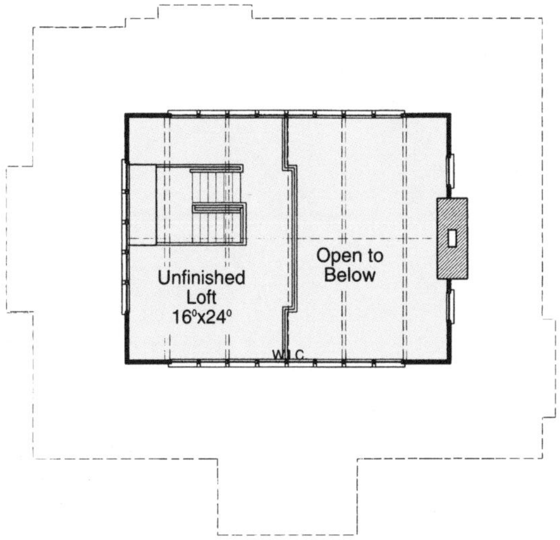

This home, as shown in the photograph, may differ from the actual blueprints. For more detailed information, please check the floor plans carefully.
Photo by Bob Greenspan

A covered porch, multi-pane windows and shingle-with-stone siding combine to give this bungalow plenty of curb appeal. Inside, the foyer is flanked by the formal living room and an angled staircase. The formal dining room adjoins the living room, and the kitchen is accessible through double doors. A large family room is graced by a fireplace and opens off a cozy eating nook. The second level presents many attractive angles. The master suite has a spacious walk-in closet and a sumptuous bath complete with a garden tub and separate shower. Three family bedrooms share a full hall bath.

Design HPT830410

First Floor: 1,205 square feet
Second Floor: 1,123 square feet
Total: 2,328 square feet
Width 57'-2" Depth 58'-7"

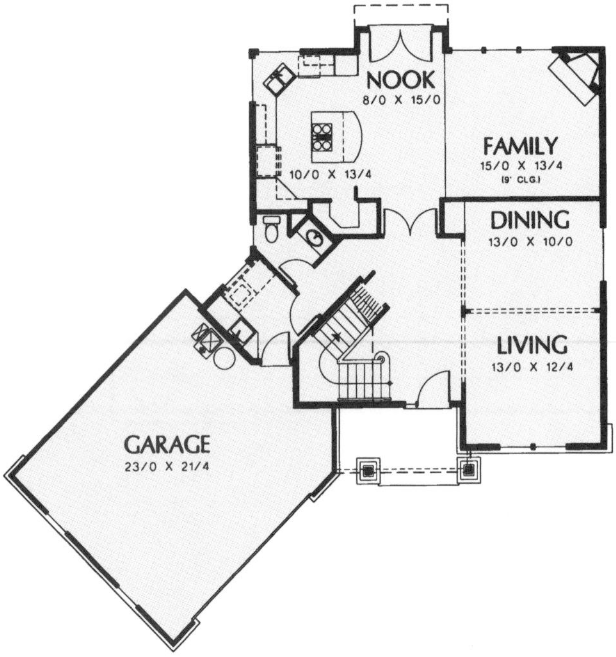

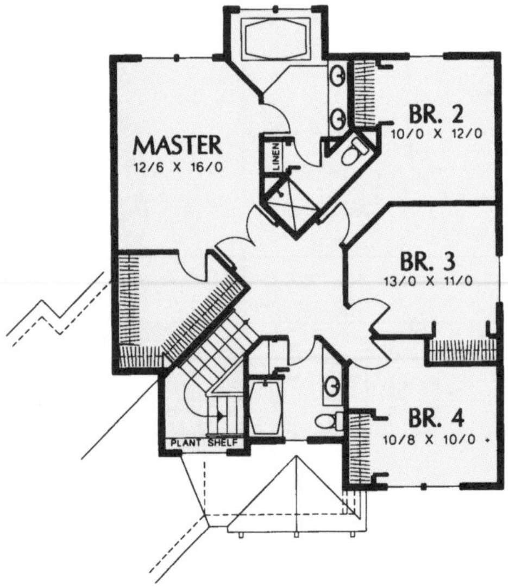

This home, as shown in the photograph, may differ from the actual blueprints. For more detailed information, please check the floor plans carefully.
Photo by Bob Greenspan

Design HPT830411

First Floor: 1,371 square feet
Second Floor: 916 square feet
Total: 2,287 square feet
Width 43'-0" Depth 69'-0"

QUOTE ONE®
Cost to build? See page 516 to order complete cost estimate to build this house in your area!

The decorative pillars and the wraparound porch are just the beginning of this comfortable home. Inside, an angled U-shaped stairway leads to the second-floor sleeping quarters. On the first floor, French doors lead to a bay-windowed den that shares a see-through fireplace with the two-story family room. The large island kitchen includes a writing desk, a corner sink, a breakfast nook and access to the laundry room, the powder room and the two-car garage. Upstairs, the master suite is a real treat with its French-door access, vaulted ceiling and luxurious bath. Two other bedrooms and a full bath complete the second floor.

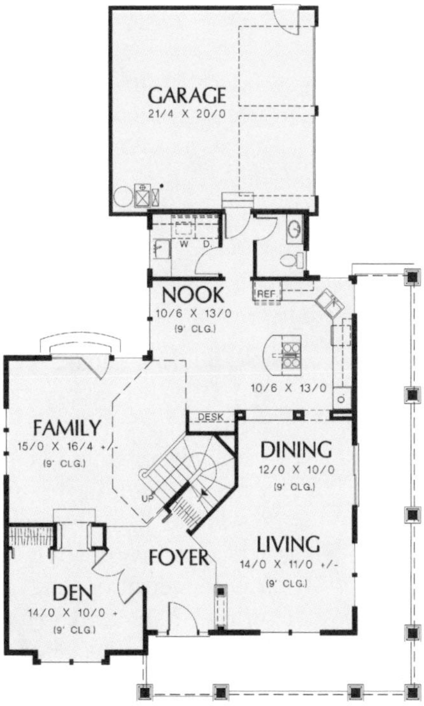

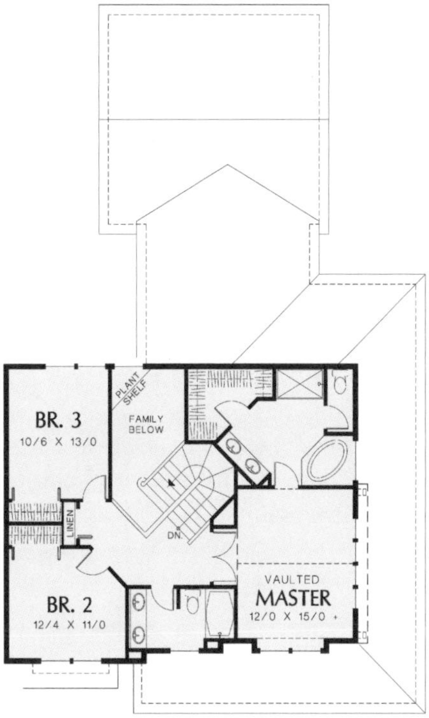

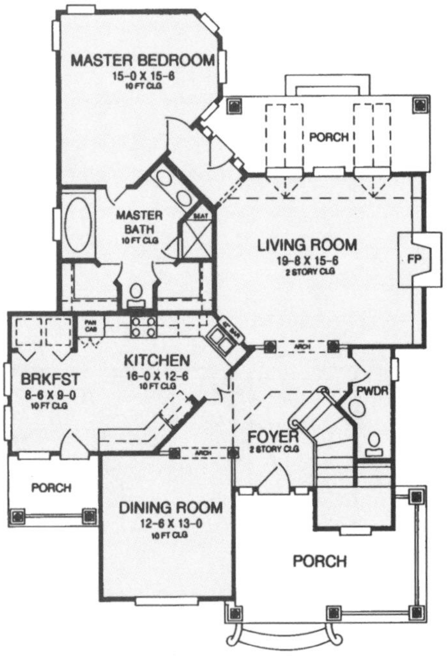

Design

HPT830412

First Floor: 1,482 square feet

Second Floor: 631 square feet

Total: 2,113 square feet

Width 41'-10" Depth 56'-5"

L

The four-square design reminiscent of the 1940s gives this home its landmark look. An inviting porch opens to a two-story foyer. Straight ahead, the living room is visible through two columns mounted on pedestals and connected by a graceful arch. Dormers located in the living room's vaulted ceiling flood the area with natural light. Enter the nearby dining room through another arched opening. A large kitchen and a sunny breakfast room invite casual conversations and lingering. The master bedroom includes a luxurious bath with His and Hers walk-in closets, a soothing whirlpool tub and a separate shower. Two additional bedrooms (one with a balcony) and a full bath share the second floor. Please specify crawlspace or slab foundation when ordering.

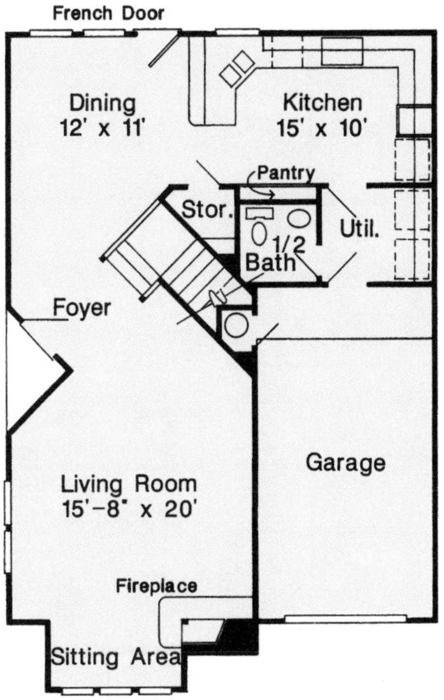
French Door
Dining
12' x 11'
Kitchen
15' x 10'
Pantry
Stor.
Util.
1/2
Bath
Foyer
Garage
Living Room
15'-8" x 20'
Fireplace
Sitting Area

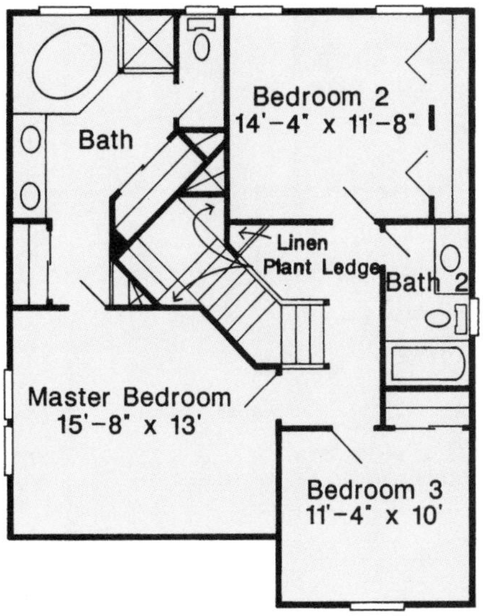
Bath
Bedroom 2
14'-4" x 11'-8"
Linen
Plant Ledge
Bath 2
Master Bedroom
15'-8" x 13'
Bedroom 3
11'-4" x 10'

Design HPT830413

First Floor: 845 square feet
Second Floor: 845 square feet
Total: 1,690 square feet
Width 28'-0" Depth 42'-4"

An angled staircase lends diversity to this cozy, three-bedroom plan. The large living room affords amenities such as a fireplace and a quaint sitting area. The roomy kitchen features a corner sink and bar that services the dining room. Here you'll find a French door opening to the rear yard. A storage closet accommodates odds and ends. With a powder room and a utility area accessing the garage, the first floor functions with convenience in mind. The second floor features a master suite with an oversized bath offering a twin vanity, spa tub and a compartmented toilet. Two secondary bedrooms and a full hall bath complete this level.

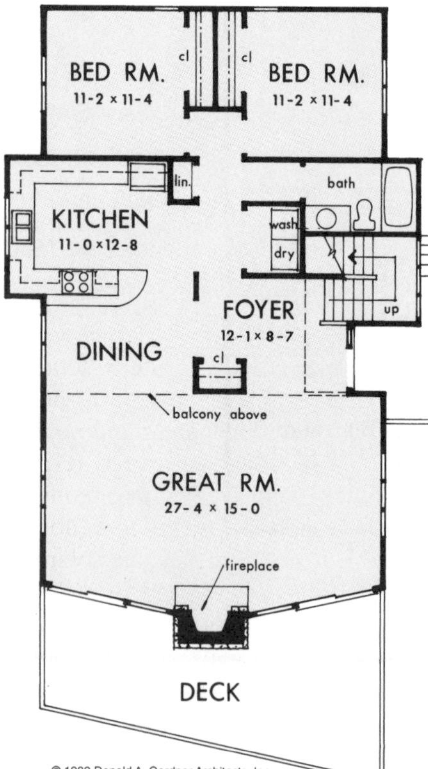
BED RM.
11-2 x 11-4
cl
cl
BED RM.
11-2 x 11-4
lin.
KITCHEN
11-0 x 12-8
bath
wash
dry
up
FOYER
12-1 x 8-7
DINING
cl
balcony above
GREAT RM.
27-4 x 15-0
fireplace
DECK

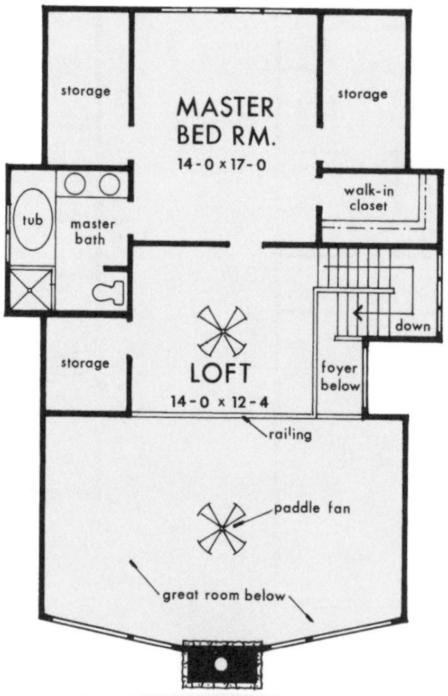
storage
MASTER
BED RM.
14-0 x 17-0
storage
walk-in
closet
tub
master
bath
down
storage
LOFT
14-0 x 12-4
foyer
below
railing
paddle fan
great room below

Design HPT830414

First Floor: 1,374 square feet

Second Floor: 608 square feet

Total: 1,982 square feet

Width 40'-0" Depth 60'-8"

This rustic three-bedroom vacation home allows for casual living both inside and out. The two-story great room offers dramatic space for entertaining with windows stretching clear to the roof, maximizing the outdoor view. A stone fireplace is the focal point of this room. Two family bedrooms on the first floor share a full hall bath. The second floor holds the master bedroom with a spacious master bath and a walk-in closet. A large loft area overlooks the great room and entrance foyer.

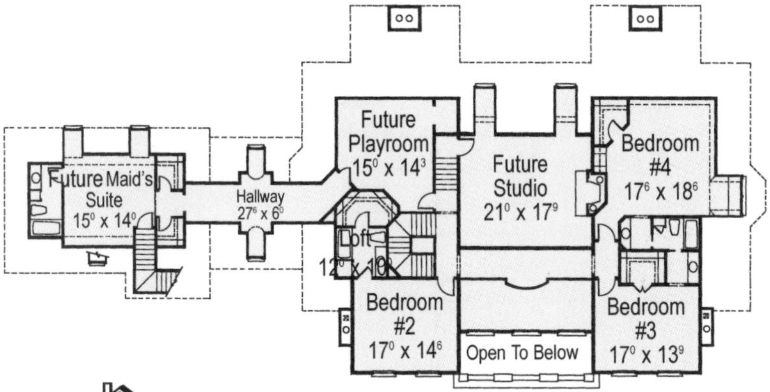
Future Maid's Suite
15⁰ x 14⁰
Hallway
27⁶ x 6⁰
Future Playroom
15⁰ x 14³
Future Studio
21⁰ x 17⁹
Bedroom #4
17⁶ x 18⁶
Loft
12⁰ x 10⁰
Bedroom #2
17⁰ x 14⁶
Open To Below
Bedroom #3
17⁰ x 13⁹

QUOTE ONE®
Cost to build? See page 516 to order complete cost estimate to build this house in your area!

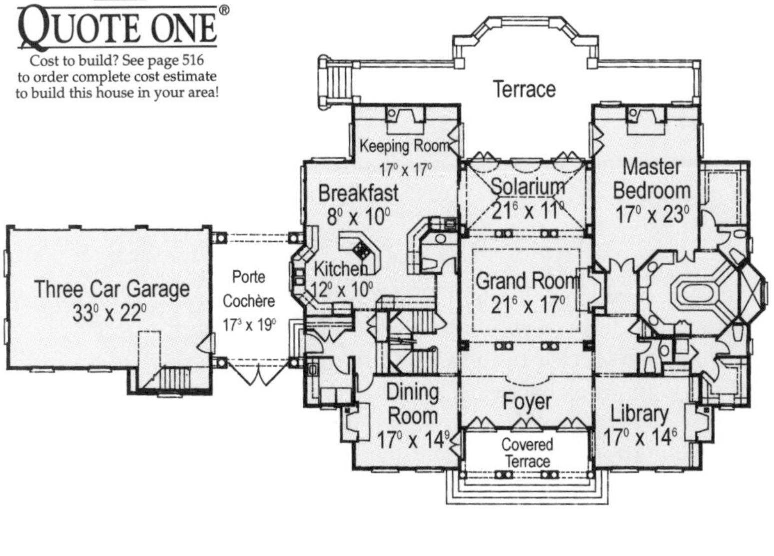
Terrace
Keeping Room
17⁰ x 17⁰
Breakfast
8⁰ x 10⁰
Solarium
21⁶ x 11⁰
Master Bedroom
17⁰ x 23⁰
Three Car Garage
33⁰ x 22⁰
Porte Cochère
17³ x 19⁰
Kitchen
12⁰ x 10⁰
Grand Room
21⁶ x 17⁰
Dining Room
17⁰ x 14⁹
Foyer
Library
17⁰ x 14⁶
Covered Terrace

Design HPT830415

First Floor: 3,703 square feet
Second Floor: 1,427 square feet
Total: 5,130 square feet
Bonus Space: 1,399 square feet
Width 125'-2" Depth 58'-10"

This magnificent estate is detailed with exterior charm: a porte cochere connecting the detached garage to the house, a covered terrace and oval windows. The first floor consists of a lavish master suite, a cozy library with a fireplace, a grand room/solarium combination and an elegant formal dining room with another fireplace. Three bedrooms dominate the second floor—each features a walk-in closet. For the kids, there is a playroom and up another flight of stairs is a room for future expansion into a deluxe studio with a fireplace. Over the three-car garage, there is a room for a future mother-in-law or maid's suite. This home is designed with a walkout basement foundation.

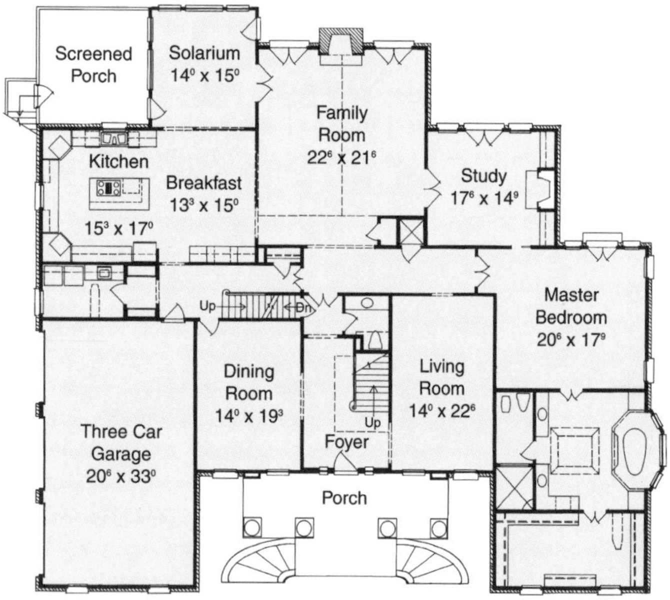
Screened Porch
Solarium 14⁰ x 15⁰
Family Room 22⁶ x 21⁶
Kitchen
Breakfast 13³ x 15⁰
15³ x 17⁰
Study 17⁶ x 14⁹
Master Bedroom 20⁶ x 17⁹
Up
Dn
Dining Room 14⁰ x 19³
Living Room 14⁰ x 22⁶
Up
Foyer
Three Car Garage 20⁶ x 33⁰
Porch

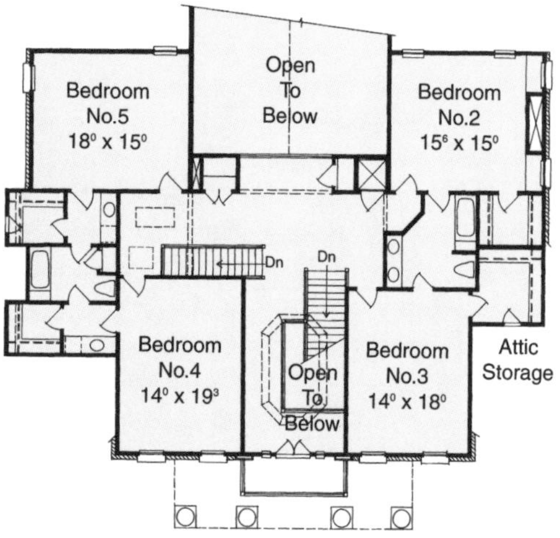
Bedroom No.5 18⁰ x 15⁰
Open To Below
Bedroom No.2 15⁶ x 15⁰
Dn
Dn
Bedroom No.4 14⁰ x 19³
Open To Below
Bedroom No.3 14⁰ x 18⁰
Attic Storage

Design HPT830416

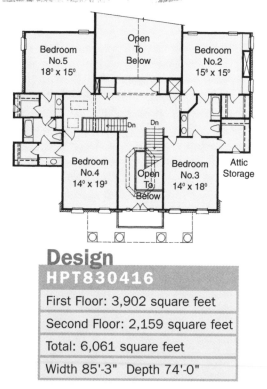

First Floor: 3,902 square feet
Second Floor: 2,159 square feet
Total: 6,061 square feet
Width 85'-3" Depth 74'-0"

The entry to this classic home is framed with a sweeping double staircase and four large columns topped with a pediment. The two-story foyer is flanked by spacious living and dining rooms. Beyond the foyer, the home is designed with rooms that offer maximum livability. The two-story family room, which has a central fireplace, opens to the study and a solarium. A spacious U-shaped kitchen features a central island cooktop. An additional staircase off the breakfast room offers convenient access to the second floor. The impressive master suite features backyard access and a bath fit for royalty. A walk-in closet with an ironing board will provide room for everything. Four bedrooms upstairs enjoy large proportions. This home is designed with a walkout basement foundation.

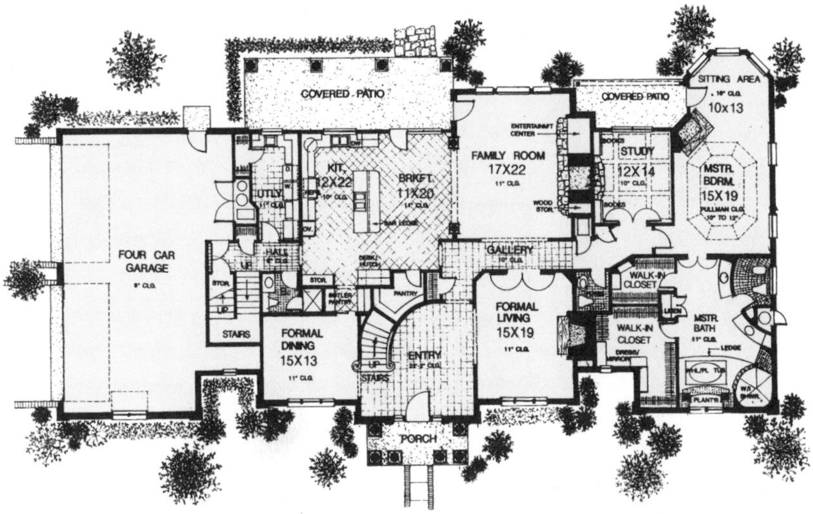

Design

HPT830417

First Floor: 3,599 square feet
Second Floor: 1,621 square feet
Total: 5,220 square feet
Bonus Space: 356 square feet
Width 108'-10" Depth 53'-10"

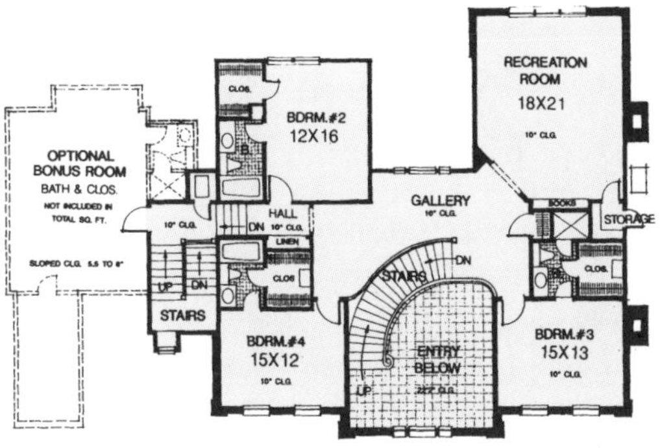

A grand facade detailed with brick corner quoins, stucco flourishes, arched windows and an elegant entrance presents this home and preludes the amenities inside. A spacious foyer is accented by curving stairs and flanked by a formal living room and a formal dining room. For cozy times, a through-fireplace is located between a large family room and a quiet study. The master bedroom is designed to pamper, with two walk-in closets (one is absolutely huge), a two-sided fireplace sharing its heat with a bayed sitting area and the bedroom, and a lavish private bath filled with attractive amenities. Upstairs, three secondary bedrooms each have a private bath and walk-in closet. Also on this level is a spacious recreation room, perfect for a game room or children's playroom.

The impressive two-story facade with a raised front pediment gives this home a stately image. Inside, the two-story foyer opens to an adjacent study and dining room. An open rail from the gallery above looks down on the foyer and living room below to give a very open appeal to the formal area of the home. The master suite—with rich appointments and access to the study—provides the perfect retreat. The kitchen is situated in a casual arrangement with the breakfast area and keeping room. Upstairs, three large bedrooms and an optional guest suite, maid's quarters or bonus room meet the needs of a growing family. This home is designed with a walkout basement foundation.

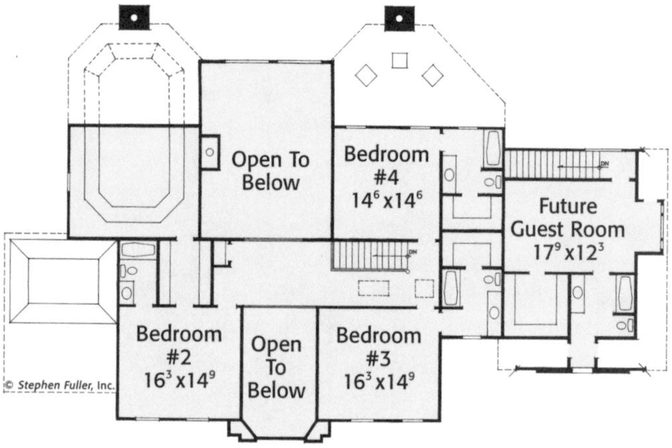

Design

HPT830418

First Floor: 2,959 square feet

Second Floor: 1,326 square feet

Total: 4,285 square feet

Bonus Space: 999 square feet

Width 90'-0" Depth 58'-8"

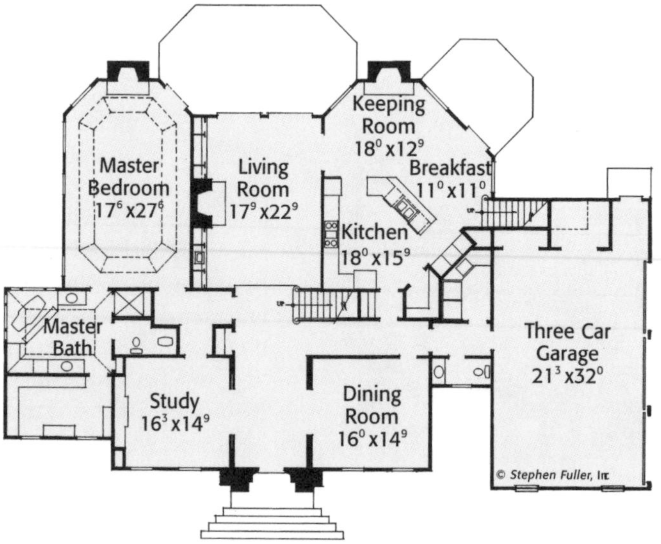

The ornamental stucco detailing on this home creates an Old World Mediterranean charm and complements its strength and prominence. The two-story foyer with a sweeping curved stair opens to the large formal dining room and study. The master suite, offering convenient access to the study, is complete with a fireplace, His and Hers walk-in closets and a bath with twin vanities and a separate shower and tub. The two-story great room overlooks the rear patio. A large kitchen with an island workstation opens to an octagonal-shaped breakfast room and the family room. A staircase located off the family room provides additional access to the three second-floor bedrooms that each offer walk-in closets and plenty of storage. This home is designed with a walkout basement foundation.

Design HPT830419
First Floor: 3,568 square feet
Second Floor: 1,667 square feet
Total: 5,235 square feet
Width 86'-8" Depth 79'-0"

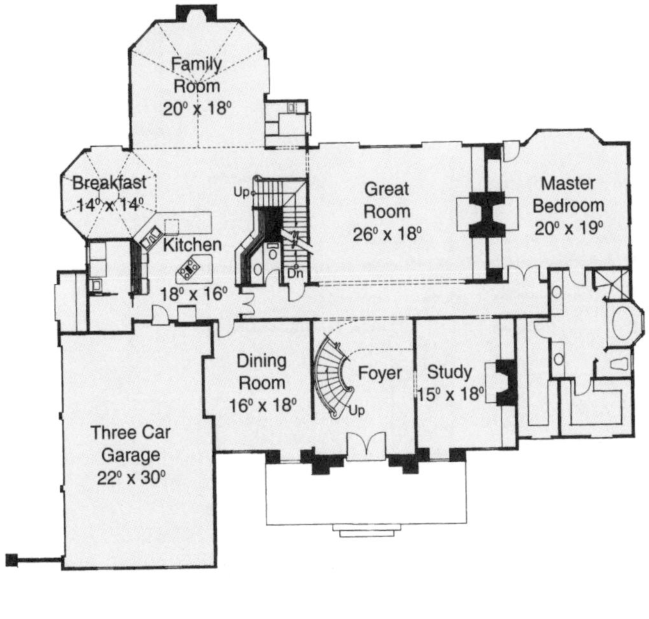

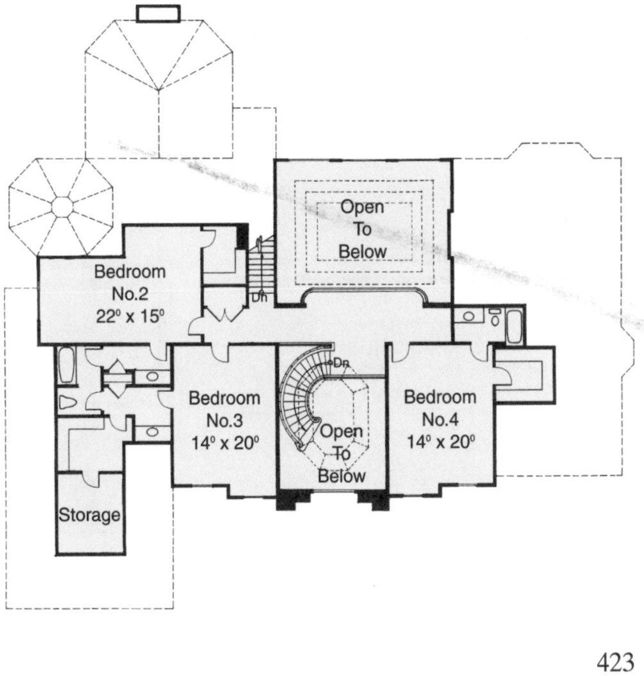

Inside this exquisite country estate, the arrangement of rooms is well-suited for a variety of lifestyles. The large dining room and great room provide the opportunity for formal receiving and entertaining. For casual living, look to the spacious kitchen, the multi-windowed breakfast room or the cozy keeping room with its welcoming fireplace. Conveniently, yet privately located, the master suite is designed to take full advantage of the adjacent study and family area. The second floor contains three bedrooms, three full baths and a bonus room that also functions as Bedroom 5. This home is designed with a basement foundation.

Design HPT830420

First Floor: 2,832 square feet
Second Floor: 1,394 square feet
Total: 4,226 square feet
Bonus Space: 425 square feet
Width 81'-6" Depth 61'-6"

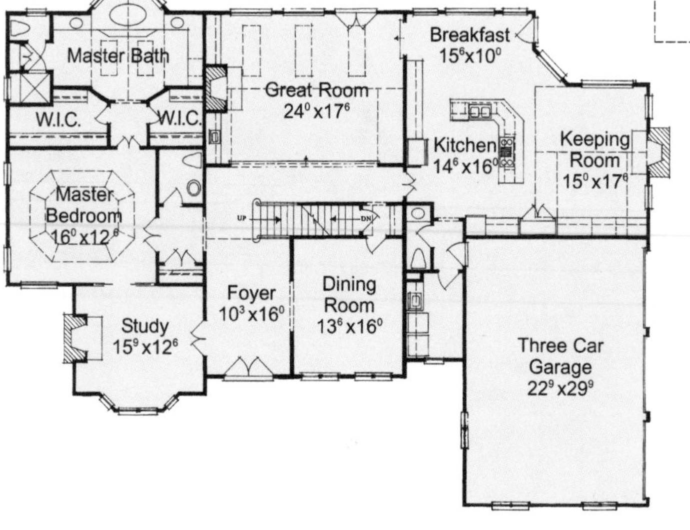

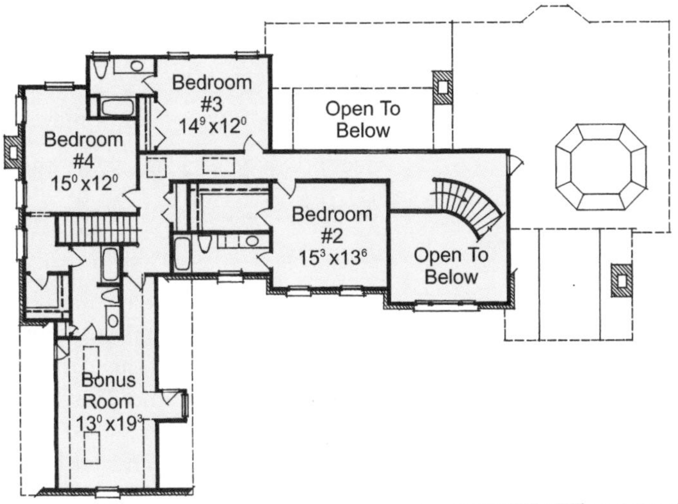

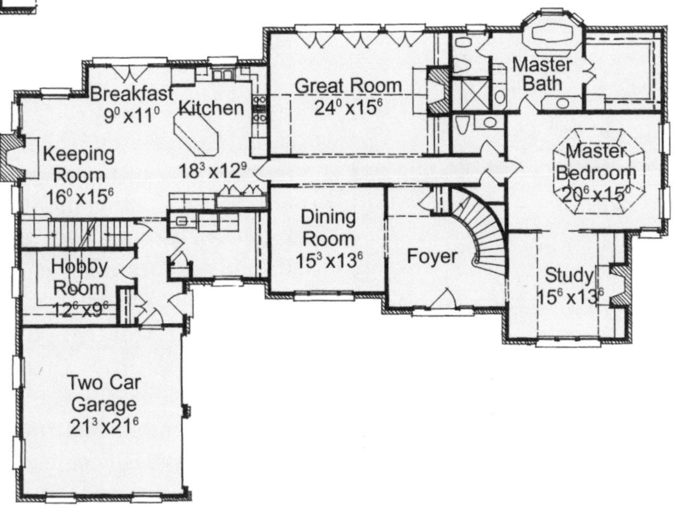

Brick details, casement windows and large expanses of glass add an Old World touch of glamour to this gracious two-story home. Sunlight streams in the two-story foyer which is highlighted by the sweeping curves of the balustrade. For formal occasions, look to the spacious dining room, the inviting study and the vaulted great room. The kitchen, breakfast room and keeping room are designed for casual family living. The master suite provides a quiet retreat with access to the study through pocket doors. Luxury abounds in the spacious master bedroom and the sumptuous bath. Upstairs, three secondary bedrooms each have private baths. This home is designed with a basement foundation.

Design

HPT830421
First Floor: 2,871 square feet
Second Floor: 1,407 square feet
Total: 4,278 square feet
Bonus Space: 324 square feet
Width 89'-3" Depth 60'-10"

This home, as shown in the photograph, may differ from the actual blueprints. For more detailed information, please check the floor plans carefully.
Photo courtesy of Stephen Fuller, Inc.

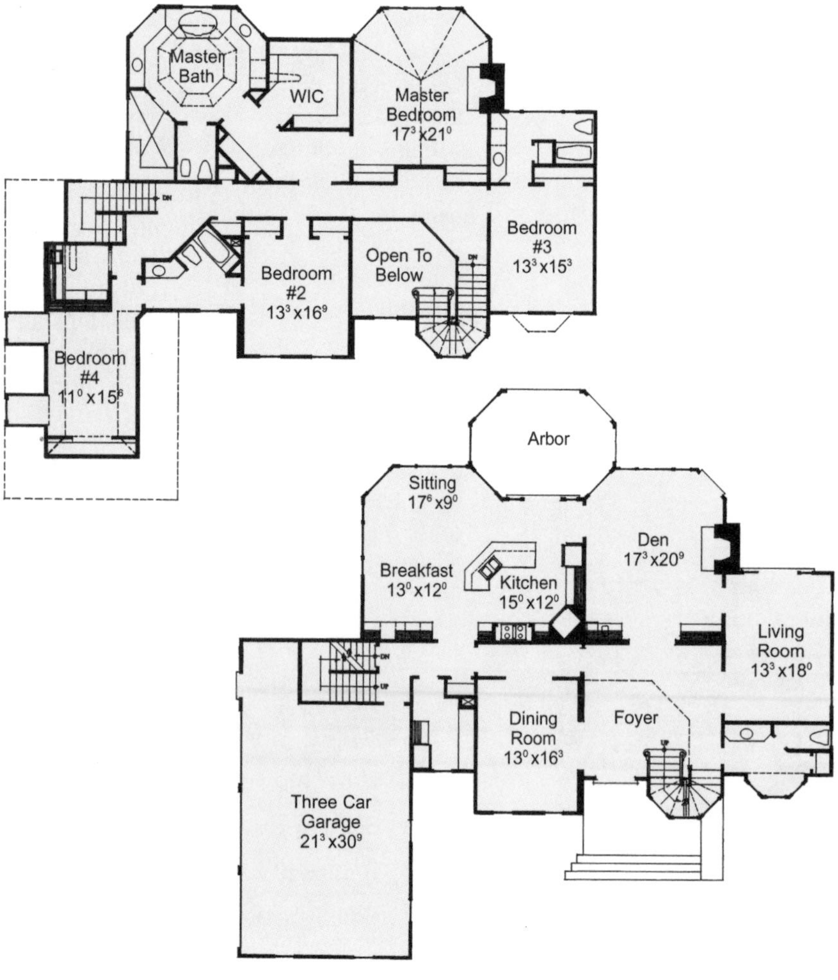

Design HPT830422

First Floor: 2,161 square feet
Second Floor: 2,110 square feet
Total: 4,271 square feet
Width 76'-2" Depth 60'-11"

A blend of stucco and stone creates the charm in this Country French estate home. The asymmetrical design and arched glass windows add to the European character. Inside, the plan offers a unique arrangement of rooms conducive to today's lifestyles. A living room and a dining room flank the foyer, creating a functional formal area. The large den or family room is positioned at the rear of the home with convenient access to the kitchen, patio and covered arbor. Equally accessible to the arbor and patio are the kitchen and breakfast/sitting area. A large butler's pantry is located near the kitchen and dining room. Upstairs, the vaulted master suite and three large bedrooms provide private retreats. This home is designed with a walkout basement foundation.

Estate and Luxury Homes

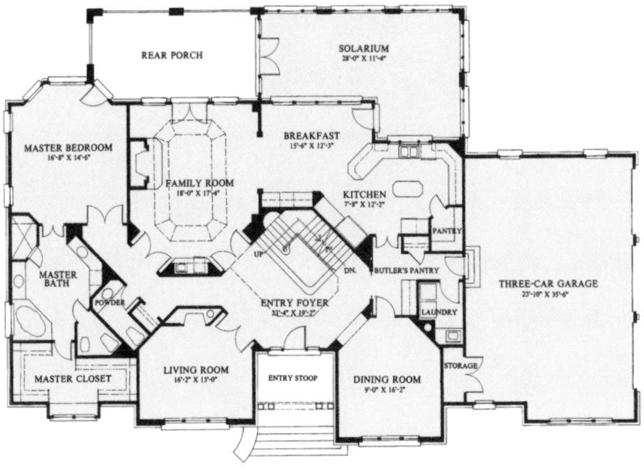

Elegance and luxury define this stately brick-and-stucco home. Creative design continues inside with a dramatic foyer that leads to the formal living and dining rooms and the casual two-story family room. A butler's pantry links the dining room to the grand kitchen. Casual gatherings will be enjoyed in the family room that joins with the breakfast room and kitchen. Here, a solarium and porch invite outdoor living. The exquisite master suite features a lush bath and sunny sitting area. Upstairs, two family bedrooms with private baths, a home office and a hobby room round out the plan. This home is designed with a walkout basement foundation.

QUOTE ONE®

Cost to build? See page 516 to order complete cost estimate to build this house in your area!

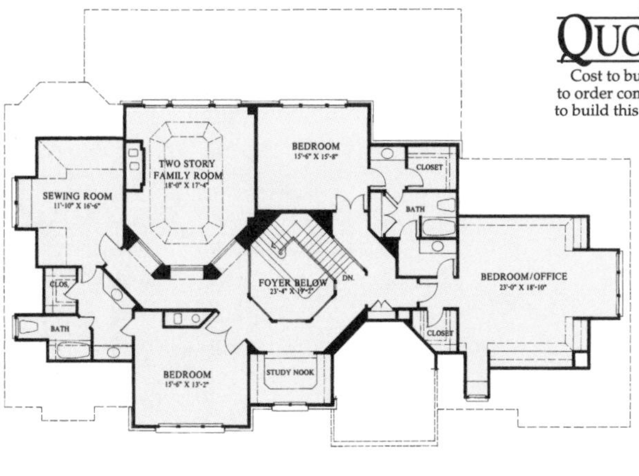

Design HPT830423
First Floor: 3,065 square feet
Second Floor: 1,969 square feet
Total: 5,034 square feet
Width 88'-6" Depth 45'-0"

Looking for style superlative? Look no farther than this quietly elegant European home. A columned entry and Palladian windows add panache and grace. The great room with a fireplace and curved staircase, a breakfast area and adjoining family room, the upstairs game room and the more formal dining and music rooms lend space for all occasions. The master suite is on the first floor, but has a loft overlook above. It has such fine appointments as an exercise room, a fireplace and a cedar closet. Two of four family bedrooms are also on the first floor. The additional two bedrooms are upstairs. Each has a private bath and walk-in closet.

Design HPT830424

First Floor: 4,383 square feet
Second Floor: 1,544 square feet
Total: 5,927 square feet
Width 113'-4" Depth 84'-5"

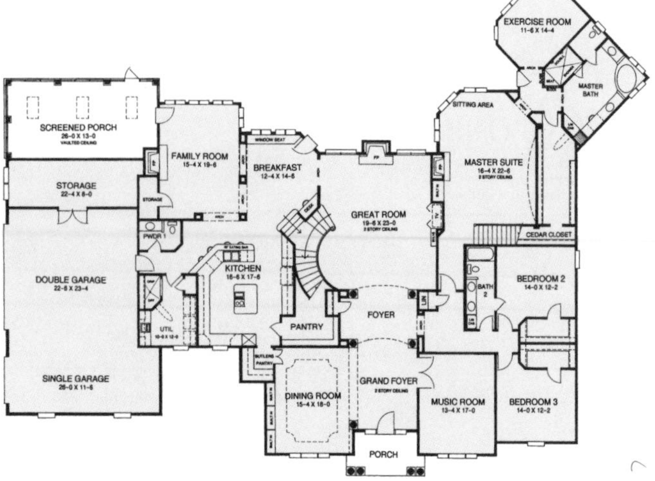

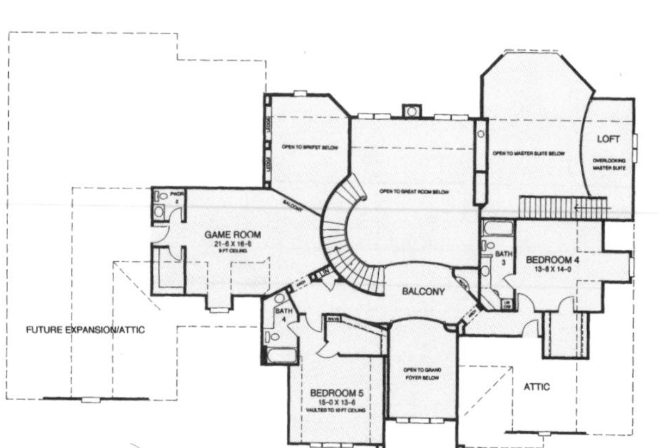

GARAGE
SCREENED PORCH
14-6 X 10-6
PORCH
PATIO WITH TRELLIS
DECK
HOT TUB
EXERCISE RM
8-4 X 11-6
10 FT CEILING
MASTER BATH
10 FT CEILING
LIN
ARCH
COVERED PORCH
BATH
3
FAMILY ROOM
15-6 X 16-0
10 FT CEILING
BREAKFAST
11-6 X 12-0
11 FT CEILING
LIVING ROOM
15-0 X 17-6
12 FT CEILING
WINDOW SEAT
STUDY/BEDROOM 3
14-6 X 13-6
10 FT CEILING
MASTER BEDROOM
15-4 X 16-6
10 FT CEILING
BEDROOM 4
11-6 X 13-0
PAN
10 FT CEILING
KITCHEN
21-0 X 13-6
UTIL
STEP
DINING ROOM
15-4 X 15-4
12 FT CEILING
FOYER
12 FT CEILING
PORCH
BEDROOM 2
12-0 X 14-0
10 FT CEILING
BATH
2

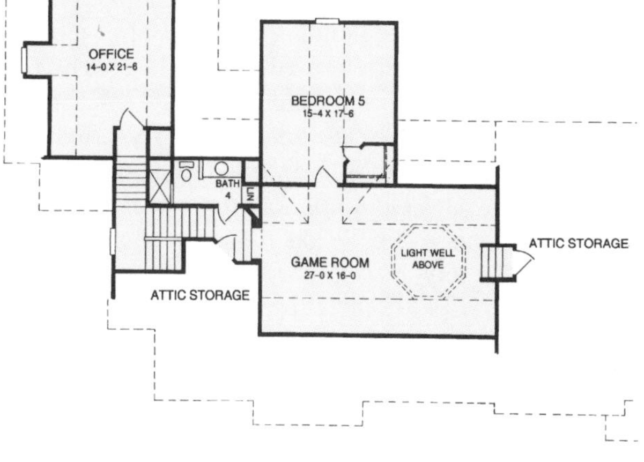
OFFICE
14-0 X 21-6
BEDROOM 5
15-4 X 17-6
BATH
4
LIN
GAME ROOM
27-0 X 16-0
LIGHT WELL
ABOVE
ATTIC STORAGE
ATTIC STORAGE

Design HPT830425

First Floor: 3,328 square feet
Second Floor: 868 square feet
Total: 4,196 square feet
Width 108'-2" Depth 61'-6"

The combination of stucco, stacked stone and brick adds texture and character to this French country home. The foyer offers views to the study, dining room and living room. Double French doors open to the study with built-in bookcases and a window seat overlooking the rear deck. The breakfast room, family room and spacious kitchen make a nice backdrop for family living. The master suite is enhanced by a raised, corner fireplace, an exercise room and a luxurious bath. Upstairs, two family bedrooms—or make one an office—and a full bath are balanced by a large game room.

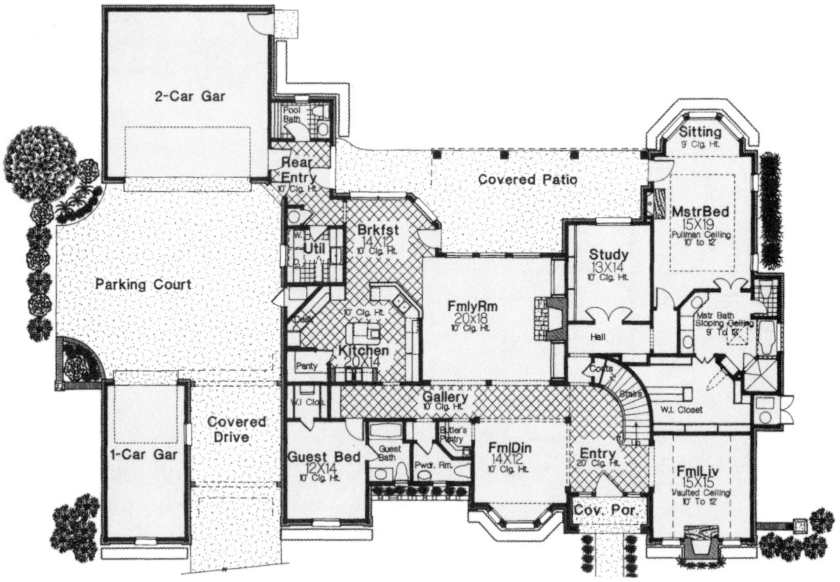

Design
HPT830426

First Floor: 3,248 square feet
Second Floor: 1,426 square feet
Total: 4,674 square feet
Width 99'-10" Depth 74'-10"

Multiple rooflines, a stone, brick and siding facade and an absolutely grand entrance combine to give this home the look of luxury. A striking family room showcases a beautiful fireplace framed with built-ins. The nearby breakfast room streams with light and accesses the rear patio. The kitchen features an island workstation, walk-in pantry and plenty of counter space. A guest suite is available on the first floor, perfect for any visitor. The master suite, also on the first floor, enjoys easy access to a large study, a bayed sitting room and a luxurious bath. Private baths are also included for each of the upstairs bedrooms.

This home, as shown in the photograph, may differ from the actual blueprints. For more detailed information, please check the floor plans carefully.
Photo courtesy of Larry E. Belk Designs, Photo by Peter Loppacher

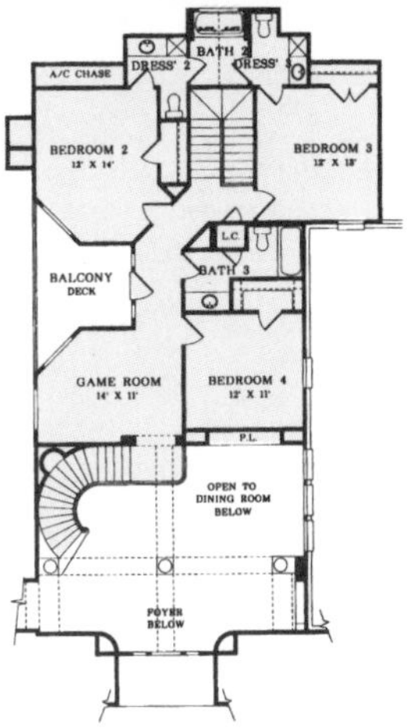

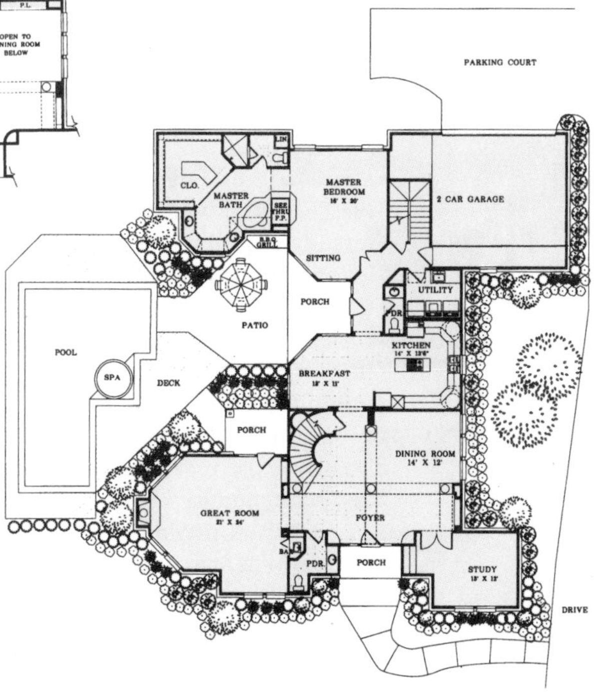

Design HPT830427

First Floor: 2,528 square feet
Second Floor: 1,067 square feet
Total: 3,595 square feet
Width 69'-2" Depth 73'-10"
L

The massive entry to this beautiful home insures that all who pass will take note of this stately elevation. Upon entering, one steps into a two-story foyer with a gallery effect created by oversized columns and connecting arches. A graceful curved staircase rises from the foyer to the second floor. The dining room is showcased off the foyer. Situated with views to the side and rear of the home, the great room is designed with an offset, perfect for a grand piano or a game table. The kitchen and breakfast room are centrally located for easy access to the rear yard. The master suite features a sitting area and a luxury bath with a two-way fireplace. The second floor completes the home with three bedrooms, two baths and a game room.

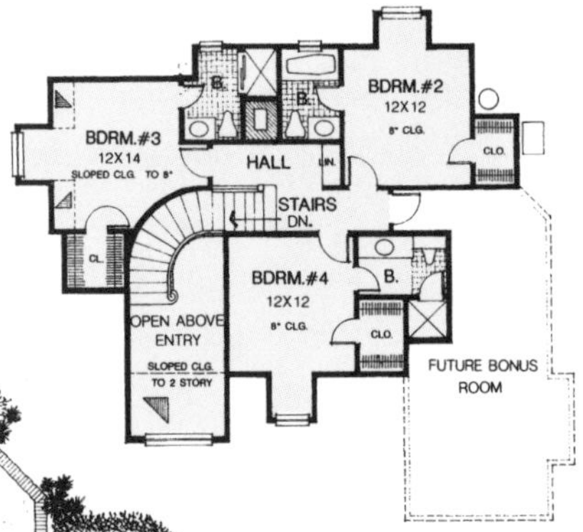

Design
HPT830428

First Floor: 2,438 square feet
Second Floor: 882 square feet
Total: 3,320 square feet
Bonus Space: 230 square feet
Width 70'-0" Depth 63'-2"

Here's a cottage that would have provided plenty of room for Goldilocks and the three bears! Wonderful rooflines top a brick exterior with cedar and stone accents—and lots of English country charm. Stone wing walls extend the front profile, and a cedar hood tops the large bay window. The two-story entry reveals a graceful curving staircase and opens to the formal living and dining rooms. Fireplaces are found in the living room as well as the great room, which also boasts built-in bookcases and access to the rear patio. The kitchen and breakfast room add to the informal area and include a snack bar. A private patio is part of the master suite, which also offers an intriguing corner tub, twin vanities, a large walk-in closet and a nearby study. The second floor is comprised of three family bedrooms and a bonus room.

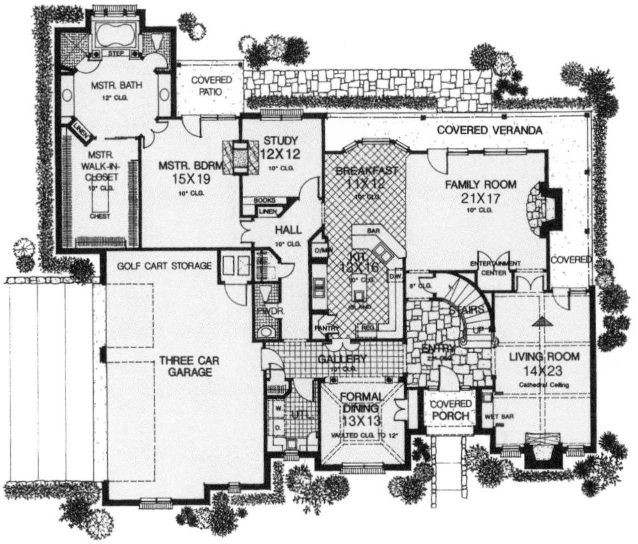

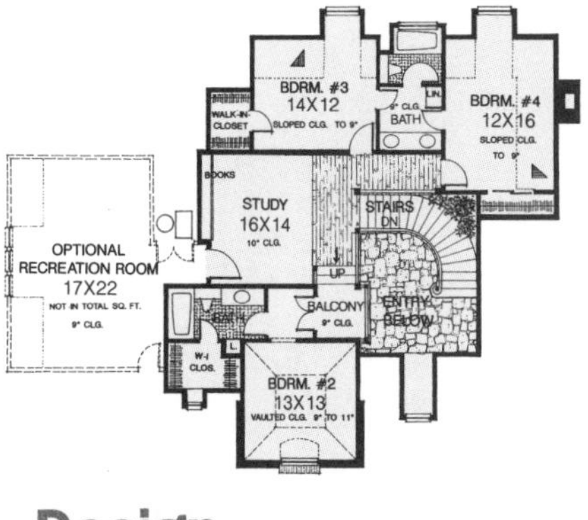

Design HPT830429

First Floor: 2,844 square feet
Second Floor: 1,140 square feet
Total: 3,984 square feet
Optional Recreation Room: 374 square feet
Width 79'-0" Depth 70'-7"

Wonderful rooflines and a stone facade lend storybook elegance to this beautiful French estate. With detailed windows and entries and decorative finial pinnacles, this home is reminiscent of 19th-Century Chateauesque architecture with a hint of Tudor charm. An uncut-stone foyer leads to the living room on the right—complete with cathedral ceiling, wet bar and extended-hearth fireplace— and the family room straight ahead, featuring a stone fireplace and access to the covered veranda. The island kitchen easily services the ample breakfast area for casual meals and the formal dining room with vaulted ceiling, perfect for entertaining. The first-floor master suite indulges with an enormous walk-in closet, step-up tub and private covered patio. Up the dramatic staircase, children and guests will delight in three large bedrooms, a study, and two full baths. An optional recreation room would make an excellent game or exercise room.

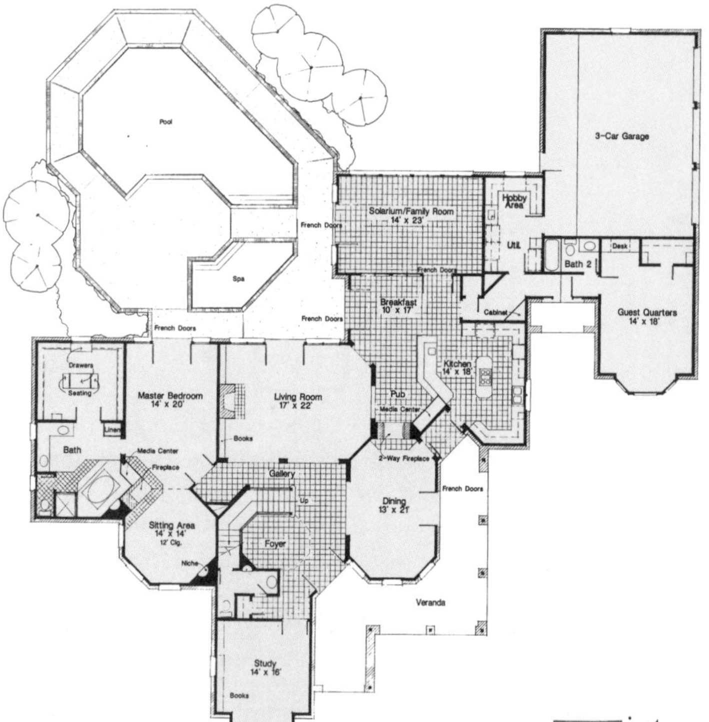

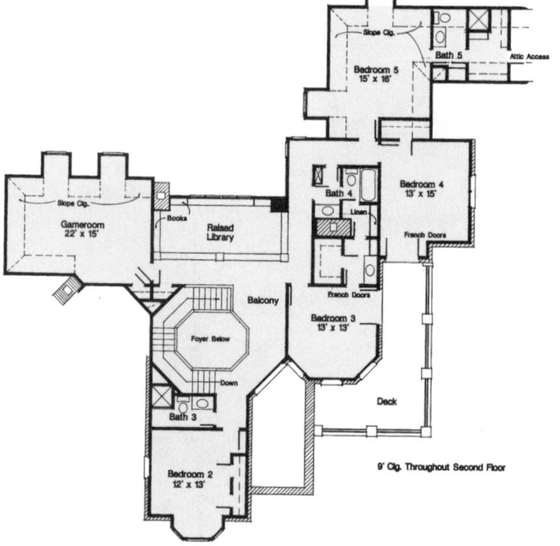

Design HPT830430

First Floor: 3,985 square feet
Second Floor: 2,278 square feet
Total: 6,263 square feet
Width 103'-4" Depth 85'-2"

First- and second-story bay windows with copper roofs and detailed brick arches at the front entry and veranda recall classic estate homes of the 1920s. The magnificent foyer features an impressive staircase and balcony. The gallery offers a view into the formal living room, which has a fireplace and French doors to the terrace. The master suite has a lovely sitting room, a corner fireplace and a lavish bath. The formal dining room shares a two-way fireplace with the pub. Charming French doors close the kitchen and breakfast area to the sun-drenched solarium and family room. Upstairs, four bedrooms with private baths are joined with a game room and library.

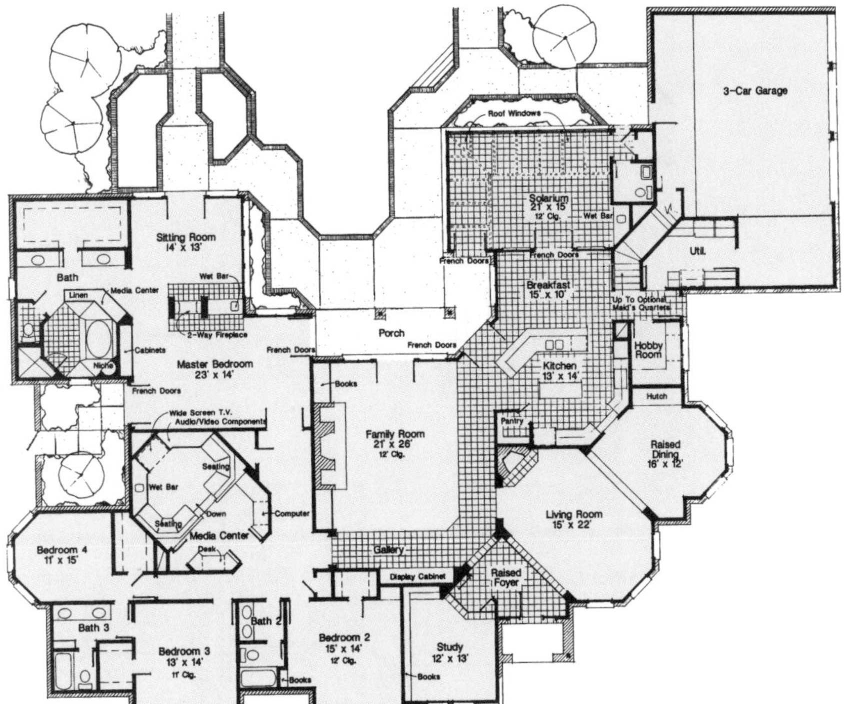

Design HPT830431

Square Footage: 4,958

Width 110'-0" Depth 96'-0"

The stately facade of this traditional estate belies the remarkably contemporary floor plan within. Surely a highlight in this open, elegant plan is the media center, just off the main gallery. Fireplaces warm the spacious family and living rooms. A study to the left of the foyer provides built-in bookshelves. The kitchen, with a work island and a large pantry, serves the family room, breakfast room and raised dining room with ease. French doors open to a commodious solarium. Three family bedrooms, one with a bay window, are accompanied by two full baths. The master suite, to the rear of the home, includes a two-way fireplace to the bedroom and the sitting room, easy access to three separate outdoor areas, a built-in media center, and a bath with a separate shower and tub.

Design HPT830432

First Floor: 3,722 square feet
Second Floor: 1,859 square feet
Total: 5,581 square feet
Width 127'-10" Depth 83'-9"
L

A richly detailed entrance sets the elegant tone of this luxurious design. Rising gracefully from the foyer, the staircase is a fine prelude to the great room beyond. The dining room sits off the entry and displays a coffered ceiling. The kitchen, breakfast room and sun room are conveniently grouped for entertaining. The master suite features an eleven foot ceiling, a sitting room and spa bath. The second level consists of four bedrooms—two with private baths and two that share a bath with private vanities—and a game room.

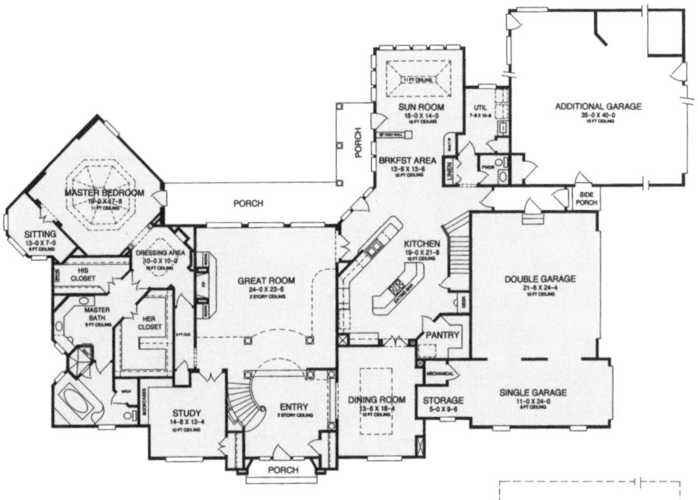

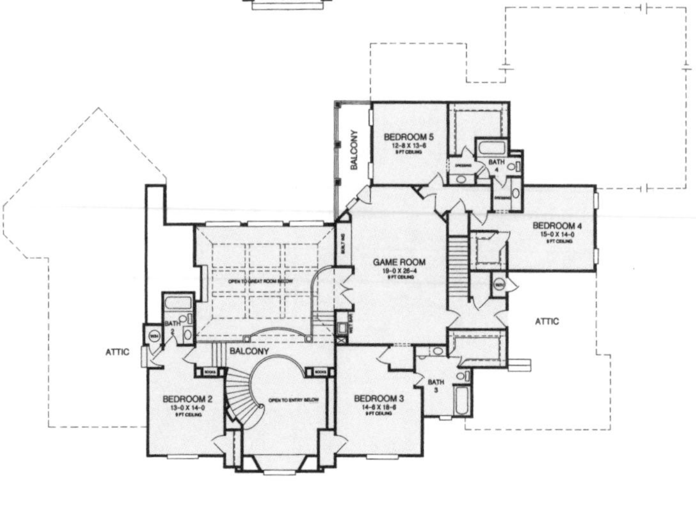

Design HPT830433

First Floor: 3,120 square feet
Second Floor: 1,083 square feet
Total: 4,203 square feet
Width 118'-1" Depth 52'-2"

The blending of natural materials and a nostalgic farmhouse look gives this home its unique character. Inside, a sophisticated floor plan includes all the amenities demanded by today's upscale family. Three large covered porches, one on the front and two on the rear, provide outdoor entertaining areas. The kitchen features a built-in stone fireplace visible from the breakfast and sun rooms. The master suite includes a large sitting area and a luxurious bath. Upstairs, two additional bedrooms and a large game room will please family and guests. Please specify crawlspace or slab foundation when ordering.

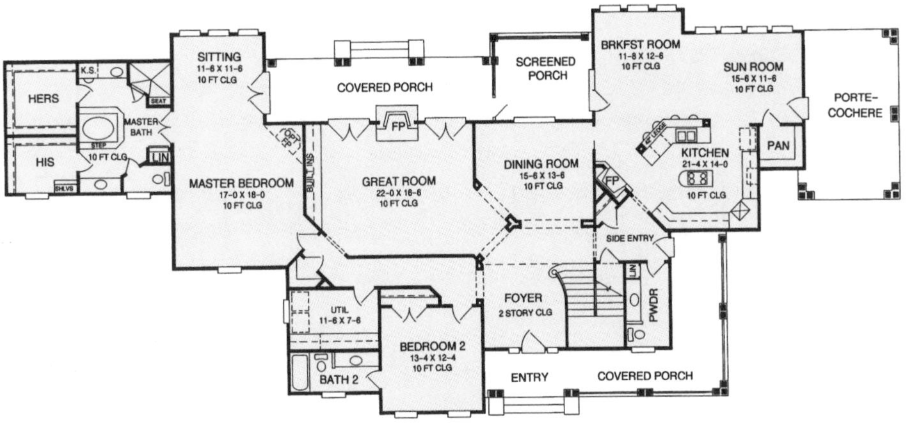

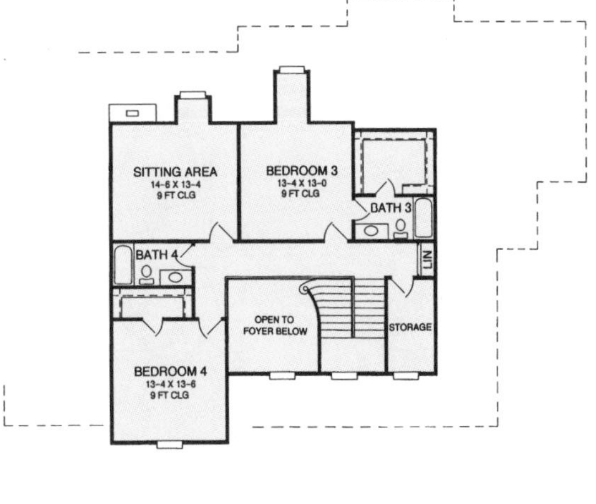

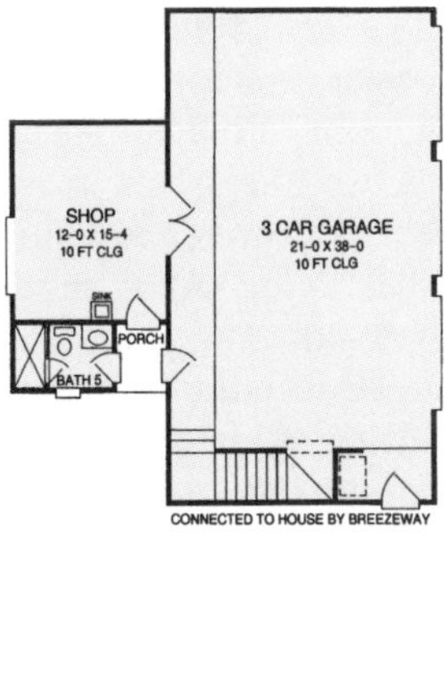

Design
HPT830434

First Floor: 3,359 square feet
Second Floor: 2,174 square feet
Total: 5,533 square feet
Width 96'-5" Depth 85'-6"
L

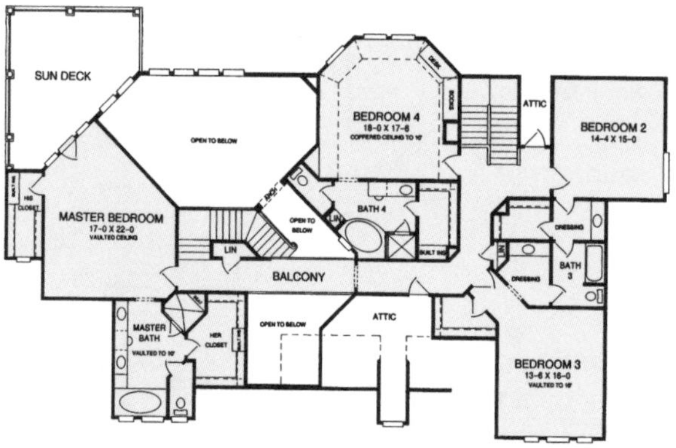

A truly unique luxury home, this farmhouse has all the amenities. The fantastic covered porch surrounds three sides of the home and provides a wonderful area for outdoor living. A two-story foyer angles to draw the eye through double arches to the elegant living room with a fireplace, built-ins and an area for the grand piano. The kitchen, breakfast room and family room join for casual living. Also on the first level: a home office, a game room and a cozy study. Upstairs, the master bedroom is luxuriously appointed and opens to a private sun deck. Three family bedrooms each have walk-in closets and bath access.

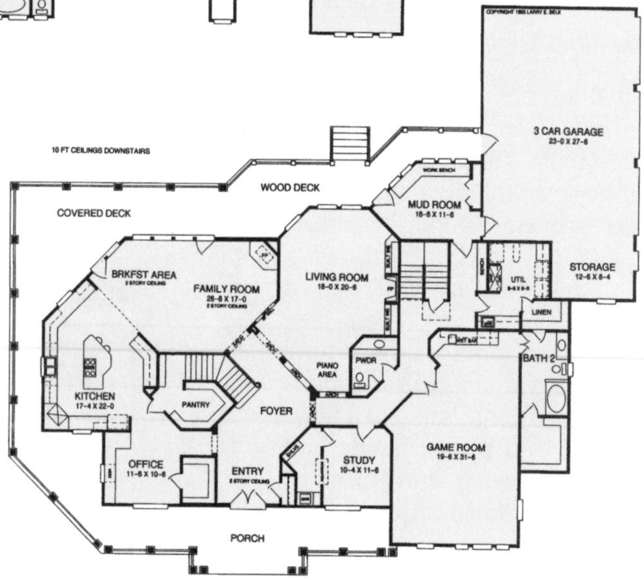

This home, as shown in the photograph, may differ from the actual blueprints. For more detailed information, please check the floor plans carefully.
Photography by Oscar Thompson Photography

Design HPT830435

Square Footage: 4,565	
Width 88'-0"	Depth 95'-0"
L	

A free-standing entryway is the focal point of this luxurious residence. It has an arch motif that is carried through to the rear using a gabled roof and a vaulted ceiling from the foyer out to the lanai. The kitchen, which features a cooktop island and plenty of counter space, opens to the leisure area with a handy snack bar. Two guest suites with private baths are just off this casual living area. The master wing is truly pampering, stretching the entire length of the home. The suite has a large sitting area, a corner fireplace and a morning kitchen. The bath features an island vanity, a raised tub with a curved glass wall overlooking a private garden, a sauna and separate closets. An exercise room has a curved glass wall and a pocket door to the study, where a wet bar is ready to serve up refreshments.

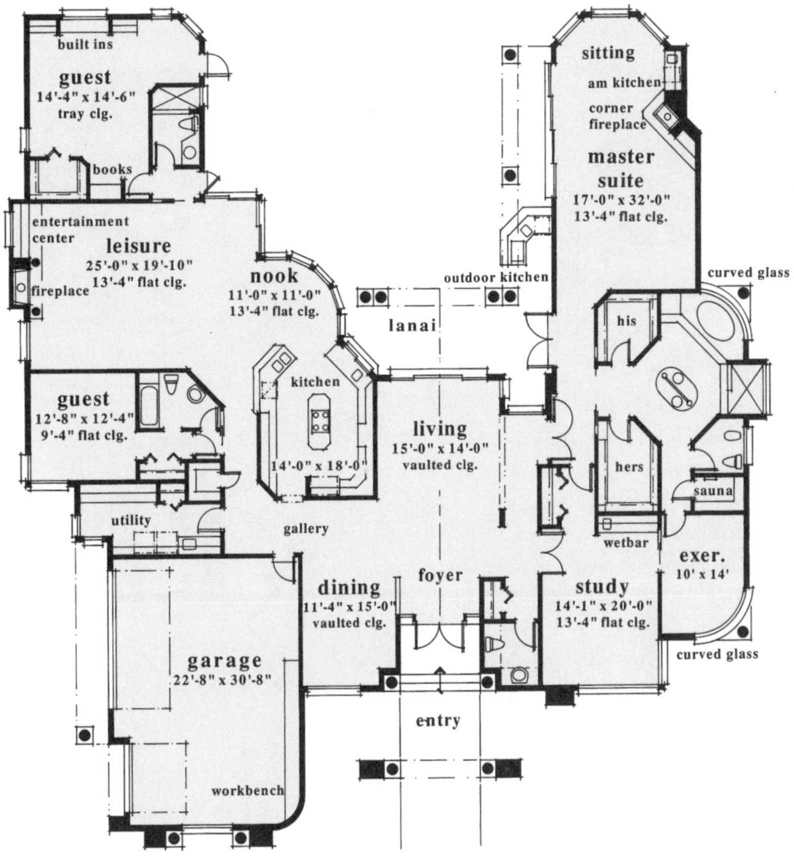

Design

HPT830436

First Floor: 3,770 square feet
Second Floor: 634 square feet
Total: 4,404 square feet
Width 87'-0" Depth 97'-6"

This fresh and innovative design creates unbeatable ambiance. The breakfast nook and family room both open to a patio—a perfect arrangement for informal entertaining. The dining room is sure to please with elegant pillars separating it from the sunken living room. A media room delights both with its shape and by being convenient to the nearby kitchen—great for snack runs. A private garden surrounds the master bath and its spa tub and enormous walk-in closet. The master bedroom is enchanting with a fireplace and access to the outdoors. Additional family bedrooms come in a variety of different shapes and sizes; Bedroom 4 reigns over the second floor and features its own full bath.

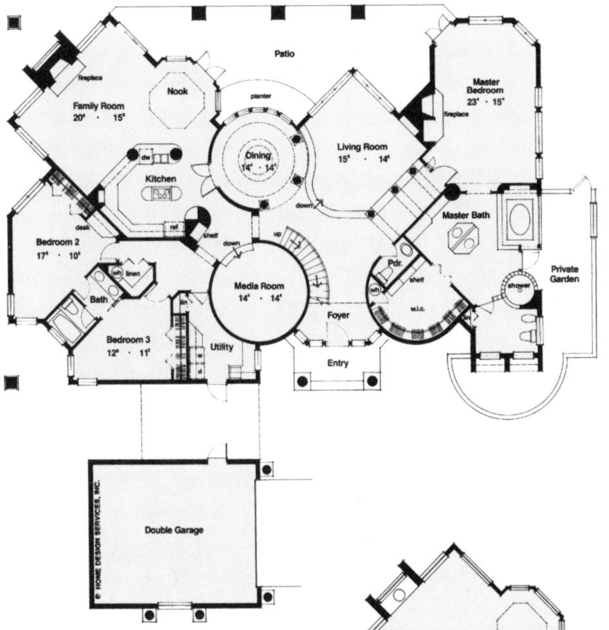

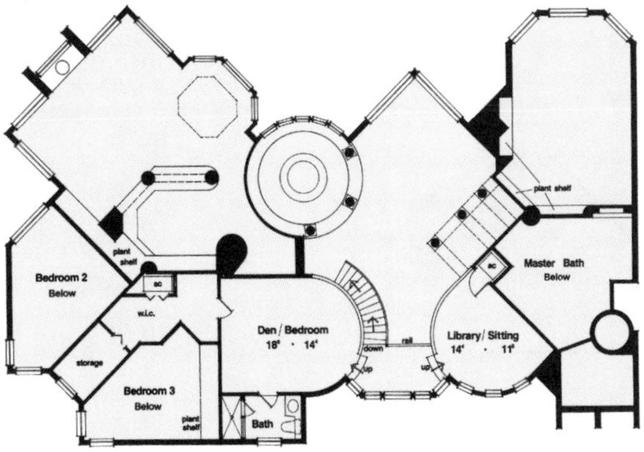

If you want to build a home light years ahead of most other designs, non-traditional, yet addresses every need for your family, this showcase home is for you. From the moment you walk into this home, you are confronted with wonderful interior architecture that reflects modern, yet refined taste. The exterior says contemporary; the interior creates special excitement. Note the special rounded corners found throughout the home and the many amenities. The master suite is especially appealing with a fireplace and grand bath. Upstairs are a library/sitting room and a very private den or guest bedroom.

Design HPT830437

First Floor: 3,236 square feet
Second Floor: 494 square feet
Total: 3,730 square feet
Width 80'-0" Depth 89'-10"

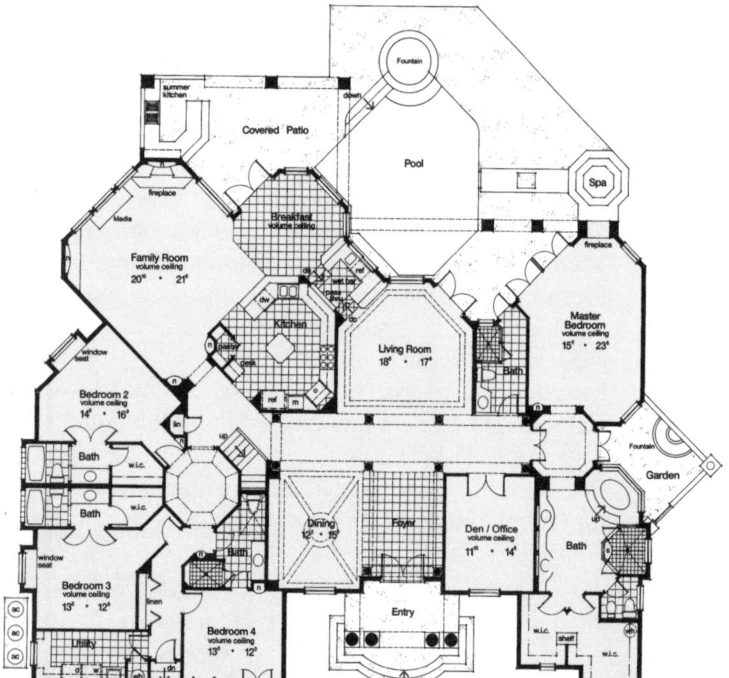

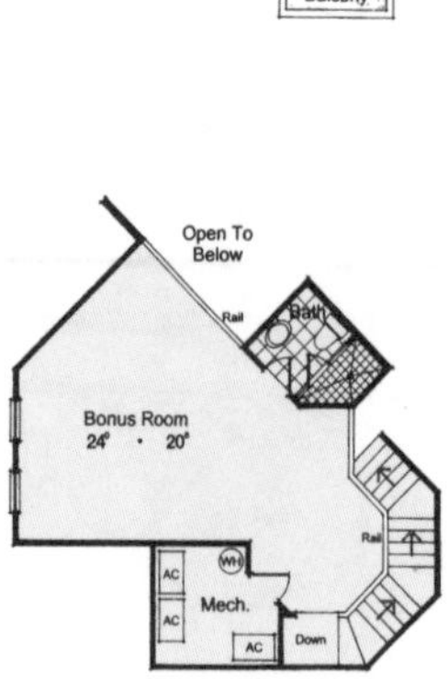

Design HPT830438

Square Footage: 4,222
Bonus Space: 590 square feet
Width 83'-10" Depth 112'-0"

The striking facade of this magnificent estate is just the beginning of the excitement you will encounter inside. The entry foyer passes the formal dining room to the columned gallery, which leads to all regions of the house, with the formal living room at the focal point. The living room opens to the rear patio and the showpiece pool lying flush against the dramatic rear windows of the house. A sunken wet bar serves the living room and the pool via a swim-up bar. The outdoor kitchen is perfect for preparing summer meals. Back inside, the contemporary kitchen has a work island and all the amenities for gourmet preparation. The family room will be a favorite for casual entertainment. The family sleeping wing begins with an octagonal vestibule and includes three bedrooms with private baths. The master wing indulges with a private garden and an opulent bath.

Design HPT830439

Square Footage: 3,556

Width 85'-0" Depth 85'-0"

A beautiful curved portico provides a majestic entrance to this one-story home. To the left of the foyer is a den/bedroom with a private bath, ideal for use as a guest suite. The exquisite master suite features a see-through fireplace and an exercise area with a wet bar. The family wing is geared for casual living with a powder room/patio bath, a huge island kitchen with a walk-in pantry, a glass-walled breakfast nook and a grand family room with a fireplace and media wall. Two family bedrooms share a private bath.

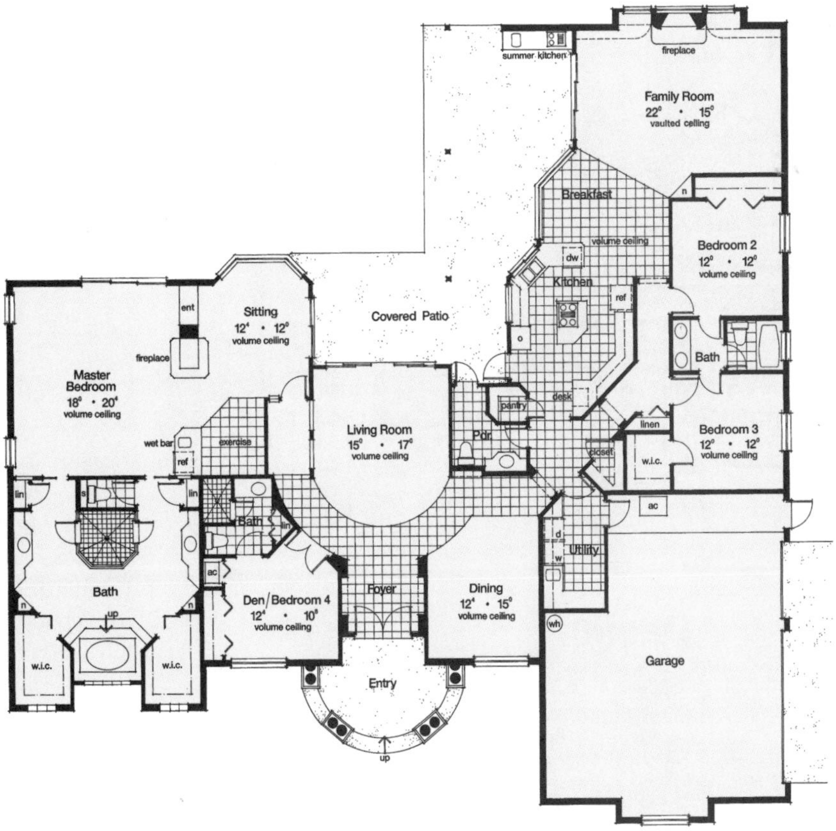

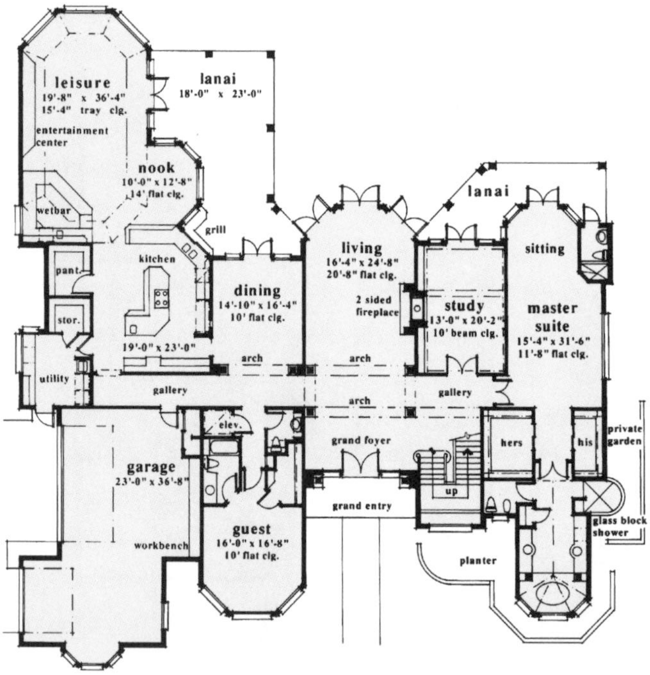

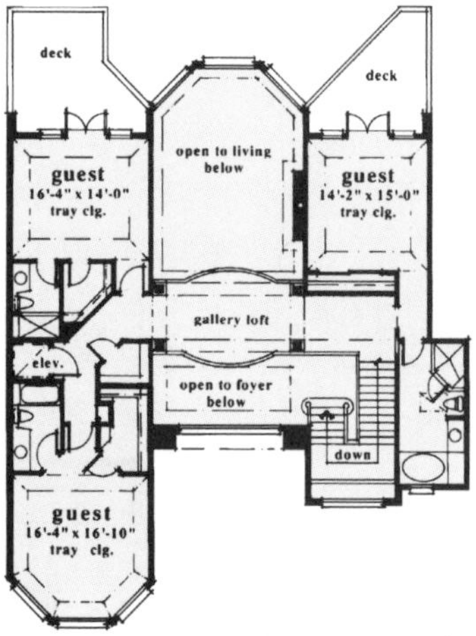

QUOTE ONE®

Cost to build? See page 516 to order complete cost estimate to build this house in your area!

Design HPT830440

First Floor: 4,760 square feet

Second Floor: 1,552 square feet

Total: 6,312 square feet

Width 98'-0" Depth 103'-8"

L

As beautiful from the rear as from the front, this home features a spectacular blend of arch-top windows, French doors and balusters. Dramatic two-story ceilings and tray details add custom spaciousness. An impressive informal leisure room has a sixteen-foot tray ceiling, an entertainment center and a grand ale bar. The large gourmet kitchen is well appointed and easily serves the nook and formal dining room. The master suite begins with a large bedroom and a bayed sitting area. His and Hers vanities and walk-in closets and a curved, glass-block shower are highlights in the bath. The staircase leads to the deluxe secondary guest suites, two of which have observation decks to the rear, and each includes its own full bath.

This grand traditional home offers an elegant, welcoming residence for the homeowner with luxury in mind. Beyond the foyer, the spacious living room provides views of the rear grounds and opens to the veranda and rear yard through three pairs of French doors. An arched galley hall leads past the formal dining room to the family areas. Here, an ample gourmet kitchen easily serves the nook and the leisure room. The master wing includes a study or home office, a luxurious bath with bumped out tub and access to the veranda. Upstairs, each of three secondary bedrooms features a walk-in closet, and two bedrooms offer private balconies.

Design HPT830441

First Floor: 3,546 square feet
Second Floor: 1,213 square feet
Total: 4,759 square feet
Width 96'-0" Depth 83'-0"

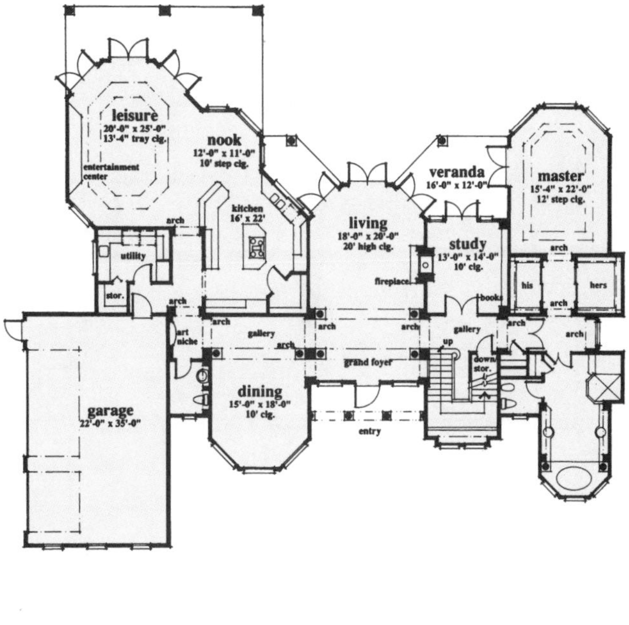

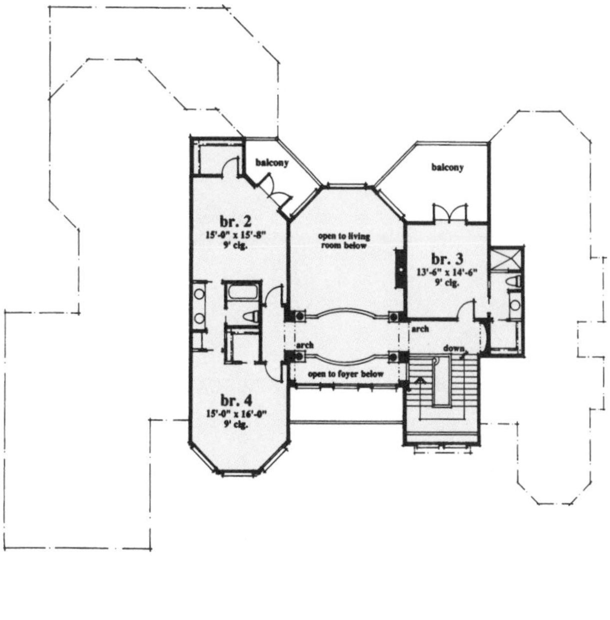

F lorida living takes off in this grand design. A grand room gains attention as a superb entertaining area. A see-through fireplace here connects this room to the dining room. In the study, quiet time is assured—or slip out the doors and onto the veranda for a breather. A full bath connects the study and Bedroom 2. Bedroom 3 sits on the opposite side of the house and enjoys its own bath. The kitchen features a large work island and a connecting breakfast nook. Upstairs, the master bedroom suite contains His and Hers baths, a see-through fireplace and access to an upper deck. A guest bedroom suite is located on the other side of the upper floor.

Design HPT830442

First Floor: 2,725 square feet
Second Floor: 1,418 square feet
Total: 4,143 square feet
Width 61'-4" Depth 62'-0"
L

QUOTE ONE®

Cost to build? See page 516 to order complete cost estimate to build this house in your area!

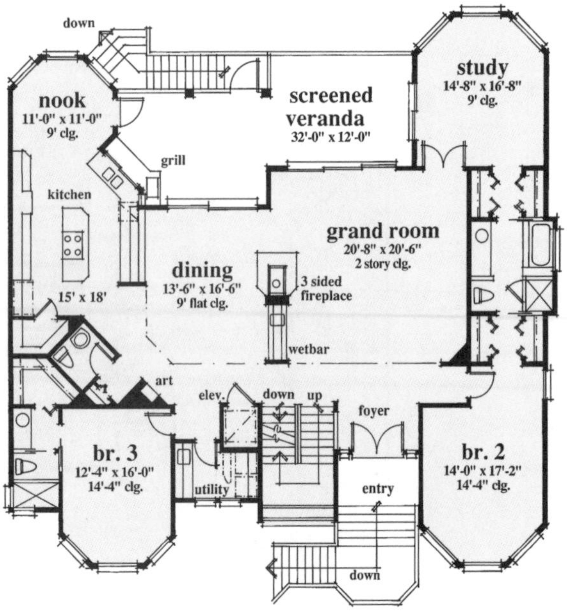

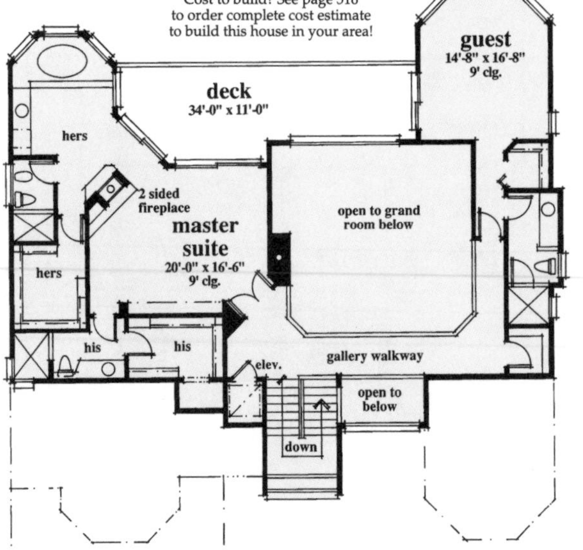

A dramatic set of stairs leads to the entry of this home. The foyer opens to an expansive grand room with a fireplace and built-in bookshelves. For formal meals, a front-facing dining room offers plenty of space and a bumped-out bay. The kitchen serves this area easily as well as the breakfast nook. A study and three bedrooms make up the rest of the floor plan. Two secondary bedrooms share a full bath. The master suite contains two walk-in closets and a full bath.

Design HPT830443

Square Footage: 2,190

Width 58'-0" Depth 54'-0"

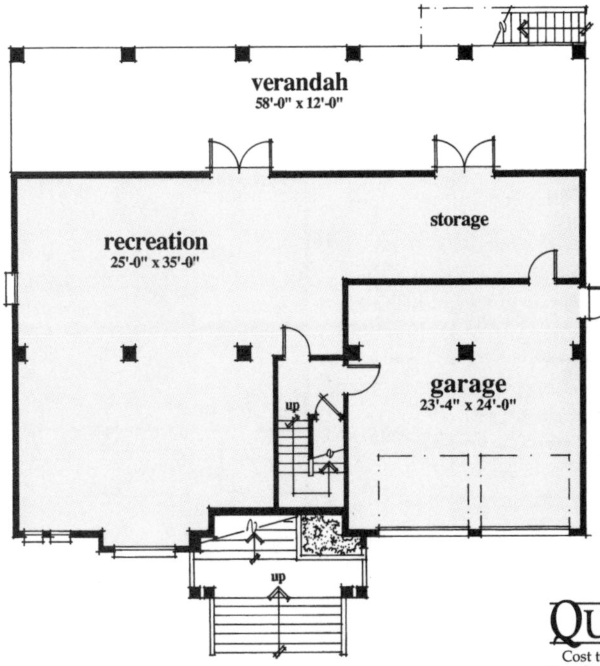
verandah
58'-0" x 12'-0"
recreation
25'-0" x 35'-0"
storage
garage
23'-4" x 24'-0"
up
up

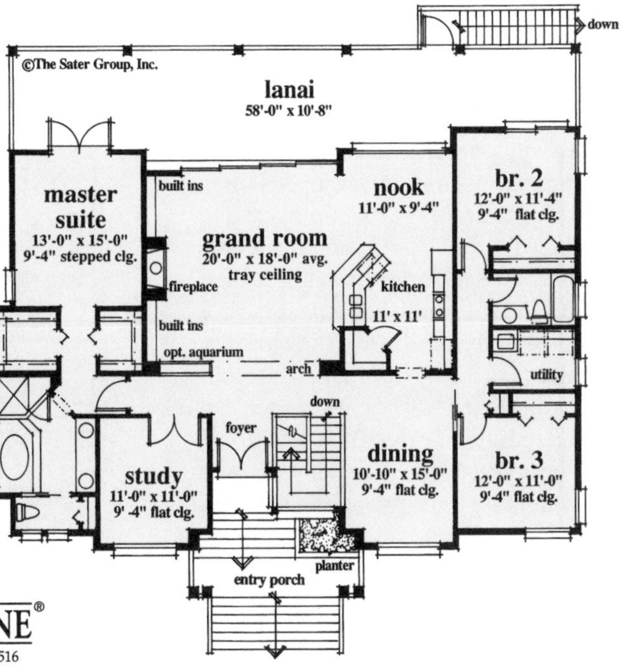
©The Sater Group, Inc.
down
lanai
58'-0" x 10'-8"
master suite
13'-0" x 15'-0"
9'-4" stepped clg.
built ins
grand room
20'-0" x 18'-0" avg.
tray ceiling
fireplace
built ins
opt. aquarium
nook
11'-0" x 9'-4"
kitchen
11' x 11'
arch
br. 2
12'-0" x 11'-4"
9'-4" flat clg.
utility
study
11'-0" x 11'-0"
9'-4" flat clg.
foyer
down
dining
10'-10" x 15'-0"
9'-4" flat clg.
br. 3
12'-0" x 11'-0"
9'-4" flat clg.
planter
entry porch

QUOTE ONE®

Cost to build? See page 516
to order complete cost estimate
to build this house in your area!

Design

HPT830444

Square Footage: 2,090	
Width 67'-0"	Depth 59'-0"

This exciting Southwestern design is enhanced by the use of arched windows and an inviting arched entrance. The large foyer opens to a massive great room with a fireplace and built-in cabinets. The kitchen features an island cooktop and a skylit breakfast area. The master suite has an impressive cathedral ceiling and a walk-in closet as well as a luxurious bath that boasts separate vanities, a corner whirlpool tub and a separate shower. Two additional bedrooms are located at the opposite end of the home for privacy and share a full bath.

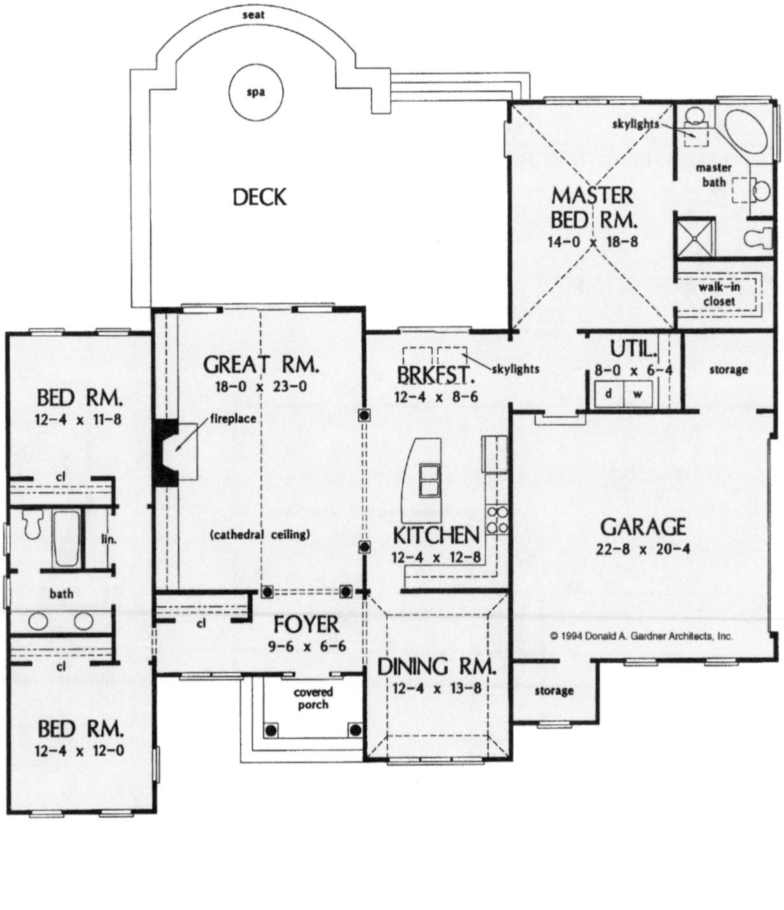

© 1994 Donald A. Gardner Architects, Inc.
B. NATHAN

Southwestern influences are evident in this design, from the tiled roof to the classic stucco exterior. A covered porch leads indoors where the great room gains attention. A cathedral ceiling, a fireplace and built-ins enhance this area. The dining room remains open to this room. In the kitchen, a pass-through cooktop counter allows the cook to converse with family and friends. Three bedrooms include two family bedrooms that share a hall bath and a master suite with skylights, a walk-in closet and a private bath.

Design HPT830445

Square Footage: 1,315

Width 66'-4" Depth 44'-4"

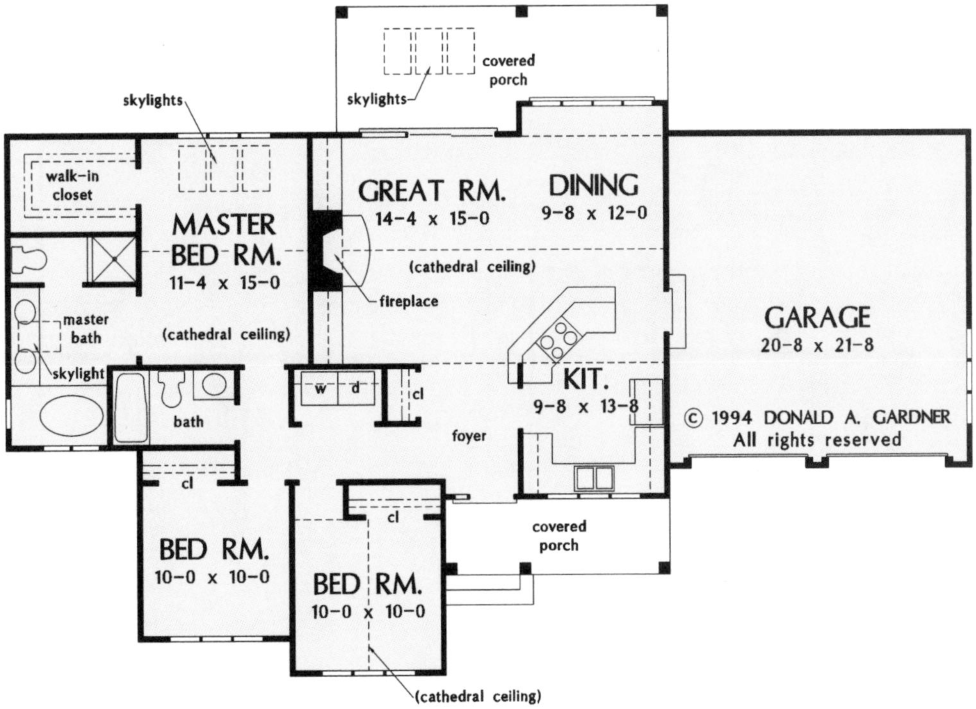
covered porch
skylights
skylights
walk-in closet
MASTER BED RM.
11-4 x 15-0
(cathedral ceiling)
GREAT RM.
14-4 x 15-0
DINING
9-8 x 12-0
(cathedral ceiling)
fireplace
master bath
skylight
bath
w
d
cl
KIT.
9-8 x 13-8
foyer
GARAGE
20-8 x 21-8
© 1994 DONALD A. GARDNER
All rights reserved
cl
cl
covered porch
BED RM.
10-0 x 10-0
BED RM.
10-0 x 10-0
(cathedral ceiling)

This country home offers a fresh face and plenty of personality, starting with its sunny bay with transom windows and a two-story turret. Inside, the foyer opens to a quiet den—the lower bay of the turret—through French doors. A formal living room with a tray ceiling leads to the vaulted dining room, which is served by a gourmet kitchen. To the rear of the plan, a spacious family area offers its own fireplace with a tiled hearth. Upstairs, a secluded master suite boasts a corner tiled-rim spa tub and an angled walk-in closet. Two family bedrooms share a full bath and a hall that leads to a sizable bonus room.

Design HPT830446

First Floor: 1,586 square feet
Second Floor: 960 square feet
Total: 2,546 square feet
Bonus Space: 194 square feet
Width 63'-0" Depth 50'-0"
L

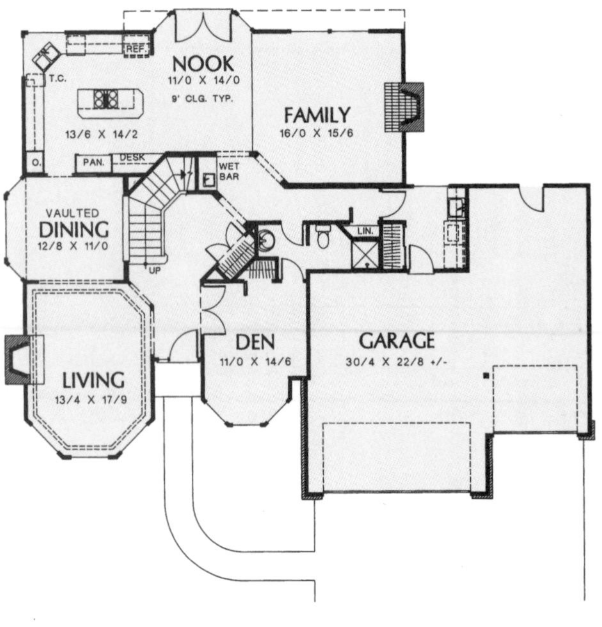

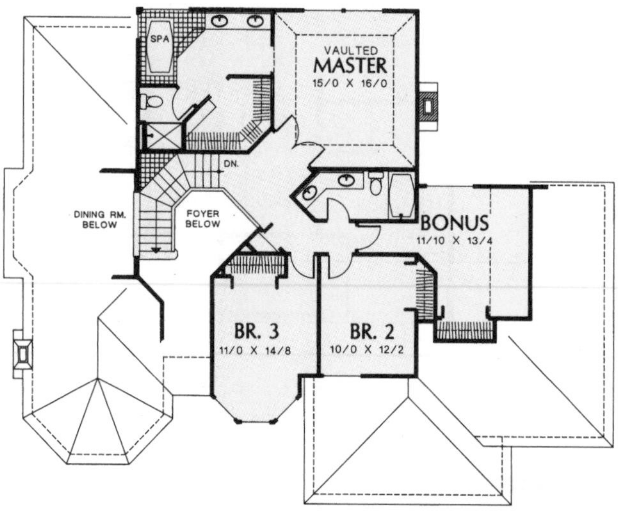

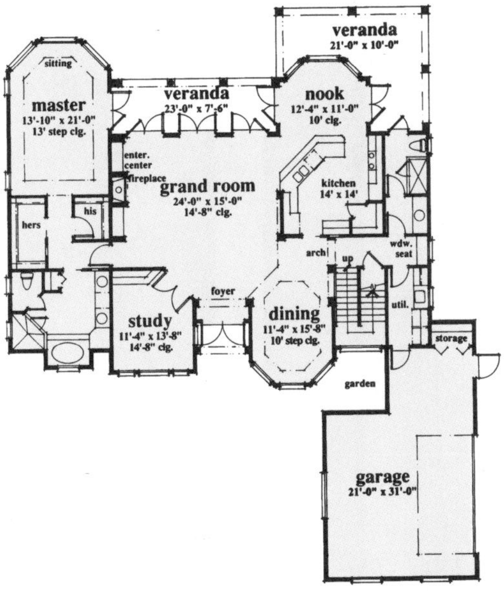

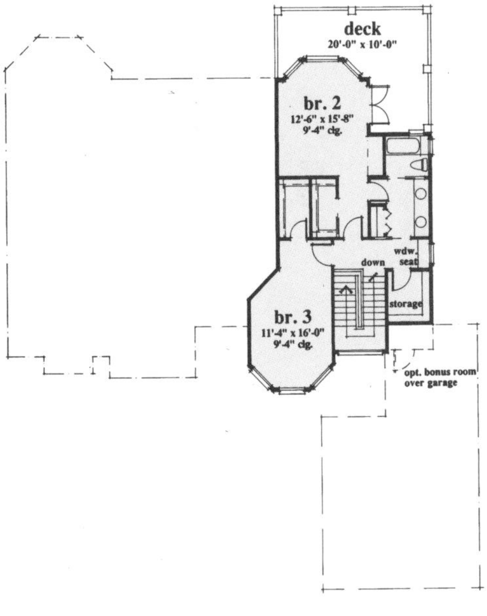

Design HPT830447

First Floor: 2,181 square feet
Second Floor: 710 square feet
Total: 2,891 square feet
Bonus Space: 240 square feet
Width 66'-4" Depth 79'-0"

An arched, covered porch presents fine double doors leading to a spacious foyer in this decidedly European home. A two-story tower contains an elegant formal dining room on the first floor and a spacious bedroom on the second floor. The grand room is aptly named with a fireplace, a built-in entertainment center and three sets of doors opening onto the veranda. A large kitchen is ready to please the gourmet of the family with a big walk-in pantry and a sunny, bay-windowed eating nook. The secluded master suite is luxury in itself. A bay-windowed sitting area, access to the rear veranda, His and Hers walk-in closets and a lavish bath are all set to pamper you. Upstairs, two bedrooms, both with walk-in closets, share a full hall bath that includes twin vanities.

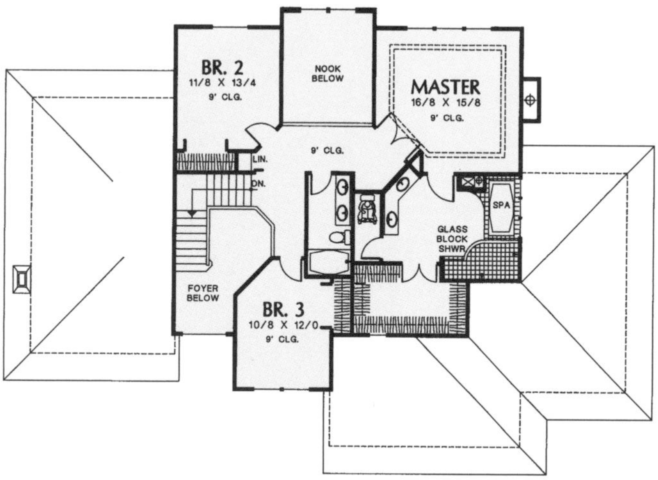

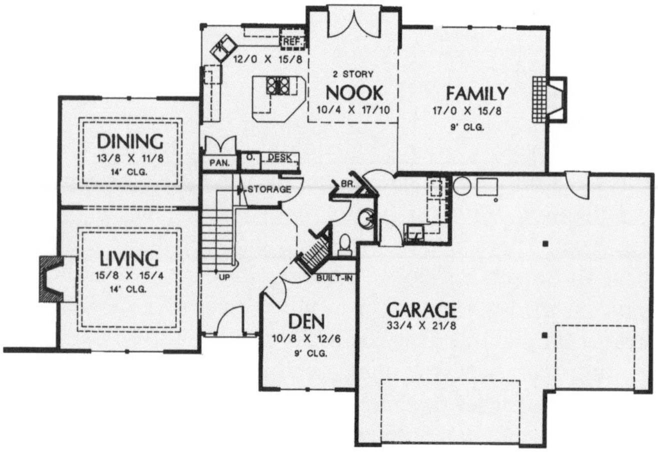

Design HPT830448

First Floor: 1,600 square feet

Second Floor: 1,123 square feet

Total: 2,723 square feet

Width 68'-0" Depth 48'-0"

L

Beyond the contemporary facade of this home lies a highly functional floor plan. First-floor living areas include formal living and dining rooms, a private den, and a large family room that connects directly to the breakfast nook and island kitchen. The upper level contains three bedrooms, including a master suite with a nine-foot tray ceiling and a sumptuous master bath which encompasses a huge walk-in closet, whirlpool spa and double vanity. A fine hall bath completes this floor.

Inside the grand entrance of this contemporary home, a large foyer offers a gracious introduction to the formal living and dining rooms. Nearby, the L-shaped island kitchen serves formal and informal areas with equal ease. A two-story family room with a built-in media center and a corner fireplace shares space with a sunny nook. The private master suite features a walk-in closet and a luxurious bath. The second floor contains two bedrooms and a full bath.

Design
HPT830449

First Floor: 1,896 square feet
Second Floor: 568 square feet
Total: 2,464 square feet
Width 45'-0" Depth 64'-0"

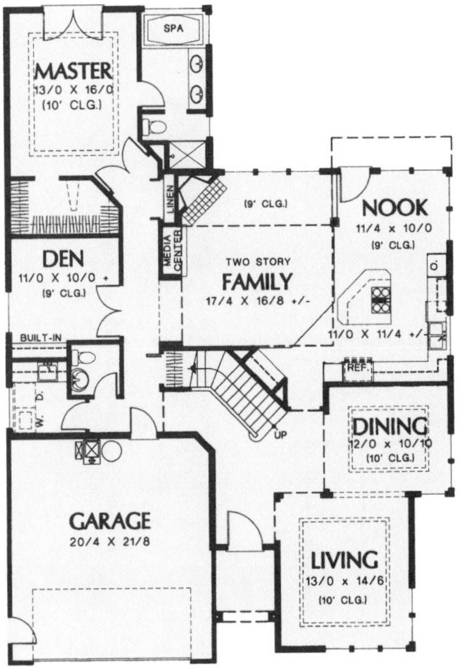

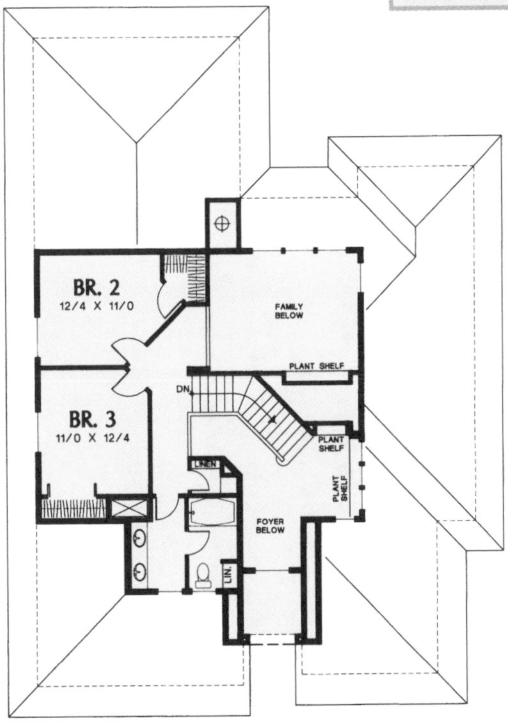

Here's a contemporary home with a French country spirit! Comfortably elegant formal rooms reside to the front of the plan, with a focal-point fireplace, a bay window and decorative columns to help define the space. A central hall leads to the family area, which includes a gourmet kitchen with an island cooktop counter, a bayed breakfast nook and a vaulted family room with an inglenook. Upstairs, a lavish master suite opens through French doors to a private deck, and a spacious bath boasts a windowed, tile-rimmed spa tub, twin vanities and a generous walk-in closet. Three family bedrooms cluster around a central hall, which opens to a quiet den and enjoys a balcony overlook.

Design
HPT830450

First Floor: 1,466 square feet

Second Floor: 1,369 square feet

Total: 2,835 square feet

Width 50'-0" Depth 60'-6"

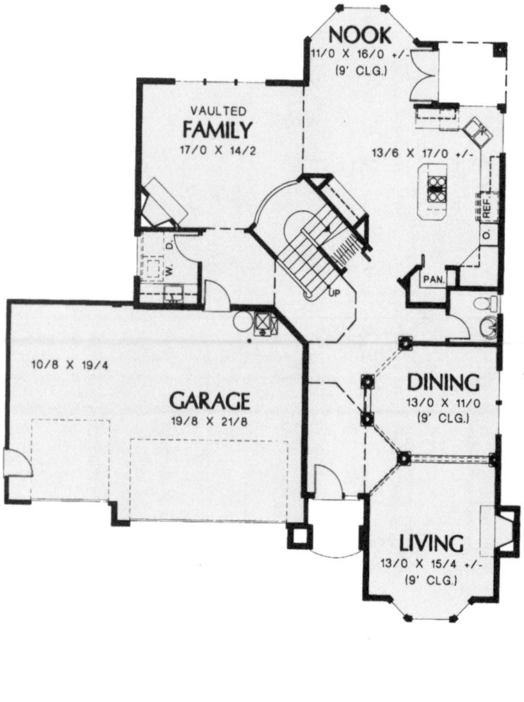

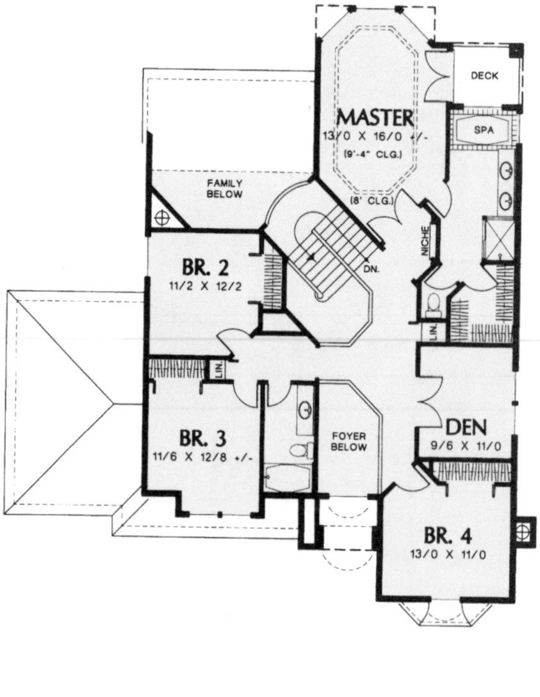

A grand entry porch combines with a wealth of windows to make a notable first impression for this traditional stucco home. The foyer brings you the dining and living rooms on the right, preceded by the private den. The oversized kitchen is the center of the family living zone. Complete with a cooktop island and extensive cabinet space, the kitchen is open to the breakfast nook and the large family room—even the cozy fireplace is visible to the cook! Up the dramatic, open staircase is the master suite and the two family bedrooms that share a full hall bath. The master suite is a welcome retreat with special touches such as the scenic corner window, a lavish master bath and French doors.

Design HPT830451

First Floor: 1,322 square feet
Second Floor: 1,000 square feet
Total: 2,322 square feet
Width 50'-0" Depth 54'-10"

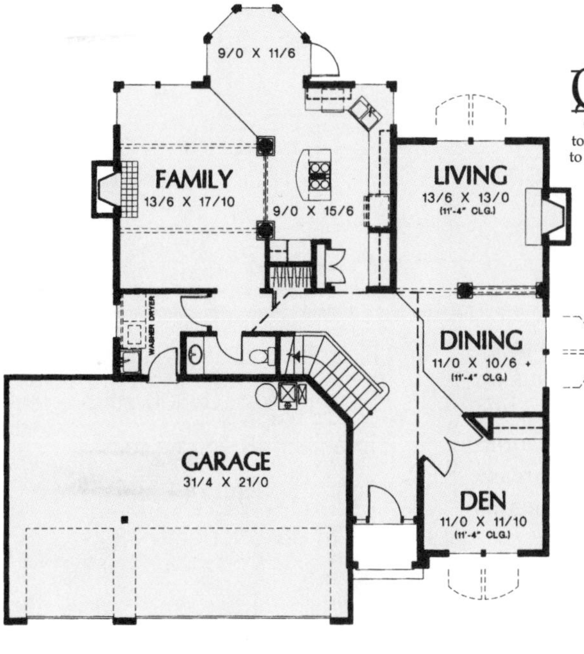

QUOTE ONE®
Cost to build? See page 516 to order complete cost estimate to build this house in your area!

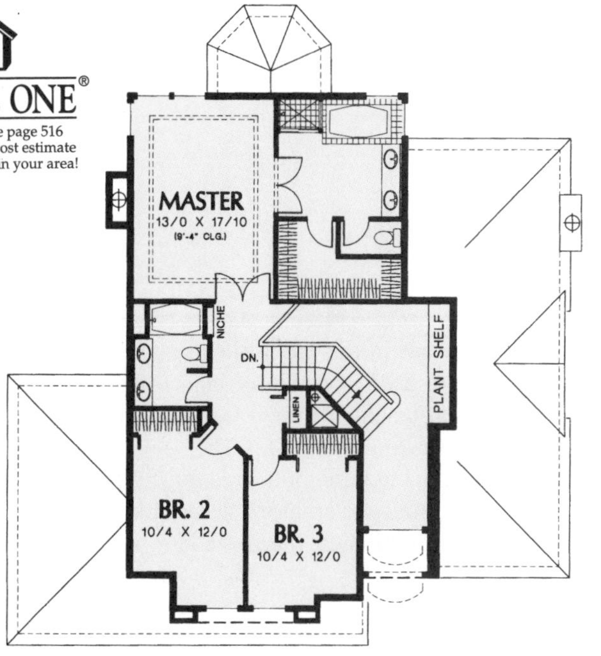

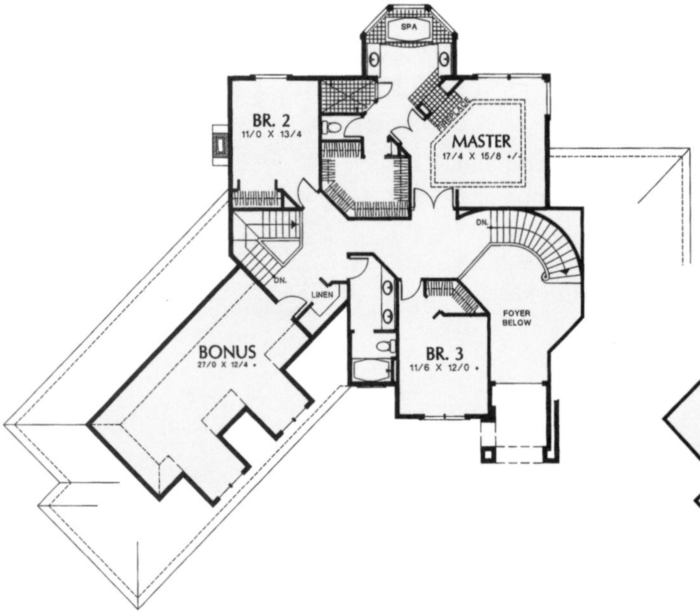

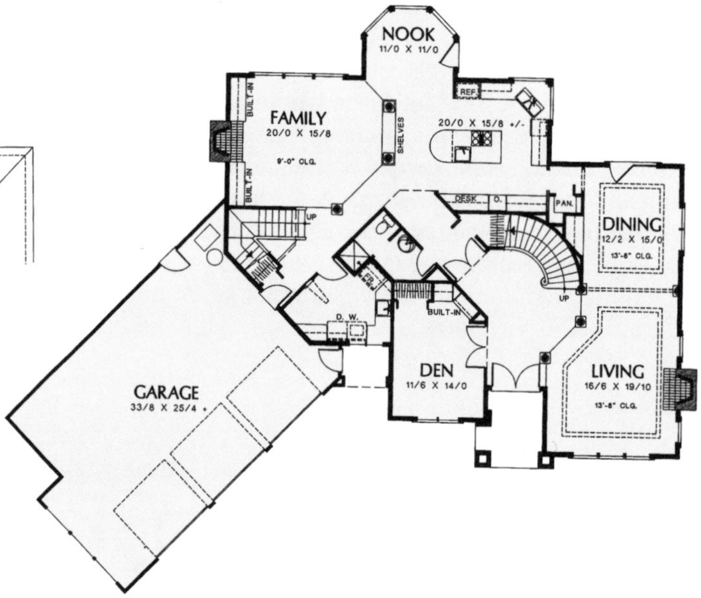

Luxury abounds in this magnificent contemporary plan. The entry foyer gives way to a den on the left and formal living and dining rooms on the right. A curving staircase leads upstairs to the master suite and two family bedrooms sharing a full bath. The rear of the plan holds a family room separated from the kitchen/nook area by built-in shelves. A back staircase here makes the upstairs even more accessible. Note special features such as the prep island in the kitchen, the three-car garage and the bonus room.

Design
HPT830452

First Floor: 2,148 square feet

Second Floor: 1,300 square feet

Total: 3,448 square feet

Bonus Space: 444 square feet

Width 86'-0" Depth 73'-0"

L

This striking stucco home incorporates fine design elements throughout the plan, including a columned formal living and dining area with a boxed ceiling and a fireplace. A gourmet kitchen accommodates the most elaborate—as well as the simplest—meals. The large family room is just off the kitchen for easy casual living. A lovely curved staircase leads to a balcony overlooking the foyer. The master bedroom contains many fine design features, including a luxury bath with a vaulted ceiling and a spa-style bath. Three comfortable family bedrooms share a full hall bath.

Design HPT830453

First Floor: 1,317 square feet
Second Floor: 1,146 square feet
Total: 2,463 square feet
Width 50'-0" Depth 54'-0"

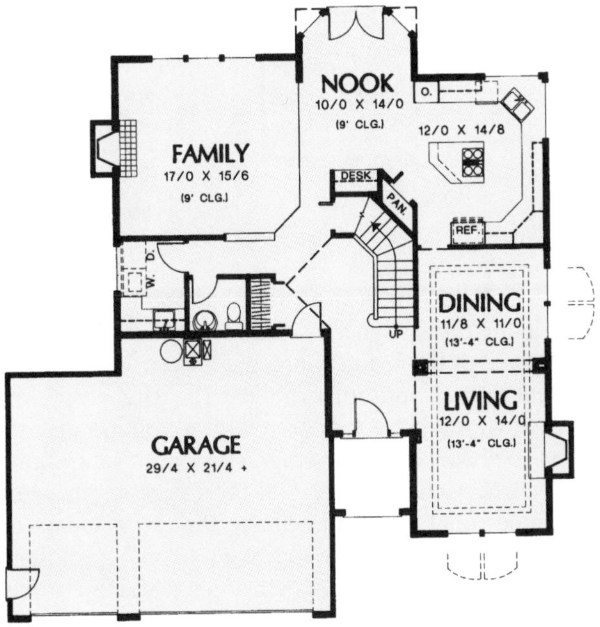

QUOTE ONE®
Cost to build? See page 516 to order complete cost estimate to build this house in your area!

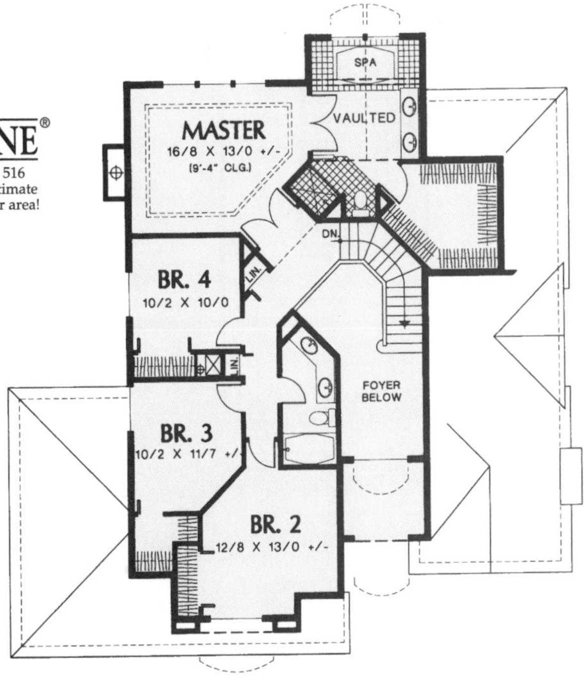

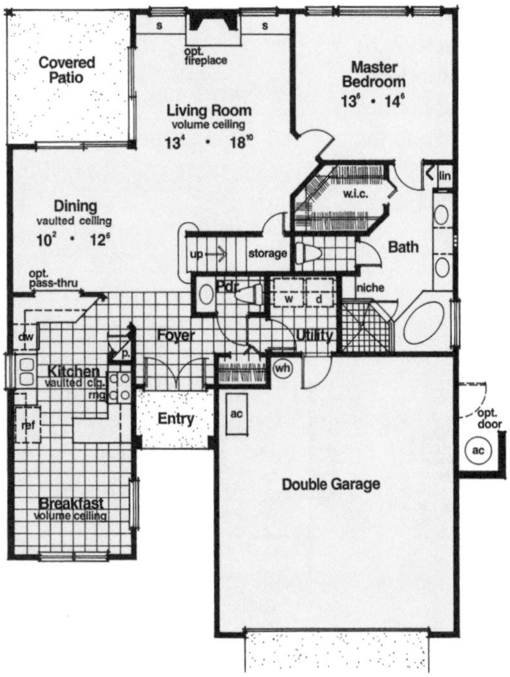

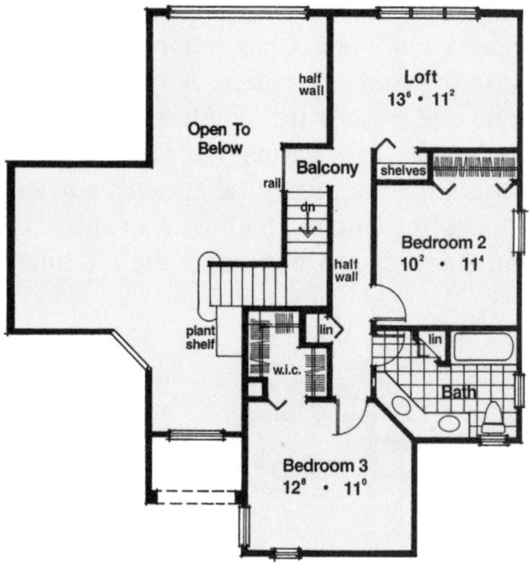

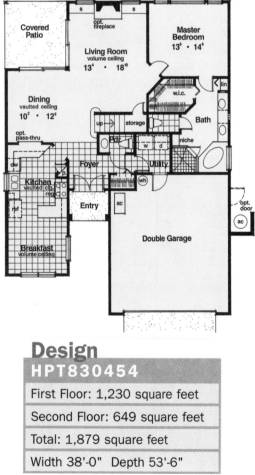

Design HPT830454

First Floor: 1,230 square feet

Second Floor: 649 square feet

Total: 1,879 square feet

Width 38'-0" Depth 53'-6"

The tiled foyer of this two-story home opens to a living/dining space with a soaring ceiling, a fireplace in the living room and access to a covered patio that invites outdoor livability. The kitchen has an oversized, sunny breakfast area with a volume ceiling. The master bedroom offers privacy with its sumptuous bath; a corner soaking tub, dual lavatories and a compartmented toilet lend character to the room. Upstairs, a loft overlooking the living spaces could become a third bedroom. One of the family bedrooms features a walk-in closet. Both bedrooms share a generous hall bath.

Design

HPT830455

Square Footage: 3,477	
Width 95'-0"	Depth 88'-8"
L	

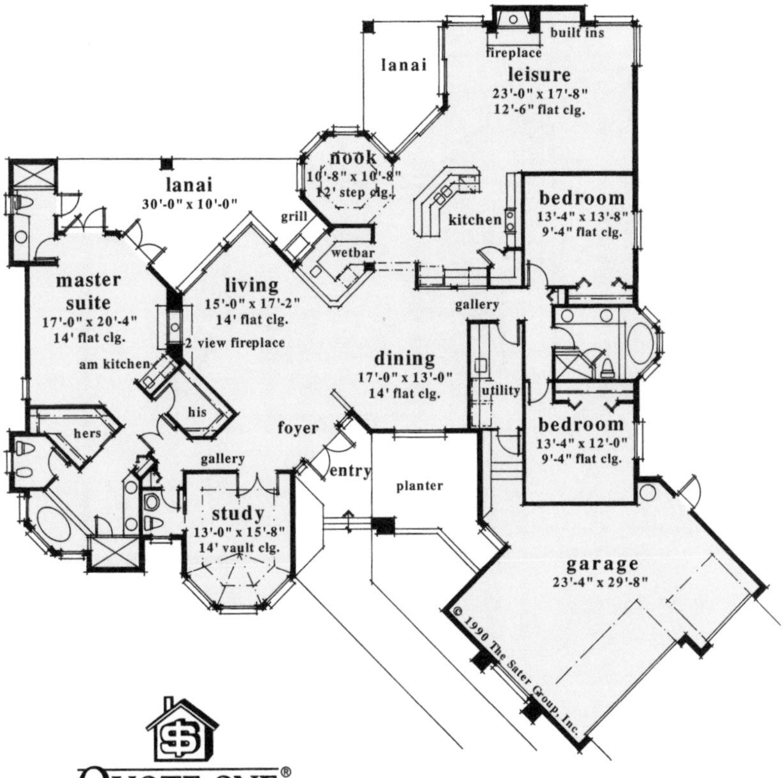

built ins
fireplace
lanai
leisure
23'-0" x 17'-8"
12'-6" flat clg.
nook
10'-8" x 10'-8"
12' step clg.
lanai
30'-0" x 10'-0"
grill
wetbar
kitchen
bedroom
13'-4" x 13'-8"
9'-4" flat clg.
master
suite
17'-0" x 20'-4"
14' flat clg.
living
15'-0" x 17'-2"
14' flat clg.
2 view fireplace
gallery
am kitchen
dining
17'-0" x 13'-0"
14' flat clg.
utility
his
hers
foyer
bedroom
13'-4" x 12'-0"
9'-4" flat clg.
gallery
entry
planter
study
13'-0" x 15'-8"
14' vault clg.
garage
23'-4" x 29'-8"
© 1990 The Sater Group, Inc.

QUOTE ONE®

Cost to build? See page 516 to order complete cost estimate to build this house in your area!

Classic columns, circle-head windows and a bay-windowed study give this stucco home a wonderful street presence. The foyer leads to the formal living and dining areas. An arched buffet server separates these rooms and contributes an open feeling. The kitchen, nook and leisure room are grouped for informal living. A desk/message center in the island kitchen, art niches in the nook and a fireplace with an entertainment center and shelves add custom touches. Two secondary suites have guest baths and offer full privacy from the master wing. The master suite hosts a private garden area, while the master bath features a walk-in shower that overlooks the garden, and a water-closet room with space for books or a television. Large His and Hers walk-in closets complete these private quarters.

Design

HPT830456

Square Footage: 2,962
Width 70'-0" Depth 76'-0"

Enter the formal foyer of this home and you are greeted with a traditional split living-room/dining-room layout. But the family room is where the real living takes place. It expands onto the outdoor living space, which features a summer kitchen. The ultimate master suite contains coffered ceilings, a "boomerang" vanity and angular mirrors that reflect the bayed soaking tub and shower. Efficient use of space creates a huge closet with little center space.

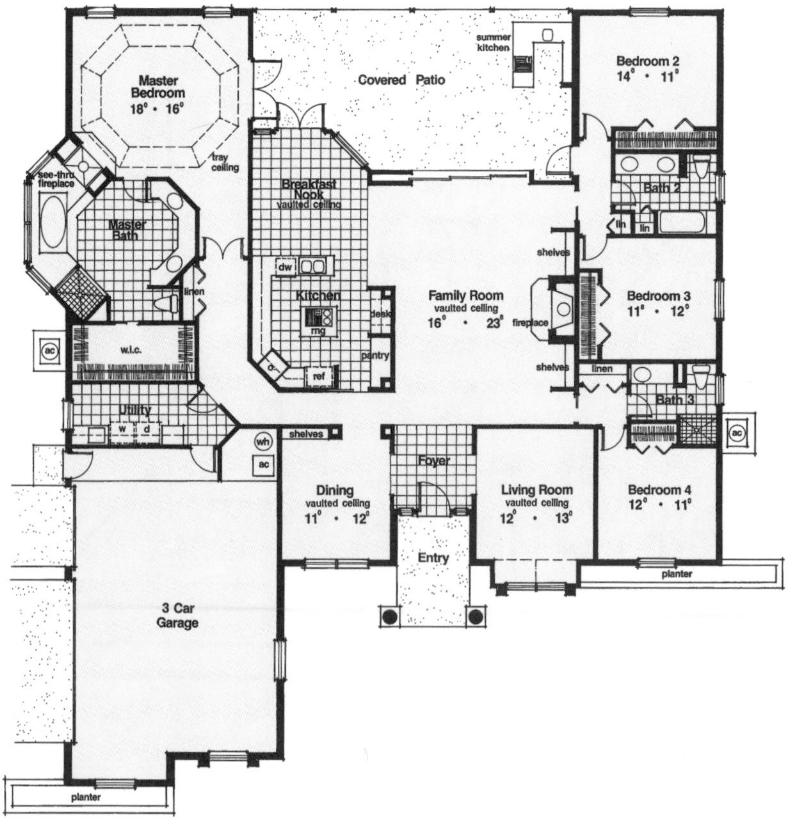

Design

HPT830457

Square Footage: 2,691

Width 78'-6" Depth 73'-10"

Italianate lines add finesse to the formal facade of this home. Strong symmetry, a soaring portico and gentle rooflines are the prized hallmarks of this relaxed, yet formal design. To the right of the foyer, columns and a stepped ceiling offset the dining room. A plant shelf heralds the living room, which also has a twelve-foot ceiling. An angled cooktop counter adds flair to the kitchen, which includes a desk and a walk-in pantry and serves the breakfast nook. A corner fireplace, high ceiling and patio enhance the family room. An arch opens the entry to the lavish master suite. Two additional bedrooms come with separate entries to a full bath.

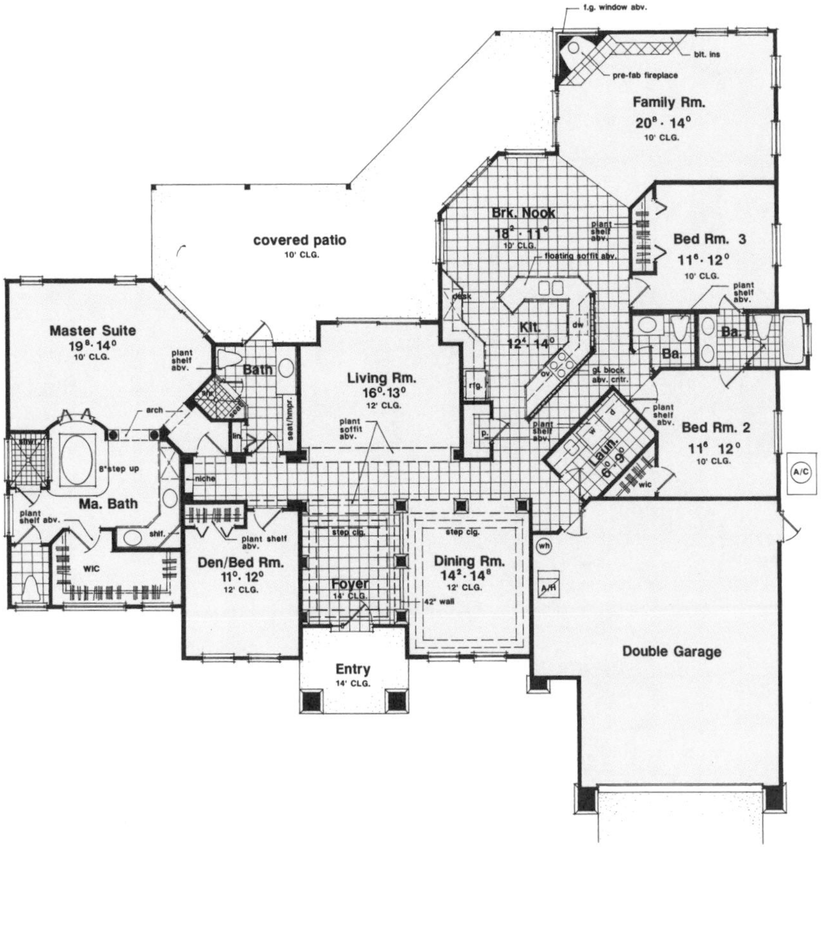

Design

HPT830458

Square Footage: 2,656

Width 92'-0" Depth 69'-0"

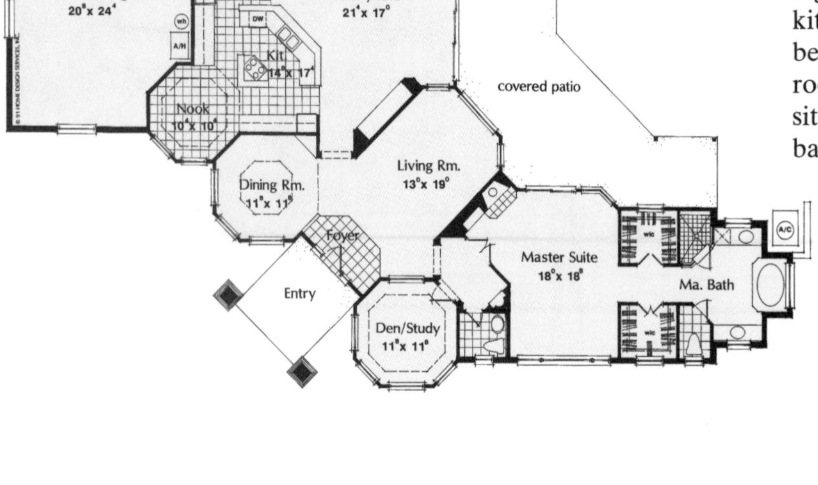

A graceful design sets this charming home apart from the ordinary and transcends the commonplace. From the foyer, the dining room branches off the sunny living room, setting a lovely backdrop for entertaining. Casual living is the focus in the oversized family room, where sliding doors open to the patio and the eat-in, gourmet kitchen is open for easy conversation. Two family bedrooms and a cabana bath are just off the family room. The master suite has a cozy fireplace in the sitting area, twin closets and a compartmented bath. A large covered patio adds to the living area.

Design

HPT830459

Square Footage: 2,986	
Width 82'-8"	Depth 76'-4"
L	

Tradition takes a bold step up with this Sun Country exterior—a bright introduction to the grand, unrestrained floor plan. Double doors lead to the formal rooms, which include an open living room with a two-view fireplace, a bayed dining room and a parlor or study with its own bay window. A secluded master suite with a compartmented bath complements family sleeping quarters, located for privacy.

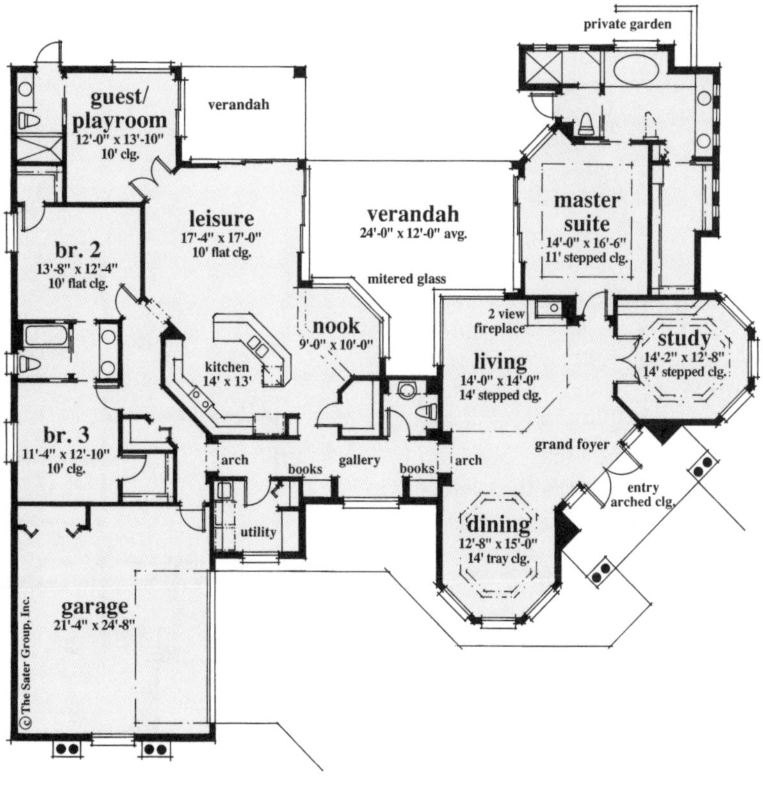

Design HPT830460

Square Footage: 1,712	
Width 67'-0"	Depth 42'-4"

A stylish stucco exterior enhances this home's curb appeal. A sunken great room offers a corner fireplace flanked by wide patio doors. A well-designed kitchen features an ideal view of the great room and fireplace through the breakfast-bar opening. The rear patio offers plenty of outdoor entertaining and relaxing space. The master suite features a private bath and walk-in closet. The master bath contains dual vanities, while the two family bedrooms each access a bath. A spacious two-car garage completes this plan.

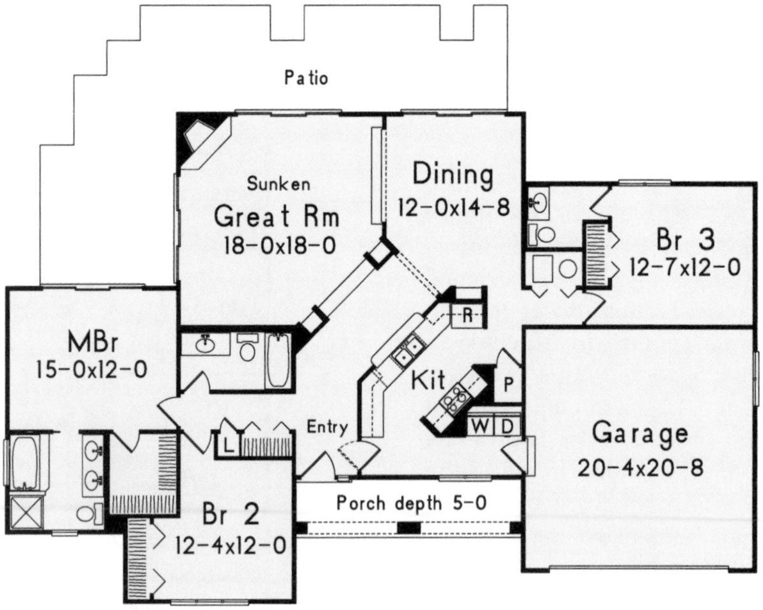

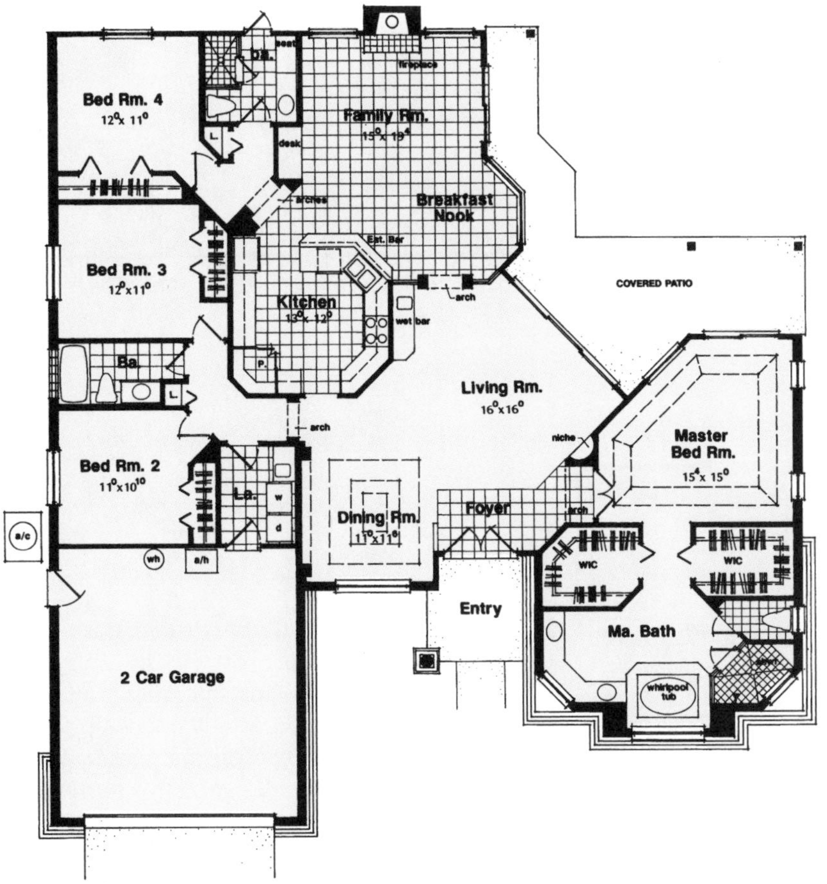

Design

HPT830461

Square Footage: 2,352

Width 61'-8" Depth 64'-8"

An array of varied, arched windows sets off this striking contemporary home. Double doors reveal the foyer, which announces the living room accented by a wet bar, niche and patio access. The spacious kitchen features plenty of work space and opens into the bright breakfast nook and family room. Double doors open to the coffered master bedroom, a private sanctuary. Its sumptuous bath has two walk-in closets, a dual vanity and a spa tub. Blueprints include an alternate elevation.

ALTERNATE ELEVATION

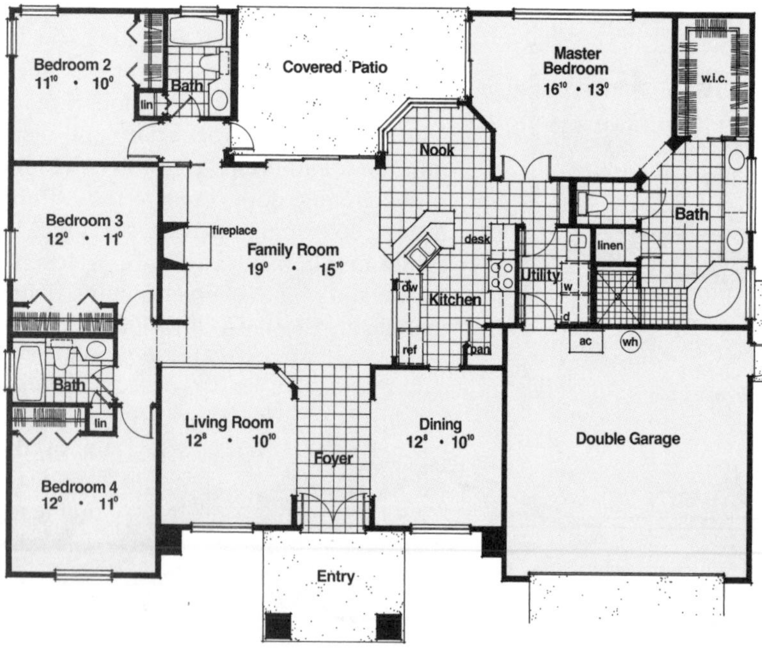
Bedroom 2
11¹⁰ · 10⁰
Bath
lin
Covered Patio
Master Bedroom
16¹⁰ · 13⁰
w.i.c.
Nook
Bath
Bedroom 3
12⁰ · 11⁰
fireplace
Family Room
19⁰ · 15¹⁰
desk
linen
dw
Kitchen
Utility
w
d
ac
ref
pan
ac
wh
Bath
lin
Living Room
12⁸ · 10¹⁰
Dining
12⁸ · 10¹⁰
Double Garage
Foyer
Bedroom 4
12⁰ · 11⁰
Entry

Design

HPT830462

Square Footage: 2,089	
Width 61'-8"	Depth 50'-4"

This four-bedroom, three-bath home offers the finest in modern amenities. The huge family room, which opens up to the patio with twelve-foot pocket sliding doors, provides space for a fireplace and media equipment. Two family bedrooms share a full bath while one bedroom has a private bath with patio access, making it the perfect guest room. The master suite, located just off the kitchen and nook, is private yet easily accessible. The double-door entry, bed wall with glass above, the step-down shower and private bathroom, walk-in linen closet and lavish vanity make this a very comfortable master suite!

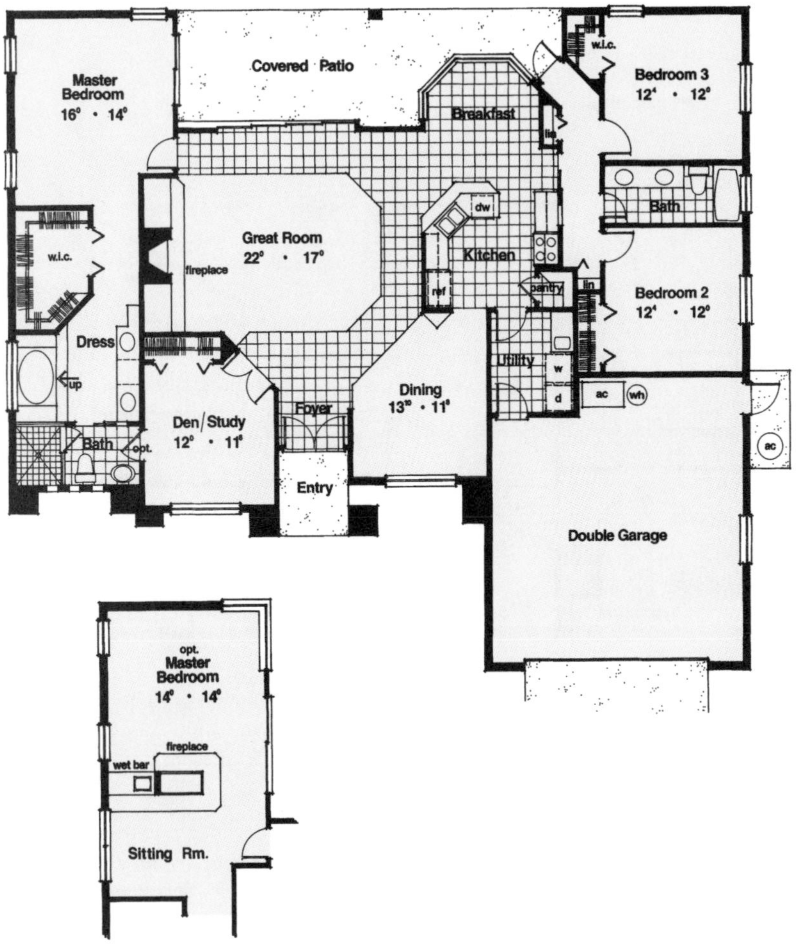

Design HPT830463

Square Footage: 2,125

Width 65'-0" Depth 56'-8"

A luxurious master suite is just one of the highlights offered with this stunning plan—an alternate plan for this suite features a sitting room, wet bar and fireplace. Two family bedrooms to the right of the plan share a full bath that includes a dual vanity and a gallery hall that leads directly to the covered patio. Tile adds interest to the living area and surrounds the spacious great room, which offers a fireplace and access to the rear patio. A formal dining room and a secluded den or study flank the foyer.

Design

HPT830464

Square Footage: 2,278

Width 57'-9" Depth 71'-8"

The grand entrance of this one-story home offers a fine introduction to an open, spacious interior. A delightful formal living and dining room sized for large get-togethers, extends from the foyer. To the left, a short hall accented with a decorator's niche, precedes the master suite, which includes a sitting area, two walk-in closets and a spa-style bath. Family will gather in the kitchen where wrapping counters, a walk-in pantry and an angular snack bar balance out the spacious family room and breakfast nook. Two family bedrooms are separated from the master suite and share a full hall bath.

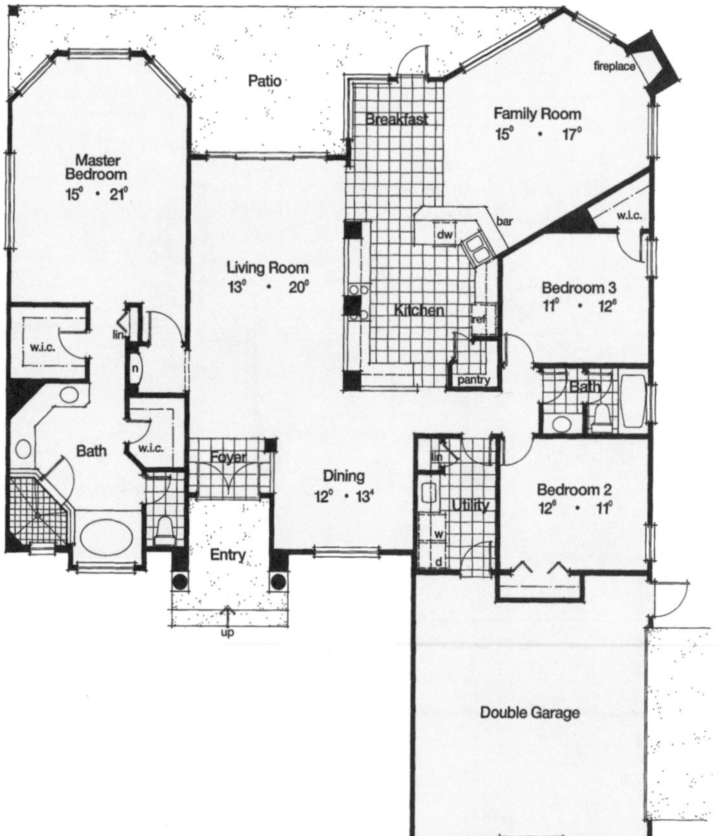

Design

HPT830465

Square Footage: 2,636

Width 71'-8" Depth 71'-4"

A towering entry welcomes all into the foyer of this soaring contemporary design with a multitude of elegant volume ceilings. The open dining room and living room each have sunny bay windows and built-in features. The spacious family room has a charming corner fireplace, plenty of windows and a breakfast nook easily in reach of the roomy kitchen. Three family bedrooms are just off the family room. The master suite has a sitting area, twin closets and an oversized bath designed for relaxing.

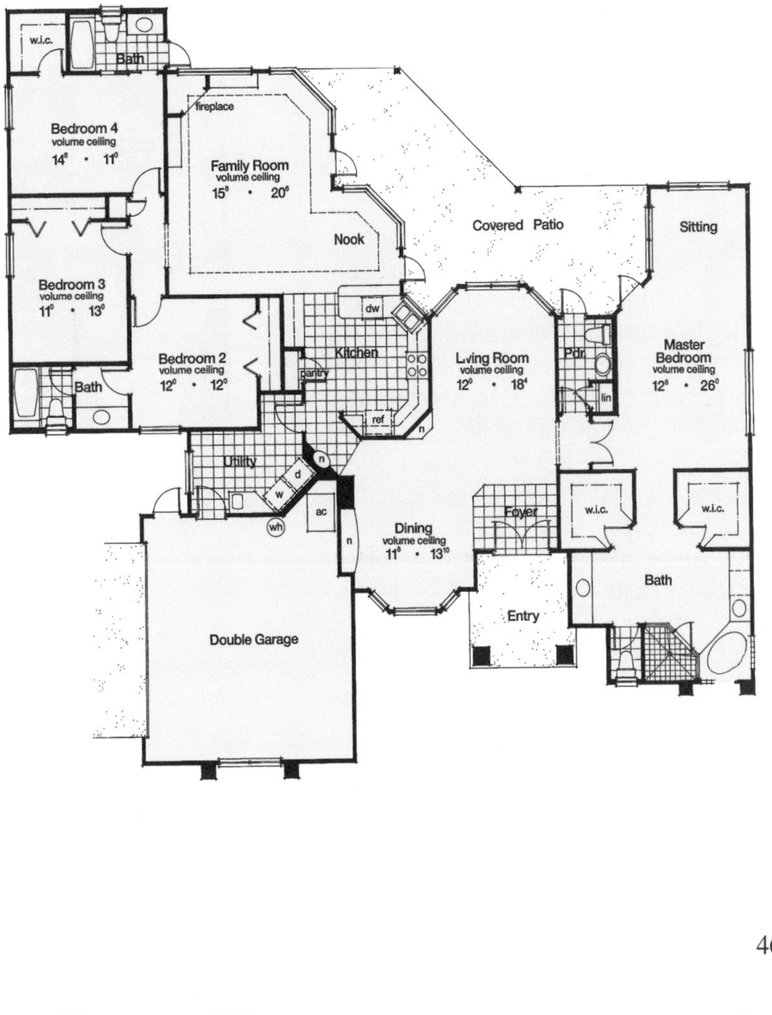

Design HPT830466

Square Footage: 2,931

Width 70'-8" Depth 83'-0"

Quoins and keystone accents lend a French country flavor to this stucco exterior, as brick contrasts and a glass paneled entry give it a fresh face. A tiled foyer leads to a gracefully curved gallery hall. The heart of the plan is the vaulted living room, which overlooks the covered patio and rear grounds, but friends may want to gather in the family room, where a centered fireplace offers cozy niches. A gourmet kitchen is designed to handle casual meals as well as planned occasions, with a service kitchen on the patio for outdoor events.

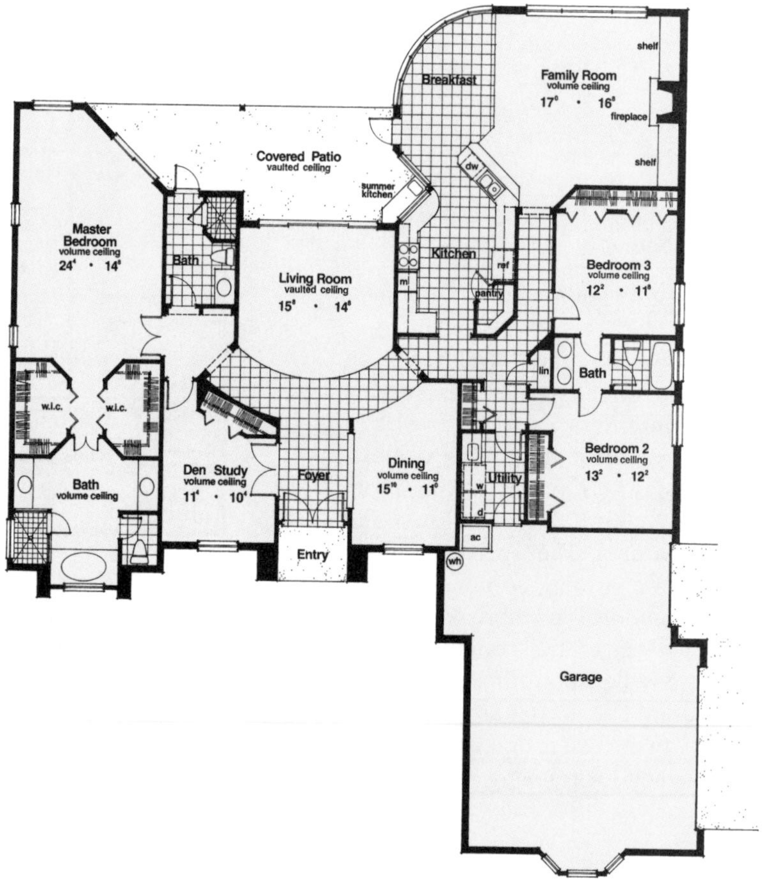

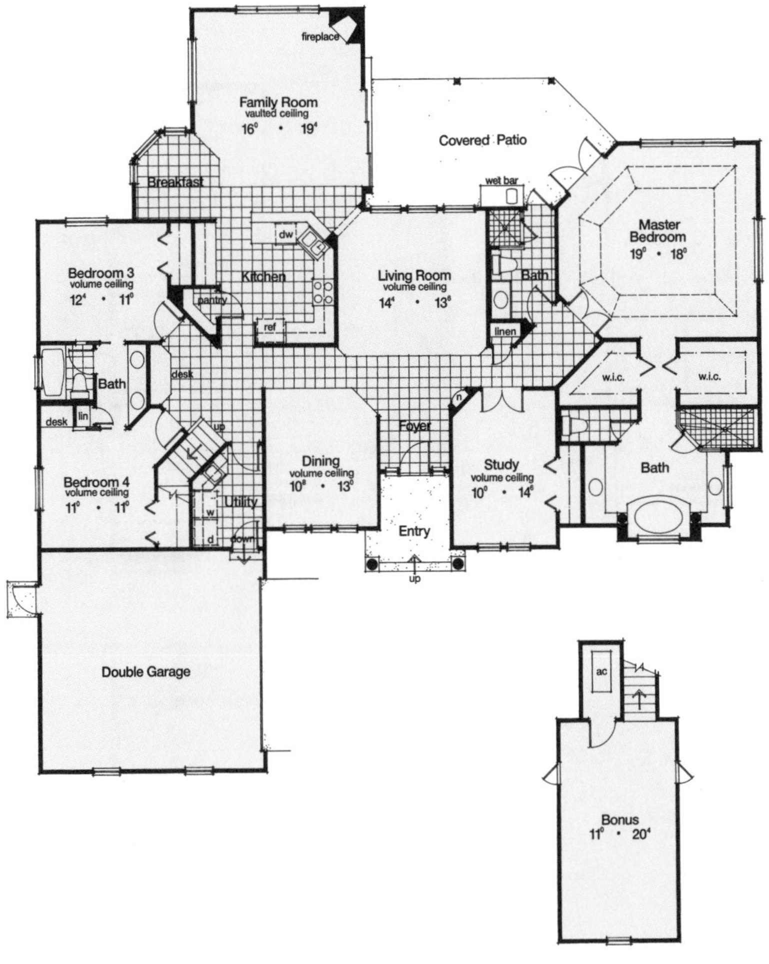

Design

HPT830467

Square Footage: 2,551
Bonus Space: 287 square feet
Width 69'-8" Depth 71'-4"

Shutters and multi-pane windows dress up the exterior of this lovely stucco home. Formal and informal areas flow easily, beginning with the dining room sized to accommodate large parties and function with the adjacent living room. A gourmet kitchen is complete with a walk-in pantry and a cozy breakfast nook. Double doors lead to the spacious master suite. The lavish master bath features His and Hers walk-in closets, a tub framed by a columned archway, and an oversized shower. Off the angular hallway, two bedrooms share a Pullman-style bath and a study desk. A bonus room over the garage provides additional space.

Design

HPT830468

Square Footage: 2,005	
Width 58'-0"	Depth 60'-0"

Vaulted and volume ceilings soar above well-designed living areas in this spectacular move-up home. Open spaces create interior vistas and invite both formal and informal gatherings. An elegant dining room, defined by columns, offers views to the front property through multi-level muntin windows. To the left of the foyer, an extensive living room offers plans for an optional fireplace as well as privacy for quiet gatherings. The great room offers a vaulted ceiling and views to outdoor areas, and opens to the breakfast room with patio access and the kitchen with its angled counter. Two family bedrooms, each with a volume ceiling, and a bath with twin lavatories complete the right side of the plan. The master bedroom enjoys its own bath with a whirlpool tub, separate shower, dual vanity and compartmented toilet.

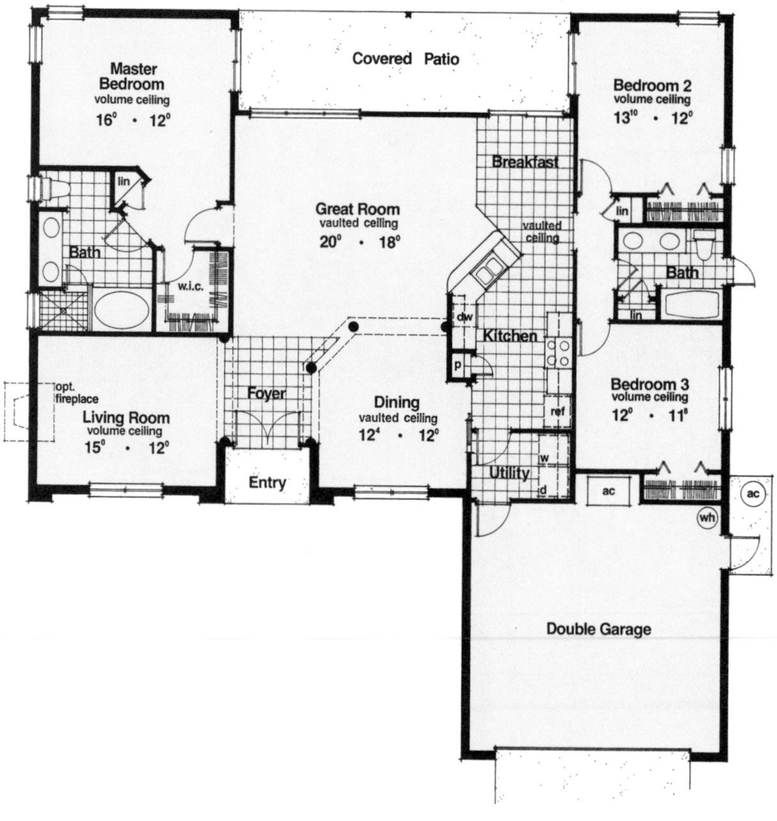

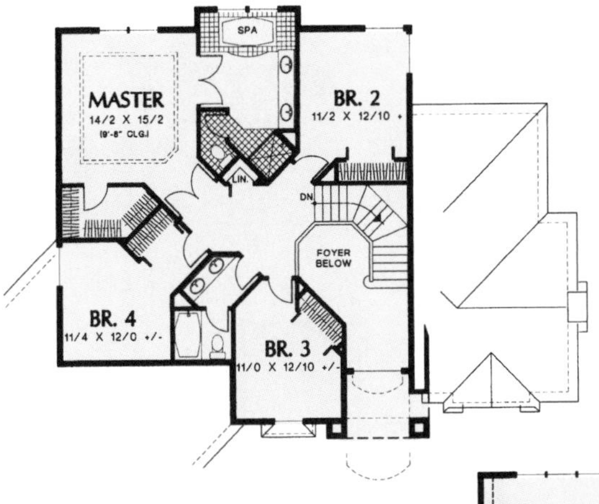

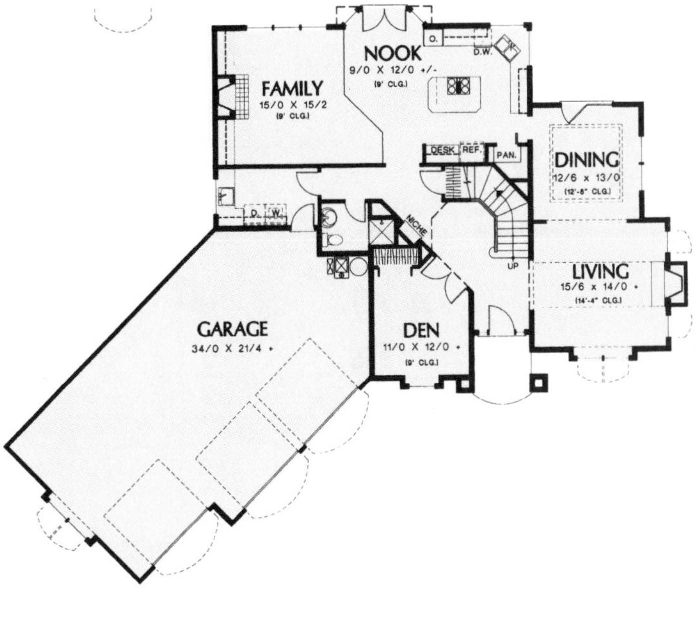

Design HPT830469

First Floor: 1,592 square feet
Second Floor: 1,178 square feet
Total: 2,770 square feet
Width 77'-5" Depth 64'-7"

The angular placement of this home's three-car garage creates an expansive and very stylish facade. The foyer is punctuated with a dramatic staircase and opens on the right to formal living areas before continuing back into the inviting family room. A fireplace and plenty of windows in the family room are a nice balance to the country kitchen. Amenities here include a breakfast nook, cooktop island and rear access to the formal dining room. Three family bedrooms and a full hall bath join the luxurious master suite on the second floor.

This modern home adds a contemporary twist to the typical ranch-style plan. The turret study and bayed dining room add a sensuous look from the streetscape. The main living areas open up to the lanai and offer broad views to the rear through large expanses of glass and doors. The family kitchen, nook and leisure room focus on the lanai, the entertainment center and an ale bar. The guest suites have separate baths and also access the lanai. The master bath features a curved-glass shower, whirlpool tub, and private toilet and bidet room. Dual walk-in closets and an abundance of light further the appeal of this suite.

Design
HPT830470

Square Footage: 3,866

Width 120'-0" Depth 89'-0"

L D

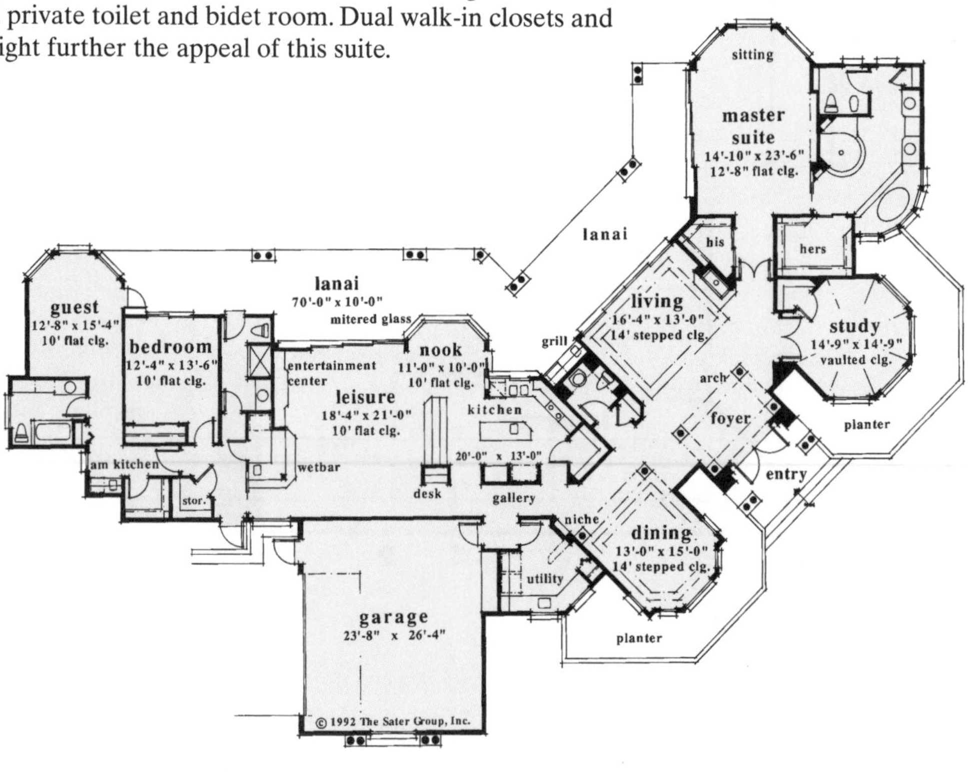

Design HPT830471

Square Footage: 3,944	
Width 98'-0"	Depth 105'-0"
L	

Innovative design and attention to detail create true luxury living. This clean, contemporary-style home features a raised, columned entry with an interesting stucco relief archway. The foyer opens to the formal living room, which overlooks the lanai through walls of glass. The formal dining room has a curved wall of windows and a built-in buffet table. Two guest suites each boast a walk-in closet and a private bath. The master suite features a foyer with views of a fountain, and a sunny sitting area that opens to the lanai. The bath beckons with a soaking tub, round shower and large wardrobe area.

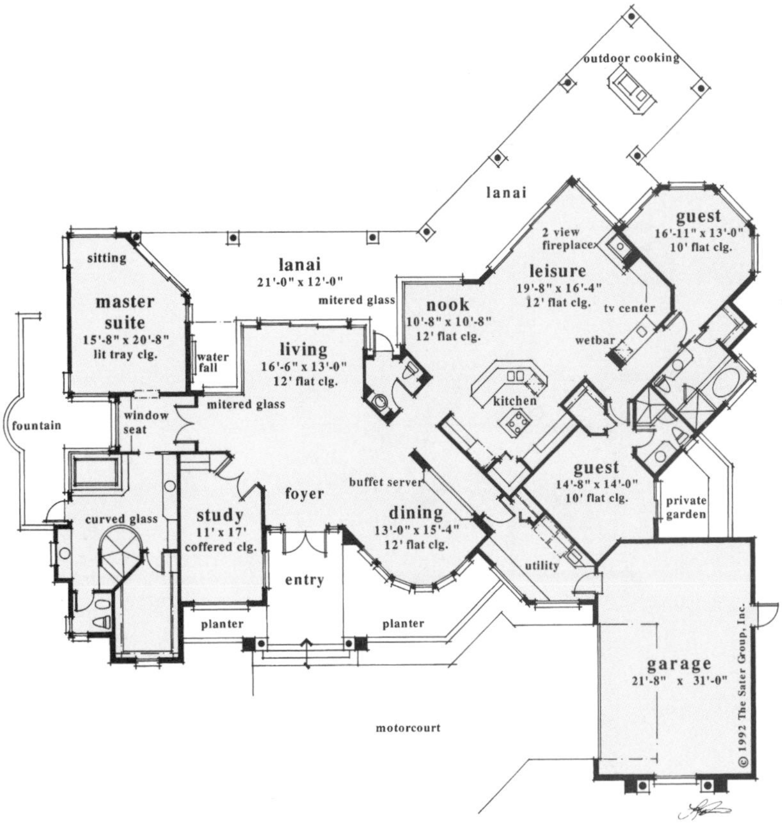

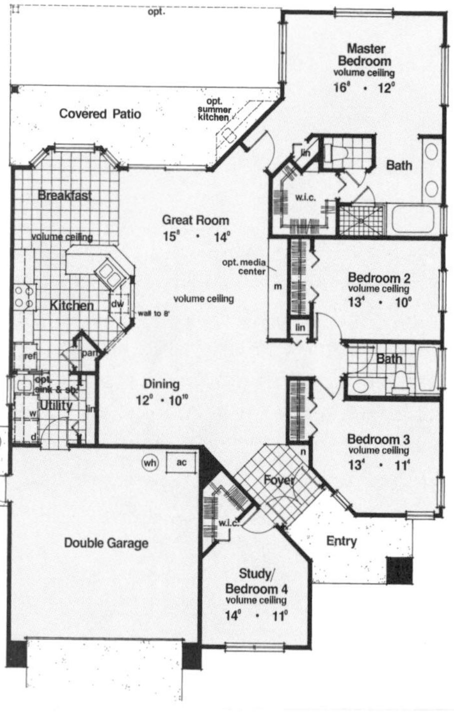

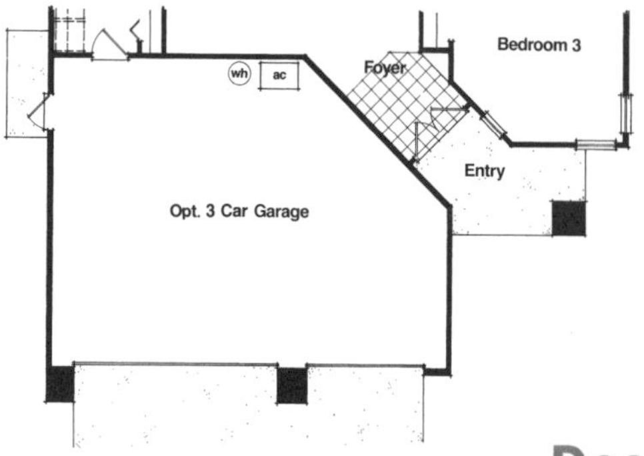

Design

HPT830472

Square Footage: 1,865	
Width 45'-0"	Depth 66'-0"

This innovative plan takes advantage of an angled entry into the home, maximizing visual impact and making it possible to include three bedrooms and a study. The joining of the family and dining space makes creative interior decorating possible. The master suite also takes advantage of angles in creating long vistas into this private environment. The master bath is designed with all the amenities usually found in much larger homes. The kitchen and breakfast nook overlook the outdoor living space where you can even have an outdoor kitchen area—a great design for entertaining.

ALTERNATE ELEVATION

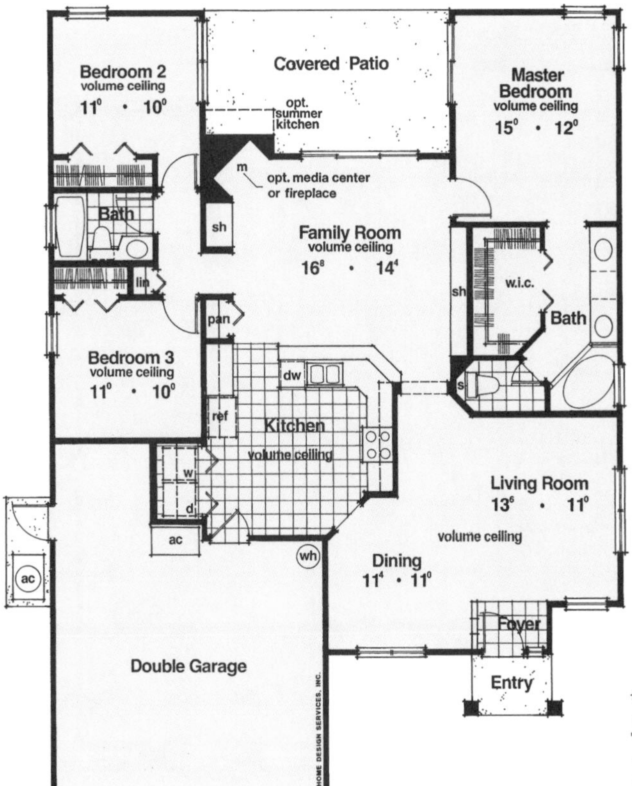

Design

HPT830473

Square Footage: 1,550

Width 43'-0" Depth 59'-0"

Enjoy resort-style living in this striking Sun Country home. Guests will always feel welcome when entertained in the formal living and dining areas, but the eat-in country kitchen overlooking the family room will be the center of attention. Casual living will be enjoyed in the large family room and out on the patio with the help of an optional summer kitchen and view of the fairway. Built-in shelves and an optional media center provide decorating options. The master suite features a volume ceiling and a spacious master bath.

ALTERNATE ELEVATION

Design

HPT830474

Square Footage: 2,214	
Width 63'-0"	Depth 72'-0"
L	

The dramatic entry with an arched opening leads to the comfortable interior of this delightful one-story home. Volume ceilings highlight the main living areas, which include a formal dining room and a great room with access to one of the verandas. In the turreted study, quiet time is assured. The master suite features a bath with a double-bowl vanity and a bumped-out whirlpool tub. The secondary bedrooms reside on the other side of the house.

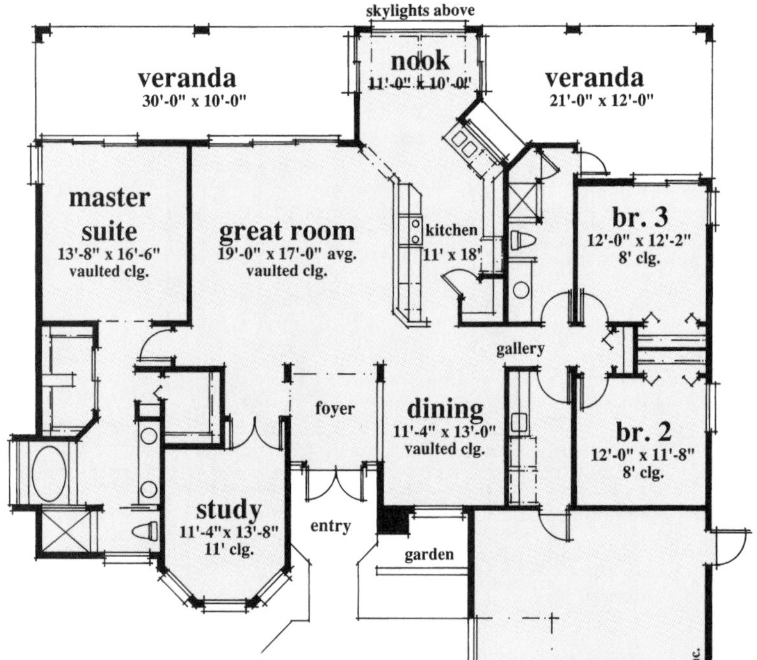

skylights above
nook
11'-0" x 10'-0"
veranda
30'-0" x 10'-0"
veranda
21'-0" x 12'-0"
master suite
13'-8" x 16'-6"
vaulted clg.
great room
19'-0" x 17'-0" avg.
vaulted clg.
kitchen
11' x 18'
br. 3
12'-0" x 12'-2"
8' clg.
gallery
foyer
dining
11'-4" x 13'-0"
vaulted clg.
br. 2
12'-0" x 11'-8"
8' clg.
study
11'-4"x 13'-8"
11' clg.
entry
garden
garage
21'-4" x 27'-8"
© The Sater Group, Inc.

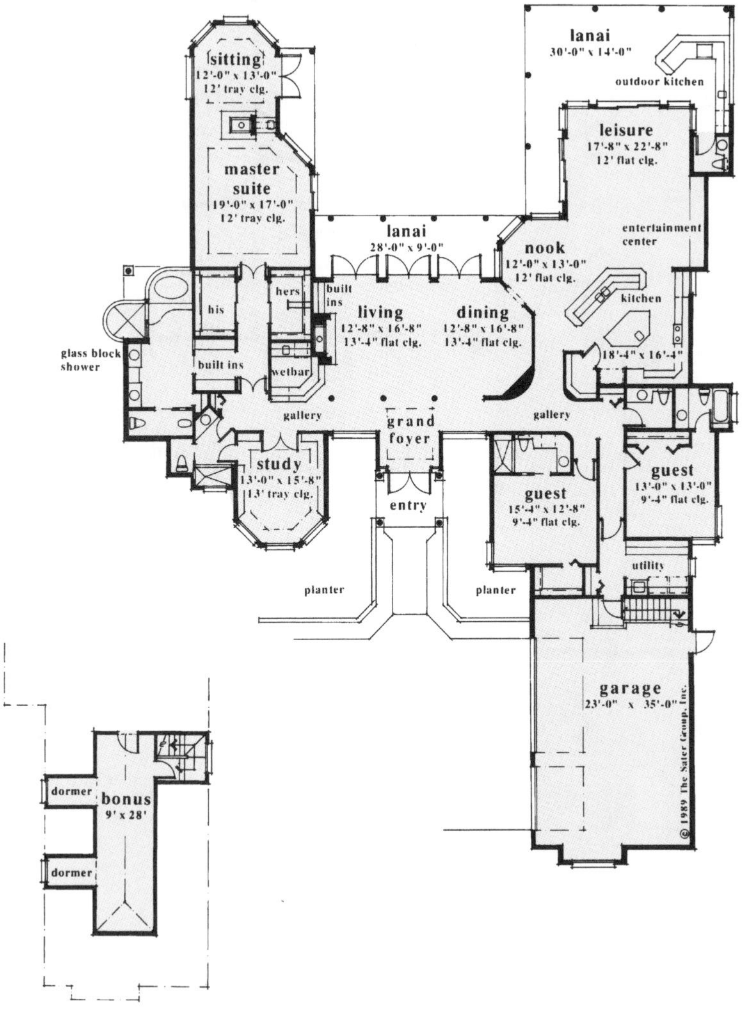
sitting
12'-0" x 13'-0"
12' tray clg.
master suite
19'-0" x 17'-0"
12' tray clg.
lanai
28'-0" x 9'-0"
lanai
30'-0" x 14'-0"
outdoor kitchen
leisure
17'-8" x 22'-8"
12' flat clg.
entertainment center
nook
12'-0" x 13'-0"
12' flat clg.
kitchen
18'-4" x 16'-4"
his
hers
built ins
built ins
wetbar
glass block shower
living
12'-8" x 16'-8"
13'-4" flat clg.
dining
12'-8" x 16'-8"
13'-4" flat clg.
gallery
grand foyer
gallery
study
13'-0" x 15'-8"
13' tray clg.
entry
guest
15'-4" x 12'-8"
9'-4" flat clg.
guest
13'-0" x 13'-0"
9'-4" flat clg.
utility
planter
planter
garage
23'-0" x 35'-0"
© 1989 The Sater Group, Inc.
dormer
bonus
9' x 28'
dormer

Design

HPT830475

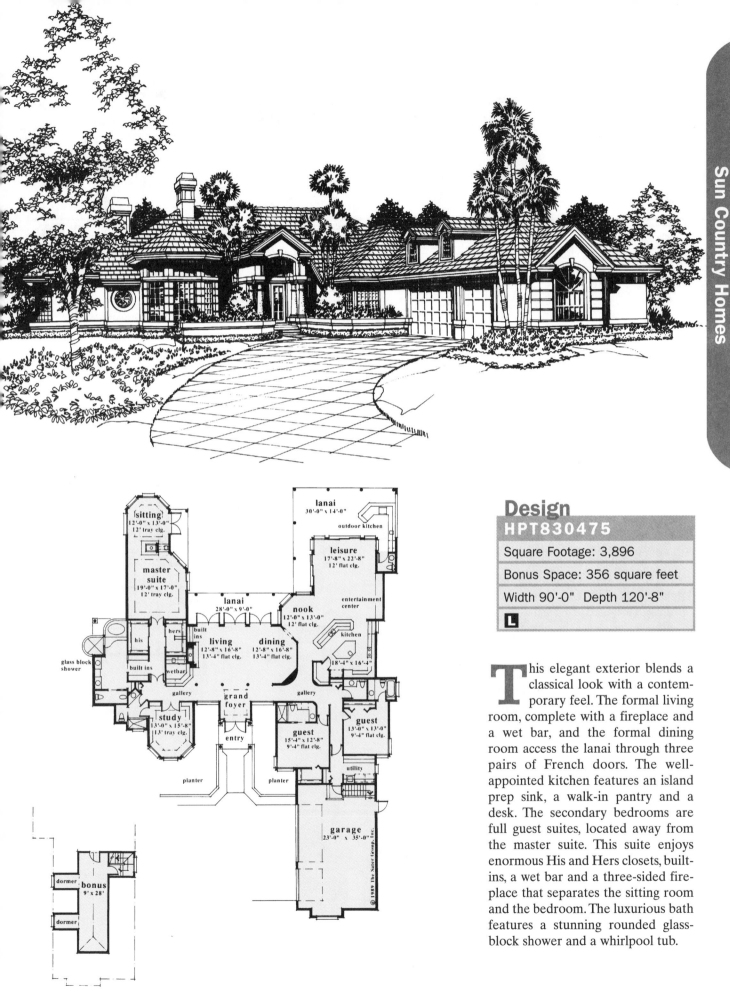

Square Footage: 3,896
Bonus Space: 356 square feet
Width 90'-0" Depth 120'-8"
L

This elegant exterior blends a classical look with a contemporary feel. The formal living room, complete with a fireplace and a wet bar, and the formal dining room access the lanai through three pairs of French doors. The well-appointed kitchen features an island prep sink, a walk-in pantry and a desk. The secondary bedrooms are full guest suites, located away from the master suite. This suite enjoys enormous His and Hers closets, built-ins, a wet bar and a three-sided fireplace that separates the sitting room and the bedroom. The luxurious bath features a stunning rounded glass-block shower and a whirlpool tub.

Design

HPT830476

Square Footage: 1,647

Width 58'-0" Depth 58'-0"

This glorious Sun Country cottage gives you the option of two elevations: choose from a hipped or gabled roof at the front entrance. Designed for casual living, the foyer opens to the dining and grand rooms while providing great views of the rear lanai and beyond. The grand room includes a built-in entertainment center and a snack bar served from the kitchen. The galley kitchen has a gazebo dining nook with a door to the lanai. The master suite is split from the family sleeping wing and features a walk-in closet and a compartmented bath. Two secondary bedrooms, a study and full cabana bath complete this luxurious home.

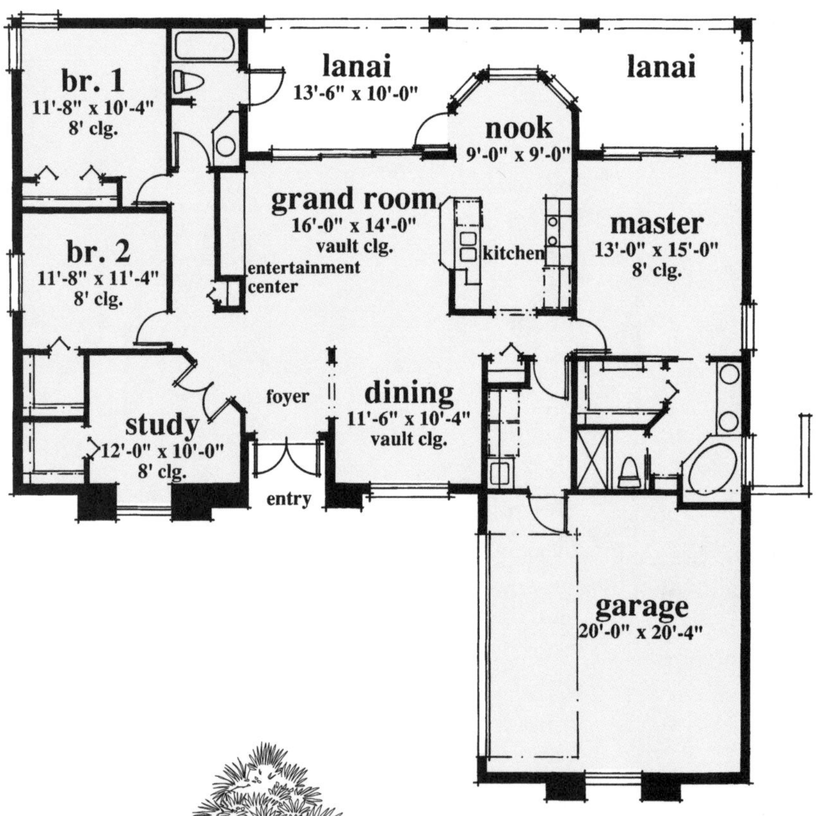

br. 1
11'-8" x 10'-4"
8' clg.
lanai
13'-6" x 10'-0"
lanai
nook
9'-0" x 9'-0"
grand room
16'-0" x 14'-0"
vault clg.
kitchen
entertainment
center
br. 2
11'-8" x 11'-4"
8' clg.
master
13'-0" x 15'-0"
8' clg.
foyer
dining
11'-6" x 10'-4"
vault clg.
study
12'-0" x 10'-0"
8' clg.
entry
garage
20'-0" x 20'-4"

ALTERNATE ELEVATION

Design

HPT830477

Square Footage: 3,265

Width 80'-0" Depth 103'-8"

A turret study and a raised entry add elegance to this marvelous stucco home. A guest suite includes a full bath, porch access and a private garden entry, making it perfect for use as an in-law suite. Secondary bedrooms share a full bath. The master suite has a foyer with a window seat overlooking another private garden and fountain area; the private master bath holds dual closets, a garden tub and a curved-glass shower.

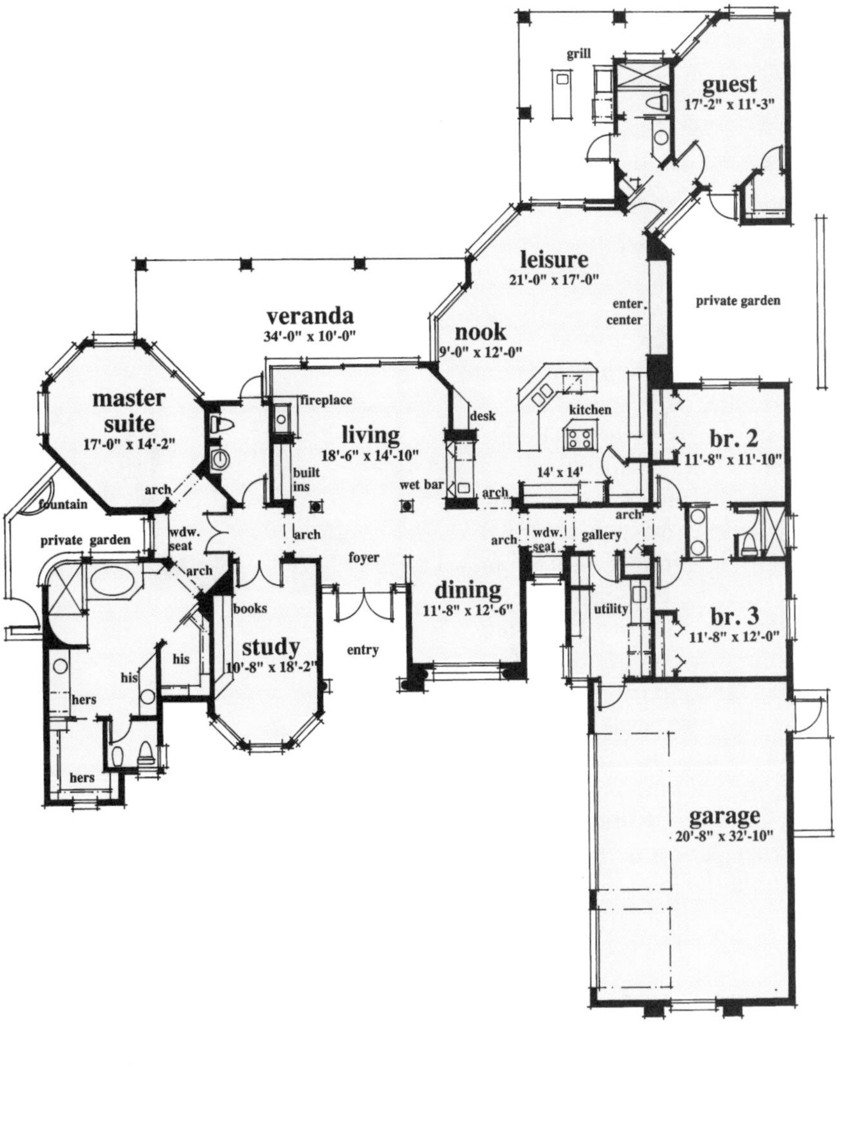

Design

HPT830478

Square Footage: 1,487	
Width 58'-0"	Depth 58'-0"
L	

Here's an offer too good to pass up! A wealth of modern livability is presented in this compact one-story vacation home. Inside, a great room with a vaulted ceiling opens to the lanai, offering wonderful options for either formal or informal entertaining. Step in from the lanai and savor the outdoors from the delightful kitchen with its bay-windowed breakfast nook. Two secondary bedrooms (each with its own walk-in closet) share a full bath. Finally, enjoy the lanai from the calming master suite, which includes a pampering bath with a corner tub, separate shower and large walk-in closet.

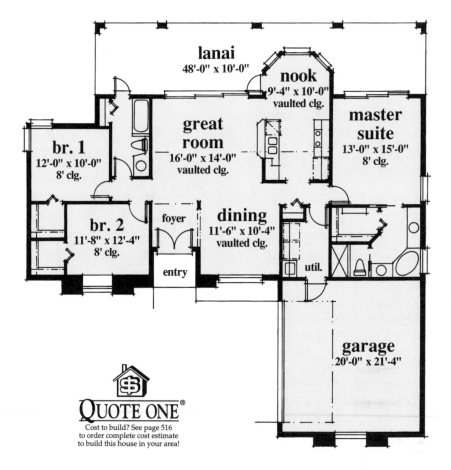

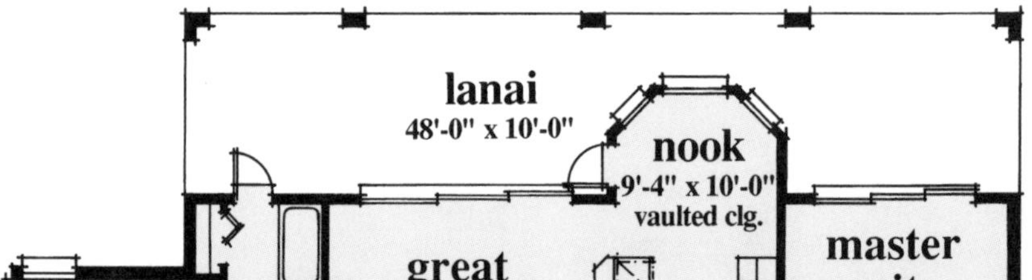

lanai
48'-0" x 10'-0"
nook
9'-4" x 10'-0"
vaulted clg.
great
room
16'-0" x 14'-0"
vaulted clg.
master
suite
13'-0" x 15'-0"
8' clg.
br. 1
12'-0" x 10'-0"
8' clg.
br. 2
11'-8" x 12'-4"
8' clg.
foyer
dining
11'-6" x 10'-4"
vaulted clg.
entry
util.
garage
20'-0" x 21'-4"

QUOTE ONE®

Cost to build? See page 516 to order complete cost estimate to build this house in your area!

Design
HPT830479

Square Footage: 2,589	
Width 64'-0"	Depth 81'-0"
L	

This plan has a contemporary Mediterranean look that gives it an Old World feel. The formal living areas are off the foyer; an archway leads to the family areas and the large living and dining room easily access the stylish wet bar. An ample kitchen has an island, walk-in pantry and desk message center. The sunlit nook and leisure room face the rear. The master wing features a bayed study with bookshelves, large sleeping quarters and a bayed sitting area. The bath has His and Hers walk-in closets, a glass shower and a garden tub. Two additional bedrooms share a full bath.

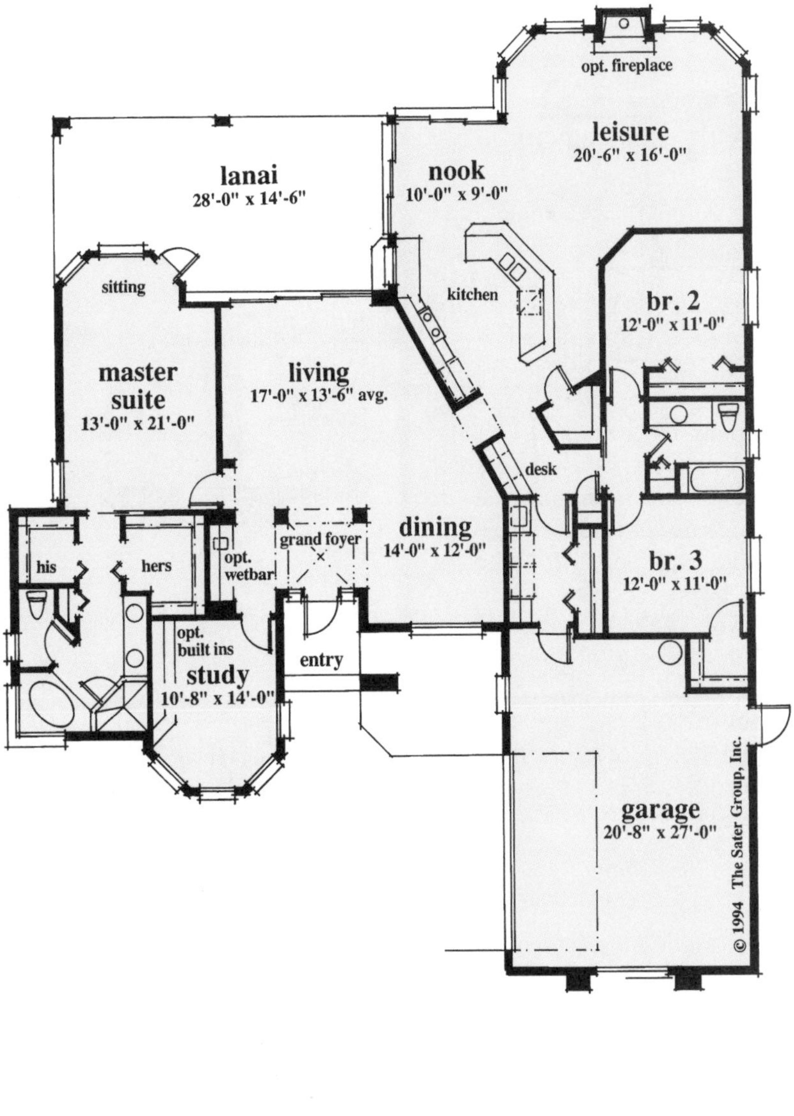

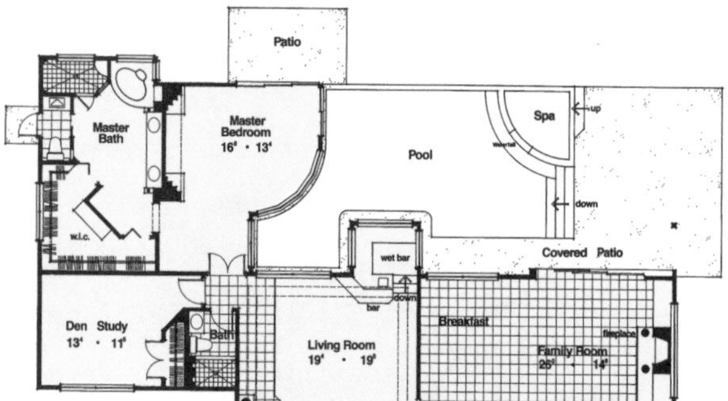

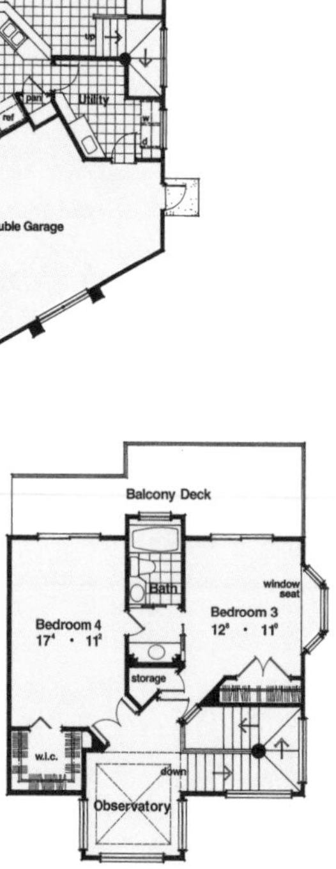

Design

HPT830480
First Floor: 2,212 square feet
Second Floor: 675 square feet
Total: 2,887 square feet
Width 70'-0" Depth 74'-1"

As you drive up to the porte cochere entry of this home, the visual movement of the elevation is breathtaking. The multi-roofed spaces bring excitement the moment you walk through the double-door entry. The foyer leads into the wide glass-walled living room. To the right, the formal dining room features a tiered pedestal ceiling. To the left is the guest and master suite wing of the home. The master suite with its sweeping, curved glass wall has access to the patio area and overlooks the pool. The master bath with its huge walk-in closet comes complete with a columned vanity area, a soaking tub and a shower for two. Two large bedrooms on the second floor—one with a bay window and one with a walk-in closet—share a sun deck, a full bath and an activity area.

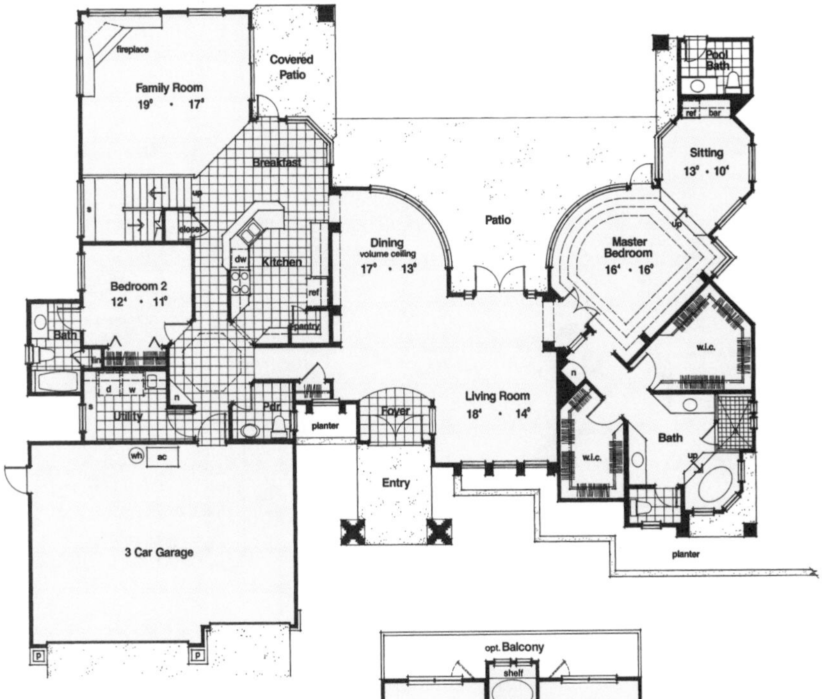

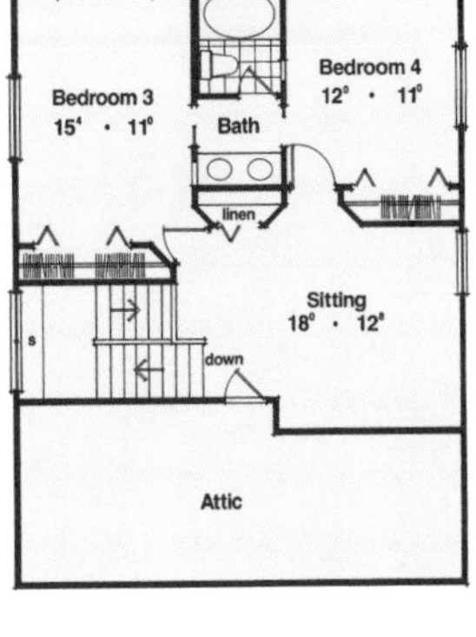

Design

HPT830481
First Floor: 2,531 square feet
Second Floor: 669 square feet
Total: 3,200 square feet
Width 82'-4" Depth 72'-0"

This exquisite brick-and-stucco contemporary home takes its cue from the tradition of Frank Lloyd Wright. The formal living and dining areas combine to provide a spectacular view of the rear grounds. The private master suite is best described as unique, highlighted by a mitered bow window, a raised sitting area complete with a wet bar, oversized His and Hers walk-in closets and a lavish, secluded bath with a relaxing corner tub, a separate shower and twin vanities. The family living area encompasses the left portion of the plan, featuring a spacious family room with a corner fireplace, access to the covered patio from the breakfast area and a step-saving kitchen. Bedroom 2 connects to a private bath. Upstairs, two bedrooms share a balcony, a sitting room and a full bath.

Design

HPT830482

Square Footage: 1,898

Width 60'-0" Depth 59'-4"

Easy living is at the heart of this brick one-story home inspired by the design of Frank Lloyd Wright. To the left of the foyer, double doors open to a den/study, which easily converts to a media room. The master suite is conveniently located nearby. Separated from family bedrooms for privacy, it features a spacious bedroom and a pampering bath with a large walk-in closet, a separate shower and a relaxing tub. Centrally located, the family room, with its cozy fireplace, combines well with the kitchen and the bay-windowed breakfast nook for casual family gatherings. The sleeping wing to the right has two secondary bedrooms that share a full bath and patio access.

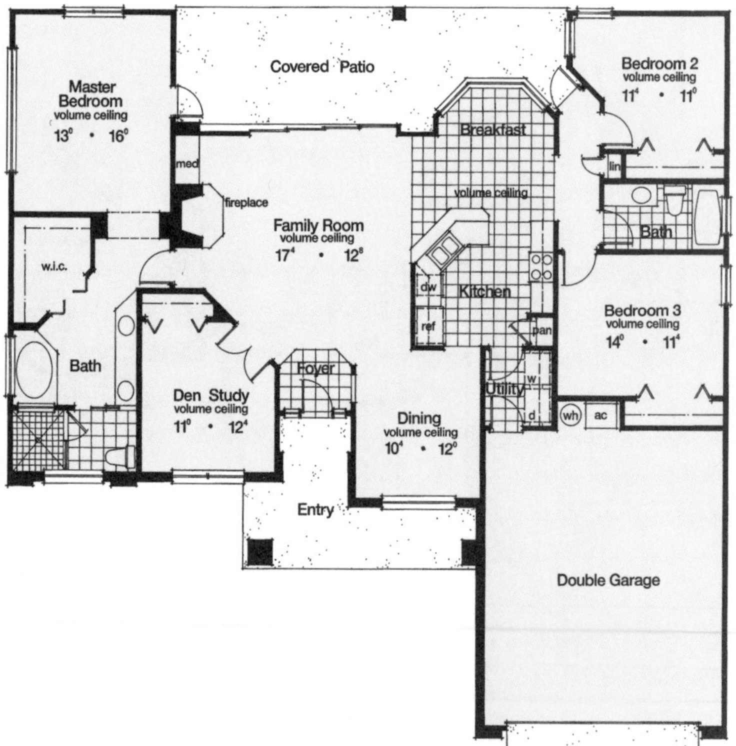

The angles in this home create unlimited views and space. Majestic columns of brick add warmth to a striking elevation. Inside, the foyer commands a special perspective on living areas including the living room, dining room and den. The island kitchen serves the breakfast nook and the family room. A large pantry provides ample space for food storage. Nearby, in the master suite, mitered glass and a private bath set the tone for simple luxury. Two secondary bedrooms share privacy and quiet at the front of the house. The den may also convert to a fourth bedroom, if desired.

Design HPT830483

Square Footage: 2,597
Width 96'-6" Depth 50'-0"

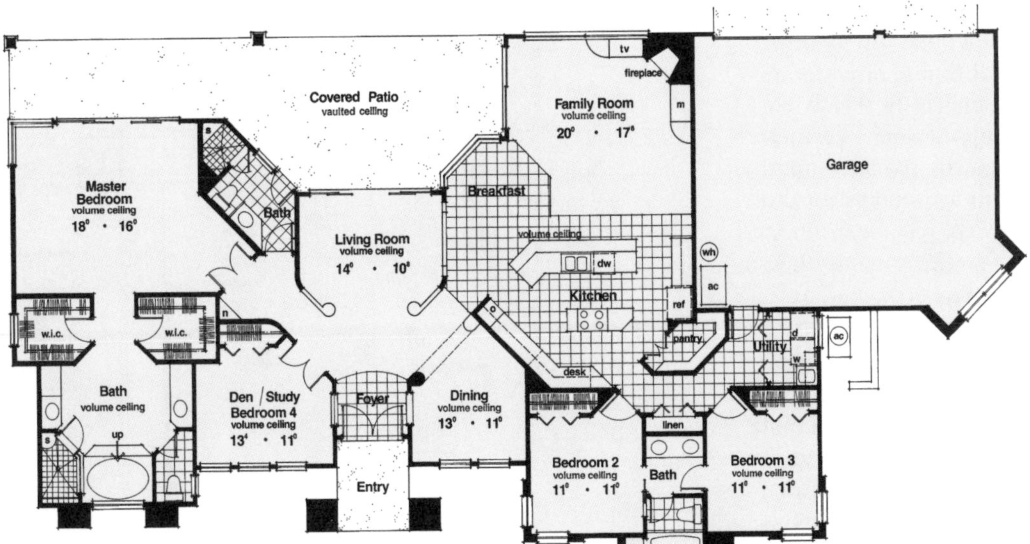

Design HPT830484

Square Footage: 2,224
Width 58'-6" Depth 74'-0"

Arches crowned by gentle, hipped rooflines provide an Italianate charm in this bright and spacious, family-oriented plan. A covered entry leads to the foyer that presents the angular, vaulted living and dining rooms. A kitchen with a V-shaped counter includes a walk-in pantry and looks out over the breakfast nook and family room with a fireplace. The master suite features a sitting room, two walk-in closets and a full bath with a garden tub. Two additional bedrooms share a full bath located between them. A fourth bedroom, with its own bath, opens off the family room and works perfectly as a guest room.

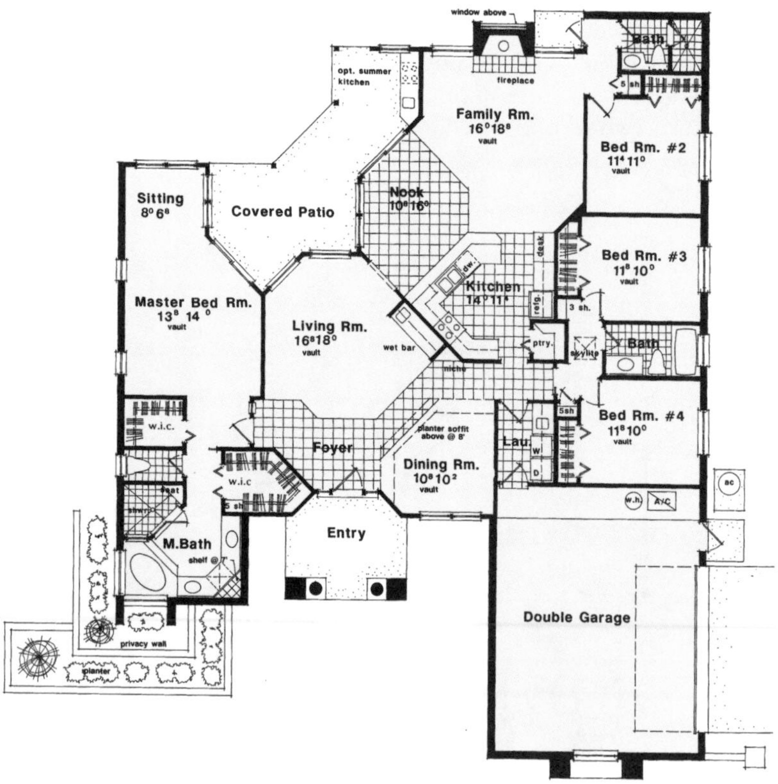

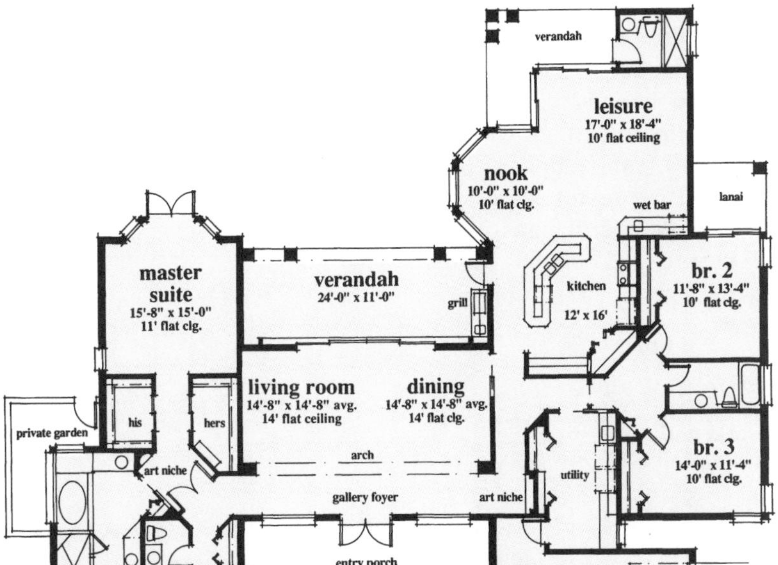

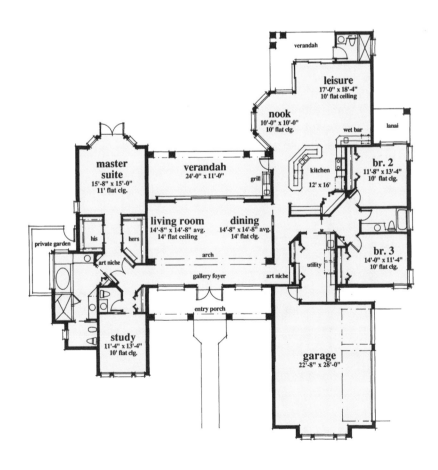

Design
HPT830485

Square Footage: 2,978

Width 84'-0" Depth 90'-0"

This home is designed to be a homeowner's dream come true. A formal living area opens from the gallery foyer through graceful arches and looks out to the veranda. The veranda hosts an outdoor grill and service counter—perfect for outdoor entertaining. The leisure room offers a private veranda, a cabana bath and a wet bar just off the gourmet kitchen. Walls of windows and a bayed breakfast nook let in natural light and set a bright tone for this area. The master suite opens to the rear property through French doors and boasts a lavish bath with a corner whirlpool tub that overlooks a private garden. An art niche off the gallery hall, a private dressing area and a secluded study complement the master suite. Two family bedrooms occupy the opposite wing of the plan and share a full bath and private hall.

This two-story home's pleasing exterior is complemented by its warm character and decorative "widow's walk." The covered entry—with its dramatic transom window—leads to a spacious great room highlighted by a warming fireplace. To the right, the dining room and kitchen combine to provide a delightful place for mealtimes, with access to a side sun deck through double doors. A study, bedroom and full bath complete the first floor. The luxurious master suite on the second floor features an oversized walk-in closet and a separate dressing area. The pampering master bath enjoys a relaxing whirlpool tub, double-bowl vanity and compartmented toilet. This home is designed with a pier foundation.

Design
HPT830486

First Floor: 1,136 square feet

Second Floor: 636 square feet

Total: 1,772 square feet

Width 41'-9" Depth 45'-0"

L

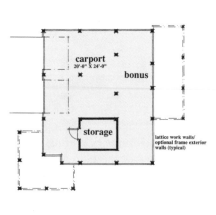

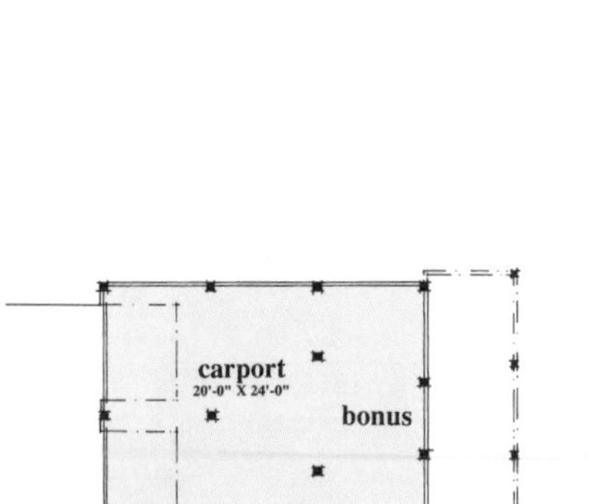
carport
20'-0" X 24'-0"
bonus
storage
lattice work walls/ optional frame exterior walls (typical)

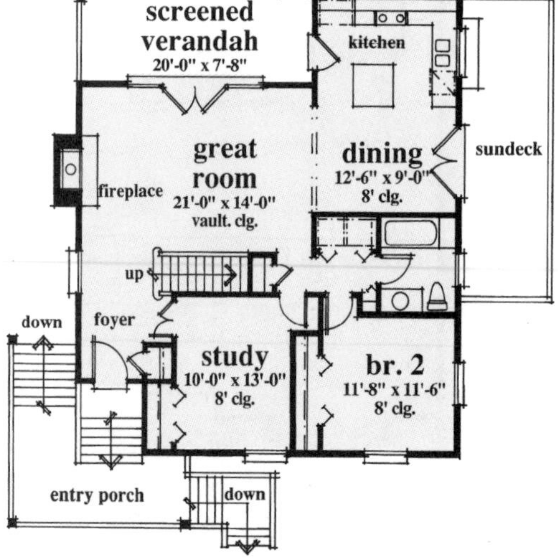
down
screened verandah
20'-0" x 7'-8"
kitchen
great room
21'-0" x 14'-0"
vault. clg.
fireplace
dining
12'-6" x 9'-0"
8' clg.
sundeck
up
down
foyer
study
10'-0" x 13'-0"
8' clg.
br. 2
11'-8" x 11'-6"
8' clg.
entry porch
down

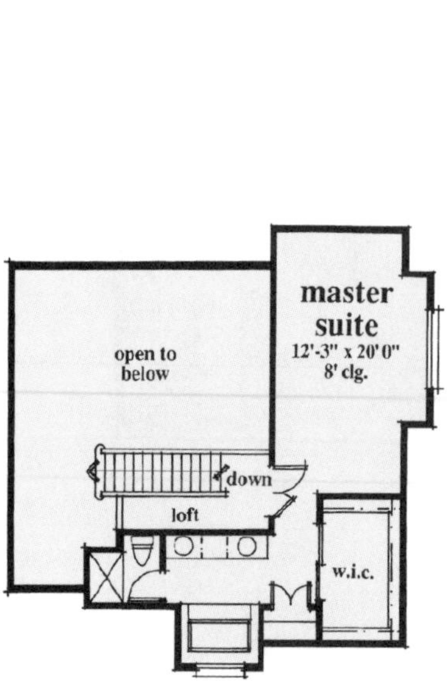
open to below
master suite
12'-3" x 20'0"
8' clg.
down
loft
w.i.c.

Amenities abound in this delightful two-story home. The foyer opens directly into the fantastic grand room, which offers a warming fireplace and two sets of double doors to the rear deck. The dining room also accesses this deck and a second deck shared with Bedroom 2. A convenient kitchen and another bedroom also reside on this level. Upstairs, the master bedroom reigns supreme. Entered through double doors, it pampers with a luxurious bath, walk-in closet, morning kitchen and private observation deck. This home is designed with a pier foundation.

Design HPT830487

First Floor: 1,342 square feet
Second Floor: 511 square feet
Total: 1,853 square feet
Width 44'-0" Depth 40'-0"

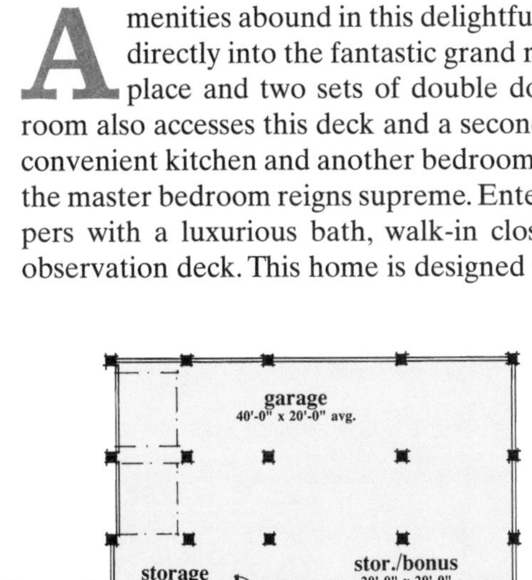

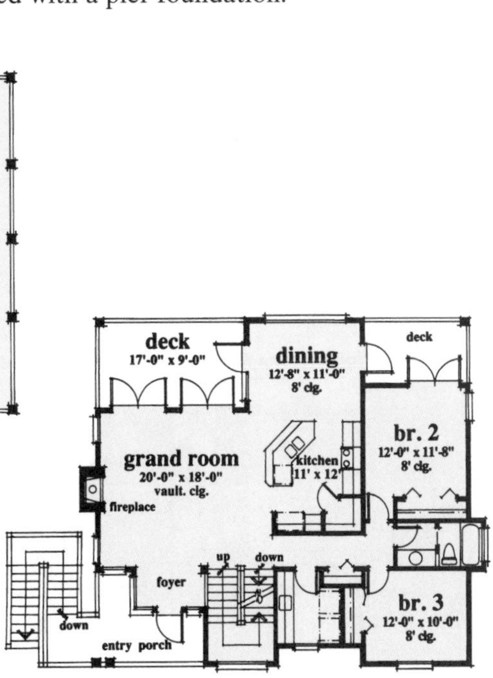

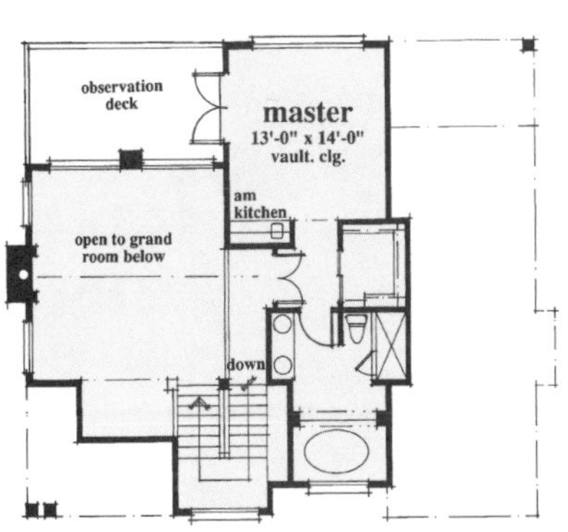

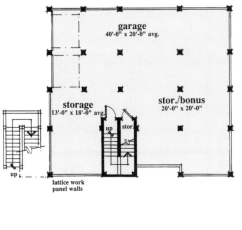

Luxury abounds in this Floridian-style home. A recreation room greets you on the garage level. Up the stairs, an open grand room, a bayed nook and a deck stretch across the back of the plan. Two bedrooms occupy the right side of this level and share a full hall bath with dual lavatories and a separate tub and shower. The master retreat on the upper level pleases with its own reading room, a morning kitchen, a large walk-in closet and a pampering bath with a double-bowl vanity, a whirlpool tub and a shower that opens outside. A private deck allows outdoor enjoyments.

Design HPT830488

First Floor: 1,642 square feet
Second Floor: 927 square feet
Total: 2,569 square feet
Finished Basement: 849 square feet
Width 60'-0" Depth 44'-6"
L

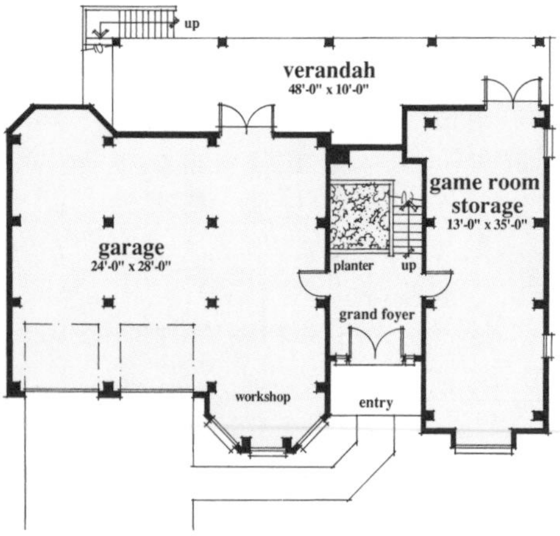

QUOTE ONE®

Cost to build? See page 516 to order complete cost estimate to build this house in your area!

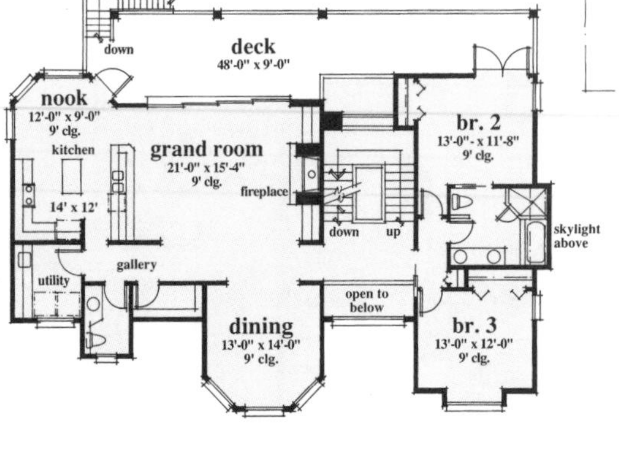

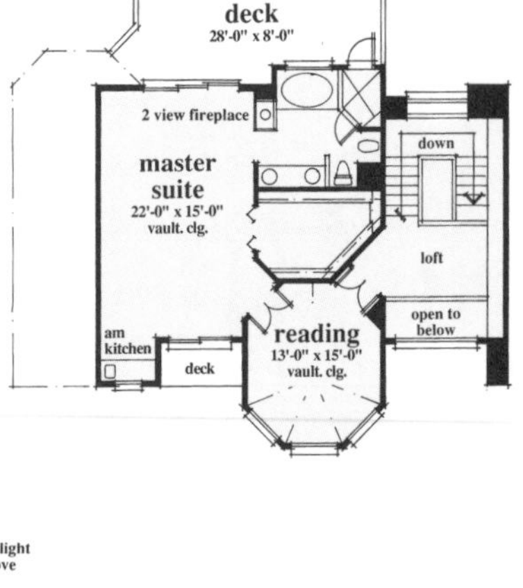

This home is quite a "looker" with its steeply sloping rooflines and large sunburst and multi-pane windows. This plan not only accommodates a narrow lot, but it also fits a sloping site. The angled corner entry gives way to a two-story living room with a tiled hearth. The dining room shares an interesting angled space with this area and enjoys easy service from the efficient kitchen. The family room offers double doors to a refreshing balcony. A powder room and laundry room complete the main level. Upstairs, three bedrooms include a vaulted master bedroom with a private bath. Bedrooms 2 and 3 each take advantage of direct access to a full bath.

Design HPT830489

First Floor: 1,022 square feet
Second Floor: 813 square feet
Total: 1,835 square feet
Width 36'-0" Depth 33'-0"
L

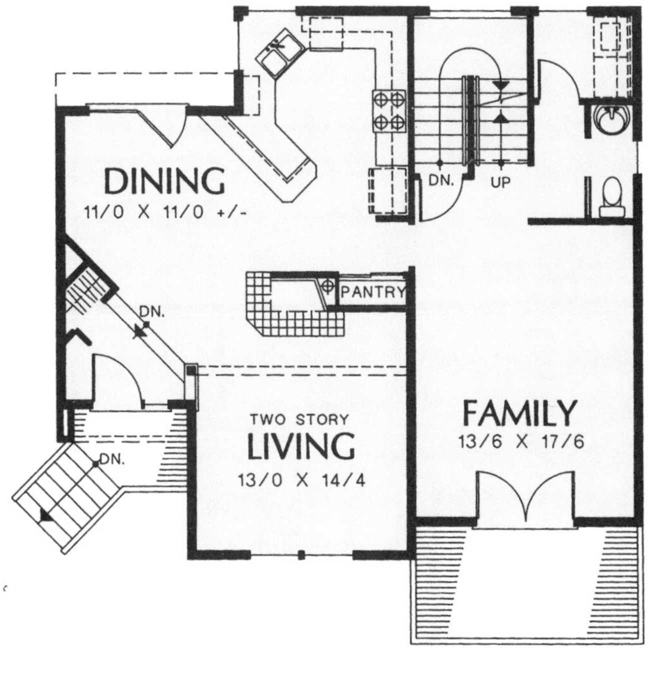
DINING
11/0 X 11/0 +/-
DN.
UP
PANTRY
DN.
TWO STORY
LIVING
13/0 X 14/4
FAMILY
13/6 X 17/6
DN.

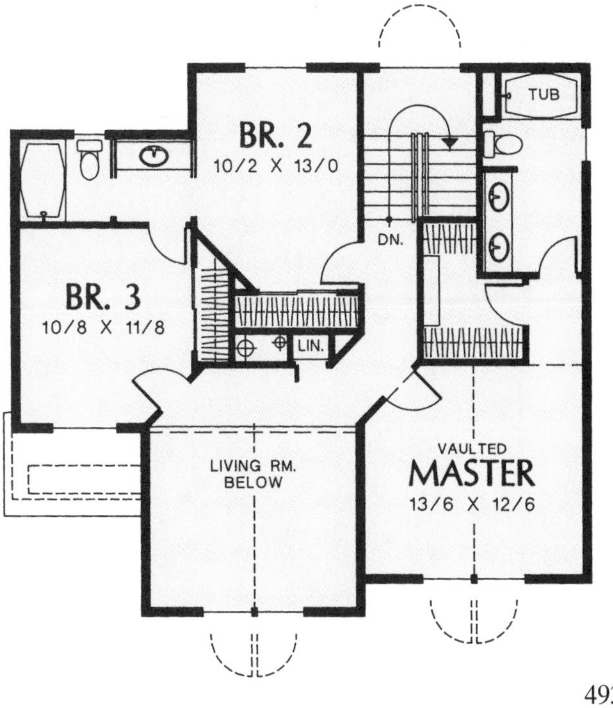
BR. 2
10/2 X 13/0
TUB
DN.
BR. 3
10/8 X 11/8
LIN.
LIVING RM.
BELOW
VAULTED
MASTER
13/6 X 12/6

The grand Palladian window lends plenty of curb appeal to this charming home. The wraparound country porch is perfect for peaceful evenings. The vaulted great room enjoys a large bay window, stone fireplace, pass-through to the kitchen and awesome rear views through the atrium window wall. The master suite features double entry doors, a walk-in closet and a fabulous bath. The optional lower level includes a family room.

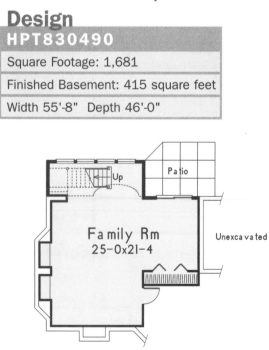

REAR ELEVATION

Design

HPT830490

Square Footage: 1,681

Finished Basement: 415 square feet

Width 55'-8" Depth 46'-0"

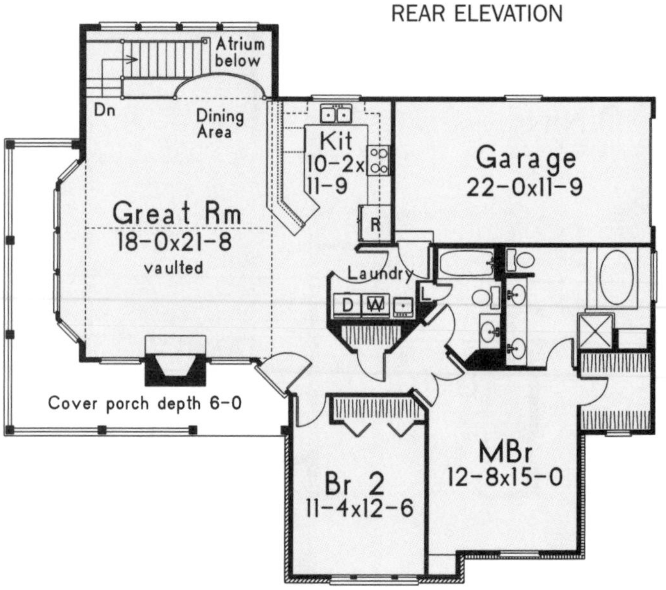
Atrium below
Dn
Dining Area
Kit
10-2x
11-9
Garage
22-0x11-9
Great Rm
18-0x21-8
vaulted
R
Laundry
D W
Cover porch depth 6-0
Br 2
11-4x12-6
MBr
12-8x15-0

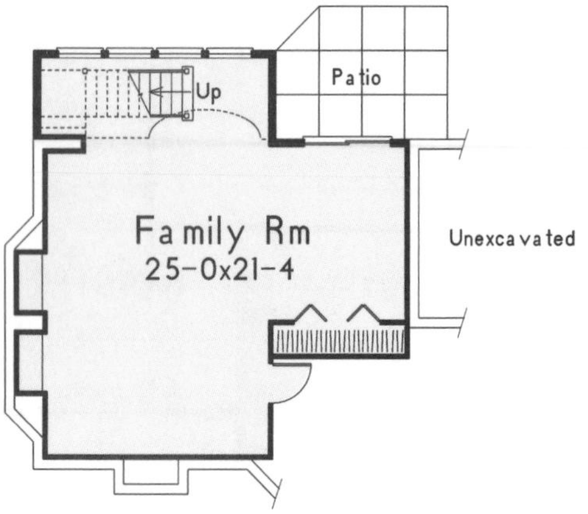
Up
Patio
Family Rm
25-0x21-4
Unexcavated

This small family home offers many traditional features and efficient amenities within. A petite porch enters into a spacious living room area with a fireplace. An open dining room for formal or casual occasions connects to the U-shaped kitchen and overlooks the rear deck. The master bedroom with a walk-in closet privately accesses the full hall bath. Two additional family bedrooms located nearby overlook the front of the property.

Design HPT830491

Square Footage: 1,252
Finished Basement: 151 square feet
Width 47'-0" Depth 32'-0"

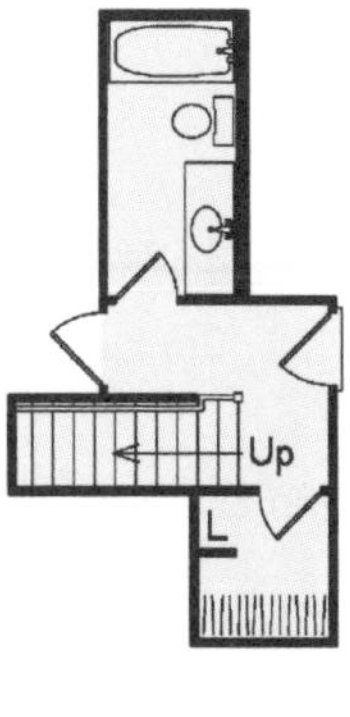

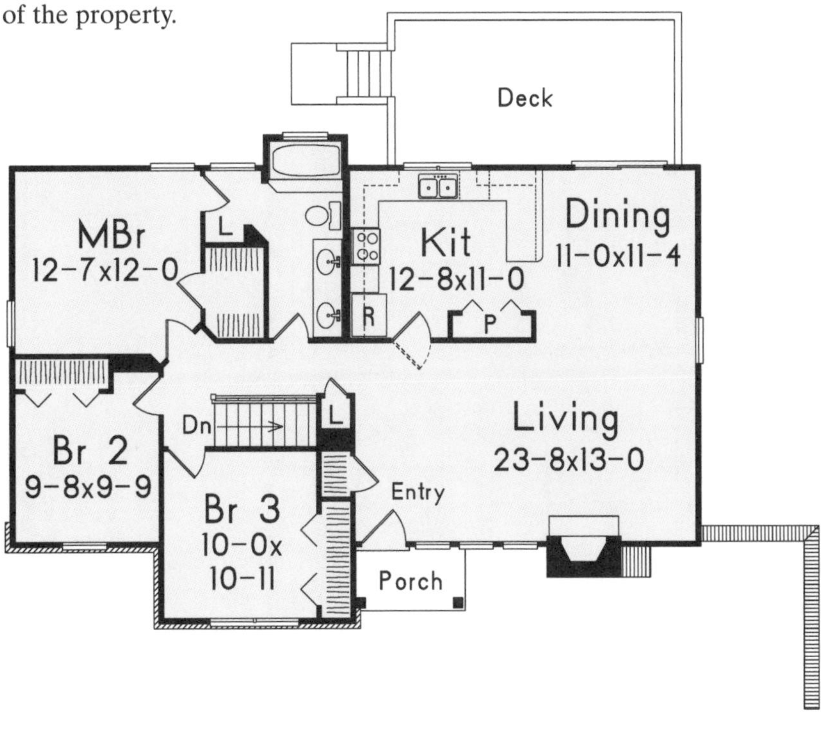

A roomy front porch gives this home a country flavor. The expansive rear view of this home offers plenty of windows. The vaulted great room boasts a fireplace, TV alcove, pass-through snack bar to the kitchen and an atrium with a bayed window wall and a stair to the lower-level family room. The oversized master bedroom features a vaulted ceiling, double entry doors and a large walk-in closet.

Design HPT830492

Square Footage: 1,777
Finished Basement: 557 square feet
Width 50'-0" Depth 56'-0"

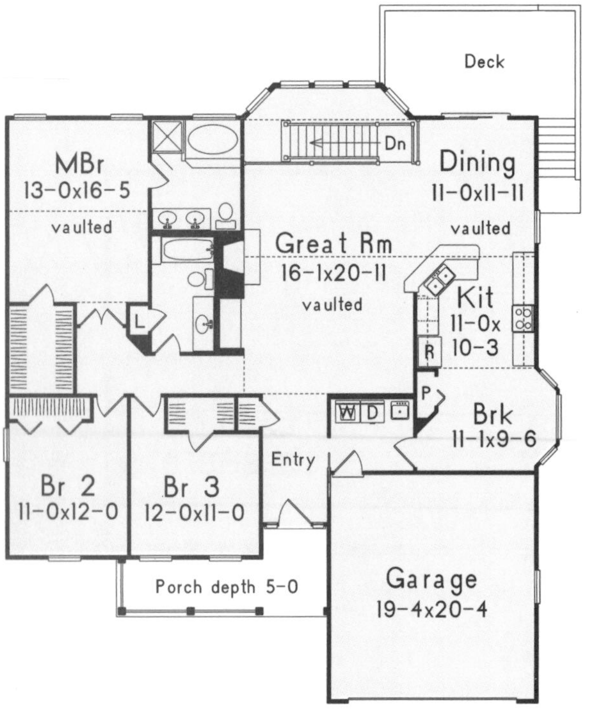
Deck
Dn
MBr
13-0x16-5
vaulted
Dining
11-0x11-11
vaulted
Great Rm
16-1x20-11
vaulted
L
Kit
11-0x
10-3
R
P
W D
Brk
11-1x9-6
Entry
Br 2
11-0x12-0
Br 3
12-0x11-0
Porch depth 5-0
Garage
19-4x20-4

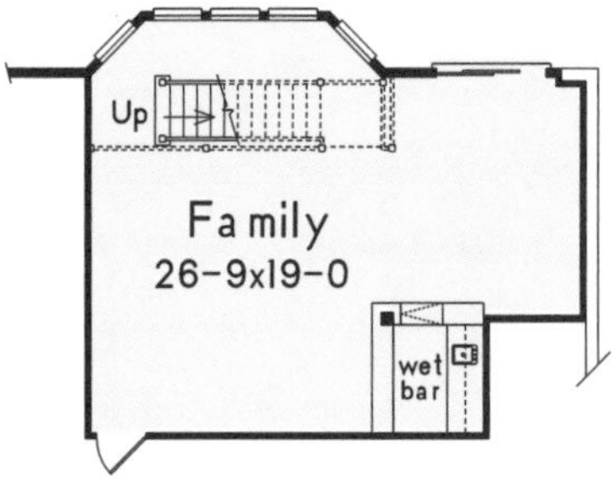
Up
Family
26-9x19-0
wet bar

REAR ELEVATION

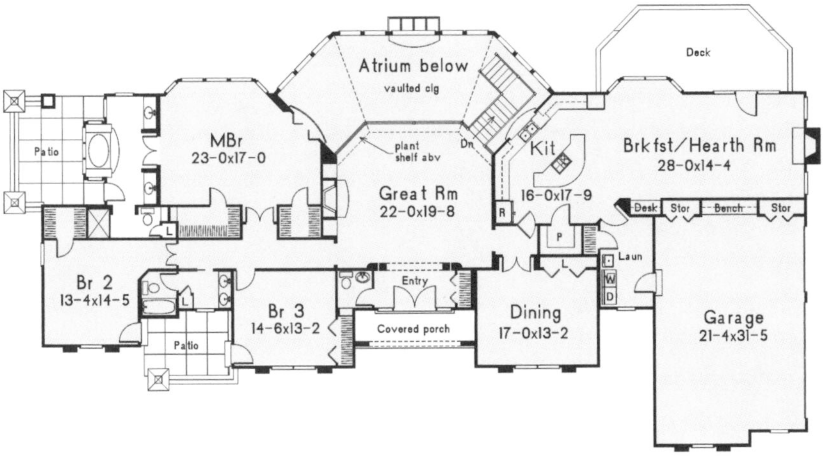

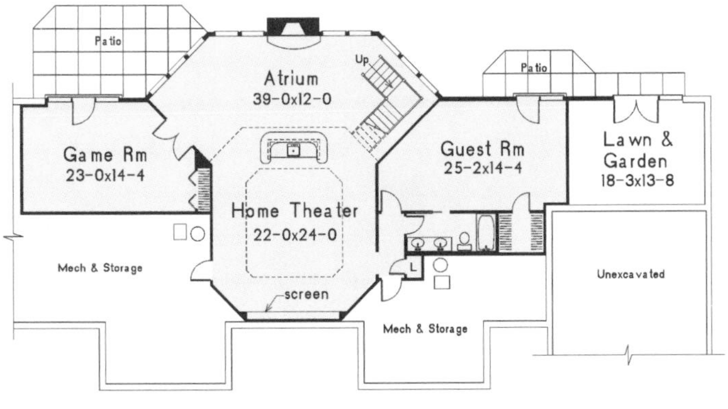

Design HPT830493

Square Footage: 3,050
Finished Basement: 1,776 square feet
Width 109'-0" Depth 57'-6"

The grand facade on this home is accented by the large window details. Sunbursts, keystones and lintels decorate the arches of the windows. The brightly lit entry connects to the great room with a balcony and a massive bay-shaped atrium. The kitchen features an island snack bar, walk-in pantry, computer area and atrium overlook. The master suite includes a sitting area, two walk-in closets, an atrium overlook and a luxury bath with a private courtyard. The family room/atrium, home theater, game room and guest bedroom comprise the lower level.

Although the facade may look like a quaint country cottage, this home's fine proportions contain formal living areas, including a dining room and a living room. At the back of the first floor you'll find a spacious kitchen and breakfast nook. A great room with a fireplace and bumped-out window makes everyday living very comfortable. A rear porch allows for outdoor dining and relaxation. Upstairs, four bedrooms include a master suite with lots of notable features. A boxed ceiling, lavish bath, large walk-in closet and secluded sitting room (which would also make a nice study or exercise room) assure great livability. This home is designed with a walk-out basement foundation.

Design HPT830494

First Floor: 1,567 square feet
Second Floor: 1,895 square feet
Total: 3,462 square feet
Width 63'-0" Depth 53'-6"

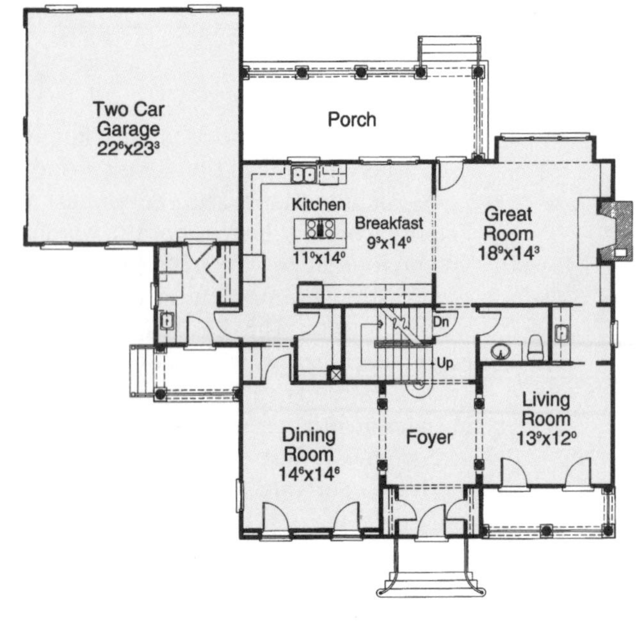

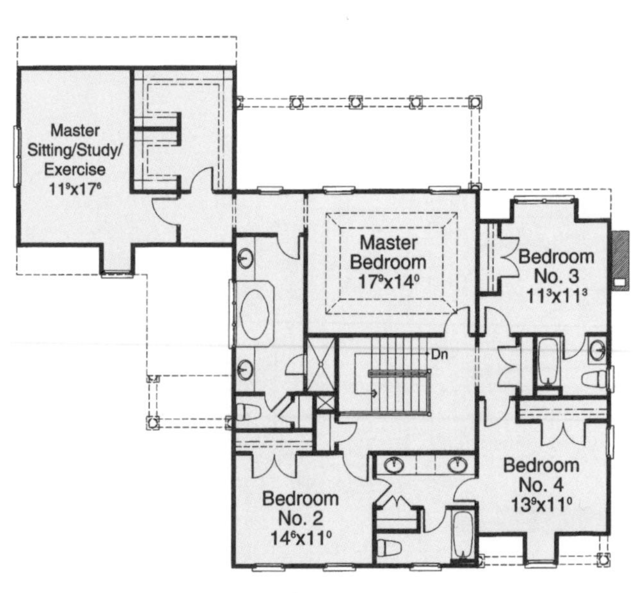

Front and back porches and a dash of Southern charm give this home its warm appeal. The living room (or study) and dining room flank the foyer. You'll also find a great room with a fireplace and easy access to the kitchen and breakfast nook for family livability. The first-floor master suite contains porch access, a luxurious private bath and a large walk-in closet. Upstairs, secondary bedrooms accommodate family or guests. This home is designed with a walkout basement foundation.

Design HPT830495

First Floor: 2,174 square feet
Second Floor: 1,113 square feet
Total: 3,287 square feet
Width 73'-6" Depth 67'-0"

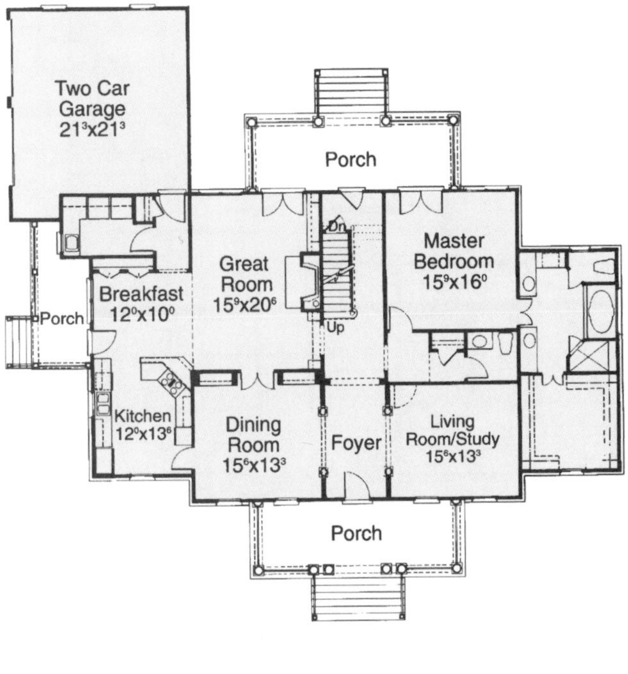

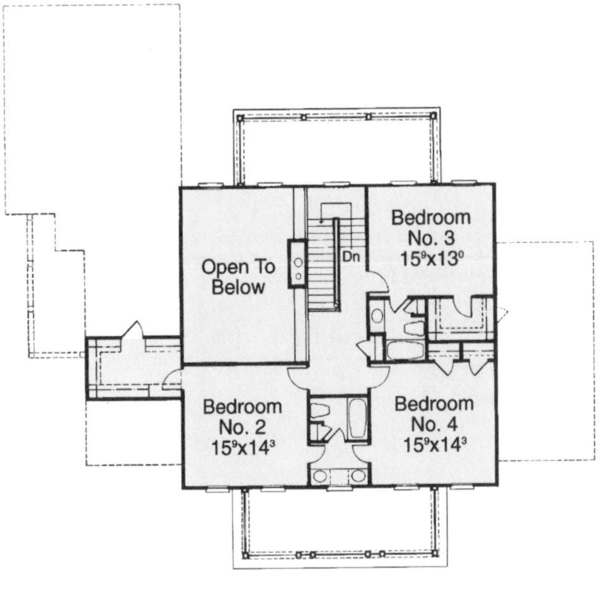

Design HPT830496

Square Footage: 1,770
Width 48'-0" Depth 47'-5"

Wood frame, weatherboard siding and stacked stone give this home its country cottage appeal. The entry opens to a great room with a cathedral ceiling and a formal dining room with a ten-foot ceiling. The spacious kitchen features a corner sink and shares a snack bar with the breakfast area. The bedroom wing has convenient laundry access. Choose the formal dining room or, if needed, make this room into a fourth bedroom. The master suite is well appointed with French doors, a volume ceiling, walk-in closet and sunny whirlpool bath. This home is designed with a walkout basement foundation.

DECK
W.I.C.
BREAKFAST
11'-4" X 7'-6"
MASTER BATH
MASTER BEDROOM
12'-6" X 16'-0"
GREAT ROOM
14'-0" X 16'-0"
KITCHEN
11'-4" X 12'-0"
W.I.C.
W.I.C.
UP
DN.
LNDR.
BEDROOM NO. 3
12'-0" X 11'-0"
FOYER
5'-0" X 8'-6"
DINING ROOM
11'-4" X 13'-6"
POWDER
BATH
BEDROOM NO. 2
12'-4" X 11'-4"

© Stephen Fuller, Inc.

Design HPT830497

Square Footage: 1,770
Width 49'-6" Depth 47'-0"

With European charm and functional floor planning, this fine family home will be a delight for years to come. A recessed front door opens to a columned dining room that shares space with the family room. A fireplace, tiered ceiling and French doors are just a few of the features that lend elegance to the plan. A bayed breakfast nook enjoys expansive rear views and direct service from the kitchen. Up a half-flight of stairs, three bedrooms include two family bedrooms and a master suite. In the master suite, French doors lead to a private deck. An expansive, secluded bath offers dual lavatories, a corner garden tub and a walk-in closet. This home is designed with a walkout basement foundation.

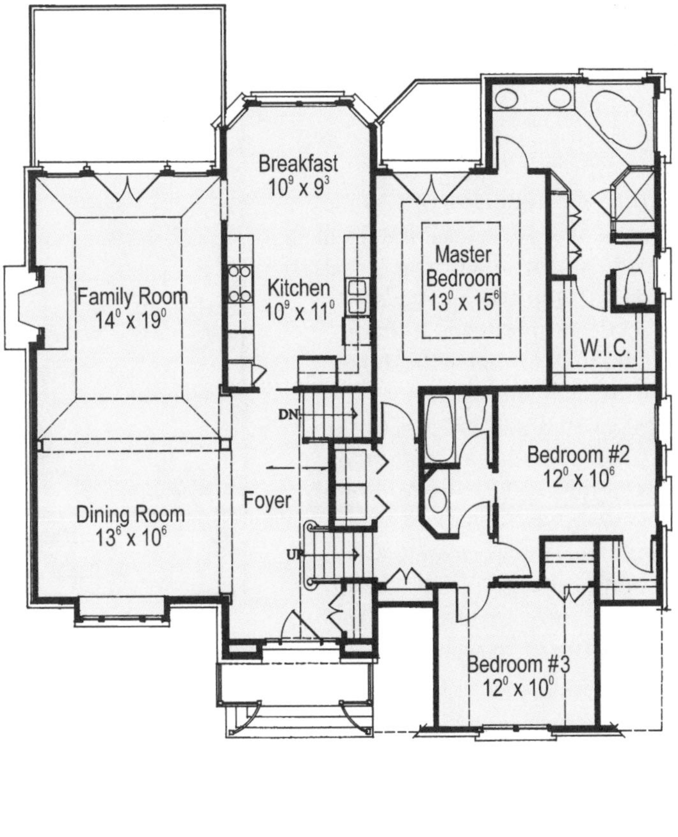
Breakfast
10⁹ x 9³
Master Bedroom
13⁰ x 15⁶
Family Room
14⁰ x 19⁰
Kitchen
10⁹ x 11⁰
W.I.C.
DN
Bedroom #2
12⁰ x 10⁶
Foyer
Dining Room
13⁶ x 10⁶
UP
Bedroom #3
12⁰ x 10⁰

Design

HPT830498

Square Footage: 1,770

Width 48'-0" Depth 47'-5"

Perfect for a sloping lot, this European one-story home includes living areas on one level and bedrooms on another. The great room contains a fireplace and access to the rear deck. Close by are the U-shaped kitchen and breakfast room with a boxed window. The formal dining room completes the living area and is open to the entry foyer. Bedrooms are a few steps up from the living areas. The master suite enjoys two walk-in closets and a sumptuous bath with a compartmented toilet. Secondary bedrooms share a full bath that includes a double-bowl vanity. This home is designed with a walkout basement foundation.

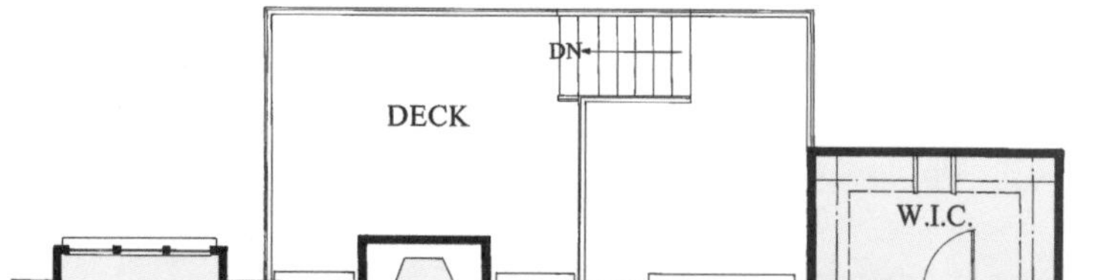

QUOTE ONE®

Cost to build? See page 516 to order complete cost estimate to build this house in your area!

Gables and a multi-level roof create the soft charm of this design. The foyer provides views into both the great room with a warming hearth and the dining room with a vaulted ceiling. The great room features a fireplace and access to the rear deck. The kitchen offers a spacious work area and opens to the adjacent breakfast room. Enter the master suite through large double doors and behold a tray ceiling and French doors leading to a private deck. Bedrooms 2 and 3 share a full bath. This home is designed with a walkout basement foundation.

Design HPT830499

Square Footage: 1,770	
Width 48'-0"	Depth 47'-0"

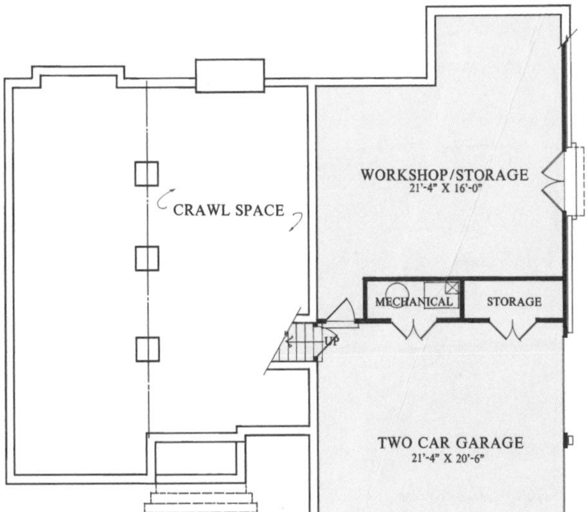

European style takes beautifully to a sloped lot. This design tames a slight grade by making use of a hillside garage. The main floor splits into two levels accessed from the foyer. The spacious great room and dining room open from the entry. Columns and windows give an open, inviting look. The eat-in kitchen has a glorious window in the nook that looks out to the deck. The upper level of the main floor holds the ultra-comfortable master suite and two family bedrooms that share a full bath. The walkout basement includes a two-car garage and a storage area.

Design
HPT830500

Square Footage: 1,725

Width 47'-6" Depth 45'-6"

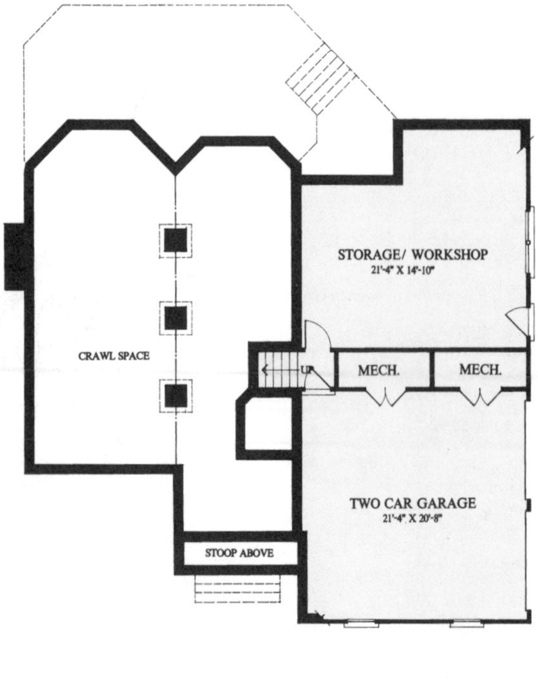

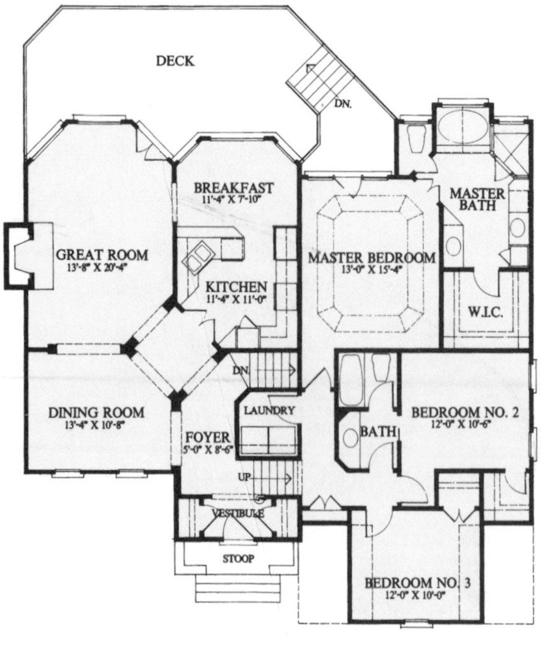

This elegant home makes the most of the hillside lot by using the lower level for a two-car garage and expandable basement space. A striking stair leads to the entry where another half-flight continues up inside. The vaulted dining room has an open rail that overlooks the entry. A vaulted ceiling in the great room accents the fireplace. A modified galley kitchen provides a snack bar and a breakfast nook. The master suite features a sitting room, compartmented bath and walk-in closet. Two family bedrooms share a full hall bath.

Design
HPT830501

Square Footage: 1,717
Finished Basement: 1,026 square feet
Width 50'-0" Depth 39'-4"

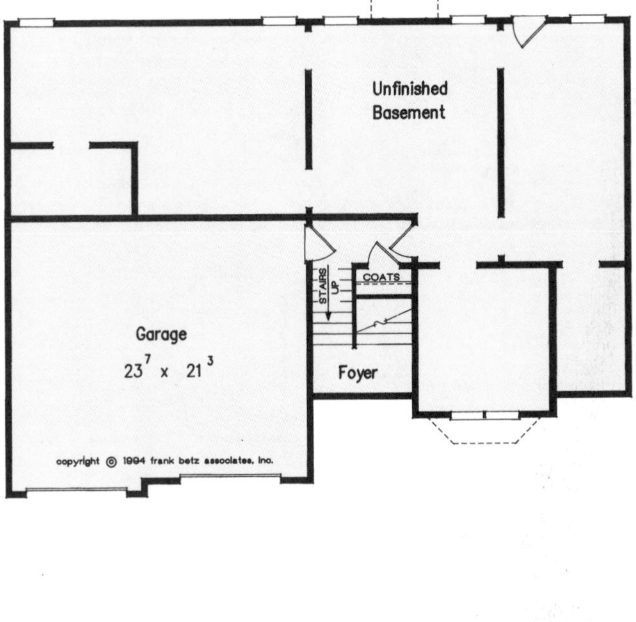

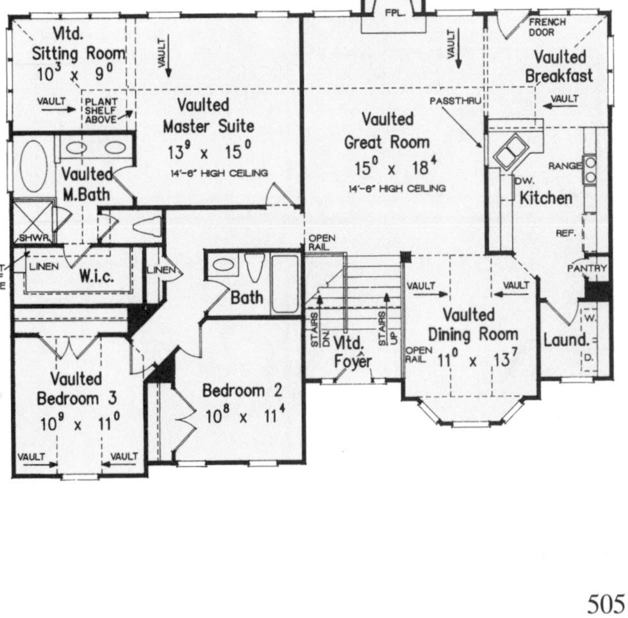

This home, as shown in the photograph, may differ from the actual blueprints. For more detailed information, please check the floor plans carefully.
Photo by Bob Greenspan

This impressive Tudor is designed for lots that slope up slightly from the street—the garage is five feet below the first floor. Just to the right of the entry, the den is arranged to work well as an office. Formal living areas include a living room with a fireplace and an elegant dining room. The family room also offers a fireplace and is close to the bumped-out nook. On the second floor, all the bedrooms are generously sized, and the master suite features a tray ceiling and a huge walk-in closet. A large vaulted bonus room is provided with convenient access from both the family room and the garage. Three family bedrooms and a full bath complete the plan.

Design HPT830502

First Floor: 1,484 square feet

Second Floor: 1,402 square feet

Total: 2,886 square feet

Bonus Space: 430 square feet

Width 63'-0" Depth 51'-0"

L

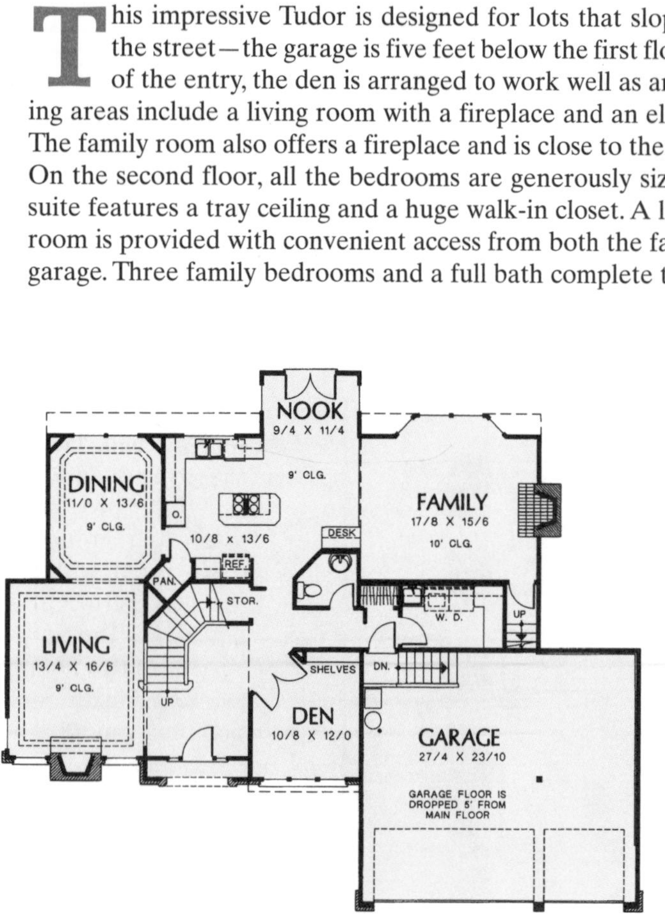

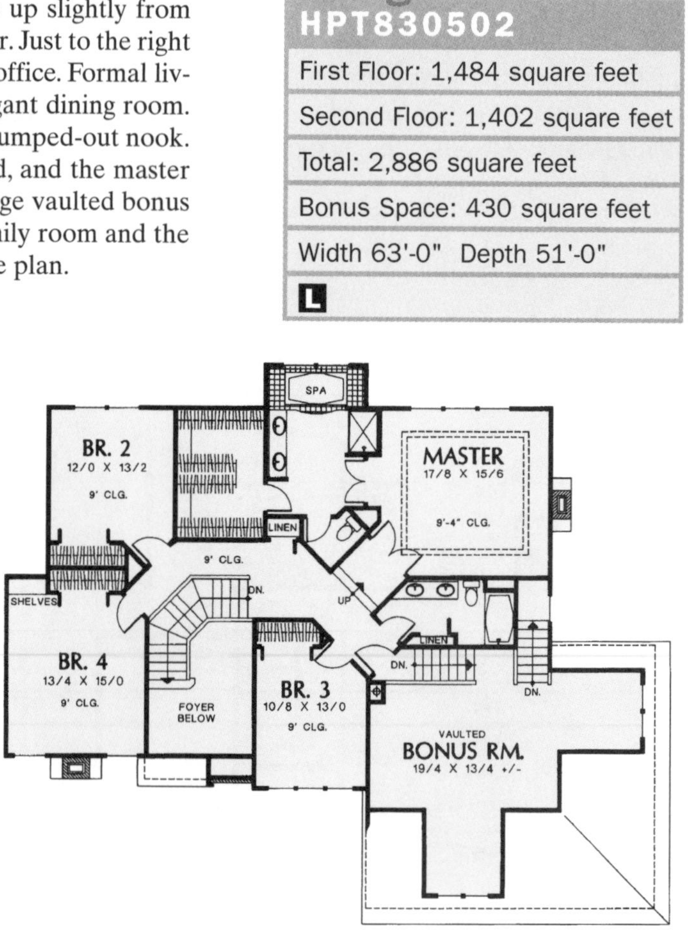

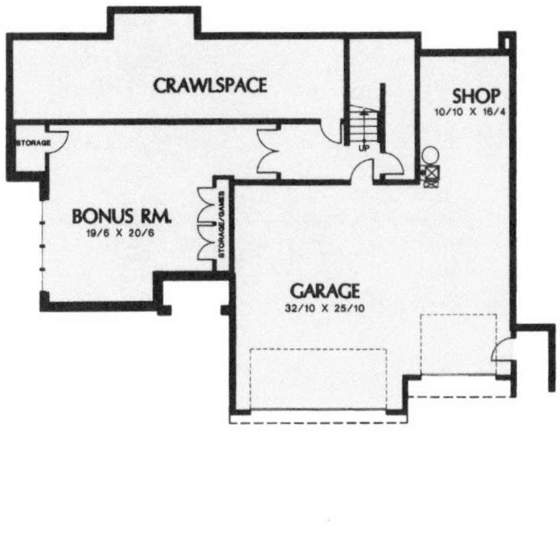
CRAWLSPACE
SHOP
10/10 X 16/4
STORAGE
UP
BONUS RM.
19/6 X 20/6
STORAGE/GAMES
GARAGE
32/10 X 25/10

Design
HPT830503

First Floor: 1,989 square feet
Second Floor: 1,349 square feet
Total: 3,443 square feet
Finished Basement: 105 square feet
Bonus Space: 487 square feet
Width 63'-0" Depth 48'-0"

Dramatic balconies and spectacular window treatments enhance this stunning luxury home. Inside, a through-fireplace warms the formal living room and a restful den. Both living spaces open to a balcony that invites quiet reflection on starry nights. The banquet-sized dining room is easily served from the adjacent kitchen. Here, space is shared with an eating nook that provides access to the rear grounds and a family room with a corner fireplace—perfect for casual gatherings. The second floor contains two family bedrooms and a luxurious master suite that enjoys its own private balcony. The basement accommodates a shop and a bonus room for future development.

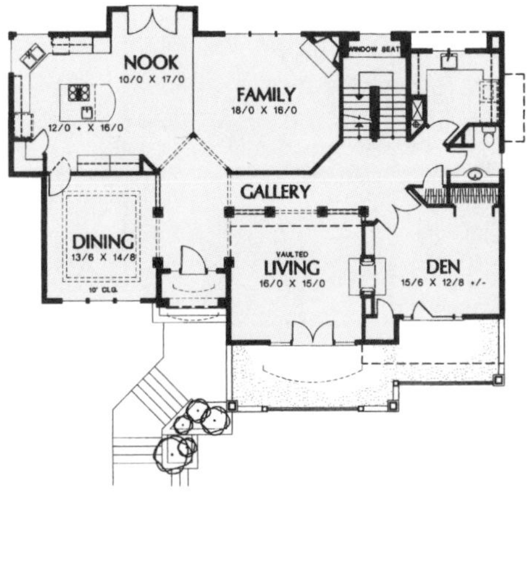
NOOK
10/0 X 17/0
12/0 + X 16/0
FAMILY
18/0 X 16/0
WINDOW SEAT
GALLERY
DINING
13/6 X 14/8
10' CLG.
VAULTED
LIVING
16/0 X 15/0
DEN
15/6 X 12/8 +/-

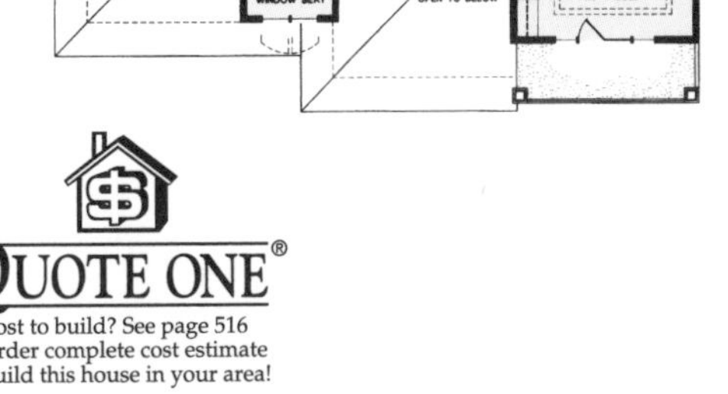
LINEN
BR. 2
12/0 X 13/0
WINDOW SEAT
DN.
BR. 3
12/0 X 11/0 +
MASTER
16/6 X 14/8
WINDOW SEAT
OPEN TO BELOW

QUOTE ONE®
Cost to build? See page 516 to order complete cost estimate to build this house in your area!

Sleek, contemporary lines define the exterior of this home. Steps lead up a front-sloping lot to the bright entry. A front-facing den is brightly lit by a curving wall of windows. Built-ins enhance the utility of this room. A two-story living room offers a fireplace and lots of windows. The kitchen serves a sunny breakfast nook, an oversized family room and the nearby dining room that invites dinner parties with its elegant ceiling. The family will find plenty of sleeping space with four bedrooms on the second level. The master bedroom suite is a real attention getter. Its roomy bath includes a spa tub and a separate shower.

Design HPT830504

First Floor: 1,894 square feet
Second Floor: 1,544 square feet
Total: 3,438 square feet
Width 64'-0" Depth 61'-6"

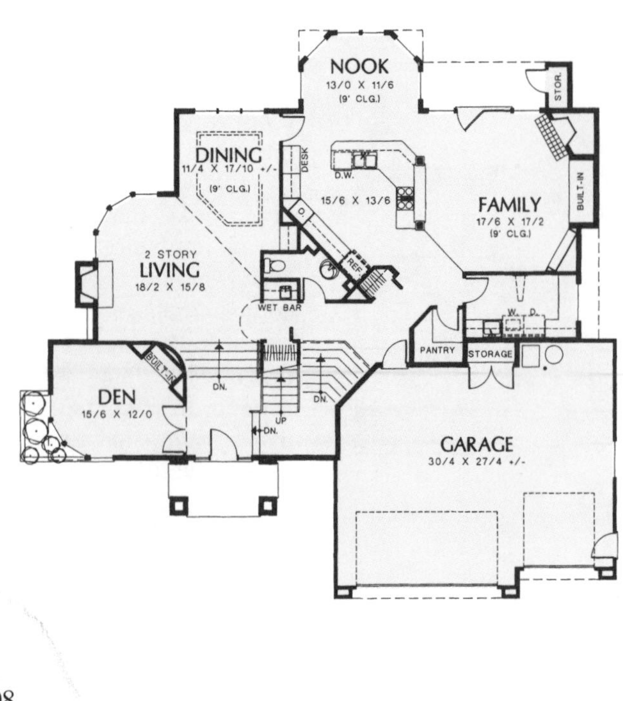

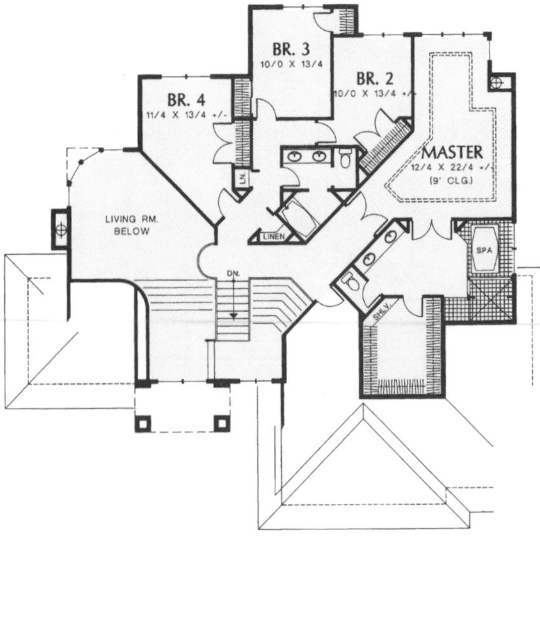

This refined hillside home is designed for lots that fall off toward the rear and works especially well with a view out the back. The kitchen and eating nook wrap around the vaulted family room where arched transom windows flank the fireplace. Formal living is graciously centered in the living room, situated directly off the foyer and the adjoining dining room. A grand master suite is located on the main level for convenience and privacy. Downstairs, three family bedrooms share a compartmented hall bath. Please specify basement or crawlspace foundation when ordering.

Design

HPT830505

Main Level: 2,196 square feet
Lower Level: 1,542 square feet
Total: 3,738 square feet
Width 71'-0" Depth 56'-0"
L

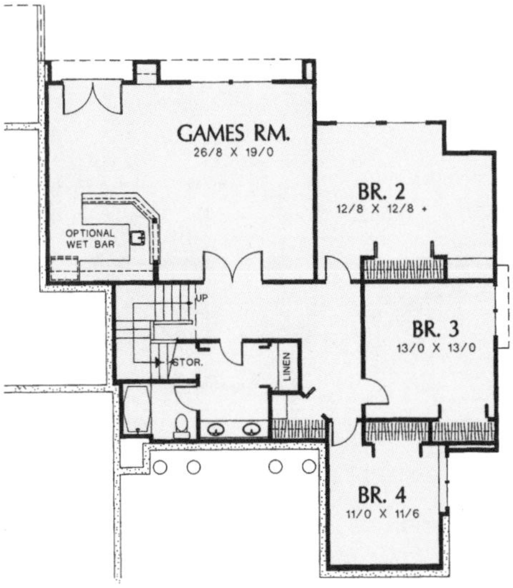

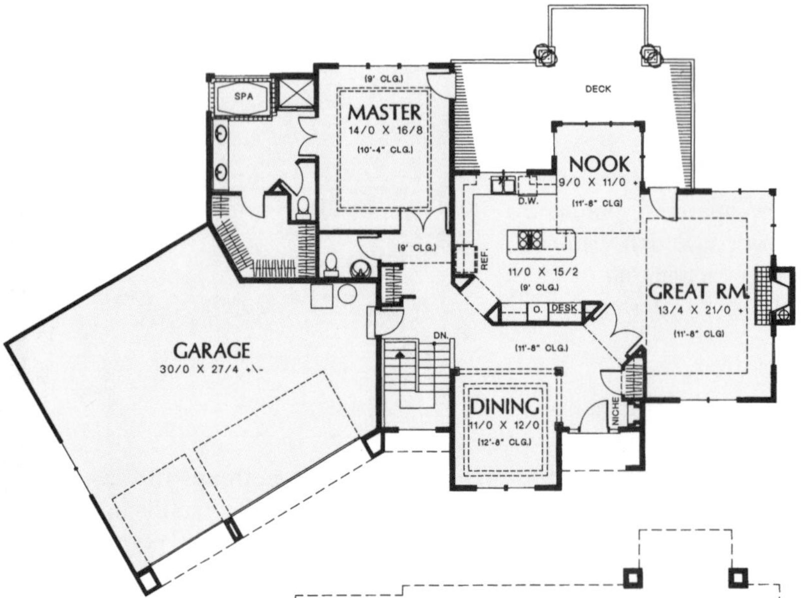

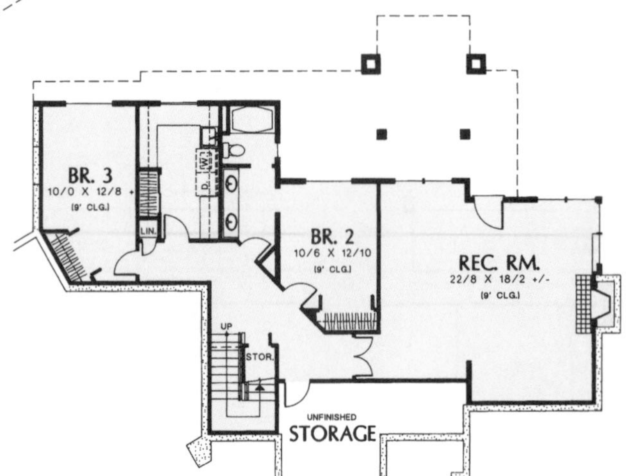

Design HPT830506

Main Level: 1,687 square feet	
Lower Level: 1,251 square feet	
Total: 2,938 square feet	
Width 82'-7" Depth 54'-9"	
L	

This striking home is perfect for daylight basement lots. An elegant dining room fronts the plan. Nearby, an expansive kitchen features plenty of cabinet and counter space. A nook surrounded by a deck adds character. The comfortable great room, with a raised ceiling and a fireplace, shares space with these areas. The master bedroom suite includes private deck access and a superb bath with a spa tub and dual lavatories. Downstairs, two bedrooms, a laundry room with lots of counter space and a recreation room with a fireplace cap off the plan.

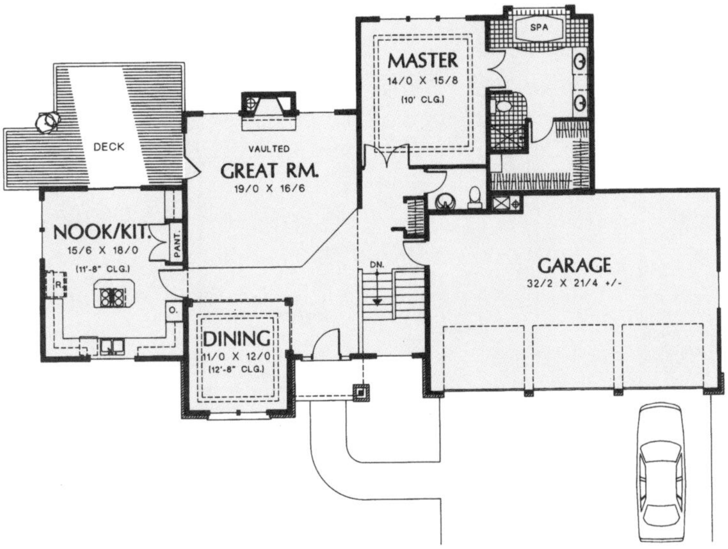
MASTER
14/0 X 15/8
(10' CLG.)
SPA
DECK
VAULTED
GREAT RM.
19/0 X 16/6
NOOK/KIT.
15/6 X 18/0
(11'-8" CLG.)
PANT.
DN.
GARAGE
32/2 X 21/4 +/-
DINING
11/0 X 12/0
(12'-8" CLG.)

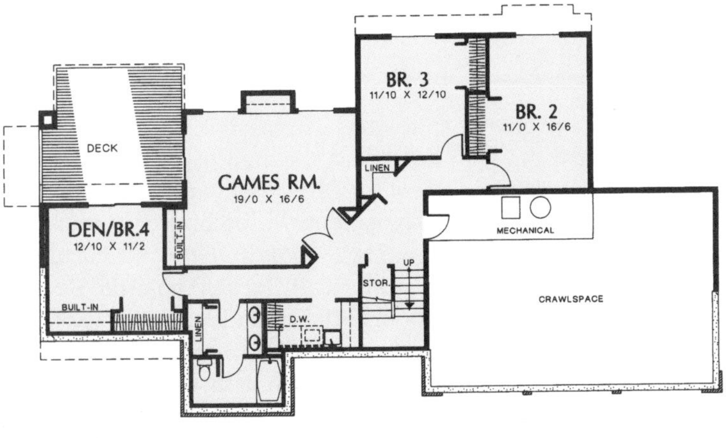
BR. 3
11/10 X 12/10
BR. 2
11/0 X 16/6
DECK
GAMES RM.
19/0 X 16/6
LINEN
DEN/BR.4
12/10 X 11/2
BUILT-IN
MECHANICAL
UP
STOR.
CRAWLSPACE
BUILT-IN
LINEN
D.W.

Design HPT830507

Main Level: 1,573 square feet
Lower Level: 1,404 square feet
Total: 2,977 square feet
Width 76'-0" Depth 43'-0"
L

There's something for every member of the family in this captivating hillside plan. The first floor holds a huge great room for family and formal gatherings, a dining room distinguished by columns, an island kitchen with attached nook and an outdoor deck area. The master suite has a lavish bath. The game room downstairs is joined by three bedrooms, or two bedrooms and a den. Look for another deck at this level. Please specify basement or crawlspace foundation when ordering.

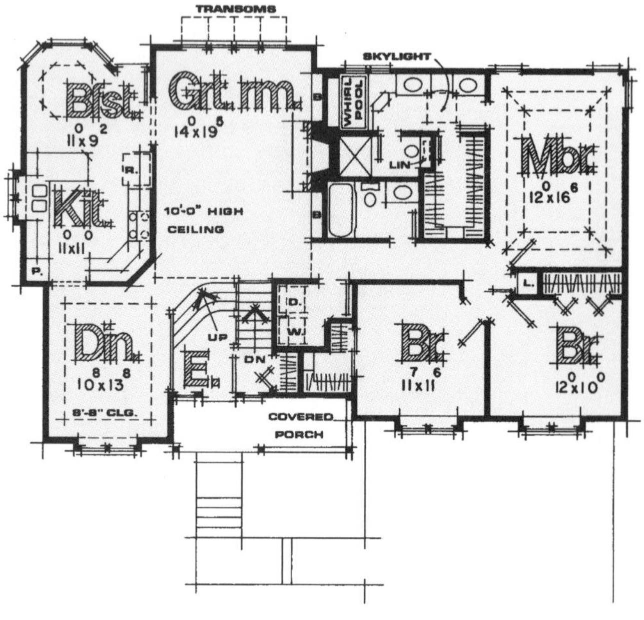

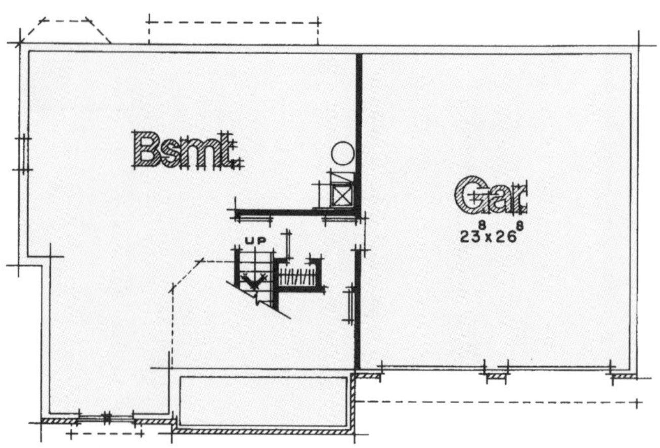

Design
HPT830508

Square Footage: 1,696

Finished Basement: 1,696 square feet

Width 54'-0" Depth 34'-0"

This convenient split-entry traditional home features a great room with a fireplace flanked by bookcases and a floor-to-ceiling view of the backyard. The efficient kitchen includes a sunny bay window in the breakfast area. Box ceilings grace both the breakfast nook and the formal dining room. The laundry room is strategically located near the sleeping wing. Two secondary bedrooms offer abundant closet space and a shared full bath. The deluxe master bedroom offers a vaulted ceiling, a large walk-in closet and a bath with a whirlpool tub.

Design HPT830509

Square Footage: 2,809
Finished Basement: 837 square feet
Width 62'-0" Depth 45'-0"

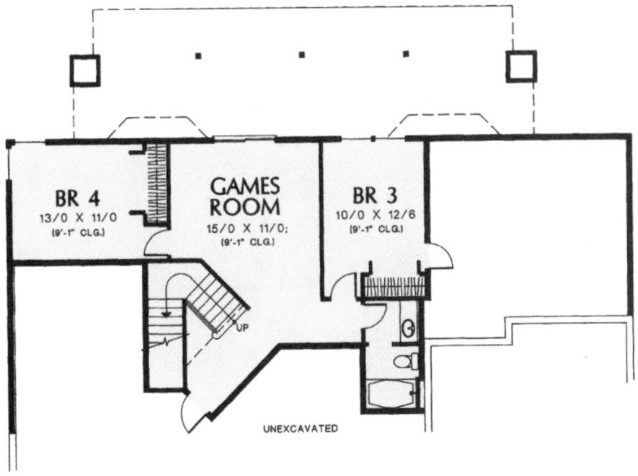
BR 4
13/0 X 11/0
(9'-1" CLG.)
GAMES ROOM
15/0 X 11/0;
(9'-1" CLG.)
BR 3
10/0 X 12/6
(9'-1" CLG.)
UP
UNEXCAVATED

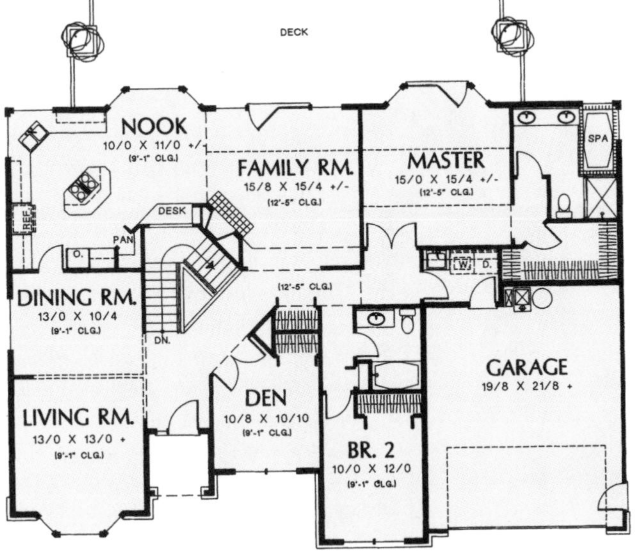
DECK
NOOK
10/0 X 11/0 +/-
(9'-1" CLG.)
FAMILY RM.
15/8 X 15/4 +/-
(12'-5" CLG.)
MASTER
15/0 X 15/4 +/-
(12'-5" CLG.)
SPA
REF.
DESK
PAN
DINING RM.
13/0 X 10/4
(9'-1" CLG.)
(12'-5" CLG.)
DN.
LIVING RM.
13/0 X 13/0 +
(9'-1" CLG.)
DEN
10/8 X 10/10
(9'-1" CLG.)
BR. 2
10/0 X 12/0
(9'-1" CLG.)
GARAGE
19/8 X 21/8 +

A gracious facade welcomes all into this delightful family plan. A formal area, consisting of living and dining rooms, greets you at the foyer. To the right, a double-doored den provides a peaceful place to work or relax. The spacious kitchen has a cooktop island, a pantry and a window-laden breakfast nook. The family room offers passage to the rear deck. The master suite provides access as well and features a private bath and a walk-in closet. Bedroom 2 is nestled in front by a full hall bath. Downstairs, two bedrooms flank a game room. A two-car garage opens to a laundry room.

COPYRIGHT DOS & DON'TS

Blueprints for residential construction (or working drawings, as they are often called in the industry) are copyrighted intellectual property, protected under the terms of United States Copyright Law and, therefore, cannot be copied legally for use in building. However, we've made it easy for you to get what you need to build your home, without violating copyright law. Following are some guidelines to help you obtain the right number of copies for your chosen blueprint design.

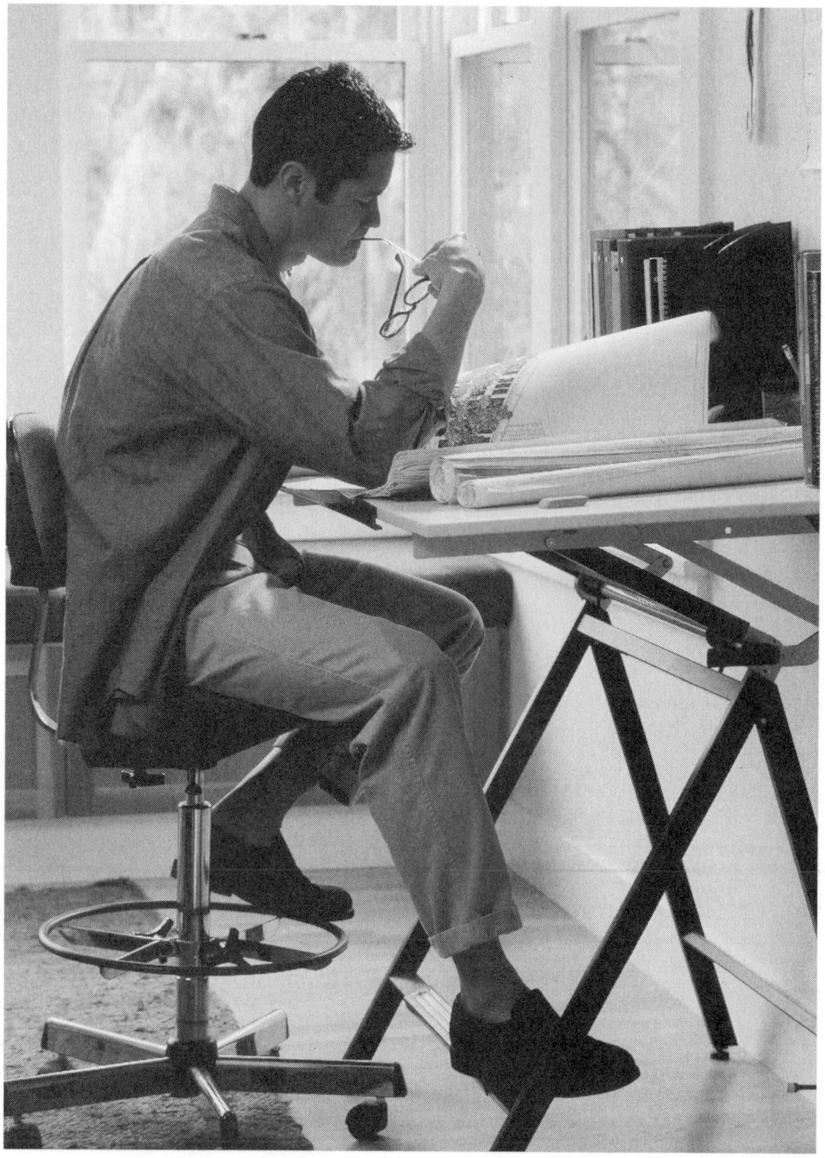

COPYRIGHT DO

■ Do purchase enough copies of the blueprints to satisfy building requirements. As a rule for a home or project plan, you will need a set for yourself, two or three for your builder and subcontractors, two for the local building department, and one to three for your mortgage lender. You may want to check with your local building department or your builder to see how many they need before you purchase. You may need to buy eight to 10 sets; note that some areas of the country require purchase of vellums (also called reproducibles) instead of blueprints. Vellums can be written on and changed more easily than blueprints. Also, remember, plans are only good for one-time construction.

■ Do consider reverse blueprints if you want to flop the plan. Lettering and numbering will appear backward, but the reversed sets will help you and your builder better visualize the design.

■ Do take advantage of multiple-set discounts at the time you place your order. Usually, purchasing additional sets after you receive your initial order is not as cost-effective.

■ Do take advantage of vellums. Though they are a little more expensive, they can be changed, copied, and used for one-time construction of a home. You will receive a copyright release letter with your vellums that will allow you to have them copied.

■ Do talk with one of our professional service representatives before placing your order. They can give you great advice about what packages are available for your chosen design and what will work best for your particular situation.

COPYRIGHT DON'T

■ Don't think you should purchase only one set of blueprints for a building project. One is fine if you want to study the plan closely, but will not be enough for actual building.

■ Don't expect your builder or a copy center to make copies of standard blueprints. They cannot legally—most copy centers are aware of this.

■ Don't purchase standard blueprints if you know you'll want to make changes to the plans; vellums are a better value.

■ Don't use blueprints or vellums more than one time. Additional fees apply if you want to build more than one time from a set of drawings. ■

LET US SHOW YOU OUR HOME BLUEPRINT PACKAGE.

BUILDING A HOME? PLANNING A HOME?

OUR BLUEPRINT PACKAGE HAS NEARLY EVERYTHING YOU NEED TO GET THE JOB DONE RIGHT,

whether you're working on your own or with help from an architect, designer, builder or subcontractors. Each Blueprint Package is the result of many hours of work by licensed architects or professional designers.

QUALITY

Hundreds of hours of painstaking effort have gone into the development of your blueprint plan. Each home has been quality-checked by professionals to insure accuracy and buildability.

VALUE

Because we sell in volume, you can buy professional quality blueprints at a fraction of their development cost. With our plans, your dream home design costs substantially less than the fees charged by architects.

SERVICE

Once you've chosen your favorite home plan, you'll receive fast, efficient service whether you choose to mail or fax your order to us or call us toll free at 1-800-521-6797. After you have received your order, call for customer service toll free 1-888-690-1116.

SATISFACTION

Over 50 years of service to satisfied home plan buyers provide us unparalleled experience and knowledge in producing quality blueprints.

ORDER TOLL FREE 1-800-521-6797

After you've looked over our Blueprint Package and Important Extras, call toll free on our Blueprint Hotline: 1-800-521-6797, for current pricing and availability prior to mailing the order form on page 525. We're ready and eager to serve you. After you have received your order, call for customer service toll free 1-888-690-1116.

Each set of blueprints is an interrelated collection of detail sheets which includes components such as floor plans, interior and exterior elevations, dimensions, cross-sections, diagrams and notations. These sheets show exactly how your house is to be built.

SETS MAY INCLUDE:

FRONTAL SHEET
This artist's sketch of the exterior of the house gives you an idea of how the house will look when built and landscaped. Large floor plans show all levels of the house and provide an overview of your new home's livability, as well as a handy reference for deciding on furniture placement.

FOUNDATION PLANS
This sheet shows the foundation layout including support walls, excavated and unexcavated areas, if any, and foundation notes. If slab construction rather than basement, the plan shows footings and details for a monolithic slab. This page, or another in the set, may include a sample plot plan for locating your house on a building site.

DETAILED FLOOR PLANS
These plans show the layout of each floor of the house. Rooms and interior spaces are carefully dimensioned and keys are given for cross-section details provided later in the plans. The positions of electrical outlets and switches are shown.

HOUSE CROSS-SECTIONS
Large-scale views show sections or cut-aways of the foundation, interior walls, exterior walls, floors, stairways and roof details. Additional cross-sections may show important changes in floor, ceiling or roof heights or the relationship of one level to another. Extremely valuable for construction, these sections show exactly how the various parts of the house fit together.

INTERIOR ELEVATIONS
Many of our drawings show the design and placement of kitchen and bathroom cabinets, laundry areas, fireplaces, bookcases and other built-ins. Little "extras," such as mantelpiece and wainscoting drawings, plus molding sections, provide details that give your home that custom touch.

EXTERIOR ELEVATIONS
These drawings show the front, rear and sides of your house and give necessary notes on exterior materials and finishes. Particular attention is given to cornice detail, brick and stone accents or other finish items that make your home unique.

IMPORTANT EXTRAS TO DO THE JOB RIGHT!

INTRODUCING IMPORTANT PLANNING AND CONSTRUCTION AIDS DEVELOPED BY OUR PROFESSIONALS TO HELP YOU SUCCEED IN YOUR HOME-BUILDING PROJECT

MATERIALS LIST

(Note: Because of the diversity of local building codes, our Materials List does not include mechanical materials.)

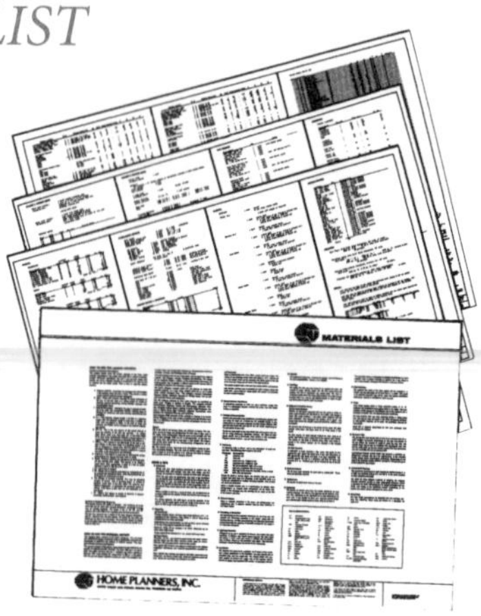

For many of the designs in our portfolio, we offer a customized materials take-off that is invaluable in planning and estimating the cost of your new home. This Materials List outlines the quantity, type and size of materials needed to build your house (with the exception of mechanical system items). Included are framing lumber, windows and doors, kitchen and bath cabinetry, rough and finish hardware, and much more. This handy list helps you or your builder cost out materials and serves as a reference sheet when you're compiling bids. Some Materials Lists may be ordered before blueprints are ordered, call for information.

SPECIFICATION OUTLINE

This valuable 16-page document is critical to building your house correctly. Designed to be filled in by you or your builder, this book lists 166 stages or items crucial to the building process. It provides a comprehensive review of the construction process and helps in choosing materials. When combined with the blueprints, a signed contract, and a schedule, it becomes a legal document and record for the building of your home.

QUOTE ONE®

SUMMARY COST REPORT **MATERIAL COST REPORT**

A product for estimating the cost of building select designs, the Quote One® system is available in two separate stages: The Summary Cost Report and the Material Cost Report.

The **Summary Cost Report** is the first stage in the package and shows the total cost per square foot for your chosen home in your zip-code area and then breaks that cost down into various categories showing the costs for building materials, labor and installation. The report includes three grades: Budget, Standard and Custom. These reports allow you to evaluate your building budget and compare the costs of building a variety of homes in your area.

Make even more informed decisions about your home-building project with the second phase of our package, our **Material Cost Report.** This tool is invaluable in planning and estimating the cost of your new home. The material and installation (labor and equipment) cost is shown for each of over 1,000 line items provided in the Materials List (Standard grade), which is included when you purchase this estimating tool. It allows you to determine building costs for your specific zip-code area and for your chosen home design. Space is allowed for additional estimates from contractors and subcontractors, such as for mechanical materials, which are not included in our packages. This invaluable tool includes a Materials List. A Material Cost Report cannot be ordered before blueprints are ordered. Call for details. In addition, ask about our Home Planners Estimating Package.

If you are interested in a plan that is not indicated as Quote One®, please call and ask our sales reps. They will be happy to verify the status for you. To order these invaluable reports, use the order form.

CONSTRUCTION INFORMATION

IF YOU WANT TO KNOW MORE ABOUT TECHNIQUES— and deal more confidently with subcontractors — we offer these useful sheets. Each set is an excellent tool that will add to your understanding of these technical subjects. These helpful details provide general construction information and are not specific to any single plan.

PLUMBING
The Blueprint Package includes locations for all the plumbing fixtures, including sinks, lavatories, tubs, showers, toilets, laundry trays and water heaters. However, if you want to know more about the complete plumbing system, these Plumbing Details will prove very useful. Prepared to meet requirements of the National Plumbing Code, these fact-filled sheets give general information on pipe schedules, fittings, sump-pump details, water-softener hookups, septic system details and much more. Sheets also include a glossary of terms.

ELECTRICAL
The locations for every electrical switch, plug and outlet are shown in your Blueprint Package. However, these Electrical Details go further to take the mystery out of household electrical systems. Prepared to meet requirements of the National Electrical Code, these comprehensive drawings come packed with helpful information, including wire sizing, switch-installation schematics, cable-routing details, appliance wattage, doorbell hook-ups, typical service panel circuitry and much more. A glossary of terms is also included.

CONSTRUCTION
The Blueprint Package contains information an experienced builder needs to construct a particular house. However, it doesn't show all the ways that houses can be built, nor does it explain alternate construction methods. To help you understand how your house will be built—and offer additional techniques—this set of Construction Details depicts the materials and methods used to build foundations, fireplaces, walls, floors and roofs. Where appropriate, the drawings show acceptable alternatives.

MECHANICAL
These Mechanical Details contain fundamental principles and useful data that will help you make informed decisions and communicate with subcontractors about heating and cooling systems. Drawings contain instructions and samples that allow you to make simple load calculations, and preliminary sizing and costing analysis. Covered are the most commonly used systems from heat pumps to solar fuel systems. The package is filled with illustrations and diagrams to help you visualize components and how they relate to one another.

THE HANDS-ON HOME FURNITURE PLANNER

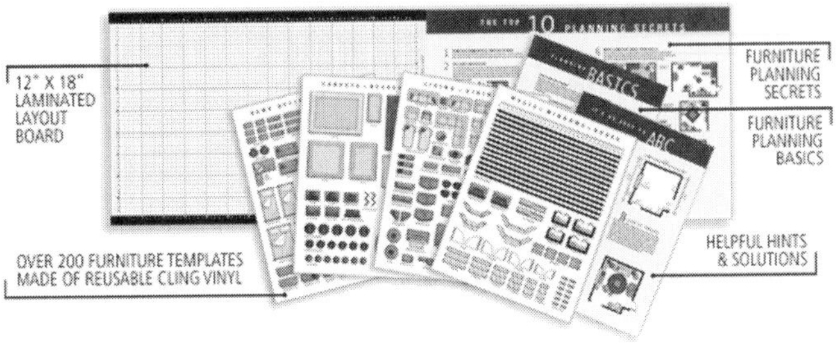

Effectively plan the space in your home using The **Hands-On Home Furniture Planner**. It's fun and easy—no more moving heavy pieces of furniture to see how the room will go together. And you can try different layouts, moving furniture at a whim.

The kit includes reusable peel and stick furniture templates that fit onto a 12" x 18" laminated layout board—space enough to layout every room in your home.

Also included in the package are a number of helpful planning tools. You'll receive:

- ✓ Helpful hints and solutions for difficult situations.
- ✓ Furniture planning basics to get you started.
- ✓ Furniture planning secrets that let you in on some of the tricks of professional designers.

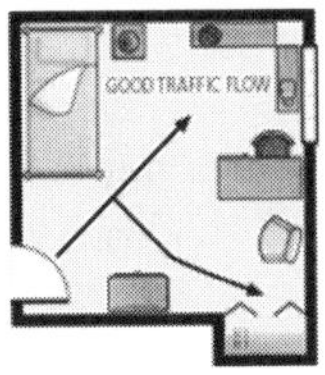

The **Hands-On Home Furniture Planner** is the one tool that no new homeowner or home remodeler should be without. It's also a perfect housewarming gift!

To Order, Call Toll Free 1-800-521-6797

After you've looked over our Blueprint Package and Important Extras on these pages, call for current pricing and availability prior to mailing the order form. We're ready and eager to serve you. After you have received your order, call for customer service toll free 1-888-690-1116.

THE DECK BLUEPRINT PACKAGE

Many of the homes in this book can be enhanced with a professionally designed Home Planners Deck Plan. Those homes marked with a **D** have a complementary Deck Plan, sold separately, which includes a Deck Plan Frontal Sheet, Deck Framing and Floor Plans, Deck Elevations and a Deck Materials List. A Standard Deck Details Package, also available, provides all the how-to information necessary for building *any* deck. Our Complete Deck Building Package contains one set of Custom Deck Plans of your choice, plus one set of Standard Deck Building Details, all for one low price. Our plans and details are carefully prepared in an easy-to-understand format that will guide you through every stage of your deck-building project. This page shows a sample Deck layout to match your favorite house. See Blueprint Price Schedule for ordering information.

THE LANDSCAPE BLUEPRINT PACKAGE

For the homes marked with an **L** in this book, Home Planners has created a front-yard Landscape Plan that is complementary in design to the house plan. These comprehensive blueprint packages include a Frontal Sheet, Plan View, Regionalized Plant & Materials List, a sheet on Planting and Maintaining Your Landscape, Zone Maps and Plant Size and Description Guide. These plans will help you achieve professional results, adding value and enjoyment to your property for years to come. Each set of blueprints is a full 18" x 24" in size with clear, complete instructions and easy-to-read type. A sample Landscape Plan is shown below. See Blueprint Price Schedule for ordering information.

CONTEMPORARY LEISURE DECK
Deck ODA021

CAPE COD COTTAGE
Landscape OLA003

REGIONAL ORDER MAP

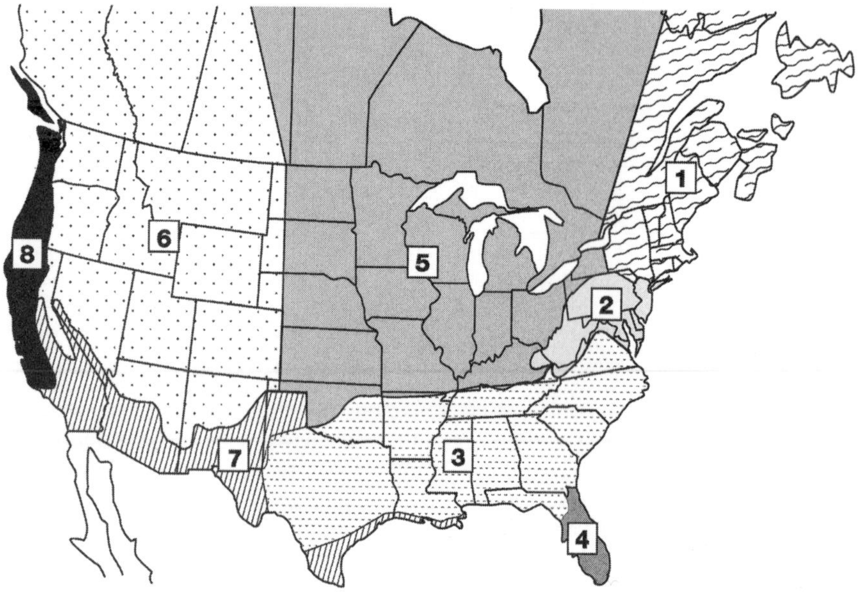

Most Landscape Plans are available with a Plant & Materials List adapted by horticultural experts to 8 different regions of the country. Please specify the Geographic Region when ordering your plan. See Blueprint Price Schedule for ordering information and regional availability.

Region	1	Northeast
Region	2	Mid-Atlantic
Region	3	Deep South
Region	4	Florida & Gulf Coast
Region	5	Midwest
Region	6	Rocky Mountains
Region	7	Southern California & Desert Southwest
Region	8	Northern California & Pacific Northwest

BLUEPRINT PRICE SCHEDULE

Prices guaranteed through December 31, 2003

TIERS	1-SET STUDY PACKAGE	4-SET BUILDING PACKAGE	8-SET BUILDING PACKAGE	1-SET REPRODUCIBLE*
P1	$20	$50	$90	$140
P2	$40	$70	$110	$160
P3	$70	$100	$140	$190
P4	$100	$130	$170	$220
P5	$140	$170	$210	$270
P6	$180	$210	$250	$310
A1	$440	$480	$520	$660
A2	$480	$520	$560	$720
A3	$530	$575	$615	$800
A4	$575	$620	$660	$870
C1	$620	$665	$710	$935
C2	$670	$715	$760	$1000
C3	$715	$760	$805	$1075
C4	$765	$810	$855	$1150
L1	$870	$925	$975	$1300
L2	$945	$1000	$1050	$1420
L3	$1050	$1105	$1155	$1575
L4	$1155	$1210	$1260	$1735
SQ1				.35/sq. ft.

* Requires a fax number

OPTIONS FOR PLANS IN TIERS A1–L4

Additional Identical Blueprints in same order for "A1–L4" price plans .... **$50 per set**

Reverse Blueprints (mirror image) with 4- or 8-set order for "A1–L4" plans .... **$50 fee per order**

Specification Outlines .... **$10 each**

Materials Lists for "A1–C3" plans .... **$60 each**

Materials Lists for "C4–L4" plans .... **$70 each**

OPTIONS FOR PLANS IN TIERS P1–P6

Additional Identical Blueprints in same order for "P1–P6" price plans .... **$10 per set**

Reverse Blueprints (mirror image) for "P1–P6" price plans .... **$10 fee per order**

1 Set of Deck Construction Details .... **$14.95 each**

Deck Construction Package .... **add $10 to Building Package price**

(includes 1 set of "P1–P6" plans, plus 1 set Standard Deck Construction Details)

IMPORTANT NOTES

- SQ one-set building package includes one set of reproducible vellum construction drawings plus one set of study blueprints.
- The 1-set study package is marked "not for construction."
- Prices for 4- or 8-set Building Packages honored only at time of original order.
- Some foundations carry a $225 surcharge.
- Right-reading reverse blueprints, if available, will incur a $165 surcharge.
- Additional identical blueprints may be purchased within 60 days of original order.

TO USE THE INDEX, refer to the design number listed in numerical order (a helpful page reference is also given). Note the price tier and refer to the Blueprint Price Schedule above for the cost of one, four or eight sets of blueprints or the cost of a reproducible drawing. Additional prices are shown for identical and reverse blueprint sets, as well as a very useful Materials List for some of the plans. Also note in the Plan Index those plans that have Deck Plans or Landscape Plans. Refer to the schedules above for prices of these plans. The letter "Y" identifies plans that are part of our Quote One® estimating service and those that offer Materials Lists.

TO ORDER, Call toll free 1-800-521-6797 for current pricing and availability prior to mailing the order form. FAX: 1-800-224-6699 or 520-544-3086.

PLAN INDEX

PLAN INDEX

DESIGN	PRICE	PAGE	MATERIALS LIST	QUOTE ONE®	DECK	DECK PRICE	LANDSCAPE	LANDSCAPE PRICE	REGIONS
HPT830058	C2	62	Y	Y					
HPT830059	C2	63							
HPT830060	A3	64							
HPT830061	A3	65							
HPT830062	A3	66	Y	Y					
HPT830063	A3	67	Y	Y					
HPT830064	A4	68							
HPT830065	C1	69	Y						
HPT830066	C1	70	Y						
HPT830067	C1	71							
HPT830068	A3	72							
HPT830069	C2	73	Y	Y					
HPT830070	C1	74							
HPT830071	C1	75	Y	Y					
HPT830072	C2	76	Y	Y					
HPT830073	C2	77							
HPT830074	A3	78	Y						
HPT830075	C1	79	Y	Y					
HPT830076	C1	80	Y						
HPT830077	A2	81	Y						
HPT830078	A4	82	Y						
HPT830079	A4	83	Y						
HPT830080	A4	84	Y						
HPT830081	A3	85	Y						
HPT830082	A4	86	Y	Y					
HPT830083	A4	87	Y	Y					
HPT830084	A3	88							
HPT830085	C1	89	Y	Y					
HPT830086	A4	90	Y	Y					
HPT830087	A3	91							
HPT830088	A4	92							
HPT830089	A3	93	Y	Y					
HPT830090	A4	94							
HPT830091	A4	95							
HPT830092	A4	96	Y	Y					
HPT830093	A3	97							
HPT830094	A3	98							
HPT830095	C1	99							
HPT830096	C1	100	Y				OLA008	P4	1234568
HPT830097	C1	101	Y				OLA008	P4	1234568
HPT830098	C1	102	Y				OLA004	P3	123568
HPT830099	A4	103							
HPT830100	C2	104	Y	Y					
HPT830101	A4	105							
HPT830102	C3	106	Y	Y					
HPT830103	C3	107	Y	Y					
HPT830104	C2	108							
HPT830105	C1	109							
HPT830106	C3	110							
HPT830107	A4	111	Y	Y					
HPT830108	C2	112							
HPT830109	C2	113					OLA008	P4	1234568
HPT830110	C2	114							
HPT830111	C2	115							
HPT830112	C1	116	Y						
HPT830113	C2	117	Y						
HPT830114	C2	118	Y						
HPT830115	C2	119	Y						
HPT830116	C2	120	Y						
HPT830117	A4	121							
HPT830118	A4	122	Y						
HPT830119	C1	123							
HPT830120	A4	124	Y						
HPT830121	C2	125	Y						
HPT830122	C1	126					OLA012	P3	12345678
HPT830123	C3	127							
HPT830124	C3	128	Y						
HPT830125	C3	129					OLA008	P4	1234568
HPT830126	C2	130							
HPT830127	A4	131	Y	Y					
HPT830128	C4	132	Y	Y					
HPT830129	C1	133	Y						
HPT830130	C1	134	Y						
HPT830131	C1	135	Y						
HPT830132	C1	136	Y						
HPT830133	C1	137	Y						
HPT830134	A4	138	Y						
HPT830135	C2	139	Y						
HPT830136	C3	140	Y						
HPT830137	C3	141	Y						
HPT830138	A4	142	Y	Y					
HPT830139	A3	143	Y	Y					
HPT830140	C1	144	Y	Y					
HPT830141	A3	145	Y						
HPT830142	A3	146	Y						
HPT830143	C1	147	Y						
HPT830144	C1	148	Y						
HPT830145	A4	149	Y						
HPT830146	C1	150	Y						
HPT830147	A4	151	Y	Y					
HPT830148	C3	152	Y						
HPT830149	C1	153	Y						
HPT830150	C3	154							
HPT830151	C3	155	Y	Y					
HPT830152	C3	156							
HPT830153	C2	157	Y	Y					
HPT830154	A3	158							
HPT830155	A3	159	Y	Y					
HPT830156	C1	160	Y	Y					
HPT830157	C1	161	Y	Y					
HPT830158	C1	162					OLA010	P3	1234568
HPT830159	C3	163					OLA014	P4	12345678
HPT830160	A4	164	Y						
HPT830161	A3	165	Y				OLA001	P3	123568
HPT830162	C3	166							
HPT830163	C1	167							
HPT830164	C2	168	Y						
HPT830165	C3	169							
HPT830166	A4	170	Y	Y					
HPT830167	A4	171	Y	Y					
HPT830168	A4	172	Y	Y					
HPT830169	C1	173	Y						
HPT830170	C3	174					OLA010	P3	1234568
HPT830171	C4	175	Y	Y					

PLAN INDEX

DESIGN	PRICE	PAGE	MATERIALS LIST	QUOTE ONE®	DECK	DECK PRICE	LANDSCAPE	LANDSCAPE PRICE	REGIONS
HPT830172	C1	176							
HPT830173	A3	177							
HPT830174	A4	178	Y				OLA001	P3	123568
HPT830175	A4	179	Y	Y					
HPT830176	A4	180	Y				OLA004	P3	123568
HPT830177	A4	181	Y						
HPT830178	A4	182	Y						
HPT830179	A4	183	Y						
HPT830180	C2	184							
HPT830181	C3	185		Y					
HPT830182	C4	186	Y	Y					
HPT830183	A4	187	Y				OLA004	P3	123568
HPT830184	C2	188							
HPT830185	C3	189	Y	Y					
HPT830186	C2	190	Y	Y					
HPT830187	C1	191	Y	Y					
HPT830188	A4	192	Y	Y					
HPT830189	A4	193	Y	Y					
HPT830190	C1	194							
HPT830191	A3	195							
HPT830192	C2	196	Y						
HPT830193	C2	197					OLA014	P4	12345678
HPT830194	C1	198	Y						
HPT830195	C3	199	Y						
HPT830196	C1	200	Y						
HPT830197	C4	201	Y						
HPT830198	C3	202					OLA005	P3	123568
HPT830199	A4	203	Y						
HPT830200	A4	204	Y						
HPT830201	C1	205	Y						
HPT830202	C1	206	Y				OLA004	P3	123568
HPT830203	SQ1	207							
HPT830204	C4	208							
HPT830205	C2	209							
HPT830206	C1	210					OLA004	P3	123568
HPT830207	C1	211							
HPT830208	C4	212							
HPT830209	A4	213	Y				OLA004	P3	123568
HPT830210	C1	214							
HPT830211	C4	215							
HPT830212	C1	216							
HPT830213	C2	217	Y	Y					
HPT830214	C1	218	Y						
HPT830215	C1	219	Y						
HPT830216	C1	220	Y						
HPT830217	A4	221	Y	Y					
HPT830218	C2	222	Y						
HPT830219	A3	223	Y						
HPT830220	A3	224							
HPT830221	A2	225	Y	Y					
HPT830222	L1	226							
HPT830223	C1	227							
HPT830224	C4	228							
HPT830225	C4	229							
HPT830226	C3	230	Y	Y					
HPT830227	C2	231	Y	Y					
HPT830228	C2	232		Y					

PLAN INDEX

DESIGN	PRICE	PAGE	MATERIALS LIST	QUOTE ONE®	DECK	DECK PRICE	LANDSCAPE	LANDSCAPE PRICE	REGIONS
HPT830229	C4	233	Y	Y					
HPT830230	C1	234							
HPT830231	C1	235	Y	Y					
HPT830232	C3	236	Y	Y			OLA014	P4	12345678
HPT830233	A4	237	Y	Y					
HPT830234	C2	238							
HPT830235	C3	239	Y						
HPT830236	A4	240	Y						
HPT830237	C4	241							
HPT830238	C2	242							
HPT830239	C3	243							
HPT830240	L1	244					OLA008	P4	1234568
HPT830241	C3	245					OLA008	P4	1234568
HPT830242	C1	246					OLA001	P3	123568
HPT830243	C3	247	Y	Y			OLA008	P4	1234568
HPT830244	C2	248							
HPT830245	C2	249							
HPT830246	C2	250	Y	Y					
HPT830247	C1	251	Y	Y					
HPT830248	C2	252	Y	Y					
HPT830249	C1	253	Y	Y					
HPT830250	A3	254	Y	Y					
HPT830251	C2	255	Y	Y			OLA008	P4	1234568
HPT830252	C3	256							
HPT830253	C2	257	Y	Y					
HPT830254	L1	258							
HPT830255	L1	259		Y					
HPT830256	C2	260							
HPT830257	L2	261							
HPT830258	C4	262							
HPT830259	C3	263							
HPT830260	C4	264							
HPT830261	C4	265	Y	Y					
HPT830262	C2	266	Y	Y					
HPT830263	L1	267							
HPT830264	C1	268							
HPT830265	C1	269	Y	Y					
HPT830266	A2	270	Y	Y					
HPT830267	A3	271							
HPT830268	A4	272	Y	Y					
HPT830269	C2	273	Y	Y					
HPT830270	C3	274							
HPT830271	C3	275	Y	Y					
HPT830272	C3	276							
HPT830273	C2	277							
HPT830274	C2	278							
HPT830275	A4	279	Y	Y					
HPT830276	C4	280	Y						
HPT830277	C3	281	Y						
HPT830278	C3	282					OLA001	P3	123568
HPT830279	C2	283					OLA012	P3	12345678
HPT830280	C4	284							
HPT830281	C4	285	Y	Y					
HPT830282	C3	286	Y	Y					
HPT830283	C2	287	Y	Y					
HPT830284	C1	288							
HPT830285	C1	289							

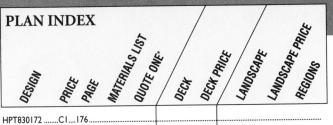

PLAN INDEX

DESIGN	PRICE	PAGE	MATERIALS LIST	QUOTE ONE®	DECK	DECK PRICE	LANDSCAPE	LANDSCAPE PRICE	REGIONS
HPT830286	C1	290					OLA005	P3	123568
HPT830287	C3	291	Y	Y					
HPT830288	C3	292							
HPT830289	C3	293	Y	Y					
HPT830290	C3	294	Y	Y					
HPT830291	C4	295							
HPT830292	C3	296	Y	Y					
HPT830293	C1	297					OLA010	P3	1234568
HPT830294	L1	298	Y	Y					
HPT830295	A3	299	Y	Y					
HPT830296	A4	300							
HPT830297	C1	301	Y						
HPT830298	C3	302							
HPT830299	L1	303	Y	Y					
HPT830300	C4	304							
HPT830301	C4	305							
HPT830302	A4	306							
HPT830303	C4	307	Y						
HPT830304	C3	308							
HPT830305	C3	309	Y	Y					
HPT830306	C2	310	Y	Y					
HPT830307	C2	311							
HPT830308	C3	312							
HPT830309	C2	313	Y	Y					
HPT830310	A4	314	Y	Y					
HPT830311	SQ1	315	Y	Y					
HPT830312	C3	316					OLA024	P4	123568
HPT830313	C1	317	Y						
HPT830314	C1	318	Y	Y					
HPT830315	A4	319	Y	Y					
HPT830316	C3	320							
HPT830317	C1	321	Y	Y					
HPT830318	A4	322	Y						
HPT830319	A4	323	Y	Y					
HPT830320	C2	324		Y					
HPT830321	C2	325	Y	Y					
HPT830322	C1	326	Y						
HPT830323	C1	327	Y						
HPT830324	C2	328	Y						
HPT830325	C2	329	Y						
HPT830326	C2	330	Y	Y					
HPT830327	C2	331	Y	Y					
HPT830328	A4	332	Y						
HPT830329	A4	333	Y	Y					
HPT830330	C2	334	Y	Y					
HPT830331	A4	335	Y						
HPT830332	A3	336							
HPT830333	SQ1	337	Y	Y					
HPT830334	C1	338	Y						
HPT830335	C1	339	Y						
HPT830336	A4	340	Y						
HPT830337	C2	341	Y						
HPT830338	C1	342	Y	Y					
HPT830339	C1	343	Y	Y					
HPT830340	C1	344					OLA001	P3	123568
HPT830341	A3	345	Y						
HPT830342	A4	346	Y						

PLAN INDEX

DESIGN	PRICE	PAGE	MATERIALS LIST	QUOTE ONE®	DECK	DECK PRICE	LANDSCAPE	LANDSCAPE PRICE	REGIONS
HPT830343	A4	347	Y						
HPT830344	C1	348	Y	Y					
HPT830345	C2	349	Y						
HPT830346	A4	350	Y	Y					
HPT830347	A4	351	Y	Y					
HPT830348	C1	352	Y						
HPT830349	C1	353	Y	Y					
HPT830350	C2	354	Y	Y					
HPT830351	L1	355							
HPT830352	A4	356	Y	Y					
HPT830353	C2	357	Y						
HPT830354	A4	358	Y	Y					
HPT830355	C1	359	Y						
HPT830356	A4	360	Y						
HPT830357	C1	361	Y	Y					
HPT830358	C1	362	Y						
HPT830359	C2	363	Y						
HPT830360	C1	364	Y	Y					
HPT830361	C1	365	Y						
HPT830362	C1	366	Y						
HPT830363	C2	367	Y						
HPT830364	A4	368	Y						
HPT830365	C1	369	Y						
HPT830366	C1	370	Y	Y					
HPT830367	C3	371	Y						
HPT830368	C2	372	Y	Y					
HPT830369	C3	373	Y	Y					
HPT830370	C3	374	Y						
HPT830371	C1	375	Y	Y					
HPT830372	A4	376	Y						
HPT830373	C2	377	Y						
HPT830374	C3	378	Y						
HPT830375	C2	379	Y						
HPT830376	A4	380	Y	Y					
HPT830377	C1	381	Y	Y					
HPT830378	C2	382	Y						
HPT830379	C1	383	Y	Y					
HPT830380	C1	384	Y						
HPT830381	C1	385	Y	Y					
HPT830382	C1	386	Y	Y					
HPT830383	A4	387	Y	Y					
HPT830384	A4	388	Y	Y					
HPT830385	C1	389	Y	Y					
HPT830386	C2	390	Y	Y					
HPT830387	C1	391	Y						
HPT830388	C2	392							
HPT830389	A4	393	Y						
HPT830390	A4	394	Y						
HPT830391	A4	395	Y						
HPT830392	A3	396	Y	Y					
HPT830393	A3	397							
HPT830394	A4	398	Y						
HPT830395	A4	399	Y	Y					
HPT830396	A3	400	Y				OLA001	P3	123568
HPT830397	A4	401	Y						
HPT830398	A4	402	Y						
HPT830399	A4	403	Y	Y					

PLAN INDEX

Before You Order...

Before filling out the order form, please call us on our Toll-Free Blueprint Hotline 1-800-521-6797. You may want to learn more about our services and products. Here's some information you will find helpful.

OUR EXCHANGE POLICY

With the exception of reproducible plan orders, we will exchange your entire first order for an equal or greater number of blueprints within our plan collection within 90 days of the original order. The entire content of your original order must be returned before an exchange will be processed. Please call our customer service department for your return authorization number and shipping instructions. If the returned blueprints look used, redlined or copied, we will not honor your exchange. Fees for exchanging your blueprints are as follows: 20% of the amount of the original order...plus the difference in cost if exchanging for a design in a higher price bracket or less the difference in cost if exchanging for a design in a lower price bracket. **(Reproducible blueprints are not exchangeable or refundable.)** Please call for current postage and handling prices. Shipping and handling charges are not refundable.

ABOUT REPRODUCIBLES

When purchasing a reproducible you may be required to furnish a fax number. The designer will fax documents that you must sign and return to them before shipping will take place.

ABOUT REVERSE BLUEPRINTS

Although lettering and dimensions will appear backward, reverses will be a useful aid if you decide to flop the plan. See Price Schedule and Plans Index for pricing.

REVISING, MODIFYING AND CUSTOMIZING PLANS

Like many homeowners who buy these plans, you and your builder, architect or engineer may want to make changes to them. We recommend purchase of a reproducible plan for any changes made by your builder, licensed architect or engineer. As set forth below, we cannot assume any responsibility for blueprints which have been changed, whether by you, your builder or by professionals selected by you or referred to you by us, because such individuals are outside our supervision and control.

ARCHITECTURAL AND ENGINEERING SEALS

Some cities and states are now requiring that a licensed architect or engineer review and "seal" a blueprint, or officially approve it, prior to construction due to concerns over energy costs, safety and other factors. Prior to application for a building permit or the start of actual construction, we strongly advise that you consult your local building official who can tell you if such a review is required.

ABOUT THE DESIGNS

The architects and designers whose work appears in this publication are among America's leading residential designers. Each plan was designed to meet the requirements of a nationally recognized model building code in effect at the time and place the plan was drawn. Because national building codes change from time to time, plans may not comply with any such code at the time they are sold to a customer. In addition, building officials may not accept these plans as final construction documents of record as the plans may need to be modified and additional drawings and details added to suit local conditions and requirements. We strongly advise that purchasers consult a licensed architect or engineer, and their local building official, before starting any construction related to these plans.

LOCAL BUILDING CODES AND ZONING REQUIREMENTS

At the time of creation, our plans are drawn to specifications published by the Building Officials and Code Administrators (BOCA) International, Inc.; the Southern Building Code Congress (SBCCI) International, Inc.; the International Conference of Building Officials (ICBO); or the Council of American Building Officials (CABO). Our plans are designed to meet or exceed national building standards. Because of the great differences in geography and climate throughout the United States and Canada, each state, county and municipality has its own building codes, zone requirements, ordinances and building regulations. Your plan may need to be modified to comply with local requirements regarding snow loads, energy codes, soil and seismic conditions and a wide range of other matters. In addition, you may need to obtain permits or inspections from local governments before and in the course of construction. Prior to using blueprints ordered from us, we strongly advise that you consult a licensed architect or engineer—and speak with your local building official—before applying for any permit or beginning construction. We authorize the use of our blueprints on the express condition that you strictly comply with all local building codes, zoning requirements and other applicable laws, regulations, ordinances and requirements. Notice: Plans for homes to be built in Nevada must be re-drawn by a Nevada-registered professional. Consult your building official for more information on this subject.

TOLL FREE
1-800-521-6797

REGULAR OFFICE HOURS:

8:00 a.m.-9:00 p.m. EST, Monday-Friday

If we receive your order by 3:00 p.m. EST, Monday-Friday, we'll process it and ship within **two business days.** When ordering by phone, please have your credit card or check information ready. We'll also ask you for the Order Form Key Number at the bottom of the order form.

By FAX: Copy the Order Form on the next page and send it on our FAX line: 1-800-224-6699 or 520-544-3086.

Canadian Customers
Order Toll Free 1-877-223-6389

DISCLAIMER

The designers we work with have put substantial care and effort into the creation of their blueprints. However, because they cannot provide on-site consultation, supervision and control over actual construction, and because of the great variance in local building requirements, building practices and soil, seismic, weather and other conditions, WE CANNOT MAKE ANY WARRANTY, EXPRESS OR IMPLIED, WITH RESPECT TO THE CONTENT OR USE OF THE BLUEPRINTS, INCLUDING BUT NOT LIMITED TO ANY WARRANTY OF MERCHANTABILITY OR OF FITNESS FOR A PARTICULAR PURPOSE. **ITEMS, PRICES, TERMS AND CONDITIONS ARE SUBJECT TO CHANGE WITHOUT NOTICE. REPRODUCIBLE PLAN ORDERS MAY REQUIRE A CUSTOMER'S SIGNED RELEASE BEFORE SHIPPING.**

TERMS AND CONDITIONS

These designs are protected under the terms of United States Copyright Law and may not be copied or reproduced in any way, by any means, unless you have purchased Reproducibles which clearly indicate your right to copy or reproduce. We authorize the use of your chosen design as an aid in the construction of one single family home only. You may not use this design to build a second or multiple dwellings without purchasing another blueprint or blueprints or paying additional design fees.

HOW MANY BLUEPRINTS DO YOU NEED?

Although a standard building package may satisfy many states, cities and counties, some plans may require certain changes. For your convenience, we have developed a Reproducible plan which allows a local professional to modify and make up to 10 copies of your revised plan. As our plans are all copyright protected, with your purchase of the Reproducible, we will supply you with a Copyright release letter. The number of copies you may need: 1 for owner; 3 for builder; 2 for local building department and 1-3 sets for your mortgage lender.

ORDER TOLL FREE!

For information about any of our services or to order call 1-800-521-6797

Browse our website: www.eplans.com

BLUEPRINTS ARE NOT REFUNDABLE EXCHANGES ONLY

For Customer Service, call toll free 1-888-690-1116.

ORDER FORM

CALL FOR CURRENT PRICING & AVAILABILITY PRIOR TO MAILING THIS ORDER FORM.

HOME PLANNERS, LLC wholly owned by Hanley-Wood, LLC
3275 WEST INA ROAD, SUITE 110 • TUCSON, ARIZONA • 85741

THE BASIC BLUEPRINT PACKAGE

Rush me the following (please refer to the Plans Index and Price Schedule in this section):

___Set(s) of reproducibles*, plan number(s) ________________ $________
indicate foundation type ________________ surcharge (if applicable): $________
___Set(s) of blueprints, plan number(s) ________________ $________
indicate foundation type ________________ surcharge (if applicable): $________
___Additional identical blueprints (standard or reverse) in same order @ $50 per set $________
___Reverse blueprints @ $50 fee per order. Right-reading reverse @ $165 surcharge $________

IMPORTANT EXTRAS

Rush me the following:

___Materials List: $60 (Must be purchased with Blueprint set.) Add $10 for Schedule C4–L4 plans $________
___**Quote One**® Summary Cost Report @ $29.95 for one, $14.95 for each additional,
for plans ________________ $________
Building location: City ________________ Zip Code ________________
___**Quote One**® Material Cost Report @ $120 Schedules P1–C3; $130 Schedules C4–L4,
for plan________________(Must be purchased with Blueprints set.) $________
Building location: City ________________ Zip Code ________________
___Specification Outlines @ $10 each $________
___Detail Sets @ $14.95 each; any two $22.95; any three $29.95; all four for $39.95 (save $19.85) $________
___❑ Plumbing ❑ Electrical ❑ Construction ❑ Mechanical
___Home Furniture Planner @ $15.95 each $________

DECK BLUEPRINTS

(Please refer to the Plans Index and Price Schedule in this section)

___Set(s) of Deck Plan ________________. $________
___Additional identical blueprints in same order @ $10 per set. $________
___Reverse blueprints @ $10 fee per order. $________
___Set of Standard Deck Details @ $14.95 per set. $________
___Set of Complete Deck Construction Package (Best Buy!) Add $10 to Building Package.
Includes Custom Deck Plan ________________ Plus Standard Deck Details

LANDSCAPE BLUEPRINTS

(Please refer to the Plans Index and Price Schedule in this section.)

___Set(s) of Landscape Plan ________________ $________
___Additional identical blueprints in same order @ $10 per set $________
___Reverse blueprints @ $10 fee per order $________
Please indicate appropriate region of the country for Plant & Material List. Region ________

POSTAGE AND HANDLING *Signature is required for all deliveries.*	**1–3 sets**	**4+ sets**
DELIVERY		
No CODs (Requires street address—No P.O. Boxes)		
•Regular Service (Allow 7–10 business days delivery)	❑ $20.00	❑ $25.00
•Priority (Allow 4–5 business days delivery)	❑ $25.00	❑ $35.00
•Express (Allow 3 business days delivery)	❑ $35.00	❑ $45.00
OVERSEAS DELIVERY	fax, phone or mail for quote	

Note: All delivery times are from date Blueprint Package is shipped.

POSTAGE (From box above) $________
SUBTOTAL $________
SALES TAX (AZ & MI residents, please add appropriate state and local sales tax.) $________
TOTAL (Subtotal and tax) $________

YOUR ADDRESS (please print legibly)

Name ________________
Street ________________
City ________________State________Zip ________
Daytime telephone number (required) (_______) ________________
* Fax number (required for reproducible orders) ________________
TeleCheck® Checks By Phone℠ available

FOR CREDIT CARD ORDERS ONLY

Credit card number ________________ Exp. Date: (M/Y) ________
Check one ❑ Visa ❑ MasterCard ❑ American Express

Order Form Key
HPT83

Signature (required) ________________
Please check appropriate box: ❑ Licensed Builder-Contractor ❑ Homeowner

ORDER TOLL FREE!
1-800-521-6797

BY FAX: Copy the order form above and send it on our FAXLINE: 1-800-224-6699 OR 520-544-3086

HELPFUL BOOKS FROM HOME PLANNERS

TO ORDER BY PHONE
1-800-322-6797

1 BIGGEST & BEST

1001 of our best-selling plans in one volume. 1,074 to 7,275 square feet. 704 pgs $12.95 1K1

2 ONE-STORY

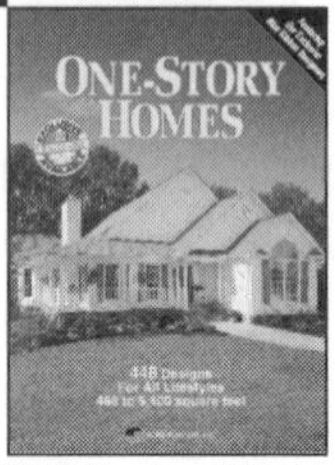

450 designs for all lifestyles. 800 to 4,900 square feet. 384 pgs $9.95 OS

3 MORE ONE-STORY

475 superb one-level plans from 800 to 5,000 square feet. 448 pgs $9.95 MO2

4 TWO-STORY

443 designs for one-and-a-half and two stories. 1,500 to 6,000 square feet. 448 pgs $9.95 TS

5 VACATION

430 designs for recreation, retirement and leisure. 448 pgs $9.95 VS3

6 HILLSIDE

208 designs for split-levels, bi-levels, multi-levels and walkouts. 224 pgs $9.95 HH

7 FARMHOUSE

300 Fresh Designs from Classic to Modern. 320 pgs. $10.95 FCP

8 COUNTRY HOUSES

208 unique home plans that combine traditional style and modern livability. 224 pgs $9.95 CN

9 BUDGET-SMART

200 efficient plans from 7 top designers, that you can really afford to build! 224 pgs $8.95 BS

10 BARRIER-FREE

Over 1,700 products and 51 plans for accessible living. 128 pgs $15.95 UH

11 ENCYCLOPEDIA

500 exceptional plans for all styles and budgets—the best book of its kind! 528 pgs $9.95 ENC

12 ENCYCLOPEDIA II

500 completely new plans. Spacious and stylish designs for every budget and taste. 352 pgs $9.95 E2

13 AFFORDABLE

300 Modest plans for savvy homebuyers.256 pgs. $9.95 AH2

14 VICTORIAN

210 striking Victorian and Farmhouse designs from today's top designers. 224 pgs $15.95 VDH2

15 ESTATE

Dream big! Eighteen designers showcase their biggest and best plans. 224 pgs $16.95 EDH3

16 LUXURY

170 lavish designs, over 50% brand-new plans added to a most elegant collection. 192 pgs $12.95 LD3

17 EUROPEAN STYLES

200 homes with a unique flair of the Old World. 224 pgs $15.95 EURO

18 COUNTRY CLASSICS

Donald Gardner's 101 best Country and Traditional home plans. 192 pgs $17.95 DAG

19 COUNTRY

85 Charming Designs from American Home Gallery. 160 pgs. $17.95 CTY

20 TRADITIONAL

85 timeless designs from the Design Traditions Library. 160 pgs $17.95 TRA

21 COTTAGES

245 Delightful retreats from 825 to 3,500 square feet. 256 pgs. $10.95 COOL

22 CABINS TO VILLAS

Enchanting Homes for Mountain Sea or Sun, from the Sater collection. 144 pgs $19.95 CCV

23 CONTEMPORARY

The most complete and imaginative collection of contemporary designs available anywhere. 256 pgs. $10.95 CM2

24 FRENCH COUNTRY

Live every day in the French countryside using these plans, landscapes and interiors. 192 pgs. $14.95 PN

25 SOUTHERN

207 homes rich in Southern styling and comfort. 240 pgs $8.95 SH

26 SOUTHWESTERN

138 designs that capture the spirit of the Southwest. 144 pgs $10.95 SW

27 SHINGLE-STYLE

155 Home plans from Classic Colonials to Breezy Bungalows. 192 pgs. $12.95 SNG

28 NEIGHBORHOOD

170 designs with the feel of main street America. 192 pgs $12.95 TND

29 CRAFTSMAN

170 Home plans in the Craftsman and Bungalow style. 192 pgs $12.95 CC

30 GRAND VISTAS

200 Homes with a View. 224 pgs. $10.95 GV

FOR FASTER SERVICE ORDER ONLINE AT
www.hwspecials.com

HEAT-N-GLO
1-888-427-3973
WWW.HEATNGLO.COM

HEAT-N-GLO®
No one builds a better fire

Heat-N-Glo offers quality gas, woodburning and electric fireplaces, including gas log sets, stoves, and inserts for preexisting fireplaces. Now available gas grills and outdoor fireplaces. Send for a free brochure.

Style Solutions™ Incorporated

Ideas for your next project. Beautiful, durable, elegant low-maintenance millwork, mouldings, balustrade systems and much more. For your free catalog please call us at 1-800-446-3040 or visit www.stylesolutionsinc.com.

ARISTOKRAFT
ONE MASTERBRAND CABINETS DRIVE
JASPER, IN 47546
(812) 482-2527
WWW.ARISTOKRAFT.COM

Aristokraft® Cabinetry
Great Ideas Made Easy

Aristokraft offers you superb value, outstanding quality and great style that fit your budget. Transform your great ideas into reality with popular styles and features that reflect your taste and lifestyle. $5.00

THERMA-TRU DOORS
1687 WOODLANDS DRIVE
MAUMEE, OH 43537
1-800-THERMA-TRU
WWW.THERMATRU.COM

THERMA TRU® DOORS
THE DOOR SYSTEM YOU CAN BELIEVE IN

The undisputed brand leader, Therma-Tru specializes in fiberglass and steel entry doors for every budget. Excellent craftsmanship, energy efficiency and variety make Therma-Tru the perfect choice for all your entry door needs.

225 GARDEN, LANDSCAPE AND PROJECT PLANS
TO ORDER, CALL
1-800-322-6797

225 Do-It-Yourself designs that help transform boring yards into exciting outdoor entertainment spaces. Gorgeous gardens, luxurious landscapes, dazzling decks and other outdoor amenities. Complete construction blueprints available for every project. Only $19.95 (plus $4 shipping/handling).

HAVE WE GOT PLANS FOR YOU!

eplans.com
Stop dreaming. Start building.

Your online source for home designs and ideas. Find thousands of plans from the nation's top designers...all in one place. Plus, links to the best known names in building supplies and services.